ASIA

IN THE MAKING OF EUROPE

ASIA

IN THE MAKING OF EUROPE

DONALD F. LACH

VOLUME

II

A
Century of
Wonder

BOOK TWO: THE LITERARY ARTS

THE UNIVERSITY OF CHICAGO PRESS

CHICAGO AND LONDON

THE UNIVERSITY OF CHICAGO PRESS, CHICAGO 60637
The University of Chicago Press, Ltd., London

Library of Congress Cataloging in Publication Data

Lach, Donald Frederick, 1917–
    Asia in the making of Europe.

    Includes bibliographies.
    CONTENTS: v. 1. The century of discovery. 2 v.—
v. 2. A century of wonder. Book 1. The visual arts.
Book 2. The literary arts. Book 3. The scholarly
disciplines. 3 v.
    1. Asia—Discovery and exploration. 2. Europe—
Civilization—Oriental influences. I. Title.
DS5.95.L3   901.93   64-19848
ISBN 0-226-46730-9 (v. 2. bk. 1)
ISBN 0-226-46733-3 (v. 2. bk. 2)
ISBN 0-226-46734-1 (v. 2. bk. 3)

To my students

Contents

Contents

BOOK THREE

PART III

The Scholarly Disciplines

Contents

Illustrations

[xi]

Preface

With Books 2 and 3 of the second volume we reach the end of the involved story of *Asia in the Making of Europe* during the sixteenth century. Over the past fifteen years and more of research and writing, I have lived as much in that *Century of Wonder* as in our own marvelous century of extraterrestrial discovery. Observing this interplanetary age has taught me many lessons which helped me to understand more empathetically the reactions of the sixteenth century. For a long time I wondered, as others have, why it took so long for the effects of the overseas discoveries to be reflected in sixteenth-century European thought, art, and institutions. It was therefore fascinating to observe that while the peaceful conquistadors of our day explored an unpopulated universe beyond the earth, the television-bound people at home only slowly, and sometimes reluctantly and unbelievingly, began to sense that basic changes were to come in man's view of his universe and that intellectual accommodations would have to be made to fuse the new to the old learning. Now I am no longer puzzled that fifty years or more had to pass before the full implications of the exploratory voyages of Columbus and Vasco da Gama began to dawn upon sixteenth-century Europe.

During the years when Americans were walking on the moon or photographing Mars, I spent most of my time earthbound in the vicinity of Chicago. Though I had traveled widely in Europe and Asia in the course of preparing my earlier studies, Books 2 and 3 of Volume II required that I should remain near my notes and the Regenstein and Newberry libraries. For the preparation of these books, unlike that of the earlier ones, I needed very little fieldwork and so undertook no extensive archival or material-collecting expeditions. The organization and evaluation of earlier experiences were combined now with the demanding and confining task of completing the project according to the plan originally set forth in the Preface to Volume I. My objective in Books 2 and 3 of Volume II is therefore to summarize the meaning of Asia for *The Century of Wonder* by isolating and analyzing Asia's influences upon Europe's learned world, national literatures, and scholarly disciplines.

For day-to-day help in the tedious tasks of locating references, making notes, finding books, and keeping the office, I am indebted to a number of graduate assistants. They tolerated, often cheerfully, my eccentricities, whims, and moods. Sister Michaela Zahner, C.S.J., labored hard in the vineyards of the University of Chicago until she was forced by illness to take a leave of absence. Peter Berger and Robert O'Neill replaced the Sister and aided me greatly by conducting a lengthy survey (chapter ii) of European libraries and their holdings. In the meantime, Sara Bobroff Bolon and I researched in the history of science, especially in the materials of biology in which she is so expert. Gloria Gibbs, Kathleen Wellman, and Lynne Oshita contributed significantly both to the research stages and to the preparation for the press of the text and the bibliographies. Theodore N. Foss, my right-hand man for three years, read and criticized the entire manuscript, planned and executed the illustration program, and thought about the problems of the project as much as I did. Foss, Oshita, and Denise Le Cocq Garfield saw the books through the press with me and helped prepare the index. To these individuals, to their predecessors mentioned in previous prefaces, and to my other students I dedicate these books with the hope that they will find in them a worthy tribute.

As in the preceding books, I have been forced by the complexities and varieties of the subjects surveyed to rely upon the cooperation and forbearance of colleagues, especially those at the University of Chicago. T. Bentley Duncan read critically the materials on Portuguese literature and, because his command of Portuguese is better than mine, provided English translations of a number of poems. J. A. B. van Buitenen, the Sanskritist and literary historian, aided me with references on the transmission of stories and tales, and read the chapter (iii) on the literary tradition inherited from India and the East. Eric Cochrane and Paolo A. Cherchi scrutinized the chapter (vi) on Italian literature and helped me to avoid mistakes of emphasis and generalization. Howard W. Winger, historian of books and printing, read the chapter (ii) on libraries and their holdings. George Haley, student of Spanish literature, kept me from erring in my discussions of the Iberian literati. The materials on Germanic literature were read by Samuel P. Jaffe and William A. Ringler, Jr. Through his meticulous reading of my section on English literature, Professor Ringler substantially improved its coverage and its interpretive accuracy. Amy Gordon of Denison University discussed with me the chapter (vii) on French literature, helped to locate materials, and contributed freely of her time and knowledge to aid in its completion. Allen G. Debus and Noel M. Swerdlow, my colleagues in the history of science, cheerfully read the science chapter (ix) and corrected my most egregious errors in biology, mathematics, and astronomy. David Woodward, director of the Hermon Dunlap Smith Cartographic Center of the Newberry Library, added to my understanding of geographical and cartographical developments by his precise emendations to chapter x; he also graciously lent me map materials from his personal collection. Ludo and Rosanne Rocher, linguists and orientalists at the University of Pennsylvania, carefully commented on the chapter (xi) on language, and corrected and added to its appendix. Edwin McClellan, professor of Japanese literature at Yale, helped me with problems relating to Chinese and Japanese characters in European manuscripts and books; Chow Tse-tung, professor of Chinese literature at the University of Wisconsin (Madison) graciously wrote me a long and informative letter on Chinese pattern poems. Walter Pagel of London, a specialist on Paracelsus, informed me about the most recent literature in his field relevant to my subject.

Because of the long time that has sometimes elapsed between my use of materials and their original preparation, I have on occasion been guilty of failing to acknowledge adequately certain debts. I owe a special apology to Harold B. Johnson, a former research assistant and now a professor at the University of Virginia, for my heavy and previously unacknowledged dependence (I, 11–19) on a paper he wrote for my seminar. To Henry Y. K. Tom, a former doctoral student and now Social Science editor of the Johns Hopkins University Press, I extend a belated thanks for the work of revision and excision he performed on the Introduction to Volume II, Book 1. Finally to Edwin Van Kley of Calvin College, who will be my collaborator in future volumes of this series, I want to express my gratitude, long overdue, for his willingness to begin working on the seventeenth century while waiting, in what must have been frustration and anguish, for me to finish in my deliberate and unhurried fashion these last two books on the sixteenth century. Though I have acknowledged the contributions of my wife, Alma S. Lach, on various previous occasions, such expressions never reflect adequately the real debt that the author owes to his spouse.

Institutions as well as individuals have contributed to the completion of this work. The University of Chicago, through its generous addition of research support to the Bernadotte E. Schmitt professorship of history which I now hold, has provided me with funds to hire research assistants and typists and to defray the numerous other expenses incidental to a project of this magnitude. In 1975 I also received financial support from the Norman Wait Harris Memorial Foundation administered through the Social Sciences Division of the university. The Regenstein Library of the university and the Newberry and Crerar libraries of Chicago have continued to be indispensable. From their administrations and staffs I have received constant and courteous help in exploiting their vast resources. Most of the illustrations here reproduced come from holdings of these libraries. I am particularly indebted to their collections of rare books, and to the staff administered by Robert Rosenthal, curator of special collections in the Regenstein Library.

In these books, as in my earlier efforts, I have brashly ventured into fields for which my qualifications are limited to the enthusiasm and dedication of the experienced general historian. As a result I have probably been guilty of committing mistakes of omission and commission of both fact and interpretation. Others have helped me to keep errors to a minimum; but for those that remain, I assume personal responsibility. I conclude with the hope, vain as it probably is, that other errors, when discovered, will prove to be funny rather than fundamental.

Introduction

Every advance into the overseas world made untenable the comfortable supposition that Europe could readily rule the earth. The optimism of the early explorers and adventurers that the riches of the East were there to be taken was quickly transformed into pessimism as merchants and missionaries confronted the stark realities of retaining precarious footholds and eliminating competition in Asia. As the Europeans pushed farther to the east, they realized that the great continental empires of India and China were not as vulnerable as the more isolated insular reaches of Asia. The men in the field consequently learned to prefer limited objectives to total conquests whether of a material or spiritual nature. Their reluctant compromise, not readily understood or appreciated in Europe, was only gradually conveyed to those at home. Once the European literati began to believe and to assimilate the reports from Asia, they became even more convinced of the need to learn what they could about the high cultures of the East and to weigh the new knowledge in their traditional intellectual balances.

Volume I of *Asia in the Making of Europe*, entitled *The Century of Discovery*, recounts the story of the Europeans' advent in the East and describes the European channels through which information was disseminated about the discoveries. From a survey of the reports received, word pictures were produced on the basis of what it was possible for sixteenth-century Europeans to know about India, Southeast Asia, Japan, China, and Asia as a whole. In Volume I, I attempted an assessment of the accuracy of the information relayed to Europe by testing it against the best of modern scholarship, in the hope of supplying a solid base from which to survey the impact of Asia's revelation upon Europe.

Volume II, entitled *A Century of Wonder*, appears in three books. The first, entitled *The Visual Arts*, reviews the arts on the basis of "silent sources": art objects, artifacts, flora, fauna, and crafts. It begins with an examination of the collections of curiosities in which ethnographical specimens, minerals, art objects, flora, and fauna were displayed side by side with the natural and artistic products of Europe. What questions did these exotic objects provoke for Europe's artists and artisans and how did they affect European creations? After a thorough examination of the major and minor arts, it becomes clear that the new knowledge of Asia did not fundamentally transform any of the art forms. It did, however, inspire imitation and contribute to the vocabulary of ornament and to the design of decoration. The growing impression of Asia as a *reality* comparable to Europe brought changes in the artistic symbolism traditionally attributed to objects and designs of Asian provenance and accelerated trends that were already developing in Naturalism and Mannerism. Asian objects as "subtle ingenia" of people in distant lands helped to produce popular wonderment, to invite contemplation, and to encourage experiment. The bounds of European art and thought were stretched to include certain of the artistic ideas and creations of Asia.

Book 2 of Volume II, *The Literary Arts*, was written in conjunction with Book 3, *The Scholarly Disciplines*. As a consequence, these two books have a continuous pagination, as well as common preliminaries and index. The general and chapter bibliographies for Books 2 and 3 appear at the end of Book 3. This complex organization was not designed to puzzle or to confuse the reader; it is rather the result of the size of the manuscript and a technical decision to print such a massive product as advantageously and economically as possible.

Book 2, following the techniques employed in Volume II, Book 1, begins with an attempt to discover the routes by which news of the East was relayed from Portugal to the rest of Europe through oral reports and literary accounts. In an effort to determine the European circulation of the number and kind of books about the discoveries, I undertook an examination of the catalogs of sixty representative and important libraries and collections in places as far apart as England and Italy, Saxony and Portugal. Before studying the individual national literatures, I survey the literary traditions about the East inherited from the pre-discovery era to show that established beliefs yielded only slowly and irregularly to the new information on Asia which filtered into all parts of Europe during the course of the sixteenth century.

The national literatures are examined in an order which follows the most consistently open and effective paths of communication. An overview of the responses of the Portuguese literati to the revelation of Asia is followed by a review of Spanish literature, for Spain was politically and intellectually closely tied to Italy, the leading center of Renaissance thought. It was mainly through Italy that the materials on Asia passed into France and Germany. Antwerp too was an important center of diffusion in northern Europe, particularly during the earlier half of the century. But the effect of Asia on Netherlandish literature itself was extremely slight until the last years of the century. The Dutch, German, and English reactions were delayed because of geographical distance from

Portugal and, most emphatically, because of the barrier erected by the Reformation between Europe's Protestant north and Catholic south.

In the analysis of each national literature I have concentrated on vernacular products but have not excluded fundamental materials that appeared in Latin versions. A systematic effort was made to study the role of the translation movement in relaying information from one country to the other. Special investigatory techniques, applicable to the peculiar types of material important to this study, were developed to analyze literary texts. In Volume II, Book 1, I experimented with special iconographical eccentricities—the features of Raphael's elephant or the dorsal horn of Dürer's rhinoceros—as tracers to detect influence of one artistic work upon the other. In literary creations I was frequently able to establish the sources for particular passages and references by using as tracers the peculiarities which appeared in the spelling of Asian names. From my knowledge of the European accounts of Asia, it was sometimes possible by studying exotic terms or names, or even turns of phrase, to locate quickly and accurately the source of passages, for example, in the works of Barahona da Soto, Arrivabene, or Bodin. The tracers did not always lead to literary sources. Writers as widely separated in time and space as Ariosto, More, Rabelais, and Marlowe followed maps to chart the itineraries of their characters. Historians and cosmographers, who often depended on all the available sources, unhesitatingly used both the old and the new materials. The spelling tracer also helped to determine and to document this fact.

The national literatures are treated in separate chapters, except for the chapter on Germanic literatures, which includes German, Netherlandish, and English literature. In northern Europe, especially in Germany and the Netherlands, the literati were less independent of Latin and the vernaculars were less developed than in the south. Although the English were relatively freer of Latin, their leading intellectuals, with the exception of Sir Thomas More, had less interest in the overseas discoveries than their Continental contemporaries until the last quarter of the century. The spread of the Reformation in northern Europe led to a hostile reaction to the exploits of the Catholics in Asia. It is for these reasons that I decided to treat the Germanic literatures in a single chapter. Also I thought that in handling them in this manner, I would prepare a backdrop for the startling growth in their importance which came at the beginning of the next century.

In Book 3, *The Scholarly Disciplines*, I concentrate my analysis upon those fields whose responses to the revelation of Asia were most apparent. The chapter (ix) on the natural sciences commences with a review of the importance of Asia to medieval technology and is followed by a brief rationale for its decline after 1500. While I survey quickly the impact of the discoveries upon navigation, astronomy, and nautics, much more original monographic research and analytical scholarship are needed to isolate and to clarify the issues. Paracelsian thought is also included in this chapter because a number of modern scholars have begun to look to Asia as the breeding ground for these ideas. Botany was the single natural science most significantly influenced by the overseas discoveries and zoology followed closely behind it. However, I omitted zoology from systematic discussion at this point in the series because I had spent so much time on animals and their representations in European art in the pages of Volume II, Book 1.

Cartography and geography, the subjects of chapter x, were the disciplines most changed by the unfolding of the world map. They were disengaged from cosmography and astronomy as they became earthbound and more independent fields of scholarly endeavor. Their practitioners were among the first to question the authority of the learned Ancients and to adopt a contemporary, empirical viewpoint. In their struggle to adapt themselves to the swift march of discovery, they were aided by interested monarchs, merchants, and printers who encouraged them with material support. The printers of Italy, the Netherlands, and the Rhenish cities played an indispensable role in preparing and in realizing the cartographic revolution of the sixteenth century. The universities, Protestant and Catholic alike, began under the pressure of events to admit the proponents of the new geography to their classrooms and libraries.

Language and linguistics, the subject of chapter xi, were the fields of scholarly activity most severely shaken by the great numbers and types of languages discovered in the overseas world. But no new scientific resolution appeared at this time as a response. Information on the Asian languages was still too often limited to the vocabulary gathered for practical purposes by untrained recorders. The missionaries, especially the Jesuits, rapidly succeeded in organizing Tamil and Malayālam, but Sanskrit remained the monopoly of the Brahmans until the seventeenth century. The confrontation of the missionaries with the languages of East Asia produced efforts to systematize those languages in terms of Latin grammar. Although the successes were notable, the linguists quickly understood that the languages written in characters presented them with challenges that they were unprepared to meet at the level of theory. The language experiments of the sixteenth century as later followed up by curious scholars did help to produce new theoretical advances in the next century. The most obvious achievement of the sixteenth century was the admission and integration into the European vocabulary of a host of exotic words, names, and terms.

In my earlier introductions of this series, I have made a number of pronouncements about the importance of studying the impact of Asia as a whole but with due attention to its related elements. I have stressed the fundamental quality of the European materials as sources for the sixteenth-century history of the various countries of Asia. Throughout I have tried to point up the interrelatedness of domestic events in Europe to the reception of the successes and failures of the expansion movement. I warned against the pitfalls inherent in image making and in tracing influence; nonetheless, I proceeded, I hope with caution, to create images and to look for influences. Not satisfied merely to study the literary materials to which the general historian usually limits himself, I tried my hand in fields usually reserved to historians of art, technology, and other specialized fields. Mostly I have sought the counsel and followed the advice of the specialists;

at times, but always with respect and deliberation, I rejected their advice and followed my own ideas and inclinations. Although I have certainly made many errors of fact, interpretation, and emphasis, I conclude my investigation of the sixteenth century firmly committed to the idea that Asia helped to shape significantly the life and mind of Europe during the first of its modern centuries.

PART

I

Portugal and the Learned Community of Europe

Introduction

Histories of expansion traditionally deal with the progress of Europeans overseas. Little attention has been given to the reverse side of the movement or to the effects of a particular nation's overseas expansion on its European neighbors. It is well known, for example, that Portugal's control over the spice trade brought its merchants and sailors intimately into touch with the markets and ports of northern Europe. But it is not often realized that individual Portuguese of various walks of life, sometimes in connection with the spice trade and sometimes not, carried news of the discoveries to other countries of Europe in their travels on official or personal business. Throughout the first half of the sixteenth century individual heralds of empire brought news of the opening of Asia to the political and cultural centers as well as to the mercantile cities of Europe. When difficulties for Portugal and the spice trade developed in the latter half of the century, the Portuguese ceased going abroad and the country turned inward. The rest of Europe thereafter followed the Portuguese and Jesuit expansion in the East mainly through the printed word. Interested bibliophiles collected the chronicles of discovery and Jesuit letterbooks. Through the availability of these materials in Latin and in the vernacular languages, Humanists, scientists, and literati of the last quarter of the century had at hand a documentation on the "new Asia" which enabled them to begin the task of evaluating its revelation for the arts and sciences of Europe.

CHAPTER I

Heralds of Empire

In the latter years of the fifteenth and in the first half of the sixteenth century Portugal expanded into Europe as well as into Africa and Asia. But its penetration of Europe was peaceful rather than bellicose. As a result of its overseas discoveries and trade, Portugal for the first time became fully involved in the complex commercial and economic life of the Continent. In the process its political and cultural ties with the other countries of Europe also became closer. Merchants, sailors, students, artists, diplomats, and curates from Portugal became more numerous and more influential than ever before in the cities of Europe. Merchants, diplomats, soldiers, navigators, and printers from the rest of Europe were attracted to Lisbon by the new prospects opening there. The Jesuits around mid-century began to work within Portugal and its overseas possessions, thereby expanding the previously limited religious and cultural dimensions of Portuguese expansion. Scholars and scientists traveled to and from Portugal to the other cultural centers of Europe. Wittingly and unwittingly the Portuguese abroad and the foreigners who visited Lisbon broadcast news about the activities of the Portuguese in Asia.

Throughout the sixteenth century the entire life of the Portuguese nation was directed to activities connected with expansion. Every family and every individual was in some measure involved in the spice trade or in matters related to it, and many of Portugal's best men left each year for posts abroad. From a population which never numbered more than one and a half million, there were some years during the reign of King John III (1521–57) when an estimated eight thousand persons went overseas.[1] This was an exceptional number, but on the average about two thousand left the country each year. The numbers who left for other parts of Europe were never as great, but the constant outflow of the

[1] Estimate of F. de Almeida, *História das instituições em Portugal* (Porto, 1903), p. 148.

[5]

first half of the century drained off to other places many of the nation's most accomplished and qualified persons. Only a few of the Portuguese who journeyed north of the Pyrenees had participated personally in the conquests overseas; however, they were all, even the students and curates, relatively well informed on the progress of empire. To the European intellectual community they were heralds from the south; the Jesuits were later to call their returnees from Asia "living letters." Throughout the century it was in part through such "living letters," both Jesuits and non-Jesuits, that the rest of Europe was to learn gradually, and sometimes reluctantly, about the opening of the East.

As early as 1503, shortly after the Portuguese opened their factory at Antwerp, Johann Kollauer (Collaurius) wrote to the Humanist Conrad Celtis:

We have arrived in this land [Antwerp] where no day passes on which I would not call upon you a thousand times. You would see here among many other noteworthy things, Portuguese sailors who relate astounding tales. You would wonder at the absurd statements of all the ancient writers who have asserted that things are not to be found in human nature, unless they themselves had discovered and seen them. . . . I am unable to write about all that we have seen and heard.²

Kollauer, a Latin secretary and a member of the Augsburg circle of Humanists, urged Celtis to visit Antwerp to observe for himself what the opening of the world meant; but he never did and he died in 1508 unshaken in his faith in the Ancients. For Celtis and Erasmus of Rotterdam the world of their concern ended at the Pillars of Hercules. But for other more open-minded and sensitive persons, like Thomas More and Albrecht Dürer,³ the stories that they heard and the new objects they saw in the Low Countries provided a stimulus to wonder and speculation.

From the return of Vasco da Gama in 1499 to the year 1511 when news reached Europe of the conquest of Goa (1510), letters of King Manuel announcing the successes of the Portuguese were sent from time to time to many of the rulers and prelates of southern Europe.⁴ Portuguese embassies of obedience were periodically dispatched to the papacy to proclaim the victories of the Portuguese in the East and to obtain the approval of Popes Julius II and Leo X to the claims of the Portuguese to exclusive control over the spice trade and to leadership in the crusade against Islam. In the meanwhile commercial agents of Flanders and the south German and Italian cities visited Portugal seeking to learn whatever they could about the spice traffic and India for the benefit of their employers and their cities. Their reports, and the accounts of German and Italian participants in the early voyages, were circulated in Flanders, Germany, and Italy, sometimes in manuscript and at other times in printed versions. But the presses of Portugal during the first two decades of the sixteenth century published nothing at all

---

² As quoted in L. W. Spitz, *Conrad Celtis, the German Arch-Humanist* (Cambridge, Mass., 1957), pp. 103–4.

³ On Dürer see *Asia*, II, Bk. 1, 17; on More, see below, p. 363.

⁴ For a brief review of these letters see *Asia*, I, 154–61; also see Virgínia Rau and E. Borges Nunes (eds.), *Carta de D. Manuel ao rei de Aragão . . . sobre a tomada de Goa* (Lisbon, 1968), pp. 11–12.

about the discoveries in Asia or on the conduct of the spice trade. What was known of these subjects in the rest of Europe was limited to the sketchy information contained in Portuguese official pronouncements and in the letters and reports of foreign merchants. When King Manuel died in 1521, the Portuguese control over printed information remained effective.[5]

The reign of John III (1521–57) was marked by numerous challenges to the Portuguese imperial monopoly in Asia. Magellan's ship, the "Victoria," circumnavigated the world and in the process invaded the Spice Islands. The other European states, especially France and England, began to challenge the claims of the Iberian powers to exclusive control of the overseas world. The maritime cities of western France sent corsairs to prey upon Portuguese shipping in the Atlantic and to prepare for the dispatch of voyages of their own to Brazil, the Indian Ocean, and the East Indies. The Turks, uncertain allies of France after 1535, extended their efforts to recapture the Portuguese strongholds of Diu and Goa and to regain control over the entrepôts of the Indian Ocean. And they also sought relentlessly to break the Portuguese hold upon Ormuz and the Persian Gulf.[6] Some of the native rulers in India and southeast Asia, occasionally stimulated by Islamic traders and sailors, made sporadic efforts to dislodge the Portuguese from their Asian footholds. Hard pressed both in Europe and Asia, the Portuguese under John III nonetheless continued to extend their overseas empire eastward and westward while establishing closer relations in Europe with other nations. But simultaneous moves of expansion in various directions could not be long maintained, and eventually the Portuguese were forced to neglect Africa and to pull back from Antwerp. At mid-century they began to concentrate the spice trade at Lisbon. Still, during the years from 1520 to 1550, the intellectuals of Portugal had become deeply involved as participants in and contributors to European culture.

I

PORTUGUESE STUDENTS AND DIPLOMATS ABROAD

Before beginning its overseas expansion of the fifteenth century, Portugal had only temporary and tenuous relations with the cosmopolitan culture of Europe.[7] The discoveries of the fifteenth century in the Atlantic and along the west coast of Africa brought the small Iberian nation into the mainstream of international commerce and made more regular and permanent its economic

---

[5] For further detail see *Asia*, I, 154–71.

[6] For a thorough resumé of this phase of the Portuguese-Turkish conflict see Salih Özbaran, "The Ottoman Turks and the Portuguese in the Persian Gulf, 1534–81," *Journal of Asian History*, VI (1972), 45–87.

[7] See J. S. da Silva Dias, "Portugal e a cultura europeia (séculos XVI e XVII)," *Biblos*, XXVIII (1952), 203–15; A. J. Saraiva *et al. História da cultura em Portugal* (Lisbon, 1955), II, 528–34.

ties with the marts of Italy, France, Germany, and the Low Countries. Portuguese diplomats and intellectuals, some of whom were also merchants, soon began to broaden their horizons by cultivating friendships with the Humanists, academicians, and artists who lived in or were visitors to the great commercial centers of Italy and northern Europe. Portuguese students in substantial numbers began to attend the universities of Italy around 1470, others appeared at Paris around 1500, and a few began to attend Louvain after 1522.[8] Over the first half of the sixteenth century, the Portuguese expansion into Europe was almost as vital for the future of the nation as were its contemporary conquests in America, Africa, and Asia.

The ties between Italy and Portugal were tightened and extended as a direct result of the overseas discoveries. The Portuguese kings were most eager to possess and retain the cooperation of the papacy, for it was on the basis of the line of demarcation drawn by Pope Alexander VI that the non-European world was given over exclusively to the Iberian powers. Prelates, diplomats, and learned nobles, as well as numerous lavish gifts, were sent to Rome with the Portuguese missions of obedience of 1501, 1514, 1560, and 1574.[9] Diogo Pacheco, an eminent Portuguese jurist, gave the formal orations for his country in 1505 and 1514, on two of the most important occasions when the Portuguese announced to the papacy their progress in Asia. In 1514 several of the Portuguese visitors were even invited to attend the May 5 session of the Fifth Council of the Lateran.

The Portuguese crown also tried to maintain permanent emissaries in Rome to keep their relations with the papacy on an even keel. Two humanistically trained clerics, Miguel da Silva (*ca.* 1480–1540) and Martinho de Portugal (d. 1547), served their king at Rome, respectively from 1514 to 1525 and from 1525 to 1535. Both men were in close touch with Italian clerics and laymen of high station, and in 1539 Martinho was elevated to.the titular post of Primate of India.[10] In their relationship with the papacy the Portuguese continued to stress, as they had from the beginning, the religious aspects of their enterprise in Asia: their dedication to the crusade against the Turk and their great contribution to the spread of Christianity.[11] The Portuguese also urged the pope to respect their treaty rights, to require other Christian princes to observe the demarcation arrangements, and to promote concord among the Christian princes in order to unite them against the enemies of the faith.

[8] Students were first sent abroad on royal scholarships in 1192, mostly to southern France. For a few glimpses of what Italian humanistic education meant to Portuguese students of the early fifteenth century see Antonio Domingues de Sousa Costa, "Estudantes portugueses na reitoria do Colégio de S. Clemente de Bolonha na primeira metade do século XV," *Arquivos de história da cultura portuguesa*, Vol. III, No. 1 (Lisbon, 1969).

[9] For a study of these missions and their accomplishments see Alberto Navarro, "*Orações obediencias*" . . .; *algumas achegas para o estudo das relações entre Portugal e a Santa Sé* (Lisbon, 1965).

[10] J. S. da Silva Dias, *A política cultural da época de D. João III* (2 vols.; Coimbra, 1969), I, 76–79, 106–11, 124.

[11] For example, see the letter (August 15, 1533) of King John to Pope Clement VII and the subsequent letter (July 20, 1536) to Pope Paul III as analyzed in F. Miranda da Costa Lobo, *A acção diplomática dos portugueses . . . destinada à realizáção de descobertas e conquistas* (Lisbon, 1937), pp. 193, 198–200.

Between 1470 and 1530 more than thirty Portuguese students traveled and studied in Italy.[12] Aires Barbosa (d. 1530), a native of Aveiro, worked at Florence with Angelo Poliziano and returned to Iberia in 1529 to teach Greek at Salamanca, to collaborate with Antonio de Nebrija, the grammarian, and to supervise the education of the children of the royal family of Portugal.[13] Hermico Caiado (d. 1509) studied first at Florence with Poliziano, then at Bologna (1495–97) and at Ferrara (1497–1501). While in Ferrara, he was associated with the literary circle of Ercole I d'Este, the duke who sponsored geographical studies and patronized Boiardo and Ariosto.[14] Among the Italians Caiado had the reputation of being one of the most gifted Latin poets of the day.[15] Sá de Miranda (1481–1558), the Portuguese poet who deprecated the materialism and greed associated with the discoveries, traveled in 1521–26 from one Italian cultural center to the other. Another of the Portuguese literati, Luís Teixeira, also in Italy during these years, later corresponded with Pietro Bembo, Tito and Ercole Strozzi, and Filipo Beroaldo.[16] Jerónimo Osório, historian of the reign of King Manuel, studied at Salamanca and Paris before entering the Spanish college of Bologna around 1527, where he became acquainted with Bembo and other celebrated Italians.[17] He was followed by André de Resende and Damião de Góis, the latter of whom spent the years 1534–38 in Italy.[18] Many physicians left Portugal in this period to study and teach in the Italian universities; among the most celebrated was Amato Lusitano, who, like many of his medical colleagues, was suspected in Portugal of being either Jewish or an unreliable New Christian.[19]

After the sack of Rome in 1527, the Portuguese were quick to return to the Eternal City. Pedro de Mascarenhas, the Portuguese ambassador to the itinerant court of Charles V, was frequently in Rome, and in 1539 he urged Pope Paul III in a public address to send missionaries to the waiting harvest in India.[20] At this same time the Portuguese architect Francisco d'Ollanda was in Rome sketching antiquities and conversing with Michelangelo.[21] A new round of relations with the papacy began in 1560 when Lourenço Pires de Tavora, the Portuguese ambassador, was presented to Pope Pius IV. On that occasion the address of obedience for the Portuguese was given by Aquilas Estaço (1524–81), the

---

[12] Silva Dias, *op. cit.* (n. 10), I, 195–98.

[13] See T. Braga, *História da litteratura portugueza* (Porto, 1914), II, 576–77.

[14] See below, pp. 504–5.

[15] See G. Bertoni, "Umanisti portoghesi a Ferrara (Hermico e Didaco)," *Giornale storico della letteratura italiana*, CXIV (1939), 49–50; and M. Bataillon, *Études sur le Portugal au temps de l'humanisme* (Coimbra, 1952), pp. 1–8.

[16] Silva Dias, *op. cit.* (n. 10), I, 198.

[17] See A. F. G. Bell, "The Humanist Jeronymo de Osorio," *Revue hispanique*, LXXIII (1928), 525–26.

[18] See below, pp. 20–21.

[19] See P. Piccinini, "Rapporti fra Italia e Portogallo nel campo delle scienze mediche," in Reale Accademia d'Italia, *Relazioni storiche fra l'Italia e il Portogallo, Memorie e documenti* (Rome, 1940), pp. 394–97; for a discussion of the Iberian attitude toward physicians see Ruth Pike, *Aristocrats and Traders: Sevillian Society in the Sixteenth Century* (Ithaca, N.Y., 1972), pp. 87–89.

[20] His pleas may have contributed to the pope's decision to send the Jesuits to Portugal and India. See P. Tacchi-Venturi, "I portoghesi e Paolo III per la diffusione della civiltà cristiana nelle Indie e nell' Estremo Oriente," Reale Accademia d'Italia, *op. cit.* (n. 19), p. 361.

[21] For details see *Asia*, II, Bk. 1, 69–70.

Latinist known as "Statius." Estaço had been taken to the East as a child and had then returned to Europe for education at Évora, Paris, and Louvain. He went to Rome in 1557 to act as librarian to Cardinal Sforza and frequently performed as an unofficial representative of the Portuguese crown.[22] A number of his Latin poems, as well as his orations of 1560 and 1574,[23] celebrated the Portuguese victories in Asia. Estaço remained in Rome until his death in 1581; he bequeathed his personal library to the Congregation of the Oratory.[24] Bartolomeu dos Martires (1514–90), the Archbishop of Braga, was entertained at dinner in 1562 at the Vatican; on this occasion he had the temerity to suggest to the Holy Father that the massive silver service should be replaced by porcelain.[25] Osório, the Portuguese historian, left his diocese secretly to escape the wrath of the court and traveled during 1576–77 in Italy.[26] From these examples it can readily be discerned that Portuguese of consequence were in almost constant touch with the Holy See, the universities, and the Humanists of Italy from the beginning of the sixteenth century to the union of the Portuguese crown with that of Castile in 1580. And it was through these Portuguese prelates, emissaries, students, scientists, and artists that the intellectual world of Italy received news of the Portuguese conquests in Asia.

The cultural and diplomatic relations between Portugal and France were particularly close during the first half of the sixteenth century. King Francis I (reigned 1515–47) of France watched carefully the progress of the Portuguese in the East and their growing control over the spice market at Antwerp.[27] The French merchant princes of the Atlantic ports took more than a passing interest in the expansion of Portuguese maritime activity as they began to lay plans for their own overseas voyages of discovery and trade. The Portuguese themselves were anxious to develop closer economic and cultural ties with France as the great nation and market which lay between the ports of Lisbon and Antwerp. Nor was such an association without historical precedent, for the French, especially the Burgundians, had played a vital role in establishing the independence of the Portuguese monarchy and in providing models, especially "the Provençal taste," for early Portuguese literary development.

Only a few Portuguese students attended the University of Paris before 1500.[28] Vasco de Lucena, who translated Quintus Curtius into French, matriculated

---

[22] For his career see J. Gomes Branco, "Un umanista portoghese in Italia: Achiles Estaço," in Reale Accademia d'Italia, *op. cit.* (n. 19), pp. 135–43.

[23] Published as *Statii Lusitani Oratio oboedientialis ad Gregorium. XIII. Pont. Max. Sebastiani. I. regis. Lusitaniae. nomine. habita, eiusdem monomachia. navis. Lusitaniae versil. descripta* (Rome, 1574). The *Oratio* is bound with the *Monomachia* in the edition in the Newberry Library. The latter describes a battle at sea between a Portuguese *nau* and the armada of Acheh in Sumatra.

[24] See Elena Pinto, "La biblioteca Vallicelliana in Roma," in *Miscellanea della R. Società Romana di Storia Patria*, No. 8 (Rome, 1932), p. 15.

[25] See *Asia*, II, Bk. 1, 412.

[20] For details see L. Bourdon, "Le voyage de Jeronimo Osorio . . . en Italie (1576–77)," *Annales . . . de Toulouse*, I (1951), 71–83.

[27] For details on Francis' personal interest in curiosities from the East see *Asia*, II, Bk. 1, 31.

[28] See L. Matos, *Les portugais à l'université de Paris entre 1500 et 1550* (Coimbra, 1950), pp. 2–7.

there along with his brother in 1454–55.[29] But it was not until 1499 that Portuguese students were granted scholarships to the Collège de Montaigu in Paris on stipends arranged by King Manuel. In 1498 the king protested officially to France the capture and sale of a Portuguese vessel by French corsairs. To appease and repay the king the French consented to provide two scholarships for worthy Portuguese students. One of the first to take advantage of this opportunity was Diogo de Gouveia the Elder (*ca.* 1471–1557), who was to become a leader among the academic luminaries and educators of Paris.

A long-time resident of Paris, Gouveia became principal in 1520 of the Collège de Sainte-Barbe, an institution founded in 1460 by Geoffroi Lenorment[30] which attracted many foreign students, especially from Iberia. By 1526 Gouveia had convinced King John III to establish a foundation at Sainte-Barbe for the training of Portuguese students. No fixed number of scholarships was set, but about one hundred fellows (*boursiers*) were actually enrolled between 1527 and 1539. Over the entire period from 1500 to 1550 a total of about three hundred Portuguese students matriculated at Paris colleges, mostly at Sainte-Barbe. In addition to those supported by the crown, students were sent to Paris by the religious orders of Portugal, especially the Dominicans and Franciscans. Between 1527 and 1547 the Portuguese had become the largest "nation" among the foreign groups studying at the University of Paris.[31] And, it should be remarked, all of this occurred at a time when France and Portugal were politically at odds over the question of freedom of maritime navigation.

Almost all the students sent to Paris at the king's expense were sons of the petty nobility, a class that had suffered severely as a result of the abrupt economic shift from agriculture to commerce. The Gouveia family itself, which had branches in Évora, Beja, and Coimbra, supplied one dozen of those who pursued their advanced academic work at Paris.[32] A number of the Gouveias, beginning with Diogo the Elder, also served the Portuguese crown by watching for the departures of French fleets, and by acting to obtain compensation for the Portuguese prizes taken by French corsairs.[33] Other Portuguese students performed similar intelligence activities for their king.

António de Gouveia (1510–66), the celebrated Humanist, studied at Sainte-Barbe from 1527 to 1534.[34] He had among his classmates in the college such later notables as Diogo de Teive (Tevius), Jean Fernel, João da Costa, Simão Rodrigues, Pierre Lefevre, Ignatius Loyola, Guillaume Postel, and Francis Xavier.

---

[29] See below, p. 97.

[30] See J. Quicherat, *Histoire de Sainte-Barbe* (3 vols.; Paris, 1860–64), I, 9.

[31] Matos, *op. cit.* (n. 28), pp. 1, 9–10. According to the Venetian ambassador, Marino Cavelli, Paris had a total of 16,000 to 20,000 students in 1546. See A. A. Babeau, *Les voyageurs en France depuis la Renaissance jusqu'à la Révolution* (Paris, 1938), p. 8, n. 3. In all probability, then as now, many of these "students" were not enrolled in academic institutions.

[32] Quicherat, *op. cit.* (n. 30), I, 122–23.

[33] Matos, *op. cit.* (n. 28), p. 31.

[34] He is most renowned for his defense in 1541 of the logic of Aristotle against the attacks of Pierre de la Ramée. For his career see J. Veríssimo Serrão, *António de Gouveia e o seu tempo (1510–66)* (Coimbra, 1966).

Four from this group of students—Loyola, Rodrigues, Xavier, and Lefevre—joined by three Spaniards in 1534, made up the famous seven who took the "oath of Montmartre" to found the Society of Jesus. Their principal, Diogo the Elder, encouraged the Jesuits to follow their aspirations and urged King John III, a patron of Sainte-Barbe, to let them be sent to Asia as missionaries.[35] For, as the king was always ready to acknowledge, one of the main reasons for training the Portuguese students at Paris was to prepare them to be missionaries and teachers in the overseas empire.

In 1534 André de Gouveia, António's brother, was requested by the city of Bordeaux to leave Sainte-Barbe and to assume the post of principal in the Collège de Guyenne. He was authorized to rebuild what was acknowledged to be a run-down institution and was granted a blank check by the municipal authorities to hire a faculty. Here he introduced the organizational and educational practices of Sainte-Barbe and brought together a faculty that during his tenure from 1534 to 1547 included the following distinguished teachers and scholars: Mathurin Cordier, Élie Vinet, Nicolas de Grouchy, João da Costa, George Buchanan, Diogo de Teive, António Gouveia, Jacques de Thou, and Guillaume de Guérente.[36] The primary subjects taught at Guyenne were grammar, classical literature, history, and philosophy. Young students flocked to the revitalized college, the most notable being Etienne La Boétie, the writer on Stoic philosophy, J. J. Scaliger, the philologist, and Michel de Montaigne, the moralist. In his *Essays* Montaigne later wrote: "André de Gouveia, our principal, . . . was beyond comparison the greatest principal in France."[37]

While the Portuguese went to Paris to study theology and the humanities, they generally matriculated at the University of Toulouse for the study of law.[38] Between 1537 and 1541 numerous Spanish and Portuguese students attended Toulouse. In the documents of the time they are indiscriminately referred to as "Hispani," possibly because many of them had earlier studied at Salamanca or simply because the registrar recognized no national difference between the foreigners from the south. Nonetheless it is clear that a number of talented Portuguese studied at Toulouse, including Diogo de Teive, Diogo Mendes de Vasconcelos, and António de Gouveia. The last received his doctorate of law in 1549 and went on to teach at the University of Cahors. Toulouse began a rapid decline in 1566, as a result of the religious wars in southern France. The only Portuguese who remained at Toulouse thereafter were New Christians (*Maranos*), Jews, and others who were dissatisfied with events taking place in their homeland.[39] A number of Portuguese joined the medical faculty of

---

[35] For Gouveia's letter of February, 1538, to King John stating that the dispatch of the men to India, "would be an invaluable asset," see M. Bataillon, *op. cit.* (n. 15), pp. 131–34. Loyola possibly first heard about India from Gouveia when both were in Italy a decade earlier. See Pedro de Rivadeneira, "Vida del padre Ignacio de Loyola," in *Obras escogidas* (Madrid, 1868), pp. 54–58.

[36] See Matos, *op. cit.* (n. 28), p. 63; and Quicherat, *op. cit.* (n. 30), I, 228–38.

[37] *Essais,* I. I, ch. xxv.

[38] See J. Veríssimo Serrão, *Les portugais à l'université de Toulouse (XIII–XVII siècles)* (Paris, 1970), pp. 53–67.

[39] *Ibid.,* pp. 99–112.

Toulouse and became some of the period's most distinguished physicians of southern France.[40] After the union of the Spanish and Portuguese crowns in 1580, Toulouse and other cities in France played host to political refugees from Portugal and the administration of Philip II. So many Portuguese advocates of "Sebastianismo" fled to France that Estevão de Sampaio (1540–1603) published at Paris in 1586 a *Thesaurus* of the refugees.[41]

As unusual as it was at this time to maintain permanent ambassadors in other countries,[42] the Portuguese kept resident emissaries at the court of France almost continuously from 1521 to 1557. In the same period, the era of John III, they sent at least eight extraordinary emissaries to France to conduct negotiations on special problems.[43] The French had a single resident at Lisbon from 1518 to 1559, Honoré de Caix, and they sent extraordinary emissaries to the Portuguese capital on at least six occasions during his tenure there. The diplomats of the uninvolved powers, such as the papal nuncios, reported on the growing tensions between the representatives of Portugal and France.[44] The main problems stemmed from efforts of the French to challenge the Portuguese monopoly of overseas trade, to prey on the ships plying between Lisbon and Antwerp, and to send voyages of their own to the East Indies and Brazil.[45] One result of the Franco-Portuguese negotiations was the Treaty of Lyons (1536), which sought to regulate maritime relations between the two states and to submit outstanding issues to mediation by a bilateral commission.[46] But matters could not be successfully resolved by diplomacy alone. It was the closing of the Portuguese factory at Antwerp in 1549, followed by the outbreak in 1560 of religious warfare in France, that brought this conflict to a halt. Paris, however, continued to be important to the Portuguese, particularly after the decline of Antwerp, as the center of the Portuguese courier system. Portuguese envoys and agents also continued the practice adopted earlier of reporting to Lisbon on economic and social conditions in France.[47]

Aside from the Portuguese students, diplomats, and refugees who went to

[40] *Ibid.*, pp. 132–53.

[41] *Ibid.*, p. 112.

[42] "What institutionally differentiates 'medieval' diplomacy from 'modern' is the employment of the resident ambassador." On this question see Charles Carter, *The Western European Powers, 1500–1700* (Ithaca, N.Y., 1971), pp. 23–24.

[43] For details see J. Veríssimo Serrão, *A embaixada em França de Brás de Alvide (1548–1554)* (Paris, 1969), p. 15. João da Silveira, a diplomat who had earlier served in India, was sent to the French court in 1510 and again in 1522. He was one of the few diplomats active in northern Europe who knew the East by personal experience. See M. E. Gomes de Carvalho, *D. João III e os Francezes* (Lisbon, 1909), pp. 7–8.

[44] For example, see the letter of Cardinal Rodolfo Pio di Carpi of February 27, 1536, as published in J. Lestocquoy (ed.), *Correspondance des nonces en France, Carpi et Ferrerio, 1535–1540* ... (Rome, 1961), pp. 140–41.

[45] On these issues see *Asia*, I, 125, 177–78. Also consult Michel Mollat, "Passages français dans l'Océan Indien au temps de François Ier," *Studia* XI (1963), pp. 239–50.

[46] See Veríssimo Serrão, *A embaixada*, p. 19.

[47] See M. Mollat, "Quelques aspects de la vie économique et sociale de la France dans la première moitié du XVIe siècle vus à travers la correspondance des diplomates portugais," *Bulletin des études portugaises et de l'Institut français au Portugal*, XII (1948), 224–53.

France, others left Portugal for more personal reasons. Some went to enjoy the cosmopolitan life of Paris, while others sought more remunerative or congenial employment. Many Jewish or New Christian physicians left the Iberian states for the more tolerant atmosphere of France. Diogo de Sá, who had been a soldier in the Indies around 1530, went to Paris after his return to Europe. In 1549 he published there a critique of the *De navigatione liber* of Pedro Nunes, the great Portuguese cosmographer and nautical theorist.[48] Lúis Nunes de Santarem was also in Paris around mid-century where he served as physician to the queen of France. Among the clerics who visited the city on the Seine there was Teotónio de Bragança (1530–1602), later the Archbishop of Évora and a great friend of the Jesuit missions.[49] A number of Portuguese navigators and sailors who felt underpaid or unappreciated at home took service with the French.[50] A Portuguese pilot and interpreter apparently sailed in 1529 from Dieppe to Sumatra with Jean and Raoul Parmentier. Around 1538 Francis I employed João Pacheco, a Portuguese expert in maritime matters. Cosmographers and cartographers also became expatriates. André Homem, the cartographer, accepted employment in 1565 as cosmographer to King Charles IX. Shortly thereafter he left for England, and his brothers, who had been in France with him, thereupon returned to Portugal. Bartolomeu Velho, an excellent cartographer, offered his services to the French king "to show you those parts of the unknown lands which are of great importance and consequence."[51] But he was not to make good on this offer, for he died at Nantes less than one year after his arrival in France.[52]

The advent of the Portuguese in France was paralleled by their appearance at Antwerp as purveyors of spices. From 1503 to the closing of their factory in 1549 the Portuguese were leading participants in its bustling commercial life.[53] The Portuguese factors and their associates were usually very young men of good families in search of quick fortune. But many of them soon became involved in the workaday affairs of the port, married into Flemish or Dutch merchant families, and settled down to become comfortable burghers of Antwerp. As part of their adaptation to the new environment, the Portuguese burghers dissociated themselves gradually from the Portuguese "nation" and became a part of the social, cultural, and intellectual life of the Low Countries.[54] They still sometimes acted as hosts to the numerous Portuguese who passed through Ant-

[48] See Matos, *op. cit.* (n. 28), p. 103. Also see below p. 419.

[49] See *ibid.*, pp. 103–4.

[50] L. Matos, *Les portugais en France au XVIᵉ siècle* (Coimbra, 1952), pp. 13–14, 18. Also see *Asia*, I, 676, 692, 701, and L. Bourdon, "Deux aventuriers portugais, Gaspar Caldeira et Antão Luis (1564–1568)," *Bulletin des études portugaises et de l'Institut français au Portugal*, XVIII (1954), 5–33.

[51] As quoted in Armando Cortesão and A. Teixeira da Mota, *Portugaliae monumenta cartographica* (5 vols.; Lisbon, 1960–62), II, 239.

[52] For details on his activities at Nantes see J. Mathorez, "Notes sur l'histoire de la colonie portugaise de Nantes," *Bulletin hispanique*, XV (1913), 318–19.

[53] On the conduct of trade at Antwerp see *Asia*, I, 121–24.

[54] See J. A. Goris, *Études sur les colonies marchandes méridionales (Portugais, Espagnols, Italiens) à Anvers de 1488 à 1567* (Louvain, 1925), pp. 27–32.

werp on their way to other places and introduced their guests to members of
the highly active Italian merchant community resident in Antwerp. They also
entertained and feted the leading intellectuals and artists of the time, such as
Erasmus and Dürer, and helped to inform them about the Portuguese activities
in the East. The Portuguese also became involved in the religious strife that
swept the Netherlands. The New Christians and Jews, unpopular in Portugal
and distrusted by the orthodox Catholics of Antwerp, were among the first to
applaud the ideas of Luther and to suffer from the Catholic reaction to the
spread of Protestant heresy.[55]

The participation of Portugal, indirect as it was, in the affairs of nothern
Europe was to leave deep and permanent imprints upon its own intellectual and
religious life. Among those who were later to become involved in educational
reform at Coimbra, there were a number who had received their training at
Louvain, the leading university in the Netherlands and one of the first European
institutions to establish a trilingual (Latin, Greek, and Hebrew) college.[56] More
than forty Portuguese matriculated at Louvain between 1522 and 1556.[57]
Included in their numbers were two of the most influential Portuguese intellectuals of the sixteenth century: André de Resende (1498–1573) and Damião de Góis
(1502–74). Resende, who had previously studied at Alcalá, Salamanca, and
Paris, matriculated at Louvain in 1532.[58] While in the Low Countries, Resende
enjoyed the protection of Pedro de Mascarenhas, the Portuguese ambassador to
the court of Emperor Charles V, then resident at Brussels. A number of eminent
Portuguese friars also studied at Louvain, including Brás de Barros (or Braga)
who later organized language studies in Portugal and eventually became Bishop
of Leiria. Through these individuals and those Netherlanders who went to
Portugal, a number of firm intellectual ties were established between Portugal
and the Low Countries that were to be of lasting significance.[59]

2

DAMIÃO DE GÓIS, PUBLICIST OF EMPIRE

It is in the story of the peregrinations and activities of Damião de Góis (1502–74)
that it is possible to perceive most clearly how the Portuguese became associated
with and influential in the intellectual community of Europe.[60] At the age of

[55] *Ibid.*, pp. 549–63.

[56] For its growth and influence see Henry de Vocht, *History of the Foundation and Rise of the Collegium Trilingue Lovaniense, 1517–1550* (4 vols.; Louvain, 1951–55).

[57] Silva Dias, *op. cit.* (n. 10), I, 350, n. 5.

[58] On Resende's career at Louvain see Vocht, *op. cit.* (n. 56), II, 399–402.

[59] See below, pp. 355, 357.

[60] The fullest and most analytical biographies are: M. Lemos, "Damião de Goes," *Revista de história*, IX (1920), 5–19, 208–26; X (1921), 41–66; XI (1922), 34–66; A. F. Bell, *Un humanista Português: Damião de Góis*, trans. from English by A. A. Doria (Lisbon, 1942); Elizabeth F. Hirsch, *Damião de Gois: The Life and Thought of a Portuguese Humanist, 1502–1574* (The Hague, 1967).

nine Góis became a page at the court of King Manuel. He served the king at a time when the court was agog over the capture of Goa and Malacca, and about the progress of the Portuguese in Ethiopia and Brazil. In 1513 he saw the Brazilian Indians shoot their bows and arrows, a thrilling spectacle to a boy of twelve. He was then in the company of a Malabar youth, baptized with the name of João da Cruz, who spent five years (1512–18) at Lisbon learning the Portuguese language.[61] Cruz, who was "not too dark" in Góis' estimation, returned to India before the Portuguese lad left the king's service. In later years, Góis also recalled, though he dated it incorrectly, the famous combat held in Lisbon on June 3, 1515, between the Indian elephant and rhinoceros.[62] If we assume that the Malabar youth was also present at this spectacle, it makes one wonder whether he was as entranced by the peculiar customs of the Portuguese in producing the combat as by the outcome itself.

Shortly after King Manuel's death in 1521, Góis evidently left the court. In 1523 he was sent to Antwerp to act as notary (*escrivão*) to the Portuguese factory there. Among his associates at the factory were João Brandão, the royal factor who had been at Antwerp since 1509 and who was widely acquainted in the commercial and intellectual circles of Flanders and in its German and Italian communities.[63] During Brandão's period as factor, Albrecht Dürer visited Antwerp and became acquainted with the Portuguese community. Góis was also friendly with Rui Fernandes de Almada, whose portrait was sketched by Dürer.[64] Almada was to become factor himself in 1529, and was later to represent the Portuguese crown at the court of France. Through these men of distinction Góis learned to know Archduchess Margaret of Austria, the ruler of Flanders from 1524 to 1530 and a collector of Chinese porcelain.[65] In these years Góis was befriended by Cornelius Grapheus (1482–1558), the poet, Humanist, and admirer of Luther. The young Portuguese employed Grapheus to teach him Latin, a language in which Góis never became proficient even though he later wrote several books in it.[66] Góis sought out sailors and navigators

---

[61] Lemos, *loc. cit.* (n. 60), IX (1920), 11–13. According to Lemos (p. 13), João da Cruz returned to Goa in 1518 with the fleet of Diogo Lopes de Sequeira. Georg Schurhammer, the famous Jesuit historian, in his study of the letters of João da Cruz (in *Varia, Anhänge* I [Lisbon, 1965], pp. 57–59) contends that João da Cruz was a *Chetty* rather than a *Nāyar*, and that he spent but three years (1513–16) at the court of Lisbon. Also see V. B. Nair, "A Nair Envoy to Portugal," *Indian Antiquary*, LVII (1928), 157–59.

[62] See *Asia*, II, Bk. 1, 161–62.

[63] Brandão, like the other factors, acted as both commercial agent and diplomat. From 1509 to 1514 and from 1520 to 1525 he was officially the factor at Antwerp. In 1517, he was secretary to a Portuguese embassy sent to the court of Emperor Charles V. See Goris, *op. cit.* (n. 54), p. 215.

[64] See for details *Asia*, II, Bk. 1, 17. Dürer, in all probability, was not the engraver of the Góis portrait sometimes attributed to him (see *ibid.*, I, following p. 164). Certainly, Góis arrived in Antwerp only after Dürer had left and there is no evidence that the two men ever met elsewhere before Dürer's death in 1528. Some recent scholars attribute the Góis portrait to Phillipe de Galle. See Mario de Sampio Ribeiro, *O retrato de Damião de Góis por Alberto Dürer; processo e história de uma atoarda* (Coimbra, 1943), p. 100; others attribute it to Quentin Massys. See Hirsch, *op. cit.* (n. 60), pp. 25–26n. None of the attributions so far advanced is completely convincing.

[65] For details see *Asia*, II, Bk. 1, 19.

[66] Hirsch, *op. cit.* (n. 60), pp. 23–24.

who had served in the Portuguese East. One of these was Rutgeste Geldres of Antwerp, who had seen action as a gunner at Goa, Kilwa, Cannanore, Mombasa, Diu, and Dabul.[67] Through his intercourse with people of various stations in life Góis acted as an intermediary between the commercial and learned worlds, between the merchants interested in material gain from the discoveries and the Humanists and artists who were most concerned about the consequences of expansion for Europe's own culture and well-being.

In 1528, after six years in Antwerp and its environs, Góis was sent on a special mission to England. While little is known of the details of this visit, Góis was certainly befriended by John Walop, the collaborator of Thomas Cromwell and a former soldier in the Portuguese service.[68] It is possible that Góis met Thomas More, a supposition made more likely by More's acknowledged interest in the Portuguese discoveries, by the fact that More's son later translated one of Góis' Latin pamphlets into English, and by Góis' grief on hearing of the execution of More in 1535.[69]

Góis was sent by his king to Poland in 1529 to try to arrange a marriage between Sigismund's daughter and John's brother, the object being an economic alliance with a leading supplier of the timber, ship's stores, and grain needed in Portugal. Though Góis started out confident of success, his mission proved fruitless. In the course of it, however, he renewed old acquaintances and widened his own circle of interest and influence. John Tarnowski, a Polish diplomat who had earlier been in Lisbon, received Góis at Cracow. A hero of the wars against the Tartars, Tarnowski in 1529 was an advocate of conciliation of the Protestants and of church reunion.[70] Góis was also received by Christopher Szydlowiecki, the king's chancellor, with whom he evidently held conversations about the projected marriage alliance.[71] Before the end of 1529, Góis was back in Antwerp.

Two years later (1531) Góis was sent to Poland again to work out the marriage alliance. Many more details are available about this trip and Góis' relations with other persons. His first stop was at Copenhagen where he negotiated with King Frederick of Denmark, presumably about the Portuguese Baltic trade. The Protestant king sent Góis to Schleswig to converse with one of his councillors, a vitriolic enemy of Catholicism and an ardent follower of the reformers. At Lübeck Góis met with Johann Bugenhagen, a leader of the Reformation in that city. From the Hanseatic city Góis proceeded to Wittenberg where he dined and held extended debate on religious issues with Luther and Melanchthon.[72] These conversations, though there is no evidence to substantiate it, might well have included discussion of the spice trade, for Luther had earlier

---

[67] Lemos, *loc. cit.* (n. 60), p. 213.
[68] Luis de Matos, "L'Humanisme portugais et ses relations avec l'Europe," *Bulletin des études portugaises et de l'Institut français au Portugal*, XXVI (1965), 63.
[69] Hirsch, *op. cit.* (n. 60), pp. 18–19. Also see below, p. 368.
[70] Hirsch, *op. cit.* (n. 60), p. 62.
[71] Lemos, *loc. cit.* (n. 60), p. 215.
[72] Hirsch, *op. cit.* (n. 60), pp. 31–35.

attacked its monopolists.[73] At Danzig Góis met John Magnus (1488–1544), the exiled archbishop of Upsala, who encouraged the young Portuguese to continue his humanistic studies and to prepare a book Góis had in mind which would advocate that the Ethiopian church be accepted as a member of the Western Christian community.[74] Here he also met with the leading merchants of the city.[75] At Marienwerder in East Prussia he met Paul Speratus, the Protestant bishop of Pomerania, and about the same time he somehow became acquainted with Tiedemann Giese (1450–1549) of Danzig, the Catholic canon of Frauenburg and an intimate of Copernicus. From East Prussia he went on to Posen and eventually to Russia where he evidently hoped to explore trading possibilities. Following his official visit, Góis, possibly inspired by his friend Tarnowski, may have undertaken an arduous and bold journey to the Don River to visit the Tartar tribes of that region.[76] About his return voyage to Antwerp nothing is known except that he was back in Flanders in December, 1531, in time to attend, along with the entire Portuguese community and their guests, a performance given in Brussels of one of Gil Vicente's plays.[77]

Góis' career as a diplomat ended with his unsuccessful missions to Poland. A growing fortune from commerce enabled him to devote time to study and writing. Long aware of his lack of formal academic training, he started in 1532 to study at Louvain. He also began to write with the aid of Grapheus his Latin account of the legation to Portugal in 1513 of Matthew, the envoy who brought letters from Ethiopia to King Manuel and the pope. Góis' *Legatio Magni Indorum Imperatoris Presbyteri Joannis ad Emanuelem Lusitaniae Regem in 1513* (Antwerp, 1532), a first literary effort, was designed to awaken the interest of the European learned community to the importance of non-European Christians. Dedicated to John Magnus, the *Legatio* helped to create an interest among Catholics and Protestants alike in the plight of overseas Christians and in the crusading activities of the Portuguese. Indicative of the general curiosity of Europe about

[73] See *Asia*, I, 122.

[74] See below, p. 19. Góis also met John's brother, Olaus Magnus (1490–1557), on this occasion. See A. E. Beau, *As relações germânicas do humanismo de Damião de Góis* (Coimbra, 1941), p. 80. The Magnus brothers brought to Góis' attention the plight of the Laplanders who resisted conversion to the Christianity of their Swedish overlords.

[75] For his later relations with the merchants see A. H. D. Oliveira Marques, "Damião de Góis e os mercadores de Danzig," *Arquivo de bibliografia portuguesa*, IV (1958), 133–63.

[76] So much is known about his trip to Poland because of his conversations with the reformers. Góis was put on trial for heresy by the Portuguese Inquisition in 1571, and it is mainly from this testimony that his itinerary in the Protestant countries has been reconstructed. For the record of the trial see Vol. II of W. J. C. Henry (ed.), *Inéditos Goesianos* (2 vols.; Lisbon, 1896–99). For his visit to the Tartars, we have only his own testimony in the *Chronicle of Manuel* and the poems of André de Resende and Grapheus who were certainly told by Góis himself that he had visited the Tartars. That such a trip was not impossible is evident from the fact that Paracelsus seems to have earlier visited the Tartars (see below, p. 423) and that Sigismund von Herberstein undertook such a trip in 1526. Hirsch, *op. cit.* (n. 60), pp. 21–22, is too inclined to accept without question the veracity of these unsubstantiated sources.

[77] The *Jubileu de amores*, performed in Portugal since 1525, was played at Brussels in the residence of the Portuguese ambassador to celebrate the birth of Prince Manuel. See A. Forjaz de Sampaio, *História de literatura portuguesa* (3 vols.; Paris and Lisbon, n.d.), II, 77. Also see below, p. 123.

the overseas world is the fact that Góis' little book was quickly translated in 1533 into Italian, English, and German.[78] As testimony to the persistence of interest in his subject is the Dutch translation which appeared at Dordrecht in 1616.[79] A number of Góis' contemporaries so highly regarded the young traveler and author that they dedicated certain of their works to him.[80]

At Louvain Góis slipped into the place that was vacated by André de Resende, the Portuguese Humanist, even to the point of taking over his lodgings. For eight months Góis apparently devoted himself to study when he was not discharging his commercial responsibilities. He joined the same circle of Erasmian Humanists to which Resende had belonged and became the intimate of Conrad Goclenius (d. 1539), a close friend and collaborator with Erasmus. But Góis did not long remain the sedentary student and merchant; he complained of headaches and eyestrain until his physician advised him to take a trip. Curious to learn what the religious reformers were doing, he went to southern Germany. In Strassburg he met and dined with Martin Bucer and Caspar Hedio, and among other matters they talked about his little book on the Ethiopians.[81] Armed with a letter of introduction from Rutger Rescius, printer and professor of Greek at Louvain, Góis visited Erasmus at Freiburg in March, 1533. He presented Erasmus with a copy of the *Legatio*, and the two had a brief meal and a conversation. Though Erasmus was favorably impressed by Góis, the modest young Portuguese some two months later sent Erasmus a fine silver tankard by which "to remember him."[82] From Freiburg Góis went to Basel where he met Bonifacius Amerbach (1495–1562), a friend of Erasmus; Sigismund Gelenius (or Ghelen) (*ca.* 1498–1534), the lexicographer; Sebastian Münster (*ca.* 1488–1552), the cosmographer; Simon Grynaeus (1493–1541), the collector of travel literature; and Heinrich Glareanus (1480–1563), the Swiss geographer.[83]

But of all the people he met on this trip, Góis was most pleased to make the acquaintance of Erasmus. The great Humanist himself was pleased to meet a young Portuguese of learning who also had influence with the king of Portugal. Like many of his scholarly and artistic contemporaries, Erasmus needed a generous patron. At the urging of Erasmus Schets, a wealthy Antwerp spice merchant, Erasmus had written a flattering dedication to King John III in the

---

[78] The Italian translation appeared at Bologna. See Bell, *op. cit.* (n. 60), p. 109; the English translation by John More exists in just two examples under the title *The Legacye or Embassate of the Great Emperour of Inde Prester John, unto Emanuel Kynge of Portugal in the yere of our lorde M.V.C. XIII . . .*; for reference to a German translation see Hirsch, *op. cit.* (n. 60), p. 226.

[79] On the relationship of this book to the ideas of the Humanists of Louvain see Vocht, *op. cit.* (n. 56), III, 57–58.

[80] Beau, *op. cit.* (n. 74), p. 121.

[81] Cf. Hirsch, *op. cit.* (n. 60), pp. 66–67.

[82] See P. S. Allen, M. H. Allen, and H. W. Garrod (eds.), *Opus epistolarum Des. Erasmi Roterdami* (12 vols.; Oxford, 1906–58), X, 251–53.

[83] The encounters with Münster and Grynaeus were apparently accidental and brief. Góis testified in 1571 before the Inquisition that he "spoke with Münster at the door of a bookshop . . . and did not see him more than that one time"; and that he "held a discussion with Simon Grynaeus, who was reading philosophy at the door of an inn but he did not go to his house." See Henry (ed.), *op. cit.* (n. 76), II, 33; also see Beau, *op. cit.* (n. 74), p. 94.

preface to his *Chrysostomii lucubrationes* (1527). Here he praised the king and his father, King Manuel, for having opened the water route to the East and for having widened the influence of Christianity; but Erasmus was unable to suppress his desire to criticize the monopolists for the high price of spices. The agents of the king were evidently so outraged by such a reproof that they did not send the book to Lisbon and so Erasmus never received the stipend he hoped for. Erasmus was especially offended because the king never acknowledged his dedication; and he also knew that John had granted a generous allowance to Juan Luis Vives (1492–1540), the Spanish Humanist, who later dedicated *De disciplina* (1531) to the Portuguese ruler. Erasmus dropped the dedication to the king in the second edition (1530) of his work, presumably out of pique.[84] He evidently also spoke to Góis of his disappointment, for the young Portuguese promised on his return to Portugal in 1533 "to serve you effectively as a true friend."[85] But Góis, although he was recalled to Lisbon to act as treasurer of the Casa da India, was unable to press the case for Erasmus successfully because he declined the proffered post and quickly returned to Louvain.[86]

Back at Louvain late in 1533, Góis devoted himself fully to his studies and to the cause of Erasmus. Finally, in the spring of 1534, Erasmus invited the young Portuguese to stay with him at Freiburg, and from April 11 to August 18, 1534, Góis enjoyed the intimacy of the great Humanist in his home. Erasmus had become acquainted with Portuguese intellectuals during his stay in Italy, the poet Hermico Caiado among them. He corresponded with other Portuguese and was particularly pleased by the adulation of André de Resende. But Erasmus never relented in his disapproval of the depredations of the Portuguese in the overseas world or of the avarice of the spice monopolists and its effect in Europe.[87] Erasmus did express concern over the fate of the repressed Lapps in northern Sweden, but the extent of his geographical interest and imagination was evidently confined to Europe, Ethiopia, North Africa, the Levant, and Russia. Despite his friendship for Góis and other Portuguese, and despite his own cosmopolitanism, he expressed no desire to learn about the overseas world. He was more interested in the ethical consequences of the discoveries for Europe than he was in exotic peoples and ideas. An examination of his published works and of the more than three thousand letters preserved of his correspondence yields not a single substantive query or reference relating to the lands and peoples east of Persia.

Góis left Freiburg and Erasmus to continue his education in Italy for four years. On his way to the fount of Renaissance learning, Góis stopped at Geneva for a short meeting with Guillaume Farel, the reformer. In November, 1534, Góis arrived at Padua with a letter of introduction from Erasmus to Pietro Bembo

[84] See M. Bataillon, *op. cit.* (n. 15), pp. 52–54, 60–79.

[85] Letter of June, 1533, No. 2826, in Allen *et al.*, *op. cit.* (n. 82), Vol. X.

[86] Góis did speak to the king about Erasmus, and John even suggested that Erasmus might be interested in a teaching post at the university that was then being planned for Coimbra. See Hirsch, *op. cit.* (n. 60), p. 70.

[87] Cf., *ibid.*, p. 72.

(1470–1547), the arbiter of letters in Italy. Góis rented an apartment in Padua that he shared with two of his acquaintances from Louvain, Splinter van Hargen and Joachim Polites. Through Bembo, the rich and learned Góis was immediately presented to the leaders of culture and education at Padua. Lazzaro Buonamico (1479–1552) befriended the young Portuguese, encouraged him, and guided his readings in classical history and thought. Góis attended public lectures in nearby Venice, and traveled widely in other parts of Italy. Under the influence of Buonamico he became a disciple of Cicero and turned his attention to the study of history.[88]

Bembo and Buonamico, unlike Erasmus, were avidly curious about contemporary affairs and their relationship to the historical process. They were particularly fascinated with the discoveries as a new act in the constantly unfolding historical drama. Bembo, according to Góis, urged the young Portuguese to become the historian of the Portuguese expansion to distant lands. Góis himself had long cherished the hope of becoming the historian of Portugal's exploits and had even begun to think about writing a history of "India." Buonamico was likewise impressed by the lasting significance of the discoveries for the history of the world and for the better understanding of the universal qualities in human nature. He wrote to Góis at a later date: "Do not believe that there exists anything more honorable to our or the preceding age than the invention of the printing press and the discovery of the new world; two things which I always thought could be compared not only to Antiquity, but to immortality."[89]

After leaving Italy permanently in 1538, Góis began to publish a number of works relating to the discoveries. On his return to Louvain he married a Flemish girl of noble, Catholic background, the sister of Splinter van Hargen. Góis again enrolled at the University of Louvain as he settled down to married life and its responsibilities. And he quickly published in Latin translation a Portuguese report of the conquest of Diu in 1538. The *Commentarii rerum gestarum in India 1538 citra Gangem* (Louvain, 1539) was dedicated to Bembo, for Góis credited the Italian with encouraging him to translate the Portuguese account of the siege into Latin.[90] In his letter of thanks from Rome in 1540, Cardinal Bembo remarked: "What can be more pleasant and delightful than to read the description of those deeds which our people have courageously performed in distant lands?"[91]

Certainly the book was "delightful" to a European Humanist, for the author

---

[88] See *ibid.*, pp. 91–93, 99–101. On Buonamico see G. Maranzoni, "Lazzaro Buonamico e lo studio Padovano nella prima metà del cinquecento," *Nuovo archivio veneto*, 3d ser. I (1901), 118–51, 301–18; II (1902), 131–96.

[89] As quoted in Hirsch, *op. cit.* (n. 60), p. 103. When Góis returned to Louvain in 1538, he sent Buonamico a globe as a memento. For further details on his career in Italy see L. de Matos, "Un umanista portoghese in Italia, Damião de Goes," *Estudos italianos em Portugal*, No. 19 (1960), pp. 48–51.

[90] For Bembo's relations with others interested in the overseas world see S. Grande, *Le relazioni geografiche G. Gastaldi* (Rome, 1906). This work was extracted and reprinted from *Memoria della Società italiana*, Vol. XII (1905).

[91] As quoted in Hirsch, *op. cit.* (n. 60), p. 102.

adulates the Portuguese as noble, virtuous, and prudent and their Turkish and Mughul enemies as adepts in trickery and ruthlessness. Following humanistic practices in writing history, impassioned speeches of exhortation are placed in the mouth of the Portuguese commander as he seeks to raise the morale of his outnumbered and discouraged forces. Any defeat of the Turk and Islam was bound to be greeted enthusiastically in a Europe where the looming menace of the infidel was a source of general anxiety. The Latin version was extravagantly praised by others of Góis' friends to whom he sent inscribed copies. It was lauded because it showed dramatically how an aggressive Christian nation could defeat the hated Turk. And Góis was also complimented by Sigismund Gelden (1497–1554), for presenting a first-hand account of events in India by a contemporary rather than falling victim to the fantasies about the East perpetrated upon an unsuspecting public by the fabricators of Antiquity. The *Commentarii* was quickly translated into Venetian (1539) and German (1540), and in 1544 the original version was reprinted with but a few stylistic revisions.⁹² Whatever else Góis' book may have done, it was responsible for making the intellectual community of Europe aware of the importance of the war in distant India to the deterrence of the Turk, and of the clear relationship of events occurring in India to the safety of Europe.

Published with the *Commentarii* was a brief tract called *De rebus et imperio Lusitanorum ad Paulum Jovium disceptatiuncula*; this was Góis' response to the criticisms of the spice monopoly by Paolo Giovio published in the *De Moschovitarum legatione* (Rome, 1525), a description of Muscovy and the lands to the east of it. Giovio, like Erasmus, attributed the rising price of spices to the Portuguese monopoly. In the English translation (1555) of Richard Eden, Giovio complained that the Portuguese

who havynge by force of arms subdued a great parte of India, and possessed all the marte townes, takynge holy [wholly] into their handes all the trade of spices to brynge the same into Spaynge [Iberia], and nevertheless to sell them at a more grevous and intollerable price to the people of Europe then ever was hard [heard] of before: and furthermore kepte the coastes of the Indian sea so straightly with continuall navies, that those trades are thereby lefte of [off], which were before exercised by the goulfe of Persia . . . and in fine owre sea [Mediterranean]: . . . since the Portugales had the trade in theyr handes with so manye incommodities of such viages whereby the spices are so corrupted by . . . filthyness of the shippes, that theyr naturall savour, taste, and qualitie, as well hereby as theyr longe reservying in the shoppes, sellers, and warehouses in Lussheburne [Lisbon], . . . they sel only the woorst and most corrupted.⁹³

In his reply Góis justified the exclusive policy of the Portuguese by reference to the huge outlays in money and men required for the exploration and main-

⁹² In the edition of his collected works published by the printer Rescius of Louvain.
⁹³ See R. Eden, *The Decades of the New World* (London, 1555), p. 278. Giovio follows this attack on the Portuguese by suggesting that better spices could be purchased more cheaply through the dukes of Muscovy.

tenance of the routes and for the protection and extension of the trade in the East and in Europe. The high cost of spices, he averred, could not be blamed upon the crown or the spice syndicate, but rather upon the gouging practices of mercenary shopkeepers and retailers. Góis, like Konrad Peutinger before him, was an outspoken defender of the merchant princes in whose circles he traveled.[94] Góis also reminded Giovio that Portugal was spreading Christianity and fighting the Turk, both efforts being of general benefit to the European community. For its overseas activities the Portuguese nation deserved the respect and cooperation of all nations, including a willingness to pay for the spices.

During his short stay at Lisbon in 1533, Góis had conversed with the Ethiopian emissary whom he called "Zagazabo."[95] The Negus of Ethiopia, Lebna Dengel, had dispatched Zagazabo to Lisbon in 1527 in the company of the Portuguese ambassador to win recognition for the Ethiopian church as a member of the Western Christian community. Although the officials of church and state in Europe ignored or dismissed the overtures of the Ethiopians, Góis became a champion of their cause. In Italy from 1534 to 1538, Góis was occupied with collecting more information on the faith of the Ethiopians. At Padua he translated from Portuguese into Latin the exposition written by Zagazabo of the principles, practices, and rituals of the Ethiopian Christians. Once he had returned to Louvain in 1538 he prepared for publication his own history of Portugal's relations with Ethiopa as an introduction to the translation, and added to it letters on the Ethiopians previously published by Paolo Giovio. When printed this work was entitled *Fides, Religio, Moresque Aethiopum sub Imperio Preciosi Joannis degentium Damiano a Goes ac Paulo Jovio interpretibus* (1540).[96] It was reprinted at Paris in 1541, and at Louvain in 1544 in the collected works of Góis. While extracts from this work later appeared in the collections of Peter Martyr and Richard Eden, it contained too many references to rituals and practices considered shocking and heretical for it to receive acceptance by the leaders of Christendom.[97] It did serve, however, to arouse more general interest in the overseas activities of the Portuguese and to underline the substantial differences which still separated Eastern from Western Christians.

Góis enhanced his reputation as a controversialist and as a spokesman for

---

[94] On the controversy over the monopoly in Germany see *Asia*, I, 122–23; also see C. Bauer, "Conrad Peutingers Gutachten zur Monopolfrage," *Archiv für Reformationsgeschichte*, XLV (1954), 1–43, 145–96. Góis visited Peutinger's library on one of his trips to Augsburg, and scanned a book on India that he saw there. This was probably the collection of materials sent to Peutinger around 1508 by Valentim Fernandes (cf. *Asia*, I, 159). Later Góis asked Johann Jakob Fugger to try to obtain the book for him, but Peutinger refused to part with it. See Hirsch, *op. cit.* (n. 60), pp. 26–27.

[95] Saga Zaab or Saga-za-Ab are probably better renditions of the name of this monk. See Lemos, *loc. cit.* (n. 60), X, 42.

[96] For a more complete discussion of the background of this work see F. M. Rogers, *The Quest for Eastern Christians* (Minneapolis, 1962), chap. vii.

[97] For further bibliographical detail see Hirsch, *op. cit.* (n. 60), pp. 226–27; for differences in rituals see *ibid.*, p. 149. For its reception in Portugal see below, p. 40. Certain historians who were interested in native sources found Góis' translation a valuable and believable document. See D. Klatt, *David Chytraeus als Geschichtslehrer und Geschichtschreiber* (Rostock, 1908) p. 87.

Iberia with the publication at Louvain in 1541 or 1542 of his *Hispania* (Iberia).[98] Shortly after his return to Louvain, the edition of *Ptolemy* (1540) prepared by Sebastian Münster, the cosmographer of Basel, was brought to his attention. To this work there was appended a brief essay comparing France to Spain. Since relatively little was known in northern Europe about the geography, institutions, and economy of the Iberian states, Münster obtained his information about them wherever he could. His main source was the comparison of France and Spain written by the Spanish physician and exile, Miguel Servet (Servetus).[99] Since Servetus was a refugee from the Spanish Inquisition, his view of Spain was jaundiced and full of biases, distortions, and inaccuracies. Münster, a fiery Protestant and a Swiss republican, uncritically accepted as correct the strictures of the exiled anti-Trinitarian and lent his name to what was truly a misinformed and defamatory critique of Spain.[100] Góis, urged by Peter Nannius (1500–1557) of Louvain, prepared the *Hispania* as a response to Münster and as a survey designed to correct many mistaken impressions current in northern Europe and to inform the learned community about the Iberian states.

While chiding Münster for writing about a place he had never visited, Góis hastily wrote a tract that is rich in detail from official sources and in impressions from his own experiences. He was particularly offended by Münster's slighting remarks about the low productivity of Iberian agriculture, the inferior quality of its exports, and its dearth of great individuals. In both the text of *Hispania* and in his essay "Defense of Spain against Münster," Góis attributes the decline of agriculture to Iberia's preoccupation with war and expansion. He shows how inadequately Münster was informed on commerce by itemizing the native and overseas products exported to northern Europe from the Iberian states. Góis also extols the great scholarly achievements of Spain, especially the Complutensian Polyglot Bible, and lists the overseas conquerors among its national heroes. In his famous *Cosmographei* (1550) Münster later quoted Góis on commerce and toned down his most generalized criticisms of Spain. But Münster retained his basically hostile attitude toward Iberia, supported Paolo Giovio in his attacks on the spice monopoly, and remained personally bitter towards Góis.[101]

---

[98] See Hirsch, *op. cit.* (n. 60), pp. 130–39. It was later reproduced in the collection of Robertus Belus (comp.), *Rerum Hispanicarum* (2 vols.; Frankfurt-am-Main, 1579), II, 1235–58. For an even more comprehensive compendium of writings on Spain and Portugal see Andreas Schott, *Hispania illustrata . . .* (4 vols.; Frankfurt-am-Main, 1603–8).

[99] See below, p. 449 n.

[100] For an evaluation of Münster's motives see K. Burmeister, *Sebastian Münster: Versuch eines biographischen Gesamtbildes* (Basel and Stuttgart, 1963), pp. 170–74; also see Beau, *op. cit.* (n. 74), pp. 150–75, for further details on the Münster-Góis controversy. For Münster's other works see below, p. 339–41.

[101] See Hirsch, *op. cit.* (n. 60), p. 133, n. 21. On the otherwise cordial reception of Góis' book by members of the learned community, such as Beatus Rhenanus, see Vocht, *op. cit.* (n. 56), III, 66. In a letter of June 20, 1549, Münster wrote to his teacher, Konrad Pelikan: "I should like to direct my pen against that one, Damião à Góis, who wrote so impudently against me and Paolo Giovio." See K. H. Burmeister (ed.), *Briefe Sebastian Münsters* (Frankfurt-am-Main, 1964), p. 148.

Events conspired in 1542 to distract Góis from his studies and writing. Captured by the French in the siege of Louvain he was carried off as a prisoner; he was held for fourteen months and released only after the king of Portugal intervened on his behalf and arranged for his ransom. John III then ordered Góis to return home. But in 1543–44, before Góis left Louvain, he inveighed against the city for its indifference to his captivity and planned with Rutger Rescius to publish his collected works as arranged by himself.[102] It was not until August, 1545, that Góis with his Flemish wife and three sons sailed up the Tagus to disembark in Lisbon.

The king had avowedly recalled Góis to supervise the education of young Prince John. But his appointment to this influential post was blocked by Simão Rodrigues, the Jesuit Provincial. While at Padua, Góis had met Rodrigues and had clashed with him on religion. Seriously dubious of Góis' orthodoxy, Rodrigues denounced him to the Inquisition. Initially the Jesuit was successful only in barring Góis' entrance to the inner circles of the royal court. So Góis and his family retired to his native village of Alenquer, north of Lisbon. Being independently wealthy, Góis was able to devote his time fully to study and writing. Occasionally he was still called on, however, to advise the king on economic and commercial questions. He also continued to correspond for a long time with his friends abroad, and he often entertained foreign visitors in his home or met with them in Lisbon.

From his retreat in Portugal, Góis wrote two more books in Latin to inform the learned community of Europe about his countrymen and their fabulous conquests overseas. The second siege of Diu in 1546 resulted in a major triumph for João de Castro, viceroy of India, and for the revival of Portuguese arms in the East. Coming at a time when Portuguese fortunes were ebbing fast in Europe, Castro's victory was greeted as a harbinger of a brighter future. Diogo de Teive and Góis both celebrated the victory in print. In 1549 Góis published at Louvain his *De bello Cambaico ultimo commentarii tres*, a description of the siege based on the reports of the Portuguese commander at Diu and of other participants in the war.[103] Góis' account was later used as a source by Simon Goulart in his *Histoire de Portugal* (Paris, 1587).[104]

Góis' last book directed to an international audience was his *Urbis Olisiponis descriptio* (Évora, 1554).[105] Even though it was published in Portugal and dedicated to Cardinal Henrique, Góis' description of Lisbon was designed to appeal to a broader public. It surveys Lisbon's past and glorifies the city's part in the rise of Portugal to world prominence. In good humanistic fashion Góis sets out to establish Lisbon's connections with the classical past and to provide etymologies

---

102 Published as *Aliquot opuscula* (Louvain, 1544). For the hostile reception of Münster's books in Iberia see below p. 42.

103 For example, see the letter dated 1546 of Miguel Rodrigues, the commander, to the king in the pamphlet published at Lisbon in 1837. A copy of this scarce work is in my personal library.

104 On Goulart see below, pp. 282–83.

105 For a recent Portuguese translation of this work see Raúl Machado (trans.), *Góis' Lisbôa de quinhentos* (Lisbon, 1937).

based on Latin for the names of Portugal's towns and cities. He unquestion-
ingly accepts many traditional stories of marvels, including fantasies about the
mermaids and mermen who supposedly had once lived on the beaches of
Portugal. His subject was the city of Lisbon, but he was unable to pass up the
opportunity of recounting the history of Portugal's overseas discoveries and of
their contributions to the growth of the city. His description of the Lisbon he
knew reads like a guidebook to its places of interest. To impress his audience
with Lisbon's wealth and size he glorifies the riches of the king and credits the
city with having twenty-thousand buildings!

When Góis published the description of Lisbon, he was fifty-two years of
age and about to undertake his serious historical work on the reign of King
Manuel.[106] He was also living somewhat under a cloud because of the enmity of
the Jesuits and the jealousy of parochial Portuguese who resented his associations
with distinguished names of the outside world. In Portugal he was visited by
foreigners like Jean Nicot, the French ambassador, and Charles de L'écluse, the
eminent Netherlandish botanist. But Góis' Jesuit enemies were not content to
let him live and work in peace. Rodrigues finally convinced the Inquisition to
put him on trial as a heretic, and in 1572 he was found guilty. After a period of
confinement, he died near Alcobaça on January 30, 1574.

Góis' career was certainly an extraordinary one for a man of his times. Other
Portuguese (especially André de Resende and Jerónimo Osório) had traveled
widely in Europe and had won the respect of their contemporaries in the great
centers of Renaissance civilization.[107] But there was no other Portuguese of
Góis' day who stayed abroad for such a long period—almost uninterruptedly
for twenty-two years—and who was such a forthright promoter of the discoveries and Iberian civilization. Góis was perhaps unique also in the range of
activities he pursued, from commercial agent to diplomat, to student, to writer,
to historian. He was not a profound thinker, linguist, or cloistered scholar. He
was a man who evidently had a talent for making money and keeping it, and
for making friends and keeping them. He was an amateur of Latin learning, but
never a stylist. His Latin books were tracts of the times directed to the educated
public. Most of his books achieved a modicum of popularity because of their
controversial and novel subject matter. Contemporaries, like Joachim Polites,
clearly recognized Góis as the spokesman of Portugal and its discoveries.[108]
And, so far as anyone knows, he carried out this aspect of his mission through his
personal efforts and at his own expense. In terms of individual achievement
alone, Góis deserves to be ranked as a Renaissance man.

---

[106] See below, p. 144.

[107] Diogo de Teive and João da Costa lived in France almost uninterruptedly from 1527 to 1547.
While they both traveled extensively within France, they apparently never visited Italy or Germany.
Teive and Costa were only mild propagandists for the Portuguese empire; they were mainly in-
terested in humanistic learning and in teaching.

[108] This was true as early as 1540 when Polites wrote congratulating Góis on his first book on Diu.
See Hirsch, *op. cit.* (n. 60), pp. 94–95. Also see the remarks of Christopher Madruzzo, Bishop of
Trent, on this same tract (*ibid.*, pp. 105–6).

3

FOREIGNERS, RETURNEES, AND JESUITS IN PORTUGAL

The repatriation of Góis in 1545 occurred at a time when Portugal began to experience a rapid new influx of returning students, foreign scholars, and Jesuit pioneers. Most of the foreign intellectuals who had previously visited Iberia went there on missions relating to the spice trade. Northern Italians, especially from Venice, Genoa, and their environs, were among the first foreigners to appear at Lisbon and Seville after the opening of the sea trade. Particularly important for their reports on Portugal, Spain, and the overseas world were Giovanni Camerino (Il Cretico), Leonardo da Ca' Masser, Antonio Pigafetta, and Andrea Navagero.[109] But other Italians were also in Lisbon early in the century. Jacobo Caviceo (1443–1511), the author of a popular romance called *Libro del Peregrino*, was possibly in Lisbon before 1508 and he may have had an interview with King Manuel.[110] On his return from the East in 1508 Ludovico di Varthema of Bologna landed at Lisbon where he was welcomed by the king, who kept him at the court for several days "in order to know about the things of India."[111] Francesco Guicciardini (1483–1540), the famous historian, represented his native Florence at the court of Castile in 1512–13. To inform his compatriots on Iberia, about which so little was known in the rest of Europe, Guicciardini wrote a relation of Spain. In this study, he identifies Portugal as the "third part" of Spain, as a small country that lies between Castile and the Atlantic Ocean, and as a place that "is best known for the merchandizing that takes place at Lisbon" in the commodities of the East.[112]

The Germans were the first among the northern intellectuals to take a direct interest in the affairs of the Iberian peninsula.[113] Valentim Fernandes, a Moravian printer, systematically sent reports from Lisbon to the German Humanists of Augsburg during the first decade of the sixteenth century.[114] Honoré de Caix,

---

109 For further details on these early reporters see *Asia*, I, 105–7, 173–76. On the unique career of Navagero see M. Cermenati, "Un diplomatico naturalista del Rinascimento, Andrea Navagero," *Nuovo archivio veneto*, XXIV (1912), 164–205. For a portrait of him see pl. 43.

110 In his romance published at Parma in 1508, Caviceo tells of a visit to Lisbon. He had been in Constantinople at an earlier date. For his remarks on Lisbon in the edition of 1533 see pp. 199ᵛ–200ʳ.

111 See *Asia*, I, 165–66. Quotation from end of Varthema's account.

112 See A. M. Fabié y Escúdero (ed. and trans.), *Viajes por España* ... (Madrid, 1879), p. 195. Agostino Nettuci, secretary to a Florentine embassy, was in Iberia from 1513 to 1516. In the unpublished account of his experiences there, he tells of seeing an ostrich and an "Indian elephant." And he reports on Portuguese activities at Malacca. See R. Almagià, "Un fiorentino in Spagna al principio del seculo XVI," in *Studi in onore di G. Luzzatto* (2 vols.; Milan, 1950), II, 141, 143n. Nettuci's manuscript account is preserved in the Vatican Library.

113 For a brief survey of Luso-German relations see E. A. Strasen and A. Gandara, *Oito séculos de história Luso-Alemã* (Lisbon, 1944); also B. de Fischer, *Dialogue Luso-Suisse: Essai d'une histoire des relations entre la Suisse et le Portugal du XVᵉ siècle à la Convention de Stockholm de 1960* (Lisbon, 1960). On the voyage to Iberia of Hieronymus Münzer see below, p. 328.

114 See *Asia*, I, 158–63. Also see A. Brásio, *Uma carta inédita de Valentim Fernandes* (Coimbra, 1959).

the French ambassador, took up his post in Lisbon during 1518. In the same year
Pierre Brissot, the physician, left his job at the University of Paris to take up
residence at Évora. Brissot hoped eventually to go to India to study medicinal
plants, but died in Portugal in 1522 without ever leaving there.[115] Scholars
from the Low Countries began to appear in Iberia only after 1530. Nicolas
Clénard (1493-1542), the linguist known as Clenardus, taught Greek and Hebrew
at Salamanca in 1531-32 before going to Portugal in 1533 to supervise the education of the Infante Henrique and to lecture for the next five years in various
Portuguese educational institutions.[116] Joannes Was (Vasaeus), a student of
Clénard, also arrived in Spain in 1531 to take service with Ferdinand Columbus,
the bibliophilic son of Christopher Columbus who was responsible for establishing the Bibliotheca Colombina at Seville. After 1535 Vasaeus acted for a time
as curator of this rich collection.[117] From 1538 to his death in 1561 Vasaeus
taught languages at Braga (1538), Évora (1541), and Salamanca (1550-61).[118]

The Portuguese diplomats and students who returned home from abroad
received a mixed reception. Miguel da Silva and Martinho de Portugal returned
from their embassies in Rome, respectively in 1525 and 1535, only to find that
the king was not satisfied with their achievements and was suspicious of their
foreign attachments.[119] Sá de Miranda, the lyric poet, returned in 1526 after five
years in Italy with a new conception of the function of poetry and the poet. His
efforts to introduce the "Italian style" to Portuguese literature met with indifference from the court. He retired to a country estate and in his writings
criticized the preoccupation of the Portuguese with constant war and expansion
so costly in lives and treasure.[120] When abroad André de Resende spent most
of his time in Spain (1512-22) and at Louvain (1522-31). After two years of
service with Pedro de Mascarenhas, the Portuguese ambassador to the court of
Charles V, he returned home in 1533 to take charge of the literary education of
the royal children. Although he was an outspoken advocate of Erasmus' ideas,
Resende retained the favor of the court throughout the remainder of his life.
Resende, unlike Sá de Miranda, celebrated the heroic deeds of the Portuguese
overseas, especially in his *Epitome* . . . (1531).[121] Francisco d'Ollanda (1517-84),
the artist who went to Italy to study and sketch the antiquities of Rome, returned
to Lisbon in 1541 imbued with a desire to "modernize" Portuguese architecture

[115] See Matos, *op. cit.* (n. 28), pp. 53-54.

[116] See Alphonse Roersch (ed.), *Correspondance de Nicolas Clénard* (3 vols.; Brussels, 1940-41), I,
xi-xii. He also studied Arabic, at the suggestion of André de Resende, with a Portuguese physician
of Évora. See V. Chauvin and A. Roersch, *Étude sur . . . Clénard* (Brussels, 1900), p. 23.

[117] See H. Harrisse, *Fernand Colomb, sa vie, ses oeuvres, essai critique* (Paris, 1872), p. 19. For comments
on the library see below, pp. 45-46.

[118] Vocht, *op. cit.* (n. 56), II, 474-75. He was also a historian of ancient and medieval Spain. See his
Hispaniae Chronicon as reproduced in Belus (comp.), *op. cit.* (n. 98), I, 437-611. For a detailed summary
of his career see Alphonse Roersch, *L'Humanisme belge à l'époque de la Renaissance: Études et portraits*
(Louvain, 1933), pp. 85-93. Also see below, p. 46.

[119] See Silva Dias, *op. cit.* (n. 10), I, 76-79, 106-11, 124.

[120] Saraiva, *op. cit.* (n. 7), II, 608-9.

[121] See Silva Dias, *op. cit.* (n. 10), I, 353-58.

and painting and to elevate the social and intellectual position of the artist. He did not suffer from royal disfavor even though his aesthetic ideals were not accorded the attention he thought they deserved.[122]

By the time Góis arrived at Lisbon in 1545, the intellectual and religious atmosphere had become rigidly hostile to unorthodox ideas and innovations. The spread of Lullist and Erasmian ideas of negotiation with and proselytizing of the Turks had increasingly aroused the fears of the Iberian rulers that their great military and naval conquests might be undermined at home by a Christian pacificism that would grow and thrive on war-weariness and disillusionment. Other ideas from abroad that filtered into the Iberian peninsula, such as the Humanist ideas of education being embraced by the Dominicans of Seville, were also viewed with suspicion. The security of the empire and the continued monopoly of overseas commerce seemed to require increased vigilance, national solidarity, and religious orthodoxy.

Portugal began to turn inward around 1540 with the establishment of the Inquisition, the repressive censorship of books, the reform of higher education, and the founding of the Portuguese Province of the Society of Jesus. What the Portuguese apparently did at this time was to extend the crusade against the Muslim to a crusade against heterodoxy at home, a departure that was officially justified by the need of the crown to preserve the empire, to extend the benefits of Christianity to the heathen, and to defeat the Muslims and heretics everywhere. The Inquisition guaranteed the fundamental official ideology and made certain that it could not safely be attacked or suborned. To the orthodox the Jews, New Christians, Protestants, and foreigners threatened the monopoly of overseas empire and the economic control of the syndicate over the spice trade. To check the decline of the empire, it was believed in many quarters that extraordinary measures were required: revival of the crusade in the East, withdrawal from northern Europe, centralization of the spice trade at Lisbon, and reinforcement at home of the bastions of education and religion.

This change of direction in the cultural and economic policies of the crown occurred piecemeal and over the decade from 1540 to 1550. In many ways the new policy was but the culmination of tendencies toward parochialism and nationalism that had surfaced occasionally in the past. The earlier Portuguese monopolies of eastward navigation, of the spice trade, and of information about the discoveries constituted a foundation for the new programs of royal control over religion and education. It was precisely because cracks were appearing in the older monopolies that the crown decided after 1540 to cooperate more closely than ever with the ecclesiastical orders in weeding out heresy and enforcing conformity. As the Society of Jesus grew in numbers and influence, the crown came increasingly to rely on it for supervision of overseas missions and higher education. King John III was the first European ruler to choose a Jesuit to be his confessor.[123]

---

[122] Cf. *Asia*, II, Bk. 1, 69–70; also see Saraiva, *op. cit.* (n. 7), II, 658–71.

[123] Luís Gonçalves da Câmara (1520–75) was unhappy about his selection as confessor, but he

The Dominicans in Portugal, as in Castile, dominated the Inquisition and the censorship of books. In 1541, Cardinal Seripando officially visited Lisbon and Portugal as part of his program for enforcing a reform of the Augustinian order.[124] The Jesuits, fresh from their victories in Rome and Lisbon, founded a college at Coimbra in 1542 for the training of missionaries. Students soon came to the new Jesuit college from Italy, Castile, and France.[125] At the court the king's chaplain, Francisco de Monzón, composed a "mirror for the prince" that spelled out the Christian duties of the king. The *Libro primero del espejo del principe Christiano* (Lisbon, 1544) extols the achievements of Prince Henry the Navigator, lists the Portuguese fortresses from Morocco to India, and reminds the king of his responsibility for maintaining the expansion, protecting its outposts, and sending missionaries to the waiting harvest. The crown, meanwhile, was moving toward the establishment at Coimbra of a royal university that was intended to rival in secular learning the great Renaissance universities of northern Europe and Italy.

The modernization of higher education in Portugal on the initiative of the crown began in 1504 with King Manuel's decision to reform the University of Lisbon.[126] The model he accepted was the University of Paris, and so, as we have seen,[127] he encouraged and subsidized Portuguese students to study there. A second reform was instituted in 1537 by John III who removed the University of Lisbon to Coimbra and merged it there with the school of the Augustinian convent of Santa Cruz, a center of French Humanism. Students returning from Paris were thereafter encouraged to teach at Coimbra, and distinguished foreigners, such as Clenardus, were also invited to lecture there. In 1540 the college was moved from the convent to the royal palace of Coimbra, and in 1547 the king formally proclaimed it to be the royal college in which would be taught mathematics, rhetoric, humanities, and languages. He invited André de Gouveia, principal of the Collège de Guyenne at Bordeaux, to head the royal college and to collect a faculty for it. In response to his monarch's bidding, in 1548 Gouveia brought to Coimbra a group of foreign and Portuguese scholars who had been trained in Paris, mainly at Sainte-Barbe. But the Guyenne group had developed independently, and the Paris Portuguese headed by Diogo de Gouveia the Elder resented the king's decision to give the principal's post to André. The foreign group at Coimbra included George Buchanan, the cele-

---

accepted the post on the urging of Loyola and Diogo Mirão, the Jesuit Provincial. See B. Duhr, *Die Jesuiten an den deutschen Fürstenhöfen des 16. Jahrhunderts* (Freiburg-im-Breisgau, 1901), pp. 2–3. Câmara traveled with Bernard, the young Japanese convert, from Rome to Lisbon in 1555. He was also in active correspondence thereafter with the Jesuits in the East. See *Asia*, I, 432 n., 673.

[124] See H. Jedin, *Papal Legate at the Council of Trent, Cardinal Seripando* (St. Louis, 1947), pp. 150–51.

[125] Among the most important of these original students for the India mission were Nicolo Lancillotto and Antonio Criminale. See F. Rodrigues, *História da Companhia de Jesus . . . de Portugal* (5 vols.; Porto, 1931), I, Pt. I, 304–11.

[126] On Manuel's efforts see T. Braga, *História da universidade de Coimbra* (2 vols.; Lisbon, 1892, 1895), I, 247–333.

[127] Above, pp. 10–11.

brated Scottish Humanist, and his brother Patrick; Nicolas de Grouchy (1520–72), the logician; and his friend Guillaume Guérente, a distinguished French educator; as well as Élie Vinet (1519–87), the mathematician and Humanist, and Arnauld Fabrice. Aside from these six foreigners, three Portuguese were added to the faculty—Diogo de Teive, João da Costa, and António Mendes—who were all former teachers at Guyenne.[128]

The advent of humanistic educators from Bordeaux produced a reaction from the "Parisians" and the Jesuits. The foreigners soon found themselves in a particularly vulnerable position because of the death of André de Gouveia shortly after their installation at Coimbra. Three of their number were denounced before the Inquisition at Lisbon on charges of heterodoxy and of sympathy for Protestantism. In making these charges the "Parisians" evidently received support from Diogo de Gouveia the Elder, an avid proponent of the Counter-Reformation. In response to these attacks, the foreigners began to leave Coimbra in 1549 for France. Grouchy, the last to leave, returned to the vicinity of Dieppe in 1551. The attack on the newcomers won a complete victory by 1555 when the king directed the Society of Jesus to take over the administration of the royal college.[129]

The French-trained Humanists, despite their difficulties at Coimbra, were responsible for helping to spread interest in the Portuguese empire and the overseas world. In 1548 Diogo de Teive published at Coimbra his commentary in Latin prose on the Portuguese victory in 1546 at Diu.[130] This work, which follows the tradition of siege literature established by Resende in his *Epitome* (1531)[131] and by Góis in his *Commentarii* (1539), justified the Portuguese expansion by pointing out the benefits in civilization and religion that it brought to both heathens and Moors. Teive's friend Grouchy meanwhile became acquainted with Fernão Lopes de Castanheda, the beadle and librarian at Coimbra. Shortly after Grouchy returned to France, Castanheda sent him the first book of his *História do descobrimento e conquista da India pelos Portuguezes* (Coimbra, 1551) with a request to translate it into French. Though initially reluctant to spend his time on such an unscholarly project, Grouchy was prevailed on by others to make a vernacular translation. Grouchy's translation was first printed at Paris in 1553 and reissued at Antwerp in the following year and in 1576. The French

128 For further detail see Braga, *História da universidade de Coimbra*, Vol. I, chap. vi.

129 See M. Brandão, *A Inquisição e os professores do Colégio das Artes* (Coimbra, 1948), *passim*.

130 Original reprinted in *Jacobi Tevii Bracarensis, Opuscula* . . . (Paris, 1762); the first edition was entitled *Commentarius de rebus gestis in India apud Dium*, and to it were added thirteen distiches of Latin verse by João da Costa, Teive's friend and long-time associate in France. George Buchanan also wrote Latin verse praising Teive's work. Quotations from his *Poemata fragmenta* are in G. J. C. Henriques, "Buchanan in Portugal," in D. A. Millar (comp. and ed.), *George Buchanan: A Memorial, 1506–1906* (St. Andrews and London, 1907), pp. 76–77.

131 For additional commentary see Francisco Leite de Faria, "Un impresso de 1531 sobre as impressas dos Portugueses no Oriente," *Boletim internacional da bibliografia Luso-Brasileira*, VII (1966), 90–109. A small book in Italian was also published at Rome in 1531 called *Impresa del gran turco*. . . . This was more of a newsletter than a full account, but it includes materials omitted from Resende's account. Both works were evidently based on the same report. For the history of Portuguese siege literature, see below, pp. 135–37.

translation was retranslated into Spanish (1554), Italian (1556), and English (1582).[132]

The Jesuits, in the meantime, had begun building their new college at Coimbra in 1547; it was not yet completed when they took over the royal college in 1555. They later moved the royal college from the lower city to the hilltop above the Mondego Valley. Other plans were meanwhile being laid to establish a Jesuit university in Évora that would likewise train young men for the Society and its missions. The University of Évora, after its formal foundation in 1557, was to become a leading center for the study of philosophy, especially Aristotle.

The Jesuit college at Coimbra was finally completed in 1560. By this time the Jesuits were also planning colleges at Porto and Braga, for there were about three hundred and fifty Jesuits then in Portugal, many of whom were preparing to become missionaries overseas.[133] The occasions when missionaries embarked for India were solemnized by processions of the Jesuits, the pious laity, and the curious. Beginning at the House of the Professed of São Roque in Lisbon, the procession, singing pious songs, would wind its way to the wharf at Belém.[134] The onlookers on these occasions often included foreign merchants, diplomats, and visitors who were here able to see for themselves how Portugal and the Jesuits were working together to spread the Christian faith throughout Asia.

The Portuguese Jesuits, some of whom traveled widely in Europe, were "living letters" who helped to spread news and information as they went about their business on behalf of the Society. Inácio Martins (1531–98), a philosophy professor of Évora, traveled to Rome in 1573 and then to Germany on diplomatic matters for Lisbon in the company of Peter Canisius.[135] Francino António (1558–1610), another Portuguese Jesuit, was, in 1576, the court preacher to the Empress Maria, the daughter of Charles V who had been brought up in Spain.[136] The biographer of Xavier, João de Lucena (1550–1600), traveled to Rome in 1578, possibly in connection with his search for materials on Xavier.[137] António de Vasconcelos (1554–1622), resident at the court of Madrid from 1588 to 1591 as representative of the Jesuit Province of Portugal, spent much time and effort vainly trying to be released from his posts in Europe and, in turn, to obtain an assignment in India or Japan.[138] From 1586 to 1592 Domingos João (1555–95) worked as a secretary in Rome, where he associated with many of the

[132] See Georges le Gentil, "Nicolas de Grouchy, traducteur de Castanheda," *Bulletin des études portugaises et de l'Institut français au Portugal*, IV (1937), 31–34. Also see *Asia*, I, 187–90, and below, pp. 274–75.

[133] Rodrigues, *op. cit.* (n. 125), I, Pt. 1, 443. On Loyola's death in 1556, it was said that the Society had a total of one thousand members. See *Asia*, I, 251. Assuming this to be so, it can readily be seen that in 1560 about one-third of all the Jesuits were located in Portugal; in 1559 there were one hundred and twenty-four Jesuits in Asia, or about one-eighth of the total. See *Asia*, I, 253.

[134] Rodrigues, *op. cit.* (n. 125), I, Pt. 2, 521.

[135] See J. Pereira Gomes, *Os professores de filosofia da Universidade de Évora, 1559–79* (Évora, 1960), p. 79.

[136] See Duhr, *op. cit.* (n. 123), pp. 15–16; also see *Asia*, II, Bk. 1, 146.

[137] Gomes, *op. cit.* (n. 135), p. 114.

[138] *Ibid.*, pp. 136–37.

city's leading intellectuals.[139] Nicolau Godinho (1556–1616), a professor at Évora, obtained his first teaching assignment in 1587 by acting as a substitute for Paulo de Oliveira (1556–1607), a Portuguese Jesuit born in India who suffered constantly from ill health while in Portugal. When Oliveira finally embarked for India in 1599, Godinho was beginning to make plans for a journey to Italy finally realized in 1604. He spent the remaining twelve years of his life in Naples and Rome writing theological tracts and corresponding with the members of the Society in Europe and overseas.[140]

The death of King John III in 1557 had again focused international political attention on Portugal. A joint regency of Queen Catherine and Cardinal Henry, the Inquisitor-General, at once assumed control of the government on behalf of Sebastian, the three-year-old grandson of the queen. The question of Portugal's future was of particular concern to the courts of Spain and France as these two arch-rivals began to jockey for new positions of influence at Lisbon. The French in particular sought to follow events closely. The Chevalier Michel de Seure was sent immediately to Lisbon to evaluate the situation. In 1559 he was replaced by Jean Nicot (1530–1604), a young courtier and Humanist who was delegated to arrange for a marriage between Margaret of Valois and the young Sebastian. Shortly after Nicot's arrival, in 1560, the French fleet stopped at Lisbon. In the meantime João Pereira Dantas acted as the accredited Portuguese representative to the court of France from 1559 to 1563.

Although Nicot's diplomatic mission failed, he was himself much impressed by what he saw and heard in Portugal. A master of classical learning, Nicot had associated in Paris before going to Portugal with members of the Pléiade.[141] While in Lisbon, he applied his talents to learn as much as he could for his compatriots about the Portuguese empire in the East. He explained to the French king in his letters the differences still existing between Spain and Portugal over the question of the Moluccas.[142] Nicot informed the king about the conquests of Portugal in Gujarat and of the revenues derived therefrom,[143] and sent him and the Cardinal of Lorraine, through the Ruiz merchants of Medina del Campo, some orange, lemon, and banana trees of the Indies.[144] Nicot raised the question of importing indigo from the East for use in the textile dyeing industry, and claimed that the renowned dyers of Segovia used nothing else for blueing.[145] He acquired books and manuscripts for himself, and prepared a memoir on the progress of the Portuguese in the Indies.[146]

By 1560 tensions between the courts of Castile and Portugal began to mount over the problem of the Spiceries. The Castilians had never been happy about

[139] *Ibid.,* p. 142.
[140] *Ibid.,* pp. 150–53. On the phenomenon of Jesuit letter-writing see *Asia,* I, 314–28.
[141] See below, pp. 276–77
[142] See especially his letter of November 5, 1559, in E. Falgairolle (ed.), *Jean Nicot, ambassadeur de France en Portugal au XVIe siècle, sa correspondance diplomatique inédite* (Paris, 1897), pp. 107–15.
[143] *Ibid.,* pp. 53–54.
[144] *Ibid.,* p. lxv.
[145] *Ibid.,* pp. lxxix–lxxx.
[146] *Ibid.,* p. xcix. On his library see below, p. 67.

the retreat from the Moluccas that Charles V had agreed to at Saragossa in 1529.[147] In the New World, especially, the conquistadors and missionaries were regularly agitating for a resumption of the Pacific expeditions. The retirement of Charles V (1556) followed by the death of John III (1557), the two monarchs who had earlier mediated the conflict over the Moluccas, acted as a signal to frustrated Castilians to move quickly and forcefully to regain a position in insular southeast Asia. The plans being advanced in Mexico and Castile immediately caused reactions within Portugal and at its outposts in the Moluccas. The French, long frustrated by their exclusion from direct participation in the spice trade, took the opportunity created by the reopening of the Moluccan dispute to fish for themselves in the muddied waters of Spanish-Portuguese relations.

Nicot returned to France in October, 1561, from his mission to Lisbon with the latest about the machinations of the Spanish party in Portugal and about the resumption of controversy over the Moluccas. King Charles IX of France (reigned 1560–74) thereafter kept himself informed about the plans of Philip II through his emissary to Madrid.[148] M. de Fourquevaux, the French ambassador, arrived at Madrid in 1565, the year when the Spanish began their conquest of the Philippine Islands.[149] In his dispatches to France over the next seven years, Fourquevaux kept Charles IX informed about the arrival of treasure fleets in Europe, about the Spanish advances in the Philippines, and about the growing tensions between the Spanish and Portuguese in Europe and Asia over the renewed Spanish activity in the southwestern Pacific region. He also reported on the revival of the overland spice trade to Venice, the hopes that were being stirred in Madrid about a northwest passage to China, and the defections of Portuguese pilots to their country's competitors. Finally, in 1570, he began to report that open war had broken out between the Spanish and Portuguese in insular southeast Asia. Throughout his stay in Madrid, Fourquevaux pressed for a renegotiation of the partition of the overseas world as recognition of the fact that the Tordesillas arrangements of 1494 were unrealistic and unenforceable. France, in his estimation, could not legitimately be excluded from participation in the division of the vast new world that the Iberians had revealed to Europe during the sixteenth century.[150] But France, burdened by its own civil wars from 1560 to 1590, was in no position to challenge Spain.

Emperor Rudolf II was kept informed on what was happening in Spain and its far-flung empire by Hans Khevenhüller, his ambassador in Madrid from 1573

[147] On the conflict over the Moluccas that followed Magellan's expedition (1521–29) see *Asia*, I, 114–19.

[148] It should be recalled that Charles IX was the patron of the Pléiade.

[149] Jean Erbard, the predecessor of Fourquevaux at Madrid, had reported very little on imperial questions or on the Portuguese–Spanish rivalry, possibly because of the direct negotiations that were then being conducted between Paris and Lisbon. See E. Cabié, *Ambassade en Espagne de Jean Ebrard, Seigneur de St. Sulpice, de 1562 à 1565 et mission de ce diplomate dans le même pays en 1566* (Albi, 1903).

[150] See M. Douais (ed.), *Dépêches de M. de Fourquevaux, ambassadeur du roi Charles IX en Espagne, 1565–72* (3 vols.; Paris, 1896–1904), I, 82, 142, 193, 288–89, 358; II, 132–33, 223.

to 1606.[151] The Fugger correspondents also provided northern Europe with reports on developments in the Iberian peninsula during the last generation of the sixteenth century. In connection with their commercial interests, the Fuggers sought to keep abreast of all events—political, social, and cultural—which might have a bearing upon business. Of particular moment to the rest of Europe was the death of King Sebastian of Portugal in 1578, which left the way open for the merging of the Spanish and Portuguese crowns under Philip II. The Fugger correspondents were particularly concerned about the effects of the union of 1580 upon the overseas empire and trade. In a letter from Cochin one writer frankly admitted that "things [in India] are no longer what they were twenty years ago."[152] Correspondents from Lisbon complained in 1582 that "uncertainty makes business slack," and in 1585 that "trade is almost entirely quiet."[153] The sea was unsafe for trade because of the wars in the Netherlands and France and the plundering missions of the English under Drake. The defeat of the Armada in 1588 followed by the English raids of the following year on Lisbon and the Spanish port cities disrupted business completely in the peninsula. News from India in 1590 was not much better for the Portuguese: the Turks were again active in the Indian Ocean, local resistance to Portuguese rule was increasing at Goa and Malacca, and the Spanish in the Philippines had become more numerous and menacing. About the only place the Portuguese prospered was in Japan, where the missionaries reported in 1590 that they were still making converts in spite of the growing hostility of Hideyoshi toward them.[154] But what was most distressing to the correspondents of the Catholic Fuggers was the appearance in Eastern waters of vessels sent out by the Protestant English and Dutch.

Rudolf's Czech subjects, distant as they were from the Atlantic Ocean, were kept informed about overseas progress through the regular reports collected all over Europe by the Rožemberk family. Petr and Vilem Vok of Rožemberk were the leading figures of this wealthy commercial family of south Bohemia. Like the Fuggers, the Rožemberks maintained a special service to collect and relay to them weekly reports on commerce and those events affecting it. A study of the newsletters still extant in the archives at Třeboň reveals that they watched closely the Iberian wars against the Turks, the commercial recovery of Venice, the political tensions in the Low Countries, and the progress of the Christian missions in Asia.[155] Reports from Venice and Rome of 1585 to the Voks dwell on the reception accorded the Japanese emissaries in Spain and Italy. Bernardius Stefanutius in his newsletter from Rome of March 23, 1585, gives

---

[151] Their correspondence also contains details on exotic art objects that were acquired for Rudolf's collection. See R. J. W. Evans, *Rudolf II and His World* . . . (Oxford, 1973), pp. 50, 181.

[152] See G. T. Matthews (ed.), *News and Rumor in Renaissance Europe* (New York, 1959), p. 71.

[153] *Ibid.*, pp. 96, 107.

[154] *Ibid.*, pp. 185–87.

[155] Based on Z. Šimeček, "Rožmberské zpravodajstír o nových zemích Asie a Afriky v 16. stoleti," ["Rožemberk Reports about the New Lands of Asia and Africa in the Sixteenth Century"] *Československý časpois historický* (Prague), XIII (1965), 428–43; for America see the same author's article, "L'Amérique au 16e siècle à la lumière des nouvelles du service de reseignements de la famille des Rožemberk," *Historica* (Prague), XI (1966), 53–93.

rich detail on the embroidered costumes of the Japanese. Contemporary reports taken from Antwerp newspapers concentrate on the arrivals in Europe of fleets from India, the capture by the English of the "Madre de Dios," and of the efforts being made by the Dutch and English to break the Iberian monopoly of the spice trade. Like the Fugger letters, the emphasis in the Rožemberk collection is upon matters which were of primary importance to commerce, to Catholicism, and the Habsburg family. After all, Bohemia's own economy, especially its silver-mining industry, had suffered dislocations as a result of the economic tremors produced in Europe by the overseas discoveries.

Other foreigners also continued to watch carefully the events unfolding in the Iberian states and in their overseas possessions. Thomas Nicholas, an English merchant who was at Seville from 1560 to 1565, later translated into English several Castilian accounts of affairs in the East.[156] Pierre de Bourdeille (*ca.* 1540–1614), the distinguished abbot of Brantôme, spent several months at Lisbon in 1564 where he was shown, as he later recalled, "tout plain de singularitez."[157] Shortly thereafter, Charles de L'écluse (Clusius), the renowned botanist, toured Portugal as the companion of young Jakob Fugger. Pope Pius V in 1571 sent his nephew, the Cardinal Alexandrino, as his legate to Portugal. The papal delegation, whose activities were recorded by a certain Giovanni Battista Venturino, saw the Host covered by an Indian cloth and was presented by Indians living in Lisbon with offerings of waxen plants, fruits, and flowers of India as symbols of springtime. In the palace of King Sebastian they observed a small table from India covered with black leather and a tapestry depicting King Manuel and his council deciding to embark on the conquest of India. The guardian of the royal treasury proudly showed them a saddle with a golden seat that was studded with precious stones which had been created for an Indian prince.[158] Six years later the Italian military engineer and architect Filippo Terzi (1520–97) arrived in Portugal for a stay of twenty years. Terzi sent back rare books, porcelains, medicinals of India, and exotic birds as gifts to Francisco Maria della Rovere, the duke of Urbino.[159]

Numerous diplomatic and commercial agents from Italy and Germany were dispatched to Portugal during the period of Philip II's takeover. Two representatives from Venice, Tron and Lippomani, were sent to Lisbon in 1580 to

[156] Cf. *Asia*, I, 212.

[157] See J. B. Aquarone, "Brantôme à la cour de Portugal et la visite à Lisbonne du Grand Prieur de Lorraine," *Bulletin des études portugaises et de l'Institut français au Portugal*, XI (1947), 66–79. See K. usti, *Miscellanean* . . . (Berlin, 1908), II, 99.

[158] Venturino's account is in manuscript in the Vatican Library (Codex 1.607). Extracts of it were translated into Portuguese and edited by Alexandre Herculano. See "Viagem do Cardeal Alexandrino, 1571," in Herculano, *Opusculos* (10 vols.; Lisbon, 1873–1908), VI, 64, 76–77, 83, 88–89.

[159] See H. Trindade Coelho and G. Mattelli (eds.), *Documentos para o estudo das relações culturaes entre Portugal e Italia* (4 vols.; Florence, 1934–35), III, xii–xiii. In Spain, too, the rarities of the Indies were collected and put on display in the courts and churches. For example, an anonymous French traveler to Spain in 1612 remarks on the exquisite Oriental textiles in the church of Montserrat near Barcelona. See C. Claverie (ed.), "Relation d'un voyage en Espagne (1612)," *Revue hispanique*, LIX (1913), 453. On Urbino see below, pp. 216–17.

congratulate Philip on his elevation as king of Portugal. An anonymous manuscript summarizes their observations in the Portuguese capital. They reported to Venice that the shops in the Rua Nova which specialized in merchandizing porcelains and other Eastern products were charging higher prices than previously because of the ravages of the plague and of the Castilian soldiery and because stocks were low owing to the failure, for the previous two years, of fleets to arrive from India.[160] The most influential of the Italians from the viewpoint of cultural relations was Filippo Sassetti, representative of the Bardi of Florence, who remained in Portugal from 1578 to 1583 before departing for India.[161] Jesuits from all over Europe were likewise active in Portugal, the most notable being G. P. Maffei, the historian of the mission in Asia, who was in Iberia gathering material from 1578 to 1584.[162] And, it was in 1584–86 that the Japanese emissaries visited Catholic Europe and aroused new hopes for the success of the Jesuits and the Iberians in proselytizing in the East.[163]

Throughout the last years of the sixteenth century, the Jesuits in Portugal extended their influence over most aspects of higher education. In their schools the professors of moral theology, like those at Salamanca, wrestled with the moral problems arising from the extension of European power over non-Christian peoples.[164] Portuguese theologians trained at Salamanca in the principles expounded by Francisco de Vitoria brought their moral concern about expansion to Coimbra and Évora. Martin de Azpilcueta and Martin de Ledesma stressed at Coimbra the obligation of both conquerors and missionaries to observe and protect the human rights of the "Indians" of the East. Luis de Molina (1535–1600), whose teachings later provoked much controversy, spent the most fruitful years (1568–83) of his life in Portugal during which he prepared his five-volume treatise on justice and law. He, like other theologians, speculated on the morality of trading with infidels, of taking Chinese and Japanese slaves, and of employing the techniques of mass and forced conversions among the highly civilized peoples of the East.[165] Even in the books of readings prepared for their schools, the Jesuits introduced excerpts from lay and ecclesiastical writers which served to illustrate the moral dilemmas produced by expansion.[166] Elsewhere in Europe similar questions were being raised by both religious and secular writers.

[160] Pertinent excerpts from this manuscript were translated into Portuguese and published as "Viagem a Portugal dos Cavalleiros Tron e Lippomani, 1580," in A. Herculano (ed. and trans.), *op. cit.* (n. 158), VI, 115–16.

[161] See *Asia*, I, 137–38, 475–77.

[162] See *ibid.*, pp. 324–25.

[163] See *ibid.*, pp. 688–706.

[164] For the debates between Las Casas and Sepulveda at Valladolid in 1550–51 see Lewis Hanke, *Aristotle and the American Indian* (Chicago, 1959).

[165] See J. Beckmann, "Die Universitäten von 16. bis 18. Jahrhundert im Dienste der Glaubenverbreitung," *Neue Zeitschrift für Missionswissenschaft*, XVII (1961), 43–46. Also see Pereira Gomes, *op. it.* (n. 135), *passim.*

[166] For example, the *Sylvae illustrum autorum* (1587) of Luis de Granada contains two pieces by Jerónimo Osório, the historian of King Manuel's reign (see *Asia*, I, 196), and another excerpt from a letter about Japan by Aires dos Santos (see Silva Dias, *op. cit.* [n. 10], II, 903).

The conquest of Asia heralded by the first two generations of Portuguese who went abroad had lost its triumphant ring by the last generation of the sixteenth century. The Portuguese, for all their victories in Asia, had been forced to relax their control of the spice monopoly in Europe and had watched helplessly while losing their political independence to Philip II. What had begun as a glorious national effort and a Portuguese monopoly was now all but taken over by others. For Portugal little remained but the memory of a glorious epoch of expansion. Its retreat from Europe in the latter half of the century, when coupled with its subordination to Spain after 1580, meant that Portugal was never again to be a leader among the states of Europe. Its expansion into Europe has indeed been all but forgotten by historians. But brief as the moment was, it should still be recalled that the Portuguese were the first to transmit the new knowledge of Asia to the learned community of Europe.

CHAPTER II

Books, Libraries, and Reading

The published books and reports on Portugal's overseas empire were not numerous in the first half of the sixteenth century. Even though important material existed in manuscript books and maps, very little was put into print before 1550 for circulation to the reading public. In Portugal and elsewhere controls on information limited carefully the distribution of writings on sensitive subjects. The rulers of church and state employed their spiritual and physical power to censor or suppress literature deemed to be subversive of faith, morals, civil order, or state security. Most of the measures of preventive censorship taken in the fifteenth century had been local in character. With the invention of printing, followed in the sixteenth century by a wider diffusion of cheaper books, a need was felt for even greater precautions. In 1467 Pope Innocent VIII decreed that all books had to be submitted to the local ecclesiastical authorities before being issued for general reading.[1] The Lateran Council of 1515 went further to decree that no work should be printed anywhere without prior examination by the appropriate ecclesiastical authorities.[2] The spread of Protestantism after 1520 stimulated further action within Catholic Europe to prevent the printing, selling, and reading of heretical and pernicious books. Beginning in the 1540's lists of forbidden books began to be drawn up on orders of the papacy, the Sorbonne, the Council of Trent, and a number of secular rulers. The Protestant states likewise imposed limits on reading and printing.

On matters of censorship the Iberian states stood at the forefront of developments. In Castile, Ferdinand and Isabella established the censorship of books as a state institution in 1502, and control over it quickly passed into the hands of the

[1] See R. A. Burke, *What Is the Index?* (Milwaukee, Wis., 1952), p. 6.
[2] For details consult Donald H. Wiest, *The Precensorship of Books* (Washington, D.C., 1953), pp. 19–20.

Inquisition.[3] A list of prohibited books was prepared at the University of Louvain in 1546 at the request of the Spanish Inquisition. In Portugal meanwhile the state had in 1504 clamped tight control on dissemination of information about the discoveries, including the publication of books about the routes to the East and the sources of the spices.[4] Very few books of any sort were published in Portugal between 1521 and 1536; there was but one printer in the country. The establishment of the Inquisition in Portugal in 1536 was followed by its gradual assumption of control over the censorship and circulation of books. At the end of 1540 the administration of the censorship was entrusted by the Inquisitor-General to three Dominican friars. Still book production increased rapidly from 1536 to 1565, most works being printed in Lisbon and Coimbra.[5]

The books published or circulated in Portugal after 1540 had to be approved by the Inquisitorial commission.[6] They were subject to censorship on an individual basis before they could appear in print or be sold. The first victim of the Portuguese censorship was the book on the Ethiopians written by Damião de Góis.[7] Presumably it was condemned for its generous treatment of the religious practices of the Ethiopians, which were generally thought to be heterodoxical by the hierarchy of the Latin church. The censorship forbade both its importation and its publication in Portugal. The Portuguese censors, who were former students at Paris and Salamanca, evidently were following in this and other cases the guidelines of literary orthodoxy being framed at the Sorbonne and by the Spanish Inquisition.[8] To substantiate this coordination among the various censorships, there is the case of the cosmography of Joachim de Watt (1484–1551), also called Vadianus, which appeared at Zurich in 1534. His *Epitome trium terrae partium Asiae, Africae et Europae* was one of the first books to be included on the *Index* (1544) of the Sorbonne.[9] Shortly thereafter it appeared on Portuguese (1547),[10] Venetian (1549),[11] and Spanish (1551)[12] lists of prohibited books.

A new Portuguese *Index*, issued and printed in 1551, was based on a Louvain catalog (1550) of printed books and on the *Bibliotheca universalis* (2 vols.; Zurich, 1545, 1548–49) of Konrad Gesner.[13] Gesner's bibliography was a treasure house for the compilers of prohibited books because it gave them the most complete list available of the writings of the Protestants, their sympathizers, and those suspected of being sympathizers. From the Louvain list the

[3] For details consult A. Sierra Corella, *La censura de libros y papelos en España y los indices y catalogs españoles de los prohibidos y expurgados* (Madrid, 1947), *passim*.

[4] See *Asia*, I, 151–54.

[5] In 1551 there were five printers in Lisbon, and in 1567 this number rose to six. See A. J. Saraiva, *História da cultura em Portugal* (3 vols.; Lisbon, 1950–62), II, 128–30.

[6] See I. S. Révah, *La censure inquisitoriale portugaise au XVIᵉ siècle* (Lisbon, 1960), pp. 19–20.

[7] *Ibid.*, p. 40. On the content of Góis' work see above, p. 18.

[8] Révah, *op. cit.* (n. 6), p. 42.

[9] F. H. Reusch, *Die Indices Librorum Prohibitorum des sechzehnten Jahrhunderts* (Stuttgart, 1886), p. 99.

[10] Révah, *op. cit.* (n. 6), p. 98.

[11] Reusch, *op. cit.* (n. 9), p. 139.

[12] *Ibid.*, p. 74.

[13] Révah, *op. cit.* (n. 6), p. 104.

Portuguese included on their new *Index* the *Concordia mundi* of Guillaume Postel, the *Bibliotheca* of Gesner, the *Cosmographia universalis* of Sebastian Münster, and the complete works of Joachim Camerarius the Elder (1500–1574). Naturally, the great majority of the prohibited titles were the writings of reformers and Jews. Vadianus, Gesner, Münster, and Camerarius were all avowed Protestants, and so, it may be assumed, their descriptions and conceptions of the world would not please orthodox Catholics. Postel, who was in trouble with the church for his interest in all types of pagan, Jewish, Islamic, and heterodoxical lore, was likewise thought to be a potentially dangerous foe of orthodoxy. But it is striking, at so early a time, that books relating to geography and the discoveries, like those of Góis and Vadianus, were also finding their way onto these lists.

The Council of Trent (1545–63) was meanwhile deliberating the problem of ecclesiastical control of literature and formulating the general rules which would govern the reading of Catholics for the following three hundred years. But even before the Council adopted its rules, Pope Paul IV issued an *Index* of his own in 1558–59 that was so comprehensive and prescriptive that it produced a veritable panic in the Catholic world among intellectuals, printers, and booksellers. For example, it forbade *all* the works of Gesner and Münster, two of the most widely read authors of the day.[14] In most of the Catholic countries the *Index* of Paul IV remained unpublished or was only partially enforced. In Portugal it was published at Coimbra in 1559 and was presumably put into effect in some of the Portuguese dioceses. The only permanent contribution of Paul IV was his system of dividing the prohibited writings into three classes: the complete works of certain authors, such as Erasmus; individual writings of particular authors; and books deemed heretical or immoral of unnamed authors or those writing under pseudonyms. The Portuguese *Index* of 1561 adopted these divisions, but mitigated somewhat the proscriptions and punishments included in Paul's harsh document. In its turn the Portuguese *Index* of 1561 influenced the Tridentine *Index* and the rules of reading that were published in 1564. Outside Italy itself, the only Catholic states to accept immediately the Tridentine *Index* and the rules of reading were the Low Countries, Bavaria, and Portugal.[15] Still, the arm of control proved to be exceedingly long. Matteo Ricci, writing from China in 1606, complained to Rome that he was unable to obtain the church's permission to publish his books in Chinese and in China.[16]

Examination of the available lists of forbidden books published in the course of the sixteenth century indicates that many works relating to the discoveries were prohibited to Catholic readers, especially if their authors were Protestants,

[14] See Reusch, *op. cit.* (n. 9), p. 181.

[15] See Révah, *op. cit.* (n. 6), pp. 50–57. The ten general rules formulated to guide the Catholic reading public detail the classes of books, such as unauthorized translations of the Bible, books on magic, and the writings of avowed heretics, which were automatically forbidden whether they appeared on any formal list or not.

[16] Letter of August 5, 1606, to Claude Acquaviva in P. Tacchi-Venturi (ed.), *Opere storiche del P. Matteo Ricci, S.J.* (Macerata, 1913), II, 302.

Jews, or persons suspected of unorthodox activity or behavior. The Iberian lists, particularly those published after 1559, were especially comprehensive. For example, they prohibited not only all the writings of Gesner and Münster but also those of the German botanists Leonhard Fuchs, Otto Brunfels, and Joachim Camerarius.[17] In the lists published in 1581, after Philip became king of Portugal, many influential works of imaginative and didactic literature were added. Prohibited were the works of Boccaccio, Gil Vicente, Torres Naharro, and Rabelais, presumably because of their satirical and immoral character. But also forbidden were the *Orlando* of Boiardo and Ariosto, the *Utopia* of More, the *Supplementum chronicorum* of Foresti da Bergamo, the *Methodus* of Jean Bodin, the *Ropica Pfnema* of Barros, and the *Republicas* of Hieronymus Roman. It was furthermore permissible to read only expurgated versions of the scientific writings of Mercator, Cardano, Amato Lusitano, and Huarte de San Juan. Most of these works were added to the papal *Index* of 1590 along with several Jesuit letterbooks that were compiled and published by non-Jesuits or that appeared without the proper imprimatur.[18]

To what extent were the authorities of the church and state successful in curtailing the distribution of books on the overseas world and Asia in the various countries of Europe? In an effort to answer this question as empirically as possible, many sixteenth-century catalogs and inventories have been searched for entries of manuscripts and printed books relating to Asia. The works of twenty-four authors—ranging in time from Marco Polo to Linschoten (at the end of the sixteenth century)—were the ones mainly sought in these inventories. It was discovered that around sixty of the extant inventories contain from one to several of the authors being charted, as the Appendix to this chapter shows. Listings of many other books less directly related to Asia, including the writings of relevant ancient authors, are noticed in the textual discussion of collections.

Much can be inferred about the availability of books by examining literary production. Too much reliance on such deductions, however, can be extremely dangerous. For example, an examination of Hans Sachs' catalog shows that he had several of the most important books on the East; but an analysis of his writings reveals that he apparently never used them as sources.[19] A study of Rabelais' famous work clearly exhibits, on the other hand, the author's dependence on contemporary travel literature for certain of his descriptions and episodes; but we have no inventory of his library. The following discussion of the distribution of books in European collections should provide a context within which more accurate deductions and inferences can be drawn about the availability and use of European books on Asia. In absolute terms the numbers of books on Asia, even the popular ones of Mandeville, Varthema, and Osório, never formed a large percentage of the total in any of the collections. But what is most impres-

[17] In his *De rebus turcis commentarii* (Frankfurt, 1598), Camerarius discusses the relations of the Turks and Cambay in their common struggle against the Portuguese (p. 75).

[18] List derived from Reusch, *op. cit.* (n. 9), *passim*.

[19] See below, p. 342.

sive is the simple, demonstrable fact that the works of most of the important authors could be found in sixteenth-century collections in places as far apart as Seville, Paris, Antwerp, Venice, Frankfurt, and London. Equally clear also is the fact that many of the great collectors—Ferdinand Columbus, Jacques Auguste de Thou, and John Dee—allowed others access to their libraries. While mere possession of books means little, the history of book collecting is nonetheless a first, if faltering, step to take when making an effort to perceive how the intellectual community began to learn about Asia through literary materials.

I

PORTUGAL AND SPAIN

The limits imposed on reading were apparently very effective in Portugal. Yet this is not to say that books were unavailable. In 1581 on the Rua Nova in Lisbon, many stalls sold books in Portuguese, Castilian, Latin, and Italian. But, as a Venetian reporter observed, the books were so extremely expensive that students and others were accustomed to renting them by the day rather than buying them.[20] This practice probably helps to account for the fact that so few inventories of Portuguese libraries are now extant. Still it is also true that the intellectual climate was not conducive to reading. Aside from the limits imposed by the strict rules of reading and censorship, very few Portuguese were devoted to the cultivation of letters. The merchants concentrated on business, the nobility on exploits of arms, and the clergy on maintaining orthodoxy at home and on evangelizing abroad. Aside from a few notable writers and scholars, the Portuguese of the last generation of the sixteenth century, in contrast to their forerunners who went abroad, were not vitally interested in learning for its own sake.[21]

When King Manuel died in 1521, the royal library itself housed only ninety-eight items that were thought worthy of being listed. Included were two manuscripts of Marco Polo, the *Speculum historiale* of Vincent of Beauvais, and a large Ptolemy.[22] It also housed a maritime map of India, an illuminated manuscript celebrating the triumphs in India, and an exhortation by Duarte Galvão directed to those going to India.[23] By 1534 King John III had added nothing else to the royal library except devotional works, a Latin vocabulary, and a romance. Of the works in the library of the later kings of Portugal bearing a publication date between 1540 and 1599, slightly under 10 percent of those printed in Portugal

[20] Anon., "Viagem a Portugal dos Cavalleiros Tron e Lippomani, 1580," in A. Herculano (trans. and ed.), *Opusculos* (10 vols.; Lisbon, 1873–1908), VI, 116.

[21] Cf. *ibid.*, p. 122.

[22] See F. M. Sousa Viterbo (ed.), *A Livraria Real, especialmente no reinado de D. Manuel* (Lisbon, 1901), p. 12 (item 8), p. 13 (item 10), p. 19 (item 58).

[23] *Ibid.*, p. 15 (item 27), p. 18 (item 31), p. 23 (item 97). See Barros on the book by Galvão in H. Cidade and M. Múrias (eds.), *Asia de João de Barros* (4 vols.; Lisbon, 1945), Vol. III, Bk. 2, chap. iv.

were devoted primarily to the East. These included the chronicles, accounts of sieges and shipwrecks, Jesuit letterbooks, the *Lusiads* (1572), and the *Xavier* (1600) of Lucena.[24]

The holdings of the libraries of the Portuguese universities, like those of many sixteenth-century universities elsewhere, were limited almost entirely to copies of the texts prescribed for courses: the standard works on theology, canon and Roman law, medicine, and grammar and rhetoric. The *Rol dos libros da livraria* of the University of Coimbra prepared in 1598 by André de Avellar reveals that its library had but 182 titles in 377 copies.[25] Not a single book on the discoveries, or one even remotely related to them, appears on this list, a fact that is made more startling when it is recalled that Fernão Lopes de Castanheda, the historian of Portugal's overseas conquests, was the librarian at Coimbra from 1538 to his death in 1559. Even when the collection of Father Francisco Suarez, the eminent Spanish Jesuit, was added to the university library in 1603, this condition did not alter appreciably. Of the 605 titles in the *Lista* of his library, the only work relating to Asia was the Jesuit Luis de Guzman's *Historia de las missiones*...(Alcalá, 1601).[26]

Such a dearth of material in the university library is particularly hard to understand when it is recalled that books on the East were regularly being printed in Portugal after mid-century. That such books circulated is sustained by the fact that later authors clearly depended in their own writings on the works of their predecessors. The private libraries of Góis, Camoëns, Orta, and other secular intellectuals, if their contents were known, would certainly reveal a selection of works on the East. The *Itinerario* of Linschoten, especially in its geographical, historical, ethnical, and botanical elements, is heavily indebted to earlier published works, many of which must have been available in Portuguese Goa.[27] But such conclusions receive only partial support from the evidence extant on private library holdings. Diogo de Murça, rector of the University of Coimbra from 1543 to 1555, had a library of 284 books which included retrospective materials on Asia: the works of Pliny, Ptolemy, and the story of Barlaam and Josaphat attributed to St. John of Damascus. The only contemporary book on the overseas discoveries in the rector's library was a *Novus orbis*, probably the collection of travel accounts published at Basel in 1532.[28] The inventory of Diogo da Azam-

---

[24] Figures based on an analysis of King Manuel II, *Livros antigos Portugueses, 1489–1600, da biblioteca da Sua Magestade Fidelissima* (3 vols.; London, 1929–32), Vols. II and III. For further details on printing in Portugal see *Asia*, I, 182–83, and Saraiva, *op. cit.* (n. 5), II, 128–30. Saraiva stresses that the number of titles, totaling over 1,300, printed in Portugal during the sixteenth century was small compared to the 4,100 that appeared in Italy. When other factors, such as population, literacy, and tradition, are put into the balance, I am impressed by the fact that the Portuguese come off this well—even if only quantitatively!

[25] For this list see T. Braga, *História da universidade de Coimbra* . . . (2 vols.; Lisbon, 1892, 1895), II, 250–53.

[26] On Suarez' library see M. Brandão, "Contribuições para a história da universidade de Coimbra: a livraria do Padre Francisco Suarez," *Biblos*, III (1927), 341. On Guzman see *Asia*, I, 328.

[27] See G. M. Parr, *Jan van Linschoten: The Dutch Marco Polo* (New York, 1964), pp. 100–1.

[28] J. A. Carvalho, "A livraria dum letrado do seculo XVI. Frei Diogo de Murça," *Boletim bibliografico da universidade de Coimbra*, Nos. i–viii (1927), pp. 1–27. For detail on the *Novus orbis* of 1532 see *Asia*, I, 179–80.

buja, a Portuguese soldier and officer who died at Madeira shortly before 1600, shows that he possessed the *Itinerario* of Linschoten and a work by Ortelius in Spanish translation.[29]

In Spain, which had interests and problems paralleling those of Portugal, the dissemination of books on the discoveries was evidently much freer. Spain, as part of Charles V's empire, was less parochial and defensive than Portugal. Ferdinand Columbus (1488–1539), the natural son of the great discoverer, was certainly the most enlightened Iberian bibliophile and collector of his day. After making several voyages to the West Indies, Ferdinand became an adviser to Charles V on overseas problems. With his ruler's financial encouragement, Ferdinand traveled to Italy, northern Europe, and England collecting books of every kind. He was also named in 1524 to represent Charles in the negotiations at Badajoz-Elvas with the Portuguese about their conflicting claims to the Moluccas.[30] Over the next two years he wrote four memoirs on behalf of his king's claims, and in the process he was obliged to accumulate and review all the literature that was then available on the Moluccas. After negotiations were temporarily broken off between the competing powers, Ferdinand returned in 1526 to his home in Seville to arrange his library and to help train pilots for the new fleets that Charles was preparing for dispatch to the Moluccas.[31]

Like many of his contemporaries, Ferdinand did an extraordinary amount of traveling in northern Europe. He visited most of the major cities from London to Venice in his unflagging search for books. He purchased everything from ancient Greek manuscripts to contemporary printed newsletters. On the last page of each item he wrote the place and date of acquisition and often noted its price. On his trips abroad he encouraged foreign scholars to visit and work in Spain. He met Johannes Was (Vasaeus) at Bruges in 1522, and was responsible for bringing him and Nicolas Clénard to Spain a decade later. Around 1535 Ferdinand, with Vasaeus as his librarian, settled down at his house at Seville to arrange his collections and to organize an Imperial College for the teaching of mathematics and navigation. When Ferdinand died in 1539, his library with its 15,370 books and manuscripts was one of the largest in Europe. In 1551 it became the property of the Cathedral Chapter of Seville. The present collection, called the "Colombina," is housed in the Cathedral library, but it now numbers only about 4,000 volumes.[32]

The truncated Colombina of today remains rich in materials relating to the life and activities of Christopher Columbus and in many other types of manuscript and printed materials. An examination of the catalog shows that Ferdinand collected almost everything he could find about cosmography and geography,

---

[29] See Braga, *op. cit.* (n. 25), II, 254–55n. On Ortelius and the epitomes of his work in the various European vernaculars see below, p. 477.

[30] For details on the conflict over the Moluccas see *Asia*, I, 114–19.

[31] For Ferdinand's activities see H. Harrisse, *Fernand Colomb, sa vie, ses oeuvres; Essai critique* (Paris, 1872), pp. 22–27. For the location of his library in Seville see pl. 11.

[32] For the history of the Colombina see H. Harrisse, *Excerpta Colombieniana . . .* (Paris, 1887), introduction.

the navigation to the East, Asia, and the Portuguese empire.[33] Among the retrospective and pre-discovery works we find the *De situ orbis* of Pomponius Mela in the edition of Hermolao Barbaro and Joachim Vadianus, Quintus Curtius' history (1494) in Latin of the exploits of Alexander the Great,[34] Marco Polo in Latin, Venetian, and Spanish, Aeneas Sylvius Piccolomini's (Pope Pius II's) *Historia*,[35] and Laurentius Corvinus' *Cosmographia* (1496) based on Ptolemy. On the Portuguese exploits in Asia we find three of the published letters of King Manuel,[36] and the *Itinerario* (1510) of Varthema. Among the French works of interest are *Le mirouer du monde* (1517) by François Buffereau and *L'histoire des successeurs d'Alexandre le Grand* (1530) extracted from Diodorus Siculus by Claude de Seyssel.[37]

During his lifetime the library of Ferdinand was open to all interested scholars and it was used by a distinguished list of them. Peter Martyr, Oviedo, and Gomara, personal friends of Ferdinand, consulted his books in preparing their histories of the discoveries.[38] Although certain of his contemporaries were hostile to Ferdinand, Oviedo described him in the *Historia* (Vol. I, Bk. III, chap. iv, p. 71) as a virtuous, noble, and affable gentleman, and there must have been a more general agreement on this favorable opinion. Among others, Ferdinand had as personal friends and as users of his library the controversialists over natural slavery, Juan Ginés de Sepúlveda and Bartolomé de las Casas. The librarian Jean Vasaeus (1511–61), in writing his *Hispaniae chronicon* (Frankfurt, 1579), certainly availed himself of Ferdinand's library. The text of Vasaeus' work, of which only the first part on history to A.D. 1020 was actually completed, is preceded by a catalog of the works he proposed to consult in writing the second part. Vasaeus indicates in this list that he planned to use as sources on Spain, Portugal, and the Iberian conquests, the works of Góis, Resende, Diogo de Teive, and the first five books of Oviedo. He also lists the first book of Castanheda, a work originally published in 1551 and in a revised version in 1554.[39] Its inclusion indicates that Vasaeus, long after the death of Ferdinand, persisted in his interests in Iberian bibliography.

The second important Spanish bibliophile was Benito Arias Montano (1527–98), Humanist, linguist, biblical scholar, and chaplain to King Philip II. A

---

[33] For the present holdings see S. Arlolí y Farando *et al.* (comps.), *Biblioteca Colombina: Catálogo de sus libros impresos* (7 vols.; Seville, 1888–1948).

[34] For further discussion of this book see below, p. 96.

[35] On this book see *Asia*, I, 70–71.

[36] These were the letters printed at Rome in 1506, 1513, and 1514. Though it does not figure in the modern catalog of the Colombina, it should be observed that Martin Fernández de Figueroa published in 1512 an abridged version in Castilian of one of Manuel's letters. See Frederick J. Norton, *Printing in Spain, 1501–20* (Cambridge, 1966). Of the books printed in Spain up to 1520 about fifty-three editions, or 4 percent of the total, deal with cosmography, geography, and activities in the East.

[37] See J. Babelon, *La bibliothèque française de Fernand Colomb* (Paris, 1913), pp 133–34, 200–1.

[38] See Harrisse, *Excerpta* . . . , pp. 32–34; on the writings of these Spanish chroniclers see *Asia*, I, 184–85.

[39] From the *Hispaniae chronicon* included in R. Bell (Belus), *Rerum hispaniscarum scriptores aliquot . . .* (2 vols. in 3; Frankfurt, 1579–81), I, 443–44; on Castanheda's book see *Asia*, I, 187–88.

reconstruction of his personal library reveals that in 1548 he already owned 128 books.[40] Listed under "books of mathematics," we find the Pirckheimer edition of Ptolemy's *Geography*, Strabo's *Geography* (Basel, 1552), the *Cosmographicus liber ... Petrus Appianus* (Landshut, 1524), and a *Descriptio novi orbis*. Under "books of history and humanities" are entered the classical histories of Pliny and Quintus Curtius, while under "books of romance" are found the first part of Oviedo's *Historia*, the *Arte de Navegar* (Valladolid, 1545) of Pedro de Medina, and the "Orlando Furioso en Toscano." In the mind of this Renaissance cataloger the Ancients alone apparently wrote "history" and evidently "romance" was not limited to fiction! A list of 1553 provides another 101 entries for his library, but they are less precise and too often the entry is simply given as "diverse navigations."[41] What is most striking about these lists is the fact that they include a larger than usual number of secular and contemporary works for a cleric's library, about 10 percent of the whole.[42]

Montano was active in his later years in helping Philip II to find rare manuscripts and books for the library of El Escorial, especially while it was being built between 1563 and 1584. The king's agents sought all over Europe for rare books for the new library. Montano, on his trips to Antwerp in 1568–70 to work out with Christopher Plantin the arrangements for publishing the second Spanish polyglot Bible, bought two manuscript books on Asia for the Escorial collection.[43] The king's agents in the Philippines and in India sent numerous Chinese books for his library, as well as copies of the new books and maps being prepared and printed at Manila.[44] After Philip became king of Portugal in 1580, he began to collect books in the Portuguese language to prepare his son and heir for the day when he would come to control Portugal and its overseas empire.[45] The collection of El Escorial, however, like that of the Vatican, stressed the acquisition of valuable manuscript books rather than the writings of

---

[40] See A. R. Rodríguez-Moñino, *La biblioteca de Benito Arias Montano, noticias y documentos para su reconstitución, 1548–98* (Badajoz, 1929), pp. 14–29.

[41] *Ibid.*, pp. 29–32.

[42] Cf., for example, the library of Antonino Augustin (1517–86), Archbishop of Tarragona, which included nothing about Asia except for a Latin version of the Barlaam and Josaphat legend and nothing about cosmography except for the works of Peter Apian. Consult his *Bibliothecae* (Tarragona, 1587), reputedly the first printed catalog of a private library in Spain.

[43] He bought a manuscript book on parchment entitled *Ung traicté de l'estat et conditions des 14 royaumes de Asia ...*, and another on paper called *Historia Indorum et regionis Aethiopum. ...* See R. Beer (ed.), "Niederländische Büchererwerbungen des Benitos Arias Montano für den Eskorial im Auftrage König Philip II von Spanien," *Jahrbuch der kunsthistorischen Sammlungen des allerhöchsten Kaiserhauses*, XXV (1905), Pt. 2, pp. vi, x.

[44] Cf., *Asia*, I, 693, 779 n.; II, Bk. 1, 13. Also see James J. Y. Liu, "The *Fêng-yüeh Chin-nang*: A Ming Collection of Yüan and Ming Plays and Lyrics Preserved in the Royal Library of San Lorenzo, Escorial, Spain," *Journal of Oriental Studies* (Hongkong), IV (1957–58), 79–107. Also see below, pp. 496–500 for printing in Asia, and W. E. Retana, *Tablas cronológica y alfabetica ...* (Madrid, 1908), pp. 7–9.

[45] In 1582 Philip sent his son a book in Portuguese "to help him learn the language (see L. P. Gachard [ed.], *Lettres de Philippe II à ses filles les infantes Isabella et Catherine écrites pendant son voyage en Portugal (1581–83)* [Paris, 1884], p. 186)." This was probably the little reading book by João de Barros called *Grammatica da lingua Portuguesa* (Lisbon, 1540).

contemporary European authors. Philip even sold off many of his father's books on "the Indies," presumably to help pay for his own rare acquisitions.[46]

Inventories to the libraries of Spanish literati of the sixteenth century are few. Of particular interest is the list (1595) of over four hundred books that belonged to the poet Luis Barahona de Soto.[47] Aside from the standard editions of classical philosophers, his collection was filled with retrospective and contemporary books on medicine and natural science as well as purely literary works in Spanish and Italian. Twenty-seven of his books, or about 6.5 percent of the total, were titles relating to the discoveries and to the East. He owned some of the pertinent geographical and historical works of Antiquity: Pomponius Mela, Solinus, Quintus Curtius, and Plutarch.[48] Of medieval writings he possessed a manuscript of the encyclopedia of Isidore of Seville, and a printed version of Sacrobosco on the sphere.[49] Among his scientific titles were two cosmographies, Rondelet's book on marine life, Vesalius on the China root, several herbals, Nicolas Monardes and Cristobal de Acosta on simples and drugs of the overseas world, one of Mattioli's editions of Dioscorides, Fracastoro on syphilis, and an unidentified discourse on navigation.[50] His contemporary works on the overseas conquests included the Spanish histories of Gomara and Oviedo, the chronicles of Castanheda (probably the Spanish edition of the first book published at Antwerp in 1554) and Osório, the *Lusiads* of Camoëns, José de Acosta's natural and moral history of the Indies, a general description of Africa, Francesco Sansovino's book on the governments of the world, and two Jesuit letterbooks about the successes of the mission in Japan.[51]

2

ITALY

Among the Italian bibliophiles the first to begin collecting books on Asia and the overseas world were members of the famous Este family, the rulers of Ferrara and Modena. Ercole I (1431–1505) was married to the Spanish Eleanor of Aragon, a princess noted for her religious devotion. Her husband, like his predecessors, was a man who cultivated the secular interests that had done so much to make the Este court a center of Renaissance learning. Ercole's eldest

---

[46] See J. J. Martín González, "El palacio de Carlo V en Yuste," *Archivo español de arte*, XXIII (1950), 246–47.

[47] See F. Rodríguez-Marín, *Luis Barahona de Soto: Estudio biográfico, bibliográfico y critico* (2 vols.: Madrid, 1903), pp. 520–51. For his career see below, pp. 179–83.

[48] *Ibid.*, pp. 526 (no. 65), 534 (172), 538 (235), 551 (418).

[49] *Ibid.*, pp. 537 (no. 207), 539 (244).

[50] *Ibid.*, pp. 531 (no. 128), 534 (167), 535 (183), 536 (191), 537 (212, 219), 538 (225), 541 (280), 546 (349), 547 (362), 549 (381).

[51] *Ibid.*, pp. 530 (no. 106), 540 (252), 543 (308), 544 (319), 545 (333), 548 (368, 375), 550 (413). The description of Africa was probably that of Mármol Caravaial published at Granada in 1573.

brother, Lionello (1407–50), had cultivated the classics and was a collector of ancient manuscripts. Borso (1413–71), the second brother, was not a skilled Latinist; so his taste in books turned toward translations and contemporary authors. Ercole, an adventurous spirit, preferred history, romance, and great feats of arms. Borso gave away to one of his courtiers in 1467 a book of Marco Polo's adventures. Ercole kept in his own study the history of Florence by Jacopo di Poggio, the *Lives of the Caesars* by Suetonius, and a copy of Marco Polo.[52] And in his dressing room, close at hand, according to an inventory of 1494, he kept the history of Alexander the Great.[53]

From the fragmentary catalog of the Este library dated 1467, it may be surmised that Borso had nothing about Asia in his library but the work on geography of Pomponius Mela.[54] The inventory of Ercole's library dated 1495 has 512 entries, a large number of which were printed books in the vernacular languages. Of relevant ancient authors he possessed printed versions of Arrian's history of Alexander, the universal history of Diodorus Siculus, two copies of the natural history of Pliny, the *Lives* of Plutarch, and the cosmography of Ptolemy. Of medieval authors he owned the *Fiore de historie doriente*, a Marco Polo, a Mandeville, and a version of Sacrobosco's (John Holywood's) *Tractatus de sphera mundi* (written *ca.* 1233). Among contemporary works he possessed a copy of the *Supplementum chronicarum* by Jacopo Filippo Foresti da Bergamo, a voluminous book on Eastern marvels that was first published at Venice in 1483. As early as 1488 it is noted in marginalia to the inventory that he owned a "'mapamondi' in a great sheath of leather."[55] But what is most revealing about his awakening interest in the discoveries are the two items dealing with the islands newly found by Spain, one enclosed in brazilwood and the other in stamped yellow leather.[56] Since the inventory does not indicate whether these were printed books, it is impossible to know their character. Certainly they might have been either literary or cartographic descriptions of the Spanish exploits in the New World. And, equally unidentifiable, is another entry which simply reads: "India per Ludovico de Mario de le sue cose mirabili."[57] Whatever else might be inferred from these entries, it must be concluded that Ercole and his circle were acutely aware of the maritime discoveries and interested in their progress.[58]

Shortly before Ercole's inventory was prepared, he arranged in 1490 for his daughter Isabella (1474–1539) to marry Francesco Gonzaga (d. 1519), the ruler of Mantua. Eleven years later Ercole had Alfonso (1476–1534), his son and heir,

[52] For details see G. Bertoni, *La biblioteca estense e la coltura ferrarese ai tempi del Duca Ercole I* (1471–1505), (Turin, 1903), pp. 18–19, 51 n. 3, 262.

[53] *Ibid.*, p. 51 n. 3. In a catalog of 1474 two Alexander manuscripts in French were listed as belonging to the Este library (*ibid.*, p. 81).

[54] Catalog reproduced in *ibid.*, pp. 213–15.

[55] *Ibid.*, p. 261.

[56] *Ibid.*, p. 243.

[57] *Ibid.*

[58] In 1598 the Este library was moved from Ferrara to Modena, its present location. See G. A. E. Bogeng, *Die grossen Bibliophilen: Geschichte der Büchersammler und ihrer Sammlungen* (3 vols.; Leipzig, 1922), I, 66–67.

marry Lucrezia Borgia, thus maintaining the Spanish connection of the house of Este. After Alfonso succeeded his father in 1505, the court of Ferrara continued to be a brilliant center of literary and intellectual activity despite Alfonso's embroilment in war. But it was Isabella and her son Federico (1500–1540) who most closely resembled Ercole in his taste for art treasures and books. Isabella's small library of 133 items contained a manuscript of Pliny and of the *Gesta Romanorum*, a medieval romance many of whose stories relate to India.[59] It also housed the printed works of Peter Martyr and something called "News of the new India ('Nove delle Indie nove')," possibly one of the newsletters that circulated widely before the age of the periodical and newspaper. From her experiences at Rome in 1514, she possessed two mementos of the Portuguese embassy and its visit there: a copy of Aretino's "Last Will and Testament of the Elephant" and a copy of the *Propalladia*, a collection of plays by Torres Naharro, one of which was presented in Spanish at Rome to celebrate the Portuguese conquest in the East.[60] Federico Gonzaga's larger library of 179 items included a number of relevant classical works in Spanish. It also housed a summary of Pigafetta's account of Magellan's voyage around the world,[61] Oviedo's *Historia general*, and Francisco Pizarro's *Relatione*. What is also striking about Federico's collection is its relatively small number of books in Latin (just 22) and the presence of so many books in Spanish, French, and Italian.[62]

Much less is known for this period about the contents of the library of St. Mark's in Venice and the university and private libraries of neighboring Padua. The scarcity of information on these libraries is particularly regrettable since it is clear from the works of Venetian printers, engravers, cartographers, and *letterati* that a wide range of materials on Asia was available in the region.[63] The library of St. Mark's, compared by Guillaume Budé (1468–1540) in 1521 to the famous library of ancient Alexandria, was superintended by Andrea Navagero from 1515 to 1523, the date when he was dispatched to Spain as a representative of the *Signoria*. He was evidently sent there to learn at first hand about the results of the Magellan expedition, news of which had been relayed to the Senate

[59] See below, p. 110 for discussion of the *Gesta Romanorum*.

[60] For the inventory of Isabella's library see A. Luzio and R. Renier (eds.), "La coltura e le relazioni letterarie di Isabella d'Este Gonzaga," *Giornale storico della letteratura italiana*, XLII (1903), 75–81, 89. For discussion of the work of Torres Naharro see below, pp. 166–68; for extracts from Aretino's satirical piece see *Asia*, II, Bk. 1, 139.

[61] For Pigafetta's correspondence with and reception by Isabella see *Asia*, I, 173–74. It may be that the reference in the inventory of Federico's books that reads "Il viaggio fatto dal Spagnolo atorno al mondo" (item 65) is to the summary account, previously unlocated, of the voyage especially prepared in 1522 by Pigafetta for Isabella, or it might also be a reference to the truncated version of Pigafetta's work which appeared at Venice in 1536.

[62] For Federico's library see A. Luzio and R. Renier, *loc. cit.* (n. 60), pp. 81–87; for the later acquisitions of the Este library, now at Modena, see D. Fava, *La biblioteca Estense nel suo sviluppo storico* (Modena, 1925), pp. 306–7, 318.

[63] For example, see the large number of works on the discoveries included in the list compiled by Maria Cristofari in "La tipografia vicentina nel secolo XVI," in *Miscellanea di scritti di bibliografia ed erudizione in memoria di Luigi Ferrari* (Florence, 1952), pp. 191–214.

directly by Pigafetta himself.[64] From 1530 to 1543 Pietro Bembo was the official librarian of St. Mark's and historian of Venice. Because of his frequent absences from Venice, Bembo was aided as librarian by Giovanni Battista Ramusio (1485–1557), the secretary of the Senate and the great collector of travel literature.[65] From their literary works and correspondence it is plain that Navagero, Bembo, and Ramusio were all deeply interested in the overseas activities of the Portuguese and Spanish. But there are no inventories extant for the public or private libraries of Venice comparable to those for the Este collections.

Even after becoming the librarian of St. Mark's, Bembo spent much of his time in Padua. He was there when Góis arrived in 1534. In his letters to Ramusio from Rome and elsewhere, Bembo mentions in 1541 and 1543 his correspondence with Oviedo, the Spanish historian.[66] Giacomo Gastaldi, the cartographer, applied in 1550 for permission to publish in Venice a map of Asia that would include everything eastward from the Mediterranean to Cathay and southward to India and the Moluccas.[67] Diego Hurtado di Mendoza (1503–75), Spanish emissary of Charles V to Venice and Rome, collected one of the finest libraries of the day, the most valuable items of which passed on his death into the library of El Escorial. From these and other materials it is obvious that the learned of Padua and Venice had available in the first half of the century the latest materials on Asia even though no detailed inventories exist to support and amplify this conclusion.

The greatest collector of books at Padua in the latter half of the sixteenth century was Gian Vincenzo Pinelli (1535–1610), son of a wealthy Neapolitan merchant. At Naples, where Spanish influence was traditionally important, the youthful Pinelli assembled a botanical garden of rare plants. When he moved to Padua in 1559, Pinelli took his collecting zeal with him. Like most wealthy Humanist collectors, Pinelli had agents who sought rare manuscripts and ancient artifacts for him. He was also fortunate enough to inherit the library of Paolo Aicardo, his friend and fellow Padovan. Although no inventory exists of his collections, we know from the biography written by his friend, Father Paulo Gualdo, that Pinelli's library included globes, spheres, maps, and books on the latest geographical discoveries.[68] His library and museum were open to his scholarly friends and acquaintances. Upon his death the best of his

---

[64] On Navagero's report see E. A. Cicogna (comp.), *Delle inscrizioni veneziana* (6 vols.; Venice, 1824–53), VI, 310–18.

[65] See C. Castellani, *Pietro Bembo, bibliotecario della libreria di S. Marco (1530–43)* (Venice, 1896), pp. 1–15. Also see *Asia*, I, 205.

[66] Castellani, *op. cit.* (n. 65), pp. 31–32. Oviedo's first book was translated into Italian by Andrea Navagero and published at Venice in 1534. See H. F. Brown, *The Venetian Printing Press* ... (London, 1896), p. 103. Also see below, pp. 171–72.

[67] Brown, *op. cit.* (n. 66), p. 102. Gastaldi's map published in 1561 was based on the Portuguese maps in its general layout, but its toponomic features derive from Marco Polo. See A. Cortesão, *History of Portuguese Cartography* (Coimbra, 1969), I, 295.

[68] See Paulo Gualdo, *Vita Joannis Vincentii Pinelli, patritii Gesuiensis* as reproduced in William Bates, *Vitae selectorum aliquot virorum* ... (London, 1681), p. 334.

manuscripts went to Venice. Most of the remainder of his books were sent to Naples where they were kept in storage until purchased by Cardinal Federico Borromeo for the great Ambrosiana in Milan.[69] At Padua the tradition of collecting was maintained into the seventeenth century by Lorenzo Pignoria (1571–1631).[70]

The Medici rulers of Florence in the fifteenth century were intent solely upon collecting the works of the ancient writers. The catalog dated 1495 of their library lists only the life of Alexander the Great and nothing else that refers directly to Asia.[71] The involvement of Florentine merchants and bankers in the spice trade led gradually, however, to the collection of books and maps on the maritime routes and the overseas countries. The inventory of the Rosselli art shop dated 1526–28 reveals that it had a substantial stock of sea charts and world maps.[72] Cosimo I (reigned 1537–74) and Francesco I (reigned 1574–87) were themselves collectors of maps and books on navigation. On the basis of the routiers acquired by Cosimo, as well as from other sources, Ignatio Danti (1536–86) prepared a huge map of the world that was one of the first to show Japan.[73]

The Humanists, artists, and *letterati* of Florence were among the earliest of the city's citizens to collect retrospective and contemporary materials on the East. Pico della Mirandola (1463–94), the eclectic philosopher, possessed a world map, the *Peregrinatio* and a book on the nations of the Levant by Ricole de Montecroix (d. 1309), the overland travels of Marco Polo and Odoric of Pordenone, and the versified *Geografia* (*ca.* 1480) of Francisco Berlinghieri (*ca.* 1450–80) based on Ptolemy.[74] Leonardo da Vinci (1452–1519) owned a world map, Pliny's *Natural History*, a *Treatise on the Sphere*, Albertus Magnus on plants and animals, and the travels of Mandeville.[75] Anton Francesco Doni (1513–74), the Utopian writer, acquired during his years of restless travel the *Historia* (1461) of Aeneas Sylvius Piccolomini, Mandeville, Quintus Curtius, the *Itinerario* of Varthema, and an account of a voyage to the king of Persia which might well have been the *Viaggi fatti alla Tana*...(Venice, 1543).[76]

---

[69] See Bogeng, *op, cit.* (n. 58), pp. 71–72.

[70] For Asian items in his collections see J. P. Tomasino, *V. C. Laurentii Pignorii ... bibliotheca et museum* (Venice, 1632), pp. 25–29. For more on his Asian interests see *Asia*, II, Bk. 1, 89 n. 172. He kept a portrait of Pinelli in his museum.

[71] E. Alvisi (ed.), *Index bibliothecae Mediceae* (Florence, 1882), p. 29. The physician of Lorenzo the Magnificent had only a Strabo and a Ptolemy in his personal collection. See Léon Dorez, "Recherches sur la bibliothèque de Pier Leoni, médicin de Laurent de Medicis," *Revue des bibliothèques*, VII (1897), 91.

[72] See H. Brockhaus, "Ein altflorentiner Kunstverlag," *Mitteilungen des kunsthistorischen Instituts in Florenz*, I (1910), 97–98. Also see below, p. 475.

[73] See *Asia*, II, Bk. 1, 39–40; and below, p. 463. For an example of the Medici wardrobe maps see pl. 76.

[74] Pearl Kibre, *The Library of Pico* (New York, 1936), pp. 109–10.

[75] E. McCurdy (trans.), *The Notebooks of Leonardo* (2 vols. in 1; New York, 1958), II, 1164–68, 1176.

[76] For Doni's collection see *La libraria del Doni Florentino: Nella quale sono scritti tutti gl'autori vulgari con 100 discorsi sopra quelli* (Venice, 1550).

In 1500 Rome had one pope and thirty-nine cardinals; consequently, it boasted forty episcopal palaces each of which housed at least one combined museum and library. The pope was Alexander VI (reigned 1492–1503) of the Spanish family of Borgia who had himself drawn the line of demarcation between the Spanish and Portuguese zones in the overseas world. The Vatican library, begun by Pope Nicholas V (reigned 1447–55), was notable not for the number but rather for the rarity and value of its manuscripts and books. In the sixteenth century, beginning with the pontificate of Leo X (1513–21), the Vatican library began to acquire a fine collection of Oriental manuscripts, mainly Hebrew, Chaldean, and Syrian. By 1590 there were almost twenty thousand books in the library, mostly in manuscript, and including a few in "Indian" languages.[77] This is possibly a reference to the Chinese books which had earlier been presented to the popes, or to those which the Jesuit Michele Ruggiero, brought back to Rome with him in 1590.[78] Whatever interpretation may be given to the word "Indian," it is clear that the librarians of the Vatican in the last decade of the sixteenth century would have been happy to include Chinese books within their select classical collection, an indication perhaps of the relationship that some savants perceived between the "Antiquity" of the West and that of China.[79]

Very few contemporary printed books, including those on the discoveries, were collected for the Vatican library. The private libraries of some of the richest and most learned cardinals were also severely limited to rarities of both Western and Oriental provenance. That books were often collected for their rarity alone is attested by an exchange of gifts which took place between Cardinal Girolamo Aleandro (1480–1542) and his patron Evrard de La Marck (1475–1538), the bishop-prince of Liége. In return for several books that he received as gifts from La Marck, Aleandro in 1533 presented the prince with two Chinese vases.[80] But not all the episcopal collectors were connoisseurs like Aleandro. Cardinal Niccolo Ridolfi (1501–50) had a number of printed books in his library on Ethiopia, on the victories of Alexander, and on cosmography.[81]

That the Romans, clerics and laymen alike, were eager for fresh information on the overseas world can be readily established. Giovanni Ricci de Montepulciano, the legate to Portugal of Paul III, reportedly acquired around 1550 from João de Barros at least three books on Asia. Montepulciano had requested

---

[77] M. Pansa, *Della libraria Vaticana* (Rome, 1590), pp. 318–19. This author, when describing the reception of the Japanese emissaries by Sixtus V, refers to them as "tre Giovani Indiani" (p. 39). At other points in his discussion (pp. 39–46) he refers to them as "Japanese." This broad sense of the word "Indian" persists into the eighteenth century. Also notice his reference to a painting in the Vatican library of the reception of the Japanese by the pope.

[78] See below, p. 528.

[79] Cf. the collection of Chinese books at El Escorial (see above, p. 47).

[80] L. Dorez, "Recherches sur la bibliothèque du Cardinal Girolamo Aleandro," *Revue des bibliothèques*, VII (1897), 57 n. 4.

[81] See Roberto Ridolfi, "La biblioteca del Cardinale Niccolo Ridolfi (1501–50)," *Bibliofilia*, XXXI (1929), 190–93.

these for the use of Paolo Giovio in writing the history of his own time.[82] The engravers and print sellers of Rome, Antonio Salamanca and Antonio Lafreri, reproduced Mercator's double cordiform map of the world with great fidelity shortly after its appearance at Louvain in 1538.[83] Newsletters printed in Portugal called *Avvisi* were sold in 1571 on the streets of Rome.[84] Seventy-eight items describing the Japanese mission were published from 1585 to 1587, most of them in Italy.[85] Philips van Winghe, the Belgian artist, wrote from Rome in 1592 to Ortelius, the Antwerp geographer, about his efforts to obtain a large map of China from an Arabian printer who had promised him one.[86] The inventory of Girolamo Muziano (1529–92) dated 1592 likewise reveals a preoccupation with the East. Of the 147 titles in this artist's library, seven deal with Oriental subjects, including Gualtieri's *Relationi* (1585) about the Japanese embassy, an *Avvisi della Cina et Giappone*, and a *Raguaglio d'un naufragio del Indie*.[87] Muziano's interest in the East is easily explained for he worked along with a number of other artists on the *Galleria delle carte geografiche* of the Vatican.[88]

St. Charles Borromeo (1538–84) was perhaps the greatest Italian bibliophile of the latter half of the sixteenth century. The wheelhorse in the final deliberations of the Council of Trent, this nephew of Pope Pius IV was politically and intellectually one of the most influential men of his day. On the death of Pius IV in 1566, Borromeo settled down in his diocese of Milan. Here he put together one of the finest private libraries of his century. In his collection were to be found the major classical and Renaissance works of geography, cosmography, and navigation. Next to the *De situ orbis* of Solinus is listed the *Theatrum orbis terrarum* of Ortelius. Of the works on the discoveries this churchman possessed histories of the navigation to India and to America, as well as the *Itinerarium portugalense . . .* (Milan, 1508) of Arcangelo Madrignano.[89] Upon his death Borromeo's library passed to his nephew, Federico, and was eventually incorporated into the Ambrosian library whose holdings were further enriched by the acquisition of G. V. Pinelli's collection from Naples.[90]

[82] H. Cidade and M. Múrias (eds.), *op. cit.* (n. 23), I, 361. It is conceivable that it was from these books that the so-called Chinese alphabet was derived (below, p. 513) for Barros refers to one of these as "um libro da escritura dos Chis."

[83] See R. Almagià, "La diffusion des produits cartographiques flamands en Italie au XVIᵉ siècle," *Archives internationales d'histoire des sciences*, XXXIII (1954), 46.

[84] See. J. Delumeau, *Vie économique et sociale de Rome dans la seconde moitié du XVIᵉ siècle* (Paris, 1957), p. 29.

[85] See A. Boscaro, *Sixteenth Century European Printed Works of the First Japanese Mission to Europe* (Leyden, 1973), p. xii.

[86] On the Arabian printer see below, p. 463. For Winghe's letter see J. H. Hessels (ed.), *Abraham Ortelii . . . epistulae . . . (1524–1628)* (Cambridge, 1887), p. 522.

[87] Ugo da Como, *Girolamo Muziano, 1528–92: Noti e documenti* (Bergamo, 1930), pp. 193–95.

[88] See. R. Almagià, *Monumenta cartographica Vaticana* (4 vols.; Vatican City, 1944–55), III, 1–11. Also see below, p. 464.

[89] Agostino Saba, *La biblioteca di S. Carlo Borromeo* (Florence, 1936), pp. 41–48.

[90] See above, p. 51, and below, p. 237.

3

THE GERMANIES

The princely bibliophiles of the House of Habsburg were, like the popes, primarily selective collectors of rare manuscripts.[91] The emperors Maximilian I (reigned 1459-1519), Ferdinand I (1558-64), and Maximilian II (1564-76) were the Habsburgs most responsible for laying the foundations of the Hofbibliothek in Vienna. The history of their book collecting activities is a long and involved tale.[92] Ferdinand I began to centralize the Habsburg book collections at Vienna and was responsible for establishing there a library independent of his art and curiosa collections. The first register of the Vienna library was completed in 1576 by Hugo Blotius (1534-1608), the guardian of the collection. In this list of 7,379 titles he makes only a slight effort to distinguish between manuscript and printed books.[93] An examination of his register shows that the Habsburgs owned manuscript books on parchment and papyrus of retrospective writings on the deeds of Alexander, the life of Barlaam, and the geography of Ptolemy.[94] They also possessed a manuscript book of Marco Polo and the *De varietate fortunae* of Poggio describing the marvels of India as related to him by Nicolò de' Conti.[95] Of the writings pertaining to the discoveries of the sixteenth century the Habsburgs possessed both manuscript and printed books.[96] But from the listings it is difficult to determine precisely what they were, as for example in the entry: "Indicanae navigationis historia manuscripta in folio."[97] Blotius lists a number of items under "Turcica" which refer to the books and manuscripts acquired by Busbecq and others in Constantinople. The "Indian books" acquired by the Habsburgs were kept in their collections of curiosities rather than in the library.[98]

While Blotius compiled his catalog, Archduke Ferdinand (1520-95) of Tirol was building his great collection of curiosities at the castle of Ambras near

[91] On their collections of curiosities see *Asia*, II, Bk. 1, 22-30.

[92] See Theodor Gottlieb, *Büchersammlung Kaiser Maximilians I . . .* (Leipzig, 1900); and A. Lhotsky, *Die Geschichte der Sammlungen* (Vienna, 1945), pp. 139-40.

[93] Blotius estimated that the library contained at least twenty thousand individual volumes, and he claimed that a full inventory would reveal that the Vienna collection was richer in rare books than the Vatican library. See J. Stummvoll, *Geschichte der österreichischen Nationalbibliothek* (Vienna, 1968), pp. 109-15.

[94] H. Menhardt, *Das älteste Handschriftenverzeichnis der Wiener Hofbibliothek von Hugo Blotius, 1576* (Vienna, 1957), pp. 33, 36, 40, 83.

[95] *Ibid.*, p. 82; on Poggio's book see *Asia*, I, 62-63.

[96] Menhardt, *op. cit.* (n. 94), pp. 52, 60, 68, 69.

[97] *Ibid.*, p. 69.

[98] See the inventories of the Prague collections of Rudolf II in *Asia*, II, Bk. 1, 46-54. It should also be noticed that the library of the Jesuit College in Vienna possesses Chinese, Malabar, and Japanese manuscripts. It is not possible, however, to know when they were acquired. See E. Gollob, "Die Bibliothek des Jesuitenkollegiums in Wien XIII (Lainz) und ihre Handschriften," *Sitzungsberichte der philosophisch-historischen Klasse*, CLXI (1909), Pt. vii, 31.

Innsbruck.[99] His personal book collection, which evidently included the books of Maximilian I that were long stored in the Hofburg of Innsbruck, was augmented by books that he purchased from his neighbors or that were acquired for him by Georg Willer, the famous book dealer of Augsburg. In 1576 he received as a gift almost three hundred printed books and sixty-nine manuscripts from the library of Count Wilhelm Werner von Zimmern (1485–1575), the Swiss collector. Gerard van Roo, a learned Dutchman, was put in charge of the Ambras library as it rapidly grew in size. In the year following Ferdinand's death in 1595, an inventory was made of the "Bibliotheca oder Pücher Kunst Camer." But this list has so far not been published, and I have not consulted the manuscript catalog in the National Library at Vienna.[100] Ferdinand's library remained at Ambras until 1665 when Emperor Leopold I united the Tirol with his other hereditary lands. Peter Lambeck (1628–80) was then sent to Ambras to inventory the collection anew and to arrange for its removal to the Hofbibliothek in Vienna. Lambeck found 569 manuscripts and 5,880 printed books in the collection. The manuscripts and 1,489 of the printed books were moved to Vienna. It is not possible today to identify the printed books then incorporated into the Vienna library or to know in detail what happened to the remainder of them. It is clear, however, that Ferdinand and his wife, Philippine Welser, collected printed contemporary accounts of the discoveries as well as a number of manuscript maps of the overseas world.[101]

While the Habsburgs concentrated on acquiring rare manuscripts, many private bibliophiles in south Germany were inclined by their interests in contemporary affairs to collect printed books. At Nuremberg, for example, the physicians Hieronymus Münzer (1437–1508) and Hartmann Schedel (1440–1514) built up substantial libraries while they watched closely the tightening of communication between their city and the Iberian states.[102] The catalog of Schedel's library prepared in 1514 lists a copy of Manuel's letter to Pope Leo X published at Rome just the year before, an entry which illustrates how swiftly news traveled to the south German cities. Schedel published his *Liber chronicarum* (1493) just one year before Münzer left on a trip to Spain. From Münzer's

99 See Menhardt, *op. cit.* (n. 94), pp. 26–27.

100 Codex 8228, fols. 485ʳ–635ᵛ. See Vienna, National Library, *Ambraser Kunst und Wunderkammer: Die Bibliothek. Katalog der Ausstellung im Prunksaal 28. Mai bis 30. September 1965* (Vienna, 1965), p. 30, item 33.

101 On some of the maps, probably from Ambras originally and now in the map collection of the National Library, see O. Quelle, "Die ibero-amerikanischen Länder in Manuscriptatlanten des 16. und 17. Jahrhunderts der Wiener Nationalbibliothek," *Ibero-Amerikanisches Archiv*, XIII (1939), 135–38. One of these (Codex ser. nov. 2630 [Ambraser Atlas]) is a book of twelve excellent sea and land maps on thick parchment from the end of the sixteenth century. They are probably Italian in origin. For a portrait of Philippine Welser see Innsbruck, Katalog, *Oesterreich-Tirol, 1363–1963* (Innsbruck, 1963), pl. 21. It is estimated that Ferdinand's library of natural history included 3,430 volumes; and they were placed at the disposal of Georg Hoefnagel, the artist, and a number of visiting scholars. See G. Händler, *Fürstliche Mäzene und Sammler in Deutschland von 1500 bis 1620* (Strassburg, 1933), pp. 49–50.

102 On the circulation of news about the discoveries in the south German commercial cities see *Asia*, I, 161–63; for Schedel's catalog see R. Stauber, *Die Schedelsche Bibliothek* (Freiburg, 1908), pp. 154–225, especially pp. 170, 174.

diary[103] it appears that he was accompanied on his eight months' (August, 1494–April, 1495) journey by three sons of rich merchants: Anton Herwart of Augsburg and Kaspar Fischer and Nikolaus Wolkenstein of Nuremberg. While in Spain and Portugal, Münzer displayed a lively interest in strange Iberian geographical features and exotic flora and fauna. He was moved to describe in his diary the black slaves he saw being sold at Lisbon. He also records that a young camel was then wandering about the royal park of Évora. While he learned of the progress of the discoveries in Africa at first hand, Münzer derived some of his information on the geography of the East from the classical authorities and from the cosmographies of Aeneas Sylvius (Venice, 1477) and Laurentius Corvinus (Basel, 1496) in his personal library.[104]

At Augsburg the German merchants, printers, artists, and Humanists were meanwhile gathering information from their commercial agents in Lisbon and Antwerp and encouraging the publication and dissemination of newsletters (*Flugblätter*), books, and engravings relating to overseas expansion.[105] Conrad Peutinger, the Humanist, collected manuscript reports from Lisbon which he bound together between wooden covers and entitled *De insulis et peregrinationibus Lusitanorum.*[106] He also collected maps of the East, one of which was possibly acquired later by the library of Wolffenbüttel.[107] In the library of Willibald Pirckheimer were nine books relating to overse᷄᷄ voyages, one of which was a copy with his own bookplate in it of the *Itinerarium* (Milan, 1508) of Montalboddo.[108]

The Fuggers of Augsburg, whose economic interests and social life were closely tied to overseas expansion,[109] were avid bibliophiles. The history of the Fugger libraries in the sixteenth century is about as complicated as the genealogy of the house and much less well documented. Raimund the Elder (1489–1535) was the first of his line to begin systematically collecting rare manuscripts and books.[110] In the middle years of the century his eldest son, Hans Jakob (1516–75), formed the vast collection that came to be called the Proto-Fuggerana. Beginning with the small library inherited from his father in 1535, Hans Jakob traveled around western Europe, including visits to the

103 For a digest see E. P. Goldschmidt, *Hieronymus Münzer und seine Bibliothek* (London, 1938), pp. 59–97.

104 He had a library of 185 titles, mainly of printed books written by classical and Renaissance authors. See *ibid.*, pp. 125–38.

105 See *Asia*, II, Bk. 1, 79–80.

106 For details see *ibid.*, I, 159.

107 See R. Uhden, "The Oldest Portuguese Original Chart of the Indian Ocean, A.D. 1509," *Imago mundi*, III (1939), 7.

108 He had a library of 276 titles. See Emile Offenbacher, "La bibliothèque de Wilibald Pirckheimer," *La bibliofilia*, XL (1939), 241–63.

109 For example, when Charles V returned from Tunis in 1536 the Fuggers reputedly gave a banquet in his honor in a hall heated by a fire of Ceylon cinnamon wood. See C. B. Petitot (ed.), "Mémoires de Jacques-Auguste de Thou," in *Collection complète des mémoires relatifs à l'histoire de France* (15 vols.; Paris, 1824–27), 1st ser. XXXVII, 281 n. 1.

110 Jakob the Rich (1459–1525) is often incorrectly credited with being the founder of the Fugger libraries. Anton the Elder (1493–1560), brother of Raimund, was also a bibliophile. See Paul Lehmann, *Eine Geschichte der alten Fuggerbibliotheken* (Tübingen, 1956), Pt. I, pp. 4–5.

Netherlands and Spain, in search of books. Well versed himself in both ancient and modern languages, Hans Jakob and his friends and agents acquired rare items of all types whenever they appeared on the market. In 1552 he bought Hartmann Schedel's library of 670 printed books, a collection rich in Latin works on the natural sciences, and in 1563 he acquired the smaller library of Oswald Eck.[111] In 1571 the library of Hans Jakob Fugger was acquired by Duke Albrecht of Bavaria (reigned 1550–79) and added to the Wittelsbach collections.

The library amassed at Munich during Albrecht's reign totaled about 11,000 volumes.[112] The books of the Orientalist Johann Albrecht Widmanstetter (1506–57) were incorporated into it in 1558 and those of Duke Ernst (1500–1560) of Bavaria in 1561. Ernst's collection numbered around 2,500 bound and unbound books and manuscripts. The collection of Hans Jakob Fugger acquired one decade later numbered around 7,000 items. From Widmanstetter the ducal library gained two books by Góis, a cosmography of Ptolemy, and notes on a sea chart.[113] From Schedel's library, included in the Fugger collection, it received a manuscript copy of Marco Polo and the letter of King Manuel to Pope Leo X announcing the conquest of Malacca which was printed at Rome in 1513.[114] From Oswald Eck came a manuscript, possibly by Ulrich Schmidel, described simply as "Iter Indicum et Hispanicum germanice chart."[115] The Fugger collection also included two copies in manuscript of a translation from Spanish into German of Duarte Barbosa's description of India made at Augsburg in 1530 by Hieronymus Seitz.[116] A small atlas of sea charts by Battista Agnese acquired from Fugger was added to the collection of forty maps and atlases which the library boasted in 1577.[117] Among the relevant printed books from Fugger were the first two decades of Barros' *Asia* (Lisbon, 1552–53) and the *Historia* (2 vols.; Antwerp, 1554) of Francisco Lopez de Gomara.[118]

Abraham Ortelius, the geographer, and Georg Hoefnagel, the animal painter, visited the library and art collections at Munich in 1577. Perhaps on that occasion they saw the Chinese book kept in the library of the Kunstkammer which is described as a book that "opens from back to front with all kinds of Indian

---

[111] *Ibid.*, chaps. ii–iii.

[112] See Felix F. Strauss, "The 'Liberey' of Duke Ernst of Bavaria (1500–1560)," *Studies in the Renaissance*, VIII (1961), 128–43.

[113] Catalog in O. Hartig, *Die Gründung der Münchener Hofbibliothek durch Albrecht V und Johann Jakob Fugger . . .*, "Abhandlungen der königlich-bayerischen Akademie der Wissenschaften, philosophisch-philologische und historische Klasse," Vol. XXVIII (Munich, 1917), pp. 180, 185, 190, 192.

[114] Also another unidentified item on India by "Malherio[?]" printed in 1507. See *ibid.*, pp. 334–38; also Stauber, *op. cit.* (n. 102), pp. 116, 169, 174.

[115] Hartig, *op. cit.* (n. 113), pp. 61–62, n. 4.

[116] *Ibid.*, p. 275. On Barbosa see *Asia*, I, 170.

[117] Hartig, *op. cit.* (n. 113), pp. 275, 352–56. The library then held the world maps of Waldseemüller, Vopell (1556), Ortelius (1564), and Gerhard de Jode (1575).

[118] *Ibid.*, pp. 330–31. On the Asia of Barros see K. L. Selig, "A German Collection of Spanish Books," *Bibliothèque d'humanisme et renaissance*, XIX (1957), 76. Fugger collected a substantial number of Spanish literary works as well.

figures which are not unlike hieroglyphic writing."[119] The Munich librarian, Wolfgang Pommer, noted in 1588 that the tutor of Prince Maximilian withdrew from the library for the instruction of his student the *Theatrum* (1570) of Ortelius, the *Res gestae Emmanuelis* of Osório, and a work on the two Indies by Johannes Metellus.[120] From these bits of evidence it can readily be adduced that the Munich collection was used by persons eager to acquire more information on the overseas world.

Interested scholars would also have been well advised at this period to visit at Augsburg the library of Ulrich Fugger (1526–84), the younger brother of Hans Jakob. It numbered over 10,000 items, and it remained in Augsburg until the vagaries of the Thirty Years' War brought its removal to Rome. Ulrich, a pious Catholic, was not as universal or contemporary in his interests as was his brother. He concentrated upon collecting the writings of Antiquity and orthodox theological works and studiously avoided much of the controversial Reformation material being circulated in his day. Still he possessed a number of works, both ancient and contemporary, on navigation and the overseas world. His library included Greek and Latin manuscript versions of the legend of Barlaam and Josaphat.[121] Among his other manuscripts were three relating to the overseas world and to navigation, and a fourth intriguingly entitled "Descriptio elephantis terrestris et marini."[122] His holdings of printed books included literally all the major works of Antiquity dealing with Asia as well as the *Supplementum chronicorum* (1485) of Bergamo, the collected works (Antwerp, 1544) of Góis, and the cosmographical writings of Amerigo Vespucci, Sebastian Münster, and André Thevet.[123] He also possessed the *Weltbuch* of Sebastian Franck, the *Epitome* of Vadianus, and a "description of the New World and previously unknown places" by Jorg Albrich von Anlau.[124]

The Augsburger most central to book-collecting activities in south Germany was Georg Willer (1514–93), a leading book dealer of the day. He had a branch in Tübingen and sent an agent on weekly business trips to Vienna. Aside from books, Willer was evidently one of the main dealers in maps printed at Venice and Antwerp. A catalog published in 1573 let his clientele of small bookshops and individual collectors know that he had for sale in Augsburg Gastaldi's maps of the world in two different editions, Ortelius' map of Asia, and a variety of other maps.[125] Willer also compiled in 1564, "for the convenience and use of book-sellers everywhere and all students of literature,"[126] a catalog of the books

[119] From Fickler's inventory (1598), as quoted in Hartig, *op. cit.* (n. 113), p. 122.

[120] *Ibid.*, p. 348.

[121] See Lehmann, *op. cit.* (n. 110), Pt. II, pp. 85, 180, 290.

[122] *Ibid.*, pp. 203, 209, 313.

[123] On classical Greek and Latin works see *ibid.*, pp. 85, 101, 109, 118, 123, 140, 176, 181, 183, 202, 223, 240, 285, 290; for the Renaissance titles see *ibid.*, pp. 199, 264, 275, 346, 348, 367, 428.

[124] *Ibid.*, pp. 184–85.

[125] See L. Bagrow, "A Page from the History of the Distribution of Maps," *Imago mundi*, V (1948), 57–59.

[126] As quoted in A. Ehrman and B. Pollard, *The Distribution of Books by Catalogue from the Invention of Printing to A.D. 1800* (Cambridge, 1965), p. 80.

that were on sale at the Frankfurt fair. The Fuggers, the Habsburgs, and the Wittelsbachs were among Willer's best clients. It was possibly from Willer, or one of his agents, that Hans Sachs (1496–1576), the leading poet of the Nuremberg school, obtained many of the books in his private library. Among the sixty-seven titles listed in his catalog, prepared by the poet himself, are a *Gesta romanorum* (Augsburg, 1489), the German translation of Varthema (Augsburg, 1515), and the *Weltbuch* of Sebastian Franck.[127]

Basel, a leading trade and printing center, was a nexus of scholarly activity in Protestant Switzerland.[128] From 1530 to 1560 this Rhenish city which stood athwart the commercial routes linking the Netherlands and Italy played host to many foreign merchants and to numbers of refugees from the wars of religion. Scholars resident in Basel and its environs included Simon Grynaeus (d. 1541), Konrad Gesner (1516–65), Sebastian Münster, Beatus Rheanus, and Sebastian Franck. It was in this distinguished company that Gesner began compiling the work that would earn for him the title of "father of bibliography." But Gesner was not limited to his contacts in Zurich, Basel, and other Swiss towns. He traveled widely on the Continent. At Montpellier he became acquainted with the naturalist Guillaume Rondelet (1507–66) and with Petrus Jacobius, a Spanish physician and botanist. At Leipzig in 1543 he met Arnold Peraxyles Arlenius, a Dutch Humanist who was the guardian of Diego Hurtado di Mendoza's library at Venice.[129] On the invitation of Arlenius, Gesner went, in the summer of 1544, to Venice where he was given an opportunity to consult Mendoza's library freely.[130]

Gesner, while pursuing his linguistic and natural scientific studies, somehow found time to compile and publish the *Bibliotheca universalis . . .* (Zurich, 1545). It is an author catalog, alphabetically arranged in the medieval style by forenames, of all the books known to him in Latin, Greek, and Hebrew. He lists in this first edition about ten thousand titles and three thousand authors. Among these are very few contemporary writers on the discoveries, probably because they wrote mainly in the vernacular languages. Included are a Latin version of the Barlaam legend and the book by Góis on the religious beliefs of the Ethiopians.[131] No significant additions to this slight list appear in Gesner's *Appendix*

---

[127] See M. Sondheim, "Die Bibliothek des Hans Sachs," *Sondheims gesammelte Schriften* (Frankfurt, 1927), pp. 259–60. Also see below, p. 342.

[128] See K. H. Burmeister, *Sebastian Münster* (Basel, 1963), pp. 135–40. On the library of Johannes Steiger (1518–81) as a center of scholarly activity, see C. F. de Steiger, "Die Bibliothek des Berner Schultheissen Johannes Steiger," *Stultifera navis*, X (1890), 44–54. Also consult J. Wicki, "Der älteste deutsche Druck eines Xaveriusbriefes aus dem Jahre 1545, ehemals im Besitz des Basler Humanisten Lepusculus," *Neue Zeitschrift für Missionswissenschaft*, IV (1948), 105–9. This is an "Indianische Missive" written in 1544 that was translated into German and published at Basel in 1545. The volume here discussed is inscribed with the name of "Sebastiani Lepusculi," a professor of Greek and Hebrew at Basel.

[129] See above, p. 51. Also J. E. Bay, "Conrad Gesner, the Father of Bibliography," *Papers of the Bibliographical Society of America*, X, Pt. 2 (1916), 63–64.

[130] On Gesner's travels see H. Fischer *et al.*, *Conrad Gessner, 1516–1565, Universalgelehrter, Naturforscher, Arzt* (Zurich, 1967), pp. 9–32.

[131] Pp. 131ᵛ and 192ᵛ. A facsimile of Münster's first edition and the *Appendix* was published by Hans Widmann at Osnabrück in 1966.

published a decade later.[132] It was only in the revised edition published in 1574, nine years after Gesner's death, by Josias G. Simmler (1530–76) that vernacular works appear in the *Bibliotheca*, and then only in Latin renditions of the titles and names. Among many other relevant works Simmler lists all of Góis' books in Latin, the Italian translation of the first and second decades of Barros' *Asia*, and the edition of Mandeville's travels published by Matthias Dresser (1536–1607).[133]

Much more contemporary in their orientation than the Gesner editions were the catalogs of books for sale at the Frankfurt book fairs which took place twice annually from 1564 to 1592. The individual catalogs printed by Willer of Augsburg beginning in 1564 were compiled in 1592 into one large volume by Nicholaus Bassaeus (Basse), the Frankfurt bookseller and publisher through whom most of the books listed could also be purchased.[134] This compendium is divided into separately paged sections on medical books in Latin and German, histories in Latin and German, and books on all subjects in Italian, Spanish, and French. An analysis of these offerings reveals that the major botanical works in Latin were available. For the plants of the East most of the herbalists depended exclusively for their information upon Orta's *Colloquies* (1563) and Cristobal de Acosta's *Compilation*.[135] Under histories in Latin, among many other relevant titles, are found the *De rebus Emanuelis* (Cologne, 1574) of Osório, the *Historia rerum in Oriente* (Frankfurt, 1587) of Sigismund Feyerabend, ten Jesuit letter-books, the *Historiarum Indicarum* of Maffei in three separate editions, and the *Lusitanorum navigatio in Indiam orientalem* (Leipzig, 1580), a poem by Martin Chemnitz.[136] Under histories in German there are listed several Jesuit letter-books, a German translation (1589) of Mendoza's book on China, a *Historia von Calecut und andern Königreichen, Landen und Insulen in India und dem Indianischen Meer* (1565), a German description (Dillingen, 1587) of the Japanese embassy to Rome as well as many other pertinent items.[137]

Books in Romance languages apparently began to appear at the Frankfurt fair only in 1568 and thereafter. Among the works in Italian the listings show

---

132 Cf. the list of books that the Basel publisher, Johannes Oporinus, had for sale at his shop in 1552. He lists over 700 titles, all but 6 of which are in Latin and Greek. See M. Steinmann, *Johannes Oporinus* (Basel and Stuttgart, 1967), p. 60.

133 *Bibliotheca instituta et collecta primum a Conrado Gesnero ... locupletata ... per Iosiam Simlerum Tigurinum* (Zurich, 1574), pp. 154–55, 344, 393. The edition of 1583 prepared by J. J. Fries is somewhat more complete but Simmler's is more accurately printed.

134 *Collectio in unum corpus, omnium librorum ... qui in nundinis Francofurtenibus ab anno 1564, usque ad nundinas autumnales anni 1592 ... venales extiterunt: desumpta ex omnibus Catalogis Willeranis singularum nundinarum ... meliorique ratione quam hactenus disposita ...* (Frankfurt, 1592). Two years earlier Bassaeus had printed a volume of pictures of exotic plants. For further discussion of the book fair catalogs see Ehrman and Pollard, *op. cit.* (n. 126), chap. iii.

135 *Ibid.*, pp. 304, 307, 314, 320, 322. Also see below, pp. 433–39, for discussion of the botanical books.

136 *Ibid.*, pp. 346, 352, 369, 375, 382, 384, 385, 391, 392, 393, 398, 406, 409, 420. On Chemnitz see below, p. 346.

137 *Ibid.*, pp. 272, 273, 274, 280, 281–82, 284–85, 299–300, 318–19. It has not been possible to identify further the *Historia von Calecut* from this entry alone.

an *Avisi della Cina e Giappone dell' anno 1586* (Antwerp, 1588–89), the *Itinerario di Marc' Antonio Pigafetta . . . Londra, appresso Giovanni Wolfio in 4°* (n.d.), the *Herbario nuovo di Castore Durante . . .* (Rome, 1585), and the *Historia dell' Indie Orientali in libri vii . . . composto dal S. Fernando Lopetz dé Castagnela* (Venice, 1577). Among the works in French are a world history (Paris, 1572), a translation (1581) of Osório, and a *Miroir de la navigation de la mer Occidentale et Orientale pratiqué et assemblé par Lucas fils de Ian Chartier . . .* (Antwerp, 1591).[138] It certainly reveals something about German ignorance of the Spanish and Portuguese languages that the titles of the Iberian works on this list appear only in Latin, or in German, Italian, and French translations.[139]

Leipzig, mainly as a result of its central position in the Reformation, had declined as an international book mart. Even so, an examination of the mid-century stock lists of three Leipzig booksellers reveals that they had on hand eighteen copies of Varthema in German.[140] The scholarly Protestant princes of Anhalt were among the leading collectors of books in the middle-German region. Prince Georg (1507–52), who studied Hebrew at Leipzig as well as the classical languages, began in 1527 to form a polyglot library at Dessau.[141] He collected classical works in contemporary editions as well as humanistic and Reformation writings. Georg and his brothers included in their library several of the contemporary cosmographies and works on the natural sciences that incorporated the latest information from the East in their respective fields. At Dresden meanwhile the Saxon princes were adding maps and books about the non-European world to their collections of oddities.[142] Their relatives, friends, and associates at the other small courts of central and northern Germany likewise collected books and curiosities which conveyed to them a growing sense of the activities of the Portuguese in the East and of their own indirect involvement in the overseas expansion. But most of the princely collectors of Germany, like the popes and Philip II, were primarily intent upon acquiring rare European manuscripts for their collections and were only incidentally concerned with adding printed books on the affairs of the day to their libraries.

[138] *Ibid.*, pp. 19, 25, 30, 33, 35, 36, 38, 39, 55, 61.

[139] But it should also be noticed that no books in English or Dutch are listed.

[140] For a general sketch of Leipzig's decline see Albrecht Kirchhoff, "Die Leipziger Büchermesse von 1550 bis 1650," *Archiv für Geschichte des deutschen Buchhandels*, XI (1888), 183–203. The inventories are dated 1548, 1551, and 1558. The dealers had on hand at that time many copies in all sizes of Münster's *Cosmography* and Ptolemy's geography. They also stocked a wide selection of books in the natural sciences. But, as might be expected, their warehouses overflowed with religious tracts and biblical studies. A reference to "6 Schiffart Vartomannj in 4°" therefore stands out prominently from the other titles. For the references to Varthema in these lists see Albrecht Kirchhoff, "Leipziger Sortimentshändler im 16. Jahrhundert und ihrer Lagervorräte," *ibid.*, 216, 260. The first printed catalog for the Leipzig book fair was issued in 1594 by Henning Gross. See Ehrman and Pollard, *op. cit.* (n. 126), p. 82.

[141] *Georgsbibliothek* is one of the few sixteenth-century libraries that remained intact into the twentieth century. For an analysis of this library see K. Haebler, *Deutsche Bibliophilen des 16. Jahrhunderts: Die Fürsten von Anhalt, ihre Bücher und Bucheinbände* (Leipzig, 1923), pp. 1–25, 44–47, 64, 67–70.

[142] See G. Klemm, *Zur Geschichte der Sammlungen für Wissenschaft und Kunst in Deutschland* (Zerbst 1837), p. 177. On the museum at Dresden see *Asia*, II, Bk. 1, 24.

4

The Low Countries, France, and England

The rulers of the Netherlands, on the contrary, were attentive to the collection and preservation of contemporary printed books and maps. This was, of course, a consequence of their direct interest in overseas expansion, trade, and printing. In 1550 Philip II ordered his agents to bring together the books in the various royal residences of the Netherlands and to deposit them in the royal palace at Brussels. In 1594 the Archduke Ernst, regent of the Netherlands, ordered that one copy of every book printed should be bound in leather and placed in the Brussels collection.[143] Viglius de Ziuchem (1507–77), president of the Privy Council of Louvain and the agent of Philip who first brought the books together at Brussels, owned a fine personal collection of maps and atlases. From his map inventory dated 1575 it can readily be seen that he possessed a number of world maps, two charts of the "great sea," and two maps of Asia, one drawn on parchment and the other printed in 1567.[144] Cardinal Antoine Perrenot de Granvelle (1517–86), Philip's closest adviser, collected for himself a magnificent library of 1,306 books in all languages, even some in "unknown tongues." Of the total, 172 volumes were cataloged as histories, some about distant countries.[145]

Netherlandish nobles, like Viscount Henri de Bréderode (d. 1568), also had substantial collections of books and maps. In his château at Vianen, on the river Eck east of Rotterdam, Bréderode had a gallery that was evidently lined with maps and decorated with an engraving of the bourse in Lisbon. In his library there were at least one volume of Ramusio, Münster's cosmography in French, and works listed as "Description de Linde orientale" and "Les Histores [sic] de Indes et Portigale."[146] Some other libraries in the northern Netherlands, for which inventories also exist, possessed maps and books about the East.[147] When the library of Philips van Marinix was auctioned in 1599, it included the cosmographies of Münster and Thevet, the *Weltbuch* (1542) of Sebastian

[143] See G. A. E. Bogeng, *op. cit.* (n. 58), pp. 210–11. The library of Brussels was burned in 1731.

[144] See Anon., "Old Inventories of Maps," *Imago mundi*, V (1948), 18–20. The map of 1567 was probably the Gastaldi map printed at Venice. For an overview of the maps available in Amsterdam in 1607 at the shop of Cornelis Claesz see A. A. van Schelven, "Een catalogus . . . ," *Het Boek*, XI (1922), 329–34.

[145] For a discussion of the unpublished catalog of 1607, now in the municipal library of Besançon, see M. Piquard, "La bibliothèque d'un homme d'état au XVIᵉ siècle," *Mélanges d'histoire du livre . . . offerts à M. Frantz Calot* (Paris, 1960), pp. 227–35.

[146] Bréderode was one of the leaders of the Gueux, or the "beggar's party," who opposed the repressive policies of Philip II and his agents in 1566. He escaped to Germany in 1567 where he died. His château and its contents were evidently confiscated. For its contents see C. R.," Inventaire des meubles et effets du château de Vianen en 1567," *Le bibliophile belge*, 3d ser. IX (1874), 106–14, 274–79. I conclude that the reference to "La bourse de Lisbonne" was an engraving because another is recorded for the "cabinet de Madame."

[147] See G. B. C. Van der Feen, "Noord-nederlandsche boekerijn in der 16ᵉ eeuw," *Het Boek*, VII (1918), 81–92, 318–34; VIII (1919), 219–24.

Franck, Ortelius' *Theatrum* (1575) and Georg Braun's *Civitatis orbis terrarum* (1572).[148] One of the greatest of the private libraries was owned by J. J. Scaliger of Leyden. He collected Chinese books as well as materials in other Asian languages.[149] In the collection of 1,382 items sold by Louis Elzevir after Scaliger's death, there were books on the discoveries as well as a number of sea charts, maps, and globes.[150] The library of the University of Utrecht, according to a catalog of 1608, possessed an extensive collection of the latest navigational literature in Dutch—a most unusual collection for a university library.[151] The library of the Protestant University of Leyden, first opened in 1587, included by century's end a palm-leaf manuscript from Java, several Chinese books, two globes, and a few cosmographies and navigational works.[152]

In Antwerp the intellectuals of the latter half of the sixteenth century generally centered their activities at the residence of Christopher Plantin, the printer. Here they had access to the products of his press and to his personal library. Plantin began to build his library in 1563 and by 1592 it contained 728 titles.[153] When Ortelius died in 1598, a number of works from his library were purchased for the Plantin collection. Before Ortelius' death, he and his intellectual associates consulted Plantin's library. Those who helped with the preparation of the polyglot Bible—Arias Montano, Andreas Masius, and Guy le Fèvre de la Boderie (1514–98) among others—lodged at Plantin's residence and used his library.[154] Theodor Poelman (1512–81), the Humanist, and Philippe Galle (1537–1612), the engraver, consulted the numerous classical and contemporary books on the natural sciences available at Plantin's. Ortelius and Mercator contributed to the Plantin collection some autographed copies of their own cartographic works. The scholars also bought books, maps, and engravings from Plantin for their own libraries and cabinets of curiosities. For example, Mercator in Duisburg bought Nicolas di Nicolai, *Les quatres premiers livres de navigation & perégrinations orientals* (Lyons, 1567) and Lucas J. Waghenaer, *Spieghel der Zeevaerdt . . .* (Leyden, 1585).[155] That Mercator had a substantial collection of books on the East is attested by a letter to Ortelius from Mercator's son written in 1596

[148] See C. Koemans, *Collections of Maps and Atlases in the Netherlands, Their History and Present State* (Leyden, 1961), p. 20; on Braun see *Asia*, II, Bk. 1, 88–89.

[149] Five of his Chinese books as well as his *Doctrina Christiana lingua Malabarica . . .* (Goa, 1577) were acquired by the library of the University of Leyden. See E. Spanheim, *Catalogus . . .* (Leyden, 1674), pp. 256, 258.

[150] See Reiffenberg, "Bibliothèque de Joseph Scaliger," *Le bibliophile belge*, IV (1847), 229–30. For a portrait of Scaliger see pl. 36.

[151] Koemans, *op. cit.* (n. 148), p. 27.

[152] See E. Hulshoff Pol, "The Library," in Th. H. Lunsingh Scheurleer and G. H. M. Posthumus Meyjes (eds.), *Leiden University in the Seventeenth Century: An Exchange of Learning* (Leyden, 1975), pp. 406, 416–17, 455. Houtman donated the palm-leaf manuscript to the library on his return from Java in 1597. Also see pl. 37.

[153] See Leon Voet, *The Golden Compasses: A History and Evaluation of the Printing and Publishing Activities of the Officina Plantiniana at Antwerp* (2 vols.; Amsterdam, 1969), I, 338–44, 350–52.

[154] *Ibid.*, pp. 367–68.

[155] See L. Voet, "Les relations commerciales entre Gerard Mercat et la maison Plantinienne," *Duisburger Forschungen*, VI (1962), 221–24.

explaining that he was unable to find in his father's library an item that Ortelius had requested. He remarks: "I have even searched through the authors of Indian travels and epistles."[156]

The rulers of France, like most other princely collectors, concentrated on acquiring manuscript books and the classical authors in printed editions. But they, unlike other royal collectors, were inclined also to collect contemporary manuscripts, printed books, and maps relating to Asia. Their interest in works on expansion certainly derived from a determination to participate directly in the opening of the overseas world and the spice trade. King Francis I's library which was housed in the Château of Blois until 1544 contained 1,896 titles.[157] Among its retrospective works were Ptolemy, Pliny, and Quintus Curtius in several editions. Relevant medieval works housed there were Marco Polo in French and Italian, the *Golden Legend* of Voragine, Barlaam and Josaphat, the letter of Aristotle supposedly written to Alexander, the *Speculum historiale* of Vincent of Beauvais, and Hayton's chronicle with a world map at the end of the book.[158] Of later works there were the *Supplementum chronicarum* of Foresti da Bergamo, "a world map for navigating,"[159] and two globes.

The sixteenth-century successors of Francis more than doubled the number of books in the royal library which was located after 1544 at Fontainebleau before being moved to Paris. King Henry IV finally installed the royal library in 1595 in the Collège de Clermont, now the Lycèe Louis-le-Grand of Paris. On this occasion a new inventory was prepared, a study of which reveals that numerous items relating to Asia had been added in the interim to the royal collections.[160] King Henry II (reigned 1547–59) acquired the *Itineriŭ Portugallensiŭ e Lusitania in India* (Milan, 1508) and the cosmography of Sebastian Münster.[161] His queen, Catharine de' Medici, possessed a copy of Arrian on Alexander, the legend of Barlaam, the Koran in Latin, "Chinese letters" (probably Jesuit letterbooks), and a cartographic collection which included special maps of Calicut, the Moluccas, and other islands of the East.[162] King Henry III (reigned 1574–89) acquired the French translation of Barlaam by Jean de Billy (Billius)

---

[156] From the letter of Rumoldus Mercator, Duisburg, March 26, 1596, in J. H. Hessels (ed.), *op. cit.* (n. 86), p. 682. Mercator's library was sold at Leyden in 1604. A catalog which has never been located was prepared for the occasion by Thomas Basson. See B. Van't Hoff, "De catalogus van de bibliothek van Gerard Mercator," *Het Boek*, XXXV (1961–62), 25–27.

[157] For the holdings of Blois there are two inventories extant, one of 1518 and the other of 1544. See H. Omont, *Anciens inventaires et catalogues de la Bibliothèque nationale* (5 vols.; Paris, 1908–21), I, 1–256.

[158] *Ibid.*, p. 7.

[159] *Ibid.*, p. 51. It is possible that this item was obtained for the king by Guillaume Pelicier, his envoy to Venice. In his own library Pelicier had a map of Asia and a book on "Insulares" in Italian. See H. Omont, "Inventaire de la bibliothèque de Guillaume Pelicier, évêque de Montpelier (1529–1568)," *Revue des bibliothèques*, I (1891), 161–72.

[160] See Omont, *op. cit.* (n. 157), I, 285–466.

[161] See E. Quentin-Bauchart, *La bibliothèque de Fontainebleau et les livres des derniers Valois à la Bibliothèque nationale* (Paris, 1891), pp. 128, 139.

[162] On the books see Omont, *op. cit.* (n. 157), I, 446, 447, 466; on the maps see E. Bonaffé, *Inventaire des meubles de C. de Medicis en 1589* (Paris, 1874), pp. 65–66.

published in 1578.[163] Among the other more interesting items added to the library by the royal collectors and the curators were a copy of Mandeville and several manuscript descriptions of the navigation to overseas islands.[164] Particularly interesting is the heading in the catalog "Folles enterprises" under which is listed "Le nouveau monde. Le chevalier deliberé."[165]

The French, like the Venetians, translated or adapted to their own ends several of the Portuguese accounts of Asia. A newsletter published at Rouen in 1539 purportedly presented a copy of the letters sent to Portugal from India on the defeat of the Turks at Diu in 1538.[166] Nicolas de Grouchy's translation of Castanheda's unrevised first book was published in French at Paris in 1553 and in Spanish at Antwerp in 1554.[167] Jesuit letterbooks in Latin and French thereafter soon began to be printed at Paris. Joachim de Centellas' account of the Portuguese conquests in the East appeared in 1578 to be followed two years later by Simon Goulart's history of Portugal based on Osório and Castanheda. In 1588 appeared a French translation of Mendoza's *China* by Luc de la Porte in which the translator shows knowledge of earlier writings on China. The mere fact that such materials appeared in French indicates that interest in the overseas activities of the Portuguese was persistent and broad. It is also quite obvious from studying the sources of Rabelais and others that they were acquainted with the most recent literature on the discoveries.[168] But an examination of the holdings in the available library inventories gives only partial support to this conclusion.

The greatest French collector of the earlier half of the sixteenth century was Jean Grolier (1479–1565), the antiquarian, Humanist, and patron of Italian and French scholarship. A native of Lyons, Grolier came of a merchant family of substance; his father was treasurer to the French army in Milan. Beginning in the first decade of the sixteenth century, Grolier began to collect the writings of his favorite ancient authors in the major publication centers of northern Italy. He also collected many Renaissance authors in fine editions. It has been estimated that his library finally included 3,000 titles, mostly in Latin. A recently reconstituted catalog of his holdings lists 562 entries in 616 volumes. Examination of this catalog shows that Grolier owned most of the ancient authors who wrote on the East, the works (Basel, 1538) of Poggio Bracciolini, the travels (Basel, 1551) to Moscow of Siegmund von Herberstein, the *Novus orbis* (Basel, 1537), and the letter of André Vesalius on the "China root" published at Basel in 1546.[169] Grolier, whose taste ran to Latin books, probably had so few of the works

163 Quentin-Bauchart, *op. cit.* (n. 161), p. 169. On Billy see below, p. 105.

164 When in Paris in 1585, Philips van Winghe noticed that André Thevet, the cosmographer and guardian of the royal cabinet of curiosities, "had in hand a book on Islands." See letter of Winghe to Ortelius (Rome), September 1, 1590, in Hessels (ed.), *op. cit.* (n. 156), p. 444.

165 Omont, *op. cit.* (n. 157), I, 289.

166 See J.-P. Seguin, *L'information en France de Louis XII à Henri II* (Geneva, 1961), p. 107.

167 For further details see below, p. 275.

168 See below, p. 264.

169 For the list see Gabriel Austin, *The Library of Jean Grolier: A Preliminary Catalogue* (New York, 1971), pp. 45–81. See especially items 148, 221, 223, 228, 403, 423a, 452, 454, 527.

relating to overseas expansion because they were usually written in vernacular languages. Other French collectors of his day exhibited a similar taste. For example, the library begun by Cardinal Antoine du Prat (1463–1535), chancellor under Francis I, contained a selection of Latin works as well as a few cosmographies in French.[170]

A change takes place in the character of the French collections after midcentury. Jean Nicot (1530–1604), the French legate to Lisbon in 1559, acquired treatises on navigation, routiers for the voyages to the East, and an account of Magellan's voyage. He probably also possessed copies of the first and second decades of Barros, Castanheda in Grouchy's French translation, and the *Commentarios* of Albuquerque.[171] Montaigne, who kept about 1,000 volumes in his study, collected ancient and modern histories in both Latin and the vernacular languages. The great essayist had the habit of putting his signature on the title page of his books, of underlining them, and of writing marginalia.[172] He had a more than ordinary interest in Portugal because his mother was of Portuguese background and because he had attended the Collège of Guyenne where Portuguese teachers were prominent.[173] His copy of Quintus Curtius is covered with annotations and a final note of 1587 summarizing his impressions of Alexander's exploits in India.[174] Among the histories that he owned and most appreciated was Osório's book on the reign of King Manuel (Cologne, 1574).[175] He also had the translation of Castanheda prepared by Grouchy, his former teacher at Guyenne, and the history of Portugal by Simon Goulart that was derived from Osório and Castanheda.[176] Montaigne's contemporary Pontus de Tyard (1521–1605), a poet of the Pléiade, likewise possessed a respectable collection of materials on Asia, including the third volume of Ramusio, two books on the navigation to the East, and a book of Jesuit letters from Japan.[177]

[170] M. Connat and J. Megret, "Inventaire de la bibliothèque des Du Prat," *Bibliothèque d'humanisme et renaissance*, III (1943), 84, 86, 88, 103, 108, 109, 113. Also see the discussion of Jean Le Feron's library in R. Doucet, *Les bibliothèques parisiennes au XVIe siècle* (Paris, 1956), and that of the Cardinal de Granvelle's library in M. Piquard, *loc. cit.* (n. 145), pp. 227–35.

[171] Nicot died without direct heirs and his books were scattered. Today some of them are in the national libraries of Paris and Copenhagen. For discussion see G. Le Gentil, "Les français en Portugal," *Bulletin des études portugaises*, I (1931), 3; and Matos, *Les portugaises en France au XVIe siècle* (Coimbra, 1952), pp. 96–99. Also see above, p. 33.

[172] Of his personal library there are but seventy-six items which have come down to us, and thirty-one of these are works of history. See P. Bonnefon, "La bibliothèque de Montaigne," *Revue d'histoire littéraire de la France*, II (1895), 314–17.

[173] See above, p. 12.

[174] Bonnefon, *loc. cit.* (n. 172), pp. 314, 341.

[175] *Ibid.*, pp. 355–56.

[176] See Pierre Villey-Desmeserets, *Les livres d'histoire moderne utilisés par Montaigne* ... (Paris, 1908), pp. 238–48.

[177] See S. F. Baridon, *Inventaire de la bibliothèque de Pontus de Tyard* (Geneva, 1950), pp. 34, 35, 40. Pierre Cabat, a Paris book dealer, had in his private library a copy of the *Voyages* (Paris, 1596) of the Seigneur de Villamont. See A. H. Schutz, *Vernacular Books in Parisian Private Libraries of the Sixteenth Century According to the Notarial Archives* (Chapel Hill, N.C., 1955), p. 72. For other small collections see U. D. Ilic, "Book Ownership in Sixteenth-Century France: A Study of Selected Notarial Inventories" (M.A. thesis, Graduate Library School, University of Chicago, 1967).

The greatest private library in Renaissance France was assembled by Jacques-Auguste de Thou (1553–1617), the historian of France and magistrate of Paris. He began to collect books systematically in 1572: over the next forty years he amassed a library estimated at 1,000 manuscripts and 8,000 printed books. The son of the president of the Parlement of Paris, De Thou was acquainted with the elite of French society and with the literati of most of western Europe. In 1581 he visited Montaigne when the essayist was beginning to read widely on the overseas world.[178] At Paris De Thou opened the treasures of his collection to all scholars, held regular meetings of literati at his residence, and employed Pierre and Jacques Dupuy as his librarians. Established as the leading bibliophile of his day, De Thou was appointed superintendent of the royal collection by Henry IV in 1593, a position from which he was able to survey all facets of French intellectual life.[179]

The catalog of De Thou's library was prepared after his death and published only in 1679 along with the list of acquisitions added to it by his descendants.[180] Eventually most of these books found their way into the national library, where they are included in the Dupuy and Colbert collections. An examination of the seventeenth-century catalog reveals that De Thou and his immediate descendants owned about 90 printed books dealing with Asia. Of the books printed before 1600 the library included almost all relevant works: Castanheda in Portuguese, French, and Italian, Barros in Portuguese and Italian, G. B. Peruschi's *Informatione . . .* (Brescia, 1597), Albuquerque's *Commentarios* (Lisbon, 1557), the collection of Ramusio, Maffei's *Historiarum indicarum* and a substantial number of Jesuit letterbooks.[181] After De Thou's death in 1617 his descendants continued to acquire materials on Asia, especially on Jesuit activities in China.

Sixteenth-century England could boast of no library—ecclesiastical, university, or private—that equaled in number of volumes De Thou's collection at Paris. In 1500 the ecclesiastical institutions of England had been the principal holders of books.[182] The dissolution of the monasteries by King Henry VIII and the dispersal of their libraries in 1538–39 brought an abrupt end to the church's control of books and put many on the market for the universities and private individuals to purchase. But foreign books were not otherwise easy for Englishmen to acquire, even though there were two importers operating in London.

---

[178] See below, pp. 294–95.

[179] For his biography see C. B. Petitot (ed.), *loc. cit.* (n. 109), pp. 189–530; also J. Collinson, *The Life of Thuanus with Some Account of His Writings* (London, 1807), pp. 238–40, and Antoine Teissier, *Les éloges des hommes savans, tirez de l'Histoire de M. de Thou* (4 vols.; Leyden, 1715), *passim*.

[180] *Catalogus bibliothecae Thuanae a clariss. viv. Petro et Iacobo Puteanis, ordine alphabetico primum distributis . . .* (Paris, 1679). It is clearly impossible to know exactly what was acquired by De Thou himself. On the basis of manuscript catalogs in the National Library at Paris, Harrisse estimates that the collection numbered 6,600 volumes in 1617, 8,000 in 1643, 11,000 in 1653, 13,000 in 1659, and about 13,178 in 1679. See H. Harrisse, *Le Prèsident de Thou et ses descendants, leur célèbre bibliothèque . . .* (Paris, 1905), pp. 73–74.

[181] *Catalogus* (n. 180), pp. 5, 6, 7–9, 31.

[182] See Sears Jayne, *Library Catalogues of the English Renaissance* (Berkeley and Los Angeles, 1956), p. 39.

It was mainly those Englishmen who traveled on the Continent, or who had business at Antwerp, Lisbon, and Seville, who brought foreign books home with them. As a consequence of the internal problems wracking Reformation England and of its physical separation from the Continent, it was not until the latter half of the century that books on the discoveries in the East began to appear in English translations for public sale and in the libraries of private collectors.[183]

Richard Eden, the pioneer English collector and translator of travel literature, had Thomas Smith as his tutor at Cambridge. Unlike most of his contemporaries in the age of Henry VIII, Smith collected a geographical library. In it were included both the major studies of the ancient authors and a few by contemporaries. His library catalog dated 1566 shows that Smith possessed three copies of Ptolemy's geography, Münster's *Cosmographia*, Eden's *Decades*, and Barros' *Asia*.[184] But what is most striking about Smith's library is the fact that it was perhaps the earliest private library to concentrate so heavily on geography and related disciplines. The library of James VI, king of Scotland, likewise boasted many geographical and cosmographical works, namely most of those published before 1583. This Scottish collector owned a French translation (1556) of Marco Polo, the *Novus orbis* of Simon Grynaeus, and the "Propalladia" of Torres Naharro in Spanish.[185] Martin Frobisher purchased for his voyage of 1576 a copy of Mandeville, the cosmographical writings of Thevet, Cunningham, and Recorde, and Pedro de Medina's famous text on navigation.[186] Three years later Drake reportedly had aboard his ship several books on navigation, an account of Magellan's voyage, and a world map made in Portugal.[187]

The most remarkable of the English students of geography and a great collector of books on navigation and the overseas world was John Dee (1527–1608), the mathemetician and occultist. Dee studied navigation as a young man with Gemma Frisius and learned to know Mercator.[188] While at Louvain from 1548 to 1550 Dee became interested in geography and probably met Ortelius in Antwerp.[189] On the Continent again in 1562–63, he stayed once more at Antwerp before proceeding to Zurich where he visited with Konrad Gesner. After touring in Italy and Hungary, Dee returned to England in 1564 to settle down for the next two decades at Mortlake, his residence in Surrey.[190] Here he

---

[183] See E. G. R. Taylor, *Tudor Geography, 1485–1583* (London, 1930), p. 25. On the translation of travel literature into English see *Asia*, I, 189, 209–15, 477–82.

[184] See Taylor, *op. cit.* (n. 183), pp. 35–36. It is possible that he had the first three *Decadas* of Barros in Portuguese, the third of which was published at Lisbon in 1563; or he might have owned the Italian translation of Alfonso Ulloa of the first two published at Venice in 1562.

[185] G. T. Warner (ed.), "The Library of James VI, 1573–83," *Miscellany of the Scottish Historical Society* (Edinburgh), I (1893), xxxi, xxxvii, xliv.

[186] For a copy of the bill paid by Frobisher for these books and for nautical instruments see D. W. Waters, *The Art of Navigation* (London, 1958), pp. 530–31.

[187] See *ibid.*, p. 536.

[188] See P. J. French, *John Dee: The World of an Elizabethan Magus* (London, 1972) pp. 24–25. Also see below, pp. 471–73.

[189] *Ibid.*, pp. 28–32.

[190] *Ibid.*, pp. 36–40.

began to assemble his collections of instruments, manuscripts, and books. As he gained fame as a promoter of overseas navigation, Dee was visited at Mortlake by Queen Elizabeth (1575), Sir Francis Drake (1581), and repeatedly by Adrian and Humphrey Gilbert. Foreign savants like Ortelius also enjoyed his hospitality. His library, which was not the least of the attractions at Mortlake, numbered in 1583 about 170 manuscripts and 2,500 printed books. And this was at a time when the library of Corpus Christi College at Oxford could claim only 379 volumes.[191]

Dee's library was especially rich in both manuscript and printed works on geography, astronomy, and voyages.[192] He likewise possessed the standard ancient books on India, several medieval encyclopedias, and the most recent accounts of navigation to the East. Nor did he neglect the natural histories, for he recognized their importance to students of travel and overseas countries. He had a sizable collection of Jesuit letterbooks and he endorsed them for the use of Protestant Englishmen by including them in his list of books important for navigation. Clearly Dee with his predilection for magic and strange religious beliefs did not esteem the Jesuit letters for their edifying qualities! The basic collections of travel literature, foreign and domestic, were on his shelves, as well as the atlas of Ortelius, several editions of Ptolemy's geography, and other world geographies and histories. In terms of works relating to overseas expansion Dee's library was as comprehensive as any collection of the century.[193]

The only book collection in England comparable to Dee's was the Lumley library. Its history begins with Archbishop Thomas Cranmer, whose books formed the nucleus of a collection built by the Earl of Arundel, Lord Chamberlain to Henry VIII. Arundel's daughter married Lord Lumley in 1557, and the young nobleman and his bride went to live at Nonesuch Castle with Arundel. Lumley shared the bibliophilic enthusiasm of his father-in-law, and both were aided in their collecting activities by Humphrey Lloyd, an Oxford graduate and physician. After Arundel's death in 1579, all of his possessions passed into Lumley's hands. For the next seventeen years, Lumley collected with even greater zeal, especially books on geography and cosmology. His collection was completed to his satisfaction in 1596, the year when he had the library fully cataloged. The catalog that appeared in 1609 on Lumley's death is a copy of the document of 1596.[194]

The Lumley library in 1596 housed about 3,000 separate works. Books on theology numbered 936 and included Quintus Curtius (Strasburg, 1518), Barlaam and Josaphat (Cologne, 1593), and the travels of Benjamin of Tudela (Antwerp, 1575) translated from Hebrew into Latin by Arias Montano.[195] Cataloged under "History" were 591 titles of which 54 (or about 9 percent)

191 *Ibid.*, pp. 43–44.
192 For a list of relevant manuscripts in his library see Taylor, *op. cit.* (n. 183), pp. 191–92.
193 See the catalog of English holdings, in which relevant works from Dee's library are included, in Taylor, *op. cit.* (n. 183), pp. 193–243.
194 S. Jayne and F. R. Johnson, *The Lumley Library: The Catalogue of 1609* (London, 1956), pp. 2–9.
195 *Ibid.*, items 132, 245a, 293.

were works relating to the East. These include the usual array of ancient authors in contemporary editions, the travel accounts of the Middle Ages, and many rare sixteenth-century books on navigation to the East and life there. Lumley had three copies of Mandeville: a manuscript in English, an Italian version printed at Venice in 1537, and an English edition of 1568.[196] Iberian authors were particularly well represented with works by Góis, Lopez de Gomara, Peter Martyr, Pedro de Medina, Osório, Barros in Italian, and Mendoza in Latin (Frankfurt, 1589).[197] He also had a representative collection of Jesuit letterbooks and histories.[198] Most interesting to modern bibliophiles are the Latin edition (Cologne, 1523) of the letter of Maximilian of Transylvania on the Magellan expedition and the *Generall and Rare Memorials Perteininge to the Arte of Navigation* (London, 1577) by John Dee, his competitor in book collecting.[199] Private English collectors, such as Gabriel Harvey (1550–1630) and William Drummond (1585–1649), continued into the seventeenth century to collect books on navigation, geography, and travel and tended to include in their libraries relatively larger numbers of books in the vernacular languages.[200]

From Italy to England the book collectors of the latter half of the sixteenth century concentrated on acquiring larger numbers of books in the vernacular. Some of these were retrospective materials, such as the *History of Alexander the Great* (1553) of Quintus Curtius which was presented to the public in the hope "that we Englishmen might be found as foreward in that behalf as other nations, which have brought all worthy histories into their national language."[201] In other places, especially Venice, the contemporary writings in Latin and in the Iberian languages were translated into the vernacular. The tradition of translating from the vernacular languages into Latin for purposes of obtaining a wider circulation among the lettered readers was never completely abandoned. The Jesuit letterbooks, for example, were regularly issued in both Latin and vernacular versions. Many Continental Humanists, like Nicolas de Grouchy, undertook only reluctantly the task of translating contemporary books.[202] But it should be noticed that the histories of the overseas expansion that were translated into Italian, German, and French were among those works which appeared most regularly at the Frankfurt book fair, in the inventories of book dealers, and in private libraries.

The works which appeared most frequently in the collections of the first half of the sixteenth century were those reports on the discoveries published in Italy. The Colombina and the library of Hartmann Schedel were the only two

[196] *Ibid.*, items 1258, 1260, 1269.

[197] *Ibid.*, items 1074, 1077, 1107, 1128, 1157, 1205, 1273, 1363, 1364, 1386, 1404, 1428.

[198] *Ibid.*, items 978, 1103, 1104, 1107, 1272.

[199] *Ibid.*, items 999a, 1801.

[200] See Virginia F. Stern, "The Bibliotheca of Gabriel Harvey," *Renaissance Quarterly*, XXV (1972), 1–62; and Robert H. McDonald (ed.), *The Library of Drummond of Hawthornden* (Edinburgh, 1971).

[201] As quoted in F. O. Matthiessen, *Translation: An Elizabethan Art* (Cambridge, Mass., 1930), pp. 25–26.

[202] See below, pp. 295–96.

collections found to include copies of King Manuel's letters. The libraries of savants, like Erasmus, were ordinarily limited to Greek and Latin books, including therein the great geographies, histories, and natural histories of Antiquity in both manuscript and printed versions.[203] Among the ancient authors the history of Alexander by Quintus Curtius and the works of Ptolemy were most prominent in the humanistic collections of the first half of the century. The contemporary history of the Portuguese in the East which was most widely circulated and best represented in the book collections throughout the century was the *Itinerario* (1510) of Varthema in both its original Italian and in its German, Spanish, and English translations.[204] The popularity of Varthema's book was rivaled only by the *Itinerarium* (1508) and the *Novus orbis* (1532), the Latin collections of materials on the overseas discoveries. In the later years of the century the chronicle of Castanheda in translation and that of Osório in Latin were conspicuously important. Such works were to be found mainly in the private libraries of literati, merchants, and students of geography.

The great royal and ecclesiastical collectors concentrated on acquiring ancient manuscripts and rarities for their libraries. Increasingly over the course of the century, particularly at the Vatican and at El Escorial, manuscripts and books of Eastern provenance were admitted to the collections because of their rarity and curiosity. Manuscript maps, and a few printed ones as well, of distant or hitherto unknown places were accorded a similar status in the great collections of the Valois, Habsburgs, Fuggers, and Wittelsbachs. The manuscript collection of Hans Jakob Fugger even included a German translation of the book of Duarte Barbosa that was made in 1530. By the end of the century both the Vatican and El Escorial collections included books printed in the East.[205]

The contemporary accounts relating to overseas expansion and to Asian life and products were found generally in private libraries, both great and small. The Colombina with its collection of over 15,000 books and manuscripts was the largest private library of the sixteenth century and one of the richest in contemporary materials. Until the middle of the century it was open to interested scholars and was extensively used by them. The libraries of the Fuggers at Augsburg were consulted by literati and artists at mid-century and afterward. In the latter half of the century the libraries of De Thou, John Dee, and Lumley performed similar functions for those interested in the overseas world. Among the smaller collectors whose libraries were open to others were the Estes, Mendoza in Venice, and the Cardinal de Granvelle.

The gentlemen book collectors whose libraries held significant materials on

---

[203] On the collection of Erasmus see "Die Bibliothek des Erasmus," in *Gedenkschrift zum 400. Todestage des Erasmus von Rotterdam* (Basel, 1936), pp. 228–59. Only a very few books by contemporary authors, such as More's *Utopia*, appear on this list. It strangely does not include reference to the books which Góis presented to Erasmus (see above, pp. 19–20). The likelihood is that they were either lost or thought to be unworthy of inclusion.

[204] For a complete list of translations see *Asia*, I, 165–66.

[205] On European printing activities in Asia see below, pp. 496–500.

the expansion into Asia included Grolier, Sir Thomas Smith, Bréderode, the Fuggers, and Lord Lumley. Among the publishers who sold and collected maps and books on Asia the most important were Georg Willer of Augsburg, Nicholas Bassaeus of Frankfurt, Christopher Plantin of Antwerp, and Cornelis Claesz of Amsterdam. That books on the discoveries were regularly available at the book fairs attended by these publishers and their representatives is amply proved from the catalogs of the Frankfurt fairs, and that they were in local shops, from the inventories of book sellers. Most of the purchasers of these books must have been private collectors, for such works are conspicuous by their scarcity in the great royal collections and by their almost complete absence from university libraries. Aside from Utrecht the libraries of most European universities, like the library of Coimbra, were collections of textbooks, often in multiple copies.

Certain savants and literati in all European countries were cosmopolitan and contemporary in their tastes and in their book purchases. In Italy, for example, the personal libraries of Pico, Leonardo, A. F. Doni, and G. Muziano contained both retrospective and contemporary materials on Asia. In Germany the learned collectors were Schedel, Münzer, Peutinger, Pirckheimer, and Hans Sachs. In France, works on Portugal and its exploits in Asia appeared in the libraries of Nicot, Montaigne, Pontus de Tyard, and De Thou. In Spain and the Netherlands the smaller private collectors included Arias Montano, Ortelius, and Mercator. In their libraries the discipline most strongly represented is geography and cartography, but the collectors also included philosophy, art, poetry, linguistics, theology, literature, and history.

What is most apparent is the effectiveness of the censorship in Portugal itself and its relative ineffectiveness elsewhere. It is likely, however, that this is a biased conclusion since relatively little material is available on the private libraries of Portugal, particularly those of its great historians and literati. It is perhaps wiser to suggest that the books on the East printed in Portugal were, like those in other parts of Europe, likely to be in the private libraries of scholars, merchants, and artists who had the interest and the money to buy them. It is unlikely, however, that the Portuguese collected books on the overseas activities of their compatriots that were printed elsewhere in Europe. But even this surmise is open to doubt for we know that the rector of the University of Coimbra had on his shelves a *Novus orbis* that was probably produced in Basel. Clearly, however, Portuguese chronicles produced in the latter half of the century (especially those of Castanheda and Barros), circulated widely in Europe in Portuguese and in translation. The Latin history of King Manuel by Osório was known everywhere, but the Portuguese history by Góis on which it was based was not found in any of the catalogs. The chronicle of Góis appears to have circulated only in Portugal itself and perhaps not very generally there. It was primarily through the Latin histories and the Italian translations of Portuguese works that Europe at large followed the expansion into Asia.

★

The discovery of the sea route to India was followed by a Portuguese expansion into Europe that was to have disruptive and permanent consequences for Lusitania and eventually for the rest of Europe. In the first half of the century the news about Asia was carried to the rest of Europe by word of mouth; in the latter half it was relayed by the printed word. Information on overseas expansion was carried abroad until 1540 mainly by individual Portuguese students, teachers, artists, diplomats, and merchants. Written materials emanating from Portugal itself in this period were limited to the official pronouncements of the king, a few documents presented at Badajoz-Elvas by the Portuguese to substantiate their claim to the Moluccas, and isolated maps and routiers that escaped Lisbon's surveillance and were smuggled abroad. Venice and Augsburg got their information through their own diplomatic and mercantile agents in the Iberian peninsula, but their concern was mainly with the operation of the spice trade. Portuguese intellectuals who went abroad and stayed there for extended periods established a bond with the leading artists, scholars, scientists, and literati of Italy, France, and the Netherlands. The churchmen of Portugal also played an important role in maintaining close working relations between Portugal and the papacy. Adventurers, political malcontents, and religious refugees from Portugal also carried stories abroad about the successes and failures of the Portuguese in India that were often given unquestioned credence by their unwary hosts.

Once it became clear between 1540 and 1550 that all was not well with the Portuguese empire, or its trade in spices, the character of Portugal's intercourse changed. The withdrawal of Portugal into itself was stimulated by events beyond Lisbon's control: the resurgence of Turkish power in the East, the spread of Protestantism and religious war in Europe, and the determination of France to break the maritime monopoly of the Iberian states. Portuguese intellectuals rarely went abroad on their own after 1550: there was no Góis or Resende to publicize the empire in the second half of the sixteenth century. Most of those Portuguese who went abroad at this time were on religious or political assignments, or were refugees from the state or the Inquisition. Within the decade the Portuguese attitude toward the rest of Europe changed from one of cautious fraternization to one of suspicious and defiant retreat.

The major writings on the discoveries by Castanheda, Barros, and Góis were completed and published during a period of tightening control over reading and the dissemination of books. The tracts of Góis and Resende written in Latin and published in northern Europe were translated at once into the vernacular languages to make them available to a larger audience. The chronicles, originally written in Portuguese, had necessarily to be translated before they could be circulated to a general audience; indeed, it was the Portuguese crown itself which urged Osório to prepare his elegant Latin adaptation of Góis' work on the deeds of King Manuel. The Italian, French, and Latin translations and adaptations of the Portuguese chronicles and travel accounts circulated widely to non-Iberian intellectuals in the last quarter of the sixteenth century. Throughout Catholic

Europe, and in some Protestant countries as well, interested readers were best able to keep abreast of the year-to-year progress of the Europeans in the East by reading the Jesuit letterbooks.

The Jesuits, the diplomats of church and state, the correspondents of the great merchant and banking houses, and the political refugees from Philip II acted, in Jesuit language, as "living letters" to the outside world about events in Iberia and its overseas possessions. Equally important were their written reports on the resumption of rivalries between Castile and Portugal in the Spiceries, the ill-fated African expedition of King Sebastian in 1578, the Spanish conquest of Portugal in 1580, the subsequent decline of the spice trade, and the new juris-dictional rivalries between Castilians and Portuguese in both Iberia and Asia. But this type of information remained the monopoly of official political, com-mercial, and religious circles. The European public knew only the chronicles with their accounts of the founding of the Portuguese empire in Asia and the contemporary successes of the Jesuits that were extolled and widely circulated in the letterbooks. To the average reader it must have appeared that the Europeans had won a great, almost universal, military victory in Asia during the first half of the sixteenth century, followed by an equally great spiritual conquest during the second half of the century under the leadership of the Jesuits.

To interested members of the intellectual community of northern Europe and Italy the revelation of the East produced more questions than answers. A wide range of raw materials were available by 1600 in travel accounts, chronicles, histories, works of natural science, cosmographies, and maps. Most of the newer literature was in printed form, and it was for sale at the fairs and in the book shops. The private libraries of the great book collectors were also open to interested investigators. By the end of the sixteenth century enough concrete material was at hand about Asia to make it possible for individual writers and observers to begin assessing the meaning of overseas expansion for themselves, their disciplines, their nations, and their culture.

Books on Asia in Sixty Sixteenth-Century Collections

Work	Collection	Number of Collections
Marco Polo	King Manuel (two manuscripts) Colombina (copies in Latin, Spanish, and Venetian) Ercole Este Borso Este (a pre-1467 copy) Mirandola ("the overland travels of Marco Polo and Odoric of Pordenone") Hofbibliothek (manuscript) Wittelsbach (manuscript) Francis I (copies in French and Italian) De Thou Dee Lumley	12
Mandeville	Ercole Este Da Vinci Doni Henry III De Thou Dee Lumley (printed copies in Italian, [Venice, 1537], in English [1568], and a manuscript in English)	7
Corvinus' *Cosmographia*	Colombina (edition of 1496) Münzer (Basel, 1496)	2
Aeneas Sylvius Piccolomini (Pius II), *Historia*	Colombina Doni (edition of 1461) Münzer (Venice, 1477)	3
Foresti da Bergamo, *Supplementum Chronicarum*	Ercole Este Ulrich Fugger (edition of 1485) Francis I	3
Madrignano, *Itinerarium Portugalensium*	Borromeo (Latin edition: Milan 1508) Pirckheimer (Latin edition: Milan, 1508) De Thou Dee Lumley	5

Work	Collection	Number of Collections
Varthema, *Itinerario*	Colombina (edition of 1510) Doni Hans Sachs (German edition, [Augsburg, 1515]) Leipzig Book Fair (18 copies in German) De Thou Dee Lumley	7
Letters of King Manuel	Colombina ("three of the published letters") Schedel ("the letters to Leo X on the conquest of Malacca") Wittelsbach-Duke Ernst (Rome, 1513)	3
Buffereau, *Le mirouer du monde*	Colombina (French edition of 1517)	1
Maximilian of Transylvania, *De Moluccis insulis*	Lumley (Latin edition, [Cologne, 1523])	1
Pigafetta, *Itinerario*	Federico Gonzaga ("summary") Frankfurt Book Fair Nicot	3
Novus Orbis[1]	Montano (*Descriptio novi Orbis*) Diogo de Murça (Basel, 1532[?]) Grolier (edition of 1537)	3
Oviedo, *Historia general*	Colombina (first five books) Montano (first part) Barahona de Soto Federico Gonzaga De Thou Dee	6
Góis	Colombina Wittelsbach ("two books by Góis") Ulrich Fugger ("Góis' collected works," edition of Antwerp, 1544) De Thou Lumley	5
Castanheda, *História*	Colombina (editions of 1551 and 1554[?]) Barahona de Soto (Spanish edition of the first book, [Antwerp, 1554(?)] Frankfurt Book Fair (Italian edition: Venice, 1577) Henry III (French edition of 1553, Spanish edition of the first book, [Antwerp, 1554]) Nicot (copy in French) Montaigne (copy in French)	

[1] Other catalogs have vague references to a work which may in fact be *Novus Orbis*.

Work	Collection	Number of Collections
	De Thou (copies in Portuguese, French, and Italian)	
	Dee (copy in Italian)	
	Lumley	9
Barros, *Asia*	Proto-Fuggerana	
	Wittelsbach-Duke Ernst	
	Wittelsbach-Duke Ernst (Lisbon, 1552–3)	
	Nicot (the first and second decades)	
	De Thou (copies in Portuguese and Italian)	
	Smith	
	Dee	
	Lumley (copy in Italian)	7
Ramusio, *Delle navigationi et viaggi*	Bréderode (at least one volume)	
	De Tyard (third volume only)	2
Camoëns, *Lusiads*	Later Kings of Portugal (1572)	
	Barahona de Soto	2
Ortelius, *Theatrum orbis terrarum*	Diogo de Azambuja (copy in Spanish)	
	Borromeo	
	Wittelsbach-Duke Ernst (edition of 1570)	
	Van Marinix, (edition of 1575)	
	Dee	5
Jesuit Letterbooks	Later Kings of Portugal	
	Barahona de Soto ("two Jesuit letterbooks on the mission to Japan")	
	Muziano (*Avvisi della Cina et Giappone*)	
	Frankfurt Book Fair (ten copies in Latin; several copies in German; *Avisi della Cina e Giappone dell'anno 1586* (Antwerp, 1588–9)	
	Catharine de' Medici ("Chinese letters")	
	De Tyard ("a book of letters from Japan")	
	De Thou ("a number of Jesuit letterbooks")	
	Dee	
	Lumley ("a representative collection of Jesuit letterbooks and histories")	9
Maffei, *Historiarum Indicarum*	Frankfurt Book Fair (three separate editions)	
	De Thou	
	Dee	
	Lumley	4

Work	Collection	Number of Collections
Osório, *Res gestae Emmanuelis*	Barahona de Soto Wittelsbach-Duke Ernst Frankfurt Book Fair (copy in French, [1581] and Latin edition, [Cologne, 1574]) Montaigne (Cologne, 1574) De Thou Dee (two copies) Lumley	7
Mendoza, *Historia*	Frankfurt Book Fair (copy in German, 1589) Lumley (copy in Latin)	2
Linschoten, *Itinerario*	Diogo de Azambuja	1

PART

II

The National Literatures

Introduction

Facts, motifs, and ideas derived from the Portuguese discoveries in Asia were incorporated into the various vernacular literatures as they developed over the course of the sixteenth century. Themes from the Alexander romance and the Indian fables inherited from medieval tradition were given more realistic dimensions in the versions of sixteenth-century authors. Writers of literature in the national languages were inclined, in contrast to the devotees of Latin Humanism, to embellish their romances, poems, and stories with exotic touches from strange lands. Names of Asian places, peoples, and products, many of which were totally unfamiliar to European readers, were frequently employed to lend sonority, urbanity, or alien charm to line, verse, or scene. The Orient as a milieu for romance continued throughout the century to appeal to imaginative writers of poetry and prose, even as it was gradually transformed from a totally fanciful region into a realm of real people with genuine achievements to their credit. China, in particular, as it replaced medieval Cathay, was praised in all the national literatures as a model society with the longest continuous history on record.

Interest in Asia was general among the literati of all countries, but their reactions to it were not uniform. In nations heavily involved in expansion, controversy over the expense, morality, and necessity of expansion often beclouded victories and hopes. Literary and intellectual responses were more profound in Italy and France than elsewhere, because of their primacy in Renaissance learning and their relative freedom from direct involvement in the grosser material aspects of the expansion movement. For Portugal the story of the "conquest" of Asia became an epic theme. Elsewhere the reactions were less direct and intimate, but often more consequential. The new knowledge of the East, as it fanned out from Iberia to Italy, France, and northern Europe, influenced significantly the development of secular literature and contributed universal dimensions to history as well as comparative aspects to political theory. By 1600 the East in all its manifestations had become an integral part of European literature and learning.

CHAPTER III

The Inherited Themes

The literati of the sixteenth century possessed literary traditions which had to be reconciled in their thought and writings with the contemporary view of Asia. The themes and stories which had passed from Asia into Europe before 1500 had produced stereotypes of the imagination, particularly with respect to India. Its Brahmans were wise, simple, and pure Gymnosophists, who had been admired by Alexander and Aristotle. A land of magic and mystery, India was a golden country peopled by Amazons, monsters, and devils. Miracles, marvels, and prodigies were common there, and might even be expected. Tales of intricate plot and moral example were associated with the deeds of India's rulers, nobles, and wise men. China was so remote before 1400 that it was simply known, under one name or another, as "the land of silk." The accounts of the Franciscan missionaries, Marco Polo, and Mandeville created the "Cathay" of the fifteenth century which in Europe vied with the older image of India as a remote land of great wealth, wise people, and long history. Little of consequence was known of the island world of Southeast Asia or the kingdom of Japan before they were uncovered by the Portuguese in the sixteenth century.

I

ANTIQUITY

India, unlike China, was never entirely isolated in remotest Antiquity from contacts with the West.[1] In their descriptions of society in the Epic age the

[1] For India in the general Greek tradition see *Asia*, I, 5–12, and Jean W. Sedlar, *India and the Greek World: An Essay in the Transmission of Ideas*, forthcoming.

Homeric and the Vedic poems exhibit striking similarities. Accounts of the conduct of war by chariot, rather than by horsemen or foot soldiers, are common to both Homer and the *Mahābhārata*, the older of India's two great epics.[2] The Persian conqueror, Darius the Great, was responsible in the early sixth century B.C. for first bringing Indians and Greeks into direct contact. Thereafter the literati of India and Greece became more aware of each other as stories and tales from both East and West were diffused throughout the Persian empire. In the *Suppliants* of Aeschylus (525–456 B.C.) the king remarks: "Moreover I hear tell of Indians, of women that go roving on camels, mounted horse-fashion . . . , them that are citizens of a land neighboring the Ethiopians."[3]

Herodotus, who was born (484 B.C.) just one year before the traditional date for the death of Gautama Buddha, incorporates into his *Histories* certain stories which were possibly derived from the *Jātaka*, the tales relating to the birth of Buddha.[4] The story of India's gold-burrowing ants, relayed to Herodotus by one of his informants, was possibly based on a misunderstanding of the Sanskrit word *pipīlaka*, a term applied to alluvial gold from its resemblance to the earth of ant-hills.[5] Herodotus lent the great weight of his authority to the traditions already established in his day that the Indians of the south were black and were related to the Ethiopians, an identification that was to remain firmly imbedded in European popular thought until the sixteenth century.[6]

Some intellectuals of the Hellenistic age thought that philosophy originated in India and that certain tenets of Pythagoreanism resembled Indian religious doctrines. Recent students of Greek and Indian thought have expressed similar views. The idea of the transmigration of the soul is normally identified in Greek thought with Pythagoras (born *ca.* 580 B.C.). Herodotus attributes its origins to the Egyptians, though it is doubtful that the Egyptians ever believed in metempsychosis. In his discussion of Indian tribes Herodotus also observes of one of them that its members "will not take life in any form, sow no seed, and have no houses and live on a vegetable diet."[7] While it is more likely that metempsychosis had Indian rather than Egyptian roots, no evidence has so far been adduced to prove that Pythagoras borrowed his ideas from India,[8] even though he has been

---

[2] While the Greeks of the Homeric epoch probably did not know of India, the resemblances in these epics have been frequently noticed. For a more detailed discussion of the similarities see H. G. Rawlinson, "India in European Literature and Thought," in G. T. Garratt (ed.), *The Legacy of India* (Oxford, 1962), p. 2.

[3] As quoted in E. J. Rapson (ed.), *The Cambridge History of India* (Delhi reprint, 1962), p. 354.

[4] Rawlinson, *loc. cit.* (n. 2), p. 3.

[5] See J. W. McCrindle, *Ancient India as Described in Classical Literature* (Westminster, 1901), pp. 44, 51. Gold-digging ants are also mentioned in the *Mahābhārata* (2.98.9). For a plausible identification of the "ants" with miners see Sedlar, *op. cit.* (n. 1), p. 29. Also see pl. 3.

[6] Scylax of Caryandra and Hecataeus of Miletus had earlier made this assertion. For Herodotus' remarks see Aubrey de Selincourt (trans.), *Herodotus: The Histories* (Edinburgh, 1960), p. 217.

[7] For the attribution to the Egyptians see *ibid.*, pp. 150–51; for the quotation see *ibid.*, p. 217. Commentary in Rawlinson, *loc. cit.* (n. 2), pp. 4–7.

[8] A. B. Keith, "Pythagoras and the Doctrine of Transmigration," *Journal of the Royal Asiatic Society* (1909), pp. 569–79; but also see A. A. Macdonell, *History of Sanskrit Literature* (London, 1928), p. 422. Also see below, p. 407.

referred to as the "Buddhist *guru*" of the Greek world.⁹ Since the doctrine of transmigration remained firmly implanted in ancient Greek thought, modern scholars never tire of trying to find Indian sources for it. Even Plato, who never mentions India in the *Republic*, has been assigned an Indian intellectual ancestry, partially because his famous utopian work concludes with an apologue describing how disembodied souls choose their next incarnations.¹⁰

About 400 B.C. Ctesias of Cnidus, a critic of Herodotus' work, wrote treatises entitled *Persica* and *Indica*, the latter being the first separate European book on India. Although he spent twenty years at the Persian court of Susa, Ctesias added little to Europe's factual picture of India. His *Indica*, fragments of which survive in the abridgments of Photius (A.D. *ca.* 820–*ca.* 891) and others,¹¹ was essentially a collection of fabulous stories about the monstrous peoples and strange animals of India. Some of these grotesque legends were probably derived from stories and beliefs originating in India itself, and from the sixth-century reports of Scylax of Caryandra, a Greek in the employment of Persia. The fabulous races of India mentioned by Ctesias, and other more sober-minded Greek commentators, are the pygmies, the noseless men, people who sleep on their ears, men whose feet turn backwards, the *Anthropophagi* or cannibals, and the *Skiapodes* or men who use their giant feet as umbrellas.¹² Ctesias' animals of India, except for the elephant, the jackal, and the parrot, are either entirely mythological or so inaccurately described as to be virtually unidentifiable. His descriptions of plants are relatively clear and satisfactory. In the opinion of certain ancient writers, the *Indica* was nothing more than a collection of tall tales invented by Ctesias.¹³ Still, Pliny the Elder relayed many of these fabulous stories to later writers who then adapted them to their own literary purposes.

The question of the possible relationship between Indian and Greek fables has provoked a long and fruitless scholarly debate. Herodotus identifies the Greek stories with "Aesop the fable-writer,"¹⁴ who traditionally is assigned the dates 620–560 B.C. Modern scholars, particularly those interested in the diffusion of fables and myths, have pointed to the parallels between Aesop's fables and the stories from the *Jātaka* and other Indian collections. Some contend that the stories were transmitted orally from India to Greece; others hold that the flow was in the reverse direction; and still others propose Egypt or Lydia in Asia Minor as common sources for both the Greek and Indian tales. The entire matter is

⁹ D. P. Cassel (ed.), *Mischle Sindbad, Secundus Syntipas* (Berlin, 1891), p. 32.

¹⁰ See Edward J. Urwick, *The Message of Plato: A Re-Interpretation of the "Republic"* (London, 1920), chap. ii, and pp. 204–7.

¹¹ For the "reigning" editions see E. Manni, *Introduzione allo studio della storia greca e romana* (Palermo, 1951–52), pp. 201–2.

¹² For the relation of these peoples to their Indian equivalents see Rawlinson, *op. cit.* (n. 2), pp. 65–66.

¹³ *Ibid.*, pp. 29–30; for example, Aulus Gellius, the Roman bibliophile, in his *Noctes Atticae* (A.D. 169) tells of buying a copy of Ctesias and of how disgusted he was to find it full of ridiculous stories (IX.4). For further discussion see St. Augustine, *The City of God*, trans. M. Doak (New York, 1950), XVI.8.530–32.

¹⁴ Selincourt (trans.), *op. cit.* (n. 6), p. 155.

highly conjectural and the question of diffusion versus independent development for such an early date must be left open for lack of specific data on oral transmission or on translation.[15] Subsequent collections of tales attributed to Aesop, particularly of the later Middle Ages, were certainly accompanied by collections of stories that were definitely Indian in origin. [16] With this example in mind it might be conjectured that there was possibly an exchange of European and Indian fables during the period of active relations between India and the West when Babrius (second half of first century A.D.) wrote down in verse his collection of Aesopian fables.[17] But so far it cannot be demonstrated that a single Greek fable was derived either directly or indirectly from an Indian source.[18]

The campaign of Alexander the Great into India from 326 to 324 B.C. brought the subcontinent for the first time into direct communication with Asia Minor and the Greek world. Once the wall of separation had been leveled, the Greeks enjoyed long, intimate, and fruitful relations with some of the leading princes and courts of northern India. Through the historians of Alexander and the account of Megasthenes, the Greeks and Syrians received vivid impressions of the high culture and opulence of Indian courtly life. Megasthenes was greatly impressed that "in many points their [Indian] teaching agrees with that of the Greeks," and observed that "like Plato, they too interweave fables about the immortality of the soul." The highest class in India is called the "philosophers," and it comprises both Brahmans and Sramanas (ascetics), who follow a "dogmatic system."[19] These acute observations were preserved and expanded upon for posterity by later historians, such as Diodorus Siculus (*fl.* second half of first century B.C.), Strabo (*ca.* 63 B.C.–A.D. 21), and Arrian (A.D. 96–180).[20] But their realistic delineations did little to dispel the popular notion of India as a hot country to the east inhabited by barbaric tribes and monstrous animals, a conception which emerged from books written before the middle of the third century

[15] For a more detailed analysis of this question see A. B. Keith, *A History of Sanskrit Literature* (reprint of 1st ed. of 1920; London, 1961), pp. 352–57. For an elaborate effort to relate the comedy of Aristophanes called *The Birds* to Indian legend see Eugène Lévêque, *Les mythes et les légendes de l'Inde et la Perse . . .* (Paris, 1880), pp. 1–106. The criteria in this and other similar efforts appear to be too subjective to justify definite conclusions about influence in either direction.

[16] For their relationship to the *Book of Syntipas* (i.e., *The Seven Wise Masters*) during the fourteenth and fifteenth centuries see B. E. Perry, *Studies in the Text History of the Life and Fables of Aesop* (Haverford, Pa., 1936), pp. 185–90. Fragments from *Kalilah and Dimnah*, a book derived from the *Panchatantra*, were combined in certain of its later recensions with Aesop's *Fables* (*ibid.*, p. 173). Also see Elinor Husselman, *Kalilah and Dimnah* (London, 1938), p. 12.

[17] A. A. Macdonell, *India's Past . . .* (Oxford, 1927), p. 125.

[18] The conclusion of B. E. Perry in *Babrius and Phaedrus* (London, 1965), p. xix.

[19] As quoted in E. J. Rapson (ed.), *The Cambridge History of India* (Delhi reprint, 1962), pp. 376–77. For commentary on the "philosophers" in Megasthenes and others see Barbara C. J. Timmer, *Megasthenes en de indische Maatschappij* (Amsterdam, 1930), pp. 70–105. The distinction between Brahmans and Sramanas seems to originate with Megasthenes, perhaps because he knew some of their writings. See S. K. Viksit, "Was the Bhagavad-Gītā Known to Megasthenes?" *Annals of the Bhandarkar Oriental Research Institute* (Poona), XXX (1949), 298.

[20] For their accounts see R. C. Majumdar (ed.), *The Classical Accounts of India . . .* (Calcutta, 1960), chaps, iii, iv, v.

B.C. to become a stock feature of the Western mentality.[21] Vergil (70–19 B.C.), like other poets more fascinated by the myth than the reality of India, refers to its people as the "Ethiopians of the East."[22]

From the first century B.C. to the fall of Rome, the relations between India and the Mediterranean world were extended through increased trade and by diplomatic missions. Aside from new information on trading relations with India and China, the Latin writers had little to add to Greek conceptions of Eastern civilization.[23] In Antioch, Rome, and Alexandria, the presence of Indians, possibly some of whom were Buddhist monks,[24] helped to enlighten certain Western thinkers about Indian philosophy and religion. Those Westerners of the early Christian centuries who had become disenchanted with Greek rationalism willingly turned their eyes eastward in the search for a more intimate and purer knowledge of the divine. Neo-Platonists, Gnostics, and Manichaeans were apparently attracted by Indian and Buddhist ideas and beliefs. Hippolytus, a writer of the early church, in his *Philosophoumena* (*ca.* A.D. 230) included a section devoted to a refutation of the Brahmanical heresy. But the increase in factual knowledge about India, and the trickle into Europe of Hindu and Buddhist teachings, did very little to help Westerners separate myth from fact, or to alter the fantastic European conception of India.

For later generations the most important Roman writer on India was Pliny the Elder (A.D. 23–79). His *Natural History*, an encyclopedic work which deals with geography, ethnography, anthropology, physiology, zoology, and various other subjects, was long a major source of information. Pliny's notices of India are drawn from the available Greek books and from current merchant reports.[25] About the Greek authors, Pliny comments: "There is no room for a careful examination of their statements, they are so diverse and incredible." But he still goes on to quote them and to enumerate from their accounts the list of "fabulous races," the social classes of India, and the wonderous flora and fauna. Aelian (*fl.* second century A.D.) in his book *On the Peculiarities of Animals* deals with a substantial number of Indian birds and animals.[26] Caius Julius Solinus (*fl.* first half of the third century A.D.) compiled his *Collectanea rerum memorabilium* from Pliny's *Natural History* and from the geography of Pomponius Mela.

The Christian writers were not content to accept unreservedly the authority of pagan Antiquity on India. The older stories about India were quickly Christianized, perhaps in deference to the suggestion of St. Augustine that God may have created "fabulous races so that monstrous births among Christians should not be attributed to lapses in his wisdom."[27] The fifth-century compilers of the

---

[21] See Albrecht Dihle, "Indische Philosophen bei Clemens Alexandrinus," in *Mullus: Festschrift Theodor Klauser* (Münster, 1964), p. 70.

[22] See J. Andrée, "Vergile et les Indiens," *Revue des études latines*, XXVI (1949), 158–63.

[23] See *Asia*, I, 12–19, for more detail.

[24] P. Slepčevič, *Buddhismus in der deutschen Literatur* (Vienna, 1920), p. 4.

[25] For a collection of some of his references to India consult Majumdar, *op. cit.* (n. 20), pp. 337–50.

[26] For extracts see *ibid.*, pp. 413–21.

[27] Cf. *The City of God* (n. 13), XVI.8.532.

Physiologus, or *The Naturalist,* transformed the marvelous animal stories from Pliny, Aelian, and Solinus into allegorical Christian sermons. The bestiaries of the Middle Ages in turn derived their conceptions of the physical characteristics, moral virtues, and symbolism of the animals from the sermons of the *Physiologus.* Stories extracted from these compendia became a part of medieval lore and some of them were incorporated into later recensions of Aesop's *Fables* and the romance of Alexander.

The early Greek tradition of the "good Brahmans" was amplified and Christianized by later writers.[28] Apollonius of Tyana (*fl.* first century A.D.), a Neo-Pythagorean philosopher, was the first Greek to travel in India for purposes other than those of war, diplomacy, or trade. He was entertained by princes and Brahmans and he reported to Europe that the "wise Brahmans" are "more Greek than Indian."[29] The early Christian writers, following the Cynic views, celebrated the ascetic qualities of the Brahmans. Of particular importance to some Christian writers was the report of Bardaisan (Bardesanes), a teacher of Christianity born at Edessa in A.D. 154.[30] Bardaisan met and interviewed an Indian deputation to the Roman emperor led by Dandamis, or Sandanes, which reached Syria in the reign of Emperor Elagabalus (A.D. 218–22). From the Indians he learned about "the order of the holy sages, whom the Greeks are wont to call Gymnosophists, and of whom there are two sects—the Brachmans and the Samanaeans."[31] His work on the "good Brahmans" was lost, but extracts from it have been preserved in the fourth book of Porphyry's (A.D. 233–306) *On Abstinence from Animal Food* and in the collection of Greek texts compiled by Joannes Stabaeus (*fl.* early sixth century A.D.). From these and other accounts of the early Christian era, the idea was firmly implanted in Europe that the Gymnosophists were sages of high moral character who lived in purity while subsisting on fruits, nuts, and berries in a land of milk and honey.

Three different "Indias" existed for Antiquity. The first of these was south India, which bordered on Ethiopia, or was connected by a land bridge with Africa. All that was known about its people was that they were black and primitive. Still, by the fourth century A.D. men of education began to suspect that the Indians and Ethiopians were two different sets of peoples. The second "India," located to the east of the Persian empire, was recognized by serious historians from Megasthenes onward to be a cultivated and highly complex society. The "fabulous India" of Homer, the historians of Alexander, Pliny, and others was located at the edge of the world and was inhabited by grotesque peoples and monstrous beasts. Naturally these conceptions of India were not hermetically sealed off from one another in the popular imagination or in the

---

[28] F. Pfister, "Die Brahmanen in der Alexandersage," *Berliner philologische Wochenschrift,* Vol. XLI, (1921), col. 569.

[29] Philostratus' biography (*ca.* A.D 217) of Apollonius reproduced in Majumdar, *op. cit.* (n. 20), pp. 383–412. Also see A. Dihle, *loc. cit.* (n. 21), pp. 60–61; and Elizabeth H. Haight, *More Essays on Greek Romances* (New York, 1945), pp. 81–112.

[30] Text in Majumdar, *op. cit.* (n. 20), pp. 425–29.

[31] See *ibid.,* p. 432.

literary accounts. But as relations between medieval Europe and the East were severely distended, the fabulous view of India became increasingly dominant, particularly as the more reliable histories of India, such as Arrian's, were neglected or lost. In the Middle Ages the India of reality was increasingly ignored; the India of legend became a fundamental source for all writers.

2

THE ROMANCE OF ALEXANDER

From Antiquity to the Renaissance the ordinary European drew his conception of India mainly from the stories and illustrations attached to the fictional biography of Alexander the Great. The feats of the great Macedonian conqueror had been embellished into legends even in his own lifetime. Cleitarchus of Colophon, one of his contemporaries, composed a romanticized version of his deeds which was but the first of a series of imaginary Alexander biographies. An epistolary romance, fragments of which survive in papyrus, and a series of letters attributed to Aristotle perpetuated the tradition of the East as the homeland of marvels. An account of Alexander's encounter with the Gymnosophists, preserved also in papyrus fragments, established his presumed relations to the sages of India. And immediately after the conqueror's death in 323 B.C. a political pamphlet was prepared celebrating the exploits of his last days while purporting to give his last will and testament.

These materials, and possibly others as well, fell into the hands of an Alexandrian during the third century A.D. He combined them with certain Egyptian legends to produce a nameless book which became the basic source for the medieval romance of Alexander and for a mass of translations and adaptations extant in most of the literary languages of the Western world.[32] The original work survives only in five later Greek redactions and in numerous derivatives of one lost version. To these various Greek texts and the traditions attached to them the world of scholarship has given the generic name "pseudo-Callisthenes."[33] None of the extant Greek texts appears to be a duplicate, or even a fair representation, of the original book. For at an early date it was subject to modifications and revisions by transcribers who epitomized stories, or excised

---

[32] For the early history of the romance see F. P. Magoun, *The Gestes of Alexander of Macedon* (Cambridge, Mass., 1929), pp. 15–24; David J. A. Ross, *Alexander Historiatus: A Guide to Medieval Illustrated Alexander Literature* (London, 1963), pp. 5–6; George Cary, *The Medieval Alexander* (Cambridge, 1967), pp. 9–10.

[33] Isaac Casaubon saw a Greek manuscript of the romance in Paris which bore an ascription to Callisthenes, a Peripatetic philosopher of Alexandria. He judged correctly that the attribution was false and in a letter of 1605 to J. J. Scaliger he refers to the manuscript as the pseudo-Callisthenes, an appellation taken up by later scholars when referring to the Greek texts. The most authoritative study of the pseudo-Callisthenes texts is Reinhold Merkelbach, *Die Quellen des griechischen Alexanderromans* (Munich, 1954).

and added materials to it. The derivatives which scholars consider to be closest to the original is the A version,[34] and from it comes most of the later adaptations and translations.

The earliest and most important Latin translation of the pseudo-Callisthenes (A version) is that made in the early fourth century by Julius Valerius entitled *Res gestae Alexander Macedonis*. While but two complete manuscripts of Valerius' work are extant, an *Epitome* prepared in the ninth century survives in sixty-seven manuscripts. The epitomizer excised certain of the Indian adventures recounted in the original Valerius, but appended to his more popular version the famous apocryphal letter of Alexander to Aristotle telling of the marvels of India. A number of vernacular derivatives of the Valerius and the *Epitome* appeared in the twelfth century. Two of the most important of these were the Old French *Roman d'Alexandre: Alberic* in dodecasyllabic or Alexandrine verse, and its descendant, the *Alexanderlied* of Pfaffe Lamprecht in Middle High German verse. The independent and lengthy poem of Lambert le Tort of Chateaudun known as *Alexandre en Orient* was revised and combined with other poems in about A.D. 1185 by Alexandre de Paris into a vulgate text that became a standard source for later adapters.[35] In Le Tort's poem the story is recounted at length of Alexander's expedition to India, his rout of King Porus, and his adventures with the monsters and marvels. Numerous adaptations of the standard *Roman d'Alexandre* were made in poetry and prose during the fourteenth and fifteenth centuries in French, Latin, Spanish, Dutch, and English.

The second Latin translation fundamental to the diffusion of the Alexander romance in Europe was that of Archpriest Leo of Naples. Around A.D. 950 Leo was sent on a diplomatic mission to Constantinople by the learned Duke John III of Campania. While at the Byzantine court, he located and transcribed a Greek manuscript of the pseudo-Callisthenes.[36] On Leo's return to Naples the duke ordered him to translate it into Latin. Leo's version in mediocre Latin prose, now lost, was entitled *Nativitas et victoria Alexandri Magni regis* (ca. 952) and is generally known today as the *Historia de Preliis* (eleventh century) from the title of its first interpolated redaction.[37]

The *Preliis* and subsequent versions of it became the most popular and influential of the Alexander books produced in the later Middle Ages. The Bamberg manuscript (ca. 1000), the version judged to be closest in substance to Leo's original, is unique among the early forms of the *Preliis* in that it has appended to it four tractates dealing primarily with life in India, the Christianization of the subcontinent, and the wonders of the East. The interpolations and additions to two *Preliis* versions prepared around 1150 are moralistic in message

---

[34] It has been translated into English in E. H. Haight, *Life of Alexander of Macedon* (New York, 1955).

[35] See Ross, *op. cit.* (n. 32), pp. 9–12.

[36] This was a manuscript of the D type which probably was derived from an independent reworking of an A type redaction. See Magoun, *op. cit.* (n. 32), p. 38.

[37] Three textual traditions in Latin derive from Leo's book. See Ross, *op. cit.* (n. 32), p. 48.

and appear to be Oriental in origin.[38] From the *Preliis* books are descended a majority of the prose versions of Alexander that circulated widely in the thirteenth and fourteenth centuries. Most of the Italian Alexander books in prose were printed between 1472 and 1502, the three last being published at Venice. A Czech translation of the *Preliis* was made in 1433 and published at Pilsen in 1513. This version of the Alexander legend was translated into Polish and published at Cracow in 1550, a work which was reprinted nine times between 1611 and 1766.[39]

The Alexander story also entered Europe through a third conduit, an Arabic version of the pseudo-Callisthenes which was translated into Spanish and then into French around 1400. Stephen Scrope translated the French into English in 1450, and this translation was revised in 1472 by William Worcester. A version of the French manuscript was retranslated by Earl Rivers under the title *The Dicts and Sayings of the Philosophers*. This work, published by Caxton, was the first dated book printed in England in the late fifteenth century.[40] In these Christianized versions Alexander is portrayed as a philosopher king who is determined to suppress idolatry in India.[41]

The Alexander books in all their incarnations were used in the later Middle Ages as sources by historians, encyclopedists, poets, preachers, and collectors of myths. The earliest version of the popular French universal history called *Histoire ancienne jusqu'à Caesar* (1206–30) contains an account of Alexander's exploits in India based exclusively on certain of the romance texts. In Book IV of the *Speculum historiale* (mid-thirteenth century) Vincent of Beauvais provides a chronicle of Alexander derived partly from the romance sources and partly from the more reliable historical accounts of Justin, Quintus Curtius, and others.[42] Gautier de Châtillon based his popular heroic epic, the *Alexandereid*, written between 1178 and 1182, upon both historical and romance sources, and Rudolf von Ems in his *Alexander* (post 1250) followed a similar method. But Thomas of Kent in his lengthy poem called *Le Roman de toute Chevalerie* (second half of the twelfth century), while relying chiefly upon the standard Alexander stories, supplemented that source with marvels collected from Solinus and other mythmongers of Antiquity. The thirteenth-century *King Alexander* in Middle English is an adaptation of *Le Roman de toute Chevalerie*.[43] From these examples

[38] The tractates are: *Commentarium Palladii, Collatio Alexandri cum Dindimo per letteras facta,* and *Epistola Alexandri ad Aristotelem.* See Magoun, *op. cit.* (n. 32), pp. 44–49; also Cary, *op. cit.* (n. 32), pp. 12–16.

[39] See Ross, *op. cit.* (n. 32), pp. 50–64.

[40] *Ibid.,* p. 7.

[41] Cary, *op. cit.* (n. 32), pp. 22–23. For an example of this characterization see M. E. Schofield (ed.), *The Dicts and Sayings of the Philosophers: A Middle English Version by Stephen Scrope* (Philadelphia, 1936), p. 154.

[42] Vincent's work was translated into Dutch by Jacob van Maerlantz and printed at Gouda (1477), Delft (1479, 1488, and 1491), and Antwerp (1515). It was translated into French by Jean de Vignay in the fourteenth century and printed at Paris in 1495 and 1496. It was mainly through the translations of Vincent that the Alexander story entered popular literature. See F. Pfister, "Das Nachleben der Überlieferung von Alexander und den Brahmanen," *Hermes,* LXXVI (1941), 163–64.

[43] See Ross, *op. cit.* (n. 32), pp. 18, 21, 25–27, 71–73.

it can be discerned that certain historians and poets sought to collate the Alexander stories with the more reliable histories. But it is significant that the stories were usually taken at face value as records of genuine events, the most fantastic of which took place in the East.

The four "Indian tractates" which had been interpolated into the romance of Alexander at various points in its history were apparently accepted in the later Middle Ages as reliable literary portraits of the Indians, especially the Brahmans.[44] These were not folk stories transmitted from India, but literary productions of European authorship which became sources for later tellers and writers of fables. The first of these treatises, *Commonitorium Palladii*, is derived from the history *On the Races of India and the Brahmans* (*ca.* 375) usually attributed to Palladius (*ca.* 363–*ca.* 430), the first bishop of Ireland.[45] Today it exists in two Greek and two Latin versions, one of which is attributed to St. Ambrose and is known as *De moribus Brachmanorum*. The treatise called "Dindimus on the Brahmans," sometimes incorrectly attributed to Palladius, includes a comparison of the Indians and the Macedonians in which the Westerners come off second best. A third treatise, *Collatio Alexandri cum Dindimo per letteras facta*, consists of five letters supposedly exchanged between Alexander and Dindimus, king of the Brahmans. In this correspondence the Indians attack the Macedonians for their worldliness and sensuality. Alexander responds by heaping ridicule on the Brahmans for their weakness and asceticism. Finally, there is the renowned *Epistola Alexandri ad Aristotelem*, a fictitious letter allegedly addressed by Alexander to his teacher, in which he describes the wonders of the East. The *Collatio* and the *Epistola* became popular after A.D. 1000 as both were prepared in a large number of separate versions and circulated independently of the Alexander books.[46]

Medieval historians, who believed their fanciful maps to be true images of the world, had very little hesitation about accepting the Indian tractates as real history.[47] Bishop Otto of Freising (d. 1158) in his world history quotes the stories from the *Epistola* as facts, but then remarks: "Therein the careful student of events will find the perils he [Alexander] endured . . . , and many matters so strange that they seem actually beyond belief."[48] Jacques de Vitry (*ca.* 1181–1239) traveled to the coastal cities of Syria on a mission for the papacy in 1217.

---

[44] For these texts see the edition of F. Pfister, *Kleine Texte zum Alexanderroman*, No. 4 in W. Heraens and H. Morf (eds.), *Sammlung vulgärlateinische Texte* (Heidelberg, 1910).

[45] This is one of the fullest ancient accounts of India, the most reliable part being the materials derived from Arrian. See J. D. M. Derrett, "The History of Palladius on 'the Races of India and the Brachmans,'" *Classica et mediaevalia*, XXI (1960), 73–74.

[46] For further discussion of the Indian tractates see Cary, *op. cit.* (n. 32), pp. 12–16; Magoun, *op. cit.* (n. 32), pp. 44–49. For the Anglo-Saxon *Wonders of the East* (*ca.* 1000), a rendition of the letter to Aristotle, see Stanley Rypins (ed.), *Three Old English Prose Texts in MS. Cotton Vitellius A XV* (London, 1924). Translations of the letter were later made also into Middle Irish, French, Icelandic, Middle English, and German.

[47] See Rudolf Wittkower, "Marvels of the East," *Journal of the Warburg Institute*, V (1942), 179–80.

[48] C. C. Mierow (trans.), *Otto, Bishop of Freising, The Two Cities: A Chronicle of Universal History to the Year 1146 A.D.* (New York, 1966), p. 183.

Upon his return to Rome he composed, in 1219–20, a *Historia orientalis* which is based on his own experiences in the Levant and on the stories about India enshrined in Solinus, Isidore of Seville, and the romance of Alexander.[49] Other respected commentators who seriously used the *Epistola* as historical sources include Walter of Metz, Fulcher of Chartres, and Albertus Magnus.

The numerous stories of Alexander's relations with the philosophers of India have a history in European literature that runs from Onesikritos and the other early historians of Alexander to the end of the sixteenth century.[50] According to Onesikritos, a certain Cynic philosopher was sent by Alexander in 326 B.C. to the Gymnosophists who lived near Taxila to become acquainted with the wisdom of the Brahmans. One of the oldest and wisest of the Brahmans called Dandamis was then sent to visit Alexander to discuss philosophical issues with him. The ascetic viewpoints expressed by Dandamis became a part of Cynic philosophy, and he was used as a mouthpiece by the Cynics for their attacks on Alexander. Megasthenes, following Onesikritos, lent his authority to this story and refers to an exchange of letters between Alexander and Dandamis. These reports were taken up by later writers who provided details, letters, and conversations from their own imaginations that became firmly established as fact in medieval literature. The interpretation of these stories by Europeans was altered from time to time to conform to the views of particular authors or schools of thought.

In the Indian tractates the Brahmans appear in two guises: as a recalcitrant group troublesome to Alexander and as a community of wise men whose leader tendered advice so sage that it impressed the conqueror. The correspondence between Alexander and Dindimus (Latin spelling of the Greek Dandamis) likewise has two sides. In the older pseudo-Callisthenes tradition the Indian emerges the victor as he upholds the greater virtues of asceticism, rejects the intellectual life, and deplores the exaltation of personality. The Brahman, or ascetic, viewpoint was admired by early Christian writers, such as Tertullian, St. Jerome, and Origen. Dindimus continues to be praised in the later Middle Ages by Christian writers of sermons, morals, and *exempla*. Abelard lauds him as one of the four pagan kings who foresaw the coming of Christ. But other theological and secular writers of the later Middle Ages eagerly adopted Alexander's view of the Brahmans as weak, unenterprising, and apathetic. Still the belief persisted that the Brahmans were pagan people of high cultivation and infinite wisdom. In 1569 the Christian Humanist Joachim Camerarius the Elder (1500–1574) published a Latin translation of Palladius entitled *Libellus gnomologicus* which celebrates the Brahmans as practitioners of the ascetic life advocated by the Protestant reformers.[51]

[49] See G. Zacher, *Die "Historia orientalis" des Jacob von Vitry* (Königsberg, 1885), pp. 5–7.

[50] See above, p. 88. The best discussions of Alexander and the Brahmans are to be found in Cary, *op. cit.* (n. 32), pp. 91–94, 167; F. Pfister, *loc. cit.* (n. 42), pp. 143–69; and J. D. M. Derrett, *loc. cit.* (n. 45), pp. 64–135. Also see R. Bernheimer, *Wild Men in the Middle Ages* (Cambridge, Mass., 1952), pp. 107–12.

[51] On Camerarius' book see Derrett, *loc. cit.* (n. 45), pp. 66–68, 85–86.

The popular conception of India in the Middle Ages is perhaps best adduced by analysis of the romance of Alexander. From these materials emerges a picture of the East as a region of vivid and startling contrasts. India is a land of opulence decorated with gorgeous palaces. The palace of Porus has golden pillars, gold-plated walls, golden vines with grapes of precious stones standing between golden pillars, and artificial birds of great beauty singing in golden trees. The idols of India are made of ivory, and the courtiers eat from priceless vessels and plates. But the climate of India is severe and unpleasant: the heat of the desert on the route to India is so hot that water boils in the vessels and the soldiers lick ice or drink oil and wine to slake their thirst. The valleys are intensely cold and violent storms wreck the soldiers' tents. Beautiful Amazons clad in silver armor live on a warm river and for protection are surrounded by dangerous animals. When naked the Amazons are hairy, without breasts, and some have boarlike tusks, others the tail of a bullock or horselike feet. The Gymnosophists live in isolation and utter simplicity, and occupy their time performing good works. The later German poets who extol Alexander add material to their plaudits from the more reliable histories or describe India's cities and palaces on the basis of their own perceptions of Europe's counterparts. The courtly romances of the crusading era glorify Alexander as the hero who defends Christendom against the Moor, an equation which identifies India as a homeland of Islam. The Moors, Egyptians, Ethiopians, and Indians are black in color like the devil. Indeed the devil was sometimes called "Niger," "Aegyptus," or "Aethiops." The invasion of Europe in the thirteenth century by the Mongols shifted to them for a time the onus of being the legions of Antichrist, the demons of hell, and the heralds of the world's end.[52]

A transition in the European conception of Alexander began to take place in the fifteenth century with the rediscovery and translation of the Greek non-legendary, or historical, accounts. These relations divide into two distinct groups: those known in whole or in part throughout the Middle Ages which were exploited by writers of the vernacular Alexander books; those only available again in the Renaissance which were soon widely diffused in printed translations.

To the first group belong the writings of Quintus Curtius Rufus,[53] Justin's *Epitome* of the *Historiae Philippicae* of Trogus Pompeius, and the universal history of Paulus Orosius entitled *Seven Books of Histories Directed against the Pagans* (early fifth century). The important but somewhat romanticized Alexander biography by Curtius was first translated in 1438 into a vernacular language by the Humanist Pier Candido Decembrio; his Italian version was shortly thereafter translated into Castilian and Valencian. A French translation of

---

[52] Description based on J. Brummach, *Die Darstellung des Orients in den deutschen Alexander-geschichten des Mittelalters* (Berlin, 1966), *passim*. Also see J. Baltrušaitis, *Le moyen-âge fantastique* (Paris, 1955), pp. 183–88.

[53] An English translation of the extant, incomplete text is to be found in Majumdar, *op. cit.* (n. 20), pp. 103–61.

Curtius was prepared in 1468 by Vasco Fernandez, Count of Lucena, a Portuguese noble attached to the Burgundian court. Fernandez deliberately rejects the fictions of the romance and extols the veracity of the ancient historian; his translation was extremely popular in both its manuscript and printed versions. It was printed seven times between 1500 and 1555 in expensively illustrated editions for the delectation of the princely and noble members of European society.[54] Solinus and Orosius likewise continued to be popular in the Renaissance, both being printed many times in the fifteenth and sixteenth centuries.

The historical accounts of Alexander which first became available in the fifteenth century included Arrian's, still considered to be the most reliable source on the conqueror's career, Plutarch's *Parallel Lives*, and the important Books XVI and XVII of the *Bibliotheca historica* of Diodorus Siculus. Arrian was first translated into Latin by Pier Paolo Vergeri, probably in the 1430's, and, was then revised and improved upon in the latter half of the fifteenth century by Bartolomeo Facio and Giacomo Curlo. Plutarch was translated piecemeal from the late fourteenth to the middle of the fifteenth century, when a standard Latin version was prepared by Guarino da Verona. The Greek text now considered to be the reigning version was published only in 1517. In the early sixteenth century Claude de Seyssel produced a French version of Books XVIII–XX of Diodorus Siculus called *L'Istoire des successeurs d'Alexandre*.[55]

The "historical Alexander" gradually emerged from the translations and printed editions of the Greek historians, especially from the Humanists of Italy and France. To those enamored of the works of Greek Antiquity, Alexander henceforward became a missionary to India in the cause of Greek civilization. Vasco de Lucena asserted that Alexander had shown that the East could be conquered without vast sums of money; certainly, he implies, it should be even easier for a prince armed with the Christian faith to subject the Orient to his will.[56] For the quattrocento Alexander was no longer merely a chivalric hero: he increasingly became the martial and philosophical king who realized by his personal efforts and genius the full expression and glory of his colossal individuality.[57]

While some Humanists denied the historical veracity of the Alexander legend, the stories and tales it enshrined continued to attract both the common people and the literati. The *Historia de Preliis* had first been translated into Italian verse by Qualichius di Spoleto in the thirteenth century. In public squares its stories were thereafter recited or sung for the entertainment of the common people.[58]

---

[54] It was prepared as a *speculum princeps*, "mirror of the prince," for the young Charles the Bold, grandson of John II of Portugal, whom Fernandez called "the Alexander of his day." See R. Bossuot, "Vasque de Lucene, traducteur de Quinte Curce (1468)," *Bibliothèque d'humanisme et renaissance*, VIII (1946), 215–17.

[55] See Ross, *op. cit.* (n. 32), pp. 80–81.

[56] See Bossuot, *loc. cit.* (n. 54), p. 216.

[57] See Cary, *op. cit.* (n. 32), pp. 240, 274.

[58] See C. Searles, "Some Notes on Boiardo's Version of the Alexandersagas," *Modern Language Notes*, XV (1900), 48.

An anonymous native of Gubbio in 1430 wrote *Alessandreida in rima*, a poem in twelve cantos first printed in 1512 and reprinted several times during the cinquecento.[59] Boiardo in his *Orlando Innamorato* seems to assume by the brevity and casualness of his references to the characters and themes of the Alexander stories that his audience was familiar with them. Such an assumption is supported by the fact that no fewer than six Alexander books were printed in Italy between 1472 and 1502,[60] the years when Boiardo was writing his romance. The career of Alexander was the subject of a poetic burlesque published in 1521 for the enjoyment of Pope Leo X's convivial court. From the pen of Domenico Falugio, it was entitled *Trionfo Magno*, and the title page of the only extant edition is graced with a woodcut showing Alexander in a triumphal car drawn by elephants.[61] A few years later, in 1529, an Alexander book was issued at Venice in Greek verse as a political satire.[62] Clearly Alexander was no longer being taken seriously in Italy, except by a few Humanists interested in collecting and preserving the extant manuscripts of the romance.[63]

The northern Europeans were slower to lose their interest and confidence in the Alexander stories. In the "Monk's Tale" Chaucer wrote:

> Alisaunder's storie is so commune
> That everie wight that hath discrecionne
> Hath herde somewhat or al of his fortune.[64]

In 1472 at Augsburg, Johann Hartlieb published his translation of the *Historia de Preliis* called *Das Buch der Geschichte des grossen Alexander*, which was reprinted many times. A German "mirror of the prince," or manual of moral guidance, was later prepared in which "King Dindimus" and his teachings were elevated to be a princely exemplar, a model which Alexander failed to follow, as Hartlieb stresses, much to the conqueror's own regret.[65] In 1558 Hans Sachs used Hartlieb's book as a major source for his tragedy of *Alexander*.[66] Willibald Pirckheimer, the German Humanist, meanwhile admitted to the great appeal

---

[59] See Cary, *op. cit.* (n. 32), p. 55.

[60] Ross, *op. cit.* (n. 32), p. 63. Also see below, pp. 202–4.

[61] *Ibid.*, p. 73.

[62] *Ibid.*, p. 43. It was reprinted in 1553 and 1600, and numerous times thereafter.

[63] For example, Piero Vellori (1499–1585), the celebrated Florentine classicist, once owned the fourteenth-century vellum manuscript of the *Historia de Preliis*, now at Munich. See Magoun, *op. cit.* (n. 32), p. 115. Vellori was also interested in geographical expansion and the India of reality as is attested by the *Ristretto*, a manuscript (Munich, Cod. ital. 160, Vict. 8) which he prepared for Cosimo on all of the states and princes of the world then known in which he includes notices of the Grand Khan, the Great Mogul, Malacca, the Philippines, Calicut, China, Japan, Siam, and Borneo. See W. Rüdiger, *Petrus Victorius aus Florenz* (Halle, 1896), pp. 96–97.

[64] *The Canterbury Tales*, l. 3821.

[65] This manuscript book of the fifteenth century was bound in 1557 and decorated with the portrait and arms of Elector Otto Heinrich (reigned 1556–59), the great bibliophile of Heidelberg. See H. Becker, "Zur Alexandersage," *Zeitschrift für deutsche Philologie*, XXIII (1891), 424–25.

[66] For an analysis of the relationship of Hartlieb's book to the tragedy of Hans Sachs see S. Hirsch, *Das Alexanderbuch Johann Hartliebs* (Berlin, 1909), pp. 133–34. Hartlieb's book was also translated into Danish in 1584. See Magoun, *op. cit.* (n. 32), pp. 42–44. Both the manuscript and printed versions of Hartlieb are well illustrated. See Ross, *op. cit.* (n. 32), p. 49.

the Brahmans had for him after reading about the relations of Apollinius of Tyana with the sages of India.[67] In the special language concocted for Sir Thomas More's *Utopia* the word "gymnosophaon" is used to mean "philosophia."[68] Sebastian Münster, whom contemporaries called the Strabo of Germany, in his famous *Cosmographei* (German, 1544; Latin, 1550) used seriously certain of the legendary materials (*Epitome* of Julius Valerius, the letter to Aristotle, and the *Collatio*) for his account of Alexander's adventures in India and for his meeting with the Amazons and Brahmans. Münster wrote: "The ancients have devised many peculiar monsters which are supposed to exist in India. . . . However, there is nobody here [in Europe] who has ever seen these marvels. But I will not interfere with the power of God, he is marvelous in His work and His wisdom is inexpressible."[69] This seems to be the last use of the romance as a historical source. Melanchthon, who promised to write a history of Alexander but never did, was quite open in questioning the value of the romance for history.[70] At the end of the sixteenth century Gabriel Rollenhagen translated the Alexander stories into German as a linguistic exercise, and in the seventeenth century his book enjoyed a considerable popularity under the title *Wahrhaffte Lügen* (*True Lies*)![71]

3

THE WESTWARD MIGRATION OF STORY

India, since ancient times, has remained an "ocean of story" pouring out many more tales over the centuries than have trickled into it. The *Rawi*, or professional storytellers, entertained social gatherings in India with a host of traditional stories to which they added local color and individualistic embellishments. Many of the popular tales were adapted by Buddhist teachers to their religious purposes and had become a part of Buddhist lore by the time of Asoka (*ca.* 269–*ca.* 232 B.C.). The large Buddhist collection called the *Jātaka* was incorporated into the Pali canon and its stories were used and adapted by Buddhist missionaries for didactic purposes as they spread the teachings of their Master to surrounding lands.[72] Wherever they went, to Ceylon, China, or Mediterranean Europe, the Buddhist missionaries inaugurated the oral transmission of the traditional Indian tales. Like most storytellers, then and now, they were

[67] Letter of Pirckheimer to Konrad Celtis (Nuremberg, November 17, 1503) in E. Reicke (ed.), *Willibald Pirckheimers Briefwechsel* (2 vols., Jena, 1930), I, 198.
[68] See E. Surtz and J. H. Hexter (eds.), *The Complete Works of St. Thomas More* (New Haven, 1965), IV, 18.
[69] *Cosmographei* (Basel, 1551), p. 1166. Also see pl. 4.
[70] See Pfister, *loc. cit.* (n. 42), pp. 167–68.
[71] See K. T. Gaedertz, *Gabriel Rollenhagen, sein Leben und seine Werke* (Leipzig, 1881), pp. 5–6.
[72] See H. Kern, *Manual of Indian Buddhism* (Delhi, 1968), pp. 2, 7.

probably content to pass on that which had been received with but few changes and in so doing to remain the anonymous and faithful purveyors of the values and beliefs of the past.[73]

Students of literature have long debated the problems surrounding the migration of Indian tales to the West. Along with the development of Sanskrit studies in nineteenth-century Europe, the conviction grew that the originals of the European folktales could probably be found in India. Theodor Benfey, the translator of the *Panchatantra (Five Treatises)*, pronounced the dictum in 1859 that a great number of folktales, except for Aesop's *Fables*, had spread westward from India. Only a small number of Indian stories reached Europe, according to Benfey, by oral transmission before the tenth century. The largest collections of Indian stories arrived there after the tenth century, he argued, as a result of the literary migration of stories through translation. Buddhist materials were also carried into Europe by the Mongol invaders and by the intercourse they promoted in the thirteenth and fourteenth centuries.[74] Emmanuel Cosquin, a distinguished French folklorist, followed Benfey's lead by studying in detail scores of tales and motifs with the deliberate design of finding their analogues in India.[75] Cosquin departed from Benfey's thesis on just two points: he argued that Benfey exaggerated the importance of the Mongols as transmitters of stories,[76] and he was inclined, unlike Benfey, to view ancient Egypt as a competing source.

Most recent students of the folktale recognize the primacy of India as the source of story, but they also discern wellsprings in other great centers of invention and dissemination.[77] Like Cosquin, they define the geographical region from India westward as a territory possessing a common tradition of folktales. Some regard the stock of tales common to the entire region as a nucleus of story from which tales spread westward by oral transmission during the Crusades.[78] The folkloric homogeneity of the territory is shown by cataloging the repetitions of incidents (motifs) and combinations of incidents rather than by noting vague similarities in plot or characters.[79] Tales which originated in one part of the Indo-European region seem normally to have traveled to other parts but had a tendency to fade out at the frontiers, and were rarely to be found east of India.[80] It is striking how few are the coincidences

---

[73] See Stith Thompson, *The Folk Tale* (New York, 1946), pp. 4–5; also see C. H. Tawney and N. M. Penzer, *The Ocean of Story: Somadeva's Kathā Sarit Sāgara* (10 vols.; Delhi reprint, 1968), I, x–xi.

[74] T. Benfey (ed. and trans.), *Pantschatantra: Fünf Bücher indischer Fablen, Märchen, und Erzählungen* (2 vols.; Leipzig, 1859), introduction.

[75] Consult especially E. Cosquin, *Les contes indiens et l'occident* (Paris, 1922).

[76] E. Cosquin, "Les mongols et leur prétendu rôle dans la transmission des contes indiens vers l'Occident européen," *Revue des traditions populaires*, XXVII (1912), 337–73, 393–430, 497–526, 545–66.

[77] Thompson, *op. cit.* (n. 73), p. 379.

[78] See Joseph Jacobs, *Indian Fairy Tales* (London, 1892), p. 235; W. R. Halliday, "Notes upon Indo-European Folk-Tales and the Problem of Their Diffusion," *Folk-Lore*, XXXIV (1923), 118–19.

[79] See Tawney and Penzer, *op. cit.* (n. 73), I, 29n.; VIII, xiv–xv.

[80] Thompson, *op. cit.* (n. 73), p. 14.

between the literary folklore of the classical European tradition and the corpus of Indo-European folktales.[81] But whatever the case may be for the oral transmission of tales, it is certain that it must rest on similarities and conjectures, particularly on questions of dates.

Many common folktales of the oral as well as the literary tradition can be traced back to a written source.[82] It is not possible, however, to be certain that the literary text is the original of the story or to make the quick assumption that the gift of imagination is a monopoly of the literati. But it is also an unwarranted assumption to insist that the oral tradition stretches back into the furthest reaches of Antiquity. Indeed the only substantial evidence for the existence of an oral tradition is to be found in written texts. Still the contingent evidence for the antiquity and persistence of the oral tradition is so persuasive, even in the written texts, that it is safe to assume that tales were exchanged from the earliest times. And it is also cogent to argue that it was the casting of the folktales into literary form which gave the popular stories the permanent, datable form essential to a study of their history.[83]

Firmer ground is reached with the appearance in Europe from the tenth century onward of collections of Indian tales. Most of the stories came to the languages of Europe through intermediary Arabic, Syrian, and Persian translations. These were rendered into Greek and Hebrew versions from which the Latin versions were usually made. From the Latin texts the tales were translated into the vernacular languages and incorporated in whole or in part into literary works and collections of stories. Some of them in their vernacular guise quite evidently entered the mainstream of the European oral tradition, thus perpetuating what might be called a cycle of literary rebirths or transmigrations from oral to written and back to oral.

The Christian legend of Barlaam and Josaphat includes as subordinate tales within its frame story the first collection of Indian parables to penetrate the literary world of medieval Europe.[84] The Indian hermit, Barlaam, and his royal pupil, Prince Josaphat, were supposed to have converted India to Christianity at some unspecified date in the remote past. The story of Josaphat's moral education by Barlaam is infused with fourteen ingenious and charming parables which soon became stock items as medieval *exempla*. The figure of Abenner, the king of India and father of Josaphat, is that of the recalcitrant heathen who tried by means fair and foul to prevent his gifted son from abjuring his native faith and accepting the teachings of Christianity. Josaphat with the help of God finally triumphs over himself, his enemies, and the machinations of the king. Ultimately the king himself recognizes the superiority of the Christian faith and turns his kingdom over to Josaphat. Four years later Josaphat relinquishes the

---

[81] See Tawney and Penzer, *op. cit.* (n. 73), VI, x–xi.

[82] Thompson, *op. cit.* (n. 73), pp. 176–77.

[83] Cf. Tawney and Penzer, *op. cit.* (n. 73), VIII, xviii–xx.

[84] For an English translation of its fourteen parables see Robert Chalmers, "The Parables of Barlaam and Josaphat," *Journal of the Royal Asiatic Society*, N.S. XXIII (1891), 423–49. For a "portrait" of Josaphat see pl. 1.

crown to his minister to be free to join Barlaam in the desert. Eventually they both die in the desert after leading lives of exemplary abstinence, meditation, and prayer.

For the faithful of the late Middle Ages Barlaam and Josaphat were moral exemplars. The churches celebrated their feast days, and their relics were thought to be imbued with healing powers. The Albigensians were inspired to such a degree by the legend's advocacy of the ascetic life and renunciation of the world that they sometimes assumed it to be a Cathar document. In 1571 the Doge of Venice presented King Sebastian of Portugal with what was allegedly a bone and a part of the spine from Josaphat's back, and these relics were later donated to the Cloister of St. Salvator in Antwerp. The Georgian and Greek churches elevated Barlaam and Josaphat to sainthood (feast day August 16), and in 1583 the Latin church fixed their feast day on November 27 in the *Martyrologium Romanum*. Morality dramas based on the legend were presented at Jesuit colleges both in Europe and overseas.[85] In Palermo a church was dedicated to "Divo Josaphat" at the end of the sixteenth century.[86]

In the mid-sixteenth century the Buddha story was relayed from Japan to Europe by a Jesuit missionary.[87] But it evidently made no impression on those who read it. Diogo de Couto, the Portuguese historian, first recognized at the beginning of the seventeenth century the striking similarity between the story of the Buddha's life he had heard in India and the career of Josaphat.[88] He also speculated that Josaphat was the Buddha, though he thought finally that the Buddha story was but an imitation of the Christian legend. Perhaps it was for this reason, among others, that no closer identification of the two stories was attempted until the nineteenth century. Eduoard de Laboulaye and Felix Liebrecht recognized simultaneously in 1859, the year of Benfey's remarkable introduction to the *Panchatantra*, that the legend of Barlaam and Josaphat was a version of the story of the Buddha's "enlightenment" which took place around 600 B.C.[89] Their discovery, like that of Benfey, sparked literary and linguistic scholarship. The historical reconstruction of the transmission of the Buddha story to Europe has since consumed the time of numerous scholars in many lands; others have devoted much energy to comparative study of the

---

[85] See G. Moldenhauer, *Die Legende von Barlaam und Josaphat auf der iberischen Halbinsel* (Halle, 1929), pp. 140, 155n.; E. Kuhn, "Barlaam und Joasaph," *Abhandlungen . . . der bayerischen Akademie der Wissenschaften*, XX (1897), 87.

[86] For further details see E. Kuhn, *loc. cit.* (n. 85), pp. 53–54; also H. Peri, *Der Religionsdienst der Barlaam-Legende* (Salamanca, 1959), pp. 22–23, and n. 25. King Abenner figures on the Roman calendar too, his feast day being August 3. Modern Catholic scholarship has accepted the secular opinion that Barlaam, Josaphat, and Abenner never existed (see *Enciclopedia cattolica*). For a comparable example of the earlier Middle Ages, relating to the acceptance in the West of the cult of the Archangel Michael, see Wolfgang von Rintelen, "Kult- und Legendenwanderung von Ost nach West im frühen Mittelalter," *Saeculum*, I (1971), 71–100.

[87] See Slepčević, *op. cit.* (n. 24), p. 5.

[88] *Década quinta da Ásia* (Lisbon, 1612), I, 123–24.

[89] See Laboulaye's note in the *Journal des débats* (July 26, 1859), and Liebrecht's scholarly article "Die Quellen des Barlaam und Josaphat," *Jahrbuch für romanische und englische Literatur*, II (1860), 314–34. Also see Max Müller, *Chips from a German Workshop* (New York, 1890), IV, 174–80.

multitude of Christianized versions which survive in the countries of Christendom from Iceland to Ethiopia, from Poland to the Philippines.

The Barlaam and Josaphat legend, for all its similarities and clear relationships
to the Buddha story, is not a direct translation of any original Indian text or
texts. From one of the lives of Buddha the news evidently migrated in fanciful
form to eastern Persia where the story was written down in Pahlavī (Middle
Persian) of the conversion of a prince by a hermit. From this Pahlavī text the
Buddha story received its Manichean form in Central Asia between the third
and sixth centuries, possibly in Persian and Turkish versions. It was then
Islamized in the seventh century and again translated, possibly into Syrian and
Arabic. On the basis of one of these texts, the legend was Christianized and
translated into Greek in the seventh century by a monk who lived in a convent
near Jerusalem. This Greek work was stylistically revised and substantively
altered for edifying purposes in the eighth century by St. John of Damascus
(*ca.* 675–749), for a long time the supposed author of the whole story. In the
meantime a Georgian version was prepared, probably from an Arabic text,
which is the earliest extant version of the Christianized legend. The original
version of St. John of Damascus, no longer extant, was translated anew into
Greek by St. Euthynius of Athos (*ca.* 955–1028) around A.D. 1000, and is still
preserved under the title *Historia psychopheles.*[90]

The European versions, numbering more than one hundred, were all
derived from the Greek text of the tenth century. The names "Barlaam" and
"Josaphat," as spelled in the Greek text, probably both refer to "Buddha":
"Joasaph" from Pali "Bodhissatta" ("a future Buddha") and "Barlaam" from
"Bahgavān" ("the Lord," one of Buddha's titles).[91] The Latin text, translated
from the Greek in 1048, is extant in a manuscript of the fourteenth century.[92]
All of the vernacular versions in prose and poetry derive without exception
from either the Greek or Latin texts, from both, or from one another. Illustrations of the career of the Christians Josaphat and Barlaam, as well as portraits
of King Abenner, helped to establish them in the popular image as potentates
of Asia.[93] In popular lore their stories were kept alive by oral transmission, as
in the rustic May plays (*Maggi*) still produced in Tuscany.

The reception of the legend into the vernacular languages of the Middle
Ages has a complicated history. Some of the vernacular versions may be

[90] For this hypothetical reconstruction see Peri, *op. cit.* (n. 86), pp. 19–22, and D. M. Lang, *The Balavariani (Barlaam and Josaphat): A Tale from the Christian East Translated from the Old Georgian* (Berkeley, 1966), pp. 11–12.

[91] See Peri, *op. cit.* (n. 86), p. 18, n. 21.

[92] The translator was probably a Latin cleric of the Amalfi monastery of Mount Athos. Naples and Amalfi were both centers for translating Greek into Latin during the eleventh century. See R. Manselli, "The Legend of Barlaam and Josaph," *East and West* (Rome), VII (1957), 334. The extant manuscript version is dated 1326 and is in the Wolffenbüttel library. For a complete list of the Latin manuscripts see Jean Sonet, *Le roman de Barlaam et Josaphat: Recherches sur la tradition manuscrite latine et française* (Louvain, 1949), p. 315.

[93] For examples, see S. der Nersessian, *L'illustration du roman de Barlaam et Joasaph* (Paris, 1937), *passim.*

traced directly to the Latin vulgate text, while others derive from the abbreviated renditions included during the thirteenth century in the *Speculum historiale* of Vincent of Beauvais and in the *Legenda aurea* of Jacobus de Voragine.[94] About 1215 the legend entered Old French literature through the lengthy metrical version of Gui de Cambrai in which Indians, Chaldeans, and Egyptians are indiscriminately grouped together as the three great religious rivals of Christendom. Gui's praise of the profound learning of the heathens who dispute Christian truth is probably a literary device for making even more resounding the ultimate victory of the faith.[95] Two accurate translations of Gui's works into Castilian appeared in the thirteenth century. The legend was also the subject of three Middle High German poems, the most influential of which was the *Barlaam* of Rudolf von Ems written between 1225 and 1230. In England the legend first became known through the abbreviated version in the *Legenda aurea* (ca. 1260–70) from which the Middle English poets prepared paraphrases in verse.[96]

The numerous French versions of the thirteenth and fourteenth centuries attracted the attention of dramatists who quickly produced a host of miracle and mystery plays based on the legend. Most popular was the "Mystère du Roi Avenir" (Abenner) by Jean du Prier which employed a vast number of scenes and hundreds of characters. Don Juan Manuel (1282–1348), the great Spanish moralist, utilized parables and themes from the Barlaam legend in his prose writings.[97] In Italy the Barlaam legend appeared mainly in prose works that began to appear in the fourteenth century. A few poetic dramas also were prepared[98] which were played by members of the confraternities in the public squares of the Italian cities, notably Florence. At the end of the sixteenth century the legend finally appeared in the Spanish theater. *Thanisdoro* (ca. 1580), a tragicomedy in Spanish probably prepared for the Jesuit schools, was one of the dramas most often performed. In it the names of the characters are changed (Josaphat = Thanisdoro) and its continuity is frequently interrupted by moralistic monologues in Latin.[99] In Portugal itself the Barlaam legend was never put on the stage, but the Portuguese Jesuits probably translated the abbreviated version of the story into Japanese during the sixteenth century for the edification of their converts.[100]

Throughout the Renaissance there was considerable confusion over the authorship of the legend. The Greek text was commonly assigned to St. John of

---

[94] The abbreviated *Vita* was widely diffused in the vernaculars as a folk book in prose. A Czech version of it exists in a manuscript of 1470. Three incunabula versions of it appeared, one in Italy and two in Germany. In the sixteenth century it was printed at Pilsen (1504, 1512), Venice (1539, ca. 1600), Florence (1582), and Prague (1593). See Kuhn, *loc. cit.* (n. 85), pp. 63–75.

[95] Peri, *op. cit.* (n. 86), pp. 43–46.

[96] *Ibid.*, pp. 69–70.

[97] See M. Ruffini, "Les sources de Don Juan Manuel," *Les lettres romanes* (*Louvain*), VII (1953), 37–41.

[98] See especially the work of Bernardo Pulci (1516), and the poem of Attilio Opezzinghi (1584).

[99] Peri, *op. cit.* (n. 86), pp. 99–101. Lope de Vega completed his *Barlaán y Josafat* in 1611 (*ibid.*, p. 104).

[100] Moldenhauer, *op. cit.* (n. 85), p. 155n.

Damascus,[101] but there was dispute over the provenance of the Latin vulgate text whch appeared in Italy in two incunabula. Some Humanists identified it as the work of Giorgius Trapezientius (d. 1484), but this attribution was challenged by northern scholars concerned with publishing the works of St. John of Damascus. At Basel the first edition of the complete works of St. John in Latin appeared from 1539 to 1575. A new Latin translation of the legend was prepared for this compilation by the Dominican Henricus Gravius of Neuss. For his independent, orthodox, Latin edition of St. John's works, Abbot Jacobus Billius (Jean Billy) prepared a new translation, directly from the Greek, that first appeared at Paris in 1577. In the following year the Billius translation was published in French, a version that enjoyed a modicum of popularity among the faithful during the last two decades of the sixteenth century.[102]

The history of the migration westward of tales from the *Panchatantra* parallels that of the parables in the Barlaam and Josaphat legend.[103] The original *Panchatantra*, possibly composed between A.D. 100 and 500, is no longer extant, but it was evidently a larger work than what now passes for the *textus ornatior*. A collection of certain tales designed as a "mirror for princes" unquestionably existed in India by the mid-sixth century A.D. From it a book was soon compiled in Pahlavī. Around 750 the Pahlavī text was translated into Arabic by Abdallah ibn al Moqaffa as *Kalilah wa-Dimnah*, a title derived from distortions of the Sanskrit names of the two jackals, characters in the first book.[104] Around 1080, Symeon, the son of Seth, produced a Greek version of the Arabic that is important because it alone among the older texts contains the story of the mouse king.[105] By the thirteenth century Hebrew and Old Spanish (*ca.* 1250)[106] translations had been made from a manuscript of Ibn Moqaffa's book. The Hebrew translation, attributed to Rabbi Joel, is of great significance as a transmitter because on it is based the Latin version of John of Capua entitled *Directorium vitae humanae* (*ca.* 1270). At the suggestion of Count Eberhart of Würtemberg an excellent German version was prepared about 1480 by Anton von Pforr, a priest of

---

[101] The *Martyrologium Romanum*, for example, asserts definitely that the acts of Barlaam and Josaphat were written by St. John of Damascus.

[102] See Kuhn, *loc. cit.* (n. 85), pp. 55–60. Billius was aware of the fact that there were some in his day who doubted the historical character of the two saints, for he reasserts emphatically his belief in their historicity. Latin versions of Billius were also published at Cologne and Antwerp in 1593.

[103] The best general account is Johannes Hertel, *Das Pañcatantra, seine Geschichte und seine Verbreitung* (Leipzig and Berlin, 1914). See also the genealogical table of the *Panchatantra* prepared by Franklin Edgerton and included in Tawney and Penzer, *op. cit.* (n. 73), V, 232–42. Also see M. Müller, *op. cit.* (n. 89), 153–60.

[104] Reconstructed from later texts. See Hertel, *op. cit.* (n. 103), p. 363. Cf. Tawney and Penzer, *op. cit.* (n. 73), foreword of Sir Denison Ross, who doubts the existence of the Pahlavī version.

[105] Circulated widely under the title *Stephanites and Ichnelates*, but not translated into the vernacular until 1583. See below, p. 106, and L. O. Sjöberg, *Stephanites und Ichnelates: Überlieferungsgeschichte und Text* (Stockholm, 1962). For an interesting suggestion about the possible influence of the story of the monkey king upon zoological literature of the sixteenth century see H. W. Janson, *Apes and Ape Lore* (London, 1952), p. 353, n. 74.

[106] The only known descendant of this version is the Latin manuscript text prepared by Raymond de Béziers *ca.* 1313.

Rottenburg on the Neckar. It was published at Ulm in 1483 under the title *Das Buch der Beispiele der alten Weisen* as a princely mirror, and reissued at Strassburg in 1536 and again in 1539. In the seventeenth century Pforr's text was translated into Danish, Dutch, and Yiddish.

The second translation into Spanish, unlike its predecessor, derives from John of Capua rather than from an Arabic text. By its anonymous author it was called *Exemplario contra los engaños y peligros del mundo* (Saragossa, 1493). On thirteen different occasions it was reissued in Spain and at Antwerp over the next century. Agnolo Firenzuola in 1548 published an abbreviated Italian adaptation based on the Spanish text of 1493. In his *Discorsi degli animali ragionanti tra loro* (Venice) the scene is laid in Italy rather than in India and the two jackals of the original become two sheep.[107] Firenzuola's work was repeatedly reissued in Italian, and was a source for the French renditions of Gabriel Cottier (1556) and Pierre de la Rivey (1577).[108] In the meantime the Latin book of John of Capua was translated into Czech by Nikolaus Konac and published at Prague sometime between 1507 and 1540.[109]

At Venice in 1552 there appeared an Italian translation of the Latin text by Francesco Doni that was issued in two parts. The first was entitled *La moral filosophia del Doni*, and the second *Trattati diversi di Sendebar Indiano filosopho morale*.[110] Doni, like Firenzuola, lays the scene in Italy, makes the personages Italian, and replaces the two jackals of the first book of the *Panchatantra* with an ass and a mule. Only the first part of Doni's work was reissued, and these new printings came in 1567, 1594, and 1606. The second printing was translated into English by Sir Thomas North as *The Morall Philosophie of Doni* (London, 1570) and was reprinted in 1601.[111] The *Trattati* of Doni was translated into French and published in 1577 by Pierre de la Rivey. Finally in 1583, Giulio Nuti included an Italian translation of the eleventh-century Greek text by Symeon Seth in his work called *Dal governo dè regni* (Ferrara).

Considered as frame stories, these Westernized collections of tales in whatever guise they appeared may be classified as "mirrors for princes." Each chapter contains a story which was supposedly related to the king of India by his philosopher to elaborate a moral or to emphasize a rule of conduct. The characters of the stories are animals in the image of men, a feature which distinguishes the Indian fables from those of Aesop. It has been suggested that

---

107 It was in print by 1483. See I. G. N. Keith-Falconer, *Kalilah and Dimnah or the Fables of Bidpai: Being an Account of Their Literary History . . .* (Cambridge, 1885), p. lxxiii.

108 Cottier's work was called *Plaisant et facécieux discours sur les animaux* (Lyons). De la Rivey's *Deux livres de philosophie fabuleuse* (Paris, 1577; Lyons, 1599; Rouen, 1620) appeared in two books: the first is a translation of Firenzuola's *Discorsi*; the second is taken from Doni's *Trattati*. See Hertel, *op. cit.* (n. 103), p. 399.

109 Hertel, *op. cit.* (n. 103), pp. 399–400.

110 The name of the Indian sage underwent change from Vishnucorman to Bidpai (Pilpay) to Sendebar in the Latin edition and its derivatives.

111 For a modern reprinting see Joseph Jacobs (ed.), *The Morall Philosophy of Doni: Drawne out of the Auncient Writers, Englished out of Italian by T. North. With Introductory Essay upon the Buddhistic Origin and Literary History of the 'Fables of Bidpai' . . .* (London, 1888).

this treatment of animals is related to the Indian belief in metempsychosis.[112] In art the relation between men and animals of the Indian stories is paralleled by the composite minatures of India and by the *têtes composées* of Giuseppe Arcimboldo (1527–93) and other European painters.[113] Certain of the Italian translators dropped all references to India from their adaptations, perhaps to avoid charges of heterodoxy. The Indian moral tales, though not drawn exclusively from the *Panchatantra* as we now know it, can certainly all be traced to one Indian collection or the other, such as the *Jātaka* and the *Mahābhārata*. But whatever the sources of the stories, there can be no doubt that the European translators from John of Capua in the thirteenth century to the middle of the sixteenth century clearly stated in their prefaces and commentaries that these were Indian stories, and they unhesitatingly retained in one distorted form or another the Indian names of personages, places, and animals.[114] Over the course of five centuries, however, the stories were modified, acclimatized, moralized, and Christianized until their Indian features were almost impossible to recognize in some of the adaptations which began to appear in the latter half of the sixteenth century.

The European story cycle called generically *The History of the Seven Wise Masters* derives ultimately from an Indian or Buddhist original.[115] All the extant versions of the *Book of Sindibad*, as this cycle is called in some of its recensions, seem to stem from a lost Arabic text which is referred to in Arabic writings of the tenth century. The extant Greek text called *Syntipas* was translated in the last years of the eleventh century by Michele Andreopulo from a Syriac version.[116] The first European adaptation of the Greek text was composed around 1184 in Latin prose by a monk called Jean de Hautesville. His Latin text is entitled *Dolopathos; sive, de rege et septem sapientibus;* its frame story corresponds closely to that of the *Syntipas*, but the subordinate tales, except for one, are different. *Dolopathos* was rendered into French verse around 1210 by Herbert;[117] thereafter a number of prose versions of it appeared in Latin and French. A Spanish

---

[112] Benfey (ed. and trans.), *op. cit.* (n. 74), pp. xx–xxi.

[113] Cf. *Asia*, II, Bk. 1, 77–78.

[114] Huet, the learned bishop of Averanches and friend of La Fontaine, traced the wanderings of the Indian fables by studying their prefaces in his *Traité de l'origine des Romans* (Paris, 1670). See Müller, *op. cit.* (n. 89), IV, 151. For the illustrations as sources see M. Avery, "The Miniatures of the Fables of Bidpai," *Art Bulletin*, XXIII (1941), 103–16.

[115] For the scholarship on this derivation and the adaptations see T. Benfey, "Einige Bermerkungen über das indische Original der zum Kreise der Sieben Weisen Meister gehörigen Schriften," *Mélanges asiatiques* (St. Petersburg Academy of Sciences), VIII (1858), 188–90; Domenico Comparetti, *Ricerche intorno al Libro di Sindibad* (Milan, 1869); Cassel, *op. cit.* (n. 9), introduction; William A. Clouston, *Popular Tales and Fictions, Their Migrations and Transformations* (2 vols.; London, 1887), I, 9–10; Tawney and Penzer, *op. cit.* (n. 73), V, 258–66; and A. H. Krappe, "The Seven Sages," *Archivum Romanicum*, VIII (1924), 386–407; IX (1925), 345–65; XI (1927), 163–76; XVI (1932), 271–82; XIX (1935), 213–26.

[116] See F. Baethgen (trans.), *Sindban, oder die Sieben Weisen Meister: Syrisch und Deutsch* (Leipzig, 1879), p. 5.

[117] For the contributions of the *Dolopathos* to the Old French *fabliau*, or droll story, see U. T. Holmes, *A History of Old French Literature from the Origins to 1300* (rev. ed.; New York, 1962), pp. 200–204.

imitation was made from an Arabic text in the mid-thirteenth century, contemporaneous with the early Spanish translation of *Kalilah and Dimnah*.

The name *Sindibad* has been traced to the Sanskrit *siddhapati* ("Siddhattha" being one of the Pali names of Buddha), and to Persian *Sinderbadhjāja* meaning an "Indian teacher." [118] In most of the early texts the story begins: "There was in India a king by the name of Kurush . . ." [119] The name "Kurush" has been identified as an Arabic distortion of "Porus," the Indian king who fought Alexander. [120] The frame story tells of a young prince who, after resisting the advances of one of his father's favorite women, is accused by the woman of attacking her. The king condemns his son to death. The prince is unable immediately to reply to his accuser because his horoscope requires him to observe a period of silence for seven days. The seven sages of the king, convinced of the son's innocence, try to save him by each in turn telling on each of seven days a story relating to the perfidy of women. Each night the woman counteracts the effects of their tales by recounting to the king stories of the deceit and depravity of men. Finally, when the prince is free to speak again, the woman's guilt is discovered and she is duly punished. The prince's period of self-imposed silence and the immorality attributed to women have been cited repeatedly as motifs foreign to European literature and as evidence for the Oriental provenance of the frame story. The analogue between the motif of "the woman who is scorned" and the story of Asoka and his son Kunala has repeatedly been noted.

The European versions of the *Sindibad* cycle became intertwined with a parallel tradition known as the *Seven Sages of Rome*. [121] The parent version of this cycle, which seems to date from before 1150, is lost. But the popularity of the cycle was enormous, for forty different versions of it are still preserved. In this cycle the scene is shifted to Rome and the number and names of the sages vary considerably. Nine versions of the *Seven Sages* exist in Middle English. From a Latin version of the cycle John Rolland derived his metrical romance of *The Seuin Seages* (1560) from which descend numerous later English versions of *The Seven Wise Masters*. In these later works all trace of the Indian heritage is lost for the reader. Only the scholarly analysis links these stories to Indian prototypes.

The European adaptations of *Barlaam and Josaphat*, *Kalilah and Dimnah*, and *The Seven Wise Masters* brought a host of Indian tales into the religious and secular literature of Europe. Until the sixteenth century the tales in most cases remained associated with India, its places, personages, and products. Even though the proper names were often changed as the tales passed from one language to the other, the transformed names could always be recognized as being of

---

[118] Cassel (ed.), *op. cit.* (n. 115), pp. 65–66.

[119] In the *Syntipas* the country is omitted; in a later text it is transformed into "Sina" (China). See Camporetti, *op. cit.* (n. 115), p. 5.

[120] Cassel (ed.), *op. cit.* (n. 115), pp. 61–63.

[121] See Killis Campbell, *The Seven Sages of Rome* (Boston, 1907), p. xv.

foreign origin. Even when the tales were Christianized, India remained the scene of the marvelous occurrences they related. This identification of India as the scene of wonderous events also conformed to the popular conception of India derived from the romance of Alexander. The translated tales were used throughout the period from the twelfth to the sixteenth centuries both for edification and entertainment. During the quattrocento they were more commonly transformed quite specifically into manuals for the moral guidance of reigning princes. It was only in the sixteenth century, as the India of reality became a fact of life in Europe, that the locales were shifted and the characters Europeanized. The acculturation of the moral tales was possibly attributable to a fear felt by the European adapters that orthodox Christians, always on the watch for heresy, might charge them with subversion of the true faith by diffusing ethical precepts of heathen or infidel origins. Increasingly during the sixteenth century, as rationalism and orthodoxy became more firmly established, Europeans were inclined to disparage the tales and to employ them in burlesques and satires. Nonetheless they still continued to appeal to the populace and to inspire the writers of romances.

4

RENAISSANCE FORMS AND FASHIONS

From the thirteenth to the sixteenth centuries the stories about India from the Alexander romance and from the collections of fables were incorporated into Europe's popular literature. The attachment of the moral stories and parables to India was reinforced for Europeans by the persistence of the Christian legends about St. Thomas and Prester John in India.[122] Little was accomplished by the Crusades that was as important as bringing home to all of Europe the fundamental conflict and radical differences which existed between East and West. The Mongol invasion of Europe in 1240–41 added new elements to the European view of Asia. The subsequent opening of overland relations between Europe and eastern Asia between 1240 and 1350 resulted in the production of a series of travel books by merchants and friars on mission which helped to dispel some of the myths of the past, to shift their locale from known places to regions still unknown, or to introduce new fables.[123] As a consequence of these overland relations, and because Europe had no clear image of China before this time, Cathay tended to be less fabulous than India to the writers of the fourteenth century.[124] In the fifteenth century, as Europe concentrated on recovering

---

[122] For details on these two related legends see *Asia*, I, 25–27.

[123] See H. Goetz, "Der Orient der Kreuzzüge in Wolframs *Parzifal*," *Archiv für Kulturgeschichte*, XLIX (1967), 6–7.

[124] See *Asia*, I, 30–48.

its classical past, little new was added to the European image of Asia before the beginning of the great overseas discoveries.[125] The stereotypes of India and Cathay which prevailed until the sixteenth century included both mythical and factual dimensions which contemporaries found it impossible to separate. For the facts about Asia were often as wondrous as the fables told about it.

The wave of Oriental stories that had swept into Europe during the eleventh, twelfth, and thirteenth centuries helped to transform the content, intent, and form of the Christian sermon book. The use to which Christian teachers had put the fables of classical Antiquity may readily be discerned in the bestiaries and lapidaries of the Middle Ages. The Oriental tales were likewise employed as parables and apologues for religious instruction. Public preaching, at first the exclusive function of bishops, was only slowly included within the priest's responsibilities. The foundation in the thirteenth century of the Dominicans and Franciscans as preaching orders brought the sermon to the popular audience. A sermon for the common people had both to entertain and edify. Jacques de Vitry (d. 1240), one of the most influential compilers of sermon books, remarked in this connection: "The keen sword of subtle argumentation has no power over the layman. To the knowledge of the Scriptures, without which one cannot take a step, must be added examples which are encouraging and amusing, and yet edifying."[126] From his time onward the *exempla* were regularly added at the end of the sermon to waken the audience when attention began to flag and to leave the layman with a final, concrete moral message that he could remember.

Books of sermons and *exempla* were prepared in increasing numbers in all countries of Europe in the thirteenth to fifteenth centuries both in Latin and vernacular versions. The *exempla* were drawn in large measure from the collections of Oriental tales. The vast number of tales that thereby became available led to an increase in the use of *exempla* in the sermons. The sermon book, which originally emphasized a moral message, increasingly became more concerned with a good story than with the moral it presumably illustrated. In the extremely popular *Gesta Romanorum* (thirteenth to fourteenth centuries) the moral is of far less interest to the writer than a new story.[127] Indeed some of its stories could hardly be called edifying in any age. Eventually the abuse of the *exempla* in sermons led the Council of Sens in 1528 to outlaw under pain of

[125] See *ibid.*, pp. 59–65.

[126] From T. F. Crane (trans. and ed.), *The Exempla . . . of Jacques de Vitry* (London, 1890), preface. For examples of Oriental tales included in this compendium see E. W. Burlingame (trans. and ed.), *Buddhist Parables Translated from the Original Pali* (New Haven, Conn., 1922), p. xxiii. Also see W. F. Bolton, "Parable, Allegory, and Romance in the Legend of Barlaam and Josaphat," *Traditio*, XIV (1958), 360.

[127] Most of the stories in this great collection appear to be of Oriental provenance. For examples, see A. A. Krappe, "The Indian Provenance of a Medieval Exemplum," *Traditio*, II (1944), 499–502; Burlingame (trans. and ed.), *op. cit.* (n. 126), p. xix; and Tawney and Penzer, *op. cit.* (n. 73), II, 295–97. Nothing is known of its author, or place and date of origin. About two hundred manuscript versions are still extant. See J. Bolte and L. Mackensen, *Handwörterbuch des deutschen Märchens* (2 vols.; Berlin and Leipzig, 1930–40), II, 599–606.

interdict "those ridiculous recitals, those stories of good wives having for their end laughter only."[128]

The "mirrors of princes," like the sermon books, were influenced by the ethical message of the Indian tales and the romance of Alexander. The moral adage and the politically pointed fable became a stock feature of the *Fürstenspiegel* prepared after 1250. The *Secretum Secretorum*, falsely attributed to Aristotle, was a compilation of political advice allegedly given to Alexander by his teacher. The earliest known version of this book, probably based on Indian tales,[129] was prepared in Syria in the seventh and eighth centuries. From an Arabic text (*ca.* 800) it was translated into Latin in the twelfth century. A flood of translations and adaptations thereafter appeared in the vernacular languages. Using its maxims, the "mirrors" told the prince to control himself at all times, never to go back on his word, to be most careful in his choice of advisers, and to entrust no secrets to women. The political message contained in the fable books was even more realistic. The political leader, it was stressed, must know his people well, must study the habits and secret faults of those about him, and must not be bound in his decisions and acts by the moral precepts governing ordinary men.[130] Advisers to the king were instructed in some of the late medieval books on how to survive and advance themselves under the rule of a tyrant. While most Europeans were certainly unaware of the social context in which the Indian stories had evolved, their stress on the need of the ruler for great personal strength and acute study of his advisers was not lost upon the European authors. The fifteenth-century adapters of the Alexander story to princely manuals portrayed the king as a Renaissance man of strong personality, philosophical bent of mind, and dedication to military achievement.[131] The "mirrors" of the fifteenth and sixteenth centuries derived from the *Kalilah and Dimnah* and *Seven Wise Masters* traditions follow their sources in emphasizing the prince's need to watch his counselors closely, to maintain his own dominance by playing them off against each other, and to place the success of his own policies and programs above all abstract moral concerns.[132]

Even before the appearance of the great overland travel accounts of the later thirteenth century, the works written in vernacular languages for lay consumption continued to use as sources on India the various renditions of the Alexander

---

128 As quoted in T. F. Crane, "Medieval Sermon-Books and Stories," *Proceedings of the American Philosophical Society*, XXI (1883), 57.

129 Tawney and Penzer, *op. cit.* (n. 73), II, 290–97. For example, the motif of the "poison-damsel" (the woman reared on poison who can kill with a kiss, a look, a bite, a breath, and a variety of other acts) passed along this route into European literature and into both imaginative and didactic writings.

130 See W. Berges, *Die Fürstenspiegel des hohen und späten Mittelalters* (Stuttgart, 1952), pp. 109–12.

131 For example, see the *Dicts and Sayings of the Philosophers* (*ca.* 1450), the French translation of Curtius (1468) by Vasco Fernandez, and the German "mirror" (1472) based on Hartlieb. For further details see above, pp. 105–6.

132 For example, see Anton Pforr, *Das Buch der Beispiele der alten Weisens* (1483) and the numerous other subsequent adaptations of the Indian cycles in the vernacular languages. See above, pp. 105–6. It should also be recalled that the *Panchatantra* (*ca.* A.D. 100–500) was originally an Indian princely mirror.

romance, the collections of Indian fables, and the legends of St. Thomas and Prester John.[133] In the thirteenth-century encyclopedic collections by Vincent of Beauvais, Jacobus de Voragine, and Roger Bacon, the most commonly available materials on India, as well as its fables, were reproduced in both full and abbreviated versions. Later writers of story and romance regularly extracted materials for their works from these handy compilations. The appearance after 1250 of the travel accounts of the friars on mission to Asia and of Marco Polo's *Description of the World* (1298–99) provided a wealth of new materials, both factual and fictional, for imaginative writers.[134] Dante and Chaucer both exhibit a traditional and vague knowledge of India, and a somewhat less fantastic idea of Tartary. Both appear to have known the fables of the East, and to have incorporated a few Oriental ideas and themes into their major works.[135] But it was mainly the later writers of stories and romances who borrowed Oriental literary motifs, concepts, and forms.

Most important for the development of European literature was the Indian form of presentation called the tale-within-tale. The collections of stories had clearly brought out the flexibility and adaptability of the literary device of the frame story, which included subordinate tales within it. The tale-within-tale collections offered opportunities to translators, compilers, editors, and authors to remove, change, or replace the subordinate stories without altering the frame story. Some of the Eastern collections were so radically altered in transmission that nothing was left of the original except for the frame. The first European author to adopt the frame technique was Boccaccio in his *Decameron* (*ca.* 1350). This great work with its frame structure, its narrative moods, and its sophisticated literary techniques spawned a host of imitators in all the countries of Europe. Many of the themes and motifs of Boccaccio were likewise imitated and adapted by later authors, and some of them were incorporated in one form or other into the greatest poetical and dramatic creations of Renaissance literature.[136]

The large body of medieval literature, rather than the materials inherited from Antiquity, provided innumerable tales to inspire European writers of imaginative literature, both before and after the writing of the *Decameron*. Boccaccio himself was moved principally by the tales well established in the literary tradition of his time rather than by the stories recounted in travel accounts or by word of mouth. He was particularly indebted to the Indian tales for a large number of his plots and motifs. Some of them have been traced back directly to Europeanized versions of stories derived ultimately from

---

[133] For further elaboration see *Asia*, I, 28–30.

[134] See *ibid.*, pp. 30–48. It should not be forgotten that Polo's book was probably given romanticized elements by Rustichello.

[135] See *ibid.*, pp. 74–76. Also see Edgar Blochet, *Les sources orientales de la Divine Comédie* (Paris, 1901); A. de Gubernatis, "Le type indien de Lucifer chez le Dante," *Giornale dantesco*, III (1896), 49–58.

[136] See W. P. Friedrich and D. H. Malone, *Outline of Comparative Literature from Dante Alighieri to Eugene O'Neill* (Chapel Hill, N.C., 1954), pp. 70–71.

the *Panchatantra, Mahābhārata,* and the *Rāmāyana.*[137] The "Apologue of the Caskets" (*Decameron,* tenth day, first story) was adapted from one of the moral tales in the legend of Barlaam and Josaphat. Indeed most of the tales of the tenth day seem to be imitations of Indian, and possibly Buddhist, prototypes.[138] The motif of the woman who entraps three or more suitors and holds them up to ridicule before her husband and the entire city (eighth day, eighth story) exists in its oldest known form in Somadeva's *Kathā Sarit Sāgara* (tenth century?). From the *Decameron* this story, like many others, was transmitted and anthologized in the later compendia of Bandello, Sansovino, and Straparola. In the hands of Boccaccio and his imitators the Indian tales were transformed from moral examples into entertaining adventures. They were completely adapted to the European environment so that little but the plot or motif remains to attest to their Indian origin. In spirit the European tales seem to follow more closely the naturalistic bent of the tales of the *Panchatantra* than the didactic emphasis of the Buddhist tales and those of the Barlaam and Josaphat tradition.[139] Some of these naturalistic and secularized tales found their way in later years into the writings of Hans Sachs, Shakespeare, and Cervantes.

The romance, a fictitious narrative which usually deals with stories of chivalry and love, was in its origins an adaptation or imitation of the Latin epic. From the twelfth century onward the French romances were embellished with marvels and conceits derived from history, traditional folktales and fables, and the imagination of the author. None of the early romances was more influential than the *Roman d'Alexandre* (compiled in its present form by A.D. 1177), which includes Alexander's expeditions to India, his love affair with Queen Candace of Ethiopia, and his victory over the Amazons. The romance, as it subsequently developed, became less restricted to themes or plots inherited from Greek and Roman Antiquity. Subjects of a more general and contemporary character increasingly became common, particularly colorful knightly adventures connected with the Crusades. The romance of adventure and love was, of course, infiltrated with subjects from other traditions such as the Arthurian cycle and the Tristan legend. With Boccaccio the romance in both prose and verse was brought into Italian literature by his *Filocolo* (1337–39) and *Filostrato* (1339–40). The central story in these romances is embellished with materials from a host of sources, including contemporary geographical lore and maps. In his faithful use of geographical nomenclature, Boccaccio set a tradition among writers of romance that would long endure.[140]

[137] See Levêque, *op. cit.* (n. 15), pp. 516–30; and A. C. Lee, *The Decameron, Its Sources and Analogues* (London, 1909), pp. 25–26, 110, 170, 222–23.

[138] Tawney and Penzer, *op. cit.* (n. 73), II, 76, n. 1.

[139] See W. F. Bolton, *loc. cit.* (n. 126), pp. 360–66; and D. Radcliff-Umstead, "Boccaccio's Adaptation of Some Latin Sources for the *Decameron,*" *Italica,* XLV (1968), 185–86.

[140] Bardi merchants informed Boccaccio of the discovery of the Canary Islands in 1336. See Giorgio Padoan, "Petrarca, Boccaccio e la scoperta delle Canarie," *Italia medioevale e umanistica,* VII (1964), 263–77; Boccaccio used the map of Marino Sanudo the Elder for the localities mentioned in his *Filocolo.* See V. Bertolini, "Le carte geografiche nel 'Filocolo,'" *Studi sul Boccaccio,* V (1969), 224–25. For geography in Boiardo and Ariosto see below, pp. 205–8.

One of those who followed Boccaccio's lead in this regard was Andrea de' Magnabotti (1370–1431), the Florentine *cantastórie* (professional storyteller) usually known as Andrea da Barberino. His prose romance called *Guerrino il Meschino* (*ca.* 1409) proved to be one of the most popular products of Italy's rich and varied literary tradition. Guerrino, a prince of Albania, was the off-spring of Andrea's imagination. According to the story, Guerrino was kid-napped as a child and sold in slavery to a merchant of Constantinople. Once grown, he entered the service of the Porte and fell hopelessly in love with the sultan's sister. Before a marriage could be arranged Guerrino had to establish his royal descent. The court astrologer advised him to seek for facts about his lineage by appealing for information to the trees of the sun and the moon located in the most eastern parts of the world. In preparing his manuscript book in the early fifteenth century, Andrea derived his geographical place names of the East from the best materials then available: the Ptolemaic maps, Marco Polo, and Italian merchants and sailors. His book was printed at Padua in 1473 and seventeen times more by 1555. It was translated into French in 1530 and into Spanish in 1548. A poetic version of it appeared in Italy in 1560. For a long time it was assumed by scholars that Andrea's geography was fantastic, but a closer examination of his names and sources reveals that he used geographical terms with considerable fidelity.[141]

The writer who most fully utilized the available travel and mission literature was Andrea's older contemporary, the author of the *Travels of Sir John Mandeville* (*ca.* 1371). While his description of India remains traditional, Mandeville was the first of the writers of romance to provide a detailed discussion of the world to the east of India. For his accounts of China and southeastern Asia he depended heavily upon the travel book of Odoric of Porderone; in fact, some of his contemporaries, and others long afterwards, thought he had actually traveled to the East with Odoric. Much of the popularity of Mandeville's work derived from the sheer artistry that he displays in weaving his sources into a rich tapestry of words to attract and entertain readers in a day when most books were merely edifying, learned, or practical. His book also had appeal as a Uto-pian work, for he elevates the Great Khan to the status of a princely hero who rules benignly over a rich land, associates with philosophers, and luxuriates in the splendor of his opulent court. The printed versions of Mandeville were often profusely illustrated to make visual the monsters and marvels of the East.[142]

The publication and subsequent popularity of the factually based romances of Andrea and Mandeville helped to produce a feeling of anticipation that Christian Europe was on the eve of new relations with the fabulous East. Tales, tracts, and poems in the vernacular languages revitalized the legend of

---

[141] See H. Hawickhorst, "Über die Geographie bei Andrea de' Magnabotti," *Romanische Forschungen*, XIII (1902–4), 689–784. And R. Peters, "Über die Geographie im *Guerino Meschino* des Andrea de' Magnabotti," *ibid.*, XXII (1906–8), 426–81.

[142] For further detail see *Asia*, I, 77–80. Also cf. discussion on the "mirror of princes," above, pp. 111–12.

Prester John and celebrated the enduring accomplishments of the Christians in the East despite the most unfavorable conditions. But for many writers and scholars of the fifteenth century the growing threat from the East had the effect of diminishing its appeal as the scene of romance. Writers of romance, beginning with Luigi Pulci's *Morganti Maggiore* (1483) began to abandon the glorification of the chivalric legend and to introduce sensuous, quixotic, and satirical elements into their creations. For them the East increasingly became merely a place of opulence and sensuousness. To scholars intent upon recovering the glories of classical Antiquity, the lands to the East were distant, heathen, and foreign.

Through the rise of Islam and the Turks, the East had also become a place of darkness and danger, the seat of the enemies of the Cross. Still the church itself sought in the fifteenth century through a series of councils to reestablish ties with the Christians of the East and with the Jewish opponents of Islam. Before the Turkish capture of Constantinople, Cyriac of Ancona had traveled in the eastern Mediterranean region observing the ruins of Antiquity, copying down inscriptions, and collecting oddities. In October, 1441, he wrote a letter to the pope asking for a post as legate to Africa and India.[143] It was in this same year that Nicolò de' Conti, a Venetian, returned to Italy after a stay of twenty-five years in the East. His report on the East was summarized in dialogue form by Poggio Bracciolini in a manuscript prepared in 1448 and printed in 1492 at Cremona under the title *India recognita*. The most realistic account of India to appear in Europe since the time of Megasthenes, Conti's description became the basis for a new view of India as a land of reality.[144]

But the East as the scene of romance and mystery still retained its appeal for many writers. M. M. Boiardo (1434–94), the creator of the immortal Orlando cycle, took up residence at the court of Ferrara in 1476. The Este court had long had a special interest in books and news about geography.[145] So it is not surprising to find Boiardo making Angelica, the central figure in his long and unfinished epic, the daughter of the king of Cathay. Pico della Mirandola (1463–94), whose mother was Boiardo's sister, was fascinated by Oriental languages and systems of thought and saw in them background for the understanding of classical and biblical Antiquity. It was his concern for cabalistic and hermetic studies which inspired the Neo-Platonists of the sixteenth century to look upon the Orient as the homeland of ancient revelation and mystery and as the original source of wisdom. In his writings of 1486 to 1488 Pico sought to bring about a concordance between Oriental wisdom and Christian beliefs. He examined the teachings of the pre-Christian civilizations to discover the primitive language and the original teachings which derived directly from God and inspired the miracles of the New Testament.[146]

143 See E. W. Bodnar, *Cyriacus of Ancona and Athens* (Brussels, 1960), p. 50.
144 For further discussion see *Asia*, I, 60–65.
145 See M. Vernero, *Studi critici sopra la geografia nell' Orlando Furioso* (Turin, 1913), p. 7. On the Este family see above, p. 9, and below, p. 202.
146 For further elucidation see R. W. Meyer, "Pico della Mirandola und der Orient," *Asiatische Studien*, XVIII–XIX (1965), 311–13.

The literary pieces which most aptly illustrate the conflicting views of the East inherited by the fifteenth century from legend, romance, and travel accounts are two poems or songs in Italian by Giuliano Dati (1445–1524).[147] The first song, composed by the Florentine priest between 1493 and 1495, was called *Treatise on the Supreme Prester John, Pope and Emperor of India and of Ethiopia* and it appeared in at least four early editions. For his sources on the ten nations of Christians, including among them the Indians, he used pilgrim's voyages, chapbooks relating to the discoveries, and the *Guerrino il Meschino*. His second poem, called simply *Second Song of India*, was printed at Rome in 1494 or 1495. It was in large measure a poetic imitation of the sections on India extracted from Conti's account as published in the second edition (1485–86) of the *Supplementum chronicarum* of Jacopo Filippo Foresti da Bergamo, an Augustinian friar. The themes of these two songs when taken together summarize succinctly the mixed feelings of awe, fear, and hope which characterized the European view of India on the eve of Vasco da Gama's voyage. Dati writes:

> Oh, India, blessed and wallowing in thy glory
> May God preserve thee in His Christian faith.[148]

[147] See. L. Olschki, "I Cantàri dell' India di Giuliano Dati," *La bibliofilia*, XL (1938), 289–316; for discussion and texts of the edited versions of the two poems see Francis M. Rogers, "The Songs of the Indies by Giuliano," *Actas do Congresso Internacional de História dos Descobrimentos* (Lisbon, 1961), IV.

[148] Quoted from the translation in F. M. Rogers, *The Quest for Eastern Christians: Travels and Rumor in the Age of Discovery* (Minneapolis, 1962), p. 101.

CHAPTER IV

Portuguese Literature

The sixteenth century was Portugal's Golden Age in the development of its national language and literature. Foreign influences—Provençal, Spanish, Moorish, and Italian—predominated in Portugal's poetry and prose until the era of overseas expansion. But its earlier literature was not devoid of originality. A fervent religiosity and mysticism characterized the lyrics of the thirteenth and fourteenth centuries. Portugal's pleasant climate and the closeness of its people to the soil inspired bucolic poetry of natural warmth and earthiness. The rigors, uncertainties, and dangers of life at sea in small fishing vessels permeated its songs and stories. The language itself, striving for independence, quickly assimilated words from the neighboring vernaculars. On the eve of Vasco da Gama's great exploit, the Portuguese were ready to write the history of the national enterprise in their own language and to express in many literary forms and with sophistication their feelings of joy, triumph, and fear.

Portugal's literature and language reached maturity at the nation's greatest hour. Indeed today it is hard to imagine what Portuguese poetry and prose would be like without the theme of expansion. Poets, dramatists, and historians of the sixteenth century recognized that they were living in an age whose accomplishments cried for epic treatment and responded readily to the call. The lyric poets proudly brought the conquests into their verses. Portuguese drama, born in this century, put on the stage the hopes and fears stimulated by the opening of the overseas world. When the empire itself began to decline around mid-century, there was even more reason to commemorate the victories of the past. New literary genres were created to bring to the public the hardships and disasters of the long voyage to India and back, and the exhilaration of victorious battles against overwhelming odds in strange and remote quarters of the world. Traditional history was modified both in content and form to make room for the record of maritime expansion and overseas conquests. Finally, the poet Camoëns produced the national epic, the greatest literary feat in Portuguese history, on the theme of the opening of Asia.

I

GLORY AND DISILLUSIONMENT

Garcia de Resende (*ca.* 1470–1536), a poet and courtier who had acted in 1514 as secretary to the Portuguese embassy to Rome, compiled a collection of poems called the *Cancioneiro geral* which he published at Lisbon in 1516.[1] His anthology was probably inspired by the Castilian *Cancioneiro general* (1511) of Hernando del Castillo; certainly some of the Portuguese poets represented in Resende's collection were themselves indebted to Castilian and Italian versifiers. The best poems by over two hundred poets who wrote between the middle of the fifteenth century and the date of publication were included in Resende's miscellany of about one thousand poems. Most were written by courtiers and deal chiefly with etiquette, costume, love, and the various trivial matters associated with an ultra-refined court life. Resende's compilation also includes a few more serious poems on contemporary and retrospective topics which are important sources for the more general manners and morals of the time.

Since most of the poems in the *Cancioneiro geral* antedate the discovery of the sea route to India, few allude to the East. What is most impressive is the rapidity with which allusions to the overseas world appear in these popular verses. Resende himself, as indicated by his prologue, was acutely aware of the potentiality of the discoveries as a noble literary theme. In his dedication to the Infante Prince John, Resende deplores what he calls the "natural habit of the Portuguese" of neglecting to write about their own great accomplishments; the trivial content of the *Cancioneiro* validates this complaint. So Resende exhorts his countrymen to take up the great theme of the overseas conquests:

. . . if writers would only set to work as they should, they would find no greater exploits or more noteworthy deeds in the records of Rome or Troy or in any other ancient chronicles and histories, than those they could describe accomplished by our own countrymen, both in past and present times.[2]

Apparently he was calling for a monumental history and an epic poem, two achievements of Portuguese creativity that would appear only in the latter half of the century.

---

[1] The best modern edition is that of A. J. Gonçalves Guimarães, *Cancioneiro Geral de Garcia de Resende* (5 vols.; Coimbra, 1910–17). For Resende's biography see F. de Figueiredo, "Garcia de Resende," in *Critica do exilio* (Lisbon, 1930), pp. 77–154. For an analysis of the anthology see A. de Crabbe Rocha, *Aspectos do Cancioneiro Geral* (Coimbra, 1950).

[2] A "haughty exaltation" of Portugal in the judgment of the Italian scholar J. Scudieri-Ruggieri, *Il Canzioniere di Resende* (Geneva, 1931), p. 6.

The poems of the *Cancioneiro* provide brief, poignant, and illuminating glimpses into the reactions of the Portuguese to overseas expansion. While most poets of the court are content "to think about and to sigh [*cuydar e sospirar*]" for the love of a gentle damsel, João de Meneses sings of an earthy love for a slave woman, whom he compares to a lady of the court. He was perhaps the first modern Western poet to reveal what it means to love a woman of another race and country.[3] Many times the poets comment sadly on the negro and "Indian" slaves who are brought from distant and noble places to live in captivity and misery.[4] Others commiserate with the Portuguese who are forced to live for long periods in India and such distant places far from their loved ones: "three years they are away / Four thousand leagues from here."[5] Others remark sadly on the great number of worthy persons who lose their lives in Asia or at sea. On hearing news of the setback of Albuquerque at Goa in 1510, Bras de Costa wrote to Resende:

> To go through such storms
> So hard a life and season,
> And so nearly come to death,
> Rather would I forgo the pepper.[6]

Resende responded to the effect that he himself had no intention of ever embarking for India.

But not all is sadness and disillusionment among the poets of the *Cancioneiro*. The lyrics of Francisco de Sousa are animated by love of the sea and a yearning for the overseas world. João Rodrigues de Sá e Meneses (1465?–1576), a savant-courtier who had studied in Italy, celebrates the stellar feats of arms performed by his countrymen:

> Who from Ceuta to the Chinese,
> In the Red Sea, and the Abyssinians
> India, Malacca, and Ormuz
> With the Orb, and with the Cross
> Will not perish until the end of the end.[7]

[3] For discussion see J. de Castro Osório, *O além-mar na literatura portuguêsa* (Lisbon, 1948), pp. 92–95. See also Guimarães (ed.), *op. cit* (n. 1), IV, 118.

[4] In the time of King John III, Resende remarked: "Vemos no Reyno meter—tantos cativos." For this and other similar comments see Scudieri-Ruggieri, *op. cit.* (n. 2), pp. 14–15.

[5] "Tres anos ha q̃ sam fora
quatro mil legoas daquy."
Guimarães (ed.), *op. cit.* (n. 1), IV, 118.

[6] "Por passar tãta tormenta,
tempo, & vyda tam forte,
& tam perto sser da morte,
antes nom quero pymenta."
Ibid., III, 344.

[7] "Que de Çeita atee as Chijs,
no mar rroxo, & Abaxijs,
Yndia, Malaqua, Armuz
com a espera, & com a cruz
durarão tee fym dos fiis."
Ibid., III, 195.

In this and other poems the names of the peoples and places of the overseas world are chanted as lovingly as a litany. They stand as literary symbols of conquest, as visual and aural representations of the march of empire.[8] Calicut, Cambay, and Malacca appear more frequently than Braganza, Paris, or Rome.[9] Nor does it seem to go beyond the limits of public knowledge for a poet casually to assert:

> If you do not find *contray*
> I shall furnish you
> With a light-green garment
> Of the merchant of Cambay
> Which is a good new dress.[10]

Nor does another poet hesitate to refer to the Chinese, who "raise higher the price of silk," or to remark on a "coarse cloth that comes from the kingdom of China."[11]

The poets celebrate the heroes of the overseas conquests in their verses. Individuals like Vasco da Gama, Almeida, Albuquerque, and Diogo Lopes de Sequeira are praised and the poets, through their personal familiarity with the heroes, often hint at biographical details that are left unmentioned in the more sober accounts of the conquerors' lives and deeds.[12] While these lyrical memorials do not in themselves represent the epic Resende called for in his prologue, they constitute a primitive effort to elevate the conquerors to the status of national heroes. It is certainly possible that Luís Henriques in his poem on the victory of the duke of Braganza at Azamor (1513) is endeavoring, though rather weakly, to take the epic approach to overseas expansion.[13] Not enough time had elapsed for it to become apparent, as it was to later generations, that overseas expansion was the greatest of Portugal's national enterprises. The poets of the *Cancioneiro* were too interested in domestic affairs and in the immediate effects of expansion at home to be able to see, or foresee, the full meaning to the nation of its conquests in the East.

---

[8] António Correa at Pegu in 1519 appears to have had in his possession a copy of the *Cancioneiro Geral*. See H. Cidade and M. Múrias (eds.), *Ásia de João de Barros* (4 vols.; Lisbon, 1945–46), III, 132.

[9] See Crabbe Rocha, *op. cit.* (n. 1), p. 56.

[10] "Se nam achardes contray
vos sereys de mym seruydo
cõ hũ rroupão verdeguay
do mercador de Cambay,
quee hũ bem novo vestido."
Guimarães, *op. cit.* (n. 1), IV, 365–66. *Contray*, or *contrai*, was Flemish cloth from Courtrai.

[11] In the poem (*ibid.*, IV, 379) of Francisco de Viveiros (Biueyro) for Diogo Lopes de Sequeira, who had been sent out in 1508 with express instructions to "ask after the Chijns." See *Asia*, I, 731. Also see the reference (Guimarães [ed.], *op. cit.* [n. 1], III, 39) made by Diogo Brandão to a "mandill que vem da região China."

[12] See Guimarães (ed.), *op. cit.* (n. 1), III, 211, 344; IV, 379. For commentary see Figureido, *loc. cit.* (n. 1), pp. 147–49.

[13] Guimarães (ed.), *op. cit.* (n. 1), III, 102–11. For the suggestion that he might have been attempting an epic, see Hernani Cidade, *A literatura portuguêsa e a expansão ultramarina* (2d ed.; 2 vols.; Coimbra, 1963–64), I, 68–69.

While some of the poets were skeptical and even fearful of the consequences of expansion, others were jubilant over the "empire" that was being founded and were excited about the new products, animals, and people pouring into Lisbon. In 1519 Diogo Velho da Chancelaria wrote a long poem called "Lisbon where all hasten to the hunt," [14] in which he delights in the fact that the trophies of the chase—gold, pearls, precious stones, gums, spices and drugs—have been driven into Portugal's corral along with jaguars, lions, elephants, monsters, speaking birds, porcelains, and diamonds. He is overjoyed that the new overseas peoples, formerly hidden and unknown, have entered the portal of Lisbon and have become a part of the Christian world. King Manuel he credits with being the creator of a "new Rome" and the ruler of a new universal empire under Christ. Velho, like the poets of the *Cancioneiro*, appears to enjoy the resonance of exotic names. In addition to topographical terms, his litany teems with reverberating nouns which intone the power, wealth, and splendor of Portugal:

> Gold, pearls, stones,
> Gum and spices,
>
> . . . .
>
> Tigers, lions, elephants,
> Monsters and talking birds,
> Porcelain, diamonds—
> All are now quite common. [15]

The young João de Barros (1496?–1570), when serving as a page to Prince John, wrote in 1520 a long romance of chivalry called *Crónica do Imperador Clarimundo*. [16] Here he relates the adventures of Clarimundo, emperor of Hungary and Constantinople and mythical progenitor of Alfonso Henriques, the first king of Portugal. Written in smooth and vigorous prose this romance of the *Amadis* type was prepared by the author within the space of eight months as a sample of his skill in writing and as preparation for the history of India that he hoped some day to write. Like most of the romances of the period, *Clarimundo* is crowded with actors who perform their feats in exotic and distant locales. While the characters and adventures are generally mythical, much of the

---

[14] "Lisboa, onde toda a caça voa," in selected portions, is reproduced in J. de Castro Osório (comp.), *Cancioneiro de Lisboa (séculos xiii–xx)* (3 vols. Lisbon, 1956), I, 23–25; also see Cidade, *op. cit.* (n. 13), I, 69–72.

[15] "Ouro, aljofar, pedraria,
Gomas e especiaria,

. . . .

Onças, leõs, alifantes,
Monstros e aves falantes,
Porcelanas, diamantes
É já tudo mui geral."
From Castro Osório (comp.), *op. cit.* (n. 3), p. 24.

[16] First published in 1522 at Lisbon, a second edition appeared at Coimbra in 1553. The modern, annotated edition is M. Braga (ed.), *João de Barros: Crónica do Imperador Clarimundo* (3 vols.; Lisbon, 1953). For a summary of its materials relating to Asia see H. Y. K. Tom, "The Wonderful Voyage: Chivalric and Moral Asia in the Imaginations of Sixteenth-Century Italy, Spain, and Portugal" (Ph.D. diss., University of Chicago, 1975), pp. 114–17.

geography is real. The distant East does not figure until near the end of the book when he writes "a prophecy" in verse on "the future" of Portugal. These verses, reminiscent of those in the *Cancioneiro* and of Canto X of the *Lusiads*, summarize and celebrate the conquests in Asia:

> On to Champa and China with its city
> Which the Persians [Muslims?] will lose.
> They will pass through diverse lands
> That they see only briefly;
> They will find the Ryukus, where they trade honestly
> And carry onwards to the Borneo peoples.
> Having added all these lands they give a gift
> Of faith, love, and great loyalty.[17]

A contemporary of Resende, Velho, and Barros at the Portuguese court was the goldsmith and dramatist Gil Vicente (*ca.* 1465–*ca.* 1537).[18] He worked as the impresario of the court and took a leading role in the important guild of goldsmiths. By 1506 he had completed the famous monstrance for the Monastery of the Jerónimos at Belém from the gold brought back from Kilwa by Vasco da Gama in 1503.[19] In these same years he began writing plays and presenting them before the court. Widely known as the founder of the Portuguese theater, Gil Vicente wrote forty-four plays that are extant: sixteen in Portuguese, eleven in Castilian, and the remaining seventeen in combinations of both languages. In terms of form he presented pastoral plays following the Castilian tradition, moralities, mysteries, farces, comedies, and chivalric pieces. These dramatic works, along with songs and miscellaneous pieces, were published at Lisbon in 1562 in a compilation (*Copilaçam*) made by his son Luís.[20]

The brilliant pageants staged on state occasions at the Portuguese court were called mummeries (*momos*).[21] As early as the period of King John II (1455–95)

---

[17] "Champa, e a China com a cidade
Que perderá o povo dos Persas,
Passando por terras muito diversas
Logo virá com grã brevidade,
Em busca dos Lequeos, que tratam verdade
Levando consigo a Burnea gente,
E ajuntados todos farão um presente
De fé, e amor, e grã lealdade."
Braga (ed.), *Cronica . . .*, III, 109. On the *Lusiads* see below, pp. 151–58.

[18] The standard biography is A. Braamcamp Freire, *Vidas e obras de Gil Vicente*, "*Trovador, mestre da Balança*" (2d rev. ed.; Lisbon, 1944); for an analytical and balanced biography see J. H. Parker, *Gil Vicente* (New York, 1967).

[19] This gold was tribute paid by the local chieftain to the Portuguese crown. Manuel ordered that it should be made into an offering to the "King of Kings." Most authorities now agree that Gil Vicente, the dramatist, was the same Gil Vicente who was entrusted with the creation of the monstrance. For discussion of the monstrance see António Manuel Gonçalves, *A custódia de Belém* (Lisbon, 1958) and *Asia*, II, Bk. 1, 118; for the controversy over the dramatist and goldsmith being one and the same person see Parker, *op. cit.* (n. 18), pp. 18–19.

[20] The best modern edition, based on the compilation of 1562, is M. Braga (ed.), *Gil Vicente: Obras completas* (4th ed.; 6 vols.; Lisbon, 1968).

[21] See L. Keates, *The Court Theater of Gil Vicente* (Lisbon, 1962), pp. 25, 78–79; J. Scudieri-Ruggieri, *op. cit.* (n. 2), p. 31; and L. Stegagno Picchio, *Storia del teatro portoghese* (Rome, 1964), pp. 16–18.

these spectacles featured rich costumes, elaborate machinery, curious props, and startling dramatic effects. At a *momo* held in Évora, warships with banners flying and cannons roaring captured the viewers' imagination while pilots and merchants dressed in brocades and silks walked in the background in a dramatic representation of Portugal's exploits on sea and land. The kings themselves and members of the court, as well as actors, would sometimes take part in these performances and even play the roles of overseas rulers. Others were costumed as dragons, giants, and various mythical creatures. Live animals, especially the rarer ones, added to the exoticism of the pageants. It is probable that Gil Vicente was attracted to the court, then at Évora, in 1490 to answer the king's call for goldsmiths to make ornaments and other finery for the theatricals honoring the crown prince on his marriage.[22]

Vicente's plays, which began to be staged regularly in 1502, were more sophisticated and thoughtful than the traditional *momos*. His farces and comedies, which were among the best of his creations, often deal with everyday life and its problems. Some of his other dramas were designed primarily as spectacles to celebrate the king and the nation. They may be called literary *momos*, for enough dialogue or monologue is introduced to explain the pageant being presented. But even the lightest and the most bombastic of his *momos* were not mere entertainments; they were mirrors that reflected, if only pallidly and distortedly, the dazzling sights that could be seen everyday in the harbor, on the wharf, in the streets, and in the marketplaces of Lisbon. It took the spark of Gil Vicente's genius to transform such mundane material into legitimate drama.

Like his contemporaries, Gil Vicente was struck with wonder by the revelation of the overseas world. But, unlike most of them, he quickly began to assess its meaning for Portugal. His feelings and thoughts on the overseas enterprise were conditioned by his observations of how life had been transformed in Lisbon. The rusticity and simplicity of the Portuguese were in his eyes being debauched by vanity, ostentatious living, and hollow display. One of his own sons, much to his dismay, went to India in Tristão da Cunha's armada of 1506 and later served at Goa under Albuquerque.[23] While his plays reveal a constant concern with problems of daily life, Vicente also adopts traditional characterizations, solutions, and techniques from literature, especially from Juan del Encina (1469?–1529), the liturgy, and the New Testament.[24]

Tristão da Cunha's armada returned in 1509, the year when Gil Vicente's *Auto da India* was presented at Almada on the left bank of the Tagus before Queen Leonor and her court.[25] This farce was the first play which Vicente

[22] See Parker, *op. cit.* (n. 18), p. 19.

[23] See Braamcamp Freire, *op. cit.* (n. 18), pp. 57–58, 81.

[24] For the argument that he "turned to literature rather than to life for guidance" see W. C. Atkinson, "Comedias, tragicomedias and farças in Gil Vicente," in *Miscelânea de filologia, literatura e história cultural a memória de Francisco Adolfo Coelho (1847–1919)* (2 vols.; Lisbon, 1950), II, 271.

[25] For the text see Braga (ed.), *Vicente . . . Obras completas* (n. 20), V, 89–166; for a French translation and commentary see C. H. Frèches, "Gil Vicente: Les Indes. Avant-propos," *Bulletin des études portugaises et de l'Institut français au Portugal* (Coimbra), XIX (1955–56), 141–57.

wrote exclusively in his native tongue. It is a strictly profane piece that reflects the pressures put upon family life in Portugal by the discovery of India. A wife hypocritically laments the departure of her husband on the "Garça" in the fleet of Tristão da Cunha of 1506. When the husband is well out to sea, a Castilian lover appears. Shortly after he leaves, a Portuguese lover takes his place. When the first lover reappears, the woman explains to the second lover that the first man is only her brother. In the midst of this hectic scene the maid rushes in to report that the fleet has returned unexpectedly and that the husband is about to arrive home. The two lovers flee, the husband appears, and the wife bemoans her loneliness, proclaims her fidelity, and wonders what riches he has brought back with him.[26] Very few direct references to India appear in the dialogue, except mentions of Calicut, precious stones, and spices, and a declaration by the Castilian lover that God created India simply to make it possible for him to have his moment with the woman. It is not known how the queen reacted to this farce, but later commentators have speculated that the dramatist equated the woman to a Portugal that had been seduced to yield its spirituality and honor for sensual gratification.[27] Whatever its meaning, the *Auto da India* influenced later Portuguese playwrights and in 1905 appeared in a popular edition prepared for use in the schools.[28]

Glorification of the conquests began with the capture of Goa in 1510. King Manuel himself dictated instructions for a series of tapestries that were to be made in Flanders celebrating the conquest of India.[29] Four years later the famous embassy of Tristão da Cunha was in Rome and Garcia de Resende was with it. It is possible that some of the gold works of Gil Vicente were included among the gifts sent to Pope Leo X.[30] Certainly the dramatist-goldsmith himself was swept up by the tide of enthusiasm that engulfed Portugal in these years. His tragicomedy called *Exortação da guerra* (1513 or 1514) is a hymn to the glory of Portugal. In it he reveals an acquaintance with Hanno, the elephant sent as a gift to the pope, by having the devil Zebron ask:

> Is the fine elephant alive
> That went to Rome for the Pope to shrive?[31]

Much more reverent in tone is the *Auto da Fama* (ca. 1515) which exalts the maritime and military achievements of the Portuguese.[32] The "Fame" of Portugal, personified by a humble girl, is enviously wooed by all nations.

[26] It has been argued that these characters correspond perfectly to the *tipos* of Greek and Roman comedy. See G. Saviotti, "Gil Vicente poeta cómico," *Bulletin historique du théâtre portugais*, II (1951), Pt. 2. 202.

[27] See M. Castelo-Branco, "Significado do cómico do 'Auto da India.'" *Ocidente*, LXX (1966), 129–36.

[28] See discussion of Antonio Prestes, below pp. 136–37; also see T. Braga, *História da literatura portugueza* (Porto, 1914), II, 102 n., and Stegagno Picchio, *op. cit.* (n. 21), pp. 92–93

[29] For a transcription of this fascinating document (Torre do Tombo, Cartas missivas, maço 3°, doc. 245) see F. de Figueiredo, *A épica portuguesa no século XVI* (Madrid, 1931), pp. 42–46.

[30] T. Braga, *Gil Vicente e as origens do teatro naçional* (Porto, 1898), p. 191.

[31] Verse 195 as translated in A. F. G. Bell, *Four Plays of Gil Vicente* (Cambridge, 1920), pp. 27–28.

[32] Text in M. Braga (ed.), *Vicente . . . Obras completas* (n. 20), V, 117–40.

Suitors from France, Italy, and Castile court her in vain. She remains true to Portugal, which has shown its valor by winning victories over heathens and Muslims at the siege of Goa (1510), the capture of Malacca (1511), the victory of Azamor (1513), and the attack on Aden (1513). At the end of this courtly allegory, Fame is crowned with a laurel wreath by Faith and Fortitude amid a great scene of general rejoicing. Not in this dramatic poem, or in the *Exortação*, does Vicente mention Albuquerque, possibly because the name of the great conqueror inspired more fear than affection in his contemporaries.[33] Both dramas exhort the nation to disdain sloth and indolence and to continue the pursuit of glory in Asia.

In his later poetic dramas Gil Vicente persists in celebrating the overseas conquests, even in those plays that emphasize comedy and lyricism. The *Cortes de Jupiter*, performed on the departure of Princess Beatriz to marry the duke of Savoy, is one of his liveliest creations.[34] But even for this happy occasion, the dramatist puts Mars on the stage to laud the Portuguese achievements in Africa and Asia and to celebrate the crown prince as a second Alexander. Vicente's play called *Triunfo do inverno* was first performed in 1529 to celebrate the birth of Princess Isabel. In the triumph of winter at sea, he derides the pilots of the ships to India who by virtue of their own incompetence too often fail to reach Cochin—a reflection of growing concern over shipwrecks.[35] Studded with lyrics, songs, and dances, this piece of court entertainment includes a ballad sung by three mermaids which relates the glories of Portugal's history. About successes in Asia, the sirens sing:

> Then remember Portugal
> How the Lord God hath honoured thee,
> He gave thee lands of the rising sun,
> For traffic and to hold in fee,
> And the gardens of the Earth
> Hast thou conquered verily.
> And the orchards of the East
> Send their noble fruits to thee
> All their earthly paradises
> Enclosed in thine empery.
> Praise Him that of all the best
> Unto thee He gave the key.
> To thee alone He has revealed
> The unknown islands of the sea.[36]

After the death of King Manuel in 1521, some of the courtiers began to lose their blind enthusiasm for the discoveries. Resende, one of the leading figures among the "Peninsulares," was challenged as leader of the court's cultural life by a party of "Italianos" led by Sá de Miranda (1481–1550). With regard to the

---

[33] See Bell, *op. cit.* (n. 31), p. xlvii. It should also be recalled that he repeatedly refers to Tristão da Cunha, the enemy of Albuquerque, in his other writings.

[34] Text in M. Braga (ed.), *Vicente . . . Obras completas* (n. 20), IV, 225–60.

[35] On shipwreck literature see below, pp. 131–35.

[36] As translated in A. F. G. Bell, *Lyrics of Gil Vicente* (2d ed.; Oxford, 1921), p. 83.

discoveries the "Italianos" were inclined to stress their cost rather than their contributions to the nation. They were also prone, like many of the Castilians at Salamanca, to question the legal and moral legitimacy of what the Portuguese were doing on the seas and in Asia. Possibly it was in response to the challenge of the "Italianos" that Resende in the last years (1530–36) of his life wrote his *Miscellanea,* a variety book of memories which reveals, better than any of his other works, his personal concerns, beliefs, ideas, and tastes.[37]

It was not until 1554, eighteen years after the death of the author, that Resende's *Miscellanea* first appeared in print. Then it was published along with his chronicle of King John II in a volume entitled *Livro das obras de Garcia de Resende.*[38] Seventy-three of the 311 stanzas in this miscellany of subjects are devoted to the overseas expansion and to descriptions of the places and peoples of Africa and Asia. In his recital of the Portuguese progress in Asia, Resende follows meticulously *The Book of Duarte Barbosa,* a work that existed only in manuscript in his day. Barbosa's book was probably written around 1517, a number of years after the author's travels in India and its vicinity: it was nonetheless one of the most comprehensive narratives prepared in the first half of the sixteenth century. Certainly no other more responsible treatment of the East was available to Resende in 1530; Barbosa's work was currently recognized as a prime source of authoritative information by the diplomats who negotiated the treaty of Badajoz-Elvas (1529).[39]

Resende's stanzas devoted to expansion and to the immortality achieved by the Portuguese through their adventures in Asia contain elements of the epic idea. They are, however, neither grand enough in concept nor elegant enough in execution to be regarded as anything more than an exposition of contemporary history in verse and as an apology for conquest. Like Barbosa, Resende appears to be fascinated by the customs and dress of the overseas peoples and is quick to notice the caste system of India.[40] He passes the exotic plants and animals, spices, precious stones, and other Eastern commodities before the eyes of his reader in a steady parade of euphonious nouns.[41] About Hanno he remarks:

> We have seen elephants come here,
> And other similar beasts
> Brought from India by sea
> And we have seen them sent by sea
> To Rome in great triumph.[42]

[37] I am indebted for this description to the suggestive analysis of the *Miscellanea* in J. S. da Silva Dias, *A política cultural da época de D. João III* (2 vols.; Coimbra, 1969), I, 156–57.

[38] A modern edition of the *Miscellanea,* which reprints the full edition (later ones were excised or changed) of 1564 appears in Mendes dos Remedios (ed.), *Garcia de Resende: Miscellanea . . .* (Coimbra, 1917).

[39] For discussion see *Asia,* I, 153, 170. Also see above, p. 58, for a reference to a German translation of Barbosa made in 1530.

[40] See Stanza 62 in Remedios (ed.), *op. cit.* (n. 38), p. 24.

[41] Stanza 275 in *ibid.,* p. 95.

[42] Translation by Manuel II in *Livros antiquos portugueses* (3 vols.; London, 1921), I, 328; on Hanno's peregrinations see *Asia,* II, 136–37.

One of his stanzas includes twenty-six names of overseas cities arranged for the rhyme rather than for geographical or historical harmony. Separate stanzas celebrate particularly important places, such as Cambay, "Narsingo" (Vijayana-gar), Malabar, Pegu, and Siam; other stanzas commemorate the achievements of individual heroes: Albuquerque, Almeida, Vasco da Gama, Pedro de Mascarenhas, and others. He incidentally refers to the contemporary debate over the question whether printing was first discovered in Germany or China.[43] Resende stresses the contrast between the material wealth of Asia and the backward condition of its pagan peoples. It is Portugal's mission, ordained by God, to civilize and Christianize the peoples of Asia and to carry without guilt as much as possible of its material wealth back to Europe. It is through the performance of these necessary tasks that Portugal makes legitimate its conquest of the overseas world. But even he finally wonders whether the effort is worth it and whether the nation can stand the strain.

Francisco de Sá de Miranda (1481?–1558) and his circle of Humanists were not satisfied with Resende's rationale for empire. Upon his return from Italy in 1526 or 1527, Miranda personally sought to live an exemplary life by up-holding steadfastly the Horatian ideals of tranquility and simplicity.[44] He was devoted to the king, and John held him and his ideas about literature in high esteem. As a sophisticated Humanist, Miranda had no interest in the spectacles and poetastry of the courtiers. He forthrightly condemned as poisonous the *momos indianos* performed at court. He was one of the first moralists to denounce the spreading corruption and decadence that lay beneath the tinsel and finery of Lisbon. In 1532 he retired to a benefice in Minho where, close to nature, he carried on an active but contemplative and independent life. In the serenity of his retreat he practiced the arts, especially poetry, and corresponded in verse with fellow poets. Many younger poets became his disciples and some of them came to share his belief that preoccupation with overseas discovery, war, and trade was leading to the moral and material decline of the country.

Miranda feared especially for the future of Portugal. Around 1533 he wrote:

> I am not afraid of Castile
> From whence war has not yet sounded,
> But I am afraid for Lisbon
> Where the smell of cinnamon
> Depopulates the Kingdom,
> And some stumble or fall!
> O go far away, bad augury

---

[43] Stanza 179 in *Remedios* (ed.), *op. cit.* (n. 38), p. 63. Also see below, p. 227.

[44] See A. F. G. Bell, *Portuguese Literature* (Oxford, 1970), pp. 139–45; also A. Forjaz de Sampaio, *História da literatura portuguesa* (4 vols.; Paris, n.d.), II, 140–47; T. Braga, *História dos quinhentistas: Vida de Sá de Miranda e sua escola* (Porto, 1871), pp. 81, 122; C. Michaëlis de Vasconcelos (ed.), *Sá de Miranda: Poesias* (Halle, 1885), pp. xix–xx; and Cidade, *op. cit.* (n. 13), I, 240–45.

Speak by that shore
Of the wealth of Cambay,
Narsinga, of towers of gold.[45]

He also deplored the tendency to make up for losses of manpower by the importation of slaves. Foreign merchandise, ideas, and people were turning the Portuguese away from their traditional, rural way of life and its ancient virtues.[46] Opulence was leading to softness in character. In his last years he reacted even more bitterly against the crown's policy of overseas expansion, for his adolescent son was killed in Africa in 1553. He sadly reminded his dead child:

You will hear the Tagus, you will hear
The Indus, the Ganges, there you will listen
To the sound, which in you your father aroused.[47]

The disciples of Miranda, members of the so-called *pléiade mirandina*, echoed his fears about the adverse effects of overseas activities. Pêro de Andrade Caminha (1520–89), the first bucolic poet to become a disciple, also suffered a grievous personal loss when his brother was killed in India.[48] Like his master, Andrade Caminha saw India mainly as a place where Portuguese met death. António Ferreira (1528–69), a student and friend of Diogo de Teive at Coimbra, differed somewhat with Miranda in the degree of his hostility to the predominance of Lisbon and the preoccupation of the Portuguese with expansion. While he wrote an elegy to Miranda's dead son, he also penned many verses praising Lisbon as the center of an expanding empire, and in 1557 he celebrated the publication of the *Comentários de Afonso de Albuquerque*. Yet Ferreira, like his associates, remained uneasy about expansion.[49]

---

[45] "Não me temo de Castela
Donde guerra inda não sôa,
Mas temo me de Lisboa,
Que ó cheiro d'esta canela
O reyno nos despovôa.
E que algum embique ou caia!
O longe vá, mao agouro
Fâlar por aquela praia
Na riqueza de Cambaia,
Narsinga, das torres de ouro."
From his letter to António Pereira in Michaëlis de Vasconcelos, *op. cit.* (n. 44), pp. 237–38.

[46] For an appreciation of Miranda's viewpoint see R. Hooykaas, "The Impact of the Voyages of Discovery on Portuguese Humanist Literature," *Revista da universidade de Coimbra*, XXIV (1971), 556–58.

[47] "Ouvil-o-ha o Tejo, ouvil-o-ha
O Indo, O Ganges, là serà escuitado
O som, que em ti teu pay levantara."
As quoted in T. Braga, *op. cit.* (n. 44), p. 124. His brother, Mem de Sá, was governor of Brazil from 1557 to 1571.

[48] On his career see T. Braga, *História dos quinhentistas* (n. 44), pp. 216–44. For his sonnet on the death of Conde da Feira, viceroy of India, see J. Priebisch (ed.), *Poesias inéditas de P. de Andrade Caminha* (Halle, 1898), p. 508.

[49] See T. Braga, *História dos quinhentistas* (n. 44), pp. 183–215.

Diogo Bernardes (1530?–1605?), an avowed enemy of Camoëns, probably had ambitions of his own to write the Portuguese epic.[50] Had he done so, his topic would not have been the Portuguese East. Like Miranda, he comments only rarely in his poems on the East and on Asian peoples. In an *Elegy* written on the death of King John III in 1557, Bernardes brands the Asians as barbarians who adhere to perverse laws and who are clearly in debt to Portugal for conquering them and bringing to them the Christian faith:

> Let them tell you, so many conquered peoples
> Barbarous of nation, of laws perverse,
> By thee overcome, by thee indoctrinated.
> Moors, Turks, Arabs, Indians, Persians;
> These, and many others hast thou triumphed over,
> Of various languages, of diverse regions.[51]

But there are also other Indians, particularly of the north, who stubbornly resist the Portuguese.[52] The political and military leaders of the Portuguese East he treats with disdain when he refers to them at all. On one occasion he wrote an elegant Petrarchan sonnet dedicated "to the hairs in the beard that João de Castro, Viceroy of India, pledged to the city of Goa." This satirical effort was inspired by the viceroy's promise to the *Câmara* of Goa that he would pledge his beard as surety for funds that he badly needed to pay for repairing the fortress of Diu.[53] In 1576 Bernardes accompanied the embassy of Pêro de Alcaçova Carneiro to the court of Madrid. About the embassy he wrote a lengthy poetic account in which he points to the "problem of the Moluccas" then in dispute, and expresses the hope:

> . . . let there be a new agreement
> On the affairs of Molucca, and without struggle
> Let it be determined, once the case is examined,
> To which king this conquest belongs.[54]

Two years later he accompanied the expedition of Dom Sebastian to Africa as its poet. He was captured at the disastrous battle of Alcacer Kebir (1578) and

---

[50] See *ibid.*, pp. 268–71.
[51] "Digão-no tantas gentes conquistadas
   Barbaras de nação, de leis perversas,
   Por ti vencidas, por ti doutrinadas.
   Mouros, Turcos, Arabes, Indios, Persas;
   Destes, e d'outros muitos triumphaste
   De varias linguas, de regiões diversas."
M. Braga (ed.), *Diogo Bernardes: Obras completas* (3 vols.; Lisbon, 1945–46), III, 177.
[52] See Sonnet CXV to the Conde da Atouguia, *ibid.*, I, 91.
[53] See *ibid.*, I, 126.
[54] ". . . se tome hum novo assento
   Nas cousas de Maluco, e sem porfio,
   Se determine, sendo a causa vista
   A qual dos reis pertence esta conquista."
From Carta XXXII as quoted *ibid.*, II, 332.

returned to Lisbon only in 1581. He fared relatively well under the Habsburg dynasty, and was afforded an opportunity to write his pleasant eclogues which successfully employ the techniques of the Spanish and Italian poets so revered by the *pléiade mirandina*.

One of the most popular and successful dramas of the sixteenth century was the *Eufrosina* of Jorge Ferreira de Vasconcelos (1527?–84). This play, along with his other two *comédias*, constitutes a veritable display of national manners and morals. A comedy of the Celestine type in prose, *Eufrosina* was written in 1542–43. It is a tale of the love of a poor courtier for the rich and beautiful daughter of a nobleman. The story takes place in the rustic university town of Coimbra high above the swaying willows and blue-green waters of the Mondego Valley. The play is crowded with characters and their adventures and misadventures. It is most revealing about the attitudes of the students and townsmen of Coimbra and provides glimpses of life at the royal court and of the debates raging about India. *Eufrosina* was probably staged at Coimbra before it was first printed there in 1555, for it is decidedly a drama that was meant to be played as well as read.[55]

Throughout the numerous scenes and episodes of the drama, Ferreira de Vasconcelos repeatedly expresses his conviction that the triumphs in the East are hollow and the overseas expansion a melancholy affair. He lauds the heroic ideals which motivate his countrymen to die in the armadas to India and in the fight against the Moor. For him India is a stage for heroics rather than a country of gold; it is the land of Alexander the Great that he knew from studying Quintus Curtius. India lures idealistic youths to leave the restricting confines of their native land in search of glory. "They won India as brave knights and," he predicts, "they will lose it as greedy and corrupt merchants."[56] At Coimbra and Lisbon, it is clear from the drama, a battle rages between the ideas and attitudes of the veterans and the men of letters. The returned knights view with disgust the preachings of the Humanists and lawyers about the adverse effects of expansion. Vasconcelos himself so abhors the corruption attending the Asian conquests that he believes their final abandonment would not result in a loss to the country. To reinforce this position he includes a genuine letter from India, presumably from Silvia's brother, which is read aloud and commented upon by her friends. The letter records the hardships of the voyage, the siege of Diu in 1538, the vicious behavior of the Portuguese in India, and the homesickness of a disillusioned youth.[57] More than any of his literary predecessors, Ferreira de Vasconcelos succeeds in bringing to life the ambivalences troubling Portuguese society: the pride in overseas achievements, the weariness with war, the hopes and fears of individuals at home and in India, the desire to spread

---

[55] Another edition appeared at Coimbra in 1560, and two at Évora in 1561 and 1566. See E. Asensio (ed.), *Jorge Ferreira de Vasconcelos: Comedia Eufrosina* (Madrid, 1951), pp. vii–viii.

[56] ". . . que ganharão a India como caveleyros esforcados, e que a perderao como mercadores cobiçosos e viciosos . . . (*ibid.*, p. 122)."

[57] For the letter see *ibid.*, pp. 113–24.

Christian teachings, and the struggle with conscience about the morality of conquest.

2

MARITIME TRAGEDIES AND SIEGE TRIUMPHS

The sea voyage to India and back was more dangerous than any other lengthy navigation undertaken by the Portuguese. Disasters were frequent, especially on the return voyage when the ships were usually overloaded. Accounts of the losses by shipwreck of men, cargoes, and vessels were periodically relayed to Portugal by the publication after mid-century of vivid narratives describing certain of the maritime disasters. Written by survivors, or by interested investigators and historians, these accounts were originally printed in pamphlet form and displayed hanging from a string in bookshops. "String literature" (*literatura de cordel*) was generally sold out quickly; as with most ephemeral materials, not many copies of the originals have survived. Fortunately for posterity, twelve of these narratives were collected by Bernardo Gomes de Brito and published at Lisbon in two volumes in 1735–36 under the title *História trágico-máritima*.[58] It was not, however, until the twentieth century that these tragic stories of disaster at sea came to be regarded as exemplary pieces of classical Portuguese prose and as sources for history and ethnography.

While all of the twelve narratives published by Gomes de Brito describe shipwrecks of the sixteenth century, certain of them were not written or published until the early seventeenth century. The first extant narrative published in the sixteenth century relates to the galleon "São João" which sank in 1552 on the voyage from Cochin to Lisbon. Like most of the ships that were wrecked, the "São João" was overloaded in India and fell prey to the storms off the coast of southeast Africa at Natal. Once the ship broke up, the survivors straggled off northward along the coast in an endeavor to reach Mozambique. This account was relayed to Portugal where it was published in 1555 or 1556 in a pamphlet of sixteen unnumbered pages with a ship woodcut on the title page. As if to connect this pamphlet with earlier travel literature, the same woodcut that appeared in the *Marco Paulo* of 1502 was used to illustrate the cover. A second edition of this maritime narrative appeared at Lisbon in 1564, and a third at Évora in 1592. Both of these later editions boasted new woodcuts and altered texts. It was the version of 1592 with which Gomes de Brito initiated his eighteenth-century collection of tragic maritime histories. Jerónimo Côrte-Real (ca. 1530–90?) was inspired to compose his long narrative poem, *Naufragio*

---

[58] The best modern edition is António Sérgio (ed.), *História trágico-marítima* (3 vols.; Lisbon, 1955–56). Synopses of the Gomes de Brito tales in English may be found in James Duffy, *Shipwreck and Empire* (Cambridge, Mass., 1955), and in a corrected version in Tom, *op. cit.* (n. 16), appendix. Also see Georges Le Gentil, *Tragiques histoires du mer au XVIe siècle, récits portugais* (Paris, 1939).

de Sepúlveda (1594), by the epic quality and the popularity of this first shipwreck narrative.[59]

The story of the wreck of the "São Bento" in 1554 parallels that of the "São João." The narrative was written by Manuel de Mesquita Perestrelo, a survivor, and was first published at Coimbra in 1564. It is lengthier and more graphic than its predecessor.[60] Perestrelo, unlike many of these authors, was a distinguished naval officer who had spent several years in the East and had made two previous voyages to India and back. Then he embarked from Lisbon in 1553 on the "São Bento" in the company of Luís de Camoëns. While the poet remained in the East, Perestrelo accompanied by his father and brother set out for Portugal on the return voyage of the "São Bento." Of the 473 persons aboard the ill-fated galleon, all but 62 perished before reaching Mozambique, including the father and brother of Perestrelo. The luckier Perestrelo returned to Portugal in 1555 where he apparently wrote down at once his recollections of the disaster. It is not known why publication was delayed until 1564, but it might be suggested that it was printed then to complement a second version of the voyage of the "São João," both of which were issued by João de Barreira, one at his shop in Coimbra and the other in Lisbon.[61]

Among the most fascinating and better-documented shipwrecks (the sixth maritime disaster of Gomes de Brito) is that of the "São Paulo" of 1561. Unlike the two wrecks previously described, the "São Paulo" perished on the outward voyage, finally running aground on an uninhabited island off southern Sumatra. After many adventures and misadventures in Sumatra itself, a handful of castaways finally made their way to Malacca. Here, while waiting for passage to Goa, Henrique Dias, a pharmacist, wrote down his recollections of the wreck and its aftermath. His account was printed at Lisbon by Gaillhard in 1565. Another version of the same disaster was also written in Malacca, probably in 1561, by the Jesuit Manuel Álvares, who had likewise survived the wreck. The Jesuit, who was a celebrated painter, illustrated his manuscript with pen-and-ink sketches. His work, however, was not published in full until 1948.[62]

[59] The best bibliographical analysis of the original independent works and of their relation to the compilation of Gomes de Brito is C. R. Boxer, "An Introduction to the *História Trágico-Máritima*," in *Miscelânea . . . em honra do . . . Hernâni Cidade* (Lisbon, 1957), pp. 48–99. For discussion of this first narrative see *ibid.*, pp. 49–52. An annotated text of the version which appeared in Gomes de Brito may be found in Sérgio (ed.), *op. cit.* (n. 58), I, 14–37. In the art museum of Durban (Natal) in the Union of South Africa are preserved some pieces of Chinese porcelain reputedly recovered from the shipwreck (see *ibid.*, p. 40). For an assessment of the popularity and influence of the story of the "São João" see Tom, *op. cit.* (n. 16), pp. 195–96, and below, pp. 134–35, 284–85.

[60] Duffy (*op. cit.* [n. 58], pp. 27–28) describes this narrative as the most effective in all the *História trágica-máritima*; Boxer (*loc. cit.* [n. 59]. p. 91) does not share this opinion.

[61] For bibliographical detail see Boxer, *loc. cit.* (n. 59), p. 54, and Sergio, *op. cit* (n. 58), I, 45–46. Both these books published in 1564 are exceedingly rare today.

[62] For bibliographical details and for an English translation of the Dias account of 1565 see C. R. Boxer (trans. and ed.), *Further Selections from the Tragic History of the Sea,* "Hakluyt Society Publications," 2d ser., No. 132 (Cambridge, 1968), pp. 4–12, 56–107. The Jesuit's account was published by J. A. A. Frazão de Vasconcelos from the Vatican manuscript in his *Naufrágio da nao 'S. Paulo'* . . . (Lisbon, 1948). The edition of Dias translated by Boxer exists uniquely in the National Maritime Museum at Greenwich.

The story of the "São Paulo," as retold by Dias, provides an insight into the appeal which the shipwreck tales had for readers at home. A man of education, Dias writes an exciting and realistic tale of adventure and a homily on morality that is studded with tags from classical authors, platitudes from the Bible, and a contrived speech or two. He promises that he "will not relate anything other than what I actually saw, as briefly as possible, so that by avoiding a prolix story, I will also avoid wearying the reader."[63] In a day when light literature was not readily available, it is easy to understand how readers at home became enthralled by a vibrant adventure story of the trials and tribulations and the victories experienced by those of their compatriots who were exposed to the ravages of angry seas and to the afflictions visited upon them by strange and inhospitable lands and unfriendly peoples. The reactions of the castaways vary. A few bear their plight without complaint and help others by their ability to bring order out of chaos merely through force of character. The virtues of the Jesuits shine forth as exemplary, for they bring religion and morality into a situation where men prey upon one another without regard for the law of God or the state. Still, it is amazing how the castaways retain enough of the vestiges of civilization to accord preference to those of high social status, to elect leaders, and to draw up notarial documents agreeing to submit their disputes to one they recognize as judge or arbiter. Interest is sustained by the encounters between the Portuguese and the natives. The Portuguese, finally lulled into a false sense of security by the feigned amity of the Sumatrans, are set upon unexpectedly and perfidiously. While they fight gallantly against overwhelming odds, many of the weakened Portuguese fall in the fray. Through the mercy of God, a remnant survives which finally reaches a safe haven where they are greeted with the love, pity, and generosity of their countrymen. But the moral to the story is clear: "It is better to live ashore less desirous of riches than to traverse the sea in quest of such transitory and fleeting things."[64]

Despite such admonitions, the human losses from shipwreck remained a serious problem, reaching especially alarming proportions in the years from 1580 to 1610. The Jesuits, particularly in their letters, describe vividly the hardships of the voyage and the terrible wrecks at sea. Father Pedro Mateus, for example, wrote from Goa of the disaster which befell the "Santiago" in 1585 at Mozambique while en route to India. His letter of 1586 was translated into Italian and French and published in those languages at Rome and Paris in 1588.[65] Finally, the cosmographer of Philip II, the influential João Baptista Lavanha (mid-1500's–1625), was ordered to prepare an account of the disaster of the "Santo Alberto" in 1593 as a guide to voyagers who might in future be wrecked off Natal and be forced to trek overland to the relative safety of Mozambique.

Lavanha's *Naufrágio da Não S. Alberto* was published at Lisbon in 1597 in an

[63] Boxer (trans. and ed.), *op. cit.* (n. 62), p. 58.
[64] *Ibid.*, p. 106.
[65] For details see Boxer, *loc. cit.* (n. 59), p. 64.

octavo of 152 leaves.[66] The author based his narrative on a notebook kept by the pilot of the "Santo Alberto" which was verified and corrected for him by Nuno Velho Pereira, the elected leader of the stranded Portuguese who led them on a hundred day's march from Natal to the river of Lourenço Marques. Because this narrative was designed as an instructional manual for future castaways, it concentrates on the overland journey rather than on the sea voyage. The author, probably with royal approbation, asserts that the increased losses must be attributed to the careless careening and the irresponsible overloading of the vessels. He instructs future castaways on Natal first to salvage their arms for defense, and then the cloth, copper, and nails from the ship to barter with the natives. He points out the greater ease and safety of the inland over the coastal route northward. He lets his readers know that Nuno Velho Pereira had benefited from reading in Goa the accounts of the disasters and hardships which had earlier beset the survivors of the "São João" (1552), the "São Bento" (1554), and the "São Thomé" (1589).[67] He tells them how to live off the land and what to buy from the natives. Throughout his lengthy description of the trek northward it is implicit in his account that the natives are friendly enough so long as the Portuguese are not defenseless, possess the wherewithal for barter, and retain slaves in their company to act as interpreters.

The shipwreck narratives of the sixteenth century, in addition to their historical and ethnographical value, constitute a new literary genre. Based on actual cases, the tales are starkly realistic in that they also frankly and dramatically depict how men react to catastrophe. They follow a regular formula of exposition with stylized presentations of the voyage, the wreck, and the tortuous sequel of the fight for survival. Using essentially the same literary formula, the several authors nevertheless produce works of differing emphasis depending upon whether the narrator is a landsman, a navigator, a priest, a soldier, or a distinguished scholar. The writers who were themselves survivors tend to see the adventure in personal terms; the historians are more intent upon presenting sober and reflective accounts.

Almost all the maritime tragedies sparkle with vivid phrases and apt analogies. The most popular and influential of the tales were those, like the wreck of the "São João," which stress personal tragedies. Indeed, the deaths of Manuel de Sousa de Sepúlveda and his heroic wife, Leonor de Sá, were sufficiently moving and dramatic to inspire treatments of the theme by Camoëns, Lope de Vega, Tiro de Molina, and Calderón de la Barca. The shipwreck theme pioneered by the Portuguese was quickly taken up in the late sixteenth and subsequent centuries by German, Dutch, French, and English writers. General anthologies of shipwreck literature and commentaries likewise catered to the growing

[66] Translated into English in C. R. Boxer (trans. and ed.), *The Tragic History of the Sea, 1589–1622*, "Hakluyt Society Publications," 2d ser., No. 112 (Cambridge, 1959), pp. 107–86.

[67] *Ibid.*, p. 126. English translations of the narratives of the wrecks of the "São João" and the "São Bento" may be found in Volume I of G. M. Theal, *Records of South-Eastern Africa* (9 vols.; London, 1898–1903). A report on the "São Thomé" is translated into English in Boxer (trans. and ed.), *The Tragic History* (n. 66), pp. 53–106.

popular taste in northern Europe for armchair adventures. The eighteenth-century Portuguese collection of Gomes de Brito was, however, a strictly national anthology in which the epic and romantic qualities of the individual stories were left to speak for themselves.[68] Or, as in the words of Henrique Dias: "where my skill and my words fail, the truth is enough to ornament and embellish my narrative."[69]

The Portuguese Humanists of the first half of the sixteenth century were quick to take up a theme provided for them by the heroics performed in defense of besieged outposts in Asia. In 1539 Góis had published in Latin at Louvain a prose commentary on the first siege of Diu of 1536–38.[70] In Portugal Jorge Coelho wrote, about the same time, a Latin poem celebrating the victory of the Portuguese over the Turkish fleet that had participated in the siege.[71] King John III was thereafter hailed as the protector of the faith by those who saw the victories in the East as serious setbacks to the hated Muslims. The accolades for the king became even more resounding after the second successful defense of Diu in 1546. In 1548 at Coimbra Diogo de Teive published *Commentarius de rebus in India apud Dium gestis anno salutis nostri MDXLVI.*[72] Like Góis, Teive praises the king for abstaining from wars against Christians and for serving God by fighting Moors in distant places. While Teive believed that the Portuguese should concentrate on Africa, he speaks with pride of the conquests in India. The justification for the Portuguese crusade in the East, advanced by André de Resende in 1531,[73] was elevated to a dictum by Góis in 1549 when he published his Latin account of the great valor and the religious zeal which the Portuguese exhibited in successfully defending Diu in 1546 for a second time against the unrelenting Muslims.[74] He also called for a new Homer who would write in Latin the epic of the Portuguese exploits.

The writers of the vernacular in the latter half of the century took up the siege theme with even greater enthusiasm than the Latin writers. The first Portuguese account to appear in print was the *Livro primeiro do cêrco de Diu* (Coimbra, 1556) by Lope de Sousa Coutinho (1515–77?).[75] The author, a

---

[68] For various views on shipwreck literature as a literary genre see Boxer, *loc. cit* (n. 59), pp. 91–95; Duffy, *op. cit.* (n. 58), pp. 22–23; Cidade, *op. cit.* (n. 13), pp. 311–24; and J. G. Simões, *História do romance portugûes* (Lisbon, 1967), pp. 184–92. For their influence in northern Europe see below, pp. 290–91.

[69] Boxer (trans. and ed.), *Further Selections* (n. 62), p. 61.

[70] See above, pp. 21–22. For a contemporaneous view of Diu see pl. 9.

[71] Mentioned in Silva Dias, *op. cit.* (n. 37), I, 252.

[72] See Luis de Matos, "O humanista Diogo de Teive," *Revista da universidade de Coimbra*, XIII (1937), 241–45.

[73] See above, pp. 131–32. Resende had been invited in 1545 by João de Castro, the hero of the second siege of Diu, to go to India to act as the chronicler of the Portuguese conquests in the East. The scholar, pleading illness and familial responsibilities, turned down the invitation and a second one extended in 1546. See the letter from Resende to Castro dated Lisbon, March 16, 1547, as reproduced in J. P. Tavares (ed.), *André de Resende: Obras portuguesas* (Lisbon, 1963), pp. 189–92.

[74] See above, pp. 25–26. Also see the peroration to the second of the *Orationes* (Coimbra, 1548) of João Fernandes, which hails the victory of 1546.

[75] A copy of the first edition is in the Fernando Palha collection at Harvard. The library of the University of Chicago possesses a photographic copy of the copy preserved at Harvard.

participant in the first siege of Diu, divides his prose volume into two books. The first deals with his experiences at Diu from his arrival in 1535 with the fleet of Nuno da Cunha to the beginning of the siege in March, 1536. The subject of the second book is his recollection of the siege itself. His recital of events is straightforward and highly personal; it boasts almost no literary embellishments. Sousa Coutinho is excellent on those details which come within the range of his personal experiences, but he shares most of the prejudices current in his day about the perfidy of Moors and the benighted characters of heathens. Still his work is more of a history than a piece of imaginative literature; it was in fact used as a source by later writers of poetry, drama, and history. Diogo do Couto himself cited Sousa Coutinho as a major source on the first siege of Diu.[76]

The siege theme quickly attracted the attention of those who sought a subject of heroic proportions. Camoëns eschewed it as a major theme, though he was certainly cognizant of its epic possibilities.[77] It was left to Jerónimo Côrte-Real (1535–88) to attempt an epic based on the siege of Diu of 1546, a victory memorable to Portuguese by the overwhelming odds and by the superhuman tenacity of the defenders. His theme was noble, but the poet of the *Sucesso do segundo cêrco de Diu* (Lisbon, 1574) was not equal to it. He produced a long narrative poem in hendecasyllabic verse which is best described as a metrical chronicle surrounded by fictions, epithets, and overly elaborate similes. Côrte-Real, who had served his king on land and sea in India, was by background and inclination more nearly a chronicler than a poet or historian. He was as anxious to include the names of all the Portuguese who participated in the siege as he was to sing of their valor. The Cambayans, whom he classifies as Muslims, are the villains of his piece, for they are constantly plotting the destruction of the Portuguese. He introduces a few bits of local color through his descriptions of Indian festivals. He places in the mouth of João de Castro a long and tedious speech that hardly befits a man of action. The last two cantos, which have little connection with the rest of the poem, relate, on the basis of an examination of certain imaginary paintings, the glorious deeds of past captains and the future great achievements of King Sebastian.[78]

Francisco de Andrade (*ca.* 1535–1614), the chronicler of King John III's reign, wrote an epic-like poem possibly in connection with his researches on

---

[76] Another source on sieges is António Castilho's *Commentario do cêrco de Goa e Chaul no anno MDLXX* (Lisbon, 1573); for a careful history of the sieges of Malacca see the work of Jorge de Lemos, a native of Goa, which is entitled *Hystória dos cêrcos . . . de Malacca* (Lisbon, 1585). For discussion of Lemos' book see *Asia*, I 197. A copy of Lemos' book is in the library of the Hispanic Society of America in New York City. The first edition of Castilho's work is at Harvard; the library of the University of Chicago possesses a photographic reproduction of it. It was also reprinted in 1736. Also see A. Baião, *História quinhentista (inédita) do segundo cêrco de Diu* (Coimbra, 1925).

[77] "De Dio illustre em cêrco e batalhas" (*Lusiads*, Canto 10:35). He also refers to Diu in Canto 2:50 and Canto 10:60, 61, 62, 64, 67.

[78] The original work was reproduced in 1784 by Bento Jose de Sousa Farinha. For commentary see Bell, *op. cit.* (n. 44), pp. 187–88. F. de Figueiredo (*op. cit.* [n. 29], pp. 20–23) characterizes Côrte Real's poem as an "anti-epic." For a detailed summary and analysis of the poem see Tom, *op. cit.* (n. 16), pp. 151–65.

the first siege of Diu.[79] Textual comparison reveals that his poem of 1589 follows closely the narrative of Lope de Sousa Coutinho published in 1556 as well as Barros' *Décadas*.[80] He embellishes the chronicle by embroidering his *oitavas* with epithets, comparisons, flowery sentiments, and digressions into mythology and history. As in Côrte-Real's poem, Andrade portrays the Cambayans as devils and the Portuguese as exemplars of virtue. While he seems to sense that his "fragile bark" is hardly equipped to sustain a voyage of over two thousand stanzas, he consoles himself with the thought that even his lifeless verses cannot deaden the glory of the deeds they describe.[81] The scrupulous attention to detail and the heavy poetic tread of both Côrte-Real and Andrade led posterity to banish their works to the museum of literary mummies. Today they retain only an uncertain value as historical sources.

Andrade's poem was a major source, however, for a poetic drama by Simão Machado (*ca.* 1570–*ca.* 1640) entitled *Comédia de Dio* (Lisbon, 1601).[82] Machado originally intended to write his drama in three parts, but he compiled only the first two parts. They are concerned with the background to the first siege of Diu and are based on the descriptions relayed through Andrade's poem. The uncompleted third part was supposed to put the war and the siege upon the stage and to bring the drama to a resounding climax. Machado's is a historical piece written in *redondilhas* with occasional speeches framed in *oitavas*. A choir informs the spectators of the history behind the events. The characters, who number about thirty, are both historical and fictional personages. The fictional characters are stereotypes: the rude peasant-soldier, the polished Portuguese officer, and the fawning Cambayan courtier. The Portuguese speak in their own tongue, while the Moors speak Castilian. The rustic characters among the soldiers chatter in a Portuguese patois which lends comic relief to the piece. Two imaginary intrigues, or romantic subplots possibly borrowed from European literature, are carried on by Moors and Hindus. While the main theme is the conflict between Christian and Moor, certain Moorish characters are treated sympathetically, possibly in deference to the traditions prevailing in *littérature courtoise*. The Hindus, who frequently collaborated with the Portuguese, are esteemed more highly than the Moors. Their polytheism appears to remind Machado of the sophisticated paganism of the Greeks and Romans. Most reprehensible are the Europeans who sell their services and their souls to

---

[79] *O primeiro cêrco de Diu; poema épico* (Coimbra, 1589), reprinted in *Biblioteca portuguêsa* (Lisbon, 1852). There is also an unpublished manuscript of his that was discovered by Jorge Faro in the Ajuda library at Lisbon. It is entitled *Comentários da vitoria de Chaul*.

[80] See P. Teyssier (ed.), *Simão Machado: Comédia de Dio* (Rome, 1969), pp. 21–24; for a comparison of Andrade's and Barros' texts see Tom, *op. cit.* (n. 16), pp. 166–69.

[81] Also see the comments in Bell, *op. cit.* (n. 44), p. 189.

[82] Included in his *Comédias portuguesas* published by Pedro Cransbeck. A copy of the first edition is in the Vatican library; it has been issued in a modern reprint by Claude-Henri Frèches (ed.), *Introdução ao teatro de Simão Machado* (Lisbon, 1971). Teyssier (ed.), *op. cit.* (n. 80), provides an annotated, modern edition of the *Comédia de Dio*. For commentary also see C. H. Frèches, "Les Comédias de Simão Machado: I, Comédia do cêrco de Dio," *Bulletin d'histoire du théâtre portugais* (Lisbon), II (1951), Pt. 2, 151–80; III (1952), Pt. 1, 1–42; and Stegagno Picchio, *op. cit.* (n. 21), pp. 98–100.

the Moors. While Machado follows in many regards the dramatic tradition of Vicente and the Portuguese *auto*, he calls his work a *Comédia* in an obvious effort to bring it to the attention of the thriving Spanish theater that was contemporaneously being given its definitive form by Lope de Vega.

At a time when Portugal's fortunes were declining sharply both at home and abroad, the writers of siege literature glorified the earlier successes in Asia. While justifying the Portuguese conquests as a continuing crusade against the Moor, they adulated their countrymen for upholding under most trying circumstances the traditional Christian virtues of chivalry, love, and duty. They remained faithful to the picture sketched by Barros and other historians of a domination that neither destroys the native population nor imposes upon it a tribute too heavy to bear. Native rulers are maintained in power, the life and customs of the Asians are respected, and cooperative cities and their regions are defended against rapacious adversaries, such as the Mughuls. Local color and exoticism are injected by using the strange names of foreign persons and places, by describing alien customs, and by clothing the characters on stage in Oriental costumes. Like the maritime tragedies, the narratives, poems, and dramas based on sieges were not unique to Portuguese literature. The Portuguese were, however, pioneers in both these modest genres. And, it is obvious that these themes would not have assumed their particular shape or included their special substance without having the overseas navigation and the conquest in Asia as their inspirations.

3

THE CHRONICLE-NARRATIVE

The story of the Portuguese discoveries silenced all other histories, according to a proud Portuguese writer of the seventeenth century.[83] Although this is an exaggerated claim, it is true that no other country in Europe, except Italy and Spain, produced historical treatises comparable in number and originality to those published in Portugal during the last two generations of the sixteenth century. Over the entire century, the Portuguese wrote three types of history: reports by men in the field which describe overseas places and peoples, relate events to which the author was an eyewitness, or summarize military, commercial, and religious activities; histories by laymen in Portugal which deal mainly with secular affairs; and chronicles, narratives, and biographies by clerics which record both missionary and secular advances. The following discussion concentrates upon those histories written in Portugal which endeavor to organize the primary materials into a comprehensive and connected literary piece. No one of them is a complete history of the discoveries; rather each is a portrait

[83] See Bell, *op. cit.* (n. 44), p. 190.

of a particular epoch. As a result they all suffer from shortness of perspective, a failing common to contemporary histories written in any age.

The national adventure in the East inspired Portuguese chroniclers and historians to concentrate so directly upon Asia that they long neglected the history of their own country's growth and the story of its other conquests in Africa and America. So long as India remained Portugal's major overseas objective, this bias in historical perspective prevailed. No official historian was appointed in the sixteenth century to write about Africa and America, but João de Barros was designated by King John III to write about the expansion into Asia. Although India remained their focus, the Portuguese historians were required for clarity's sake to bring into their narratives a background of internal history and occasional excursions into the progress being made contemporaneously in Africa and America. It can thus be asserted that the national history of Portugal was first written in conjunction with the history of overseas discovery, a fact unique in the annals of historiography.[84]

The sixteenth-century chronicles of the kings, the biographies, and the histories of the Portuguese conquest, are mainly concerned with the wars and missions in the East. Details about the historians and their works have already been discussed, and so they will not be repeated here.[85] It is sufficient to recall that the histories published by Castanheda (1551–61) and Barros (1552–63) were followed by the chronicles of King Manuel in the renditions of Damião de Góis (1566–67) and Jerónimo Osório (1571). When grouped together these four chronicles provide the most comprehensive and authoritative account of the Portuguese expansion prepared in the sixteenth century. The first three are models of Portuguese historiography written by nonclerical historians. Bishop Osório's account is a model of Latin prose and was the book about the discoveries most widely read in the rest of Europe. The biography of Albuquerque in the *Comentários* (1557) and the Latin *Xavier* (1590) by João de Lucena extended the documentation on Portuguese activities in the East. While previously the interest in history was confined to clerics and nobles, these histories awakened a more general interest in the records of national achievement. From perusal of them it was possible for an interested reader to obtain a sketch of what the Portuguese had done in Asia. Many of the omissions in this outline could be filled in by reference to the other more specific accounts of individual regions, such as in the *China* (1569) of Gaspar da Cruz.

While all the historians sought to awaken general interest in the great achievements of the Portuguese nation, it was only Barros, Góis, and Osório

---

[84] For general introductions see Bell, *op. cit.*, chap. v; J. Albrecht, *Beiträge zur Geschichte der portugiesischen Historiographie des sechszehnten Jahrhunderts* (Halle a.S., 1815); A. E. Beau, *Die Entwicklung des portugiesischen Nationalbewusstseins* (Hamburg, 1945), chaps. i–iii; M. Cardozo, "The Idea of History in the Portuguese Chroniclers of the Age of Discovery," *Catholic Historical Review*, XLIX (1963), 1–19; H. M. A. Kömmerling Fitzler, "Fünf Jahrhunderte portugiesischen Kolonialgeschichtsschreibung," *Die Welt als Geschichte*, VII (1941), 101–23; and J. V. Serrão, *História breve da historiografia portuguesa* (Lisbon, 1962), chaps. i–vii.

[85] *Asia*, I, 181–98.

who sought to weld the internal development of the country to its outward growth. In this effort they met with a limited success. What is required here, then, is an estimate of what the discovery, conquest, and revelation of the East contributed to historical structure, style, and thought in sixteenth-century Portugal.

Barros, as can be shown from an analysis of his extant writings, was the only one of the Portuguese to conceive of the history of Portugal in a world setting. He evidently planned to write a history that would be divided into four parts, geographically determined. In the first part, called "Europe," he intended to narrate in his grand style the founding, rise, and external relations of Portugal in Europe. In the other three sections, "Asia," "Africa," and "Santa Cruz" (Brazil), he planned to present the great deeds of the Portuguese in these overseas regions. His basic historical narrative was to be supplemented by a volume of universal geography that would describe the places in which the historical events took place. An additional supplement was to consist of a treatise on international commerce, a task which he was admirably suited to undertake as factor (1533–68) of the Casa da India. But such a plan was evidently too large for a man to complete in the course of a single lifetime, even when he had a limited amount of aid from others. He mentions his treatises on geography and commerce, but these have so far not come to light. He possibly did not even begin to write the chronicles of Europe, Africa, and Santa Cruz. All that remains today of his grand historical design are partial versions of his *Décadas da Asia*; the fifth and last decade of this work was edited and revised for publication by Lavanha and did not appear in print until 1625. Though he failed to complete the gigantic task he set for himself, Barros was probably the first European to conceive of putting the history of expansion into a setting of universal history, geography, and trade.[86]

Góis and Osório, the chroniclers of King Manuel's reign (1495–1521), make no effort to sketch the King's activities on a broader background. Nor did Góis, who undertook in 1558 the task of chronicling the reigns of King John II and Manuel, try to discover any logic or structure beyond chronology in the annals he compiled.[87] Instead he studied the works of earlier Portuguese chroniclers and modeled his structure on theirs. Osório, who closely followed Góis in his Latin chronicle of Manuel, likewise advanced no new organizing principle.[88]

---

[86] On Barros' design see M. da Camara Ficalho, "João de Barros—historiador do império," in *Congresso do mundo português* (Lisbon, 1940), V, 383–84; also see C. R. Boxer, "Three Historians of Portuguese Asia," in *Istituto português de Hongkong, Bóletim* (Macao, 1948), I, 19–20; I. A. Macgregor, "Some Aspects of Portuguese Historical Writing of the Sixteenth and Seventeenth Centuries on South East Asia," in D. G. A. Hall (ed.), *Historians of South East Asia* (London, 1961), p. 186; Bell, *op. cit.* (n. 44), p. 195.

[87] The modern edition by David Lopes is entitled *Crónica do felicíssimo rei D. Manuel composta por Damião de Góis nova edição conforme a primeira de 1566* (4 vols.; Coimbra, 1943–55).

[88] *De rebus Emmanuelis . . .* (Lisbon, 1571); an English translation in two volumes was made by James Gibb and published at London in 1752. A Portuguese translation did not appear until our century. See Francisco Manuel do Nascimento (trans.), *Da vida e feitos de el-rei D. Manuel* (2 vols.; Porto, 1944).

Perhaps he does relate events in Portugal and overseas somewhat more closely to general trends and developments in Europe. Both Góis and Osório, by faithfully following an annalistic organization, are forced to flash back and forth in their works from Portugal to the overseas world and from one overseas region to the other. Such a problem is not unique to them; it is inherent in the chronicle form.

But it should not be assumed that the structure of the chronicle underwent no change over the course of the sixteenth century. While the Portuguese annalists, like chroniclers elsewhere in Europe, were conscious of the models presented by Livy and Thucydides, they did not follow slavishly either these ancient historians or their own immediate predecessors. The chronicler who had to deal with overseas activities was forced by his reader's lack of background to provide a fuller than normal narrative with many more explanations of settings and lengthier identifications of places, peoples, and things. As a consequence far more space is taken and far more explanation appears when the author is dealing with extra-European matters than when he is relating events which took place at home or in the rest of Europe. It is for this reason, as well as because of the greater interest inherent in distant events, that the conquests in Asia occupy far more space in the chronicles of King Manuel than all other events combined. Osório dismisses a devastating famine in Portugal with but a few sentences while he dwells at length on battle preparations for a skirmish in India. It is in this manner that events in Asia helped to produce a form of historical writing that departs from the principal models of the past. The works of Castanheda and Barros along with those of Góis and Osório are best described as chronicle-narratives organized along geographical lines.

The vertical flashbacks in time and the lateral cross references in space characteristic of the chronicle-narrative oblige the authors to invoke comparisons. Castanheda believed that the deeds of the Portuguese would be remembered as long as those of classical times celebrated by the Greek and Roman authors. Barros, Góis, and Osório, all of whom were well grounded in humanistic learning, compare with more specificity the deeds of the Portuguese to the heroic achievements recorded by ancient writers. Barros could not conceal his pleasure in the fact that his countrymen had made conquests in countries unknown to Alexander the Great. All these writers self-consciously seek to find in their sources the traces of Greek and Roman intercourse with Asia. Osório relates a story that he heard about the alleged activities of Hercules in Cambay and comments that he will let the reader decide whether this is a "fabulous romance, or a real fact."[89] Comparisons are numerous in all these writings between the individual heroes of Homer and Vergil and the great Portuguese conquerors.

Contemporary comparisons are far more numerous than those involving the ancient world. Asian cities are compared to the cities of Europe in terms of

[89] J. Gibb (trans.), *The History of the Portuguese People* (2 vols.; London, 1752), I, 345.

geographical location, size, and unique features. The military prowess of the Portuguese is compared to the weakness of their Asian foes by reference to feats of individual bravery, to use of arms, and to techniques of warfare. Osório compares the hearty eating and frivolous habits of the Chinese to those of the French and Germans.[90] Nor are the comparisons restricted to the similarities and differences between Asians and Europeans. The historians, on the basis of their limited knowledge, compare the customs of the Javans and the natives of Martaban to those of the Chinese. Such references are usually made without preparation or lengthy elaboration, but they nonetheless illustrate the fact that European historians were more inclined than previously to introduce comparative materials. In the process they raised questions, sometimes unconsciously, about the diversity of certain kinds of activity and the universality of other practices.

The introduction of comparisons into the Portuguese works resulted as much from literary style as from historical form. Barros, the most humanistically oriented of the Portuguese, wrote more self-consciously than the others as the spokesman of his country and his age.[91] Like Garcia de Resende, Barros regretted the tendency of his compatriots so to expend their energies in war that they neglected to record their splendid past. The influence of Livy, Plutarch, Ptolemy, and other ancient writers can readily be detected in the *Décadas*. The quotations from medieval authors are limited to a few of the early church fathers, to encyclopedic compendia, and to Marco Polo. Barros' acquaintance with Renaissance authors is illustrated by his references to Pico della Mirandola, Peter Martyr, Paolo Giovio, Polydor Vergil, Thomas More, Girolamo Cardano, and Antonio de Nebrija. His lofty style, which sometimes becomes pompous and monotonous as he relates the epic deeds of his countrymen, is lightened and made more interesting by his digressions, descriptions, and comparisons. Even though he wrote in Portuguese, a language that was not generally known in Europe, Barros was consciously writing a history that he hoped would compare favorably to those of the Ancients and to those of his own day being prepared in Spain and Italy.

Barros used a greater variety of sources than his contemporaries in Portugal and elsewhere. Aside from his occasional references to the historians of Antiquity and of his own day, he systematically combed the official materials available to him as factor of the Casa da India. He consulted first-hand descriptions of the Magellan expedition, the Latin version of Varthema's travels, and Galvãos' eyewitness account of the Moluccas. He was able to procure Persian, Arabic, Indian, and Chinese books and manuscripts. Some of these he had translated for his own use. He obtained special reports from missionaries and others in

90 *Ibid.*, II, 247.

91 The best modern edition of his work is H. Cidade and M. Murias (eds.), *João de Barros: Asia* (6th ed.; 4 vols.; Lisbon, 1945–46). For his biography and for brief contemporary literary criticisms see Manuel Severim de Faria, "Vida de João de Barros," in *Discursos varios politicos* (Évora, 1924), pp. 22–59. Also see Silva Dias, *op. cit.* (n. 37), I, 253–54; and Albrecht, *op. cit.* (n. 84), pp. 21–28, 67–69.

Asia. He evidently did not use Castanheda's material, since they were writing competitive histories. While he was not always critical of his sources, Barros customarily would cite them, a practice not uniformly followed by his contemporaries. But what is most impressive about the *Décadas* is the ingenuity he displays in weaving a rich diversity of materials into a smooth, readable, and informative historical fabric.

In many regards Barros followed the principles of historical writing prescribed by Renaissance Humanists. The *Décadas* is organized on the model of Livy. It possesses an epic quality in that heroic adventures play a central role. Barros contrived speeches for his characters in which Albuquerque and others declaim in a lofty and sophisticated prose befitting them as heroes if not doughty warriors. In his digressions he displays a pedantic love of definition and makes brave, if somewhat naive, efforts to provide etymological explanations for Asian names and terms. He collected the myths about the past which circulated in Asia and inserted them, sometimes with appropriate critical reserve, into his narrative. He is particularly careful to provide the pre-conquest history, geography, and ethnology of the places and peoples of Asia. Throughout the work he is supremely conscious of his duty to present a lofty and truthful narrative, to reflect the grandeur of the Portuguese conquest, to present moral lessons to posterity, and to uphold uncompromisingly the dignity of history itself.

Recent commentators have criticized Barros for his tendency to report only on the aristocrats in India, to omit the misdeeds of his prominent characters, to exhibit partiality toward certain of the actors, to provide too much detail on unimportant matters, to pass over lightly the subjects of vast significance such as commerce, and to make generalizations which occasionally run counter to or are not supported by the sources.[92] To a certain extent these charges can be answered by reference to the structure and style of the *Décadas*. The annalistic form, so basic to most pioneer histories, tempts the historian for the sake of balance to include within a given year or decade as much material as he does in every other one, irrespective of the intrinsic worth of the material itself. The annal form itself lacks an ordering principle or a measure for making distinctions about the relative importance of historical materials. The wish to moralize may also lead the well-intentioned historian to provide too much detail on an otherwise insignificant subject if he is intent upon using it to point up a lesson. The contrived speech usually provides the moralistic historian with a vehicle for introducing praises or strictures of his own into the history by putting words into the mouth of the hero or villain of the piece. Like Tacitus, Barros intentionally excluded from his noble narrative all "low" people, things, or words. From the perspective of a later age it is always difficult to assess precisely what is important and what is trivial in an earlier history, for questions of significance and balance are in no sense absolute since they usually reflect the concerns of the

---

[92] See Macgregor, *loc. cit.* (n. 86), p. 182; also Camara Ficalho, *loc. cit.* (n. 86), pp. 385–86.

writer and his epoch. It is in his use or abuse of documents that Barros deserves criticism, but even here he transgresses the basic rules of historical method only occasionally.

Barros' competitor, Castanheda, based his chronicle-narrative upon his own experiences in Asia and upon the writings and reports of others from the field. He, like Góis, was particularly insistent upon the importance of first-hand observation, perhaps because he knew that Barros had never traveled to the East. In this connection he wrote: "He who writes histories must make the efforts I made and see the land that he is to write about, as I saw it, for so was it done by ancient and modern historians.... Very supernatural must be the talented man who will know how to write about things he never saw." [93] Castanheda did not have the easy access to official materials that Barros enjoyed. Nor did he consult Barros' history while writing his own. He spent twenty years gathering his materials as he tirelessly checked and rechecked his information. Castanheda, like Barros, was convinced that it was no reflection on the dignity of history to write his narrative in the Portuguese language. Although Castanheda possessed no ambition to write a universal history of the type Barros planned, his *História* is a worthy example of the chronicle-narrative form and compares favorably in terms of accuracy with Barros' more majestic work. Castanheda wrote in a simple, straightforward style in which marks of humanistic erudition appear only occasionally. His geographical descriptions are briefer and less well-documented than Barros', but in many instances they possess the color and intimacy which only an eyewitness could give. His references to the pre-conquest history of Asia are cursory and uninterested, and he copies unhesitatingly from Duarte Barbosa without acknowledgment. In his estimates of peoples and policies he tends to be less pretentious and more impartial than Barros, perhaps because of his greater sensitivity to and understanding for the complexity of the problems that the Portuguese faced in India. While he lacks the eloquence and urbanity of Barros, Castanheda impresses the reader by the simplicity and sincerity of his narrative, by his abstention from superfluous rhetorical flourishes, and by his willingness to blame as well as to praise the conquerors. [94]

The chronicle of King Manuel by Góis is written in an unadorned style. Even though he had studied history with some of the leading Humanists of Italy, Góis was not inclined to cast his work in the frame prescribed by rhetoric. While he occasionally contrived speeches for the actors, they are relatively few and short. His main effort was directed to setting the record straight. He was in a particularly favorable position to do so, since he was superintendent of the royal archives (Torre do Tombo) from 1548 to 1571. There he studied the earlier chroniclers, consulted Castanheda's book, and combed Barros' work.

---

[93] Cardozo, *loc. cit.* (n. 84), p. 16.

[94] See the introduction in Pedro de Azevedo (ed.), *Fernão Lopes de Castanheda: História do descobrimento e conquista da India pelos portugueses* (3d ed.; 4 vols.; Coimbra, 1924–33). Also consult Albrecht, *op. cit.* (n. 84), pp. 12–18.

While he specifically eschewed ethnology as being outside his province, he was perhaps more inclined than the other historians to introduce comparisons of customs into his narrative. These reflect to a degree the broad acquaintance with Europe acquired in his earlier years. Because he adhered strictly to chronological order, Góis' history lacks focus to the point that the character of Manuel, the subject of the piece, never really emerges from the narration.[95] The history is basically a chronicle with a few asides on subjects which interest the author particularly, rather than a history which exhibits unity and a sense of proportion.

The Latin chronicle of Manuel's reign by Jerónimo Osório was based to a large extent on Góis' Portuguese book, a debt which the bishop acknowledges at the beginning of his account. Osório also refers to Ptolemy, Varthema, and Paolo Giovio but their works contributed but little to his. Essentially a revised version of Góis' chronicle, Osório's *De rebus Emmanuelis* (1571) was written in elegant Latin for the delectation of European intellectuals. The "Portuguese Cicero," as he was called in later days, injects a clerical, pious air into the narrative that is missing in Góis' straightforward, secular account. While he writes polished Latin speeches in Ciceronian periods for the actors, Osório introduces very few facts not found in Góis. The first volume begins with a brief description of Portugal's geography and history and concludes with 1510, the year when Almeida died, when Albuquerque became viceroy, and when Sequeira brought the Portuguese banner to Malacca for the first time. The second volume opens with the dramatic capture of Goa and concludes in 1521 with a description of the death and character of Manuel.

Osório, the good prelate, while he is supremely conscious of the hand of God working in history, is as enchanted as Góis with battles, sieges, and blockades. Osório, whose father was active in India, shares Góis' enthusiasm for the enterprise in the East. He is particularly attracted by the high civilization of the Chinese, possibly because he consulted the work of Gaspar da Cruz. He criticizes vehemently the attacks of the crown and the Portuguese people upon the Jews and does not hesitate to castigate the Portuguese in Asia for deeds which he deems morally reprehensible. He even deplores the fact that the king was dissuaded by his councillors from participating personally in a crusading expedition to North Africa. Perhaps it was because of his audacity in criticizing the nobles of the realm that Osório soon found himself out of favor at the court of Sebastian. It was possibly to avoid the intrigues of the courtiers that Osório left Portugal secretly in 1576 to visit Italy and Rome; without regard to consequences, he returned in the following year to his diocese.[96] Outside of Portugal his reputation was made by his chronicle. Montaigne in 1588 referred to him as the "best Latin historian of our century."[97]

[95] See E. F. Hirsch, *Damião de Góis: The Life and Thought of a Portuguese Humanist, 1502–1574* (The Hague, 1967), pp. 196–201.

[96] See L. Bourdon, "Le voyage de Jerónimo Osório . . . , en Italie (1576-77)," *Annales . . . de Toulouse,* I (1951), 71–85.

[97] *Essais,* ed. of 1588, I, 14; in the posthumous edition of 1595 (I, 40), Osório is described as being a "non mesprisable historien de nos siècles."

Osório was not the only Portuguese historian to meet disapprobation in high places. Castanheda was forced to withdraw from circulation the first book of his *História* printed in 1551. He was required to revise and to give a more favorable picture of King Manuel before he was permitted to reissue it in 1554. Barros, who was well placed himself and chary about criticizing the heroes of his epic, had no reported trouble with disgruntled readers. Góis, on the contrary, had fallen under a cloud shortly after his return to Portugal in 1545. Despite the hostility of the Inquisition, Góis refrained from praising extravagantly the ancestors of powerful persons and from including every bit of information which might add luster to the name of an illustrious family. Nor was he uncritical of the king or his nobles. Because of complaints, Góis was forced to revise his first edition and to issue a purged version of the chronicle. In 1571 Góis was tried by the Inquisition on charges of heresy and was forced to abjure the following year. Osório was well aware of the dangers of writing the recent history of Portugal "where the resentment of all is sure to fall upon him who ventures upon so bold an attempt." [98] It is perhaps for this reason, in addition to the epic quality of the subject itself, that the Portuguese chroniclers chose to write more about the history of India than about internal developments. Presumably it was far safer to write about the triumphs of arms in Asia than to report on the scheming that went on in Portugal for positions of power and influence.

How did the repressive character of life affect the view of historians about the history of Portugal and about the discipline of history itself? Without exception they expressed the firm belief that the events of the conquest were so great and glorious in themselves that they warranted recounting, even if the author himself lacked the genius of a Livy. They held in common the belief that the record had to be set straight, and stirring events had to be remembered if Portugal were ever to take pride in its magnificent achievements overseas. Barros, alone among the writers, sought to match the imperial glory with a grandiose historical structure and a lofty literary style. The others thought that great deeds should be allowed to speak for themselves, deeds greater than anything performed by the Greeks and Romans. Without qualification the historians were united in their determination to record for posterity what a patriotic, brave, and God-fearing people could achieve.

The epic approach to history also required the historian to take a moral stance. It is clear to all of them that doubt existed as to whether the pursuit of empire is a worthy cause. The simple and sincere Castanheda was originally untroubled by this question. He indicates in the prologue to the *História* that history is useful to king and subject as a lesson from life. And he was so offended by the criticisms of his first book that he might have suspended publication had the queen not encouraged him to continue his work. Barros, who was aware of all that went on around him, was determinedly oblivious of all the critics of empire. He

---

[98] Gibb (trans.), *op. cit.* (n. 89), I, 2.

holds firmly throughout his work to the conviction that he is majestically portraying the meaning of expansion for posterity. His is a universal history in which the actions of the individual are subordinated to the rush of events. Nor was he ever willing to write the history of King Manuel, even when asked to do so. His devotion to the history of empire, his slight attention to individuals, and his avoidance of internal history combined to help Barros escape the strictures of contemporaries. It should also be added that it would have required a bold man to attack the scholarship of the person in Portugal who had more materials at his command than others and who enjoyed high status and the unswerving devotion of the royal house.

The problems of Góis and Osório were complicated by the fact that they were forced by the nature of their subject to deal with internal history. Both were unswerving in their devotion to the truth and to recording it. They weighed their sources carefully, but they were still fair prey for those who wanted praise or secrecy for themselves and their families. Because they were writing contemporary history, they were forced to take a stand on controversial issues and personalities. Both gave more attention to overseas activities than was equitable, possibly in the hope of keeping their appraisal of burning domestic issues to a minimum.

Among these historians there was none who worried about problems of historical theory. Their ideas about causation in history are implicit rather than explicit in their writings. They were well aware that God moves mysteriously in history, and that men are motivated by a thirst for riches, honor, power, and glory. Barros and Osório were the only ones to exhibit tendencies toward abstract thought. Before beginning his history, Barros wrote a brief treatise called *Rópica Pnefma* (1532), a colloquy in which Time, Understanding, Will, and Reason discuss their respective qualities and in which notice is taken of the new religious and philosophical heresies.[99] Barros refuses in this piece to recognize the Ancients as the wellspring of all knowledge. Christ taught the type of wisdom of which philosophers are ignorant, so Barros regrets the superiority which the Christian world accords to the pagan ideas of Antiquity. The discovery by Iberians of New Worlds of which the Ancients were ignorant requires a new philosophical outlook. The scientific limitations of the Ancients, as well as their moral inadequacies, can and should be corrected by Moderns. While continuing to insist on the errors of the Ancients, Barros fails to produce in his writings any proposals for an alternative philosophical system. Nor does he attempt in his history of the Portuguese empire to do more than inveigh against the Ancients.

Osório, who is perhaps better known for his theological works than for his history, was completely unconcerned about accounting for historical change on human grounds. He attributes almost everything to the remarkable goodness of

[99] For a modern edition see I. S. Révah (ed.), *Rópica Pnefma, ou Mercadoria Espiritual* (2 vols.; Lisbon, 1952). For analysis see Révah, "'Antiquité et christianisme,' 'Anciens et Modernes,' dans l'oeuvre de João de Barros," *Revue philosophique de la France et de l'étranger*, CLVII (1967), 165–85.

God. Evil occurs when the faith given to Christ is broken. Ships are wrecked and lives lost because God's just anger is being directed against the evils perpetrated by men in their search for riches and glory. Portents and signs from God guide Christians to success: the pagans who follow the directions of soothsayers and wisemen are doomed to failure. Pagan religion is regarded as vile dissimulation, while the truths known to the pagans were surely brought to them in times past by Christian teachers. Often he lectures the Portuguese about their unchristian acts by putting noble moral speeches in the mouths of pagan leaders. Wicked advisers are generally held to be responsible for the merciless acts of Christian leaders and kings. At no point in Osório's lengthy history does he recognize human or impersonal secular causes as being responsible agents.

In Góis' work, on which Osório based his history, the Christian emphasis is lacking. Góis is unconcerned about the religious or ethical implications of his story. History for him is a human drama in which the actors take personal responsibility for their deeds. He describes primitive customs, delineates individual characters, and comments on battles without drawing a moral from his observations. Góis, perhaps because of his humanistic training, tends to view the historical scene impartially. It was perhaps this quality in his work, as well as his Erasmian and Protestant connections, which brought down upon him the wrath of the court nobility and the Inquisition. Góis' insistence upon the principle that history should be written exclusively from first-hand reports or from personal observations likewise won him no friends, especially among those who adulated Barros. His open admiration for the pagans, especially the Chinese, was certainly further evidence to the orthodox of his wrong-headedness. Even the Jesuit writers, who greatly admired the Chinese and Japanese, opposed Góis' proposal to visit India to see for himself how life was lived there.[100]

The revelation of Asia did not inspire the creation of new historical forms or ideas. It did give the histories a new subject matter and a new focus. While the old chronicle form remained paramount, the historians were forced to stretch it to accommodate the East. Much more on geographical and ethnological background was required to make the chronicle intelligible to the European reader. In the process long narratives on geography or digressions on native customs were inserted into the chronicle. To illustrate their points and to clarify their identifications, the historians inserted comparative words, phrases, and paragraphs into their narratives. Nor are these merely comparisons between Europe and Asia; numerous comparisons were also drawn between the various peoples and regions of the overseas world. God, as the mover in history, continued to dominate the scene, but His empire was understood to be wider than before. History, the gift of God to rational creatures, was more valuable as a guide to monarchs than was the advice of councillors subject to human error. Questions were openly and repeatedly raised about the inadequacy of

---

[100] On the trial of Góis by the Inquisition see Paul Rêgo (ed.), *O proçesso de Damião de Goes na Inquisição* (Lisbon, 1971).

ancient knowledge. A secular, naturalistic bent was added to historical writing, derived in part from the humanistic belief that everything has its history. Asia supplied the Humanist with a fertile field in which to experiment with this concept. History was still thought of in terms of rhetoric, especially in the emphasis which Barros gives to moral lessons. In historical writing, as in other fields of endeavor, the European prototype remained intact under the impress of new knowledge about new worlds. But the chronicle had to be stretched so far in a narrative direction that it virtually became a new genre of historical writing—the chronicle-narrative.

4

THE EPIC SYNTHESIS

When Luís de Camoëns (1524–80) was but nine years of age, Barros openly called for an epic. He also expressed his preference for epic over lyric poetry and romances of chivalry:

In olden times at the tables of lords and princes the notable deeds of great men were sung in verse. Thus, heroic poetry began, and even today, as I have been told, the Turks praise in their songs the bellicose acts of their captains into Spain and Europe at large, there would be more profit, I believe, in such music than in lovelorn songs and lyrics.[101]

In his *Clarimundo* (1520) Barros himself had glorified his country and its overseas discoveries in a prophecy written in ottava rima, the metrical form of heroic poetry. Many others, beginning with Garcia de Resende, had joined in the cry for a hymn lauding the achievements of the nation and its heroes.[102] A few attempted to respond in poetry, in both Latin and Portuguese, but the best heroic pieces produced before the *Lusiads* (1572) were the histories in prose. It was left to Camoëns to produce an epic poem which expounded a noble message, pulsing with vigor, that inspired his own age and all those following it.[103]

As a youth Camoëns was trained at a monastic school in Coimbra, the city idealized by Portugal's poets. Once his preliminary studies ended, he entered

---

[101] From his panegyric to King John III in M. R. Lapa (ed.), *João de Barros: Panegíricos* (Lisbon, 1943), p. 1.

[102] See above, pp. 118–20. The poet, António Ferreira, exhorted António de Castilho by asking:
"When shall I see the Lusitanian name
Through thee in history's pages so renowned
As to dull lofty Rome's enduring fame."
As quoted and translated in F. De Figueiredo, "Camões as an Epic Poet," *Romanic Review*, XVII (1926), 218.

[103] On the epic concept and on Camoëns' place in its history see C. M. Bowra, *From Virgil to Milton* (London, 1963), chap. III, and Figueiredo, *op. cit.* (n. 29), pp. 9–12. For a discussion of sixteenth-century concepts of epic theory in Italy and their reception among Iberian poets see Tom, *op. cit.* (n. 16), pp. 144–46.

the University of Coimbra where he received a fine grounding in the classics, especially in Latin literature and mythology. He also learned to write Spanish fluently, while becoming familiar with Italian language and literature. In 1544, when but twenty years of age, he migrated to Lisbon where his father worked in the warehouse of the Casa da India. Here he tutored the son of a famous nobleman, had a love affair that the king frowned upon, and continued writing poetry and light verses. His poetry soon won the attention of court circles, including the leading poets of the day. He also began writing dramas, some of which were produced in the salons of the capital. His drama based on the historical tale of King Seleucus of Syria and his son Antiochus was played before an audience that included the king and queen. The plot, indiscreetly chosen, paralleled too closely the acts of King Manuel I, the reigning king's father, who had taken as his third wife the princess earlier betrothed to his son. Some of Camoëns' lines were also interpreted to be disparaging to others of the royal ancestors. So the brash young dramatist was exiled from the capital in 1546; in the following year he took service as a common soldier in the army besieging Ceuta in north Africa.

After losing his right eye in Africa, Camoëns returned to Lisbon in 1550. Here he fell in with unruly companions, possibly the only ones left who would consort with an impoverished, one-eyed ex-soldier. Finally, in 1552, he fought in a street brawl in which he wounded an official of the court. After spending eight or nine months in jail, Camoëns was pardoned by the king on condition that he serve the crown in India. In March, 1553, he embarked on the "São Bento," the ship fated for disaster on its return voyage.[104] After an arduous voyage he arrived six months later at the bar of Goa. For the next fourteen years Camoëns remained in the Portuguese East.[105]

While soldiering in India, Camoëns found both the time and inspiration to continue writing. Personally he judged himself to be "more at peace than if I were in the cell of a Preaching Friar." As in Portugal earlier, he could not refrain from making his opinions public. For the life of the Portuguese in Goa he had little good to say. The Golden City he describes as "the mother of evil and the stepmother of honest men."[106] The arrival of a new viceroy, Francisco Barreto, in 1555 provided the occasion for merrymaking and for a production of Camoëns' play called *Filodemo*. The excesses of the Portuguese on holiday also inspired him to write nine stanzas of satirical verse called "Disparates na India," or "Follies in India," in which he lashed out against the vice and corruption of Goa. This was followed by a sonnet "Here in this Babylon, Sink of the world's iniquity" in which he upholds Portugal as the Zion from which he

---

[104] Cf. above, pp. 132–33.

[105] The best biography is by F. W. P. Storck, as translated from German and annotated by Carolina Michaëlis de Vasconcelos, *Vida e obras de Luís de Camoës: Primeira parte* (Lisbon, 1897). In English the fullest treatment of his life is in H. H. Hart, *Luis de Camoëns and the Epic of the Lusiads* (Norman, Okla., 1962).

[106] Quotations taken from a letter to a friend at home as translated in Hart, *op. cit.* (n. 105), p. 117. For the complete text of the letter as printed in the 1598 edition of his writings see H. Cidade (ed.), *Luís de Camoës: Obras completas* (3d ed., 5 vols.; Lisbon, 1962), III, 243–48.

lives in exile in an evil and doomed Goa. Such bold attacks immediately aroused resentment among the influential and well-placed, and again Camoëns suffered official displeasure. In 1556 he accepted the post offered to him as "Trustee for the Dead and Absent" in distant Macao.

En route to the farthest East, Camoëns stopped at Cochin, Malacca, and the Moluccas. Whether he ever arrived in Macao is a point scholars dispute.[107] He was evidently shipwrecked near the mouth of the Mekong River at one point in his peregrinations. He returned westward to Malacca and finally made his way back to Goa in June, 1561. After a short stay in prison, Camoëns took up life in Goa again. Things were better for him because Francisco Coutinho, the viceroy and count of Redondo, had known Camoëns in Lisbon and recognized his merits as a writer and as a man of culture. To meet his bills Camoëns obtained through Coutinho a clerkship in the government. He also made the acquaintance and enjoyed the friendship of Diogo do Couto, the historian and keeper of the archives at Goa, and Garcia da Orta, the physician and herbalist. He discussed the *Colloquies* with Orta and was party to their publication in 1563. In this work, he saw for the first time one of his own creations in print, an ode invoking the blessings of the viceroy on Orta's book.[108] The next five years of his life in Goa were passed in relative ease and quiet, conditions which enabled him to work on his epic. In 1567 he left Goa for Mozambique on his way back to Lisbon. In company with Couto he finally arrived at the estuary of the Tagus on April 7, 1570. The *Lusiads* appeared in print slightly over two years later.

Very little certain knowledge exists about the order in which Camoëns wrote the ten cantos of the *Lusiads*. It is generally argued that he prepared those parts of Cantos III and IV which deal mainly with Portuguese history before he left Lisbon in 1553.[109] Cantos I–IV, of which the leading subject is Vasco da Gama's journey to India, could only have been written, in their final form at least, after the author had himself experienced the voyage. Camoëns, who certainly wrote substantial portions of his epic while in the East, is often given credit for a prodigious memory in that he was able to imbue his entire work with

---

107 The only evidence that he was in Macao is contained in Diogo do Couto's eighth *Década*, sometimes considered to be a forgery. See C. R. Boxer, "Was Camoëns Ever in Macau?" *T'ien Hsia Monthly*, X (1940), 324–33.

108 See Cidade (ed.), *op. cit.* (n. 106), II, 144–47. An excerpt from it in Hart's translation (*op. cit.* [n. 105], p. 162) reads:

> "Behold how in your own bright years
> The fruits are ripe
> In the garden of far-famed Orta
> Where burgeon forth new plants and herbs
> Ere now to the learned world unknown.
>
> Behold, how in his fields of Ind
> An Orta [garden] caused such herbs to grow
> As Medea and Circe never knew,
> Although they both excelled in witches' magic lore."

For details on Orta's book see *Asia*, I, 192–95, and below, pp. 433–34.

109 See F. W. P. Storck, *op. cit.* (n. 105), p. 13.

obscure classical references. Or, it is sometimes argued on the basis of these classical references that he must have done his writing in Lisbon. These are unwarranted conclusions based on the assumption that European classical works were not to be found in India. Standard classics, such as the *Iliad* and the *Aeneid*, were certainly available to him in Goa, particularly during his second period (1561–67) of residency there. A bookstore had been opened in Goa during his absence in the East.[110] Orta, Couto, and the ecclesiastics of Goa had substantial private libraries, which he certainly could have consulted. Even in Lisbon, most books were held in private collections so that a man of Camoëns' limited financial means would necessarily have had to depend upon the good will of others. Indeed, with the Inquisition operative and watchful, about the only books that were absolutely safe from condemnation in both Goa and Lisbon were the established classics. That classical books were widely distributed in the East is proved by the fact that Aesop's Fables were printed in a Japanese version by 1593.[111] It is therefore not satisfactory to argue from an absence of evidence that Camoëns had to write in Portugal because of his numerous and obscure references to the classics. Nothing, as far as is known, prevented him from writing and rewriting most of the epic as we know it while he was in the East. What is most likely is that he started at home to write on Portuguese history, and then, while in the East, decided to make the theme of his epic into the story of Portugal's Eastern conquest and to adopt Vasco da Gama as his hero.

The *Lusiads*, or *Os Lusíadas*, is an exaltation of the achievements of the Portuguese nation, especially in the East. The title means "the sons of Lusus," or "the Portuguese." Lusus was a friend of the Greek god Bacchus and the mythical first settler of Portugal. In Camoëns' eyes Bacchus (Dionysius) is important also as the only one of the ancient gods who knew Asia; Bacchus had reputedly led an expedition to India and had stayed there for several years.[112] Vergil, the Latin poet who had sung of arms and soldiering in his *Aeneid*, was adulated by the classical Renaissance and his epic was adopted by Camoëns as a model. The *Lusiads* like the *Aeneid* centers on the travails and triumphs of a storm-tossed mariner. Aeneas symbolizes Rome; Da Gama represents Portugal. Both heroes are portrayed as moral exemplars rather than as men prone to suffer from human failings. Their destiny, like that of their nation, is of concern to the pagan gods. Venus, the champion of Aeneas, frustrated the efforts of the jealous Bacchus to put difficulties in the way of Da Gama. She even provided an Island of Love for the comfort and delight of the Portuguese heroes after their arduous adventures in India.

The *Aeneid* was not only a model to Camoëns: it was also a challenge. He prepared to rival it in art and to surpass it in truth and fame. While he follows

---

[110] See Hart, *op. cit.* (n. 105), p. 159.

[111] See below, p. 498.

[112] His ideas of Bacchus as the pagan god who best represents the Orient may have been derived from Valerius Flacius, *Argonautica* (III, 538–45 and V, 73–81), See H. H. Post, "Une source peu connue des 'Lusiades,'" *Boletim de filologia*, XIX (1960), 84.

the structure of his model and borrows devices from Vergil which help him to interweave past and future, his work exhibits numerous qualities which set it apart.[113] The meter, the ottava rima popularized by Ariosto, enabled him to add a modern romantic quality to the epic. His language, despite a plethora of classical allusions, is lucid, direct, and reflective of his own day. The title, unlike that of the *Aeneid*, evokes directly his concern with the history of the nation rather than with the exploits of a man. To the history of Portugal he gives more space than Vergil gives to the Roman past. The *Lusiads* is thus explicitly a national epic portraying both the grandeur of the past and the vast geographical conquests of the present. It also reveals a fresh intimacy of acquaintance with the sea and distant places.

Whatever Camoëns' debt to Antiquity might be, the *Lusiads* is the first epic poem to celebrate overseas expansion. The poem, as we know it, could never have been written without benefit of the maritime discoveries and the revelation of the East. About three-fourths of the poem relates to the overseas world.[114] Camoëns could never have written such a work without his personal experiences. His vivid word pictures of storms at sea and other maritime phenomena are credible and accurate because he had experienced them. The bitter and unrelenting hostility he displays toward the Moor was typical of most of his countrymen, whether in Europe or India. But his elevation of Portugal as champion of both Christianity and civilization receives context and reality from his personal relations with Moors and pagans in Asia. He desires nothing less than a European crusade against Islam, not because the Moors threatened his homeland any longer but because they occupied the holy places of the Near East and threatened the Portuguese empire in Asia.

He deals most directly with Asia itself in Cantos VII–X. Canto VII begins with Da Gama's arrival in India, "the land of wealth abounding."[115] Here the Portuguese carry the war directly to the Moor and do not, like other Christian nations, waste their substance on internecine struggle. As Da Gama's brave band sails into the harbor of Calicut, Camoëns describes in some detail the geographical configuration of India and notes that "to the south the country is shaped in the form approximately of a pyramid."[116] The Portuguese entrance into Calicut is eased by Moncaide, a friendly Moor, who acts as interpreter and as informant on Malabar's history and customs. Once given permission to disembark, the Portuguese are greeted by the Zamorin's men, who escort them to the royal residence. As they parade through Calicut, there is "much puzzlement in the faces of the onlookers at the strange sight, and they would have liked well to question the foreigners, had not the Tower of Babel made that impossible long before."[117] First the Portuguese are taken to a temple where they

113 See Bowra, *op. cit.* (n. 103), pp. 89–92.

114 *Ibid.*, p. 90.

115 From the English translation in prose by William C. Atkinson, *Camoëns: The Lusiads* (London, 1952), p. 161.

116 *Ibid.*, p. 164.

117 *Ibid.*, p. 169.

see "images of the country in wood and stone" which appear "abominable to Christian eyes."[118] On the wall surrounding the palace they see frescoes, paintings of Camoëns' own creation, which celebrate the conquests of the Ancients in India. Da Gama is told by his escort that the sages of Malabar had predicted a new conquest, obviously by the Portuguese, against which "no human resistance can prevail."[119] Da Gama delivers a speech in which he proposes an agreement "whereby the wealth and plenty of both kingdoms may increase."[120] While the ruler consults with his ministers, the other Malabar officials return to the ships with the Portuguese to learn whatever they can about the foreigners.

Canto VIII begins with a lengthy discourse in which the Malabars hear of the legendary and historical deeds of the Portuguese heroes. Meanwhile the local soothsayers consult their augurs only to learn that cooperation with the Portuguese "would mean their perpetual subjection to an alien yoke."[121] Warnings from Bacchus in Muslim dress inspire the local followers of Islam to denounce the Portuguese to the Zamorin and to bribe his advisers. In alarm the ruler defers any agreement and questions Da Gama about allegations that he and his men are priests and represent no legitimate authority. In a long speech Da Gama denounces the Muslim conspirators and relates the history of the early Portuguese expeditions "until now [when] we have come to set up our last landmark in this distant abode of yours."[122] Eager to profit by trade, the Zamorin permits goods to be brought ashore. But the Catual, the ruler of the city, is bribed by the hated Muslims to put delays and obstacles into the way of commerce. "And here," concludes the moralistic Camoëns, "the curious and judicious reader may consider how potent, in rich and poor alike, is depraved self-interest."[123]

Canto IX opens with two Portuguese factors offering their wares to the local traders. The Muslims do their best to bring trade to a halt until the annual fleet from Mecca arrives at Calicut and drives out the interloping Portuguese. Moncaide explains their design to Da Gama, who then calls for his two factors to return to the ships. The factors are detained on shore and in retaliation Da Gama seizes several Indian jewel merchants as hostages. When it becomes apparent to their families on shore that Da Gama is about to sail away with the hostages, a great clamor ensues. The Zamorin orders the release and return of the two Portuguese, and Da Gama responds by sending some of his hostages ashore. Da Gama sets sail to the south with his cargo, with the remaining hostages, and with Moncaide, "for the Moor, under divine inspiration, was desirous of becoming a Christian."[124] Venus, as a reward to the courageous Portuguese, guides them to the Island of Love, which she has created for them in the middle

[118] *Ibid.*, p. 170.
[119] *Ibid.*, p. 171.
[120] *Ibid.*, p. 173.
[121] *Ibid.*, p. 187
[122] *Ibid.*, p. 193.
[123] *Ibid.*, p. 197.
[124] *Ibid.*, p. 202.

of the Indian Ocean. Here they disport themselves with willing nymphs. About this adventure Camoëns moralizes: "Count nothing impossible: he who willed always found a way. In the end you too will be listed on fame's scroll of heroes, and this island of Venus will be yours."[125]

Canto X, known as the "Canto of Viceroys," differs from all the others in its preoccupation with India after Da Gama's reconnaissance. A nymph prophesies in song how the pagan rulers of India will submit to Portugal. She sings of the victories that will be won by dauntless Duarte Pacheco over Calicut with but a handful of courageous men. While awarding the palm to Pacheco over the heroes of Greece and Rome, Camoëns digresses melancholically on the bad treatment meted out to the soldier by king and country, an injustice which the poet feels he himself shares. Viceroy Francisco de Almeida "will perform wonders with his ships against the swarming enemy and his artifices."[126] Albuquerque will teach the enemy to bow the neck "from the sheer physical superiority of the Portuguese."[127] But the siren interrupts her song of praise to recall angrily the injustices perpetrated by Albuquerque in punishing his men. Tristão da Cunha, Soares de Albuquerque, and Lopes de Sequeira "will be responsible for the discovery of remote islands rich in new wonders for mankind"[128] and "will claim many another like them, winning their titles to fame and admiration in divers regions to become as so many Mars among men."[129]

Her song ended, the nymph takes Da Gama to a lofty mountain of the magic island where they see suspended in the air a transparent globe representing the celestial sphere. She then explains the Ptolemaic conception of the universe and the place of the earth in it, and points out all the places on the earth where Portuguese arms will triumph. The story of St. Thomas and his mission to the Indians she recounts in connection with this discussion. On the regions east of India she gives rich ethnographical detail as she points out Arakan, Pegu, Siam, Sumatra, Cambodia, and China:

And here now is a vast territory dotted, as you can see, with the names of a thousand nations you have never even heard of: the Laos, powerful in extent and numbers, the Ava and Bramas, who have their homes in great mountain-ranges, the Karens, savage tribes inhabiting the remoter hills who eat the flesh of their enemies and cruelly tatoo their own with red-hot irons.[130]

While much of the earth's surface will remain hidden to the Portuguese, the nymph foretells that Japan will "soon be famous too through the spreading of Christianity among its people."[131] The *Lusiads* ends with the return of

125 *Ibid.*, p. 217.
126 *Ibid.*, p. 223.
127 *Ibid.*, p. 226.
128 *Ibid.*, p. 228.
129 *Ibid.*, p. 232.
130 *Ibid.*, p. 243.
131 *Ibid.*, p. 244.

Da Gama from the Island of Love, over a sea ever calm, to the mouth of the friendly Tagus.

Camoëns' vast geographical knowledge of Asia was derived from Ptolemy, Barros, Castanheda, and personal experience. A map of the world based on the *Lusiads* shows that Camoëns was well informed and accurate in his placement of countries, waterways, and cities.[132] Naturally his knowledge was incomplete, but it was far more comprehensive and authoritative than that found in some contemporary cosmographies. His epithets are rarely hollow and usually reflect personal experience or solid physical information acquired from others: "the salty waters of the winding Cochin river," "the famous Ganges enters the sea," "Singapore where vessels find their passage narrowed to a straight," "the Mekong River [which] floods even in summer," and the "cavernous Himalayas." He likewise gives brief glimpses into economic geography: "fishing smacks hailing from Calicut," "Oraisa with its busy looms," and "Japan, famous for its fine silver." Java he describes as being so large that the southern mountainous region has not yet been explored, a simple matter of fact that can readily be observed by studying the European maps of his day.

On tropical flora the *Lusiads* is equally good, possibly because of Camoëns' acquaintance with Orta. Many species and dozens of varieties of plants are mentioned in its pages.[133] The epithets are likewise terse, accurate, and informative: "betel leaves, which he chewed," "sweet-smelling aloe," "many-hued flower of the nutmeg," "the trees shed tear-drops of a thick, resinous substance known as camphol," and the "stately coco-palm [of the Maldive Islands] is found growing under water." On tropical fauna the *Lusiads* is not equally varied, accurate, and explicit. Still it mentions forty-four kinds of animals, mainly in similes and in characterizations of different regions and places.[134] Camoëns' knowledge of the geographical distribution of the animals is essentially correct. Reference is made to the bird of paradise which never alights, a repetition of a common myth current in both Asia and Europe at least until the time of Linnaeus in the eighteenth century. Elephants are mentioned in connection with war and the dragging of logs. Notice is taken of the fact that the people of Malabar never kill an animal.

The poem is also rich in ethnographical detail, much of it obtained from personal experiences and the observations of others. The influence of the histories of Castanheda and Barros can be discerned in about one-third of the epic's verses.[135] He repeats almost verbatim some of the tales told by Barros: for example, the story by which the Burmans are said to originate from the union

---

[132] For details see A. C. Borges de Figueiredo, *A geografia dos Lusiádas* (Lisbon, 1883), pp. 26–29. For a list of all geographical names mentioned in the *Lusiads* see pp. 55–61.

[133] For a listing and evaluation by a professional botanist see Conde de Ficalho, *Flora dos Lusiádas* (Lisbon, 1880), chap. iii. Also see A. F. S. Ventura, "Subsidios para o estudo da flora Camoniana," *Biblos*, IX (1933), 128–39; XI (1935), 72–84; XII (1936), 212–22.

[134] See E. Sequeira, "Fauna dos Lusiádas," *Boletim da sociedade de geographia de Lisboa*, VII (1887), 65–68, for a complete listing of the animals in the poem.

[135] For this figure see J. M. Rodrigues, "Fontes dos Lusiádas," *O Istituto*, LII (1905), 637–38.

of a dog and a woman.[136] In Moncaide's speech delivered before Da Gama ever sets foot on Indian soil, the people of Calicut are categorized as idolaters and Moors. He identifies just two castes: "the more ancient one called Naires [Nāyars], and a lower, the Pariahs, who are forbidden by their creed to inter-marry with the others."[137] He repeats the story of the advent of St. Thomas in southern India and his troubles with the Brahmans. About the lands beyond India he refers to the beliefs of the Cambodians in transmigration and the reverence of the Sinhalese for the footprint on the rock at Adam's Peak.[138]

The publication history of the *Lusiads* reveals that it was one of the most successful books ever to appear in the Portuguese language. The first edition of 1572 was evidently pirated by a Lisbon printer who quickly reissued it in the same year. A third edition appeared at Lisbon in 1584. Two Spanish translations were published in 1580, the year of Camoëns' death and of Philip II's assumption of the Portuguese throne. The Portuguese Bento Caldeira published a Spanish translation at Alcalá de Henares and a Sevillian, Luis Gómez de Tapia, published another at Salamanca. Eleven years later, in 1591, a Portuguese, Henrique Carces, published another Spanish translation at Madrid. The *Lusiads* has since been translated into at least a dozen other languages, including Latin and Hebrew. Within a quarter-century after Camoëns' death an estimated twelve thousand copies of the *Lusiads* had been printed, an extraordinarily large number for the sixteenth century; by 1624 it is said that this number had increased to twenty thousand.[139] The *Lusiads* and its poet won the praise of Miguel de Cervantes, Luis de Gongora, and Torquato Tasso. Lope de Vega professedly placed it above the *Aeneid* and the *Illiad* in his estimation.[140] Lin-schoten used it as a source in the preparation of his *Itinerario* (1595), a fact which indicates that the fame and authority of Camoëns was known to northern Europe before the close of the sixteenth century.[141]

The *Lusiads* is a synthesis of all the elements included in the reality and myth of Portugal's overseas expansion. It captures the heroism and the suffering, the glory and the disillusionment, the generosity and the avarice which characterized the national enterprise. The author himself was the only major Portuguese poet to participate personally in the voyage, the wars, and the rigors of life in Asia. His epic successfully combines the personal with the national experience and provides thereby an intelligible, individualistic expression of the collective enterprise in which Portuguese of all walks of life had engaged either directly or

---

[136] On Barros' account see *Asia*, I, 553; for Camoëns' adaptation see Atkinson (trans.), *op. cit.* p. 242, and Cidade (ed.), *op. cit.* (n. 106), V, 246.

[137] Atkinson (trans.), *op. cit.* (n. 115), p. 168. Couto (*Décadas*, VII, Bk. x, chap. xi, p. 532) cites Camoëns on the marriage customs of the Nāyars.

[138] Atkinson (trans.), *op. cit.* (n. 115), pp. 243, 245.

[139] Bell, *op. cit.* (n. 44), p. 282.

[140] On these matters see F. de Figueiredo, "Camoës e Lope," *Revue de littérature comparée*, XVIII (1938), 160–70; W. Freitas, *Camoëns and His Epic* (Stanford, 1963), pp. 170–71; Hart, *op. cit.* (n. 105), pp. 223–25.

[141] Cf. *Asia*, I, 201, on the use which Linschoten made of the *Lusiads*. For further evidence of its fame in other countries see below, pp. 180–83.

indirectly. The *Lusiads*, while it sings the praises of the Portuguese nation, also possessed a special appeal for Christian and Renaissance Europe. It calls for a common crusade against the Turk and for more understanding of other peoples and customs, a paradox that characterized much of Renaissance thought. It teaches a love for human diversity and in Canto X shows how man and the earth are fused together within a larger universe.[142]

In a literary sense, too, the *Lusiads* is the culmination of all that preceded it. Like the poets of the *Cancioneiro*, Camoëns recognized the intrinsically poetical character of the overseas expansion; in it he saw fancy dominating calculation and sentiment mastering reason. Nor did Camoëns differ greatly from the earlier poets who were dubious about the value of expansion and deplored its heavy economic and moral cost to the nation. He uses the old man of Restelo to express his sentiments of disapprobation:

Oh, the folly of it, the craving for power, this thirsting after the vanity we call fame, the fraudulent pleasure known as honour that thrives on popular esteem. . . . It wrecks all peace of soul and body, leads men to forsake and betray their loved ones, subtly yet undeniably consumes estates, kingdoms, empires. . . . To what new disasters is it bent on leading this realm and its people.[143]

While reflecting the despair felt by contemporaries, Camoëns makes no suggestions for change. Like the earlier poets, he sings about the cruel manner in which men prey upon one another for material gain. But he, like them, evidently assumes that the human character is evil and unchanging and that people are content to live with greed and avarice. He expresses his personal disillusionment near the end of the poem:

> No more, O muse, no more,
> For now my lyre is out of tune
> And my voice grows faint.
> I weary not of singing
> But of folk whose ears are deaf to song,
> And whose hearts are hard.[144]

The *Lusiads* also includes sad reflections stimulated by the hardships of the maritime voyage and by the tragedies at sea. But because the voyage was so terrifying, he lauds the Portuguese for being bold enough to brave the hazards of the deep in their determination "to discover the sun's very cradle in the East."[145] Like the writers of siege literature, Camoëns never ceases to marvel at the ability of his hero—the Portuguese nation—to snatch victory from situations where defeat seems inevitable. He is also the inveterate foe of the

---

[142] See Cidade, *op. cit.* (n. 106), chap. v; Figueiredo, *op. cit.* (n. 29), pp. 9–11; and J. Cortesão, *Camoës e o descobrimento do mundo* (Lisbon, 1944), p. 10.

[143] Atkinson (trans.), *op. cit.* (n. 115), pp. 119–20.

[144] Hart, *op. cit.* (n. 105), p. 188.

[145] See Atkinson (trans.), *op. cit.* (n. 115), p. 43

Muslim, an attitude which he expresses with terrible clarity in one of his sonnets:

> With unflinching breast and mighty sword
> Crush the insolent roving pirates of the main.
> Make Ceylon tremble and Gedrosia shrink,
> Give new tincture to the Arab strait
> Let the Red Sea true to its color be—
> Dyed with the blood of the hated Turk.[146]

In many ways Camoëns realized in epic poetry what Barros strove for in his prose history: a truthful narrative of the acts and deeds of the Portuguese in Asia. Both men wrote in an ambiance of growing disillusionment with the present and of adulation of the recent past. The call for the writing of an epic had become more strident as the empire was forced increasingly on the defensive in Asia and Europe. Neither Barros nor Camoëns was the creator of the epic itself; it was anterior to them as the long and collective enterprise of the Portuguese nation.

The voyage to India had been Portugal's national dream of the late fifteenth century, and in the sixteenth century most Portuguese believed that the conquest in Asia was its materialization. All of those sixteenth-century poets, other than Camoëns, who sought to answer the call for an epic based their efforts on the theme of the Portuguese in the East.[147] Of the titles printed in Portugal between 1540 and 1600 more deal with the East than with any other category except for religious works and governmental decrees.[148] Even the chronicles of King Manuel concentrate on the achievements in Asia rather than on domestic, European, or African affairs. The *Lusiads*, as a synthesis of national sentiment and literary development, stands unchallenged as the epic of the Portuguese nation, and it celebrates more than anything else the voyage of Da Gama and the intrepid bravery of the Portuguese on land and sea.

Inevitably one must conclude that the flowering of Portuguese literature and its concentration on conquest in Asia owes an obvious and substantial debt to the opening of the sea route to India and to the subsequent conquests in Asia. The poets and dramatists of the earlier half of the century had responded by celebrating the victories and anguishing over the costs. The genres of maritime tragedy and siege triumphs which the Portuguese pioneered developed directly from the voyages to India and from the defenses of the outposts in the East. The chronicle as a historical form was not well suited to an exposition of

---

146 Hart, *op. cit.* (n. 105), p. 264.

147 For a list of forty-six epic-type poems in Portuguese see Figueiredo, *op. cit.* (n. 29), pp. 7–8. Even Diogo do Couto seemed to have a plan to write a romance of India. Part of it is reproduced in T. Braga, *Romanceiro geral português* (3 vols.; Lisbon, 1906–9), II, 356.

148 Cf. *Asia*, I, 182–83.

history in distant places; in response to this new literary and historical problem, the chronicle was expanded into a chronicle-narrative in which explanations and settings were provided in more detail and explanatory comparisons introduced more frequently. Finally, the epic of the *Lusiads* adopted the voyage to India as its fundamental theme in clear recognition of the crucial role played by the opening of Asia in the evolution of the Portuguese nation and its literature.

CHAPTER V

Spanish Literature

Spain of the pre-discovery era was much more intimately involved than Portugal in the affairs of the Mediterranean world. The Christian states of Spain, preoccupied by the reconquest of the peninsula between the eighth and thirteenth centuries, finally forced the Moors in 1266 to barricade themselves within the kingdom of Granada. A suspension of the crusade followed, which permitted the kings of Castile to consolidate their power in northern, southern, and central Spain and the rulers of Aragon to form their kingdom of eastern Spain. And it was not long before Aragon extended its sway to the Balearic Islands, Sicily, and Sardinia; in 1442 Alfonso V, its ruler, was formally recognized as king of Naples. The western Mediterranean was consequently dominated by the Aragonese during the period of the High Renaissance in Italy.[1]

The union of Castile and Aragon in 1479, as imperfect as it was, eventually involved all of Spain in the affairs of Italy and established a link between the two southern peninsulas of western Europe which eased material and intellectual intercourse. Even after Castile began to concentrate on the conquest and colonization of America, the kings, prelates, and nobles of Spain kept in regular touch with events in Italy. As a consequence, Spain acted throughout the sixteenth century as an intermediary between Iberia and Italy. With the accession of Charles I in 1516, Spain also became directly involved in the Netherlands, and indirectly in the Germanies and at other places in Charles' empire. Spain was therefore politically and intellectually much more fundamentally concerned than Portugal with the affairs of the rest of Europe, both before and after the opening of the overseas world.

[1] On the growth of the early Spanish empire see R. del Arco y Garay, *La idea de imperio en la política y la literatura españolas* (Madrid, 1944), chaps. iii and iv.

The Spanish attitude toward the East was conditioned by a crusading zeal which focused on the conquest of the Moors and by a missionary spirit which aspired to establish the universal rule of Christ. Ramon Lull (ca. 1236–1315), the Catalan philosopher, Franciscan zealot, and student of Arabic language and culture, in the early fourteenth century initiated a concrete program for enlarging Christendom. He advocated the peaceful conversion of Jews and Muslims by rational persuasion, and, these means failing, the destruction of the opponents of Christ by a crusade.[2] His program later provided the Spanish and the Portuguese with an inspiration and a rationale for their domestic policies of forced conversion and expulsions, and for their attacks upon Muslim strongholds in Africa. While the Iberian monarchs were certainly motivated by selfish national and dynastic interests, their crusading activities were seriously viewed by some contemporaries, such as Lefèvre d'Étaples in Paris, as a sincere effort to begin reconstituting early Christianity.

Queen Isabella, "La Católica," on her deathbed in 1504 reputedly called for her people to carry the war to Africa. In 1506 King Ferdinand, aided by the powerful Archbishop Francisco Cisneros (1436–1517), sought the support of Portugal and England for his cherished enterprise of annihilating Islam and recapturing Jerusalem.[3] While King Manuel adhered to the idea in spirit, his resources were then being stretched to their limits in India. In his pose as a modern Prester John, Manuel could always reassure his fellow Christians that he was busily cooperating outside Europe by puncturing the Islamic world in its soft underbelly, the East. In a sense, then, Cisneros' capture of Oran in Africa in 1508 could be viewed by the advocates of crusade as part of the same united Christian effort which resulted in Albuquerque's conquest of Goa in 1510 and of Malacca in 1511. From the viewpoint of the papacy these combined activities were certainly seen, particularly at the time of the Portuguese mission of obedience of 1514 to Leo X, as part of a concerted Iberian drive to extend the rule of the Vicar of Christ to Africa and the East.

Spanish literature of the late Middle Ages reflects this close relationship of Spain, the Moorish world, and Latin Europe. In Christian Spain the passionate fervor of the populace was expressed by religious plays which celebrated events from the life of Christ. Of the many mystery plays performed the only one preserved is the *Auto de los Reyes Magos*, a story of the three wise men from the East.[4] A thirteenth-century poem called *Libro dels tres reys dorient* perpetuated this subject at a time when Spanish writers were beginning to translate and adapt the Indian fables to their own ends. The moral and didactic tales of *Kalilah and Dimnah* and of *Sendabar* were first translated into Spanish around

---

[2] For a brief summary of his views and their implications for the missionary movement see W. J. Bouwsma, *Concordia Mundi: The Career and Thought of Guillaume Postel (1510–1581)* (Cambridge, Mass., 1957), pp. 80–93.

[3] See M. Bataillon, *Erasme et l'Espagne* (Paris, 1937), p. 56.

[4] See A. F. G. Bell, *Castilian Literature* (Oxford, 1938), p. 184.

1250.[5] The famous book of examples, the *Conde Lucanor* of Don Juan Manuel which was written before 1335, incorporated parables from the *Barlaam and Josaphat*, the *Sendabar*, and the *Kalilah and Dimnah* collections.[6] Before 1400 a Spanish version of the romance of Alexander appeared that had been translated from an Arabic version of the pseudo-Callisthenes. The crusades were treated in a fabulous manner in the *Gran conquista de ultramar* (fourteenth century), an early indication of the love for romance which later made it difficult for readers to distinguish between fact and fiction in stories about the East.

In the fifteenth century the realm of the factual was enlarged by two travel accounts of Spaniards who had visited the Levant and returned to tell what they had heard there about India, China, and Tartary. The narrative of the embassy to Tamerlane at Samarkand written around 1406 by Ruy González de Clavijo (d. 1412), a participant in the three-year (1403–6) voyage, was especially popular.[7] Clavijo's report was followed a generation later by the travels of Pedro Tafur entitled *Andanças e viajes por diversas partes del mundo avidos* (*1435–39*) in which the trade of India is described from the vantage point of Tana at the confluence of the Don River and the Sea of Azov.[8] Both these accounts were already circulating in manuscript before the return in 1441 of Nicolò de' Conti from the East. Conti's printed account, so popular in fifteenth-century Italy, appeared in a Spanish-language edition at the beginning of the sixteenth century.[9] From such works the vogue for books of travel and romances of chivalry took its beginnings and helped to produce a mixed genre that was to become extremely popular in the course of the sixteenth century. In the chivalric romances, whether of native or foreign provenance, the East remained the locale of fabulous beasts and wondrous deeds, and the source of profound wisdom. For example, in the prose prologue to *La Celestina* (1501) of Fernando de Rojas the elephant and the Arabic "roc" symbolize Asia. Even after the Asian geography of the writers became more certain and accurate, the fantastic East of the Alexander romance and of the Indian fables continued to permeate Spanish literature.[10]

[5] For the history of these tales in Europe at large see above, pp. 105–8.

[6] It was first printed at Seville in 1575 by the famous Andalusian historian, Argote de Molina. See J. M. Blecua (ed.), *Don Juan Manuel: El Conde Lucanor . . .* (Madrid, 1969), pp. 25, 37. It was read by Cervantes and Lope de Vega and much admired by Gracian. Also consult M. Ruffini, "Les sources de Don Juan Manuel," *Les lettres romanes* (*Louvain*), VII (1953), 41.

[7] For an English translation see G. Le Strange (trans.), *Embassy to Tamerlane, 1403–1406* (London, 1928). Also see below, p. 165. Mariana later remarked (as quoted in Bell, *op. cit.* [n. 4], p. 57) that Clavijo related "many things sufficiently marvelous, if true." For pre- and post-discovery "portraits" of Tamerlane see pls. 12 and 13.

[8] See the modern, edited version (Madrid, 1874) published as Vol. VIII in "Coleccion de libros españoles, raros e curiosos," pp. 163–66.

[9] For the history of Conti's account see *Asia*, I, 62–63.

[10] For example, Tirso de Molino's play, *El condenado por deconfiado* (1621) is based in part on a tale from the *Mahābhārata*.

I

CURIOSITY, HOPE, AND FRUSTRATION

New dimensions of myth and reality from the past became available to Spanish readers in the course of the sixteenth century through the translation and publication of older books. While the Casa de Contratación at Seville assiduously gathered and jealously guarded new information on the East learned about through its own activities and through relations with Portugal, Spanish intellectuals were busy putting before the hungry public a menu of leftovers. Rodrigo de Santaella (1444–1509), whose statue now stands in the patio of the University of Seville, was a Dominican educator and classical scholar trained at Bologna and in Sicily. In 1503 he published at Seville a work of translation in imitation of the volume issued a year earlier at Lisbon by Valentim Fernandes called *Marco Paulo*.[11] Santaella's *Marco Paulo*[12] includes a brief introduction on cosmography, based in part on Fernandes' materials. Santaella states that he is providing a Spanish version to help disseminate information on the Orient. He pointedly makes a distinction between the Portuguese discoveries in the East and the Castilian discoveries in the Atlantic as he propounds the thesis that the "Antilles" is the "Opposite-India." While he borrows certain materials on Polo from Fernandes, the translation itself of Polo's book was made independently from a Venetian manuscript that has only recently been identified. Included with Santaella's version of Marco Polo was a translation of Poggio's *India recognita* (Book IV of the *De varietate fortunae*), likewise derived from a manuscript that Fernandes had not used. In his preface to the Poggio, Santaella indicates that he is translating it to help confirm the veracity of Polo's account. Santaella's book was reissued by Juan Varela de Salamanca at Seville in 1518 and by Miguel de Eguia at Logroño in 1529. An English translation based on Santaella's version was made by John Frampton and printed at London in 1579.[13] Two other, unrelated editions of Marco Polo appeared in Spain in 1507 and 1520.[14]

A variety of other relevant manuscripts and translations were also printed in Spanish during the sixteenth century. Narcis Viñoles published at Granada in 1510 a Spanish translation of the parts of Poggio contained in the *Supplemen-*

---

[11] See F. M. Rogers, "Valentim Fernandes, Rodrigo de Santaella, and the Recognition of the Antilles as 'Opposite-India,'" *Boletim da sociedade de geografia de Lisboa*, LXXV (1957), 286–88.

[12] Title reads: *Cosmographia breve introductoria enel libro de Marco Polo. El libro de famoso Marco paulo veneciano . . . Con otro tratado de micer Pogio florentino. . . .*

[13] Reprinted and edited by N. M. Penzer (ed.), *The Most Noble and Famous Travels of Marco Polo* (London, 1929).

[14] See H. Harrisse, *Bibliotheca Americana vetustissima* (reprint; Madrid, 1958), I, 130–34.

tarum chronicarum . . . (Brescia, 1485) of Jacopo Filippo Foresti da Bergamo.[15] Varthema's *Travels*, first published at Rome in 1510, was issued at Seville in Spanish versions in 1520 and 1523. Three printed Spanish editions of the *Travels* of Sir John Mandeville, possibly derived from a Latin text, appeared in 1521 (Valencia), 1540 (Valencia), and 1547 (Alcalà de Henares).[16] At Seville in 1573 Christobal de las Casas published his translation of Solinus' ancient work as *De las cosas maravaillosas del mundo*. Two years later at Seville the *Conde de Lucanor* first appeared in print. In 1582 the *Vida del Gran Tamerlane* (Seville) of Clavijo was printed for the first time at the instance of the chronicler, Gonzalo Argote de Molina. By this time, then, most of the best ancient and medieval commentaries on Asia were available in Spanish.

Martín Fernández de Figueroa of Salamanca was the first Spaniard to work in the Portuguese East and report back on his experiences. His sojourn in Asia lasted from 1505 to the end of 1511, the period when Albuquerque won many of his most spectacular victories. Figueroa's rough notes were prepared for publication by Juan Augüro de Trasmiera, who checked them against the writings of Poggio and Marco Polo, probably in the version published by Santaella, and against a letter of King Manuel. The *Conquista de las indias de Persia & Arabie que fizo la armada del rey don Manuel de Portugal* . . . (Salamanca, 1512) lauds the Portuguese for their maritime conquests at Ormuz and Goa and for their naval victory at Diu. Figueroa describes Calicut but fails to mention the Christians of St. Thomas. This is one of the earliest books written in the sixteenth century by foreigners in the Portuguese service.[17]

Initially, the reaction of the Spanish poets to the revelation of India was one of curiosity mixed with anxiety and bewilderment. Fray Ambrosio Montesino, the favorite poet of the Catholic queen and an armchair observer, was one of those who responded to the opening of the overseas world with undisguised excitement:

> Men sail the seas and find far lands:
> When they come back we wait on shore
> And ask them what they saw;
> And if they tell us of strange things
> We scarce can sleep the whole night through
> Longing to know what they learned.[18]

---

[15] *Suma de todas las cronicas del mundo*; also see *Asia*, I, 63.

[16] A fifteenth-century Aragonese manuscript of Mandeville is also extant. For details see J. O. Marsh, Jr., "The Spanish Version of Mandeville's *Travels*," (Ph.D. diss., University of Wisconsin 1950), pp. xv–xvi, xxxvi–xxxviii.

[17] Figueroa's book is now exceedingly rare, but a copy of it exists in the Harvard College Library. For a translation and commentary see J. B. McKenna (trans. and ed.), *A Spaniard in the Indies: The Narrative of Martín Fernández de Figueroa* (Cambridge, 1967). Also see Francis M. Rogers, *The Quest for Eastern Christians: Travel and Rumor in the Age of Discovery* (Minneapolis, 1962), pp. 126–27.

[18] Possibly written as early as 1493, this verse is included in the *Cancionero* of 1508. The English translation is from O. H. Green, *Spain and the Western Tradition* (4 vols.; Madison, Wis., 1964–66), III, 35–36.

In 1508, while Cisneros was fighting in Africa, Francisco de Avila put these words into the mouth of Death:

> All powers and principalities
> Must drink of my bitter draught,
> They know me in Calicut
> And other unpleasant regions.[19]

The *Cancionero general* compiled in 1511 by Hernando del Castillo contains a poem by Quiros which calls "so sorrowful" the date on which the Portuguese took Calicut. Like some of the Portuguese, he deplores the high cost of trying to conquer distant realms.[20] Alonso Gomez de Figueroa, a Cordovan poet, published at Valencia in 1513 a book of verse called *Alcaçar imperial . . .* which tells of the travels of the author over the four parts of the world. While much of his material is fictitious, Figueroa's descriptions of south India appear to be based on recent information about the activities of the Portuguese there, possibly derived from the narrative of Martín Fernández de Figueroa.[21] Spanish poets of a decade later, when the question of the Spiceries was foremost in the minds of many,[22] were inclined to see America only as a source of drugs and natural remedies whereas Asia remained the source of spices and fabulous wealth.[23] After the discovery (*ca.* 1535) of precious metals and gems in America, Peru and Mexico likewise became poetic symbols of distant riches.

The most exuberant literary response in Spanish to the early conquests of the Portuguese in the East came from the pen of Bartolomé de Torres Naharro (*ca.* 1485–*ca.* 1520), a professional soldier and poet-dramatist. He journeyed to Rome in 1508, became an active member of the Spanish group then so prominent there, and probably won the patronage of Giulio de' Medici.[24] He was actively writing when the famous Portuguese mission to Pope Leo X arrived at Rome in 1514 to announce the conquest of Malacca and to present the elephant and other exotic gifts to the Medici pope.[25] For the occasion Torres Naharro prepared, possibly on commission from the Portuguese, his *Comedia Trophea*. This play was staged for the entertainment of the embassy and its hosts sometime during the period of the embassy's stay in Rome of March to June, 1514. Isabella d'Este was probably present on this occasion, for she later acquired a copy of the play for her library.[26] Moreover, Torres Naharro shortly thereafter wrote his *Jacinta* (1514 or 1515?), a play which exalts the lady

[19] From *La vida y la muerte* (Salamanca, 1508) as translated in Green, *op. cit.* (n. 18), III, 36.

[20] *Cancionero general . . . según la edición de 1511 . . .*, "La sociedad de bibliofilos españoles" (2 vols.; Madrid, 1882), I, 198–99.

[21] See above, p. 165, and Rogers, *The Quest* (n. 17), pp. 104–5.

[22] See below, p. 172.

[23] For example, see the *Retrato de la Lozana andaluza* (Venice, 1528) of Francisco Delicado. Commentary in M. A. Morínigo, *América en el teatro de Lope de Vega* (Buenos Aires, 1946), pp. 27–31.

[24] See Joseph E. Gillet, *Propalladia and Other Works of Bartolomé de Torres Naharro* (4 vols.; Bryn Mawr, Pa., 1943–61), IV, 401–5. Vol. IV was compiled by Otis H. Green.

[25] For details on the mission see *Asia*, II, Bk. 1, 135–39.

[26] Cf. above, p. 50.

from Mantua.[27] The *Comedia Trophea* was first published at Naples in 1517 in a collection of Torres Naharro's works that he entitled *Propalladia*. This Greek title refers to "the first things" or the early works of Pallas, one of the companions of Aeneas, the hero of Vergil's epic. *Propalladia* was reprinted with additions at Seville in 1520, 1526, 1535, 1545, and at Naples in 1524.

The *Propalladia* itself was conceived by the author as a literary caravel which carried news of strange peoples and distant lands to an eager public.[28] Most explicit in this regard is the aforementioned *Comedia Trophea*, which celebrates in five acts the achievements of the Portuguese in Africa and Asia.[29] The play opens with Fama praising fulsomely the great deeds of King Manuel and the Portuguese nation. She proudly proclaims to her listeners:

> How laudably and with what merit
> By means of what sacred wars,
> He has won and subdued more lands
> Than Ptolemy ever recorded.[30]

To still the protests of the Greek geographer on stage, and probably to quiet the doubts in the minds of a learned, humanistic audience, Fama recites one after the other the names of the outposts conquered by the Portuguese from Guinea to Malacca.[31] Most of the names chanted receive epithets: Cochin is "the flower of all the spicery," Ceylon is where the king "obtains precious stones," and Malacca "pays him tribute."[32] After a second act devoted to comic relief, Torres Naharro in the third act brings the "kings" of the recently conquered territories onto the stage to offer their obeisance to the Portuguese throne. They are presented by an interpreter who lets the audience know through a lengthy speech that the "kings" are worthy individuals, that they are anxious for baptism, and that they speak with one voice in support of the requests that the Portuguese embassy is making of the pope. "Two things they want from your hands," asserts the interpreter, "both baptism and the same laws to live by that Christians have."[33] After another interlude of comedy and satire, the final act depicts Fama, on the invitation of Apollo, taking flight to proclaim the glory of Manuel; the winged Fama scatters poems in the audience which foretell a splendid future for the young Prince John of Portugal, the heir to a splendid overseas empire.[34]

It is hard to imagine how the prelates and their distinguished guests reacted to this curious spectacle. The script in its present form seems lifeless and drab. But then it must be recalled that the Roman audience probably shared the

---

[27] See Gillet, *op. cit.* (n. 24), IV, 405.

[28] Cf. *ibid.*

[29] For the text and an introduction see F. de Figueiredo (ed.), *Comedia trofeo* (São Paulo, 1942).

[30] As translated in O. H. Green, *op. cit.* (n. 18), III, 38.

[31] Cf. the similar recital in Gil Vicente's *Auto da Fama* (*ca.* 1515). See above, p. 125.

[32] See F. de Figueiredo (ed.), *op. cit.* (n. 29), pp. 68–70.

[33] *Ibid.*, p. 94.

[34] For a more detailed summary see Gillet, *op. cit.* (n. 24), IV, 489–92.

exuberant mood which moved Torres Naharro to write his piece in the first place. They welcomed the Portuguese conquests, whatever their loyalties, as a victory of Christians over Muslims. Some undoubtedly saw the Portuguese expansion as a threat to Venice's commercial supremacy in the East. But the Medicis, under whose direction Florentine merchants were active in Lisbon, Antwerp, and the East, were probably not displeased by the turn of events.[35] The audience had also been prepared for a spectacle flattering to the Portuguese by the stir caused in Rome with the entrance of the elephant and the presentation of other fabulous gifts from the East. Still it is strange that no contemporary references or descriptions of the play's presentation have yet come to light, whereas many of the Latin poets of Rome celebrated the elephant.[36] Perhaps this is but another indication of how long it took the men of that day to grasp the implications of the discoveries, even when they were put before them in a spectacle. Whatever the case may be, it seems that Isabella d'Este was about the only person present to be attracted both by the elephant and the play.[37]

The hopes raised in Spain and Italy by the Portuguese victories over the Muslims were abruptly dashed by Turkish victories in the Levant. Egypt was captured by Sultan Selim I (reigned 1512 to 1520) in 1517, and two years later the Turks overran the Holy Land. Torres Naharro and Juan del Encina (1469?–ca. 1530), another Spanish poet living in Italy, thereafter began to call imperatively for a united Christian effort to free the Holy Land and to conquer the Turk.[38] Generally though, in Spain itself the writers of imaginative literature remained indifferent to the Ottoman threat and content to treat the Turks as the intrepid enemies of Christian heroes in the romances of chivalry.[39] Other Spaniards, however, came to look upon King Charles I, who became Emperor Charles V in 1519, as a future conquistador of the Near East and Africa.

As Spain became more intimately involved in Mediterranean and American problems, the focus of its attention did not shift entirely away from the Portuguese East. Balboa had sighted the Pacific Ocean in 1513 and had claimed all shores washed by it for the Spanish crown. In 1519 Ferdinand Magellan sailed westward in his successful effort to find the Moluccas by rounding South America and traversing the Pacific Ocean. The "Victoria" successfully completed the circumnavigation of the world by September 6, 1522, shortly after Charles V outlawed Martin Luther at the Diet of Worms and redirected his own attention to affairs in Spain and its overseas empire.

In the 1520's the international involvements of Spain extended to Italy, to Flanders, to Mexico, and to the Moluccas—a foreshadowing of the entanglements that would occur again after 1580. The significance of the Pacific Ocean to the futures of both Spain and Portugal was appreciated even before the

[35] See *Asia*, I, 168–69, and below, p. 197.

[36] See below, pp. 198–99.

[37] On her interest in the elephant, Hanno, see *Asia*, II, Bk. 1, 141–42. On the play see above, p. 167.

[38] See especially the discussion of Encina's long poem, *Tribagia, ò via sagra de Hierusalem* (Rome, 1521), in Rogers, *The Quest* (n. 17), p. 110.

[39] See A. Mas, *Les turcs dans la littérature espagnole du siècle d'or* (2 vols.; Paris, 1967), I, 31–33.

successful circumnavigation of the world. Albuquerque's conquest of Malacca in 1511 was followed two years later by Balboa's discovery of what he called "the South Sea." In Spain thereafter the opinion became current that the territories east of Malacca belonged within the Spanish demarcation. Even before Magellan set out, the *Suma de geografía* (Seville, 1519) of Martín Fernández de Enciso, voiced the Spanish claim to the easternmost parts of Asia. While Enciso knew the West Indies from his own experiences there, his information on the East Indies came from what he learned through Portuguese informants and from reading the travels of the Italians, Marco Polo and Varthema. He was possibly responsible for having Varthema's influential book translated into Spanish and published at Seville in 1520. Enciso's own book was reissued in 1530 and was translated into English by 1541.[40]

The return of Magellan's lone surviving vessel in 1522 stimulated the Spaniards in both Europe and America to new efforts to plant the Spanish banner permanently in the Moluccas. Before 1529 five Spanish expeditions to the Moluccas were attempted. Charles V meanwhile claimed officially that the Spiceries were within the Spanish demarcation. Though naval warfare went on in the Moluccas between the Spanish and Portuguese, the Spanish failed to establish a foothold there mainly because they had not yet learned enough about Pacific navigation to make the return voyage eastward to Mexico. The failure of the Spanish at this time to solve the practical problem of establishing and maintaining an outpost in the East forced Charles V, despite adverse public reaction, to agree at Saragossa in 1529 to defer his claim.[41] The subject of the rightful ownership of the Moluccas was to becloud Spanish-Portuguese relations again during the reign of Philip II, both before and after he became king of Portugal in 1580.

From the time of Columbus onward the overseas discoveries of the Spanish and Portuguese were observed, cataloged, and commented upon by Pietro Martire d'Anghiera (1457?–1526), better known in the English-speaking world as Peter Martyr. A native of Italy, Martyr was brought to Spain in 1487 by a Spanish ambassador to Rome. He remained in Spain for the rest of his life, where he took holy orders and became apostolic prothonotary, a member of the Council of the Indies, and eventually prior of the Cathedral of Granada.[42] Because of his intimacy with both the Spanish and papal courts, Peter Martyr was in an excellent position to learn the latest news about the discoveries and to relay it quickly to correspondents in Rome. He was personally acquainted with Colombus, Da Gama, Vespucci, Cortes, and Magellan, and frequently received

[40] For the English translation and adaptation by Roger Barlow see E. G. R. Taylor (ed.), *A Brief Summe of Geographie* "Publications of the Hakluyt Society," 2d ser. LXIX (London, 1932); see pp. 126–48 for Enciso's discussion of the East Indies and the interpolations of Barlow. For commentary see Zoe Swecker, "The Early Iberian Accounts of the Far East, 1550–1600" (Ph.D. diss., University of Chicago, 1960), pp. 185–86. For Marco Polo in Spanish see above, p. 164.

[41] On the negotiation and interpretation of this treaty see Swecker, *op. cit.* (n. 40), pp. 177–81.

[42] For his career see J. H. Mariéjol, *Un lettré italien à la cour d'Espagne (1488–1526): Pierre Martyr d'Anghera, sa vie et ses oeuvres* (Paris, 1887).

as visitors others who had returned from overseas voyages. In a letter written from Medina del Campo, possibly in 1499, he informed Julius Pomponius Loetus in Rome of the first voyage of Da Gama to Calicut, news which he thought the recipient would find "remarkable."[43] Later he wrote again to Pomponius from Avila relaying information obtained from the Portuguese ambassador there about Da Gama's voyage of 1502–3.[44] His letters contain nothing more about the discoveries in Asia until he reports on the return of the "Victoria" in 1522 and on the subsequent conflict between Portugal and Castile over their competing claims to the Moluccas.[45]

Four years after his death and one year after the treaty was concluded at Saragossa, Martyr's *De orbe novo* (1530) was published. This work, like his *Opus epistolarum*, was not composed at one time but is rather a compilation of reports written down as he learned about particular events. *De orbe novo* thus recounts the progress of the Spanish in the New World to 1526, the date of Martyr's death. Book VII of the Fifth Decade is devoted entirely to Magellan's expedition.[46] It is an excellent summary based on official reports, interviews with returnees, account books, and cargo lists.[47] Martyr's geography of the East, like that of the cosmographers who battled over the Spanish and Portuguese claims, is uncertain and vague. However, his vision of the world is post-Ptolemaic. Like other early commentators, he includes the Moluccas and other insular regions of Southeast Asia within his definition of the "New World."[48] It is clear from his inclusion of the Pacific region in the *De orbe novo* that he thought the Spanish demarcation included everything east of Malacca. He correctly points out that merchants from China and India frequently traded in the Moluccas.[49] The curious Martyr also obtained clove branches from members of Magellan's crew which he passed out to others while holding some in reserve "until I learn whether Your Holiness [Pope Clement VII] possesses any."[50] He also tasted the sago bread which the crew had subsisted on during the return voyage. He remarks that "nothing is sourer or of worse flavor. This bread must only be eaten by miserable creatures who possess no fields and hence cannot cultivate rice."[51] Martyr justifies the attention and space which he accords to the first circumnavigation of the earth by exclaiming: "If a Greek had

[43] See P. Gaffarel and F. Louvot (trans. and ed.), *Lettres de Pierre Martyr Anghiera* . . . (Paris, 1885), pp. 9, 21–23.

[44] *Ibid.*, pp. 23–25.

[45] *Ibid.*, pp. 40–41. For further relevant discussion of his 812 extant letters, a small part of his vast correspondence, see H. Heidenheimer, *Petrus Martyr Angherius und sein Opus epistolarum* (Berlin, 1881), pp. 50–65.

[46] For an English translation see F. A. MacNutt (trans. and ed.), *De orbe novo . . . of Peter Martyr* (2 vols.; New York and London, 1912), II, 151–71. For a "portrait" of Magellan see pl. 24.

[47] See *ibid.*, pp. 420–21. There is included an interesting list of the trading items the expedition carried from Spain.

[48] For similar definitions of the "New World" see above, p. 44, and below, pp. 279, 456.

[49] MacNutt (trans. and ed.), *op. cit.* (n. 46), p. 160.

[50] *Ibid.*, p. 166.

[51] *Ibid.*, p. 162. A certain sympathy for this reaction wells up in one who ate sago bread on the island of Ambon in February, 1973!

accomplished this what would not the Greeks have written about his incredible feat!"[52]

Others were likewise aware of the importance of Magellan's voyage to the future of Europe. The reports, both verbal and written, of Maximilian of Transylvania and Antonio Pigafetta, the official chronicler of the voyage, were relayed to the rest of Europe shortly after the return of the "Victoria" to Spain.[53] Even before Pigafetta personally appeared before the Signoria of Venice to describe his great experience, the doge had appointed two of the Republic's most important citizens to represent him at the court of Charles V. Lorenzo de Priuli (d. 1557), the future doge, and Andrea Navagero (1483–1529), the Latin poet and librarian of St. Marks', were designated legates on October 10, 1523. They arrived in Toledo only on June 11, 1525, and remained there until February 20, 1526. Navagero, in particular, sought to learn as much as he could about the Spanish voyages to the Spiceries from authorities such as Diego Colon, Peter Martyr, and Gonzalo Férnandez de Oviedo. He translated Oviedo's *Sumario de la natural historia de las Indias* into Italian shortly after it appeared at Toledo in 1526.[54] This little book probably whetted the Venetian's interest because its author foresaw a shorter spice route to Spain. Obviously confident that the Spanish would master the return from the East to Panama via the Pacific, Oviedo proposed that the spices should be carried over the narrow isthmus and taken to Europe by ships of Spain's Atlantic fleet. Since this proposal came shortly after the dispatch to the Moluccas of the Loaisa fleet in 1525, it was taken seriously in Spain and Venice where hopes remained high that Spain would eventually gain control over the Moluccas.[55] When Navagero's translation was published in 1534, it excited debates at Bologna and Padua over the assignment of a relatively short 1,600 leagues to the distance between the Moluccas and Panama. Oviedo's ideas were generally supported by Ramusio, the great Venetian collector of travel literature.[56]

To the literati of Spain the appearance of Navagero at Toledo, and later at Granada and Seville, was an event of capital significance. Both as a close friend of Pietro Bembo and in his own right Navagero was regarded by the Italianized intellectuals of Iberia as a spokesman for Renaissance high culture. Navagero himself was evidently willing to play such a role, for he urged the poet, Juan Boscán (1474?–1542), to abandon *cancionero* poetry and to begin experimenting with Italian metres and verse forms. Boscán followed this suggestion; he and his

[52] *Ibid.*, p. 166.

[53] See *Asia*, I, 172–77.

[54] See A. Lopez de Meneses, "Andrea Navagero, traductor de Gonzalo Férnandez de Oviedo," *Revista de Indias*, XVIII (1958), 63–69. Navagero traveled to many Spanish centers from Granada to Burgos, and finally crossed the border to France where he died at Blois in 1529.

[55] Oviedo's *Sumario* is in no way related, either as a preview or as an extract, to his more important chronicle published later. See Swecker, *op. cit.* (n. 40), p. 187. Also see below, pp. 200–201. O. H. Green, *op. cit.* (n. 18), III, 28, mistakenly identifies the *Sumario* as a preview of the *Historia*.

[56] See R. Ferrando, "F. de Oviedo y el concimiento del Mar del Sur," *Revista de Indias*, XVIII (1958), 478–80. On the problem of the width of the Pacific Ocean for geographers and cartographers, see below, pp. 457–58.

fellow poet, Garcilaso de la Vega (1501?–36), began to imitate Petrarch, the model prescribed by Bembo.[57] By turning away from traditional balladry to Italianate composition, the Spanish poets soon lost their interest in national traditions and enterprises, including overseas activities. Their defection coincided roughly with the failure of Charles' Moluccan venture and his subsequent return to the affairs of Italy and central Europe.

The abandonment of the Moluccan enterprise left Castile free to concentrate upon America. Events in the New World itself, especially the conquest of Peru in 1533, also directed Spanish attention to the wealth in the "Indies of the West." These developments accelerated the conversion of Seville from a port town into a thriving international metropolis. When Navagero visited Seville in 1526,[58] it was still a relatively small city trying to recover from a severe epidemic of the plague. In 1534 the population of Seville included only about 55,000 inhabitants; by 1588, the year of the Armada's defeat, it numbered over 100,000 souls.[59] All classes of Seville's society in these years were engaged in commerce, and some merchants and nobles enjoyed huge incomes from both agriculture and trade. The great lords built magnificent palaces and patronized the arts. Ferdinand Columbus (d. 1539), one of the famous bibliophiles of Europe, opened his house and fine library to scholars like Oviedo and Gomara.[60] Later, the great-grandson of Christopher Columbus, Alvaro Colon y Portugal, opened his palace as a meeting place for Fernando de Herrera (1534–97), called "el divino," and his circle of savants and poets often referred to as the "school of Seville."[61] Seville also became Spain's greatest center of printing during the sixteenth century and its presses issued most of the official publications and books dealing with the overseas world.[62] The Kromberger family of Nuremberg, which ran its famous press there from 1503 to 1557, published Torres Naharro, Peter Martyr, and the various parts of the *Historia general de las Indias* of Oviedo.

Oviedo was appointed by the king in 1532 to be "chronicler of the Indies," a post which his contemporary, João de Barros, assumed unofficially in Portugal about the same time. Oviedo and Gomara, like Barros and Castanheda, published their great histories in the middle years of the century. Both Oviedo and Gomara incorporated in their works full accounts of the Pacific expeditions of 1519 to 1529 and general information about the Spiceries.[63] Oviedo, who published in 1519 a romance of chivalry called *Claribalte*, was determined that

[57] See the excellent introduction in Arthur Terry, *An Anthology of Spanish Poetry, 1500–1700* (Oxford, 1965), pp. XV–XVII. For more detail see A. Valbuena Prat, *Historia de la literatura española* (6th ed.; 3 vols.; Barcelona, 1960), Vol. II, chap. xxii.

[58] On March 26, 1526, he wrote from Seville about the arrival at Lisbon and Sesimbra of two richly laden ships from India. See E. A. Cicogna, *Delle vita e delle opere di Andrea Navegero* (Venice, 1855), p. 187. Also see pl. 43.

[59] Based on Ruth Pike, *Aristocrats and Traders: Sevillian Society in the Sixteenth Century* (Ithaca N.Y., 1972), chap. i.

[60] See above, p. 46.

[61] See Pike, *op. cit.* (n. 59), pp. 28–29.

[62] For further detail on printing in Spain see *Asia*, I, 183–84.

[63] For an analysis of the Asian materials in their works see *ibid.*, pp. 184–85.

his *Historia* should not be considered a mere romance in Spanish, a genre that he had come to despise.[64] He feared that his natural history of the New World with its narrative of adventures and misadventures in exotic climes would be taken by the populace at large as simply another romance. He knew full well that the Spanish moralists had inveighed against the romances; the Inquisition later banned them precisely because they were too often taken to be literally true.[65]

Though he modeled his work on Pliny's natural history, Oviedo wrote it in Castilian and boldly declared that "true history" could be written in the vernacular as well as in Latin. He stresses repeatedly the veracity of his text, the exactness of his descriptions, and his dependence upon personal experience in America and the eyewitness testimony of others. He was also critical in his use of sources, usually being skeptical of fabulous stories which seemed unreasonable or were mere adaptations of traditional stories current in Europe.[66] His *Historia* is rich in narrative material, a fact which makes it, like the works of the Portuguese historians, an example of a new genre, the chronicle-narrative.[67]

Among Oviedo's contemporaries were others who likewise concerned themselves with maritime and colonial affairs. At Seville Pedro de Medina (1493–1567), a cosmographer attached to the Casa de Contratación, wrote and published practical textbooks on navigation as well as speculative tracts summarizing cosmographical theories on the nature of the universe.[68] Juan Luis Vives (1492–1540), who dedicated his *De disciplinis* (1531) to King John of Portugal, shows that men of a theoretical bent of mind were also stirred by the discoveries. In this treatise on educational theory the Spanish philospher-in-exile writes that the Portuguese, who patronized his work, have "revealed to us the existence of fabulous peoples and natives of marvelous and barbaric life, endowed with dizzying wealth that we contemplate with such eager eyes."[69] Fray Bernardino de Laredo (1482–1545) declared in 1535 that the sun gives its heat and power equally to the peoples of Yucatan, Flanders, and the Indies of Prester John. But Pedro Mexía (*ca.* 1500–1551), a native of Seville and a disciple of Erasmus, shows himself in his pseudo-historical miscellany, *Silva de varia lección* (Seville, 1540) to be almost entirely oblivious to the opening of the world. The erudite Mexía discusses Tamerlane without knowing Clavijo; he discourses on the invention of paper and printing without mentioning the Chinese.[70] Both in the

---

[64] See H. Thomas, *Spanish and Portuguese Romances of Chivalry* (Cambridge, 1920), pp. 138–39.

[65] See Bell, *op. cit.* (n. 4), pp. 59–60; also cf. above, p. 47, where his *Historia* is listed in Arias Montano's library under "books of romance."

[66] See B. Sánchez Alonso, *Historia de la historiografía española* (2 vols.; Madrid, 1941, 1944), I, 451–54.

[67] Cf. above, pp. 138–46.

[68] For his intellectual biography see the introduction to Ursula Lamb (ed. and trans.), *A Navigator's Universe: The Libro de Cosmographia of 1538 by Pedro de Medina* (Chicago, 1972).

[69] As translated in Green, *op. cit.* (n. 18), III, 39; also see M. Bataillon, *Études sur le Portugal au temps de l'humanisme* (Coimbra, 1952), p. 84.

[70] For an English translation of Mexía see Thomas Fortescue (trans.), *The Forest*. . . (London, 1576), pp. 67^r–71^r, 90^r–92^r.

Silva and in the *Dialogos* (Seville, 1547) Mexía shows an almost complete indifference to the meaning of the discoveries for current thought. It is indeed hard to believe from these writings that he was the townsman of both Oviedo and Medina.

Francisco López de Gomara (1511–66) in his *Historia general de las Indias* (Saragossa, 1552)[71] displays a much greater sensitivity than most of his contemporaries to the discoveries and their meaning for mankind. In his dedication to Charles V he exclaims: "Sire: The greatest event since the creation of the world—if we except the Incarnation and the Death of Him Who created it—is the discovery of the Indies." The text of his history also begins with words of wonder: "The world is so vast and beautiful, and contains so many things, each different from the other, that he who contemplates it well and ponders it must be moved to amazement." All the earth he declares to be habitable, contrary to traditional beliefs, and cites as authority "experience, our sure guide in everything." Despite the denial by St. Augustine and St. Isidore of Seville of the existence of antipodes, the fact is that they exist. The "Victoria" which "circumnavigated the globe and touched at the lands of both sets of antipodes, made manifest the ignorance of Antiquity and returned to Spain three years after her departure." Later he suggests that the "Victoria" should "be placed in the shipyard of Seville as a memorial" to its great achievement.[72]

While Gomara marveled about the New World and attacked outmoded geographical notions, a great debate was building to a climax in Spain over the character, treatment, and role of the American Indians.[73] This battle revolved around the Aristotelian doctrine of natural slavery, a teaching which held that a portion of mankind is destined by nature to live in subjugation and servitude. Africans and Indians as "inferior peoples" were supposed to serve the Spaniards willingly, to accept Christianity cheerfully, and to be thankful for the benefits conferred upon them by European civilization. The Dominican Fray Bartolomé de las Casas (1474–1566) had begun as early as 1519 to denounce these Aristotelian ideas and to call for an end to the forcible conversion and economic exploitation of the Indians. Slavery, he argued, was not countenanced by God or the Church. Some of Las Casas' ideas were upheld by the notable theologian and legal theorist, Francisco de Vitoria (1486–1546) of Salamanca, who credited the Indians with possessing reason, as well as a social system and a religion of their own. The traditional Aristotelian position was advocated by Juan Ginés de Sepúlveda (1490?–1573), a classical scholar of international reputation who held that the wars against the Indians were just and necessary preliminaries to their conversion.

Charles V, who evidently had long been uneasy about the morality of the Spanish conquests, decided in 1549 to suspend activities in America until a

---

[71] For his discussion of Asia see Swecker, *op. cit.* (n. 40), pp. 199–203, and *Asia*, I, 185.

[72] Quotations in this paragraph from the analysis of Gomara's work given in Green, *op. cit.* (n. 18), III, 28–31. Also see Valbuena Prat, *op. cit.* (n. 57), I, 447–49.

[73] On this subject see Lewis Hanke, *Aristotle and the American Indians* (Chicago, 1959).

council of jurists and theologians should instruct him on how to conduct overseas affairs justly. Both Las Casas and Sepúlveda appeared before a council at Valladolid in 1550 to debate the moral and philosophical issues growing out of the conquests in America. After nothing was decided definitively, the conquest resumed. Subsequent legislation, however, ameliorated the lot of the Indians slightly and punished the worst excesses which the conquerors perpetrated in the name of Spain and the Christian God. Las Casas' dictum that "all the peoples of the world are men" also had the effect in the 1580's of easing the lot of the Chinese converts of the Spanish in the Philippines.[74]

In Portugal questions relating to the treatment of native populations never became so bitter a moral and intellectual issue. Portugal's maritime empire was too scattered, too superficial, and too loosely held for such sharply defined confrontations to develop. It was also possible for the Portuguese in Asia to justify their acts by proclaiming that they were advancing the Christian cause by rooting out the Moors. Indeed it seems true that the Portuguese generally sought to enlist the natives against the Moors, to reward the local people for cooperation, and to leave relatively intact, except at Goa, most of their institutions. But it is perhaps most important to emphasize that the Portuguese in Asia were interested more in trade than in conquest for its own sake—a difference in emphasis which became patently obvious in eastern Asia after Philip became king of Portugal in 1580.[75]

From the evidence of Spanish literature the opening of Asia by the Portuguese in the first half of the sixteenth century was but a minor theme in the history of expansion. Spanish translations were made of Marco Polo and a number of other pre-discovery writers on Asia. Peter Martyr and others kept track of the early Portuguese voyages to the East. A few Spanish poets, balladeers, and dramatists noticed in their writings the help that Christendom was getting from the Portuguese in its continuing battle against Islam. Serious study of the Portuguese progress eastward began in Spain with the return of the "Victoria" in 1522, the dispatch of subsequent voyages across the Pacific, and the controversy over the Moluccas. Martyr, Oviedo, and Gomara, as historians of the Spanish empire, included sections in their works dealing with the Pacific and with distant reaches of insular Southeast Asia. But the Spanish literati were chiefly absorbed, particularly after 1525, in assimilating the Italian Renaissance into the mainstream of Spanish culture. Even at Seville, where everyone was involved at least indirectly in overseas affairs, the courtly poets typified by Herrera were more interested in imitating the sonnets of Petrarch than in singing the great exploits of the Spanish in America. Possibly the slow and indecisive character of the Spanish literary response to the opening of the overseas world reflects a preoccupation with the moral debate. With respect to

[74] See Lewis Hanke, *The Spanish Struggle for Justice in the Conquest of America* (paperbound reprint; Boston, 1965), pp. 159–61.

[75] For discussion of the conquistadorial spirit in Asia see *Asia*, I, 808–9; also see below, p. 192.

Asia it is perhaps sufficient to restate the obvious fact that Spaniards in the first half of the century could hardly be expected to react enthusiastically to the overseas victories of their Portuguese rivals, particularly when Spain's own hope of controlling the Moluccas had been so bitterly frustrated in 1529.

2

UNIVERSAL EMPIRE IN ROMANCE AND POETRY

Andrea Navagero, the influential Venetian Humanist and ambassador, was at Toledo in 1525 for the Feast of the Assumption (August 15). On that occasion, a spectacle was presented which included a dance by four black savages and their king and by four Amazons and their queen. This exotic performance was probably supposed to celebrate the victories of the Spanish in Africa and America, the return of the "Victoria," and the hopes of Spain in the Pacific. Sixty years later, in 1585, the same festival was again celebrated at Toledo but with another sort of exotic performance. On this occasion the dancers were eight "Indians" wearing cloth of taffeta in various colors decorated with silver and gold, mirrors on their breasts, jewels on their fingers, and feather decorations. According to the script, the "Indians" were supposed to enter the cathedral accompanied by an elephant, either a real one or a good imitation, which carried a monkey on its back.[76]

Notice the change in the description of the "Indians" between the first and second performances from primitive to highly sophisticated, richly appareled people. Notice that the "Indians" in 1585 are accompanied by an elephant, the symbol of Asia of which Philip II had received a live specimen as a gift on becoming king of Portugal.[77] About nine months before the festival the emissaries from Japan had spent two weeks (*ca.* October 1–15, 1584) in Toledo. Later they were received at a royal audience in Madrid and remained in Spain until April 7, 1585.[78] With these points in mind it is safe to conclude that the "Indians" of this second occasion probably represented the "Indians" of Asia rather than those of America. What had transpired in Spain in the interim to effect

---

[76] See C. A Marsden, "Entrées et fêtes espagnoles au XVIᵉ siècle," in J. Jacquot (ed.), *Fêtes et cérémonies au temps de Charles Quint* (2 vols.; Paris, 1960), II, 392. The monkey on the back of the elephant symbolizes evil on the back of good. See *Asia*, II, Bk. 1, 176. Also contrast the spectacle of 1585 with that of 1571 which highlighted the entry of Anne of Austria to Burgos. On this occasion the "Indians" were richly dressed, wore masks encrusted with precious stones, played with a rubber ball like the Indians of America, and were accompanied by chariots (see Marsden, *loc. cit.*, II, 400–401). On "feather decorations" for Asians see *Asia*, II, Bk. 1, 18, or cf. the dance by three Indians of Brazil, Japan, and Mexico in the *Examen sacrum* of an anonymous Jesuit playwright of the third quarter of the sixteenth century as cited in Morínigo, *op. cit.* (n. 23), p. 51.

[77] See *Asia*, II, Bk. 1, 154.

[78] See *ibid.*, I, 692–94.

the change in the identity of the "Indians" who appeared in these two festivals?

The forty-two years of Philip II's reign (1556–98) were marked by major gains for Spain in Asia. The early years of his rule coincided with the decline of Portugal's control over the spice trade in both Europe and Asia. The general peace concluded at Cateau-Cambrésis (1559) left Spain the arbiter of Europe, the greatest colonial power, and the champion of a resurgent Catholic orthodoxy. Philip hereafter took as his goals the strengthening of Spanish hegemony in Europe, the suppression of heresy at home and abroad, and the continuation of aggressive expansion overseas.

Miguel Lopez de Legazpi (d. 1572) was dispatched in 1564 from Mexico to discover "the islands of the West in the region of the Moluccas." The king's principal aims in sending out the Legazpi expedition were "to bring the faith" to "the inhabitants of those places," and "if it should be deemed advantageous to have it for God, our Lord, and for the advancement of the Royal Crown" to found a Spanish settlement in the Spiceries.[79] Thus began the second period of Spanish expansion across the Pacific in defiance of Portugal's claims and rights. While Legazpi himself remained at Cebu, he dispatched a ship back to New Spain. Its navigator, Fray Andres de Urdaneta, was successful in discovering how to make the return voyage across the Pacific. This route being firmly established, Spain remained in the western Pacific, principally in the islands called "Filipinas" after the king, from 1565 to 1898.

The Spanish outposts in insular Southeast Asia were periodically attacked after 1565 by the Portuguese fleets based on the Moluccas. Meanwhile in Europe diplomatic tension between Lisbon and Madrid over the Moluccan issue afforded the French, Venetians, and other foreign interests the opportunity to fish in the troubled waters of Spanish-Portuguese relations.[80] The unstable condition of the Portuguese crown, following the death of John III in 1557, contributed to Portugal's inability to deal decisively with the Spanish encroachment in the Spiceries and with the growth of privateering and revolt within its own Asian empire. The death of King Sebastian in Africa in 1578 led directly to the union of Spanish and Portuguese crowns in 1580, a fusion effected by the superior military strength which Philip possessed to support his claim to the Portuguese throne. By this act Philip became sovereign in fact, if not in theory, over Portugal and its empire. In Spain the union certainly aroused hopes of sharing the wealth that was commonly supposed to be pouring into Portugal from the Spiceries. And, when it is recalled that Spain was largely unthreatened by the Turks in the Mediterranean after the battle of Lepanto (1571), it certainly seemed clear in the 1580's that Philip's policies were everywhere successful, or on the verge of succeeding. Certainly the mutinous Netherlanders with their

[79] As quoted in Luz Ausejo, "The Philippines in the Sixteenth Century" (Ph.D. diss., University of Chicago, 1972), p. 2; for the problems faced in establishing the Spanish settlement on Cebu see pp. 232–37.
[80] See above, pp. 33–34.

English supporters hardly seemed to be in a position to challenge for long the authority and might of a ruler whose dominion was believed by many to be almost universal.[81]

Philip's military successes abroad were accompanied at home by a tightening of royal control over the provinces, the economy, and the religious and cultural life of the people. Religious orthodoxy following the principles adopted by the Council of Trent was imposed in Spain by a vigilant Inquisition and by a king who strongly believed that religious uniformity was essential to the maintenance of political stability. For the literati the tightening of royal control became most apparent in the new censorship rules adopted. The 1502 law of censorship was strengthened in 1558 by making the unlicensed importation of foreign books a capital offense. All books published in Spain were hereafter required to receive the censor's approval before being printed. The Inquisition rigorously enforced its 1551 list of prohibited books, and in 1584 it issued an expurgatory index of books that would be permitted to circulate after offending passages had been deleted.[82] But with all this legislation and restriction, both religious and secular books continued to pour off the presses; indeed the Golden Age of Spanish literature reached its apogee at a time when official control over reading and publication was thought to be operating most effectively.[83]

Light can be shed on the effects of royal control over publication by examining the history of the romance of chivalry, the dominant form of Spanish fiction in the sixteenth century. In the century following the first publication of the *Amadis de Gaula* in 1508, fifty new chivalresque works appeared in Spain and Portugal. Until 1550 a new one appeared almost every year; from 1550 to 1588 but nine were added; three more appeared between the date of the Armada and the publication of *Don Quixote* in 1605. In the latter half of the century churchmen and moralists denounced the romances as contributing to the deliquency of the laity. Their export to America was banned. In 1555 the Cortes at Valladolid singled out the romances as books to be banned in Spain itself.[84] While steady denunciation discouraged the appearance of romances on new themes, the older romances continued to be printed, circulated, and sold to a public eager for light reading. A few of the new

[81] Even Justus Lipsius (1547–1606), the Flemish scholar, seems to have thought so, for he begins after 1580 to address Philip of Austria (later King Philip III) as "Philippo Austriaco Hispaniarum et Indiarum Principi," and he refers in 1595(?) to Philip II as an "Alexander" whom the son will one day succeed in his control over Asia. See A. Ramirez (ed.), *Epistolario de Justo Lipsio y los españoles (1577–1606)* (Madrid, 1966), pp. 121–23.

[82] Cf. the history of Torres Naharro's *Propalladia*. The Toledan Index of 1559 banned it along with many other printed plays. Writers of romances and plays hereafter were constrained to respect religious doctrine and social decorum more closely. The *Propalladia* was reissued in an expurgated version at Madrid in 1573. See E. M. Wilson and D. Moir, *The Golden Age: Drama* (London, 1971), pp. 14, 18.

[83] For a general description of the Spanish system of censorship see A. Sierra Corella, *La censura de libros y papeles en España, y los indices y catalogos españoles de los prohibidos y expurgados* (Madrid, 1947). Also see above, p. 39.

[84] See R. O. Jones, *The Golden Age: Prose and Poetry* (London, 1971), pp. 53–54.

romances that quietly appeared may even have pleased the court for they celebrated in prose and peotry the resounding military exploits of the crown at Lepanto and elsewhere. The older romances were regularly refurbished to make them more credible and contemporary in their appeal both to the court and to the public.

Of particular interest are the Angelica romances that appeared in Spain after 1580. The story of Angelica, princess of Cathay, had received its original form in the celebrated Italian romances of Boiardo and Ariosto.[85] The *Orlando furioso* of Ariosto was published in its definitive Italian form in 1532; thereafter some of its Italian continuators made Ariosto's unrepentant heroine into a penitent. The Spanish writers picked up the theme from the Italians and converted the original Angelica into a brooding and brave Castilian beauty. When Ariosto's romance was first translated into Castilian in 1550, a moral exposition was added to each canto by the translator.[86] By 1584 this translation had been reprinted eleven times and various Spanish authors had imitated it in numerous prose and poetic renditions of their own.

Along with the refurbished romances there began to appear rhymed chronicles and heroic poems celebrating the conquests in America. The chief poetic product of the American experience was *La Araucana* of Alonso de Ercilla (1533–94), which appeared in three parts in 1569, 1578, and 1589.[87] Ercilla's heroic poem became a model for later poets who wrote on the American theme and its popularity helped to produce in Spain a taste for realistic deeds of greatness rather than mythical exploits. The Spanish imitators of Ariosto catered to the growing taste for realistic as well as moralistic heroics by embellishing the Angelica theme with new trappings to give it both a credibility and a reverent tone that the original legend lacked.

One of the most successful imitators of Ariosto was Luis Barahona de Soto (*ca.* 1548–95), a physician and poet who studied medicine at the University of Osuna. In 1571 he migrated to Seville where he practiced medicine and came to be on close terms with the literati of the port city.[88] He was befriended by Cristobal de las Casas, who published in 1573 a Spanish translation of Solinus' famous classical work on the marvels of the world.[89] He knew Nicolas Monardes (*ca.* 1512–88), the pharmacist, who issued in 1569 his popular two books on the products of the New World deemed valuable as medicines.[90] He was certainly acquainted with Fernando de Herrera and the members of his literary and artistic circle. Even though Barahona was enraptured with the vibrant life of Seville, he left that city in 1579 and returned to Granada where he had begun his studies. Here he lived through the terrible epidemic of 1580–81, while he

[85] See below, p. 204, and H. Y. K. Tom, "The Wonderful Voyage: Chivalric and Moral Asia . . ." (Ph.D. diss., University of Chicago, 1975), pp. 45–46.

[86] See Green, *op. cit.* (n. 18), III, 434.

[87] See M. Chevalier, *L'Arioste en Espagne (1530–1650)* . . . (Bordeaux, 1966), pp. 132, 144.

[88] See F. Rodríguez Marín, *Luis Barahona de Soto* . . . (2 vols.; Madrid, 1903), I, 75–105.

[89] See *ibid.*, pp. 138–39.

[90] *Ibid.*, pp. 158–63.

completed *Las lágrimas de Angélica*, read parts of it before the Academy of Poetry, and had it printed in 1586.[91]

Traditionally Barahona's *Angélica* has been treated as simply another continuation or imitation of Ariosto. Actually it is far more original than it might appear to be on casual reading. A hint about the complexity of the work appears in the preface by Gregorio López de Benavente, who talks about "the many secrets and mysteries which the author chose to conceal beneath a covering of such pleasant and easily understandable subject matter," and points out to the reader that the contest from the very beginning of the poem is to capture "the most beautiful and richest part of the world—China."[92] Barahona borrowed precisely one-half of his characters from Ariosto, at least in name.[93] His Angelica, however, does not resemble the brilliant, serene, and graceful lady of Ariosto; she is an unhappy young woman plagued with misfortune who is extremely moral and very faithful to her perfect love for Medoro. Angelica occupies the center of the stage consistently in Barahona's piece, a prominence which had not been accorded to the princess of Cathay by most previous writers.[94] The chivalric atmosphere disappears almost completely from Barahona's *Angélica* and is replaced by an absorption with bookish knowledge and scholarly erudition which occasionally detracts from its poetic quality.[95] Probably inspired by Ovid, Barahona overwhelms his reader with the opulence and abundance of his references. He brings to his poem flora, fauna, and geographical names and terms which Ovid never knew. His descriptions of distant places and peoples and his wonder at the fecundity of nature in all parts of the world make it clear that Barahona is writing from sources unknown to Ariosto.

Barahona organized his poem spatially through the device of the voyage from west to east: from Asia Minor to India, from India to Taprobana, and from Taprobana to China. For him the Cathay of Angelica is a port, probably the principal city, of China.[96] Since most of the scenes are laid in the Orient, he quite understandably immersed himself in the current writings about Asia. An examination of his library catalog shows that he possessed a fair selection of the ancient, medieval, and sixteenth-century works dealing with Asia.[97] Close scrutiny of his text reveals that he used many of these books in his preparation of the *Angélica*. A careful study of his spelling of Asian place names proved to be a particularly useful device for finding leads to some of his sources.

One of his major sources was the *Lusiads* of Camoëns, possibly the Spanish translation published in 1581.[98] It is perfectly clear, even when the comparison is limited to the original Portuguese and Spanish texts of the *Lusiads*, that

[91] *Ibid.*, pp. 169–225.
[92] See the reprint of 1904 called *Primera parte de la Angélica* (Granada, 1586).
[93] See Chevalier, *op. cit.* (n. 87), pp. 221–22.
[94] *Ibid.*, p. 229.
[95] *Ibid.*, pp. 223–24.
[96] See Tom, *op. cit.* (n. 85), pp. 51–52.
[97] See above, p. 48.
[98] I have not been able to locate a copy of this translation.

Barahona forthrightly borrowed or closely imitated verses, lines, and names. The itinerary followed by the fleet which escorts the princess of Cathay from the Persian Gulf to the coast of China is heavily dependent upon Camoëns' epic. A long list can be made of direct borrowings of lines from the *Lusiads*, especially from the famous Canto X which was so often to be a source of information and inspiration for poets.[99]

A study of Barahona's spellings of individual words, especially place names, reveals that Camoëns was not his only Portuguese source on the East. For example, in referring to Orissa, a province of India, he spells it "Oriza" (*Angélica*, Canto VIII, p. 167) following Camoëns' "Orixa" (*Lusiads*, X, 120); earlier in the same canto (p. 165), he spells it "Duria," a variant which is peculiar to Castanheda and his *Historia* (I, 242).[100] The discovery of this variant spelling led to a comparison of the two texts, particularly because Barahona possessed a copy of Castanheda's chronicle-narrative in his own library.[101] So, as unusual as it is, the poet Barahona borrowed directly from or imitated the prose history of Castanheda in preparing the *Angélica*. What follows are some of the more obvious examples of substantial imitation:

Angélica, Canto VIII, p. 165:
Tras el los muchos reyes, que contiene
Narsinga, que el â todos los regia,
El de Coramandél, y Telengueyo
Y el de Duria, y el de Teanragéyo.

Y los de Vengapòr, y Talinàte,
Que manda los de Honor, y de Huberrano,
Mergêu, Baticalà, y de Caramàte,
Bracelòr, Mangalòr, Manjauerràno;
Y de Cintacorà, hasta el remate
De Lancolà, y la gran Barrauerrano!
Muy fuertes todos y seguros puerros,
Y por la larga costa Indiana abiertos.

Historia, I, 242:
"Ho reyno de Narsinga he na segunda India.... A primeyra se chama Talinate: & começa da fortaleza de Cintacora ... pouco mais ou menos ate hũ lugar chamado Ancola em que ha estes lugares: Manjauarrão, Bracelor, Mangalor, Vdebarrão, Caramate, Bacanor, Barrauerrão, Baticalâ, Honor, & Mergeu que sam todos muyto grandes & bõs portos. A segũda se chama Teãrragei & he no sertão & tambẽ comarca cõ ho reyno de Daquẽ."

Angélica, Canto VIII, p. 166:
Con tocas todos, largas y parejas,
Y sus Patolas de algodon ò seda
Sus arracadas de oro en las orejas
De peso, que sufrirse à penas pueda;

Historia, I, 261:
Andam nuus da cinta pera cima, & pera baixo se cobrẽ com panos de seda & dalgodão que chamão patolas, trazem toucas nas cabeças, & nas orelhas arrecadas muy ricas douro & pedraria & aljofar grosso, de tanto peso que fazẽ estirar as orelhas, tanto que chegão ao pescoço.

[99] Such a comparative list appears in Chevalier, *op. cit.* (n. 87), pp. 226–28. However, it is not complete.

[100] Castanheda is also somewhat inconsistent, for he spells it "Doria" on the same page. What is unique here is the ellision of "de oriya" to designate "those who speak the language called Oriya." To my knowledge Castanheda is the only sixteenth-century authority on India who employs this spelling, or anything resembling it. The references to Castanheda's work are cited from P. de Azevedo (ed.), *História do descobrimento e conquista da India pelos portugueses* (4 vols.; Coimbra, 1924–33).

[101] See above, p. 48.

Angélica, Canto VIII, p. 166:
Con piedras blancas, verdes, y vermejas,
Yndignas de apreciarse por moneda,
Rubiès, Balaês, Iacintos, y Zafiròs,
Topazios, Amatistas, y Porfiros.

Iangonças, y Crisolitos, y aquellos
Que al ojo quieren parescer del gato.

Historia, I, 259:
Nace tambẽ nesta ilha muyta pedraria, assi
como rubis muyto finos, vermelhos &
brancos, balais, jacintos, çafiras, topazios,
jagonças, amatistas, crisolitas, & olhos de
gato, que os Indios estimão muyto.

Angélica, Canto XI, pp. 212–13:
Despues la rica, y varia especeria,
El malabatro, el clauo, la pimienta,
La nuez moxcada, y flor que encima cria,
Que limpia al seso, y su calor sustenta,
Despues la innumerable pedreria,
Las perlas del aljofar, que es sin cuenta,
Cera, ambar, y marfil, coral, y seda,
Sal, cobre, azogue, plata, oro, ye moneda.

Elb ermellon, la piedra y man, la grana,
Los cofres del oro, y cestos de oro orlados,
Y la luziente, y clara porcelana,
Do àn sido mas los Indios señalados,
La ropa de algodon ligera, y vana,
Las differentes mezclas de brocados,
Y brocadillos de oro, y seda, y plata,
Y el rico chamelote, y la escarlata.

Historia, I, 35:
E como erão grãdes mercadores & de muy
grosso trato, veose a fazer a mayor escala
& a mais rica de toda a India, porque nela
de achaua toda a especiaria, droga, noz, &
maça q̃ se podia desejar todo genero de
pedraria, perlas, & aljofar, canfora, almiz-
quere, sandalos, & aguila, lacre, porcelanas,
cestos dourados, cofres, & todalas lindezas
da China, ouro, ambar, cera, marfim, &
alaquecas, muyta roupa dalgodão delgada,
& grossa, assi branca como pintada, muyta
seda solta & retros & todo genero de panos
de seda & douro, & brocados, brocadilhos,
chamalotes, graãs, ezcarlatas, alcatifas, ta-
feciras, cobre, azogue, vermelhão, pedra
hume, coral, agoas rosadas, & todo ho
genero de cõseruas.

Clearly Barahona relied on Camoëns and Castanheda for his materials on
south Asia. The likelihood is that he used Mendoza's book published in Spanish
at Valencia in 1585 for his materials on China. For example, Barahona wrote in
Angélica:

> From here [Canton], the mighty empire of China
> Is shown long and wide, stretching
> From Olan which is confined by the Indies
> To the place where the sun is first adored.[102]

The place-name "Olan" is the key word to the source. Almost certainly it is a
variant spelling of "O-lâm," the name in the Amoy vernacular for the northern
province of Honan. Martín de Rada, the Spanish Augustinian who wrote a
report on his mission of 1575 to Fukien, the province in which Amoy is located,

---

[102] As translated in Tom, *op. cit.* (n. 85), p. 57. The original reads:
"De aqui el soberbio Imperio de la China
Se muestra, largo, y ancho, dilatado
De Olan, que con las Indias mas confina
Hasta do el Sol primero es adorado."
Primera Parte de la Angélica, p. 173ʳ.

uses the romanization "Olam" in his catalog of the Chinese provinces.[103] Mendoza, in turn, cites Rada's spelling, but he misplaces "Olam" as the province "which is that towards the south and nearest unto Malacia."[104] Barahona in his verse follows Mendoza in locating "Olam" incorrectly; in the process he provides strong evidence of his dependence upon Mendoza's books rather than the other sources which he might have consulted. Certainly it would be possible to show on closer examination of Barahona's poem that his debt to Mendoza was considerable.

Despite the staid, bookish quality of the quoted passages, the *Angélica* of Barahona is full of exuberance; even these passages add to the opulence and curiosity of the poem and evoke visions of magical and mysterious realms where the rarest and richest goods are abundant. The imitators of Petrarch had hesitatingly presented a pearl, a gem, or a crystal in their verses as examples of lustrous and sparkling beauty. Following Barahona, the poets of the 1580's multiply the references which they make to precious objects, to their places of origin, and to their qualities.[105] Proof that his contemporaries appreciated Barahona's *Angélica* as a work of originality and quality is attested by Cervantes himself. In *Don Quixote* he excluded *Angélica* from the flames to which he consigned the other romances of chivalry, and had his curate remark that "the author thereof was one of the most famous poets of the world, not only of Spain."[106] While this was certainly an exaggeration, it is nonetheless true that Barahona's influence upon his contemporaries in Spain was considerable.

In lyrical poetry the followers of Petrarch, from Boscán to Herrera, regularly expressed a feeling for "the splendid and copious Orient."[107] But most of the allusions to the East are incidental to the main point being made. For example, Michael de Carvojal and Luis Hurtado in *Las cortes de la muerte* (1557) allude to the Orient and its gems to illustrate how far the idea of hierarchy and common origins extends into the world of nature:

> Among the gems of the Orient
> Scholars everywhere declare
> The ruby is most excellent
> By reason of its secret virtues.
> And so great is its perfection
> That this single stone contains
> The qualities of all the others;
> God gave it such great distinction.[108]

[103] For Rada's reference and the identification of "O-lâm" see C. R. Boxer, *South China in the Sixteenth Century* (London, 1953), p. 267, n. 6.

[104] G. T. Staunton (ed.), *The History of the Great and Mighty Kingdom of China and the Situation Thereof Compiled by the Padre Juan Gonzalez de Mendoza* ("Hakluyt Society Publications," Old Series, Vols. XIV, XV [London, 1853–54]), XIV, 21.

[105] Cf. the remarks of Chevalier, *op. cit.* (n. 87), pp. 228–29.

[106] See Thomas Skelton (trans.), *Cervantes' Don Quixote*, "Harvard Classics," vol. XIV (New York, 1909), pp. 57–58.

[107] Boscán's *Leandro* (1543) begins: "En el lumbroso y fertil Oriente."

[108] As quoted in Green, *op. cit.* (n. 18), II, 17.

Others use the Orient and the Indies as synonyms for the remote, the ineffable, and the incomprehensible.[109] Fray Luis de Leon (1527–91) and Herrera add interest and color to their lyrical offerings by references to an opulent and fantastic East. No Spanish lyric poems of the sixteenth century appear to exist which have the discoveries as a major theme.[110]

Still the immersion of the Spanish lyricists in a sea of Italian poetry did not drown public interest in native traditional poetry. Successive editions of the *Cancionero general* were printed throughout the century and a number of highly regarded poets began near its end to compose in the older manner. Luis de Gongora (1561–1627), a contemporary of Barahona, began early in his career to compose short traditional verses in which he alludes realistically and jestingly to the new commitments assumed by the king in Asia in 1580. In a poem entitled "The Country-Bachelor's Complaint," Gongora quips:

> Oft boasting how the might of Spain
> The world's old columns far outran,
> And Hercules must come again
> And plant his barriers in Japan.[111]

In another poem of 1587 he outlines in broad strokes those "parts of the map over which Philip's rule extends."[112] A sonnet of 1588 satirizes the grandees of Spain as being broader than elephants and rhinoceroses.[113] This is a telling

---

[109] See *ibid.*, III, 27.

[110] See H. Capote, "Las Indias en la poesia del Siglo de Oro," *Estudios americanos*, VI (1953), 6.

[111] A free translation of Edward Churton (in *Gongora* ... [2 vols.; London, 1862], II, 157) of the verse written either in 1582 or 1585, which reads:

> "Ahora que estoy despacio
> y, hecho otro nuevo Alcides
> trasladada sus columnas
> de Gibraltar a Japon
> con su segunda *Plus Ultra*."

See J. Mille y Gimenez and I. Mille y Gimenez (eds.), *Góngora, Obras completas* (Madrid, 1956), p. 51.

[112] "porque parce ellas
trae cuanto de Indias
quardan en sus senos
Lisboa y Sevilla;
traeles de las huertas
regalos de Lima
y de los arroyos
jovas de la China

. . . .
sabe que en los Alper
es la nieve fria,
y caliente el fuego
en las Filipinas."

See Mille y Gimenez (eds.), *op. cit.* (n. 111), pp. 90, 92.

[113] "Grandes, mas que elefantes y que abadas (*ibid.*, p. 459)." Notice his use of the word "abadas," a term which had just entered the Iberian languages. For further discussion see below, p. 545.

comparison, for both an elephant and a rhinoceros from Asia were on display in Madrid beginning in 1584.[114] In describing the preparations being made for the festival of St. Hermenegild in Seville, Gongora gaily sings:

> One gives the silk of China to the breeze
> Another Persia's costly tapestries
> Hang out in sunny gladness on the walls.[115]

It was probably in 1589, shortly after the disaster of the Armada, that Gongora wrote his poem on the new Escorial palace in which he seriously remarks:

> A great Religion works this marvel rare
> Meet for the monarch, whose unquestioned sway
> The new-found West and Eastern Indians own.[116]

Gongora also wrote a poem celebrating the Spanish translation of the *Lusiads* which opportunely appeared at Seville in 1580, the year when Philip II became king of Portugal.[117]

Like Barahona and Gongora, the young Felix Lope de Vega (1562–1635) was moved by the expansionist activities of his day. After a series of escapades, he joined the Armada in 1588 and sailed off to England. In the intervals when he was not fighting the English, he wrote *La hermosura de Angélica*. This romance in poetry continues Ariosto's poem and draws some of its content from contemporary sources as well. Lope, who was well aware of the popularity of *Las lágrimas de Angélica*, evidently set out to prepare a similar work in the hope that it would enjoy an equal success.[118] But in this he was disappointed, for he was not even able to publish his *Angélica* until 1602.

Lope's Angelica resembles the beauty of Barahona's poem, but she is more obsessed by vanity. While she remains the princess of Cathay, Lope transports her along with Medoro back to Spain. A coronation is held at Seville which is attended by kings and princes from the East. The only new character added to the romance is Angelica's son, Angeloro, born in Cathay. Lope follows some of the Oriental kings back to their homelands. But his treatment of Asia is much more chivalric and commonplace and less realistic than Barahona's. Much more of the Asia of Ptolemy, Pliny, and the medieval romances remains in his depiction of countries and peoples. To a public that had feasted on the rich fare provided by Barahona and Mendoza, the Asia of Lope's *Angélica* must have seemed bland and

---

[114] See *Asia*, II, Bk. 1, 169; also cf. above, p. 176.

[115] Trans. of Churton, *op. cit.* (n. 111), II, 72; for original see Mille y Gimenez (eds.), *op. cit.* (n. 111), p. 571. For the reaction of lyric poets to America at this time see Morínigo, *op. cit.* (n. 23), pp. 53–60.

[116] Trans. of Churton, *op. cit.* (n. 111), I, 234; for original see Mille y Gimenez (eds.), *op. cit.* (n. 111), p. 461.

[117] For this poem see Mille y Gimenez (eds.), *op. cit.* (n. 111), pp. 565–66.

[118] See H. A. Rennert, *The Life of Lope de Vega (1562–1635)* (New York, 1968), pp. 146–47.

stale. To those who had traveled abroad, or who had studied geography, his confusion about places and peoples must have been irritating.[119]

That Lope knew Barahona's work is proved by his reference to Canidia, a magician of Barahona's own creation.[120] He was also well aware of the *Lusiads*, a work which he probably carried to England with him. His knowledge of classical historians like Quintus Curtius and geographers like Strabo and Ptolemy shows up clearly in his allusions in the *Angélica* and in other works as well.[121] But his reconciliation of ancient with modern geography is not clear. Classical terms like "Taprobana" and "Aurea Chersoneso" appear in the same verse with Malacca and Java.[122] He appears to be much more aware of Japan than others, perhaps because he saw or heard about the young legates who were in Spain in 1584–85. He refers to the silver, the silks, and the arms of Japan,[123] this last possibly being a reference to the swords worn by the Japanese at their audience with Philip II.[124] Like Barahona, he was fascinated by the jewels of India, especially the sapphires and rubies of Ceylon.[125] *Angélica en al Cathay*, his second attempt to portray the Cathayan beauty, was written between 1599 and 1603. In it he used the opulence of India as background for the picturesque and colorful scene in which Angelica and Medoro arrive on the banks of the Ganges.[126] But here, too, Lope's geography is confused, for he has Florida and China on either side of the "Western Ocean."[127]

Following the defeat of the Armada in 1588, a degree of disillusionment with overseas empire began to set in. The mood is dour and foreboding in poems such as Lope's *La Dragontea* (1598) based on the last voyage and death of Sir Francis Drake. Still in this poem and in the *Jerusalem*, Lope continues to employ substantial numbers of geographical names for the purpose of lending sonority to his verse.[128] Gongora in his *Polifemo y Galata* (1613) borrows references to the nefarious activities of the Malays and Javans from Barahona who possibly derived them from Camoëns.[129] But in *Soledades* (1613) Gongora, while extolling the beauty of the Spice Islands, implies that discoveries inspired by greed lead ultimately to the destruction of the discoverers.[130]

[119] Based on analysis in Tom, *op. cit.* (n. 85), pp. 69–71.

[120] See Chevalier, *op. cit.* (n. 87), pp. 352–53.

[121] For an analysis see A. K. Jameson, "The Sources of Lope de Vega's Erudition," *Hispanic Review*, V (1937), 131–34.

[122] See *La hermosura de Angélica* as reprinted in *Coleccion de las obras sueltas* . . . (Madrid, 1776), II, 104.

[123] *Ibid.*, pp. 3, 150. Lope was later on much interested in and inspired by the Dominican mission to Japan. See H. Bernard, "Lope de Vega et l'Extrême Orient," *Monumenta nipponica*, IV (1941), 278–79. More authoritative and important is J. S. Cummins (ed.), *Triunfo de la fee en los reynos del Japón of Lope de Vega* (London, 1967).

[124] See *Asia*, I, 692.

[125] *La hermosura de Angélica* (n. 122), pp. 125, 150.

[126] See Chevalier, *op. cit.* (n. 87), p. 17.

[127] As cited in Morínigo, *op. cit.* (n. 23), p. 104.

[128] See Jameson, *loc. cit.* (n. 121), pp. 133–34.

[129] See Mille y Gimenez (eds.), *op. cit.* (n. 111), p. 631. Also see A. Vilanova, *Las fuentes y los temas del Polifemo de Góngora* (2 vols.; Madrid, 1957), II, 675–77.

[130] See Jones, *op. cit.* (n. 84), p. 156.

3

New Historical Genres

The later writers of prose, like the poets, were much better informed about
Asia than their predecessors of the earlier half of the century. Antonio de
Torquemada (*fl.* 1553–70), who wrote in the tradition of Pliny and Mexía,
exemplifies the change. His *Jardín de flores curiosas*, first published at Salamanca
in 1570, brings together materials from a vast array of sources.[131] In the six
informative colloquies into which the book is divided, he refers to the following
authorities on Asia: Castanheda, Bergamo, Barros, Mandeville, Marco Polo,
Megasthenes, Plutarch, Pigafetta, Ptolemy, and Pliny.[132] From the writings of
these authors he extracted some of the curious stories which made his book so
popular throughout western Europe. Before the end of the century, it was
reprinted eight times in Spain and twice at Antwerp. It was translated into
French and issued at Lyons in 1579 and 1582, and at Paris in 1583; an Italian
version appeared at Venice in 1590. The translator of the English version of
1600 appropriately entitled it *The Spanish Mandeville of Miracles; or the Garden
of Curious Flowers . . .* (London).

Torquemada, in contrast to Mexía, displays a genuine interest in the curiosities
of the overseas world. He points out to his readers how ignorant Ptolemy was
of the geography of the world and how uninformed Pliny was of its variety.[133]
He speculates on the sources of the Nile and the Ganges on the basis of what he
read in the Portuguese writings.[134] But he is most interested in assembling from
the contemporary accounts of Asia "the many strange and pleasant Histories"
he found in them.[135] From Castanheda he relates a story about a man of 340
years of age who was brought in 1530 before Nuno da Cunha, the viceroy at
Goa.[136] He recounts the legend of St. Thomas in India and, on the basis of the
"Chronicles of Portugale," describes how the disciple's body was discovered at
Mylapore.[137] From Barros he quotes the legend of the mating of a woman and
a dog to produce the people of Burma; this story of human and animal cohabita-
tion is repeated in one form or other by Camoëns, Barahona, and Lope de
Vega.[138] At another point he tells of a sex change experienced at adolescence by
a young Portuguese girl in the East a story that he learned from reading Amato

[131] For a modern reproduction and introduction of the Lerida edition of 1573 see A. G. de Amezúa
(ed.), *A. de Torquemada—Jardín de flores curiosas* (Madrid, 1955).
[132] These names extracted from the list of authors, *ibid.*
[133] See *The Spanish Mandeville*, fol. 116.
[134] *Ibid.*, fol. 49.
[135] Quoted from the full title of *ibid.* Also see Bibliography below, chap. viii, "English Literature."
[136] *Ibid.*, fol. 26ʳ.
[137] *Ibid.*, fols. 55ᵛ–56ᵛ.
[138] *Ibid.*, fol. 33. For this story in legend and literature cf. Chevalier, *op. cit.* (n. 87), pp. 352–53, n.
83, and *Asia*, I, 553.

Lusitano.[139] Most amusing is his acceptance on the basis of Pigafetta's "authority" of a mélange of the old European tales about Eastern peoples:

Pigafetta ... said, that being in the Archipelago, which is in the Sea of Sur [the Pacific], and on the other side of the Straight, there were found Pigmees in a certain Island ... for their eares were as great as their whole body, they laid themselves downe of the one, and covered themselves with the other, and were in their running exceedingly swift, which though he himself did not see, because he could not apart himselfe from the voyage which the ship held, yet it was in the Islands thereabout, a thing notoriously knowne and manifest, and the most part of the Mariners testified the same.[140]

Serious history, as opposed to "curious history," also responded to the opening of Asia during the last generation of the sixteenth century. In conjunction with the conquest and pacification of the Philippines, information on China began to pour into Spain after 1565. Earlier a few glimpses of China had been provided by the various Jesuit letters printed at Coimbra in Castilian beginning in 1555.[141] Materials on China in Portuguese were also available to Castilians in the 1560's in the histories of Castanheda and Barros. The earliest separate book on China appeared in Portuguese, the *Tractado ...* (1569) of Gaspar da Cruz. But the first effort to synthesize into a narrative all the available sources on China was undertaken by Bernardino de Escalante in his *Discurso ... de la China* (Seville, 1577). A Spanish clergyman, Escalante had not visited China himself but based his work on the available literary sources and on interviews with Portuguese and Chinese informants. Even before Escalante's book appeared, the Spanish in the Philippines had sent proposals to Madrid urging a military expedition against China. In his simply written and straightforward narrative Escalante likewise sought to encourage his compatriots to extend their trading and missionary activities from the primitive Philippines to the much richer field of China. Escalante's book attracted readers outside of Iberia, for it was translated into English in 1579 and was consulted by intellectuals like Ortelius.[142]

The union of the Spanish and Portuguese crowns in 1580 stimulated great hopes among the imperialists of both countries and of their overseas possessions that they could by their combined efforts defeat and reduce to submission the stubborn Muslims of North Africa and the Indonesian archipelago.[143] Since some churchmen were among the staunchest advocates of military expansion, the papacy began to assess for itself what the new Iberian union foreshadowed for the future of Christendom. The Jesuit mission in Japan was flourishing, but Christian fortunes were still uncertain in other parts of Asia. The Jesuits at Macao were making friends slowly, but the mainland of China remained closed to them until 1583. In this same year, while Matteo Ricci established a

---

[139] *The Spanish Mandeville*, fol. 34. On Lusitano see below, pp. 430–31.

[140] *Ibid.*, fol. 15.

[141] See C. Sanz (ed.), *B. Escalante, Primera historia de China* (Madrid, 1958), pp. xxv–xxvii.

[142] For greater detail on Escalante's *Discurso* see *Asia*, I, 742–43, 746.

[143] See C. R. Boxer, "Portuguese and Spanish Projects for the Conquest of Southeast Asia," *Journal of Asian History*, III (1969), 118–36.

tenuous foothold in Kwangtung province, Pope Gregory XIII called upon Juan González de Mendoza, a Spanish Augustinian, to compose a "history of the things that are known about the kingdom of China."[144] Two years later, while the Japanese embassy toured in Italy, Mendoza's *Historia de las cosas mas notables, ritos y costumbres del gran Reyno de la China* was published at Rome. It was also issued at Valencia in 1585, the year of the Rome edition, and reprinted in Spanish eleven more times by the end of the century.

Mendoza, like Escalanate, compiled his book from the available written records and from personal interviews. He cites certain of his primary sources in the text, but neglects to acknowledge his heavy reliance upon the narratives of Barros and Escalante.[145] Indeed he appears to go out of his way to conceal the debt to Escalante.[146] Part I of Mendoza's book, which follows the basic outline of Escalante's, is a synthesis of what was then known in Europe about China. In form it departs abruptly from the chronicle-narrative of the Portuguese historians and Gomara. It is somewhat reminiscent of Book XX of Oviedo's history where he pauses in his chronicle of discovery to review what he knows about those parts of the East visited by Magellan and his immediate successors. In its organization and presentation Mendoza's popular description of China resembles more than anything else the ethnohistories of Mexico.[147] These works adopted as their formula the orderly discussion of geographical placement, history, customs, and religion of a particular country or region. In short, Escalante's and Mendoza's books are ethnohistories of China, the first of their kind on any Far Eastern nation and comparable to the works that were contemporaneously being produced on the Turks.[148] While the histories of the Turks helped to inspire interest in "Turqueries," it would be absurd to claim that Mendoza's book, for all its popularity, helped to produce at this time a vogue for "Chinoiseries." It did, however, become a major source for historians, social commentators, and a few writers of romances in Spain, Italy, and France.[149]

Considerable criticism of Mendoza was expressed by his contemporaries in Spain and elsewhere. He was charged with errors, exaggerations, and frivolities. Foreign readers were warned that his book was designed to extol without regard for the truth the achievements of the Iberian nations in Asia. Jerónimo Román, a fellow Augustinian, charged him with writing "as though he were some oracle."[150] Román's irritation with Mendoza was possibly inspired by personal disappointment. In 1575 Román had published a work called *Republicas*

[144] As quoted in *Asia*, I, 743.

[145] See *ibid.*, pp. 747, 750.

[146] For a detailed analysis of the relationships between the two texts, and for the charge that Mendoza falsified his documentation see J. D. Kendall, "Juan Gonzales de Mendoza and His *Historia de la China*: An Essay in Historical Bibliography" (M.A. thesis, University of Minnesota, 1965), pp. 84–86, 90–91. Also see *Asia*, I, 792–94.

[147] For a discussion of these sixteenth-century histories see Sánchez Alonso, *op. cit.* (n. 66), II, 134–53.

[148] See Mas, *op. cit.* (n. 39), I, 107–8.

[149] See above, pp. 182–83, and below, pp. 221–23.

[150] *Asia*, I, 792.

del mundo (Salamanca) which contained no material on the Far East. A second edition of this study was printed at Salamanca in 1594–95 which included treatises on the Tartars and China. Too often it is assumed, because of publication dates, that Román's account of China was written after Mendoza's. But this is not entirely clear, for the license to print his revised version is dated 1585, possibly indicating that Román had actually written the text of his final version before the appearance of Mendoza's book.[151] Whatever the case is, Román's discussion of China adds nothing new to what was already broadly available in print before 1595. His treatise on the Tartars, based on Marco Polo and other early writers, when placed in juxtaposition to his treatise on China, produces for Román a puzzling and insoluble source problem. While he believes that Cathay and China are probably the same place, he seems otherwise to be in a quandary as to how to reconcile and integrate the older sources with the new information on China.[152] In terms of its impact upon contemporaries, Román's book was much less influential than Mendoza's, perhaps because of its dated quality.

The Spanish Jesuits in their writings began to respond to the opening of Asia in various individual ways. Pedro de Ribadeneira in his biographies of Loyola (1583) and Xavier (1601) incorporates materials on the East culled from the Jesuit letters. José de Acosta (1540–1600), the Pliny of the New World, in his original and elegant *Historia natural y moral de las Indias* (Seville, 1590), is one of the first to sense the meaning for mankind of the circumnavigation of the world and the establishment of direct maritime contact between Mexico and the Far East. He precedes his description of the New World with a lengthy cosmographical discussion which examines the knowledge and opinions of the ancient biblical and medieval writers in the light of the new discoveries. From his personal experiences in America and Europe, and from his inquiries about the Far East, Acosta optimistically concludes that, no matter how vast the earth, it is still subject to man, "since with his feet he has measured it."[153] While his references to Asian geography and his discourse on religion in Japan are derived from the Jesuit letters, he does not hesitate to compare and contrast Asian and American religious beliefs and practices with each other and with Christianity and Islam. He consciously compares the pictographic languages of America and the Far East and comments on the limited character of scientific learning in China.[154] He was also of the opinion that the land of Ophir is to be found in the

---

[151] Suggestion of Swecker, *op. cit.* (n. 40), pp. 230–31. But also see F. Villarroel, "The Life and Works of Fray Jerónimo Román . . ." (M.A. thesis, University of London, 1957), pp. 230–33.

[152] For his sources see preface to Pt. III, *Repúblicas del mundo* (Salamanca, 1595). He explicitly cites Xavier's letters, Cruz, Escalante, Gomara, Hayton, Marco Polo, and Ramusio. His veiled allusion to Mendoza as an "oracle" also appears here. For commentary see C. R. Boxer (ed.), *South China in the Sixteenth Century* (London, 1953), pp. lxxxii–lxxxiii.

[153] See Francisco Mateos (ed.), *Obras del P. José de Acosta de la Compania de Jesus* (Madrid, 1954), p. 7. The first edition of the *Historia natural* was published in Latin in 1589. Cf. the declaration of Venegas in 1540 to the effect that the equatorial regions of the earth "in our time have been very adequately traversed by the feet of men." As quoted in Green, *op. cit.* (n. 18), II, 108.

[154] For detailed analysis see *Asia*, I, 806–8.

East Indies rather than in Peru.[155] But what is most significant about his natural and moral history is his willingness to put the Far East into the context of the westward expansion and thus to place it in a new historical setting.[156] Seen in this light, the geographical and ethnographical relations of the two Pacific regions become more apparent and in the process comparisons and contrasts emerge which set the stage for later speculation on cosmography and on the origins of the world and man.

While Acosta put the Far East into the westward conquest, his fellow Jesuit Juan de Mariana (1536?–1623?) brought overseas expansion into Spanish history. Mariana's was the first successfully unified and coordinated history of Spain. Written in narrative form, it begins with Tubal and ends with the year 1515. Mariana started working on his history no earlier than 1579; so most of it was written after the union of the two Iberian crowns in 1580. It was being readied for publication in 1586, but it did not appear at Toledo until 1592. The *Historia de rebus Hispaniae libri XXV* included, despite the title, just the first twenty books of Mariana's history. The others remained in manuscript for a time, possibly because publication funds ran out. The first Spanish translation appeared in two volumes as *Historia general del España* (Toledo, 1601). The earliest complete, revised edition in Latin appeared at Mainz in 1605, mute testimony to the fact that Mariana's book was more immediately popular outside of Spain than in it.[157]

Mariana states simply that he was impelled to undertake the preparation of his history because, while abroad, he perceived a widespread desire for knowledge of Spain and of the causes of its grandeur. His classical training and his intimacy with the medieval *Myriobiblon* (ninth century) and the encyclopedic writings of Isidore of Seville (*ca.* 560–636) had prepared him to undertake such a monumental task.[158] For his chapter on the New World he relied heavily on Gomara. Through his association with the Society of Jesus he was regularly kept informed on the progress of the missions in America and Asia. To bring Portugal and its Asian conquests to 1515 into his Spanish history, Mariana was initially dependent on the Latin history of Osório alone. Pablo Ferrer, a fellow Jesuit and a professor at the University of Évora, noted the thinness of his documentation on Portugal and its empire, and in a letter of June 17, 1598, Ferrer suggested that Mariana should also use the Latin writings and the *Chronicle* of King Manuel by Góis, as well as the histories of Castanheda and Barros.[159]

---

155 See L. Kilger, "Die Peru-Relation des José de Acosta und seine Missionstheorie," *Neue Zeitschrift für Missionswissenschaft*, I (1945), 24–38.

156 Cf. the definition of the "New World" as comprising all those places not known to the Ancients, including insular Asia. See above, p. 170, and below, pp. 456–57.

157 For a family tree of its complicated publication history see G. Cirot, *Mariana historien* (Paris, 1904), pp. 152, 452–69. The only compendium of Spanish history to appear in northern Europe before Mariana's was Robertus Belus (Robert Bell) *Rerum Hispaniarum* (2 vols.; Frankfurt, 1579).

158 See Cirot, *op. cit.* (n. 157), p. 305.

159 See *ibid.*, pp. 312–15.

In the final version of his history Mariana devotes three chapters to the voyages and exploits of the Portuguese in Asia based on Osório, Góis, Castanheda, and Barros.[160] While he concludes his general narrative with the year 1515, he runs on to comment on the discovery of Japan (1543) and the establishment of the Portuguese at Macao (*ca.* 1556).[161] He also has a chapter on the struggle between the Turks and the Portuguese for control of Diu,[162] and a review of Albuquerque's exploits in the East in a chapter inspired by the conqueror's death at the bar of Goa in 1515.[163] Another chapter describes the Portuguese embassy of 1514 to Rome by which the Eastern conquests were announced to the papacy.[164] In the chronology appended to the end of the book he records for the period after 1515 the treaty of Saragossa (1529), the sieges of Diu, the death in 1552 of Xavier off the coast of China, and the demise in 1580 of the Portuguese historians Osório and André de Resende.[165] Like his Portuguese sources, Mariana concentrates on the distances from place to place in the East, geographical relationships, the conditions of trade there, and a few observations on the progress of Christianity.

The first decade of the seventeenth century saw significant further additions to the Spanish documentation on Asia. In 1601 the Jesuit Luis de Guzman published his *Historia de las missiones* . . . (Alcalá de Henares), a comprehensive survey of the mission in the Far East, especially in Japan. Guzman's is one of the earliest vernacular mission histories, a genre introduced to historical writings in 1588 with Maffei's Latin history of the Jesuit endeavor in the East. It is also an ethnohistory of Japan comparable in scope to Mendoza's *China*.[166] Marcelo de Ribadeneira, a Franciscan, published at Barcelona in 1601 a polemical work on the progress and martyrdoms of the Franciscans in the Philippines, Japan, China, and continental Southeast Asia.[167] This was followed by Pedro Chirino's *Relación de las Filipinas* (Rome, 1604) which recounts the history of the Jesuits there. Antonio de Morga, a civil servant at Manila from 1595 to 1603, published at Mexico City in 1609 his *Suceos de las Islas Filipinas*, the first history by a layman of the Spanish progress in the Philippines.[168] Finally in 1609 there appeared at Madrid, the *Conquista de las islas Moluccas*, a substantial book which deals with the Spanish in both the Phillipines and the

[160] *Obras del Padre Juan de Mariana*, the "Biblioteca de autores españolas, Vol. XXXI (Madrid, 1872), II, 255–65.

[161] *Ibid.*, pp. 264–65.

[162] *Ibid.*, pp. 334–35.

[163] *Ibid.*, pp. 374–75.

[164] *Ibid.*, pp. 371–72.

[165] *Ibid.*, pp. 384, 386, 391, 402.

[166] For summary see *Asia*, I, 711–19.

[167] Entitled *Historia de las islas del archipielago Filipino y reinos de la Gran China, Tartaria, Cochin-China, Malaca, Siam, Cambodge y Japon.*

[168] See J. S. Cummins (trans. and ed.), *Antonio de Morga: Sucesos de las islas Filipinas*, "Publications of the Hakluyt Society," 2d ser. No. 140 (Cambridge, 1971). Also see C. R. Boxer, "Some Aspects of Spanish Historical Writings on the Philippines," in D. G. E. Hall (ed.), *Historians of South East Asia* (London, 1961), pp. 200–203, and W. E. Retana, "La literatura histórica de Filipinas de los siglos XVI y XVII," *Revue hispanique*, LX (1924), 293–300.

Moluccas.[169] The Spanish involvements in Asia were also incorporated into a world history celebrating the era (1559–98) of Philip II that was prepared by Antonio de Herrera y Tordesillas (1559–1625), the royal chronicler of Castile and the Indies. In his *Historia general del mundo . . .* (3 vols.; Madrid, 1599–1612), Herrera summarizes the Spanish conquest of the Philippines, the Portuguese position in the East, the Japanese embassy to Europe, and the progress of Christianity in Asia.[170]

In the thirty-five years separating the appearance of Escalante's *Discurso* (1577) and the final volume of Herrara's world history, the writers of Spanish prose provided readers with separate histories of China, Japan, the Philippines, and the Moluccas. They also furnished general histories of the missions to the East, two by Jesuits and one by a Franciscan. Most of the histories were geographically defined and were designed to inform the public about the conquests and missions of the Iberians in Asia. Only three histories, those of Escalante, Mendoza, and Guzman, were devoted in large measure to a description of the Asian setting. While the Spanish produced no epic comparable to the *Lusiads*, the Portuguese produced no ethnohistory to compete with Mendoza's. Cruz's history of China, based on his personal experiences supplemented by those of a few others, is not, like the Spanish histories, a critical synthesis in narrative form of the sources available in Europe. The national historians of Portugal neglected domestic history in their chronicles in favor of relating the history of discovery and conquest. Mariana's general Spanish history admitted the story of Portugal's conquest in the East and integrated it into the long history of Spain's rise to grandeur. The same can be said for Herrara's history of the world in the time of Philip II; it includes the conquests in the East as a significant feature of the worldwide accomplishments of the king.

The Spanish histories, unlike their Portuguese counterparts, were widely read in Europe at large. Even those which appeared only in Spanish were better known because Spanish was more generally read than Portuguese. In Spain itself the histories of the overseas world were appreciated as a new, informative, and entertaining form of literature. The historians of the New World and Asia wrote a vigorous prose that was diverting enough to produce an impression among the unsophisticated that they were reading romances of chivalry. Interest was also added to the natural histories by the comparisons in customs, thought, and beliefs that they explicitly expressed or that they implicitly invited. By the turn of the century a number of historians, both secular and clerical, had clearly become aware of the importance of Asia and hospitably accepted the treatment of it as a part of their general responsibility.

The infiltration of Asia into the Spanish consciousness came in spurts. Before 1520 a few court poets and chroniclers watched with curiosity and a degree of

---

[169] See Miguel Mir (ed.), *Conquista de las islas Malucas . . . escrita por el liceniado Bartolome Leonardo de Argensola,* "Bibliotheca de escritores aragoneses, Seccion literaria," VI (Saragossa, 1891).
[170] See II, 450–59; III, 712–17.

anxiety the progress of the Portuguese eastward. The circumnavigation of the globe, the subsequent voyages to the Moluccas, and the demarcation controversy stimulated interest in the geography of Asia, navigation of the Pacific, and the possibility of opening a new spice route through Panama. But such events were mainly of concern to technical writers: Enciso on geography, Oviedo on trade, and Medina on cosmography. The question of the Moluccas and the activities of the Spanish there also helped to inspire Oviedo and Gomara in their chronicles of discovery to extend their sights beyond America to the western Pacific region and to include materials in their histories on the Spiceries.

This initial burst of interest was abruptly stifled by disappointment and frustration over the pawning of Spain's claims to the Moluccas, the long delay in finding a route for the return across the Pacific to Mexico, and the divisions produced by the burgeoning controversy over the treatment and status of the Indians in America. In literary circles the concentration after 1525 upon assimilating Italian culture and adapting Spanish literature to its requirements had the effect of turning imaginative writers, especially poets, away from celebrating the national traditions and the conquests overseas. The new romances of chivalry that appeared before 1550 were printed by some of the same publishers who were responsible for translating and issuing Marco Polo, Mandeville, and other real and mythical voyages of times past. The reading public, always uncertain about the difference between mythical and real deeds of valor and adventure, confused romance with history, much to the dismay of serious chroniclers like Oviedo. Both the church and the state inveighed against the romances of chivalry as a threat to public morals. While discouraging the fictional romances, the moralists might have unwittingly delayed the creative responses to the exciting and real conquests overseas.

The latter half of the sixteenth century was marked by a series of new reactions to the expansion abroad. The Inquisition and the secular authorities imposed tighter controls over the reading, publication, and importation of books. These controls probably checked the search for new chivalric themes and encouraged the composition of rhymed chronicles, moralistic-heroic poems, and a less fanciful literature. The extension of the Spanish empire into the Philippines after 1565, followed by Philip's assumption of the Portuguese crown in 1580, awakened a new interest in the national enterprise overseas and in Asia. The writers of "curious histories," like Torquemada, brought stories from Asia into their productions to give a broad public a glimpse of new oddities. The revival of national pride had the effect in serious literature of turning the brightest young lights, like Gongora and Lope, away from Petrarchan imitations to a revival of traditional poetic metres and forms. In the process the poets of the 1580's began to bring Asia into their verses in celebration of the achievements of the king and the nation.

The romance of chivalry itself underwent a change in these years. The old themes were refurbished to make them more realistic, moralistic, credible, and acceptable to a public that was constantly being stimulated by real victories over ancient foes and by conquests in new lands. The *Angélica* of Barahona de Soto exemplifies the effort to produce new harmonies on an old theme. He not only changed the character of Angelica herself; he also transformed the world in which she ventured forth from a mythical Cathay to a realistic Asia. In his effort to transform the setting he drew heavily upon the verses of the *Lusiads*, the chronicle-narrative of Castanheda, and the ethnohistory of Mendoza. Lope de Vega followed suit in his *Angélica* by modeling his presentation in some ways on Barahona's romance. Both poets, like the Portuguese poets of the *Cancioneiro geral*, veneered their verses with geographical and other new terms associated with Asia to make them bright with authority, glossy with exoticism, and resonant with sonority.

Historical dimensions and forms were also changed in deference to the appearance on the spatial horizon of new lands, peoples, and cultures. The vigorous, comprehensive, and straightforward chronicle-narratives of the type written by Oviedo and Gomara gave way to special histories—or ethno-histories—of individual places in America and Asia. In the preparation of both histories and romances the Spanish writers of the last generation of the century unhesitatingly borrowed from the Portuguese: Escalante from Cruz, Mendoza from Barros, Barahona de Soto from Camoëns and Castanheda, Mariana from Osório, Lope from Camoëns.[171] The vernacular histories of foreign missions, following the lead of Maffei's Latin *Historia* (1588), likewise became a new genre with the publication in 1601 of Guzman's work. In the Spanish histories, because of Spain's involvement in both Asia and America, the materials for comparative study of customs and beliefs were especially abundant. Spain's general historians, like its writers of romances, were quick to accept the *reality* of Asia as they incorporated it painlessly into the history of Spain and its world empire.

[171] Lope might also have used the *Tractado* . . . (Burgos, 1578) of Cristobal de Acosta, which was based on the *Coloquios* . . . (Goa, 1563) of Garcia da Orta. See *Asia*, I, 192–95, and below, pp. 433–37.

CHAPTER VI

Italian Literature

Long before the discovery of the sea route to India, the eastern ports of Italy from Venice in the north to Catania in the south were involved in trade and intercourse with the Levant. Italian merchants and friars had taken advantage of the era of "Mongol peace" in the thirteenth and fourteenth centuries to venture eastward across Asia by overland and maritime routes. The Venetians especially, following the return of Marco Polo in 1295, were eager to capture and retain control over the lucrative Eastern trade. While its patricians collected precious stones, exotic plants, and Oriental rugs, the merchants and scholars of Venice sought to acquire information on the trade routes, geography, and customs of the East. Even after the Portuguese began to threaten its supremacy in Eastern trade, Venice and its satellites retained more interest in Asia than most of the other Italian cities. The Florentines, who were permitted by the Portuguese to participate directly in the spice trade in India and at Lisbon and Antwerp, only slowly began to challenge the Venetians in the sixteenth century as connoisseurs of Eastern products and as purveyors of information about Asia.

From Portugal the Italians had nothing to fear except the competition for Eastern trade. The greatest external threat to Italian independence came from France, the Empire, and Spain. The invasions and meddlings of the great powers, particularly after 1494, produced political instability, war and pillage, and a growing sense of both physical ineffectiveness and intellectual despair. From the international struggle for control of Italy the Habsburgs of Spain emerged victorious. Naples became a viceroyalty of Spain in 1503; Milan was reclaimed as an imperial fief in 1535 and was ruled by a Spanish governor after 1540. Florence, Genoa, and the papacy along with their satellites were increasingly subjected to Spanish influence and control. Venice alone was able with its powerful navy to remain relatively free of the overwhelming strength of Spain.

The Spanish political presence in Italy helped to weld close intellectual and literary ties. Italians who went to Spain as emissaries of Florence, Venice, and the papacy were sometimes leading intellectuals or courtiers with close connections to the arbiters of literature and thought. Through Spain the Italians went into Portugal and even to Asia. More than thirty Italians actually traveled in the East over the course of the sixteenth century; fourteen of them were Florentines who worked with the Portuguese.[1] Italian missionaries, like Valignano and Ricci, gradually assumed positions of primacy in the Jesuit mission in Asia with the concurrence and cooperation of the Portuguese and Spanish crowns. Literature in Spanish was regularly published in Italy, and many Iberian works, including parts of the chronicle-narratives of Barros and Castanheda were translated into Italian and published at Venice.[2]

Once the battle of Lepanto (1571) had freed the western Mediterranean from the threat of Turkish expansion, the political and military ties between Venice and Spain became tighter. For Venice this was a particularly welcome development after the Turks captured Cyprus (1571) and consolidated their control over the eastern Mediterranean. Philip II's assumption of the Portuguese crown in 1580 enabled him to solidify his political control over the entire area from Lisbon to Milan, and to reinforce Spanish influence in northeastern Italy. Although the fortunes of Philip suffered setbacks in northern Europe during the last two decades of his reign, he was able to die (1598) secure in the thought that Spain retained its preponderance in Italy.

I

REALISM IN ROMANTIC POETRY

Curiosity and disquietude about the spice trade of Portugal were felt earliest in the cities of the Venetian mainland (*Veneto*). Ferrara, Padua, Mantua, Verona, Bologna, and Vicenza, like Venice itself, had watched the steady growth of Levantine commerce in the fifteenth century and had profited indirectly from it. The fear that this trade would cease and pass permanently into the hands of the Portuguese inspired the Venetian government and its neighbors to dispatch commercial agents and spies to Iberia to determine what the prospects were for Portugal to retain control over the traffic in spices.[3] Iberian intellectuals, who

---

[1] Of the thirty-one I have counted, only five came from Venice and they were not officially associated with the Portuguese.

[2] See O. H. Green, *Spain and the Western Tradition* (4 vols.; Madison, Wis., 1966), III, 55 n. 8. At Venice alone during the second half of the century 71 works were published in Spanish, and there were 724 translations from the Spanish.

[3] For details see *Asia*, I, 104–7.

had long been going to Bologna and Padua for university training, also helped to keep northeastern Italy abreast of events taking place in the overseas world.[4] But it was their own informants in Iberia who were most trusted by the princes of the lower Po Valley and the Veneto.

Like the Venetian commercial agents, the Florentines in Iberia kept their compatriots informed on the economic details of the spice trade and on the routes to India.[5] Materials on the discoveries were collected by Amerigo Vespucci, the Florentine merchant-pilot and explorer who participated at the beginning of the century in the overseas enterprises originating at Seville and Lisbon.[6] A collection of first-hand accounts of the discoveries was also made at Vicenza by Francanzano da Montalboddo, a teacher of literature, who published them in 1507 under the title, *Paesi novamente ritrovati . . .*; in the next year this book was translated and published at Milan as *Itinerarium Portugalensium . . .*, a work that was to become popular throughout western Europe during the sixteenth century.[7] Jacobo Cavicio's *Libro del peregrino* (Parma, 1508), a popular romance dedicated to Lucrezia Borgia, likewise remarks on activities at Lisbon. The most authoritative and influential account of the Portuguese East to appear in print during the first half of the sixteenth century, the *Itinerario* of Ludovico de Varthema, was first published at Rome in 1510.[8] Through these works the first decade of the sixteenth century provided a relatively reliable and comprehensive documentation in Italian and Latin of the Portuguese spice trade in both Europe and India. What is more, the *Paesi* and the *Itinerario* were two of the most popular travel books to appear anywhere throughout the century. As mute testimony to the high regard accorded Varthema's book, there remains extant the calligraphic copy prepared in 1510 by the famous copyist Ludovico degli Arrighi as a special gift for Vittoria Colonna (1490–1549), the young wife of the Marquis of Pescara and later one of Italy's leading creative writers and savants.[9]

Italy's learned and artistic community had its eyes riveted on Rome in 1513 with the accession of Leo X, the urbane Medici pope. The arrival there in March, 1514, of the Portuguese embassy of obedience was welcomed by Leo's convivial court as another occasion for revelry.[10] The courtiers, both the serious and the frivolous, were fascinated by the exotic gifts, especially the "elephant-diplomat."

[4] See above, pp. 8–10.

[5] See above, p. 27, on Guicciardini and other Florentines in Iberia.

[6] See German Arcinegas, *Amerigo and the New World* (New York, 1955), chaps. xiii–xx.

[7] See *Asia*, I, 163–64, and above, p. 76.

[8] For bibliographical details see *Asia*, I, 164–65, and below, p. 332. Among later eminents who used Varthema as a source were the geographers Ortelius, Mercator, and Livio Sanuto. Varthema was probably also consulted by Barros, Castanheda, and Góis for his descriptions of early Portuguese sieges and battles in India. See Paolo Giudici (ed.), *Itinerario di Ludovico di Varthema* (Milan, 1928), pp. 63–65.

[9] The original calligraphic copy is in the National Library at Florence (Landa Finaly 9). See E. Casamassima, "Ludovico degli Arrighi . . . copista dell' 'Itinerario' del Varthema," *La bibliofilia*, LXIV (1962), 122, 136.

[10] See *Asia*, II, Bk. 1, 136–39.

The populace was treated along with the courtiers to exhibitions of the elephant, to displays of the valuable gifts, to receptions, speeches, feasts, and to dramatic spectacles praising the Portuguese for their conquests in the distant world east of India.[11] The bacchanalian revels of 1514, in which Isabella d'Este participated with so much gusto,[12] became the talk of Italy. The elephant, who was paraded about on these occasions, became a symbol of merrymaking as well as an exemplar of wisdom.

The rhyme smiths of the papal court celebrated the elephant in both Latin and Italian verse. Aurelio Sereno wrote verses on the elephant and collected the poems of others. These he published in his *Theatrum capitolium . . .* (Rome, 1514).[13] In his dedication to Leo X, Sereno recalls:

Early in the spring [i.e. March], when the earth is becloaked with variegated flowers which dispense everywhere their sweetest fragrances, Manuel, Most Serene King of the Portuguese sent you by Tristão da Cunha, his noble cavalier and emissary, the most sagacious of all the animals, the elephant![14]

In the poems themselves the elephant is lauded in orthodox classical terms with almost no recognition of the beast itself or of the land from which it came.[15] Many more direct references to the triumphs of the Portuguese can be found in the Latin verses praising the Portuguese orator Diogo Pacheco and in the Italian poems.[16] Other Italian commentators, like the Spanish and Portuguese moralists, were critical of the greed and rapine associated with the discoveries. Machiavelli has *The Golden Ass* (*ca.* 1517) complain: "You arc not content with one food only, as we are, but better to fulfill your greedy desires, you journey for such things [spices] to the kingdoms of the East."[17]

The return of the "Victoria," one of Magellan's ships, with Antonio Pigafetta of Vicenza aboard, provided a new focus of interest for Italian intellectuals.[18] The dispatches of Antonio Bagarotto, Mantua's emissary in Valladolid, included summaries of the "Victoria's" trials and successes. These were directed to Isabella d'Este Gonzaga by then the Marquesa of Mantua.[19] The authorities in Venice meanwhile decided to send emissaries to the court of Charles V to

---

[11] For the *Comedia* of Torres Naharro see above, pp. 166–68.

[12] See A. Luzio, *Isabella d'Este nei primordi del papato di Leone X e il suo viaggio a Roma nel 1514–1515* (Milan, 1906), p. 41.

[13] For full bibliographical information see G. Mercati, "Un indice de libri offerti a Leone X," *Il libro e la stampa*, n.s. II (1908), 43.

[14] Translated from the quotation given in L. Matos, "Natura, intelleto, e costumi dell' elefanta," *Boletim internacional de bibliografia Luso-Brasileira*, I (1960), 46.

[15] For the Latin text of some of the elephant poems see W. Roscoe, *The Life and Pontificate of Leo X* (4 vols.; London, 1805–1827), II, App. C, 103–5. Also see Filippo Beroaldo, *Carminum* (Rome, 1530).

[16] For example, *La victoria de lo serenissimo ed invictissimo Emanuele Re de Portugallo . . .* (Rome, 1515). Commentary in Matos, *loc. cit.* (n. 14), p. 47.

[17] See Allan Gilbert (trans.), *Machiavelli: The Chief Works and Others* (3 vols.; Durham, N.C., 1965), II, 771–72.

[18] For Pigafetta see *Asia*, I, 173–76.

[19] See G. Berchet (ed.), "*Fonti italiani per la storia della scoperta del nuovo mundo.*" In *Raccolta di documenti e studi publicati della R. Commissione Colombiana . . .* Pt. III, Vol. I, pp. 172–73. Rome, 1892.

evaluate the meaning of the circumnavigation for the future of the spice trade. Early in 1523 Pigafetta himself returned to Italy and was graciously received at Mantua by Isabella. She urged him to go home to Vicenza and write of his experiences. There he composed his narrative intermittently, a labor interrupted by his appearances before the Signoria of Venice (November 7, 1523) and before the pope in Rome (spring, 1524). When he completed his manuscript in 1524, he could not find the means to publish it. Epitomized versions of it were circulated, and an extract was published in Ramusio's *Navigationi* in 1554, including a sampling from the Malay vocabulary.[20]

While Pigafetta was writing at Vicenza, the Venetian emissaries to Charles V were on their way to Spain. The legate, Andrea Navagero, one of the humanistic luminaries of Venice and Padua, was made responsible for relaying to his colleagues at home whatever information he could gather on overseas activities. At Toledo he renewed his acquaintance with Oviedo, who studied in Italy from 1498 to 1502 and again at a later date, and who was first sent to the New World in 1514 as a Spanish official. Navagero translated Oviedo's *Sumario* (1525) into Italian and sent a copy to his circle of friends at Padua.[21] Like Oviedo, Navagero was an avid naturalist, and his villa with its garden on the island of Murano was a showplace in its day. In Spain he collected information about the overseas plants and animals arriving there and dispatched samples and descriptions of them to Pietro Bembo and Ramusio, two of his closest friends.

Navagero died without returning home, but his dispatches as well as his garden were of interest and value to his remarkable associates. His reports on the bird of paradise, on potatoes and bananas, as well as other odd bits and pieces of information garnered from Peter Martyr, Oviedo, and others, titillated the curiosity of his friends.[22] Bembo, Ramusio, Fracastoro, Giacomo Gastaldi, and U. Aldrovandi carried on a correspondence with Oviedo and among themselves on subjects arising from the overseas discoveries. Bembo's interests were historical, Ramusio's geographical, Gastaldi's cartographical, Aldrovandi's biological, and Fracastoro's medical.[23] In his Venetian history Bembo introduced at the beginning of Book VI a resumé of the Iberian discoveries based on information sent him by Oviedo and Navagero.[24] The renowned maps of

[20] See below, pp. 492–93. For a history of the *Navigationi* and its compilation see *Asia*, I, 204–8.

[21] See above, pp. 171–72. Also note that in 1530 Navagero's brothers applied for a copyright in Venice. Ultimately his translation was published in 1534 as the second book in the *Summario della historia delle Indie Occidentali*, probably printed by Nicolo Zoppino. See H. F. Brown, *The Venetian Printing Press* (London, 1896), p. 103.

[22] See M. Cermenati, "Un diplomatico naturalista del Rinascimento Andrea Navagero," *Nuovo archivio veneto*, N.S. XXIV (1912), 200–201; and Georgina Masson, *Italian Gardens* (New York, 1961), pp. 202–3. Also see below, pp. 428–31, and pl. 43.

[23] On their "encyclopedic interests" see S. Grande, *Le relazioni geografiche fra P. Bembo, G. Fracastoro, G. B. Ramusio, G. Gastaldi* (Rome, 1906), pp. 5–18. This is a reprint extracted from *Memorie della Società italiana*, Vol. XII (1905).

[24] *Della historia viniziana de Monsignor M. Pietro Bembo, volgarmente scritta* (Venice, 1552), pp. 72–74. Also see C. Lagomaggiore, "L'Istoria viniziana di M. Pietro Bembo," *Nuovo archivio veneto*, 3d ser., IX (1905), 40–43.

Gastaldi and the celebrated *Navigationi* (1550–56) of Ramusio, though they appeared at mid-century, owe a substantial debt to these early gropings for information. The same can be said with regard to Aldrovandi's elaborate books and collections of plants and animals.[25]

The initial responses of this learned group is best illustrated by the career and writings of Girolamo Fracastoro (*ca.* 1483–1553), a philosophical encyclopedist and poet. Like Navagero and Ramusio, Fracastoro studied philosophy at Padua under Pietro Pomponazzi (1462–1525), the eminent Aristotelian who stressed the importance of observation and experiment in the study of the natural world. Fracastoro himself wrote tracts in Latin on plants, animals, and minerals that were based largely on his own observations. He was profoundly interested in the relations between the terrestrial and celestial spheres and between the natural world and man. In his *Homocentricorum* (Venice, 1538) he attacked Ptolemy's conception of the universe and pointed up his inadequate geographical understanding. He also followed the voyages of discovery, placing the new lands on his wooden maps of the world. In Latin poems and personal letters he expressed a fierce pride in the accomplishments of the men of his own age in conquering the seas and discovering new lands.[26] His principal book, *Syphilis, sive de morbo Gallico* (Verona, 1530), denies in verse the New World origins of syphilis, a connection that was commonly accepted in his day since the appearance of the disease in Europe coincided with the discovery of America. He includes verses in this work on Columbus, the American Indians, and the Spiceries located

> Midst farthest Ind, where Ganges rolls his floods,
> And Ebon forests wave and spicy woods.[27]

That Fracastoro and his colleagues had been obliged to obtain their recent information on the geographical discoveries directly from sources in Iberia is best illustrated by reference to the curiously antiquated *Libro di Benedetto Bordone nel qual si ragiona de tutte l'Isole del mondo . . .* (Venice, 1528). Bordone (*ca.* 1450–1530) was a native of Padua who spent the last thirty years of his life in Venice, where he enjoyed a modest reputation as miniaturist, sketcher, geographer, and publisher of classics. His little book on the islands of the world, their ancient and modern names, history, fables, and modes of life is interesting as an early example of geographical specialization and of the romantic allure of islands.[28]

---

[25] See M. Cermenati, *U. Aldrovandi e l'America* (Rome, 1906), pp. 18–19. Also see below, pp. 438–39.

[26] See E. di Leo, *Scienza e umanesimo in Girolamo Fracastoro* (Salerno, 1937), pp. 40, 71–75. A similar attitude is expressed by Celio Calcagnini, the astronomer-poet of Ferrara, in his "De re nautica" in *Opera aliquot* (Basel, 1544), p. 305.

[27] As translated in Roscoe, *op. cit.* (n. 15), II, 159–60.

[28] "Insular romanticism," an attitude which associated distant islands in unexplored seas with mysteries, fables, and marvels, characterized imaginative writings of the Renaissance as well as many other works purporting to be more realistic. For discussion see L. Olschki, *Storia letteraria delle scoperte geografiche* (Florence, 1937), pp. 39–41. Also see pl. 5.

Published in 1521 [29] with the approval of Pope Leo X and of the Signoria of Venice, Bordone's materials on the islands of the Eastern seas (pp. 67–73) were derived entirely from pre-discovery works. He displays no knowledge of Pigafetta's account, even though Pigafetta had related his story before the doge in 1524. Bordone's sources are Marco Polo, Odoric of Pordenone, and Mandeville. No wonder that at the end of his work he anticipates incredulity on the part of the "philosophers." These Humanists working in his own neighborhood were certainly far better informed than he on the most recent islands discovered. But his book was reprinted at Venice in 1534 and 1547.

The Italian city most closely associated with geographical learning was Ferrara, the seat of the Este family from the thirteenth century to 1598. At their brilliant court the arts flourished, for the Este princes took a deep personal interest in secular learning. From the extant inventories of their book collections it is clear that Ferrara's quattrocento princes possessed an abiding interest in classical geographies and histories as well as in medieval travel books and cosmographies.[30] Ercole I (reigned 1471–1505) was married to the Neapolitan princess Eleanor of Aragon, an alliance which also helped to keep the Estes abreast of the overseas activities of the Iberians. The inventory of Ercole's library indicates that he collected books and maps which recorded the Iberian discoveries. Isabella (1479–1539), the daughter of Ercole and Eleanor, associated herself with the court at Rome, where interest in Spanish literature and overseas activity deepened in the last decades of the fifteenth century. She continued to learn about the discoveries as soon as they happened, even after she married Francisco Gonzaga and became Marquesa of Mantua. In 1505 she commissioned a copy of a world map housed in the pope's library which showed the new places discovered by the Iberians.[31] She also encouraged Pigafetta to write down in detail the record of his experiences with Magellan's fleet.[32]

During Isabella's early years at Ferrara, one of her father's courtiers was Matteo Maria Boiardo (*ca.* 1434–94), the count of Scandiano and author of the *Orlando innamorato*. This long romantic poem, which Boiardo left unfinished, was based on the medieval French epic recounting the adventures of Roland, a model chivalric hero. In the hands of Boiardo and his predecessors the French hero was transformed over the course of the fifteenth century from a virtuous, chaste, and pious knight into the lover of a pagan queen. Materials from the

[29] The pope's brief was issued before the return of the "Victoria," an indication that Bordone's book may have been written, though not published, before Pigafetta had returned to Italy with his news of many "islands" not heretofore known. But there were other unpublished manuscripts available in Italy before 1521. For example, Pietro di Dino, a Florentine, wrote from Cochin in 1519 a *Relazione dei suoi viaggi nelle Costi dell' Africa e dell' India* which exists in manuscript in the National Library at Florence. See P. Peregallo, *Cenni intorna alla colonia italiana in Portogallo . . .* (Genoa, 1907), p. 144.

[30] See G. Bertoni, *La biblioteca Estense e la coltura ferrarese ai tempi del duca Ercole I (1471–1505)* (Turin, 1903), pp. 18–19, 213–52. For an analysis of these collections see above, pp. 48–50.

[31] See A. Luzio and R. Renier, "La coltura e le relazioni letterarie di Isabella d'Este Gonzaga," *Giornale storico della letteratura italiana*, XXXIII (1899), 37–38.

[32] See above, p. 50, and below, p. 452.

chansons de geste and *fabliaux* were attached to individualistic heroes comparable to those associated with personalities in the English cycle of King Arthur stories.[33] In addition to secularizing and individualizing the French hero, Boiardo introduced new characters and themes drawn from various sources, including his own fertile imagination.[34] The poem itself, like the *Decameron*, embodies a series of stories for entertaining reading.[35] As his frame Boiardo uses the wars of the Saracens against Charlemagne. The wars are interrupted by fables, adventures, and romantic interludes drawn from a host of sources.

Nothing is known about Boiardo's personal library. But he certainly had access to the Este collections. Even though the inventories are not always complete and the descriptions of books not always clear, the Ferrara collections certainly included a wealth of French romances, Arthurian legends, Alexander romances, the cycle of the *Seven Wise Masters*, and the medieval travels of Marco Polo and Mandeville. It remains difficult nonetheless to identify with precision the sources that Boiardo actually used in the preparation of his marvelous romance, for he was more imaginative than imitative. Still, it is clear that he presupposed his audience to be familiar with the stories about India from the Alexander romance that had long been sung or recited in the public squares of Italy.[36] This conclusion is supported by the fact that no fewer than six Alexander books were published in Italy between 1472 and 1502.[37] Boiardo also seems to have assumed the existence of a general knowledge of the "Cathay" and the "Tartars" popularized by Marco Polo and Mandeville.[38]

In the French courtly romances and in their early Italian adaptations, the Orient was used as the setting for marvels and as an imaginative refuge from the realities of a European life regimented by feudal and ecclesiastical obligations.[39] This vague Orient of the traditional romances became more explicit in Boiardo's *Orlando*. He invented the character of Angelica, princess of Cathay, and a number of other Oriental personages associated with her.[40] He replaced the Saracens with the Tartars as the inveterate enemies of the Christians. Most notable were Agrican, emperor of the Tartars, and his son Mandricardo, a courageous and ruthless knight. He also invented Angelica's father and brother

---

[33] See H. Hauvette, *L'Arioste et la poésie chevalresque à Ferrara au début du XVIᵉ siècle* (Paris, 1927), pp. 60–64; also C. Searles, "The Leodilla Episode in Bojardo's *Orlando Innamorato*," *Modern Language Notes*, XVII (1902), 328–42, 406–11.

[34] See G. Reichenbach, *L'Orlando innamorato di M. M. Boiardo* (Florence, 1936), pp. 12–15, 64–65, 84–85.

[35] On Boccaccio see above, p. 112.

[36] See C. Searles, "Some Notes on Boiardo's Version of the Alexandersagas," *Modern Language Notes*, XV (1900), 58.

[37] See above, p. 98.

[38] Cf. R. A. Pettinelli, "Di alcune fonti del Boiardo," in G. Anceschi (ed.), *Il Boiardo e la critica contemporanea* (Florence, 1970), p. 7.

[39] See R. R. Bezzola, "L'Oriente nel poema cavalleresco del primo Rinascimento," *Lettere italiane*, XV (1963), 387–91, 396–97.

[40] For a detailed list of Boiardo's Asian characters see H. Y. K. Tom, "The Wonderful Voyage: Chivalric and Moral Asia in the Imagination of Sixteenth-Century Italy, Spain, and Portugal" (Ph.D. diss., University of Chicago, 1975), pp. 21–22.

as well as Gradasso, the pagan king of Sericana. In the epithets applied to these characters, as well as in individual references within the poem, Boiardo clearly shows that he distinguished the traditional divisions of Asia into Tartary, Serica, Cathay, and India, and that he presupposes a similar geographical knowledge on the part of his audience. The pagan world that he creates is a real place that is still sufficiently unknown for it to remain the scene of imaginary chivalric deeds. A distinction is made by the poet between the known Orient and the "Isola Lontana," a totally imaginary place of tranquillity and repose. His Oriental characters are people of flesh and blood, in every way similar to their European counterparts. Europeans and Orientals alike move freely from one side of the Eurasiatic continent to the other, apparently without difficulty. They seem to speak various languages and to share many values.[41] They are distinguished from each other mainly by their Christian or pagan beliefs.

Angelica is a central figure in Boiardo's poem.[42] She is the most beautiful of women, a sorceress whose charm and magic are irresistible. Being a pagan princess, she has no need to exhibit Christian virtue. She is free to be an immoral adventuress who takes advantage of her beauty to tempt and betray Christian knights, to titillate the elderly Charlemagne, and to conquer the chaste heart of Orlando. She spirits an unwilling Rinaldo away to Cathay to her sumptuous Oriental palace where she tempts him unavailingly with lavish hospitality. For love of her, Orlando slays Agrican, the fierce Tartar king, and delivers from siege the city of Albracca, capital of Cathay. Angelica turns Rinaldo and Orlando against each other, and the Christian knights fight for the favors of the pagan queen. Tartars and Christians alike fall prey to her wiles, testimony to the belief that all men are equal in their inability to resist a beautiful and unscrupulous woman. Boiardo left unfinished the delineation of Angelica in his uncompleted poem. Later writers were thus given an opportunity to produce their own Angelicas and to alter her character to satisfy their own moralistic or literary ends.[43]

The task of completing Boiardo's *Orlando* was first undertaken by Lodovico Ariosto (1474–1533). When Ariosto arrived at Ferrara in 1486, Boiardo was in the process of publishing what he had so far written of his work. The young Ariosto commenced his stay in Ferrara by taking up the study of law and the humanities; soon he also became proficient in writing Latin and Italian verse. From 1495 to 1503 he was on friendly terms with Bembo, then resident at the Este court. He became secretary in 1503 to the Cardinal Ippolito d'Este and two years later began to write the *Orlando furioso*. The first edition of Ariosto's version of the Orlando story appeared in 1516 and was followed five years later by a second revised edition. The definitive edition to which five new cantos were added appeared in 1532, the year before Ariosto's death. In the eyes of

---

[41] Orlando in Ariosto's words was said to be well versed in many languages, especially Arabic. See below, p. 53.

[42] See Hauvette, *op. cit.* (n. 33), p. 308.

[43] See above, pp. 179–85, for the Angelica theme in Spanish literature.

contemporaries the *Orlando* of Ariosto, technically a continuation of Boiardo's poem, was a new masterpiece glorifying the achievements of the Este family. The *Orlando furioso* quickly became the subject of literary debate and criticism in Italy and abroad, was translated in the course of the sixteenth century into many vernaculars, and provided inspiration to numerous imitators and continuators.

Ariosto, unlike Boiardo, was faithful to his sources.[44] From close examination of the text it has been possible to locate with surprising precision the inspirations of many of his tales and motifs. His personal inventions are few; his artistry emerges from the manner in which he uses and embellishes the sources.[45] The *Orlando* of Boiardo was the model for his theme, locale, and characters. Ideas merely suggested by Boiardo he amplifies with more specific references, which permit easy identification of his ultimate sources. To the Eastern materials used by Boiardo for stories and motifs, Ariosto adds other tales, particularly those dealing with the infidelity of women—from the *Thousand and One Nights*, *Panchatantra* and *Mahābhārata*.[46] The specificity of his detail makes it possible to show that in his thought and poetry Ariosto was constantly widening his view of the world from information on the overseas discoveries which became available to him during the writing of his work from 1505 to 1532.

Ariosto, like his predecessors Boccaccio and Andrea de' Magnabotti,[47] followed his geographical sources with fidelity. His conception of Asia shows clearly that for geographical information he probably drew on the Ptolemy with maps, the *Natural History* of Pliny, and Marco Polo, or some maps based on the Polo account, all in the library of Borso d'Este. He follows the traditional authors in identifying the Nile as the boundary between Asia and Africa, and the Don as the frontier between Europe and Asia. Like the medieval writers, he makes Cathay a part of India and does not fully comprehend the peninsular configuration of the subcontinent.[48] To the east of Cathay lies the island of Alcina (VI, 43), a place of delight which was almost certainly inspired by Polo's description of Zipangu (Japan).[49]

Ariosto's basic conception of the East derived from medieval sources was augmented by new information that seeped into Ferrara. Late in 1502, Alberto Cantino, the secret emissary of the Estes in Lisbon, sent to Ferrara a planisphere

[44] The most comprehensive examination of his sources is still P. Rajna, *Le fonti dell' Orlando Furioso* (2d rev. ed.; Florence, 1900). For further commentary see R. Barilli, "Il Boiardo e l'Ariosto nel giudizio del Rajna," in G. Anceschi (ed.), *Il Boiardo e la critica contemporanea* (Florence, 1970), pp. 61–72.

[45] See Hauvette, *op. cit.* (n. 33), p. 214.

[46] For details see F. L. Pullé, "Originali indiani della novella Ariostea nel XXVIII canto del *Furioso*," *Giornale della società asiatica italiana*, IV (1890), 129–64; and P. E. Pavolini, "Di alcuni altri paralleli orientali alla novella del Canto XXVIII del *Furioso*," *ibid.*, XI (1897–98), 165–73. Also see for comparative passages E. Lévêque, *Les mythes et les legendes de l'Inde et de la Perse dans Aristophane, Platon ... Arioste, Rabelais, etc.* (Paris, 1880), pp. 531–42.

[47] See above, pp. 114–15.

[48] See A. Strauch, *Die Kosmographie in Ariosts Orlando Furioso* (Bonn, 1921), pp. 8, 22, 36; also M. Vernero, *Studi critici sopra la geografia nell' Orlando Furioso* (Turin, 1913), p. 129.

[49] Simone Fornari, a Florentine literary critic, so concluded already in 1549. See S. Fornari, *La spositione sopra l'Orlando Furioso di M. Lodovico Ariosto* (2 vols.; Florence, 1549), I, 197–98. Also see *Asia*, I, 652–53 and pl. 58.

on which all the latest discoveries were recorded. This map, at present in the Bibliotheca Estense of Modena, was probably commissioned by Cantino from a Portuguese cartographer who had access to the official *padrão* (world map) kept in Lisbon. Cambay and Calicut are placed on the Indian peninsula, and the legends on India and the East Indies indicate what is known about the products of particular places.[50] This planisphere, and a copy of the map acquired by Isabella in 1505 from the papal library, may well have been available for Ariosto to consult when he started to write the *Orlando furioso*. Although Ariosto never traveled much himself, he was mentally moved by the new knowledge garnered for him by others:

> The traveler, he whom sea or mountain sunder
> From his own country, sees things strange and new;
> The misjudging vulgar, which lies under
> The mist of ignorance, esteems untrue:
> Rejecting whatsoever is a wonder,
> Unless 'tis palpable and plain to view:
> Hence inexperience, as I know full well,
> Will yield small credence to that tale I tell.[51]

Mandeville had confidently and graphically asserted that it was possible and practical for men to sail around the earth in either a westward or eastward direction and return home safely.[52] Ariosto appears to have read about Magellan's expedition, possibly in the version of Pigafetta.[53] Both Boiardo and Ariosto sent a number of their characters on world tours. In Ariosto's work Ruggiero, Astolfo, and Angelica are especially tireless as travelers. The itinerary of the voyage of Ruggiero on the hippogriff starts in Iberia and crosses the Atlantic to Alcina (Japan), then over Cathay, and back to Europe.[54] Ariosto makes no mention of America in describing this flying tour, perhaps because he did not distinguish between Asia and America.[55] On his first voyage Astolfo, an Englishman like Mandeville, returns to Europe from Alcina by sailing southward along the China coast and then westward around Malacca and Taprobane to a port (probably Ormuz) in the Persian Gulf. From there he proceeds overland to the Red Sea, Egypt, the Levant, and Europe. Such itineraries, limited as they are, indicate that Ariosto knew the major routes traditionally followed in the overland and maritime trade between Asia and Europe and possessed specific knowledge about Southeast Asia derived from contemporaries.

[50] See A. Cortesão and A. Teixeira da Mota, *Portugaliae monumenta cartographica* (5 vols.; Lisbon, 1960–62), I, 7–9; also see below, p. 451.

[51] As translated in S. A. Baker and A. B. Giamatti (eds.), *Ludovico Ariosto, Orlando Furioso, Translated by William Stewart Rose* (Indianapolis, Ind., 1968), Canto VII, verse 1, p. 54.

[52] See J. W. Bennett, *The Rediscovery of Sir John Mandeville* (New York, 1954), pp. 232, 235.

[53] Suggestion of G. Mazzoni, "Ludovico Ariosto e Magellano," *L'Ape* (Ferrara), Nos. 3–4 (March–April, 1939), pp. 2–3.

[54] As translated in A. Gilbert (trans.), *Ariosto's Orlando furioso* (2 vols.; New York, 1954), Canto X, verses 70–71.

[55] See Vernero, *op. cit.* (n. 48), p. 107; for discussions of America and its geographical relationship to Asia on early maps see below, pp. 456–58.

In Canto XV, one of those added to the *Orlando furioso* shortly before its publication in definitive form in 1532, the new maritime discoveries in Asia begin to emerge more clearly. The fleet of Astolfo coasts around "odoriferous Ind," possibly a reference to the Spice Islands, and sails westward through a sea dotted with a thousand islands toward the Land of Thomas, or the Coromandel coast of India.[56] On approaching the east coast of India, the pilot steers his ship northward and:

> Astolfo, furrowing that ocean hoar,
> Marks, as he coasts, the wealthy land at ease.
> Ganges amid the whitening waters roar,
> Nigh skirting now the Golden Chersonese,
> Taprobana with Cori next, and sees
> The frith which charges against its double shore;
> Makes distant Cochin, and with favoring wind
> Issues beyond the boundaries of Ind.[57]

On the voyage toward Africa, Astolfo asks Andronica if European vessels "ever appear in the Eastern sea, and if one who looses his cable in India can go without ever touching land to France and England."[58] Andronica replies that the sea encircles the land on all sides. But, she observes, the sailors of both Europe and Asia have heretofore feared the long voyage around Africa and have persisted in believing that no passage exists. She predicts that in a time to come the sea road will be opened to India and that "in imitation of the circular course of the sun" navigators will sail around the world to find new lands. In a poem of praise to Charles V,[59] Andronica foresees:

> The imperial flags and holy cross I know
> Fixed on the verdant shore; see some upon
> The shattered barks keep guard, and others go
> A-field, by whom new countries will be won;
> Ten chase a thousand of the flying foe,
> Realms beyond Ind subdued by Arragon;
> And see all, wheresoe'er the warriors wend,
> To the fifth Charles' triumphant captains bend.[60]

[56] The Moluccas appear clearly on the Salviati map of 1525-27 (original in Biblioteca Mediceo-Laurenziana in Florence) and on the Weimar Spanish map of 1527. Also see pl. 67.

[57] As translated in Baker and Giamatti (eds.), *op. cit.* (n. 51), Canto XV, verse 17. Golden Chersonese is possibly Sumatra; Taprobana is Ceylon; "Cori" refers either to a small island in Adanis Strait or to Cape Comorin; Cochin, the center of the Malabar pepper trade, was the place where the spice ships waited for the monsoon to carry them across the Indian Ocean on the first leg of their return trip to Europe.

[58] As translated in Gilbert (trans.), *op. cit.* (n. 54), Canto XV, verse 18.

[59] Cf. the prophecy of Venus in the *Lusiads* of Camoëns. See above, pp. 155-56. Evidently the achievements of the Spanish under Charles V, probably the voyage of Magellan in particular, led Ariosto to shift his focus away from the achievements of the Portuguese to those of the Catalans. In the 1516 edition of the *Furioso* we read: "In Lusitanian galley bound for Ind" (XXXVIII, 35). This formulation was retained in the edition of 1521. In the definitive edition of 1532 he moved this passage to Canto XLIII, verse 38, and changed the word "Lusitani" to "Catalani." For further discussion of this point see Vernero, *op. cit.* (n. 48), p. 103.

[60] As translated in Baker and Giamatti (eds.), *op. cit.* (n. 51), Canto XV, verse 23.

Ariosto's references to the East include little that he could not have learned from current geographical books as well as from maps and their legends. More than likely he worked from one of the revised Ptolemaic maps or map series which were then being published.[61] On the Cantino map the legends are particularly explicit with regard to pertinent local conditions of sailing and trade in the seas around India. Cathay, for which Angelica longs, is clearly a rich and populous region that she is proud to award to Medoro, her lover. India is a land of rare gems and sumptuous living. Magic is powerful in both Cathay and India; indeed, Astolfo always keeps close at hand the little book which Logistilla had given him in India to protect him from spells and incantations.[62] A ring, stolen in India from a queen, also wards off enchantments.[63] In India, Angelica learned surgery and medicine "for it seems that this study is in that country noble and dignified and in high esteem, and without much turning of pages, because the father leaves it as a legacy to his children."[64] For Ariosto India remains, as it had for Boiardo, a land of wealth, magic, and the healing arts—a place of escape from the realities of European life. The East had become a part of his world only to the extent that he could see it on a map. It constituted, as it had for earlier and would for later imaginative writers, a place located somewhere between the real and the imaginary worlds—in short, a setting for romance.[65]

The concerns of the first generation of the sixteenth century were closely linked to local fears and hopes relating to the future of the spice trade. At the courts of the lower Po Valley and the Veneto the progress of the Portuguese eastward was a matter of constant worry, for their representatives were strictly excluded from participating in it. In Rome and Florence the situation was different, because representatives of the Medici and the papacy were intimately involved in the Portuguese enterprise. The successful circumnavigation of the "Victoria" aroused hopes in northeastern Italy that Spain might wrest control of the Moluccas from Portugal and establish an alternate route for the spice trade, an enterprise from which the Venetians would presumably not be excluded. In Venice, Ferrara, and Rome the report of Pigafetta produced a lively interest among courtiers, merchants, and scholars. But Italian hopes for a possible share in the Iberian spice trade were dashed by Charles V's sack of Rome in 1527 and by his decision in 1529 to pawn his claim to the Moluccas.

As a side effect to these commercial concerns, the scholars of Padua and Rome began to take an interest in the flora and fauna of the overseas world. The appearance of live and stuffed Asian beasts at Rome stimulated scientists as well as poets to speculate about the meaning of the new discoveries for the arts and sciences of Europe. While the Latin poets continued to treat the East in

---

[61] On this conclusion see Vernero, *op. cit.* (n. 48), p. 129. Also see pl. 64 for a map.

[62] See Gilbert (trans.), *op. cit.* (n. 54), Canto XXII, verse 16.

[63] *Ibid.*, Canto III, verse 69.

[64] *Ibid.*, Canto XIX, verse 21.

[65] For more detail on the problem of magic in Ariosto's epic see Tom, *op. cit.* (n. 40), pp. 26–27, 34–35.

classical terms, the authors of vernacular romances were inclined to incorporate materials in their poems from the travelogues of the Middle Ages and the books, reports, and maps deriving from the Iberian discoveries. In Italy the progress of the Portuguese in Asia was of far more interest to the *letterati* than the conquests of Castile in America, a region that many still thought of as the promontory to Asia.[66] For the writers of romance Asia was a reality recognized by the revered writers of Antiquity, by the medieval travelers, and by the Portuguese of their own age. It was not, however, a clearly delineated region with a history of its own. Asia was still a semi-imaginary world, a rich locale where marvels, magic, and mystery still remained possible and likely.

2

POPULAR AND DIDACTIC LITERATURE

The coronation of Charles V at Bologna in 1530 constituted a public acknowledgment of his primacy in the political affairs of Italy. Imperial control and influence over most of the states of the peninsula was then succeeded over the course of the century by a Spanish hegemony which ultimately exerted profound influence everywhere. The Council of Trent (1545–63) meanwhile worked out a reform of the Roman Catholic Church which brought into Italian life and letters a sterner morality, a heightened religiosity, and more official control. Repression was generally limited to the realms of philosophy and theology while art and popular literature remained free. Intensified foreign and ecclesiastical control helped to produce a national reaction which brought the Italian vernaculars more commonly into use in both popular and scholarly literature. Latin was never completely abandoned by ecclesiastics and Humanists, but many reputable authors began to write more in the vernacular. The Florentine Academy was founded in 1540 for the express purpose of publishing works of science in Tuscan. Sperone Speroni (1500–1588), a vigorous proponent of the vernacular, expressed the conviction, echoed by many others, that the local language could most advantageously be employed in writing of practical, modern affairs, including "itinerarii di mondi novi."[67]

For information on activities in the East, Venice was still and was long to remain one of Italy's major channels. The Venetian printers regularly collected and published travel accounts. An abbreviated version of Pigafetta's voyage appeared at Venice in 1536 and was followed three years later by Alvise

---

[66] For a general discussion of America see R. Romeo, *Le scoperte americane nella coscienza italiana del Cinquecento* (Milan and Naples, 1954). Francesco Becutti (1509–53), known as "Il Coppetto," wrote lyrics celebrating the overseas achievements of King John III of Portugal. They were first published in his *Rime* (Venice, 1580), pp. 4–5. Also consult A. Belloni, *Il poema epico e mitologico* (Milan, 1912), pp. 290–93.

[67] See N. della Laste and M. Forcellini (eds.), *Opere* . . . (5 vols.; Venice, 1740), V, 445.

Roncinotto's *El viazo de Colocut* (1539). The famous Aldine Press published in 1543 a collection called *Viaggi fatti alla Tana* . . . , five travelogues by Venetians of their experiences in Asia.[68] Pietro Aretino (1492–1556?) was among the *letterati* residing in Venice who received letters from India, a fact which he relates to let it be known how far his fame extends.[69] The Spanish diplomat and bibliophile Diego Hurtado di Mendoza gathered intelligence in Venice from informants in the East on the state of affairs in the Portuguese empire which he relayed to his government.[70] In the meantime Ramusio was putting together his great collection of *Navigationi*, the first volume of which appeared in 1550 at the press of Tomasso Giunti.[71] Four years later the first list of prohibited books prepared by the Venetian government came off the press of Gabriel Giolito as part of a more general effort to suppress books dangerous to civil and ecclesiastical order and to public morality.[72]

In Italy, as in Spain, the *Index* in its various manifestations did not muzzle the printing press or inhibit the growth of popular literature. But a trend appeared under the influence of the Counter-Reformation for literature to become more definitely moralistic.[73] Chivalresque romances translated from or inspired by the moralistic Spanish tales of *Palmerin* and *Amadis* rolled in a steady stream off the presses of Italy during the latter half of the century. Michele Tramezzino, the Venetian publisher, apparently operated a factory in which chivalresque romances were translated and created to keep his presses running. His chief hack was Mambrino Roseo da Fabriano (*fl.* 1544–71), the alleged translator and continuator of many romances and the author of several popular histories. In 1558 Tramezzino published what purported to be the first part of the "thirteenth book" of the *Amadis* series. Actually it was the first of a series of original additions by Roseo which were printed as "parts" of the "thirteenth book" of *Amadis* between 1558 and 1565 and later reissued in revised or amplified editions.[74] The hero of this series is Prince Sferamundi of Greece, a character from the eleventh book of the Spanish *Amadis* who becomes involved in wars with Eastern kings and peoples.[75] In a sister series based on Volume III, Book 5, of the Spanish *Amadis*, the hero is Splandiano, emperor of Constantinople.[76] In the later editions of this series the king of China and his ambassadors appear on

[68] See *Asia*, I, 180–81.

[69] Letter of May 4, 1542, to Captain Francesco Faloppia in F. Nicolini (ed.), *Pietro Aretino: Il secondo libro delle lettere* (1 vol. in 2 parts; Bari, 1916), Pt. 2, p. 165.

[70] For example, see the letter of May 19, 1541, to Leon Francisco de los Cobos in A. Vasquez and R. S. Rose (eds.), *Algunas cartas de Don Diego Hurtado de Mendoza escritas 1538–1552* (New Haven, 1935), pp. 71–72.

[71] For details see *Asia*, I, 204–5.

[72] See A. F. Johnson, *Periods of Typography: The Italian Sixteenth Century* (London, 1926), p. 19.

[73] See F. Flamini, *Il cinquecento* (Milan, 1898–1902), p. 428.

[74] See H. Thomas, *Spanish and Portuguese Romances of Chivalry* (Cambridge, 1920), pp. 184, 189.

[75] I have used *La prima parte del terzodecimo libro di Amadis di Gaula* . . . (Venice, 1584), *passim*. Also see *Della historia del principe Sferamundi* . . . (Venice, 1610). Both these volumes are in the Newberry Library, Chicago.

[76] For discussion see H. Vaganay, "Les romans de chevalerie italiens d'inspiration espagnole," *La bibliofilia*, XII (1910–11), 287, 291, 298, 299.

the scene and sketchy depictions of China itself are woven into the romance.[77] A similar evolution also occurs in later additions and series printed under Roseo's name by the Tramezzino press. For example, the kings of both China and Japan figure in the series whose primary hero is Lisuarte of Greece, the son of Splandiano.[78] The "China" that appears in these romances is derived mainly from the Jesuit letterbooks and from the history of Mendoza.

The writers of *novelle* of the latter half of the sixteenth century began to bring into their compilations new stories based on the tales recounted in contemporary travelogues. Matteo Bandello (*ca.* 1480–1562), a continuator of the Boccaccio tradition, used Varthema, as he admits in the first line of the story (Part I, *Novella* 52), as his source for a tale in which Mahomet and Prester John figure.[79] Plots for other stories he derived from Peter Apian's cosmography and the travel accounts in the collection of Ramusio.[80] Bandello's dramatic and realistic tales quickly became known internationally through the French translations of Boaistuau (1559) and Belleforest (1568) and were broadly influential in providing later European writers with moral themes and plots.[81] The *Piacevoli notti* (2 parts; Venice, 1550, 1553) of Giovanni Francesco Straparola, another popular collection of tales, printed for the first time many of the stray fables from the East commonly related by itinerant storytellers. Straparola's collection was reissued sixteen times between 1550 and 1570 and was translated into French, and possibly into German, by the beginning years of the seventeenth century.[82]

Most fascinating is the collection of tales published by Michele Tramezzino called *Peregrinaggio di tre giovani del re di Serendippo* (Venice, 1557).[83] According to the title page, this book was allegedly translated from Persian into Italian by Christoforo Armeno. This was evidently not so, however, for no single source, Persian or otherwise, has yet been located from which this translation might have been made, and no trace exists of the supposed translator in either Italian or Armenian sources. The plan of the book follows the Persian poem of Nizami called *The Seven Beauties*. But the tales themselves are of ancient origin and from various sources, especially Indian. Here in refurbished form are the Indian

---

[77] M. Roseo, *Il secundo libro delle prodezze di Splandiano, imperator di Constantinopoli aggiunto al quinto libro di Amadis di Gaula* . . . (Venice, 1600), chaps. lxxxiii–lxxxvii, cxxviii–cxxix, cxl, cxlv, clviii.

[78] See M. Roseo, *Lisuarte di Grecia* (2 vols.; Venice, 1630), II, 86ʳ.

[79] "Scrive nel suo Itinerario Lodovico Varomanno romano." See G. Brognoligo (ed.), *Matteo Bandello: Le novelle* (5 vols.; Bari, 1910–12), II, 234. His contemporary, A. F. Doni, had a copy of Varthema in his personal library. See above, p. 52, and below, p. 371.

[80] See T. G. Griffith, *Bandello's Fiction* (Oxford, 1955), pp. 55, 101, 119.

[81] See below, pp. 287–88. In a number of writings Bandello blames the excessive opulence of the Spanish-dominated society of Milan upon the ready availability of the unguents, ointments, and perfumes of the East. See A. Divrengues, "La société milanese d'après Bandello au temps de la Renaissance," *Revue du seizième siècle*, XVIII (1931), 225. Also see pls. 7 and 8.

[82] See W. G. Waters (trans.), *The Nights of Straparola* (London, 1894), I, xi–xvi.

[83] For translations with critical notes see T. Benfey (trans. and ed.), *Die Reise der drei Söhne des Königs von Serendippo* (Helsinki, 1932); and T. G. Remer (ed.), *Serendipity and the Three Princes* (Norman, Okla., 1965).

stories of the magic mirror, the wine merchant, the laughing statue, and the three hypocritical virgins. The characters and places named in the story are all of Persian origin, or they are Persian variants on or corruptions of Indian names. The conclusion is inescapable that Tramezzino, his circle, and his staff put into Venetian the tales that were then current in the Persian world with flourishes of their own devising.[84]

Long after the discovery of the sea route to India, the Venetians continued to maintain overland relations with India through Persia.[85] The *Peregrinaggio* itself was dedicated to Marc Antonio Guistiniani, the son of a distinguished Venetian political family whose members had sometimes acted as emissaries to Persia.[86] Giuseppe Tramezzino, the brother of the printer and a student of Oriental languages, was evidently sent to Persia on a mission in 1555,[87] the date when the compilation of the *Peregrinaggio* began. About this same period the house of Tramezzino was working with Giacomo Gastaldi in the preparation and printing of maps of Asia.[88] With the publication in 1557 of the *Peregrinaggio* Tramezzino also began to issue translations from Spanish of the Jesuit letterbooks on overseas missions.[89] The Italian letterbooks, first published at Rome in 1552, enjoyed a great vogue, and the Venetian printers were among the leading publishers of such volumes. The popularity of the letterbooks rested in part on the persistent demand for entertaining translations of Spanish romances of chivalry and adventure. For in Italy, as in Spain at this time, the reading public was not always able to distinguish between fact and fiction about distant places.[90]

The better informed Venetians were probably aware that the king of "Serendippo" in the tales was in fact the ruler of Ceylon. The traditional Persian name for Ceylon is "Seren-dip," a corruption of Sanskrit and Hindustani words designating Ceylon as "The Golden Island."[91] The mariners of the Persian Gulf and the Turks continued to refer to "Seren-dib" rather than Ceylon, and it was probably from them that the Venetians adopted the word.[92] This name was probably linked to a literary conception of "the golden island," a distant locale which would provide a suitably remote, wealthy, and exotic background.[93]

[84] See Remer (ed.), *op. cit.* (n. 83), pp. 47–49, 179.

[85] See *Viaggi fatti alla Tana* (Venice, 1543), and M. Longhena (ed.), *Viaggi in Persia* ... (Milan, 1929).

[86] Benfey (ed.), *op. cit.* (n. 83), pp. 11–12.

[87] See A. Tinto, *Annali tipografici dei Tramezzino* (Venice, 1966), p. x.

[88] See R. Almagià, *Monumenta cartographica Vaticana* (4 vols.; Vatican City, 1944–55), II, 35–37; also Brown, *op. cit.* (n. 21), p. 102, and below, p. 462.

[89] His first two titles were *Nuovi avisi* (1557) and *Diversi avisi* (1559).

[90] See above, pp. 46–47.

[91] For details see L. A. Goodman, "Notes on the Etymology of Serendipity and Some Related Philological Observations," *Modern Language Notes*, LXXVI (1961), 455–56. Also see Benfey, *op. cit.* (n. 83), p. 31, n. 1.

[92] The Turkish *Mohît* compiled in 1554 gives "Seran-dib" as the name. See M. Bittner and W. Tomaschek, *Die topographischen Capitel des indischen Seespiegels Mohît* (Vienna, 1897), pl. XVII. Also see below, p. 343.

[93] Cf. the moralistic stories in *Le sei giornate* (Venice, 1567) of Sebastiano Erizzo (1525–85) which take place in Spain, Portugal, and Peru. See G. Gigli and F. Nicolini, *Novellieri minore del cinquecento*, *G. Barabosco—S. Erizzo* (Bari, 1912).

The suggestion has been advanced that "Serendippo" was selected as the locale because of the effort to convert Ceylon and its king to Christianity then being undertaken by the Portuguese and the Jesuits.[94] It might also be pointed out that the "princes" of Ceylon were known in Portugal, and possibly in Venice, by the golden image of Prince Dharmapala Astana which had been brought to Lisbon in 1541, by the baptism of two other Sinhalese princes at Goa in 1546, and by the kidnapping of King Dharmapala's infant son and his removal to Goa in 1551.[95] Unfortunately for these conjectures, no concrete evidence exists to support them. Examination of the Jesuit letterbooks then available in Italian reveals only passing references to wars and conversions in Ceylon and no reference at all to the Persian "Seren-dip." It therefore seems highly unlikely, even if Tramezzino himself knew from other sources about these activities in Ceylon, that the Italian public could have connected "Seren-dib" with Ceylon or the sons of the king of "Serendippo" with the Sinhalese princes. Perhaps the most that can be said for this idea is that Tramezzino and his circle, who were probably aware of such connections, were indulging themselves in a bit of intellectual whimsy that could be appreciated only by an enlightened few. The *Peregrinaggio*, however, has a respectable record in the history of collections of popular stories. It was republished in 1584 at Venice, and was translated into German and published at Basel in 1583.[96] A French translation appeared in 1610 but an English version did not see print until 1722. It was Horace Walpole who in 1754 coined the English word "serendipity," a term derived from the adventures of the "three princes" who possessed a penchant for making happy and unexpected discoveries by accident.

Tramezzino was not the only prolific producer of books in Venice. The city on the Adriatic was renowned for its scribblers, popular writers more politely referred to as "polygraphs." The publishers of Venice, by their willingness to print the polygraphs' work, encouraged the writing of books on all kinds of subjects. Books on practical matters, such as lace-making and agriculture, vied for public attention with treatises on love and courtesy. Many of the busy writers of the Venetian region met at the Castello del Catajo erected in 1570 at Battaglia Terme near Padua by Pio Enea Obizzi. Celebrated by Speroni in his dialogue called "Cathaio," this splendid villa was decorated by Battista Zelotti, the pupil of Titian and others, in a fantastic way reminiscent of the Orient.[97] Giuseppe Betussi (*ca.* 1520–*ca.* 1575) published a dialogue in 1573 in which he discusses the program of decoration for the villa including reference to a representation of the "regnum Cathai."[98] Betussi, who was friendly with

---

[94] See Remer, *op. cit.* (n. 83), pp. 41, 47.

[95] See *Asia*, I, 272–73.

[96] Translated by Johann Wetzel and published as *Die Reise der Söhne Giaffers*.

[97] The villa assertedly received its name from the region of the "Veneto" in which it was built. But it is difficult to detach the name of the region and the villa from the Cathay of Marco Polo, the Venetian traveler. See G. Mazzotti, *Ville venete* (Rome, 1963), pp. 52, 66, 68.

[98] *Ragionamento . . . sopra il Cathaio* (Padua, 1573), p. liii. Betussi had traveled to Spain in 1559–60 in the entourage of Gian Luigi Vitelli.

Aretino and A. F. Doni, had earlier exhibited his interest in the fantastic by dedicating his dialogue on love called *Il Raverta* (Venice, 1544) to Vincino Orsini, the creator of the mysterious garden of Bomarzo.[99] In this dialogue Betussi also comments on the love and regard for the dead shown by the Indians who preserve the ashes of their deceased in glass vases.[100]

Tommaso Porcacchi (*ca.* 1530–85) and Francesco Sansovino (1521–86) were leading lights among the Venetian polygraphs. Porcacchi, an editor of Ariosto's *Orlando*, was mainly a commentator on and imitator of the literary works of others. His book on the most famous islands of the world, while an improvement on Bordone's book of 1528, is a direct imitation of that earlier work. But it incorporates more recent data taken from the maps and travel books available in the print shops of Venice.[101] Sansovino, renowned for his translations, editions of earlier authors, and original works of poetry and prose, kept in close touch with contemporary events. In his work on Venice, Sansovino remarks that printing was invented in China five hundred years before it was known in Europe.[102] He also wrote a history of the Turks, celebrated the military victories of his city over them, and might well have inspired the popular collection that Luigi Groto (1541–85) made of the lyrics written by various authors on the victory at Lepanto (1571).[103] A blind poet, Groto also published a poetic tragedy of his own creation called *La Dalida* (Venice, 1572) which features a chorus of Indian women and Queen Berenice, daughter of the king of India.[104] Groto's associate, G. M. Bonardo, meanwhile compiled and published *La minera del mondo* (Venice, 1585), an alphabetical miscellany in which the plants, animals, and precious stones of Asia figure prominently.[105]

At Ferrara the epic tradition of Boiardo and Ariosto was kept alive by Torquato Tasso (1544–95), a native of Sorrento who took service with the Este family in 1565. Ten years later he completed the first version of the *Gerusalemme liberta* (1575), his personal masterpiece and one of the most celebrated poems in the Italian language. Tasso's Christian epic, as opposed to the more pagan masterpieces of Boiardo and Ariosto, is concerned with the conquest of Jerusalem in 1099 by Geoffrey of Bouillon. Particularly stirring are Tasso's descriptions of the battles fought by the crusading armies against the Saracens. The *Jerusalem Freed*, first published in full in 1581, is much more structured and much less spirited than the Orlando romances; it was nonetheless immediately

---

[99] See *Asia*, II, Bk. 1, 148–49. On Doni see above, p. 52.

[100] *Il Raverta*, "Bibliotheca rara," Vol. XXX (Milan, 1864), p. 159.

[101] See *Asia*, II, Bk. 1, 87. Also see above, p. 201, for Bordone's book. I have used Porcacchi, *L'isole piu famose del mondo* . . . (Venice, 1576). The first edition was issued in 1572, and there are later reprintings of 1590, 1620, and 1686.

[102] *Venezia città nobilissima et singolare* (Venice, 1581), p. 245. For commentary on this and his other histories see P. F. Grendler, "Francesco Sansovino and Italian Popular History," *Studies in the Renaissance*, XVI (1969), 139–80.

[103] *Trofeo della victoria sagra ottenuta della cristianissima lega contro i Turchi* (Venice, 1571).

[104] Pp. 10, 18. Several historical queens called "Berenice" were married to the Ptolemies of Egypt.

[105] Reprinted at Venice in 1589 and 1600, and at Mantua in 1591.

popular in Italy and abroad. By 1600 it had appeared in the English translation of Edward Fairfax as *Godfrey of Boulogne, or The Recoverie of Jerusalem*.

Tasso, like most of the other writers of epics, frankly modeled his masterpiece upon the works of Homer and Vergil. But, appearing as it did in the era of the Counter-Reformation, the *Jerusalem* stresses the Holy War against the Muslims and the threat to Christianity from the East. Examination of its text reveals, however, that Tasso was not concerned enough about the danger from the East to follow events there. Unlike Ariosto, he was not interested in the activities of the Iberians in Asia; he does not even see their enterprise as part of the Christian crusade against Islam. In the *Jerusalem* his knowledge of the East shows no advance over that exhibited by Ariosto fifty years earlier. In general his geography appears to be limited to the Ptolemaic traditions of the pre-Colombian era.[106]

At Ferrara it was impossible for an intellectual of Tasso's stature to remain completely oblivious to the overseas discoveries. Examination of his minor writings—lyrics, letters, and dialogues—reveals that he was sensitive to certain of the discoveries' effects upon Europe. He knew about Hanno, the elephant sent to Pope Leo X to announce the successes of Portugal in Asia, and about the confrontation staged at Lisbon between the elephant and the rhinoceros.[107] In a letter of 1572 to a friend in Ferrara, he comments upon the profits reaped by France through the spice trade with Portugal and of the losses consequently experienced by Venice.[108] The plants, precious stones, pearls, and seashells of Asia likewise engage his attention.[109] In his dialogue on nobility he discourses on the universality of the qualities of beauty and reason and points out that what is beautiful and reasonable in Europe is likewise so esteemed in Asia.[110] In his poem to Pope Sixtus V (1585–90) Tasso alludes to Magellan's voyage around the world.[111] But most surprising is his sonnet saluting Camoëns and praising his "poem in the Spanish language about the voyages of Vasco."[112]

While Tasso knew Camoëns' epic, he certainly did not use it in preparing the *Jerusalem*. The *Lusiads* first appeared in Portuguese in 1572 while Tasso was putting some of the finishing touches on his own work. The Spanish version of the *Lusiads*, the one to which Tasso probably refers in his poem, did not appear at Seville until 1580, or the year before the publication of the complete *Jerusalem*. Thus it was probably not possible, even had he cared to do so, for Tasso to incorporate material from Camoëns' epic into his own. The case for arguing that he was not seriously interested in using Camoëns as a source for his epic is

---

[106] See P. Maffi, *La cosmografia nelle opere di Tasso* (Milan, 1898), pp. 153–54. Also see G. Getto, *Nel mondo della "Gerusalemme"* (Florence, 1968), pp. 222, 227.

[107] See B. Maier (ed.), *Torquato Tasso: Opere* (5 vols.; Milan, 1963), V, 566–70. Comments on these events are in his dialogues on *imprese*. Also see *Asia*, II, Bk. 1, 86 n., 150, 167 n.

[108] Tasso accompanied Cardinal Luigi d'Este to France from November, 1570, to March, 1571. Letter to Count Ercole de' Contrari in Maier (ed.), *op. cit.* (n. 107), V, 738–39.

[109] See *ibid.*, IV, 30–31, 214; V, 595, 619.

[110] See *ibid.*, IV, 846–47.

[111] *Ibid.*, II, 109.

[112] *Ibid.*, I, 1012–13.

supported by the fact that no traces of influence from the *Lusiads* can be found in Tasso's later writings, such as *Il mondo creato* (1592) and the *Gerusalemme conquistada* (1592). In these works his view of Asia and the overseas world remains virtually what it had been in the *Jerusalem Freed*.

To Tasso the extremes of the known world were at the Pillars of Hercules and at the mouth of the Ganges. America and the countries and islands of the distant East are either mentioned in his writings not at all or only very indirectly.[113] Typical of his image of Asia is this verse:

> Then from the mansions bright of fresh Aurore
> Adrastus came, the glorious king of Inde,
> A snake's green skin spotted with black he wore,
> That was made rich by art and hard by kind;
> An elephant this furious giant bore,
> He fierce as fire, his mounture swift as wind;
> Much people brought he from his kingdom wide,
> 'Twixt Indus, Ganges, and the salt sea side.[114]

Adrastus is mentioned elsewhere in the poem merely as "the Indian,"[115] but at no place in the epic does Tasso refer to the India known to the Portuguese of his own day. Judging from a reference or two, Tasso possibly knew Varthema's *Itinerario*;[116] if he did, however, it had no perceptible influence on his view of the East—one that was essentially classical and that might have been held by Vergil himself.[117]

Not all of the Italian *letterati* of the last decades of the century were as unresponsive as Tasso to the opening of the East. The courtiers of Duke Francesco Maria della Rovere of Urbino, as well as the duke himself,[118] received gifts from Portugal of books, porcelains, medicinals, and plumages from the East. These curiosities were dispatched to Urbino by Filippo Terzi (1520–97), the Italian military engineer, who was in Portugal from 1577 to 1597.[119] The Florentine Humanist and merchant Filippo Sassetti (1540–88), was also in Spain and Portugal from 1578 to 1582 as commercial agent of the Capponi before his departure for India on April 1, 1582. Before leaving Florence, Sassetti had become a member of the Accademia Fiorentina (1573) and the Accademia degli Alterati (1574). Once Sassetti was established in Lisbon he became an adept in the new knowledge available there about geography and the natural

---

[113] "Catai" is mentioned just once, in a letter. See Maffi, *op. cit.* (n. 106), pp. 171–72.

[114] Canto XVII, verse 28, as presented in the sixteenth-century translation of Edward Fairfax in R. Weiss (ed.), *Torquato Tasso: Jerusalem Delivered* (London, 1962), p. 422. It is possible that this verse was produced in imitation of Vergil's *Giorgicas* (Bk. III, vv. 26–27).

[115] See Maier (ed.), *op. cit.* (n. 107), III, 660, 698. In Greek legend Adrastes was king of Thebes.

[116] See *ibid.*, III, 561.

[117] See S. Multineddu, *Le fonti della Gerusalemme Liberata* (Turin, 1895), pp. 169, 211.

[118] The duke, as a very young man, had spent thirty months in Madrid and was at the court of Philip II from 1566 to 1568. See. F. Cavalli, *La scienza politica in Italia* (New York, 1968), II, 161.

[119] See H. Trindade Coelho and G. Matelli (eds.), *Documentos para o estudo das relações culturaes entre Portugal e Italia* (4 vols.; Florence, 1934–35), III, xii–xiii.

sciences. From Lisbon and India he wrote lengthy letters to Baccio Valori and others in Florence about the products and peoples of Asia. His Florentine correspondents shared his letters and gifts with their friends and associates in the two academies.[120] In the meantime the Italian Jesuit historian, G. P. Maffei was active in Portugal from 1578 to 1584 gathering material for his general history in Latin of Jesuit activities in the East.[121] Terzi, Sassetti, and Maffei were all in Iberia therefore when Philip became king of Portugal in 1580, an event which made even closer the relations between Italy and Iberia in affairs both secular and ecclesiastical relating to the East.[122]

The triumphal tour of the Japanese embassy from 1584 to 1586 in Portugal, Spain, and Italy sparked a new enthusiasm in southern Europe for the Jesuit mission in Asia. Some Italian commentators compared the Japanese to Magellan and his men as the world's greatest travelers.[123] In Italy the Japanese youths visited Tuscany (March 1–20, 1585), Rome (March 22–June 3, 1585), Venice (June 25–July 6, 1585), Mantua (July 13–18, 1585), Milan (July 25–August 3, 1585), and many other smaller places en route. Their five-month tour in Italy was marked by exchanges of gifts, processions, receptions, dramas, and special church services.[124] Artists sketched the envoys, inscriptions were incised to commemorate their visit, and poets sang their praises in both Latin and Italian verse.[125] In the meantime Italian readers were also afforded a new adulatory view of China when the first edition appeared at Rome in 1585 of Mendoza's *Historia de las cosas mas notables . . . del gran Reyno dela China*. It is therefore not surprising to find a more substantial interest in the East appearing at this time and hereafter in Italian popular literature.

Asia began in these later years of the century to appeal particularly to writers of moralistic and didactic literature. Bernardino Baldi (1553–1617) of Urbino (the city kept in touch with the discoveries through Terzi)[126] was one of the

---

[120] See M. Rossi, *Un letterato e mercante fiorentino del secolo XVI, Filippo Sassetti* (Città di Castello, 1899), pp. 22–23, 35–36. Also see *Asia*, I, 475–77. For Sassetti in the Florentine context see E. Cochrane, *Florence in the Forgotten Centuries, 1527–1800* (Chicago, 1973), pp. 108, 114, 128–29.

[121] See *Asia*, I, 694–700.

[122] For an eyewitness account by an Italian of the Spanish takeover in Portugal see G. F. di Conestaggio, *The Historie of the Uniting of the Kingdom of Portugall to the Crown of Castile . . .* (London, 1600). The author describes Portugal, discusses the discovery of the sea route to India (pp. 7–8), and concludes that "this corruption and weakness of the Realme [Portugal] was brought on by the delights of the East" (p. 9). The Italian original of this work was published at Genoa in 1585.

[123] For example, see G. A. Corazzino (ed.), *Diario Fiorentino di Agostini Lapini* (Florence, 1900), pp. 240–43.

[124] The Japanese presented Pope Gregory XVI with a number of gifts. One of these was a picture of a parrot the like of which had not been seen in Europe before. For the history of this parrot in Rome see H. Diener, "Die 'Camera Papagalli' im Palast des Papstes," *Archiv für Kulturgeschichte*, XLIX (1967), 66–67.

[125] Ciro Alidosi (*ca.* 1520–89), a Florentine who had served the Medici in Madrid and Lisbon from 1577 to 1597, wrote *Carmine* celebrating the successes of the Japanese at Rome. See G. Aleandro, *Vitae et res gestae pontificum romanorum* (2 vols.; Rome, 1630), Vol. II, col. 1782. Also see Marc' Antonio Ciappi, *Compendio delle heroiche et gloriose attioni, et santa vita di Papa Greg. XIII* (Rome, 1591), pp. 61–64, who comments on their "Indian costume most delightful to see." For title pages of books published in Italy on their visit see pls. 19 and 21.

[126] See above, p. 36.

first Italian poets to adopt a maritime theme directly inspired by contemporary events. His long epic-like poem called *La nautica* (1585) is divided into four books which treat (1) of the construction of a ship and the choice of a pilot; (2) of the stars, winds, and weather at sea; (3) of the management of the voyage in fair weather and foul; and (4) of the countries and cities of the world to which the pilot should steer his ship to obtain precious merchandise.[127] Baldi, a student of Near Eastern languages, had translated the *Geography* of Edrissi from Arabic into Italian, and it was probably from this source that he first obtained information about the places and products of the East. He was also aware of the achievements of the Portuguese navigators and praises them for exemplifying the courage and caution that good pilots should have.[128] He possibly obtained some of his knowledge of maritime navigation and Iberian exploits from consulting an Italian translation of the *Libro de cosmographia* of the Spanish Pedro de Medina.[129] Baldi asserts that every country, according to its geographical placement and climate, produces its own special products. Odoriferous gums grow in India and Arabia that could never prosper in Tartary and Scythia.[130] The pilot must steer his ship to India for the pearls of Ormuz, ebony, and the crystals of Ceylon.[131] Baldi comments at length and critically on the practice of *sati* (widow-burning) in India.[132] For the precious cloves the pilot must head in the direction of China to the distant Moluccas and Taprobane.[133] After indicating the specialities of distant climes, he concludes his poem with praise for the excellence of Italy, a land that he compares favorably to all other places.[134]

India, unlike China and Japan, was criticized by the moralists. The religious and social practices of the Hindus seemed abhorrent to many sixteenth-century writers. The recalcitrance of the Hindus, especially the Brahmans, in refusing to accept Christian teachings was stressed in the Jesuit letters; the Hindus were almost always compared unfavorably to the more enlightened and tractable Japanese. News of the massacre of Rudolph Acquaviva and his four companions at Salsette near Goa in 1583 arrived in Europe about the same time the Japanese legates landed there. The Italian Jesuits were particularly outraged at the death of Acquaviva, their distinguished compatriot. Francesco Benci (1542–94), a Jesuit Latinist and an editor of the *Litterae annuae* (the annual letters from the missions which appeared in book form),[135] wrote a poem exalting the heroic sacrifice of Acquaviva and his companions—*Quinque martyres e Societate Iesu in India libri sex* (Venice, 1591)—which placed the sacrifice of the martyrs before

---

[127] See G. Romeo (ed.), *B. Baldi: La nautica* (1585) *e le egloghe* (Lanciano, 1913), preface. The editor here reproduces the edition of 1590 (Venice).

[128] *Ibid.*, Bk. III, lines 283–310, p. 61.

[129] Suggestion of A. González Palencia (ed.), *Obras de Pedro de Medina* (2 vols.; Madrid, 1944), I, xix.

[130] G. Romeo (ed.), *op. cit.* (n. 127), Bk. IV, summary, p. 72.

[131] *Ibid.*, Bk. IV, lines 222–35, p. 79; lines 259–65, p. 80.

[132] *Ibid.*, Bk. IV, lines 236–58, pp. 79–80.

[133] *Ibid.*, Bk. IV, lines 265–76, p. 80.

[134] On the voyages and explorations as an epic subject see L. Bradner, "Columbus in Sixteenth-Century Poetry," in *Essays Honoring Lawrence C. Wroth* (Portland, Me., 1951), pp. 16–17.

[135] Benci compiled the five volumes, published from 1589 to 1594.

the Society as an edifying example. Benci's solemn lines were read by many generations of Jesuits as inspirational literature. They were also read, whether consciously or not, as a condemnation of India. This Jesuit view of the perfidy of the Brahmans was likewise preserved in the paintings of the martyrdoms of Salsette.[136] But hope was also revived in the last decade of the century by the Jesuit missions to Akbar that India might yet be saved.[137]

The customs of the Indians were not universally condemned by Italian *letterati*. Pomponio Torelli (1539–1608), a native of Parma and a student at Padua, was one of the first to compare Indian to European practices. Torelli was sent to Spain in 1584–85 by the Farnese duke of Parma to negotiate with Philip II about the duke's claim to the devolution of Piacenza. Upon his successful completion of this mission, Torelli returned to Parma and his literary activities. Though best known for his tragic dramas, Torelli was also an active courtier and a leading member of the *Academia de' Innominati* of Parma. It was in his capacity as an academician that he wrote his *Trattato del debito del cavalliero* (Parma, 1596), a treatise reminiscent of Castiglione's famous *Libro del cortegiano* (1518).

Torelli's essay on the duty of the knight clearly shows that he learned from his experience in Spain and from his perusal of Portuguese literature a bit about the obligations of cavaliers in India. The knights of Asia like those of Europe believe in God, religion, and moral living as basic virtues. Where faith does not exist, the capacity for honor and noble living is lacking.[138] The Nāyars, whom he identifies as the knights of Malabar, are devotees of military exercises and the noble art of war.[139] Cavaliers should read books of great adventures and mighty deeds in distant places, such as the Orlando books and the *Lusiads* of Camoëns.[140] In Narsinga (Vijayanagar), he notes with approval, the most beautiful women accompany the men to war for the Indians believe that love of women makes warriors fight more effectively.[141] From these few scattered references it is clear that Torelli was beginning to think in terms of a code of knighthood common to Indians and Europeans, a viewpoint that certainly would have shocked the Portuguese nobles and missionaries in India. Torelli's willingness to compare the knights of Europe to those of India, and not always unfavorably to the Indians, constitutes an exhibition of tolerance for Indian customs which was completely at variance with the orthodox Jesuit view then prevailing of the unredeemable character of Indian life.

China, where the Jesuit mission seemed to be on the verge of prospering, enjoyed in the 1590's a far better reputation than India among Italian men of letters. Most explicit in its appreciation of China is *Il magno Vitei* (Venice,

---

[136] See E. Mâle, *L'Art religieux après le Concile de Trente* (Paris, 1932), pp. 119–20.

[137] See *Asia*, I, 446–60.

[138] P. Torelli, *Trattato* . . . (Parma, 1596), pp. 27^r–27^v.

[139] *Ibid.*, p. 15^v.

[140] *Ibid.*, p. 99^v.

[141] *Ibid.*, pp. 174^v–175^r. This story he derives from the chronicle of King Manuel, probably from Osório's Latin version.

1597),[142] the last literary work to appear from the pen of Ludovico Arrivabene (*ca.* 1530–*ca.* 1597). After 1589 the leading poet and literary light of the Gonzaga court at Mantua, Arrivabene was well known among contemporaries for his cosmopolitan interests. Steffano Guazzo (1530–93) comments in a letter of 1589 that Arrivabene's pronouncements on the exotic natural world constitute veritable "Indian treasures."[143] Arrivabene's dialogue written in 1592 on the Holy Land and on the Christian pilgrims in the Levant further illustrates his growing concern for events in distant places, for moralizing, and for universal justice.[144]

Il magno Vitei, a progenitor of the heroic-gallant romances of the seventeenth century, is a lengthy prose piece in which the wise and virtuous hero is celebrated.[145] The locale is China and its neighbors in the East: Cochin-China, Champa, Cambodia, Siam, Pegu, Japan, Sumatra, India, and Tartary. China is depicted as the most virtuous nation yet known to mankind. Ezonlom, a governor of ancient China, is portrayed as an exemplar of the excellent prince and the perfect captain. The eldest of his sons, the great Vitei, is the most valiant and wisest of all knights and kings. It is in the strange ambiance of China that these exemplary men live and perform their great deeds. Indeed, some literary historians have concluded that the whole Asian background was provided solely for the purpose of creating a foreign and fantastic atmosphere.[146]

Arrivabene himself, in the preliminary note to his "kind and understanding readers," recognizes that some will perhaps say that his history contains many bits and pieces of information of dubious credibility. To such skeptics he replies, "I have worked hard for the express purpose of bringing to light the fundamental qualities of the glorious Chinese nation; qualities which have lain in complete and utter darkness." That contemporaries took his assertions seriously is illustrated by the fact that when the book was reissued two years later the title was changed to *Istoria della China* (Verona).[147] Students of Italian literature have cavalierly rejected Arrivabene's own assertion about his serious study of China and its neighbors and have persisted in describing his work as a prose romance of the chivalric or Alexandrine type made popular by Boiardo and

[142] For its title page see pl. 16. It is a large volume of 578 numbered pages with 12 unnumbered preliminary pages and 11 unnumbered index pages. It is dedicated to Duke Francesco Maria della Rovere of Urbino, a collector of Eastern rarities (see above, p. 36) and in Arrivabene's words "uno Prencipe letteratissimo."

[143] *Lettere del Signor Steffano Guazzo* . . . (Turin, 1591), pp. 383–84.

[144] *Dialogo delle cose più illustri di Terra Santa* . . . (Verona, 1592).

[145] For a comparison of the ideal prince in Castiglione and Arrivabene see Tom, *op. cit.* (n. 40), pp. 85–88.

[146] See the article by S. Carando in *Dizionario biografico italiano*. For a more reasonable discussion see A. Albertazzi, *Romanizieri e romanzi del cinquecento e del seicento* (Bologna, 1891), pp. 126–33; G. Passano, *I novellieri italiani in prosa* (Turin, 1878), Pt. I, pp. 29–30. Also see A. Albertazzi, *Storia dei generi letterari italiani: Il romanzo* (Milan, 1902), p. 73.

[147] Passano (*op. cit.* [n. 146], p. 30) was the first scholar to point out that this *Istoria* of 1599 was possibly nothing more than an effort to sell the remaining copies of the first edition by changing the title and the title page. He points out that both editions have the same number of pages and identical errors in pagination. The publisher is changed from Discepolo to Tamo on the new title page.

Ariosto. Some have even asserted that the names of places and personages were contrived by the author, except for such well-known locations as China, Japan, and India. Such a conclusion is unwarranted as can easily be revealed by analysis of the text.

Il magno Vitei is actually based in large measure on Mendoza's popular book on China with additions from other contemporary European sources, the travel collection of Ramusio, and the Jesuit letterbooks. The names of Arrivabene's principal characters—Vitei, Ezonlom, and Hautzibon—are all derived from Mendoza, as are those of a number of his minor characters.[148] From Mendoza's romanizations it is next to impossible to identify the Chinese names they actually represent. This difficulty can be traced to the fact that the Chinese informants of the Spanish in the Philippines spoke the Amoy and Cantonese dialects of Chinese. It is possible, however, to conclude from Mendoza's description of Vitei's achievements that he was characterizing under Vitei's name the earliest emperors and cultural heroes of Chinese history. His reference to Vitei as "the first king of China" and as the ruler who inaugurated the principle of hereditary succession seems to lead back to Ta Yü, or Yü the Great, the founder of the traditional Hsia dynasty (ordinarily assigned the dates 2205–1766 B.C.).[149] But from Mendoza's list of Vitei's cultural achievements he seems rather to be referring to Huang-ti, the Yellow Emperor, who is said to have reigned from 2698 to 2598 B.C., or for the one hundred years attributed to Vitei.[150] Arrivabene's reference to a popular name for Vitei, the "Iddij,"[151] was not derived from Mendoza. But the practice of giving such names to the emperors was certainly in harmony with later Chinese custom. Whatever historical identity may be assigned to Vitei, no question exists that to both Mendoza and Arrivabene he stands as the first king of China and as an exemplary ruler.

Arrivabene's tale revolves around the military exploits of Ezonlom and Vitei against the Tartars, against rebels at home, on Hainan Island, in Cochin-China and Cambodia, and on land and sea against the Japanese. Most of his geographical names, including those of rivers, mountains, provinces, cities, and islands are identifiable as Ptolemaic terms or as names derived from post-discovery sources. "Argon," the Arghune of Persia, derives from Marco Polo, probably

---

[148] See G. T. Staunton (ed.), *The History of the Great and Mighty Kingdom of China . . . compiled by the Padre Juan González de Mendoza,* "Publications of the Hakluyt Society," O.S. XIV, XV (2 vols.; London, 1853–54), I, 52, 69–71. For the minor characters, such as the Chinese princes Usao, Huntzui, and Ochieutei, see pp. 51–52. Others may be found on pp. 73, 75.

[149] Martin de Rada, whose information about China came from many of the same sources as Mendoza's, refers only briefly to "Vitey." C. R. Boxer identifies "Vitey" with Yü the Great, though Rada clearly states that he "reigned for one hundred years" and in spite of the fact that none of the traditional sources assigns such a long reign to Yü. See C. R. Boxer (ed.), *South China in the Sixteenth Century,* "Publications of the Hakluyt Society," 2d ser. CVI (London, 1953), p. 297, n. 4.

[150] See H. A. Giles, *A Chinese Biographical Dictionary* (reprint: Taipei, 1964), p. 338.

[151] *Il magno Vitei,* p. 3. Possibly, but not probably, a reference to the fact that Huang-ti's surname was "chi" so that his popular name might have been "I-chi" by analogy to the popular name of Shih-huang-ti, who was called "I ti," or "First Prince."

through Ramusio's edition.[152] "Sunzien" (Shun t'ien-fu, official name of Peking and its prefecture) he takes from Mendoza.[153] The designation "voo" (probably from Japanese "O" meaning king) could easily have been adopted from any of a number of the Jesuit letterbooks in which it was used.[154] He lists in clearly recognizable form the names for six of the most important of the Spice Islands, or the Moluccas, which he apparently learned from the accounts of Maximilian of Transylvania and Pigafetta published by Ramusio.[155] His names of places in northern India, such as "Moltan" (Multan), probably came from the Jesuit letterbooks that were so full of the mission to Akbar of the 1590's, or from the accounts of India by the Venetian merchants Cesare Fedrici and Gasparo Balbi published respectively in 1587 and 1590.[156]

Vitei excelled in all the arts of peace and war. He invented artillery and a marvelous war machine which he called "stormer of the cities." He found herbs for treating snake bites and invented the craft of printing. He discoursed learnedly on painting and sculpture as well as on the natural sciences. He produced recipes for the preparation of special foods for the better nutrition of horses and birds. He consulted the oracles both natural and divine and sagely predicted the outcome of battles and other events. He revered his father, organized festivals to honor him, and invented machines to astound the spectators at these festivals. He discussed eclipses, tidal waves, earthquakes, and the horrible storms of the Eastern seas and specified ways for predicting their occurrence. He was reverent in his attitude toward god and man, prized friendship and loyalty, and held that woman's true beauty lies in her good character. Vitei, in short, was a model prince who possessed deep understanding, pride in solid accomplishments, and staunchness in moral virtue.

The landscape of Arrivabene's "Asia" is dotted with marvels, both real and fabulous. Animals figure prominently in his descriptions and great care is taken to speculate about the qualities and character of strange beasts and of their ability to reason. Horses, dogs, ants, bees, frogs, elephants, rhinoceroses, panthers, parrots, crocodiles, and other real animals compete for the reader's attention with mermaids, Amazons, giants, unicorns, monsters, and fantastic creatures part animal and part man. Palaces, cities, provinces, and countries are described but at no greater length than miracles, demons, funerals, festivals, and the supposed virtues and powers of certain precious stones. The gods include a mélange of Asian and Greek deities, including the Tartar Natigai mentioned by both Marco Polo and Mendoza.[157] In fact, most of the book deals with descriptions of people, places, and things. It includes just a few romantic or chivalric episodes, the most notable being a kind of pastoral tale revolving around Tiatira, the daughter of

---

[152] *Il magno Vitei*, p. 12.
[153] *Ibid.* Cf. Staunton (ed.), *op. cit.* (n. 148), p. 56.
[154] *Il magno Vitei*, p. 70. Also see *Asia*, I, 661.
[155] *Il magno Vitei*, p. 530.
[156] See *Asia*, I, 452–56, 468–75.
[157] *Il magno Vitei*, p. 43.

the king of Travancore and wife of Rui Bareto, who, to judge from his name, is a Portuguese adventurer![158]

From this brief summary it can clearly be perceived that *Il magno Vitei* is really a mixture of ethnohistory and romance generously sprinkled with observations on natural phenomena and morality. Its Asian setting is authentic in terms of what Europeans knew at the time. The attributes of most of its leading characters appear to be the personal creation of the author. Many places are authentic but a few are clearly mythological or defy identification. Arrivabene seeks in this work to delight his readers with descriptions of a real but exotic Asia and to transmit his moral message of the perfect prince by regarding him as the founder of China, long the model state of Asia.

That Arrivabene was justified in his elevation of China to a model for Europe can be easily observed by reading Mendoza's book, the Jesuit letterbooks of the late sixteenth century, and the works of Possevino and Botero.[159] The message that emerges from these writings supports in large part Arrivabene's enthusiasm for China. But it should also be noticed that he studiously omits from *Il magno Vitei* the criticisms expressed in his sources about the cowardice, rapacity, unreliability, deviousness, and sexual immorality of the Chinese. Arrivabene's book is a homily rather than a history or a romance. It is also the first in a long line of didactic works in prose in which China is celebrated as a model state. In short, the China that was revered by Enlightenment writers of the eighteenth century is anticipated in this work of the late sixteenth century. From this viewpoint Arrivabene had more in common with Voltaire than with Ariosto, a conclusion that highlights how far European writers had moved in their understanding and appreciation of Asia over the course of the sixteenth century.

Venice and its subject cities of northeastern Italy maintained a position of primacy in the translation, publication, and dissemination of popular literature throughout the century. To the writers of the first generation Asia was of interest mainly in terms of its commercial importance and its strange flora and fauna. For Boiardo and Ariosto it was still a semi-imaginary world, a background for heroic accomplishments in war and love. The appearance of travel collections and printed maps at mid-century had the effect of making Asia, especially India, more definitely a part of the real world. Authors and collectors of *novelle* extracted new stories as well as exotic embellishments and backgrounds from the travel books. The polygraphs regularly included new materials about Asia in their diverse encyclopedic works which became so numerous in the latter half of the century.

The main effect of the Counter-Reformation in Italy, especially after the publication of the Tridentine *Index*, was to discourage morally casual and

---

[158] *Il magno Vitei*, p. 145. For a more detailed summary of the episode in *Il magno Vitei* see Tom, *op. cit.* (n. 40), pp. 87–98.

[159] See below, pp. 235, 237.

dissolute literature and to promote writings didactic in intent. By discouraging activity in previously flourishing fields of literature, it encouraged interest in distant lands and peoples. The Jesuit letterbooks openly compared Asian to Christian manners and morals for the edification of European readers. But some lay moralists, like Tasso, were almost completely unresponsive in their writings to the new knowledge about Asia and the overseas world that had become available. While he knew and appreciated the *Lusiads*, the Portuguese East was not included in Tasso's vision of the world, for the events of the last two decades of the century had the effect of shifting interest away from India and the Spiceries to the religious and commercial opportunities which seemed to be presenting themselves in Japan and China. The appearance of the Japanese emissaries in Italy during 1585, accompanied and followed by the publication of Mendoza's *China* (1585) and Maffei's Latin history of the Eastern missions (1588) stimulated new hopes for success in eastern Asia that were reflected in the hack romances of the Venetian printers as well as in moralistic writings. Baldi compares the products while Torelli compares the social practices of Europe and Asia. In the *Vitei* of Arrivabene, China is elevated to a model kingdom where the perfect prince finds a suitable milieu in which to perform his exemplary heroics. The medieval "Cathay" of Boiardo had thus been transformed over the course of the sixteenth century into a glorious kingdom from which Europeans had much to learn.

3

HISTORY AND COSMOGRAPHY

The sages of Padua, Bembo and Buonamico, were among the first of the Italian intellectuals to bring the overseas discoveries into history. They had encouraged the young Portuguese Damião de Góis, during his stay in Padua from 1534 to 1538, to continue writing on the overseas exploits of his countrymen.[160] Bembo, as already mentioned, summarized the Portuguese discoveries on the basis of reports he received, and included a brief recapitulation of them in Book VI of his history of Venice (1551). The celebrated historian Francesco Guicciardini set out in his history of Italy (1567) to recount as objectively as possible the story of the wars that swept Italy from 1492 to 1534. Even he diverged from his analysis of Italian events and personages to comment: "It is manifest that the Ancients were mistaken in many things relating to the knowledge of the earth."[161] Other members of his family were also seeking to remedy this deficiency by studying cartography and geography and by collecting materials on the Portuguese East.[162]

160 See above, pp. 20–21.

161 From the English translation of *The History of Italy* (London, 1753), III, Bk. vi, 311.

162 M. Battistini (ed.), *Lettere di Giovan Battista Guicciardini a Cosimo e Francesco de' Medici: scritte dal 1559 al 1577* (Brussels and Rome, 1949), p. 71.

Responses of this sort by the most eminent Italian historians of the century constituted recognition of the fact that all known nations and peoples had to be brought into history. Their inclusion was necessary if comparisons were to be made and general principles derived to elucidate geography, human similarities and differences, and universal institutional norms.[163] Very expressive of the general need to know more about the rest of the world and so to provide for Europe's own security and future well-being is this comment from Cardano's *The Book of My Life* (1575):

Among the extraordinary though quite natural circumstances of my life the first and most unusual is that I was born in this century in which the whole world became known, whereas the ancients were familiar with but little more than a third part of it.

On the one hand we explore America. . . . Besides all these, towards the East under the Antarctic we find the Antiscians . . . as well as Japan, Binarchia ["double kingdom," i.e. China], the Amazons, and a region which is beyond the Island of the Demons—if these be not fabled islands—all discoveries sure to give rise to great and calamitous events in order that a just distribution of them may be maintained.[164]

Representative of the attitude of Humanist historians toward the discoveries in the East are the writings of Paolo Giovio (1483–1552), also known as Paulus Jovius. Like many of his contemporaries, Jovius took a degree in medicine at Pavia and sporadically practiced at Rome and elsewhere. Early in life Jovius began to compile a history of his own times which he wrote in Latin. In carrying out this project he was encouraged by the patronage of Pope Leo X and a number of his successors. In 1528 Jovius was awarded the bishopric of Nocera, one of the benefices that contributed to the wealth which made it possible for him later in life to live in style at his villa on Lake Como. A favorite of the Medici family, he was employed by them to undertake a number of ceremonial missions. His connections with the Vatican and the Medicis enabled him to spend many years close to the seats of ecclesiastical, political, and economic power in Italy. Through these associations he was able to keep in touch with persons from other parts of Europe who frequented the Vatican or maintained relations with the Medici.[165]

Jovius wrote many biographies and collected a musuem of portraits of the great men of his day. One of the earliest of his published works was the life of the Spanish officer Gonsalvo Hernandez de Cordova, called the "great captain." Written in 1525 and 1526, this biography includes a brief survey of the major historical events of the years immediately preceding, including the wars in

[163] See F. Gilbert, "The Renaissance Interest in History," in C. S. Singleton (ed.), *Art, Science, and History in the Renaissance* (Baltimore, 1968), p. 386.

[164] G. Cardano, *The Book of My Life* (New York, 1930), p. 189.

[165] For his biography see G. Sanesi, "Alcuni osservazioni e notizie intorno a tre storici minori del cinquecento," *Archivio storico italiano*, 5th ser. XXIII (1899), pp. 260–88; also F. Chabod, "Paulo Giovio," in *Scritti sul Rinascimento* (Turin, 1967), pp. 243–67. The most recent edition of the works was published by *Istituto Poligrafico dello Stato* and edited by G. G. Ferrero and D. Visconti, *Opera . . .* (4 vols.; Rome, 1956–64). For his relations with Florence see Cochrane, *op. cit.* (n. 120), pp. 71–72, 81–82.

Hungary and Poland, the conflicts between the Turks and Persians, and the overseas achievements of the Portuguese. He observes that the Portuguese, after subduing the kings of India, pushed eastward to Malacca, Sumatra, and the Spiceries.[166] This was probably information that Jovius gathered from the Portuguese embassy that was still the talk of Rome when he arrived there in 1516. Such a conclusion is supported by the fact that he included a description of the embassy in his *Lives of Great Men* and kept a portrait of Tristão da Cunha, its leader, in his gallery.[167] But what is most significant about this biography is Jovius' apparent determination to bring events from the non-European world into chronological juxtaposition with contemporary European happenings.

A review of Jovius' extant correspondence of the 1540's reveals his overwhelming fear of Turkish expansion, his enthusiasm for the Christian crusades in the Levant, and his preoccupation with all events and matters relating to the struggle between Europe and the Ottoman Empire.[168] He is therefore mainly aroused by those events in Portuguese expansion which could be interpreted as being reverses for Islam.[169] He is well informed about the geography of the Indian Ocean and the Persian Gulf and understands the strategic naval problems confronted by the Portuguese in controlling the maritime trade routes between India and the Mediterranean basin. Jovius apparently had a Portuguese servant, whom he refers to in his letters as "mio portoghese," who helped to keep him in touch with happenings in the overseas empire.[170] This Portuguese promised to obtain for Jovius an ebony idol with mother-of-pearl eyes and ivory teeth that was worshipped by the king of Cannanore and which was reputedly almost as large as Rodamonte, the pagan champion in Ariosto's *Orlando*.[171] From the writings of João de Barros, the Portuguese chronicler, it appears that Jovius corresponded with him directly and that Barros sent materials on Asia as well as Asian books to Jovius.[172] That Jovius was able to keep abreast of contemporary happenings in Asia is substantiated by his letter of 1547 on the Portuguese victory at Diu of the previous year in which he remarks:

In the meantime we rejoice in two great victories—one in India, where the King of Cambaya has been ejected from the city of Diu with great loss and shame, since he had

---

[166] See C. Panigada (ed.), *Le vite del Gran Capitano e del Marchese di Pescara*, translated from Latin into Italian by Ludovico Domenichi (Bari, 1931), pp. 189–90.

[167] See Paulo Giovio, *Illustrium virorum vitae* (Florence, 1551), p. 263. Also see for his gallery of portraits C. Müntz, "Le musée de portraits de Paul Jove," *Mémoires de l'institut national de France, Académie des inscriptions et belles lettres*, XXXVI (1901), 249–343.

[168] Cf. his *Turcicarum rerum commentarius* (Paris, 1538) in which he deals with the life and celebrates the victories of Scanderbeg, the Albanian national hero and foe of Turkey.

[169] Jovius probably knew the little Italian book called *Impresa del gran turco per mare e per terra contra Portoghesi* (Rome, 1531). For a reproduction and a discussion of it see Francisco Leite de Faria, "Un impresso de 1531 sobre as empressas dos Portugueses no Oriente," *Boletim internacional da bibliografia Luso-Brasileira*, VII (1966), 90–109.

[170] For examples, see Ferrero and Visconti (eds.), *op. cit.* (n. 165), I, 263; II, 160–61.

[171] From a letter to his patron, Cardinal Alessandro Farnese (Rome, September 8, 1544), as reproduced *ibid.*, I, 342. Also see *ibid.*, p. 350.

[172] See *Asia*, I, 410 n., 777.

already leveled to the ground its towers and battleworks; yet more than 600 Portuguese *fidalgos* have been killed. So, long live their king, Dom John, and his wife.[173]

In the *Historiarum sui temporis*, first published in 1550, Jovius undertook to record in forty-five books divided into two parts the most important events which occurred in every part of the world from the French invasion of Italy in 1494 to the year 1547. The materials (Bks. IX–XI) in the first part which refer to the period from 1498, the date of Vasco da Gama's first voyage, to 1513, the election of Pope Leo X, were inexplicably omitted in the sixteenth-century editions. His first notice of events in the East appears in connection with his comment on the Portuguese embassy of 1514 to Leo X. Here he seizes the opportunity to report on the victories of the Portuguese at the celebrated emporiums of Cannanore, Cochin, and Calicut in India and of Malacca further to the East.[174] Later, he refers again to Portuguese conquests in India and adds to his list "Narsingam" (Vijayanagar), whose present king is wealthy and possesses a strong mounted army. He also notes that the Portuguese sway in 1514 extends from Ethiopia to the coast of China.[175]

Jovius observes that the Portuguese carry on trade at "Cantam" (Canton), a city similar to Venice, surrounded by the sea and with buildings joined together by stone bridges.[176] Canton's lofty houses, like those of Venice, boast windows with transparent glass panes and iron trellises and here and there gardens with fruit-bearing trees and plants. Men and women alike ride about in covered boats and in horse-drawn carriages "like ours." The gentry wear colored and extravagantly long gowns and sport beards like those of the Venetians.[177] And what is most admirable to him is the presence at Canton of printers

who print according to our own method certain books containing histories and rites on a very long folio which is folded inwards into square pages. Pope Leo has very graciously let me see a volume of this kind, given him as a present with an elephant by the king of Portugal. So that from this [example] we can readily believe that others of this sort, before the Portuguese had reached India, came to us through the Scythians and Muscovites and provided us with an incomparable aid to letters.[178]

Whether Jovius concluded on his own that printing had passed overland from

---

[173] Letter from Rome (October 1, 1547) to Cardinal Nicolò de' Gaddi as reproduced in Ferrero and Visconti (eds.), *op. cit.* (n. 165), II, 113. In this same year the Portuguese Diego Pirro (also known as Didaco) wrote from Ferrara a long autobiographical letter to Jovius, a further testimony to his association with Portuguese men of letters. See G. Bertoni, "Umanisti portoghesi a Ferrara (Hermico e Didaco)," *Giornale storico della letteratura italiana*, CXIV (1939), 50.

[174] See Ferrero and Visconti (eds.), *op. cit.* (n. 165), III, 233–34.

[175] *Ibid.*, pp. 317–18.

[176] *Ibid.*, p. 320. Notice also that Odoric of Pordenone had remarked in the fourteenth century that Canton "is as big as three Venices" (*Asia*, I, 41).

[177] The comparison of Canton to Venice suggests that Jovius obtained this information from a Venetian informant, perhaps Ramusio. For a study of his admiration for Venice and of his relations with Venetians see C. Volpati, "Paolo Giovio e Venezia," *Archivio veneto*, 5th ser. XV (1934), 132–56. It is also possible, however, that his information came through his Portuguese servant, or even from Barros directly.

[178] Ferrero and Visconti (eds.), *op. cit.* (n. 165), 320. Also see *Asia*, I, 777.

China to Europe is not known. It is clear, however, that the question of priority of discovery was being discussed in Portugal before mid-century.[179]

In the second part of his *History*, dealing with the years from 1527 to 1547, Jovius is concerned primarily with the activities of Suleiman the Magnificent, sultan of the Ottoman Empire from 1520 to 1566 and the conqueror of the Hungarians at Mohacs in 1526. In his disquietude over the advance of the Turks into Europe, Jovius sees the Portuguese conquest of the spice route and of the strategic maritime locations in the East as contributing to the under-mining of a vital source of Ottoman income and as an important distraction of Turkish effort.[180] For information on strategic points such as Ormuz, Aden, and Ceylon he apparently consulted the cosmography of Peter Apian.[181] He was also impressed by the Spanish and Portuguese achievements in opening the overseas world. The accomplishments of Columbus make him more worthy of eternal fame than Hercules. The voyage of Magellan Jovius calls "miraculous," and claims for Serrano, Magellan, and Pigafetta "every ornament of praise to the perpetual fame of their names as was the custom among the ancient Greeks."[182] He evidently met Pigafetta at Rome when the world traveler was received in 1524 at the court of Pope Clement VII. Jovius lived at the Vatican then and he obtained from Pigafetta pictures of and writings about many marvelous things. Jovius was also aware, probably through the writings and letters of Peter Martyr,[183] that the Castilians were following up the voyage of Magellan to the Spiceries with other expeditions across the Pacific. Thus, the emperor as well as the Portuguese would, in Jovius' estimation, be in a position to strengthen Christendom and weaken the Turk through capturing and holding against all comers the source of the spices. But he, like Luther and Erasmus, was not happy with the spice monopoly or with the high prices charged by the Portuguese. He even suggested that better and cheaper spices could be obtained through Muscovy.[184]

Jovius treats the discoveries in the East as marginal to his main concern, the problems of security posed by Turkey in eastern Europe. He is also well aware of the importance of the spice trade and the metals of America to the prosperity and stability of Christendom.[185] His interest in Muscovy also causes him to be sensitive to the balance of power in the Levant and Central Asia. To 1550, the date of publication for his *History*, only a few written sources on Asia were available to him; the Portuguese control on information was still operative and the Jesuits had not yet begun to publish their newsletters. An eager student of geography, he sought as best he could to present accurately the locations, names, and descriptions of distant places, such as Canton. At least one gazetteer

---

179 See above, p. 127, and below, pp. 404–5.
180 Ferrero and Visconti (eds.), *op. cit.* (n. 165), IV, 302, 336, 434.
181 *Ibid.*, p. 300.
182 *Ibid.*, p. 349.
183 *Ibid.*, p. 346.
184 See above, p. 22.
185 On his treatment of America see Romeo (ed.), *op. cit.* (n. 127), pp. 30–31.

was compiled from an analysis of his *History*.[186] He was only vaguely interested in the peoples of Asia in general, mainly limiting his remarks to their natural conditions. But he was impressed by what little he knew of Chinese civilization and was sufficiently open-minded to suggest that the art of printing had traveled overland from China to Europe. He does not hesitate to place the navigators and conquerors of his own day on a pedestal as high as, or sometimes higher than, those he usually reserved for the heroes of Antiquity. Despite the fragmentary character of his interest, Jovius tried to incorporate the discoveries into general history and, as a consequence, shed for the learned community a bit of light on their meaning to the Europeans of his own day.

The polygraphs of Venice were likewise busy in writing contemporary history, usually in the form of annals. These popular historians, like the scholarly Bembo, were supremely conscious of events taking place outside Italy and were more inclined than others to compile geographical chronicles called world histories.[187] Giovanni Tarcagnota (d. 1566), a native of Morea, was probably inspired or even hired by the printer Giunti, the publisher of the Ramusio travel collection, to compile a comprehensive history of the world in annalistic form. His *Delle historie del mondo* (3 vols. in 5 parts; Venice, 1562) centers on Antiquity and the Middle Ages and concludes with the year 1513. It was continued by Mambrino Roseo in a volume published in 1573 which covers the period from 1519 to 1559.[188] Roseo, who in 1570 had published a life of Alexander the Great and a compendium of ancient writings on his successors,[189] was much better informed than Tarcagnota on contemporary events in Asia. Under 1540 he reports on Xavier's departure for the East Indies and asserts that the Jesuit learned there "a language named Malay, the universal language of the Indies."[190] He tells of the Portuguese-Turkish naval battles in the Indian Ocean and of the first siege of Diu.[191] He comments at length on the efforts of the Jesuits and the Portuguese to convert the truculent people of Goa.[192] Probably on the basis of the Jesuit letters he summarizes the progress of the Christian mission in China and Japan to 1557.[193] He expresses personal surprise that the Japanese and Chinese live in so orderly a fashion without knowledge of the "true God," a feeling which Xavier himself had also experienced.

A contemporary of Roseo was Giovanni Lorenzo d'Anania (*ca.* 1545–*ca.* 1607),

---

[186] See Carlo Passi, *Tavola della provincie, citta, castella, popoli, monti, mari, fiume, et laghi de quali il Giovio ha fatto nelle sue istorie mentione*... (Venice, 1570). Strangely he makes no mention of either Goa or Japan.

[187] See O. Logan, *Culture and Society in Venice, 1470–1790* (London, 1972), pp. 115–16. Also see W. T. Elwert, *Studi di letteratura veneziana* (Venice, 1958), pp. 36–37.

[188] *Delle historie del mondo . . . parte terza. Aggiunta alla . . . Historia de M. Giovanni Tarchagnota* (3 vols. in 5; Venice, 1598). Tarcagnota's history was later continued by others down to the date 1606.

[189] M. Rosco, *Vita di Alessandro Magno* (Venice, 1570) and *Historia de' successore di Alessandro Magno. Raccolata da diversi auttori, et in gran parte da Diodoro Siculo* . . . (Venice, 1570).

[190] M. Roseo, *Delle historie del mondo* (n. 188), pp. 125^r–125^v.

[191] Under 1539, *ibid.*, pp. 146^r–146^v.

[192] Under 1557, *ibid.*, pp. 325^v–326^r.

[193] *Ibid.*, pp. 335^r–336^v.

a native of Taverna in Calabria who spent his active years in Naples. Anania was sponsored at Naples in his extensive study of natural sciences, languages, and theology by Archbishop Mario Carafa (d. 1576). As an outgrowth of his studies, Anania published in 1573 his *L'universale fabrica del mondo* ... (Naples), a cosmography divided into four treatises. These give far more sophisticated and integrated views of the overseas world than contemporaries could obtain from the brief references in the annalistic histories. Each treatise deals with the contemporary state of knowledge on each of the four geographical regions into which he divides the world: Europe, Asia, Africa, and America. Three years after its publication at Naples, Anania's work was reprinted by I. Vidali at Venice for the printer A. San Vito of Naples.[194] It was again reprinted twenty years later (1596) at Venice, an indication of the interest that it continued to have for sixteenth-century readers.

Anania's second treatise, which deals with Asia, is almost one hundred pages long (pp. 157–253). About one-half of it centers on Portuguese Asia and Tartary (pp. 202–33). From the list of authors which he provides at the beginning of his work, it is evident that Anania assiduously combed the literature of Antiquity, the Middle Ages, and his own day for materials on Asia. It is hard to find an authority whose writing was in print before 1573 whom he does not list in his bibliography or cite in his text.[195] His Portuguese sources are Barbosa (probably in Ramusio's rendition), Góis, and Barros. Textual comparison indicates that he closely followed in many places the Italian translation of the first two *Décadas* of Barros published at Venice in 1562.[196] Among the Spanish writers, Anania cites most of those reproduced in Ramusio's *Navigationi*, including Peter Martyr, Oviedo, and Gomara. His Italian sources are naturally the most numerous; they include among others: Marco Polo, Corsali, Varthema, Vespucci, Pigafetta, Paulus Jovius, Bordone, and Porcacchi. He also cites the maps and accounts of the modifiers of Ptolemy, as well as Gastaldi, Münster, and Ortelius. He mentions "Abilfada Arabi" (possibly the Christian historian, Aboulfaradj) and refers repeatedly in his text to Levantine writers and informants. One of these was Don Filippo d'Austria, a Turkish Christian.[197] He also lists "Gioscepe Indo," probably a reference to Priest Joseph, the Syro-Malabar Christian who visited Italy in 1502 and whose comments appeared in print in 1505 and thereafter.[198] His most recent materials Anania obtained from the Jesuit letters and letterbooks circulating in Italy as well as from seamen who

194 I have used this first Venetian edition. It is dedicated to Catherine Jagellon Sforza, princess of Poland and queen of Sweden, the sister of Sigismund II of Poland who married John III of Sweden to merge the Jagellon and Vasa dynasties.

195 He apparently did not know or use the work of Castanheda, even though the first book of the *Historia* had appeared at Rome in Italian translation in 1556. See *Asia*, I, 189. Ulloa's translation of the first seven books of Castanheda's *Historia* did not appear in print until 1577–78.

196 The translation of Alfonso Ulloa entitled *L'Asia del S. Giovanni de Barros* (Venice, 1562) was published by Vincenzo Valgrisio. Anania's place names in India frequently, but not always, follow the order and spelling of those in the Italianized Barros.

197 Anania, *L'universale fabrica del mondo* ... (Naples, 1573), p. 215.

198 See *Asia*, I, 157–58.

turned up at the port of Naples. He often cites a certain "Aviadat," presumably a sailor who had seen service with the Portuguese, as an authority for his comments on places and practices in maritime southeast Asia. He describes the appearance of certain Chinese who had come from Portugal to Naples. This is the first and only reference to Chinese visitors in Naples at so early a date, that is, before 1573.[199]

In his delineation of Portuguese Asia, Anania follows the general outline provided in Barros' work. His sketch is much less detailed than Barros', but he treats the regions of Asia in the same order: India, Southeast Asia, China, and Japan. He also brings Barros up to date by amplifying and amending his remarks with more recent materials from the Jesuit letters.[200] He points up conflicts and omissions in his sources and enlivens his materials by including observations based on his own experiences. For example, when commenting on the Indian and Chinese languages he describes their "alphabet" and forms of writing on the basis of samples he had seen.[201] He delights in describing strange customs such as the Sinhalese worship of the "tooth of Buddha" and the Indian practice of chewing betel.[202] Nor does he neglect the elephant and rhinoceros, the two pachyderms which had come to symbolize "Asia" for the sixteenth century or the lory (he gives *Nuri*, the Malay word), the bird about which "Aviadat" told him many details.[203] He briefly describes the Portuguese political system in India and, on the basis of the Jesuit letters, endeavors to identify the principal officials of Japan and China.[204] He is fascinated with strange products, such as coir, rhubarb, cinnamon, tea ("chiam"), sago, and cloves. Samples of certain of them he observed and tasted at the home of Ferrante Imperato (*ca.* 1550–1631), the Neapolitan pharmacist and collector of botanicals, minerals, and precious stones.[205] He remarks in some detail on religious practices especially of the Brahmans and Yogis of India and the Buddhists of Ceylon, Siam, and Japan.[206]

In his discussions of religion, language, and products Anania regularly introduces a comparative note by observing that certain practices resemble

---

[199] Anania, *op. cit.* (n. 197), p. 225. That Chinese visitors to Europe went from Iberia to other parts is later attested by Mendoza: "there came anno 1585 three [Chinese] merchants with verie curious things, and never staied till they came into Spaine and into other kingdomes further off" (Staunton [ed.], *op. cit.* [n. 148], I, 95).

[200] In his list of authors consulted, he mentions *Lettere de'Iesuiti* and two titles (*Commentarij della Cina, e quelli dell' India Orientali* and *Somario delle cose Oriêtali*) which I take to be those of the letter-books.

[201] *Ibid.*, pp. 204, 235. Also see below, p. 205. He mentions seeing samples of Chinese writing in the Jesuit letterbooks.

[202] *Ibid.*, pp. 211, 213.

[203] *Ibid.*, pp. 210–11, 214, 228.

[204] *Ibid.*, pp. 207, 225, 234–35.

[205] *Ibid.*, p. 230. On the basis of his collection and of his experiments in his botanical garden, Imperato published his *Dell' historia naturale libri XXVIII* (Naples, 1599). It was reissued at Venice in 1610 and 1672 and translated into Latin and published at Cologne in 1695. Also see below, p. 439.

[206] Anania, *op. cit.* (n. 197), pp. 209, 211, 213, 215, 228, 234–35.

"ours," or that products are like "ours," or that Japanese resemble Flemings in their industry. Like Barros, he is interested in names and etymology; he notes that Ceylon is called "Sarandil" by the Persians and Turks, that the great maritime storms of Asia are called "Tifone," that "Cina" is derived from Greek and Latin "Sina," and that the Arabs call cinnamon "Darseni" (actually "dār-chīnī").[207] The people of India are dark in color,[208] of medium stature, refined, astute, and unstable in their ideas; the Chinese, whom he had personally seen, are about the height of a Fleming, broad, with only a slight beard, with small eyes, and a complexion "like ours"; the natives of the Spiceries are unstable in mind, of medium stature, very delicate, and, because they originally came from both China and India, some are white like the Chinese while others are as black as Ethiopians.[209] The Chinese and Japanese are far superior to all other Asians—possibly because they are white—in wealth, ingenuity, and the cultivation of the liberal and mechanical arts.[210]

Anania describes Tartary on the basis of Ptolemy and Marco Polo. He claims that Tartary was called "Magog" by the Hebrews and "Scythia" by the Greeks and Romans. He discusses the Mongol invasions of China, Russia, and eastern Europe and records that almost all of Asia recognized the rule of Genghis Khan. In contrast to his description of Portuguese Asia, his literary portrait of Tartary is filled with traditional stories told almost without regard to chronological order. He is himself aware of his source problem for he sought to verify his materials by interviewing English members of the Muscovy company when they passed through Naples. He was even willing to accept the word of an English schismatic, "Thomas Cusnibi," about Tartar customs.[211] From Richard Gray, who had been in Russia from 1555 to 1557, he learned of the fur-bearing animals of the steppe, and something about the trade between China (Cataio) and Muscovy.[212] But for all his efforts, he was able to provide only a hazy sketch of Tartary (pp. 236–52) which contrasts unfavorably with his relatively clear and accurate account of maritime Asia. Despite his obvious limitations, Anania was still far better informed about Asia than any of his Italian predecessors, and he was the first of a generation of cosmographers, historians, and political theorists who would begin to take Asia seriously and to bring it into their narrative works as an independent and civilized part of the known world.

A model for the universal histories of the last decade of the century is provided by the two works of Cesare Campana (*ca.* 1540–1606), a native of Aquila who spent most of his adult life in Vicenza. His general history of the world from

---

[207] *Ibid.*, pp. 210, 220, 222, 228, 230. On the Turkish word for Ceylon also see above, p. 212 n. On the word "typhoon" see below, p. 533. He also notices that the Chinese refer to themselves as *Tamen*, a recognizable romanization of *Ta Ming*, or men of the "great Ming" dynasty.

[208] For contemporary speculation on the reasons for diversity of complexion see G. C. Maffei, *Scala naturala* (Venice, 1564), pp. 52–57.

[209] Anania, *op. cit.* (n. 197), pp. 204, 225, 226.

[210] *Ibid.*, p. 235.

[211] *Ibid.*, p. 247.

[212] *Ibid.*, p. 249.

the foundation of Rome onward is not of direct interest.[213] But its continuation which deals with events from 1580 to 1596 contains much information on the East.[214] He is aware of the activities of the Spanish in the Philippines and of the dispatch of Augustinian missionaries to China, materials probably obtained from Mendoza's book.[215] On the basis of the Jesuit letters he comments at length on the successes of the mission in Japan and of the political strife and wars in that distant island kingdom.[216] In connection with his discussion of the martyrdoms at Salsette in 1583, he gives a brief history of Portuguese India and the problems faced there by Europeans.[217] He was most impressed, however, by the presence of the Japanese emissaries in Italy in 1585. Under that date he allots more space to Japan and the Japanese than he does to the famine and riots in Naples which resulted in a sudden political insurrection against the Spanish crown. From his observations it seems clear that he actually saw the Japanese, probably during their stay at Vicenza in July, 1585.[218] He remarks that they eat everything with chopsticks, except bread, and that they sleep fully clothed. Of the Japanese themselves he remarks: "They are of less than average stature and they have faces olive in color, an agreeable mien, and genteel; the eyes small with heavy eyelids, and the nose bulgy at the end without serious disfigure-ment."[219] Campana notes under subsequent years the arrival of the Japanese at Goa and Macao on their return trip home.[220] In connection with Spanish activities in the Philippines he reports that many seeds of plants important to human life have been brought back to Europe, even though it is not clear to him how they will be used.[221]

As illustrated in the writings of Campana and his predecessors, the conviction had become firmly rooted among Renaissance thinkers that everything has a history and that it is the function of history to provide knowledge of remote times and peoples to compare to the known present.[222] Francesco Patrizi (1529–97) compares the account of the Castilian and Portuguese "voyages" to the *Natural History* of Pliny and admits them to historiography as "mixed histories" because they recount something about the ways of living and describe

213 *Delle istorie del mondo . . . libri 4* (Venice, 1591).

214 *Delle historie del mondo . . . libri sedici; ne' quali diffusamente si narrano le cose avvenute dall' Anno 1580 fino al 1596 . . .* (Turin, 1598). For a comparison of his treatment of Asia with a contemporary work see G. N. Doglioni, *Compendio historico universale . . .* (Venice, 1605). Doglioni has almost nothing to say about the overseas world except to remark (p. 485) that Ramusio has replaced in authority the writings of Ptolemy, Strabo, and Pliny.

215 *Ibid.*, p. 13.

216 *Ibid.*, pp. 89–90, 247–48, 272–76.

217 *Ibid.*, p. 115.

218 The publisher, Perim and Angelieri, printed at Vicenza a *Descrittione* of the embassy in 1585. See Maria Cristofari, "La tipografia vicentina nel secolo XVI," in *Miscellanea . . . in memoria di Luigi Ferrari* (Florence, 1952), p. 199.

219 *Ibid.*, p. 164.

220 *Ibid.*, pp. 276, 321.

221 *Ibid.*, pp. 392–93.

222 See G. Spini, "Historiography: The Art of History in the Italian Counter-Reformation," in E. Cochrane (ed.), *The Late Italian Renaissance* (London, 1970), pp. 102–3; and Peter Burke, *The Renaissance Sense of the Past* (New York, 1970), pp. 39–49.

the world of nature in distant places.[223] The related tendency of the secular students of history to treat religion and the church merely as historical developments subject to change stirred hostility among the orthodox. The Jesuits in particular sought to build intellectual defenses against the infiltration and dissemination of ideas deemed to be dangerous to the church as a divine institution.

One of the leading Jesuit historians to undertake the task of rebutting the heretical ideas of Machiavelli, Bodin, Patrizi, and the Protestant historians was Antonio Possevino (1534–1611). A native of Mantua, Possevino entered the Society of Jesus in 1559 and spent many years leading missions in Europe. From 1573 to 1577 he acted as secretary of the Society and worked directly under General Mercurian. Pope Gregory XIII sent him to Poland and Russia in 1581–82 in an effort to effect religious concord.[224] On his return to Italy in 1586 he turned his attention to teaching at Rome and Padua and to the preparation of religious counterattacks against secular historiography. Possevino launched his campaign in 1592 by publishing a *Judicium* on the writings of Machiavelli and Bodin as well as on those of two lesser authors.[225] Here as elsewhere he attacks the political amorality of Machiavelli and argues vehemently against the dangerous ideas of Bodin and the Protestants. Although he inveighs unrelentingly against the *Methodus* of Bodin, he implicitly accepts its tripartite divisions of natural, human, and divine history. Possevino then creates a fourth division of ecclesiastical history, or the history of religious institutions and thought. It is this last field which he tries his utmost to cultivate by bringing into his view of history and into the curriculum of the Jesuit colleges what knowledge the Society possessed about Japanese religion and about the achievements of the Jesuits in converting the overseas world.

In 1593 Possevino published at Rome his *Bibliotheca selecta*, a compendium of scholarly reading and documentation which lists more than eight thousand authors as well as their works and points of view. The final pages of Book IX deal with China and are based on materials and information relayed to him by Father Michele Ruggiero, the Jesuit who had returned to Rome from China in 1590.[226] Possevino himself provides a brief but highly flattering moral portrait of the Chinese comparable to those of Arrivabene and the Sinophiles of the eighteenth century. Books X and XI include an authoritative discussion of

---

[223] *Della historia diece dialoghi* . . . (Venice, 1560), p. 8ᵛ. Patrizi, the Neo-Platonist philosopher, also displays interest in Chinese and Japanese characters as images or emblems of the things they represent. He had evidently seen examples of Chinese books and characters (*ibid.*, p. 12ᵛ). He mentions them in connection with his discussion of "fantasies," or the visual representations which remain of the human past.

[224] Possevino thought that a union between Latin and Greek Catholics was not only important in itself, but that cooperation between Rome and Muscovy might lead to the Christian conquest of all Asia. See S. Polein, "Une tentative d'Union au XVIᵉ siècle: la mission religieuse du Père Antoine Possevin, S.J., en Moscovie (1581–82)," *Orientalia Christiana analecta*, No. 150 (1957), pp. 25, 39, 90–91.

[225] *Judicium de quatuor scriptoribus* (la Nove, Bodin, Philip de Morney et Machiavelli) (Rome, 1592).

[226] On Ruggiero see *Asia*, I, 820–21, and below, p. 515.

Japanese religion, especially Buddhism, written by the able Jesuit Visitor and Humanist, Alessandro Valignano.[227] To this discussion Possevino adds a series of arguments designed to convince the Japanese of the existence of the Christian God and of their imperative need to observe the First Commandment by denying all other gods.

Possevino's *Bibliotheca selecta* was reissued in 1594 and 1603; it was revised and expanded in his *Apparatus ad omnium gentium historiarum* (Venice, 1597), a kind of guidebook to the study of geography and to different parts of the world. Possevino himself translated this work into Italian and had it published at Venice in 1598 at a time when he was teaching in the Jesuit college at Padua.[228] The bibliographies he gives for reading about the nations of Asia are more interesting than his sketchy textual materials on recent history. He provides comprehensive lists of the ancient, medieval, and modern works which will best introduce the reader to the countries and peoples east of the Indus.[229] Among the Portuguese authorities he lists Góis, Castanheda, Barros, and Osório. His Italian sources include Varthema, Vespucci, and Paulus Jovius. He stresses the importance for recent information of the Jesuit letters and makes special mention of the histories of Maffei, José de Acosta, and Peruschi.[230] He advises the reader to consult his *Bibliotheca* about China and Japan. Originally he took no notice of the popular book by the Augustinian Mendoza on China (Rome, 1585), but he finally does include mention of it in the revised edition of his *Bibliotheca* published in 1603.[231] From these indications Possevino was certainly acquainted with most of the literature on Asia available in his day, and it may be assumed that he assigned his students the task of reading it.

4

THE POLITICAL THOUGHT OF GIOVANNI BOTERO

Possevino's contemporary and acquaintance Giovanni Botero (1544–1617) was one of Europe's leading commentators on history and on political and economic theory.[232] A native of the Piedmont, Botero was educated in rhetoric and

[227] On Valignano see *ibid.*, pp. 255–57, 293–94, 685–86. This document was probably brought to Rome by Ruggiero. See also Possevino, *Bibliotheca selecta* (Rome, 1593), pp. 452–57. For commentary see H. de Lubac and H. Bernard-Maitre, "La découverte du bouddhisme," *Bulletin de l'association Guillaume Budé*," 3d ser., No. 3 (October, 1953), pp. 106–7.

[228] Translated as *Apparato all'historia di tutte le nationi. Et il modo di studiari la geografia.* It is this Italian translation which I have used.

[229] *Ibid.*, pp. 207ᵣ–208ᵥ. Most of the text relates to Greek and Roman historiography, but the final chapter deals with the sources for study of recent history. All of Asia and America come under "India" in his classification.

[230] For details on these authors and their works see *Asia*, I, 323–26, 452–53, 806–8.

[231] On p. 450 he refers to the 1587 edition of Mendoza's *Historia*.

[232] On his date of birth see the article by L. Firpo in *Dizionario biografico degli italiani*. The best study of his intellectual development and of his writings is F. Chabod, *Giovanni Botero* (Rome, 1934); this book is reprinted in the collection of Chabod's works, *Scritti sul Rinascimento* (n. 165), pp. 377–458.

philosophy in the Jesuit colleges of Palermo and Rome. In 1565 he began his teaching career at the Jesuit college of Billom near Clermont in France. Two years later he left the provinces for the college in Paris where he was at once caught up in the city's stimulating cultural and intellectual life. Two years later he returned to Italy to teach and to continue his own studies. In 1573 he was at Padua where he studied theology for the next four years as he prepared to take final vows as a Jesuit. Not happy with a sedentary life, he asked in 1575 and again in 1577 for an assignment to the mission field in "the Indies." His record, however, had been marred over the years by his political activities and by his tactlessness. He was not permitted to take final vows or become a missionary. In 1580 he was dismissed from the Society in which he had served for twenty-two years, possibly because he was a contentious and overly independent personality who had the audacity to preach a sermon in which he attacked the temporal power of the papacy.

Carlo Borromeo, the archbishop of Milan, found the ex-Jesuit a position as a secular priest. In 1582 Botero became secretary to the archbishop. After Borromeo's death in 1584, Botero was sent to France on a diplomatic mission for Savoy which was led by René de Lucinge, a disinguished author of political works. Botero was in Paris during those months in 1585 when the Japanese emissaries were touring Italy, a fact which perhaps accounts for the relatively slight attention he pays to Japan in his writings.[233] While in France he became acquainted with the works of Jean Bodin on political and historical theory. On his return to Italy in 1586, he took service with Federico Borromeo, Carlo's nephew, and accompanied the young prelate to Rome. He helped the younger Borromeo to become cardinal in 1587. Thereafter Botero enjoyed the privilege of being in constant attendance at a cardinal's court. He kept in touch with members of the curia as well as with intellectual luminaries who congregated there.[234] It was during his Roman years (1586–95) that Botero wrote and published, with the cardinal's aid and inspiration, his pioneering works in political thought and history.

Even before his friendship with Federico, Botero had begun to be fascinated with human history. While still serving Carlo in Milan, he published in five books his *Del dispregio del mondo* (Milan, 1584). The opening sentence of Book II proclaims that he will discourse on cosmography, politics, and secular history. He cites the work of Barros, probably the Italian translation of 1562, as one of his sources on Asia. Like Barros, he displays a profound admiration for China as "the greatest, richest and most populous country that is known." [235] In a Latin letter directed to Cardinal Antonio Carafa, written around 1584 on behalf of Carlo, Botero reports on the presumed vestiges of Christianity which the first navigators to Asia and America had found in those places. At the conclusion of this lengthy letter Botero lists among his sources the Jesuit letters and the works

233 See above, p. 54, on the Japanese mission.
234 See Chabod, *op. cit.* (n. 232), pp. 38–39.
235 As quoted *ibid.*, pp. 31–32.

of Peter Martyr, Ramusio, Barros, Castanheda, and Osório.[236] That Botero was interested at this period in works of a historical-geographical character is attested by a letter that he wrote to Gian Vincenzo Pinelli, the collector of exotica and bibliophile of Padua.[237] Such a connection was natural, for Botero had studied at Padua when Pinelli was there, and Carlo Borromeo, his protector, had been known throughout Italy as one of the greatest bibliophiles of the day.

In the year (1585) before the arrival of Botero in Rome, the Eternal City had received the Japanese legates and had witnessed the publication of Mendoza's book on China. In 1586 the Roman printer F. Zanetti began to publish the small collections of Jesuit letters which first let the public know that Michele Ruggiero and Matteo Ricci, both Italian members of the Society, had entered China's Kwangtung province.[238] Botero, fresh from Paris, arrived at Rome in 1586 full of the political ideas of Bodin on the influence of climate and geography on men and nations.[239] But he, like certain of his Italian contemporaries, was much more concerned about cities than nations. The history of Italy was after all the story of the growth, expansion, and decline of the city-state. Machiavelli, whose ideas about the separation of politics from morality were still very much alive, had been attacked by Botero in a number of his earlier writings. The ex-Jesuit had pointed out that Machiavelli's analysis of the prince in political life had ignored the impersonal factors at work, especially climate and economics. With all these elements in the background Botero began, probably in 1587, to write his two related theoretical treatises *Della cause della grandezza e magnificenza della città* (Rome, 1588) and *Delle ragion di stato* (Rome, 1589).[240]

His little study *The Greatness of Cities* presents a scientific theory of the character and development of the urban agglomerate. In it he stresses the relationship of city growth and prosperity to natural environment, economic resources, and population. He defines the city as "an assembly of people" who come together for the purpose of living "at their ease in wealth and plenty." The city is great not because of its size but because of the "number of inhabitants and their power."[241] Men congregate in cities in the first place for safety, work, or

---

[236] While at Paris in 1586, Botero published his *Ioann Boteri . . . Epistolarum . . . D. Caroli Cardinalis Borromaei nomine scriptarum, Libri II*. This letter appears (pp. 122ʳ–140ᵛ) under the title "De Catholicae religionis vestigiis." It was reprinted separately in Italian translation at Rome in 1588 by Angelico Fortuneo.

[237] See above, pp. 53–54, for Pinelli's collection and for reference to the fact that his books were later purchased by Cardinal Borromeo for the Ambrosiana.

[238] Jesuits, Letters from Missions, *Avvisi del Giapone de gli anni M. D. LXXXII. LXXXIII. Et LXXXIV. Con alcuni altri della Cina dell' LXXXIII. Et LXXXIV. Cavati dalle Lettere della Compagnia de Giesù. Ricevute il mese di Dicembre M. D. LXXXV* (Rome, 1586). Later collections stressed in their title the fact that they included news about the penetration of China. For example, *Avvisi della Cina, et Giappone . . . ricevute il mese d'Ottobre, 1588* (Venice, 1588). A publication essentially the same as this was issued simultaneously by Gioliti in Venice.

[239] On Bodin see below, pp. 306–9.

[240] On the relationship between the two books see Chabod, *op. cit.* (n. 232), pp. 42–45.

[241] Quotations taken from the 1606 English translation of Robert Peterson reprinted in P. J. and D. P. Waley (eds.), *Giovanni Botero: The Reason of State* (London, 1956), p. 227.

cultural satisfaction.[242] Certain cities grow great by attracting excellent workmen from other places and by providing opportunities for all classes to garner profits. A city is in a position to attract outsiders if it is strategically located, situated in a fertile area, and possesses access to river, sea, or land transportation. To keep its citizens proud and content the city must provide markets, freedom, public entertainment, and imposing buildings and monuments. A city will increase its "power and glory" if it becomes a religious, juridical, or educational center. The government of the city must be strong enough to assure the co-operation of the populace, to guarantee its safety, and to attract others within its walls.[243] A city is also helped to greatness if it is the residency of a prince or a great noble who helps to maintain the peace and who causes agriculture, trade, industry, and the arts to flourish. Cities decline when these prescriptions are neglected, or if other cities fare better and so attract or force away population and business.[244]

Botero does not limit his observations to the cities of Europe. In Asia, meaning the Levant, "the cities of account have all of them been the seats of princes."[245] But the nation with the greatest cities of all is China, "of which it can be said that there is no kingdom . . . that is either greater, or more populous, or more rich, or more abounding in all good things or that hath more ages lasted and indured."[246] The cities in which its kings have had their residences— Suntien (Hangchow?), Anchin (Nanking?), and Panchin (Peking)—are "the greatest that have been in the world."[247] Canton, about which most is known in Europe, "is greater than Lisbon, which yet is the greatest city that is in Europe except Constantinople and Paris."[248] "Sanchieo" (Chang-chow) is said to be three times as large as Seville, and "Huchou" (Huchow) is greater than both Canton and "Sanchieo." Botero declares that his information, incredible as it may be, on the greatness of China's cities comes from such reliable sources, both secular and religious, that any person who dares to question its veracity will "shew himself a fool."[249] His materials on China, though he rarely cites his sources, clearly derive in the main from Barros, the Jesuit letters, and from Mendoza's book first published in Italian at Rome in 1585.[250]

---

[242] *Ibid.*, pp. 230–31.

[243] *Ibid.*, pp. 246–47, 258.

[244] *Ibid.*, pp. 252, 261, 278, 280.

[245] *Ibid.*, p. 270. He puts Cambaluc, the Mongol capital, in this category (*ibid.*, pp. 263–64).

[246] *Ibid.*, pp. 264–65.

[247] *Ibid.*, p. 265. "Suntien" is *Shun-t'ien-fu*, or the "city obedient to heaven." From the romanizations, probably derived from the Amoy vernacular, of the other two cities I have not been able to identify or establish his source. For his reference to Suntien see Mendoza's *China* (Staunton [ed.], *op. cit.* [n. 148], I, 25). Anchin is possibly Mendoza's "Ancheo" (Foochow), or "Nanquino," and Panchin is certainly Peking. See Boxer, *South China* (n. 149), App. II.

[248] Waley and Waley (eds.), *op. cit.* (n. 241), p. 266.

[249] This information and the names of cities are taken directly from Mendoza's book (Staunton [ed.], *op. cit.* [n. 148], pp. 278–79). Whatever the correct identification of these cities may be, they are certainly Fukien ports visited by the Augustinians from the Philippines.

[250] An extract from Mendoza's book was also published in Italian in Florence in 1589. For a summary of its editions see *Asia*, I, 744. By 1600 there were nineteen additional printings in Italian.

For the satisfaction of his readers, Botero then speculates on the reasons for the greatness of China's cities.[251] He starts by laying down the proposition that the East "hath more virtue, I know not what, in the producing of things than the West" and that in the "things that are common unto both . . . , they are generally much more perfect in the East than in the West."[252] Since China is the country farthest to the East, it possesses "all those perfections that are attributed to the East." The climate of China is moderate, its land produces both necessities and "all sorts of dainty things for man's delight and pleasure."[253] The Chinese drink no wine, a practice which preserves both health and temperance. Because the country faces the sea and internally is well supplied with rivers and streams, its waters yield "an unspeakable profit and commodity for navigation and tillage."[254] China's huge population of "more than three score millions of souls," exercises "extreme diligence and pains" in the cultivation of its land and waters.[255] In no country of the world do the mechanical arts "more flourish both for variety and for excellence of skill and workmanship."[256] Perfection in the arts stems from the law of Vitei[257] which ordains that every person, including women, must work and in most cases follow the profession of the father. The Chinese waste nothing, are remarkably self-sufficient, and require no imports. They export silk in incredible quantities, and their other commodities are so plentiful and cheap that the merchants of Mexico buy them from intermediaries in the Philippines rather than purchasing the products of Spain.[258] To Botero it is perfectly credible that "China hath the means partly by the benefit of nature and partly by the industry and art of man to sustain an infinite sight of people."[259] China has become so populous that the entire country can be looked upon as being "but one body and but one city."[260] Such

---

[251] Waley and Waley (eds.), *op. cit.* (n. 241), p. 266.

[252] *Ibid.*, p. 266. As evidence for the correctness of this proposition, he points out how the spices grow in the East and not in the West and asserts that "the pearls which do grow in the West are in comparison to those of the East as it were lead to silver."

[253] *Ibid.*, p. 267.

[254] *Ibid.*

[255] *Ibid.*, pp. 267–68. This figure of more than 60 million persons corresponds almost exactly to the figure of 60,187,047 given in Martin de Rada's relation of China (see *Asia*, I, 769, n. 208) and to the "more than sixty millions" of taxpayers in Matteo Ricci's letter of 1584 (*ibid.*, p. 802). Since Rada's work was not published in this period, the conclusion is almost inescapable that Botero used Ricci as his source.

[256] Waley and Waley (eds.), *op. cit.* (n. 241), p. 268. Also see *ibid.*, p. 256. He also notices (*ibid.*, p. 236) that "the Portuguese do write that in some large and spacious plains of China they use coaches with sails, which some essayed not many years since in Spain." On "sailing chariots," see below, pp. 402–3.

[257] Botero derives this name directly from Mendoza (Staunton [ed.], *op. cit.* [n. 148], I, 70–71) as well as the association of it with the requirement that no woman should be idle. The modern English editors (Waley and Waley [eds.], *op. cit.* [n. 241], p. 368) have incorrectly substituted Wu-ti, a Chinese name they evidently recognized, for "Vitei." For the identification of "Vitei" see above, p. 221.

[258] Waley and Waley (eds.), *op. cit.* (n. 241), pp. 268–69. Cf. the remarks of Apollinare Calderini in *Discorsi sopra la ragione di stato del Signor Giovanni Botero* (Milan, 1609), p. 64.

[259] *Ibid.*, p. 269.

[260] *Ibid.*

a condition exists because the Chinese emperors are prevented by law from engaging in wars of conquest and the people are prohibited by law from emigrating.

Botero concludes by asserting that "we Italians do flatter ourselves too much . . . when we prefer Italy and her cities beyond all the rest in the world." Italy's cities will never become greater because of a paucity of navigable rivers and its location away from the great oceans of the world: "And of consequence, our trade and traffic is but poor in respect to the marts of Canton, Malacca, Calicut, Ormuz, Lisbon, Seville, and other cities that bound upon the ocean." [261] While Botero might well be charged with making generalizations based upon insufficient evidence, it is clear from this analysis that he founded his remarks on China's cities upon the best sources available: Barros, Mendoza, and the Jesuit letters. And in most instances, he reports the facts accurately, even though he is certainly inclined to select those data which best fit his belief that the city, whether Florence or Canton, is the focal point at which favorable physical condi·ions and the ingenuity of man may best be seen working together.

Delle ragion di stato, the companion study to the *Greatness of Cities*, is Botero's rather lengthy statement of the basis for a good and strong state. This contribution to political theory was but one of many similar treatises that appeared in Italy between 1550 and 1600 in response to Machiavelli's *The Prince*.[262] But Botero's work was much more influential than the others, possibly because of its broader geographical scope.[263] Many of the other accounts, like Machiavelli's, theorized about politics on the basis of the Italian experience alone. Others brought in comparative materials from the various European countries, but Botero's was the first study of *raison d'état* that endeavored to be universal in scope.

In contrast to the *Greatness of Cities*, Botero's *Reason of State* gives substantial recognition to the part played by individuals, especially the ruler, in the origin, security, and growth of the state. Although he asserts that he is writing to counter Machiavelli, Botero retains many of Machiavelli's positions in his treatment of individual questions relating to the creation and preservation of the state. Force is an approved tactic when the security of the state is in danger; Christianity as the religion of the state helps to assure obedience to the ruler. While Botero proclaims that morality and politics cannot be separated, Christian ethics rarely enter into his specific political judgments.[264] Perhaps it could not have been otherwise since he treats the princes and states of the non-Christian world so extensively and tolerantly.

[261] *Ibid.* Also cf. his earlier comments (p. 255) on the importance of "vendible merchandise" and commercial monopolies to the greatness of cities. He asserts (p. 271) that Lisbon is bigger than London or Naples because of its control of the spice traffic.

[262] There were at least sixty-six such treatises published between 1550 and 1600. See T. Bozza, *Scrittori politici italiani dal 1550 al 1650* (Rome, 1949).

[263] It was reissued many times over the next decade in Italian and was shortly translated into Spanish (1593), French (1599), and Latin (1602).

[264] Cf. Chabod, *op. cit.* (n. 232), pp. 57, 65.

One of the themes running through *Reason of State* is the problem of empire. Botero, who lived in an Italy dominated by Spain, logically concludes that "a scattered empire is as secure and lasting as a compact one." [265] The command of the sea, as is well illustrated by the Spanish and Portuguese experiences, provides enough cohesion to make a scattered empire secure. The union of the Spanish and Portuguese crowns created a world empire which meets in the Philippines and which is secured by naval predominance, strategic outposts, subject nations, and allies. The great empires throughout history have been created by peoples who live in moderate climates for they "are better endowed than others with qualities of mind and spirit, and they are most fitted to dominate and to govern" whether they are Greek, Romans, Chinese, or Spanish.[266] The Chinese, whose nation has endured longer than any other, showed far greater prudence than others in preserving themselves and their society. When they dominated the East, their rulers realized that the expense of maintaining such a dominion was too vast. So they decided "to abandon it and to withdraw to their own country, making a law against sailing to these countries, and against aggressive war." [267] The Spanish and Portuguese, he suggests, are not equally prudent. The Portuguese, it is true, have shown far greater valor in India than they have closer to home. This rests upon the fact that they fought there "with the strength of despair when they were far ... from any possible aid." [268] The Castilians and Portuguese alike receive no aid from their distant colonies but dispatch thousands of good people to them annually to provide protection.[269] Such a policy, Botero believes, must lead to decline, particularly when coupled with the intemperance, excessive luxury, and evil ways which the Portuguese have been led into by the "delicacies" of India.[270]

The Chinese, in part because they were prudent about expansion, possess the wealthiest nation in the world. The "king of China" receives revenues annually of "more than a hundred millions of gold, [a fact] which some find incredible."[271] Botero is prepared to believe this figure and he recalls for the reader the great fertility of China, the industry and frugality of its people, and the country's very

[265] Waley and Waley (eds.), *op. cit.* (n. 241), pp. 11–12.

[266] *Ibid.*, p. 38.

[267] *Ibid.*, p. 142. This is a good example of how Botero goes beyond his sources. Barros, Mendoza, and others talk about the Mongol and Ming expansion movements and about the decision of the Ming rulers to abandon their maritime enterprises. But at no time do they picture a vast Chinese empire which dominated the East. Still, it is true that they indicate that most of the Eastern nations, except India, are tribute-bearing vassals of China. Botero's so-called "law against aggressive war" is also much more specific than anything in his sources which relates to the unaggressive character of the Ming state.

[268] *Ibid.*, p. 183.

[269] *Ibid.*, p. 157.

[270] *Ibid.*, p. 70. But he is also aware that the Portuguese adopted worthwhile things from India. He mentions that "the ginger brought from India does very well [in Portugal], and indeed I remember having eaten ginger that had been grown in Paris" (*ibid.*, p. 149). On ginger in commerce see below, p. 432.

[271] *Ibid.*, p. 143. Mendoza (Staunton [ed.], *op. cit.* [n. 148], I, 82–84) surveys the income of the king and seems to come up with much more than one hundred million. So Botero is here being conservative!

favorable balance of payments. The great income of the emperor of China also supports his general theoretical position that revenues are central to and reflective of the economic well-being of the state. He is convinced that China is one of the best administered countries in the world. Its rulers insure the integrity of officials by paying them well, by promoting them according to seniority, and by forbidding them to accept presents. Officials receive "everything needed for their rank and comfort . . . so that they are able to give their whole mind to the administration of justice and the execution of their duties."[272] The conditions under which the officials operate are so severe that they may not eat or drink before holding court.[273] To control the princes of the blood royal from conspiring against the throne, the kings of China "confine them in noble and spacious quarters provided with every comfort and delight."[274] This method of isolation was, however, not always successful in preventing sedition and revolt. Rebels in times past sometimes released the princes, assassinated the ruler, and placed his kinsmen upon the throne.[275] Chinese law obliges a son to follow his father's calling, requires the blind and crippled to do whatever work they can, ordains that women must perform useful labor, and refuses to tolerate laziness and begging.[276] The king can insure himself against the poor who have nothing to gain from public peace either by driving them out of the state or by giving them a stake in internal order. All ranks of society in China have therefore a stake in internal peace and are not inclined to revolt. Subjects acquired in war are not killed or enslaved in China, but are used as soldiers to protect the frontier situated most distant from their homelands.[277]

The other nations of Asia also follow practices which catch Botero's attention. To preserve their reputations for posterity, the kings of India and Japan, like the Emperor Charles V, retire from their thrones when they become older and less effective.[278] The king of Siam, who rules over many different peoples, "uses only Siamese as troops, lest his other subjects learn his military methods and secrets."[279] He also organizes all sports and festivities as war games and exercises.[280] From the Jesuit Maffei's history, Botero learned that "the king of Siam has the exploits of his outstanding soldiers written in a book and then read to them, in order to encourage his vassals in time of war."[281] Among Europeans, the Portuguese have been more enterprising than others in chronicling the deeds of their heroes. In India, for example, they relate that the valiant João de Castro confronted his soldiers at the siege of Diu with the necessity of fighting to the

272 Waley and Waley (eds.), *op. cit* (n. 241), p. 25. Also see p. 22.

273 Cf. Mendoza in Staunton (ed.), *op. cit.* (n. 148), I, 107–8.

274 Waley and Waley (eds.), *op. cit.* (n. 241), pp. 82–83. In this practice, he avers, the Chinese are more humane than the rulers of Ormuz who blinded their relatives.

275 *Ibid.*, p. 84.

276 *Ibid.*, pp. 92–93.

277 *Ibid.*, p. 166.

278 *Ibid.*, p. 58.

279 *Ibid.*, p. 171n.

280 *Ibid.*, p. 187.

281 *Ibid.*, pp. 190–91.

death by cutting off their access to retreat.[282] The subjects acquired by conquest in India, whether heretics or infidels, should be converted, given special favors, and their children educated in Christian schools to guarantee their loyalty.[283] As Machiavellian as these last tactics are, they were generally justified by contemporaries as being necessary to the spread of Christianity in the East.

That Botero was an avid follower of the Christian enterprise is substantiated by the turn that his writing takes after the publication of his theoretical works. From 1591 to 1595 he published at Rome the first four parts of his *Relazioni universali*. Originally conceived as a statistical study of the progress of Christianity, the scope of the *Relazioni* was broadened until it became a systematic and comprehensive survey of the countries of the world in which Botero relates God, nature, and physical conditions to the progress of mankind and civilization. The first part contains a geographical description of the world and of its known countries. The second part discusses the political forms and the economic and social organization of the more important nations. The third and fourth parts deal with religion, especially Christian missionary activity.[284] The fifth part, not published in his lifetime, examines more closely the internal conditions prevailing in some of the more important states.[285] The materials for the *Relazioni* were apparently compiled for the purpose of measuring and testing the validity of the theoretical principles earlier mentioned in the *Greatness of Cities* and the *Reason of State*.[286] Botero therefore presents, especially in Parts I, II, and V, a systematic, comparative review of the physical conditions, demographic densities, economic resources, military power, and political constitutions of all the known countries of the world. The *Relazioni* established Botero as a leading authority on governance, for it was translated almost immediately into Latin (1596), German (1596), English (1601), Spanish (1603), and Polish (1609).

Botero's statistical and empirical descriptions of the various states, especially in Part II of the *Relazioni*, seem to follow the outline of the summary relations prepared by publishers on the basis of the reports of the Venetian ambassadors. These surveys usually begin with a definition of the geographical boundaries of the state, an enumeration of its overseas possessions (if any), an examination of its military and naval defenses, and a review of its political divisions, cities, population, commerce, and revenues.[287] Such factual compendiums often compare the resources in manpower, natural wealth, and military strength of the states under review. Both Anania and Botero adopted this technique

[282] *Ibid.*, pp. 198–99.
[283] *Ibid.*, p. 99.
[284] The fourth part was dedicated in 1596 to Juan Fernandez de Velasco, the Spanish governor of the Duchy of Milan who had earlier criticized Mendoza's book on China. See *Asia*, I, 790–91.
[285] The fifth part, probably not written before 1610, was first published in 1895 in C. Gioda, *La vita e le opere di Giovanni Botero* (3 vols.; Milan, 1895), Vol. III.
[286] See Chabod, *op. cit.* (n. 232), pp. 70–71.
[287] Based on "Relatione di Portugallo," in *Thesoro politici* (Venice, 1612). Also see Chabod, *op. cit.* (n. 232), pp. 192–93.

in their writings and applied it to all the countries of the world on which it was possible for them to obtain concrete data.[288] The *Relazioni* of Botero, through its fullness, its accuracy, and its author's acute observations, was much more highly regarded than any of the other compilations of this type. For almost a century following its initial appearance, the *Relazioni* was used as a geopolitical manual by European students, scholars, and statesmen.

Asia, in Botero's estimation, "is the most noble, greatest, and vastest part of the world."[289] Its "people are of excellent wit, exceedingly rich, and happy in all good things."[290] Over the centuries it has produced many extraordinary persons and has given birth to numerous powerful and prosperous empires. Contemporary Asia he divides for discussion into five empires: Muscovy, Tartary, Turkey, Persia, and "India or East India." His "India" includes "the Great Mogor" (Mughul empire), China, Siam, "Narsinga" (Vijayanagar), "Calecute" (meaning the Malabar states), and Japan. Botero's "India" is a "spacious portion of Asia" exceeded in size only by Tartary.[291] Because of its vast area, this region is "subject to diverse temperatures."[292] Still it is far better than any other part of the world "for goodness of situation, health and fertilitie."[293] Famine is rare for its soil is well watered and produces all the requisite grains and fruits, except wheat and grapes. The peoples of "India" who are "diversely dispersed into diverse Regions and Principalities, doe diversely differ in language, usage, habit, manners, and religion."[294] In addition to the natives (gentiles), there live in this region Jews, Muslims, Arabs, and St. Thomas Christians. The Portuguese "intruded by armes, prayers, and policie" but their occupation of Goa is "so farre from the name of a Conquest, as was the possession of the English from the Crowne of France, when they held nothing but Calais in Picardie."[295] Botero's "India" is not merely a part of the Portuguese empire; it comprises a number of independent states with their own histories, customs, and institutions.

On the basis of information derived from the works of Barros and Maffei, Botero presents a discussion of the history, extent, and characteristic features of the Mughul empire.[296] This sprawling empire of the Indo-Gangetic plain appears to him to be comparable to the empire of the "Great Turk."[297] The princes of "Mogor," who claim to be decendants of Tamerlane, moved out of

---

[288] For amplification of this relationship see Alberto Magnaghi, *D'Anania e Botero* (Ciriè, 1914). When Botero possesses inadequate data to discuss Cochin-China, he simply says so.

[289] Quoted from the revised translation of R. Johnson published by John Haviland, *Relations of the Most Famous Kingdomes and Common-wealths thorowout the World: Discoursing of Their Situations, Religions, Languages, Manners, Customes, Strengths, Greatnesse and Policies . . .* (London, 1630), p. 198.

[290] *Ibid.*, p. 199.

[291] *Ibid.*, p. 574.

[292] *Ibid.*, p. 575.

[293] *Ibid.*

[294] *Ibid.*

[295] *Ibid.*, p. 576.

[296] For passages from Maffei and Botero which parallel some of those in the *Relazioni* see Chabod, *op. cit.* (n. 232), pp. 151–65.

[297] Botero, *Relations* (n. 289), p. 579.

central Asia and around 1500 began systematically to conquer and occupy Hindustan and the states of India southward to the northern border of Vijayana-gar. Botero, as in other places, here stresses the huge size of Asian armies, observes that they live off the land, and concludes that "all their thoughts tend to warlike provision." [298] The "Mogor" rulers are tyrants who rule through slaves, soldiers, and vassals who "hold hard hands over the commonalty" and periodically rebel against their overlords. [299] The moral is: "Fear admitteth *no* securitie, much less perpetuity: and therefore these tyrants . . . trust whoely upon their men of warre." [300] Because they realize that their subjects hate them, the tyrants cultivate the favor of their retainers to prevent unrest at home and to discourage invasion from abroad. Such a policy means that they must constantly be planning conquests to obtain prizes for their vassals as payments for loyalty.

Great kingdoms like Cambay (Gujarat) and Bengal were in fact captured by the "Mogors." Each of these Indian nations includes more parishes and popula-tion than France and other European states. [301] Though eminently successful in conquering the states of India, the "Great Mogor" is unable to establish his dominion over the states east of India because the obstacles are too numerous and formidable both at home and abroad. Empires like the seas have a flood tide that is inevitably followed by an ebb tide. The greater the empire the more it is subject to internal sluggishness, unwieldiness, and change. Huge armies that are invincible on the field of battle "are most commonly overthrowne by famine, the forerunner of pestilence." [302] Natural obstacles, such as mountains, deserts, and seas, as well as the power of Burma, prevent the Mughuls from expanding to the east of the Ganges. Even the Portuguese with their small numbers effec-tively resisted the "Mogor" armies and forced them to waste much treasure. And still the Portuguese hold strategic places and control the seas. [303]

Botero's knowledge of China, which he had previously derived exclusively from Barros, Mendoza, and the Jesuit letterbooks, becomes more realistic and critical in the *Relazioni*, possibly because of the new information and perspective which he derived from the Jesuits, especially Maffei and Michele Ruggiero. [304] He asserts, as he had earlier, that the annals and chronicles of China record that it was once "farre larger than now it is." [305] Relics of China's conquest west-ward to the Indian Ocean can still be seen at various places, and vestiges of its earlier dominion can be discerned in the continued widespread use of the Chinese calendar and astrological system by the nations of Southeast Asia. He

[298] *Ibid.*, p. 581.
[299] *Ibid.*
[300] *Ibid.*
[301] *Ibid.*, pp. 583–84. He uses statistics for Europe derived from Guicciardini's book on the Nether-lands and Bodin's on France.
[302] *Ibid.*, p. 586.
[303] *Ibid.*, p. 588.
[304] For his references to Ruggiero see *ibid.*, p. 601.
[305] *Ibid.*, p. 589.

concludes that this extensive dominion was maintained until a recent date since the rulers of the vassal states still regularly dispatch tribute missions to China. After suffering severe losses, the Chinese prudently decided to retreat and "to containe themselves within their own boundes."[306] Their former vassals were set free, but the kings of Korea, Liu-ch'iu, Cochin-China, and Siam by their own choice decided to remain feudatories. The Chinese live in an earthly paradise under the rule of one emperor who is called "Lord of the World" or "Son of Heaven." The emperor resides in Peking ("Paquin"), a city protected from overland incursions by the Great Wall, and he never leaves it except in time of war. The emperor fears none of his neighbors except the "great Khan of Tartary" (the Mongols), who is kept out of the kingdom by the garrisons at the Great Wall and by the huge armies at the emperor's command.

While Botero still proclaims China to be "one of the greatest Empires that ever was,"[307] he here introduces many more qualifications and criticisms than in his earlier writings. The prohibition against leaving the country means that the increase in numbers is so great that China "is even pestered with inhabitation."[308] General epidemics are unknown in China, but "earthquakes are more dreadfull unto them than any pestilence to us."[309] The emperor is peaceloving and efficient but tyrannical and "his vassals obey him, not as a king, but rather as a God."[310] Printing, painting, and gunpowder are ancient and common in China, but their printing is "but stamping," their painting is "meere steyning [staining]," and their guns are inferior.[311] It is no marvel that their cities are large, for their houses are "base and low, but one story high (for fear of earthquakes) which makes them take up more roome on the ground than in the ayre."[312] The Chinese possess very little knowledge of the liberal arts and are inclined to be crafty and wily rather than wise. In their manners and morals they are "obscene and shamelesse," their idolatry is "vile and vicious," and their exorcisms "dammable."[313] From these examples, it becomes clear that the Jesuits had managed to modify Botero's earlier image of China, one that he had derived in large part from the rosy picture painted by Mendoza, the Augustinian. His new account reads almost as if he kept his earlier materials together as a foundation and included as qualifiers to it the comments the Jesuits had made upon reading it.[314] He still insists emphatically that China remains much more populous and prosperous than any nation of Europe.[315]

In the *Relazioni* Botero for the first time attempts to give a systematic treat-

[306] *Ibid.*, p. 590.
[307] *Ibid.*, p. 586.
[308] *Ibid.*, p. 594.
[309] *Ibid.*
[310] *Ibid.*, p. 596.
[311] *Ibid.*, p. 598.
[312] *Ibid.*
[313] *Ibid.*, p. 592.
[314] For example, his description of the economy (especially, *ibid.*, pp. 592–93) remains a summary of materials from Mendoza.
[315] *Ibid.*, pp. 595–96.

ment of the kingdom of Siam, one of the three most powerful continental empires of the East.[316] He derives most of his information about Siam and its satellites from Barros and the Jesuit letters.[317] Siam is a fertile and abundant land, but its inhabitants "take no great delight in manuall occupations, which causeth the Kingdome to be poore in merchandize."[318] Silver is brought to Siam from Laos and adds to the wealth and splendor of its magnificent cities. The king rules over nine states and is "absolute Lord over all the demeanes [lands] of the Kingdome."[319] In time of war he depends only on his Siamese subjects. The Arabs and Portuguese have taken away his command of the seacoast and of maritime trade, but they keep on good terms with him and refrain from invading inland. His riches in people and property enable him to outfit and maintain huge armies. It is easier in Asia than it is in Europe to raise huge levies because the needs of tropical people are simpler in terms of food, drink, and clothing. They also go to war without so much armor and other heavy equipment. Finally, the Eastern rulers, presumably in contrast to their European counterparts, were forehanded enough "to provide incredible masses of money, victuall, and such warlike provisions, before they entered into action."[320]

Botero then returns to India to recount something about the southern Hindu states which had successfully remained independent of the Mughul empire. In his treatment of Vijayanagar Botero again follows Barros. He is here most interested in the size and financing of armies. The ruler of Vijayanagar, like other Eastern princes, is not interested in peace, justice, or the welfare of his subjects. He maintains a tyrannical rule and keeps "possession [of] all the profits of the lands, woods, mines."[321] If the king of France were absolute lord of all his nation's resources, and if he wished to spend all his revenue on arms, he might also be able to raise and maintain a huge army of the kind that the rulers of Asia are reported to have. Botero introduces this comparison, not because he is advocating the Asian system, but because he wants to explain to the incredulous of Europe how it is possible for the Eastern rulers to maintain such large armies. Even in "Calecute," where the military forces employ no cavalry but only "shipping and footmen,"[322] the Portuguese face mass armies. But the "barbarians putting more confidence in their numbers than their goodnesse, have always wanted that vertue which should make armies dreadfull and fortunate, which is good order and Discipline."[323]

Japan, the last of Botero's Asian empires, is an insular state "inhabited by a people differing in manners and customes from the residue of the

[316] *Ibid.*, pp. 602–12.

[317] Cf. *Asia*, I, 522–25. He mentions a "certain Jesuit" as a source. This is probably a reference to the letter of 1554 by Fernão Mendez Pinto (*see ibid.*, pp. 530–35) in which he writes about the mid-century wars between Siam and Burma.

[318] Botero, *Relations* (n. 289), p. 603.

[319] *Ibid.*, p. 604.

[320] *Ibid.*, p. 612.

[321] *Ibid.*, p. 614.

[322] *Ibid.*, p. 618.

[323] *Ibid.*, p. 620.

Orient." [324] The inhabitants of these relatively barren islands are intelligent, ambitious, staid, resolute, courteous, fearless, upright, and patient in adversity. Their diet is simple and they drink nothing but *chia* (tea). Their buildings are wooden "partly because the Country is subject to Earthquakes." [325] In the past, for at least sixteen hundred years, the Japanese obeyed a single Prince called *Dairi* (emperor). But two of his lieutenants (Oda Nobunaga and Toyotomi Hideyoshi) revolted "so that now he resembleth the shadow rather than the King." [326] Warfare among contesting lords shortly became almost perpetual. All the wealth of the land then passed into the hands of the great warlords who increasingly proved to be tyrants. The people of Japan are kept hard at work building palaces, temples, towns, and fortresses, "the like whereof are no where to be seen." [327] Once these enterprises were completed, the supreme lord (Hideyoshi) began to build a fleet for the conquest of China. Like the Greek and Roman leaders, the Japanese ruler reveres demigods and so determined (as revealed in the expulsion edict of 1587) to banish the Jesuits and to condemn Christianity in his realm. He persecuted "true Religion" and sought "to arrogate to himselfe the Name of God." [328] Here Botero is clearly expressing the opinion of his Jesuit informants to whom he is certainly indebted for his material on Japan. In theoretical terms Botero uses the Jesuit experience in Japan to illustrate the influence of God upon political change. For, he asserts, "in the midst of these proud and unreasonable cogitations, God raised up against him [Hideyoshi] a new enemy from the Easterne parts of Japan [the Tokugawas], who as wee understand, is likely to give him his hand and head full of businesse." [329]

The unpublished fifth part of the *Relazioni* was written around 1610, four years after Botero returned from an extended visit to Spain. Much of it is devoted to a restatement of the material on the East reviewed in Book II. Changes of fact and more extended comments appear which indicate that he continued to keep himself informed on what was happening in Asia. On India he cites the travels of the Venetian Gasparo Balbi. [330] On China he provides more specific descriptions of Nanking and Peking. From the Jesuit letterbooks he narrates the progress of clan warfare in Japan and compares the island kingdom unfavorably to Europe as a place in which no Aristotle or Plato ever emerged. [331] The last section is concerned with the number of Christians in the various countries of the world. Toward the end he remarks that he has seen in manuscript the first four books of the voluminous history of the Indies that Diogo do Couto had prepared in Goa by royal order. [332]

[324] *Ibid.*, p. 621.
[325] *Ibid.*, p. 622.
[326] *Ibid.*
[327] *Ibid.*, p. 624.
[328] *Ibid.*, p. 625.
[329] *Ibid.*
[330] Gioda, *op. cit.* (n. 285), III, 212.
[331] *Ibid.*, pp. 237–41.
[332] *Ibid.*, p. 306.

Botero, unlike most of his contemporaries writing in the field of political thought,[333] was extremely sensitive to the discoveries and to their implications for Europe. In his preoccupation with the influence of climate and terrain on the character of peoples, cities, and states, Botero finds in Asia a host of examples and an abundance of unexploited data. News of the penetration of China by the Jesuits reached him at a time when he was in the process of writing his theoretical works, and when the books of Barros, Castanheda, and Mendoza were at hand in which China is described as a kind of model state. To Botero China is a moral exemplar of the state because it voluntarily renounced expansion and retired within its own confines. The prosperity enjoyed by the Chinese is the fruit of this prudent withdrawal. Prudence rather than *virtu* in the Machiavellian sense is the quality Botero most admires in rulers and states.[334]

The peaceful Chinese, unlike other peoples, are left free to cultivate their fertile land and to profit from its natural bounty. As a consequence, China's cities are the greatest, its political administration the best ordered, and its people the most industrious and ingenious in the world. Even when Botero darkens this bright picture in the *Relazioni*, he remains convinced that China is far better administered and more prosperous than the other nations of the world. The Chinese rulers may be tyrants but they are not expansionists. The other tyrants of Asia, the huge armies they maintain, and the wars they fight show what happens among "barbarians" when they are neither Christian nor prudent. The Indians, Siamese, and Japanese have their own diverse qualities, good and bad, but they can in no way approach the peaceful Chinese as exemplars. For China provides an unparalleled example, both historically and contemporaneously, of what can be achieved when a people renounces aggressive war and devotes itself utterly to the arts of peace.

The new "Asia" of the discovery era made its way but slowly into Italian popular literature, history, and political theory. Boiardo invented Angelica, princess of Cathay, but Ariosto was the first of the major poets to incorporate materials from the Portuguese discoveries into his work. The polygraphs of Venice were quick to follow suit as they included references to Asia in their imitative romances, encyclopedic books, annals, and popular histories. Historians from Paulus Jovius to Campana unhesitatingly incorporated notices of past and contemporary events in Asia into their chronicles and narratives. Cosmographers like Anania and political philosophers like Botero were quick to stress the importance for comparison and generalization of the new materials being relayed to Europe from the East. Mendoza's *China* was the first ethnohistory

---

[333] For example, Paolo Paruta (1540–98), Scipione Ammirato, and Girolamo Frachetta (1560–1620) ignore the overseas world completely in their works on political theory. G. Rosaccio (*ca.* 1530–1620), the physician and geographer who revised Ptolemy's *Geografia* (Venice, 1599), exhibits nothing comparable to the knowledge of Asia possessed by Botero. His maps and texts are also very unsophisticated when compared to the earlier works of Gastaldi and others. He shows almost no interest at all in economic geography, one of Botero's strong points.

[334] See Chabod, *op. cit.* (n. 232), pp. 60–61.

published in sixteenth-century Italy which dealt with but one country of Asia. Arrivabene's *Il magno Vitei* was the only substantial didactic work to use East Asia as its locale and to focus squarely on Asian characters, traditions, beliefs, and resources.[335] In their view of China, both Arrivabene and Botero were much closer to the Sinophiles of the eighteenth century than they were to Boiardo and Ariosto.

During the first generation of the sixteenth century the Italian interest in the Asian activities of the Portuguese was essentially limited to the papacy, to the Florentine investors in the spice trade, and to the Venetian state. News of the Christians found in India and of the easy military victories of the Portuguese in the East aroused hopes in Rome that Christian pressure upon the Muslims in the East would ease Turkish pressure upon Europe itself. But in Venice the early victories of the Portuguese produced more consternation than hope. The successful circumnavigation of the world by the "Victoria" proved that the Spiceries could be reached from Mexico and raised the prospect that Castile might establish an alternative route that would effectively undermine the Portuguese monopoly and permit Venice to take back control over a substantial portion of the spice trade. Italian literature of these years—especially the travel accounts, histories, and Ariosto's *Orlando*—reflects this general concern over the future of the spice trade, the looming Turkish threat, and the danger to Italian independence from France and the Habsburgs. The Italian learned community, convinced of its own primacy in the world of letters, was at first only slightly curious about the nature of the peoples, plants, and animals of the overseas world. But as questions were raised about accepted teachings, and as Italians increasingly felt the weight of outside political pressure, a sense of uncertainty and insecurity began to grow. To the orthodox, Italy was being punished by God, and to many who were not so traditional in their Christianity, it had become apparent by about 1530 that new solutions had to be found if Italy were to preserve what remained of its independence and its proud culture.

The Counter-Reformation in Italy began with the convocation of the Council of Trent in 1545. Censorship and the *Index* were sporadically and gradually put into effect thereafter and came to be institutionalized. The new emphasis upon orthodoxy diverted men of letters from following previously flourishing fields of literature and led them to experiment with new subjects unrelated to religious controversy. Popular literature—romances, *novelle*, travelogues, and annals— poured from the pens and presses of Italy. In all its categories literature became increasingly more didactic in tone and content. The secular romances of Boiardo and Ariosto were followed by the Christian epic of Tasso and the edifying romance of Arrivabene. The sixteenth-century imitators of Boccaccio—the writers of *novelle*—were inclined to take pagan stories from both oral and written sources and to rewrite them in Christian and European terms. Even the Jesuit letterbooks which were certainly read in part for their informational and

---

[335] Cf. the stories of the princes of Ceylon. See above, pp. 211–12.

entertainment value gradually became more obviously letters for the edification of a Christian audience.

As Italians came to be more analytical and critical of themselves, they came to be more open-minded about others. At various points in his books Botero chided Italians for believing in their own superiority, pointed out the weaknesses in their economy and governance, and upheld the superiority of China's cities and administration. While they learned about Asia through the Portuguese, the Italians were generally more interested in the Asian nations themselves than in their place in the Portuguese empire. Annalists, polygraphs, and historians increasingly brought Asia into their writings as best they could with the limited sources available to them. Jovius praises the discoverers, extols the Portuguese for their victories over the Turks in Asia, compares Canton favorably to Venice, and gives China credit for inventing printing and for passing the craft to Europe. Notices of contemporary events in the East increasingly appear in the annals, chronicles, and world histories. Anania in his cosmography (1573) and Botero in his *Relazioni* (1595) try to provide synopses of what was known about Asia and make explicit comparisons. Possevino read widely in the available European materials and put together a bibliography and an instructional manual which brought the study of Asia into the *ratio studiorum* of the Jesuits

The Italian *letterati* generally accepted the attitudes toward Asia expressed in the Portuguese chronicle-narratives, the travel collections, and the Jesuit letterbooks. They were usually hostile to India while appreciating the fact that the Hindus opposed Islam as well as Christianity. They blamed the "delights" and "delicacies" of India, like many Portuguese themselves, for undermining the virility and character of the Portuguese nation. They were unabashedly curious about the islands where most of the spices grew. Japan, which had been little more than an imaginary island to Ariosto, became a concrete reality by the end of the century. Until 1587 hopes ran high that Japan was about to accept Christianity, but Hideyoshi's change of attitude produced an almost instantaneous spate of criticisms about the island empire. The success of the Jesuits in being received at the court of Akbar again raised hopes in the 1590's for the success of the Jesuit enterprise in India. Still, all of the states of Asia, like the nations of Europe, were judged by both the Jesuits and the *letterati* to spend too much of their energy and substance on useless war.

In the last two decades of the sixteenth century the great hope of the future was China. The Italians had learned from reading Barros, Castanheda, and the Jesuit letterbooks that China was politically and culturally the predominant and the most highly respected state of Asia. Mendoza's book adulating China appeared at Rome in 1585, the year when the Japanese emissaries were there and when news was circulating that Italian Jesuits had succeeded in penetrating the Chinese mainland for the first time. The reputation of China as the most ancient of living states, as a center of superior craftsmanship, and as the home of fundamental inventions was well established in Europe. When it seemed possible that China might also open its portal—the one before which Xavier had languished and died—the impression grew stronger that God was moving in his own mysterious way to put the world's two great civilizations into direct touch with each other to the ultimate benefit of both.

What China lacked most was the sublime gift of the Christian religion. This it would finally receive from the hands of the eager Jesuits. What Europe needed, as Botero and others had pointed out, was China's prudence in international affairs, its effectiveness in social organization and control, and its devotion to the arts of peace. For Europe to learn these lessons from China, tolerance was not enough. What was needed was a deep and abiding admiration for China as a model state. Barros, Mendoza, and the Jesuits were in agreement that many Chinese practices and ideas were worthy of emulation. Others, particularly those from the field like Ruggiero, were more qualified in their high regard for China's civilization and its rulers. But to Arrivabene, China's ancient princes were exemplars, for they had personally cultivated the arts of peace and war. They had successfully established and maintained a society which was the most enduring and advanced the world had ever known. From China the nations of Europe had much to learn, provided that they were willing and foresighted enough to make the effort.

1. Josaphat's first outing. A page from the first German printed edition of *Barlaam and Josaphat* (Augsburg, 1476). Reproduced from T. Bowie *et al.*, *East-West in Art* (Bloomington, Ind., 1966), fig. 237.

2. Portrait of Marco Polo. Frontispiece of the first printed edition of his work *Das puch . . . des Marcho Polo* (Nuremberg, 1477). Reproduced from the Moule–Pelliot variorum edition of Marco Polo's *Description of the World* (London, 1938), frontis.

3. Woodcut of a gold-digging ant of India. From S. Münster, *Cosmographei* (Basel, 1550), p. mclix.

4. Woodcut of Indian "Odota," or horse-like creature, reminiscent of Ariosto's Hippogriff. From S. Münster, *Cosmographei* (Basel, 1550), p. mclix.

5. The fabled Island of Women, called "Imaugle"—one of the insular conventions followed by Camöens in the Isle of Venus. From A. Thevet, *La cosmographie universelle* . . . (Paris, 1575), p. 444ʳ.

L'HISTOIRE
DV NOVVEAV
MONDE DESCOV-
uert par les Portu-
galois,

ESCRITE PAR LE SEIGNEVR
PIERRE BEMBO.

A PARIS,

*Par Estienne Denyse, en la rue sainct
Iacque, deuant les Ma-
thurins.*

1556.

Auec Priuilege pour deux ans.

6. Title page of the adaptation prepared in Paris of Book VI of Pietro Bembo's *Della historia vinitiana* . . . (Venice, 1552). Courtesy of the Henry E. Huntington Library.

PRODIGIEVSES,
EXTRAICTES DE
PLVSIEVRS FAMEVX AVTHEVRS,
Grecz & Latins, sacrez & prophanes: mises en
nostre langue par P. Boaistuau, surnômé Launay,
natif de Bretaigne: auec les pourtraicts & figures.

Dediées à treshault, & trespuissant Seigneur,
Iehan de Rieux, Seigneur Dasserac.

A PARIS
Pour Iean Longis, & Robert le mangnier Libraires,
tenans leur boutique au Palais, en la galerie
par ou on va à la Chancellerie
M. D. LXI.
AVEC PRIVILEGE DV ROY.

7. Title page of Pierre Boaistuau,
Histoires prodigieuses . . . (Paris, 1561).

HISTOIRE PRODIGIEVSE
d'vn Oyseau qui n'a aucuns pieds, & vit en l'air
& n'est trouué que mort en la terre,
ou en la mer.
Chapitre. XXXIIII.

8. Stylized bird of paradise illustrating
Pierre Boaistuau, *Histoires prodigieuses* . . .
(Paris, 1561), p. 157ᵛ. According to
Boaistuau's caption (p. 158ʳ), woodcut
borrowed from Gesner's Latin book on
birds.

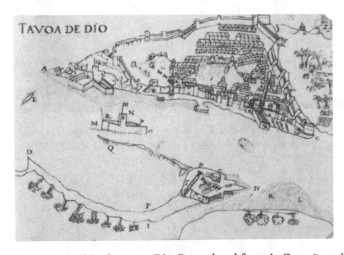

TAVOA DE DÍO

9. Drawing of the fortress at Diu. Reproduced from A. Cortesão and A. Teixeira da Mota,
Portugaliae monumenta cartographica (6 vols.; Lisbon, 1960–62), Vol. I, pl. LXII.

10. Goa from the French version of Sebastian Münster, *La cosmographie universelle* prepared by Belleforest (Paris, 1575). Notice the temple of India on the island, the ship-building yard, and the chain across the river's mouth. Courtesy of the Newberry Library.

Labels within the engraving: Santa brigita · Monasterio de S. Isidro · Seuilla la vieja · Camas · Santiponce · Monsterio de las Cuevas · Guerta de Colon · Casas de Colon · Puerta de Goles · La S. Ynquisition

11. Engraving of Seville showing the residence and library of Ferdinand Columbus. Reproduced from H. Harrisse, *La Colombine et Clément Marot* (Paris, 1886), frontis. Courtesy of the Newberry Library.

12. Tamerlane from *Nuremberg Chronicle*, 1493 (Lilly Rare Book Library, Indiana University). Reproduced from T. Bowie *et al.*, *East-West in Art* (Bloomington, Ind., 1966), fig. 294.

13. Tammerlane. From A. Thevet, *Les vrais pourtraits* . . . (Paris, 1584), p. 630^r. Courtesy of the Newberry Library.

14. The rulers of Asia and Prester John in Ethiopia on an anonymous planisphere of c. 1545 in the Österreichische Nationalbibliothek (Vienna). Reproduced from A. Cortesão and Teixeira da Mota, *Portugaliae monumenta cartographica* (6 vols.; Lisbon, 1960–62), vol. I, pl. 55.

15. Portrait of Mandelaph, King of Taprobane. From A. Thevet, *La cosmographie univer-selle* (Paris, 1575), p. 422ᵛ. Courtesy of the Newberry Library.

IL MAGNO VITEI

DI
LODOVICO ARRIVABENE
MANTOANO.

IN QVESTO LIBRO, OLTRE AL PIACERE,
che porge la narratione delle alte cauallerie del glorioſo
VITEI primo Rè della China, & del valoroſo IOLAO, ſi
hà nella perſona di EZONLOM, vno ritratto di ottimo Prencipe, & di Capitano perfetto.

*Appreſſo ſi acquiſta notitia di molti paeſi, di varij coſtumi di popo-
li, di animali, sì da terra, & sì da acqua, di alberi, di frutti, &
di ſimiglianti coſe moltiſſime.*

Vi ſi trattano ancora innumerabili quiſtioni quaſi di tutte le ſcienze più nobili.
Fatti di arme nauali, da terra, aſſedij, & aſſalti di varij luoghi, molte gioſtre.
razze di caualli, & loro mareggi. Funerali, trionfi, ragionamenti di ſog-
getti driuerſi, auenimenti marauiglioſi; & altre coſe non punto diſcare a' Let-
tori intendenti.

IN VERONA,
Appreſſo Girolamo Diſcepolo. 1597.

16. Title page of the first edition of Ludovico Arrivabene, *Il magno Vitei* (Verona, 1597).

	Northern people are	Middle are	Southern are
1 In their bodies.	High and great, phleg-maticke, sanguine, white, and yeallow, sociable the voice strong, the skin soft and hairy, great eaters and drinkers, puissant,	Indifferent and tempe-rate in all those things, as neuters or parta-kers a little of those two extremities, and partici-pating most of that regi-on to which they are nee-rest neigh-bours.	Little, melancholick, cold, and drie, blacke, Solitarie, the voice shrill, the skin hard, with little hair, and curled, abstinent, fee-ble.
2 Spirit-	Heavy, obtuse, stupid sottish, facill, light, in-constant.		Ingenious, wise, sub-tile, opinative.
3 Religion.	Little religious and de-vout.		Superstitious, contem-plative.
4 Manners.	Warriers valiant, pain-full, chaste, free from jea-lousie, cruell and inhu-mane.		No warriours, idle, unchaste, jealous, cruell, and inhu-mane.

Nothern.	Midlers.	Southern,	
The common sense,	discourse and reasoning,	Vnderstanding.	Qualities of the soul.
Force, as of Beares and other beasts.	Reason and justice of men.	Subtility of force, and religion of divines.	
Mars {Warre The moon {hunting	Mercury {Emperors, Iupiter. {Oratours,	Saturn {contemplation, Venus {love.	Planets.
Art and handi-crafts.	Prudence, knowledg of good and evill.	Knowledg of truth and falshood.	Actions and parts of the Common-weal.
Labourers, Artifi-cers, Souldiers, to execute and obey.	Magistrates, provident, to judge, command.	Prelates, Philose-phers, to contem-plate.	
Yong men, unapt.	Perfect men, managers of affaires.	Grave old men, Wise, pensive.	

17. Charts illustrating geographical determinism from Pierre Charron, *Of Wisdome* (London, 1612 [?]). Translated by Samson Lennard.

BREVE RELACION DEL

recibimiento que en toda ytalia, y España
fue hecho a tres embaxadores de los Rey
nos de Bungo, y Arima, y Omura, de Iapó
de nueuo conuertidos a la fee Catolica ǫ
fueró embiados a dar la deuida obediencia
al summo pontifice y se la dieron
como conuenia.

¶ Impresso en Seuilla por Fernardo Malderado

18. Title page of a Spanish account, taken from various Italian sources, of the reception
accorded the Japanese envoys in Italy. Printed in 1586 [?] at Seville before the departure of the envoys from Portugal. Reproduced from A. Boscaro, *Sixteenth Century
European Printed Works on the First Japanese Mission to Europe* (Leyden, 1973), pl. 52.

ACTA CONSISTORII

PVBLICE EXHIBITI

A S.D.N. GREGORIO PAPA XIII.
REGVM IAPONIORVM LEGATIS
ROMAE, DIE XXIII. MARTII.
M. D. LXXXV.

EX AVCTORITATE SVPERIORVM.

ROMAE,
Apud Franciscum Zannettum.
M. D. LXXXV.

ACTA
CONSISTORII
PVBLICE EX-
HIBITI

A. S. D. N. *GREGORIO* PA-
PA XIII. REGVM IAPONIO-
RVM LEGATIS ROMAE,
DIE XXIII. MARTII.
M. D. LXXXV.

EX ARCHETYPO ROMANO.
DILINGÆ,
Apud IOANNEM MAYER.
M. D. LXXXV.

IAPONIORVM

REGVM LEGATIO,

Romæ coram summo Pontifice,
GREGORIO XIII. 23. Martij
habita: Anno: 1585.

Addita etiam est breuis in calce descriptio
Insulæ Iaponicæ.

ROMAE, apud Franciscum Zannetum,
Et BONONIAE, *apud Alexandrum Benatium,*
Et CRACOVIAE, in Officina Lazari,
Anno Domini: 1585.

ACTA CONSISTORII
PVPLICE EXHIBITI

A S.D.N. GREGORIO PAPA
XIII. REGVM IAPONIORVM LEGATIS
ROMAE, DIE XXIII. MARTII.
M. D. LXXXV.

Cum consensu Reuerendissimj Archiepiscopj Pragensis.
PRAGAE,
Apud Michaelem Peterle,
M. D. LXXXV.

19, 20, 21, 22. Title pages from several European printed works describing the Japanese legation of 1585's activities on its European mission. All of these include the *Acta Consistorii Publice Exhibiti* as well as other matters. They illustrate how widespread in Catholic Europe was the information on the Japanese legation, all of them published in the same year in the cities of Rome, Dillingen, Prague, Bologna, and Cracow. Reproduced from A. Boscaro, *Sixteenth Century European Printed Works on the First Japanese Mission to Europe* (Leyden, 1973), pls. 2, 6, 7, and 10.

& twentie meetres, & the longest furnisheth the middle angle, the rest passe vpward and downward, still abating their lengthes by one or two sillables till they come to the point: the Fuzie is of the same nature but that he is sharper and slenderer. I will giue you an example or two of those which my Italian friend bestowed vpon me, which as neare as I could I translated into the same figure obseruing the phrase of the Orientall speach word for word.

A great Emperor in Tartary who they cal Can, for his good fortune in the wars & many notable conquests he had made, was furnamed Temir Cutzclewe, this nã loued the Lady Kermesine, who presented him returning frõ the cõquest of Corason (a great kingdom adioyning) with this Lozange made in letters of rubies & diamants entermingled thus

Sound
O
Harpe
Boil be out
Time the fleet
Ruler who with sharpe
Trenching blade of fierce steele
Hath made his fierce foes to feele
Attacher wrought him shame or harme,
The strength of, but braue right arme,
Chasing hard downe vnto the eyes
The new plaslet of her enemies,
Much honor hath he wonne
By doughtie deedes done
In Cora soon
And all this
Worke
Round.

To which Can Temir answered in Fuzie, with letters of Emeralds and Amethist mingled, cut and entermingled thus

Fine
Sore kninitie
Manfully fought so
To doughty Feild
With bright blade in hand
Hath Temir tost & fost to yeld
Many a Captaine strong and stoute,
And many a king but Temir stout,
Conquering large countrey and land,
To me my valone, I will be rie,
I spoke it to my great glorie,
Ai when I did first conquer that
O Kerms soon of all mine foes
The most cruell, of all my sweet woes
The fairest, the fairest
My proude, Can quit
My rich chest pray
Lend me thy fight
Whose only light
Keepes me not
alive.

nothing pleasant to an English care, but time and vsage wil make them acceptable inough, as it doth in all other new guise, be it for wearing of apparell or otherwise. The formes of your Geometricall figures be hereunder represented.

The Fuzie or The Triangle, called   The Square or   The Pillaster,
The Lozange spindle, called   Tricquet   quadrangle   or Cilinder
called Rombus Romboides

The Spire or   The Rondel   The egge or   The Tricquet   The Tricquet
taper, called   or Sphere   figure ouall   reuerst   displayed
piramis

The Taper   The Rõdel   The Lozange   The egge   The Lozange
reuersed   displayed   reuersed   displayed   rabbated

Of the Lozange.

The Lozange is a most beautifull figure, & fit for this purpose, being in his kind a quadrangle reuerst, with his point vpward like to a quarrell of glasse the Greekes and Latines both call it Rombus which may be the cause as I suppose why they also gaue that name to the fish commonly called the Turbot, who beareth iustly that figure, it ought not to containe about thirteene or fifteene or one and

23. Two pages illustrating pattern poems in George Puttenham, *Arte of English Poesie* (London, 1589).

CHAPTER VII

French Literature

The French, unlike the Iberians and Italians, had few direct or indirect links to the opening of the East during the sixteenth century. While the Atlantic voyages alerted Frenchmen to the existence of new lands and peoples, their awakening was at first neither sudden nor excited. Until mid-century their impressions of the outside world were gained from the travel books and encyclopedic compilations of the Middle Ages and from a few contemporary accounts which often mixed indiscriminately the factual and the fanciful. Only a few among the educated and urbane of French society began gradually to suspect from their reading of Latin, Spanish, and Italian writings, or of French translations of them, that discoveries had been made overseas which would in the course of time revolutionize Europe's view of itself and the world.

During the first two decades of the sixteenth century, the French nobility spent its energies abroad in the Italian wars. At home the people enjoyed a degree of repose and a mild economic prosperity as the country slowly recovered from the worst ravages of the English wars (1337–1453) and the Black Death. Intercourse with the leading political and intellectual lights of Italy helped to bring some of the abundant fruits of the Renaissance from Italy to France. King Francis I (1515–47), after his successful conclusion of the Concordat of Bologna (1516) with the papacy, inaugurated a policy of importing Italian artists and intellectuals. He and his sister, Margaret of Navarre, also encouraged and patronized French literati and Humanists, even as they spent huge sums on the royal residences of Chambord and Fontainebleau.

Despite a dogged determination to pursue a series of ruinous wars against Emperor Charles V, Francis managed to maintain a rich and flourishing life at his court and in certain major cities. In his efforts to offset the advances of Charles V, he unsuccessfully sought friendship with England; however, in 1535 he successfully concluded an alliance with the Turks directed against the Empire and Spain. Francis was also inclined to compete, or to permit his subjects in Normandy and Brittany to compete, with the Iberian powers for control over the fishing grounds and sea lanes of the Atlantic Ocean. Even though France was slow in becoming directly involved in overseas voyaging and trade, the reign of Francis I saw the nation become entangled in a distant and revolutionary alliance with the infidel Turk and a party to maritime activities undertaken in defiance of the Iberian claim to a monopoly of the overseas world.[1]

Lyons, Paris, and Bordeaux were the most cosmopolitan of France's cities. Strategically located astride the overland routes joining France, Switzerland, and Italy, Lyons in the early sixteenth century was heavily involved in the spice trade. Artisans from near and far poured into Lyons, especially silk weavers from Italy and printers from Germany. At Lyons, Florentines and Genoese operated branch banks and lived in sumptuous residences. Its merchant aristocracy played host to visiting Italian intellectuals and clerics. In 1523 a syndicate of Lyons merchants helped to finance the Atlantic voyage of the following year headed by their townsman Giovanni da Verrazzano, which sought unsuccessfully for a northern passage to Cathay by sailing westward.[2] Italian artists and intellectuals were likewise patronized by Lyons, particularly after Ippolito d'Este became its archbishop in 1539. In literature the École lyonnaise included a number of notables: Jean Marot, Rabelais, Maurice Scève, and Pontus de Tyard.[3] The eighty printing shops of Lyons, the chief one operated by Sebastien Gryphius, were busy in these years publishing French translations and adaptations of Latin classics and Italian travel books and popular literature.[4]

The French court had especially close commercial, diplomatic, and intellectual ties with Ferrara, the Italian city most responsive to the geographical discoveries. Renée, sister of Francis I, was married in 1528 to Ercole d'Este. A circle of French literati immediately clustered about Renée at the Ferrara court and remained there until her husband sent them away in 1536.[5] Other members of the Este family visited Paris and were possibly responsible for encouraging its printers to publish travel accounts and geographical works. Between 1480 and

[1] The most recent authoritative account of French maritime and colonial activities is C. A. Julien, *Les voyages de découverte et les premiers établissements (XVe–XVIe siècles)* (Paris, 1948); for the meaning of the Turkish alliance to French society and culture see C. D. Rouillard, *The Turk in French History, Thought, and Literature, 1520–1660* (Paris, 1938), chap. ii.

[2] See L. Romier, "Lyon et le cosmopolitisme au début de la renaissance française," *Bibliothèque d'humanisme et renaissance*, XI (1949), 32–33. While Verrazzano called himself a Florentine, he was probably born in Lyons and his voyage was certainly underwritten by some of the wealthy Florentines resident in the French city. See L. C. Wroth, *The Voyages of Giovanni da Verrazzano, 1524–28* (New Haven and London, 1970), *passim*.

[3] See H. Gambier, *Italie et renaissance poétique en France . . .* (Padua, 1936), pp. 56–57.

[4] On Lyons as a market of spices and books see R. Gascon, *Grand commerce et vie urbaine au seizième siècle: Lyon et ses marchands (environs de 1520–environs de 1580)* (2 vols.; Paris, 1971), I, 86–95, 104–6, 203–33.

[5] See A. Cameron, *The Influence of Ariosto's Epic . . . on Ronsard and His Group* (Baltimore, 1930), pp. xiii–xiv.

1530 the printers of France published forty-five geographical works, or an average of almost one each year. Twenty-eight of these were published at Paris, six at Lyons, and the remainder at Antwerp and Rouen.[6] By 1536 the Paris printers and booksellers Simone de Colines and Galliot de Pré had published the works of Peter Martyr, the *Supplementum chronicarum* of Foresti da Bergamo, the *Novus orbis regionum*, and Pius II's *Asiae Europae que elegantissima descriptio*.[7]

From the earliest days of printing the French church and government had sought to control the book trade. The printers and booksellers of Paris formed a corporation that was closely regulated as a dependency of the Sorbonne. An ordinance of Francis I issued in 1521 charged its Faculty of Theology with the responsibility of authorizing and licensing books for printing. Prepublication censorship of books was designed mainly to prevent the circulation of heretical, seditious, and defamatory texts. In 1543 the Sorbonne compiled an *Index* which tried to eliminate the publication and circulation of books favoring Protestantism. A decree of 1563 forbade the publication of all books which did not possess the "king's privilege." The French censorship, like the Italian and Spanish, had the general effect of discouraging speculative literature and of encouraging a shift toward secular themes. The turning to lay subjects was also given impetus by a sharp decline in the ecclesiastical patronage of scholars and by the state's new willingness to employ men of letters in bureaucratic and legal offices that were sometimes little more than sinecures.[8]

Some of the earliest and most consistently influential books on the discoveries appeared in Latin versions. Certain books originally issued in the vernacular were quickly translated into Latin for the international market:[9] for example, Varthema's book was translated from Italian into Latin in 1511. Maximilian of Transylvania published in 1523 at Cologne and Rome his Latin account of Magellan's voyage.[10] A compilation of retrospective travel literature called *Novus orbis regionum* was first published at Basel in 1532 with an introduction by Sebastian Münster.[11] But more broadly influential in France were the translations and adaptations in French which began to appear in print at the beginning of Francis' reign. In 1515 the *Paesi novamente ritrovati* was published in a French version to be followed the next year by Mathurin de Redoer's translation of the writings of Amerigo Vespucci. An abridged version in French of Pigafetta's account of Magellan's voyage appeared at Paris in 1525 followed

---

[6] Based on an analysis of G. Atkinson, *Les nouveaux horizons de la Renaissance française* (Paris, 1935), pp. 10–12, as rearranged and reinterpreted by V. L. Saulnier, *La littérature française de la Renaissance (1500–1610)* (8th rev. ed.; Paris, 1967), pp. 20–21.

[7] For more detail see J. Guignard, "Imprimeurs et libraires parisiens, 1525–36," *Bulletin de l'association Guillaume Budé*, 3d ser., No. 2 (1953), pp. 62, 65.

[8] See S. Kinser, "Ideas of Temporal Change and Cultural Process in France, 1470–1535," in A. Molho and J. A. Tedeschi (eds.), *Renaissance Studies in Honor of Hans Baron* (Florence, 1971), pp. 734–35.

[9] See *Asia*, I, 164.

[10] *Ibid.*, p. 172.

[11] *Ibid.*, pp. 179–80.

in 1532 by a partial translation of Peter Martyr.[12] In 1544 a French translation of Peter Apian's *Cosmographius* (originally published at Landshut in 1524) appeared; it was reprinted in 1553, 1581, and 1584.

Other books indirectly connected with the discoveries were also translated into French during this period. Many of the classical writings relating to Asia were wholly or partially translated. Cavicio's *Libro del peregrino*, the first of the Italian romances of travel to appear in French, was translated in 1528. A version in French prose of Ariosto's *Orlando* appeared in 1543, to be followed by a new and better translation of Boccaccio's *Decameron* (1545) and by the first translation of Boiardo's *Orlando* (1549-50).[13] The initial book of the Spanish *Amadis* was translated into French in 1540, and translations and adaptations of its other books, including the Italian additions, appeared later in the century. It was possibly because so much of the European chivalric literature was translated that the French poets of this century were so slow in producing romances of their own.[14]

In connection with the translation movement, a literature of compilation developed which sought to put between the covers of one book the most famous opinions and assertions of the great authors of the past. As part of the effort to vulgarize knowledge, the encyclopedia of universal learning gave way gradually to compilations of materials on particular subjects, including some on manners and morals. The earliest compilations of "prodigy" literature were translated from Latin into vernacular languages, especially French, and in the process were often enlarged.[15] The famous Latin collection of manners and customs, originally published in 1520 from classical and medieval authors by Johann Boemus, was first translated into French in 1539 as *Recueil de diverses histoires* and published at Paris by Galliot de Pré.[16] The following year it was published at Antwerp and thereafter it was repeatedly reprinted at Paris and elsewhere. Boemus' books enjoyed a good reception throughout the French-speaking world and elsewhere, perhaps because it made readily accessible to the intelligent reader a kind of literary cabinet of curiosities which enabled him to see quickly the great variety in human behavior. In the meantime newsletters from abroad were translated into French which enabled the man-on-the-street to learn a few details about the progress of the Portuguese in the East.[17] Truly, as Jacques Peletier remarked in his *Art poétique* (1555): "it is through the translations that France began to savor the good things."

[12] See J. Denizet, "Le livre imprimé en France aux XVᵉ et XVIᵉ siècles," in M. Mollat and P. Adam (eds.), *Les aspects internationaux de la découverte océanique aux XVᵉ et XVIᵉ siècles* (Paris, 1966), pp. 32-33.

[13] See A. Tilley, *The Literature of the French Renaissance* (2 vols.; Cambridge, 1904), I, 49-51.

[14] See below, pp. 284-85.

[15] See R. Schenda, *Die französische Prodigienliteratur in der zweiten Hälfte des 16. Jahrhunderts* (Munich, 1961), pp. 9-10, 12, 13.

[16] The original was called *Omnium gentium mores*. . . . A revised and expanded Latin version appeared at Lyons in 1536 from which the French translations were made. On Boemus see below, pp. 336-37.

[17] For example, a French version of the letters sent from India to Portugal telling of the victory at Diu in 1538 appeared in an eight-page pamphlet at Rouen in 1539. See Jean-Pierre Séguin, *L'Information en France de Louis XII à Henri II* (Geneva, 1961), p. 107.

I

THE CHALLENGE OF ASIA

The earliest among the French poets to exhibit more than a casual interest in the overseas world was François Buffereau, the author of a long descriptive poem in three parts called *Le mirouer du monde* (Geneva, 1517). Although his information derives entirely from pre-discovery literary sources, the poet accords more pages to "India" than he gives to any other part of the world. He describes in traditional terms its products, peoples, and topographical features. He has nothing to report on China or Southeast Asia, but the attention he lavishes upon "India" leaves the modern reader with the distinct impression that he is more than slightly aware of the growing importance of the East to the Europe of his day.

Other enterprising individuals were also aware of France's need to learn about Asia and to become a part of the expansion movement. Around 1520 the French center of interest in overseas navigation was the Norman town of Dieppe.[18] From this port in 1524, Jean Ango, its merchant-prince, sent the expedition of Verrazzano to find a northwestern passage to Cathay. After the failure of this effort, Ango began to send his vessels to India by the Cape route in defiance of the Portuguese monopoly. Two of Ango's vessels were dispatched to the East in 1529 under the command of Jean and Raoul Parmentier. Although the Parmentier brothers died in Sumatra, one of Ango's vessels returned safely to Dieppe in 1530 with the astronomer Pierre Crignon aboard. In the following year Crignon compiled and published at Paris the poetical writings of Jean Parmentier (1494–1530) in a memorial volume entitled *Description nouvelle des merveilles de ce môde.*[19] It included his *Traicté en forme d'exhortation*, a long poem written to encourage the frightened sailors on the long voyage to Sumatra.

In literary history Parmentier belongs, like Jean Marot, to the school of *rhétoriqueurs*. Most of his poems are *chants royaux* in praise of the Virgin. In those written from 1518 to 1528, a decade in which he took service with Jean Ango and worked with sea charts and globes, his poems reflect clearly his growing interest in the sea, navigation, exploration, and trade. In an allegorical poem the Virgin is likened to a well-provisioned ship which carries men safely across the sea of life. Other poems express the sorrows of the men who go to sea and their joys on returning home; these lines are studded with technical words taken from the nautical and cartographical vocabularies. In his *Traicté* he exhorts his compatriots to undertake maritime enterprises for the glory of king

---

[18] See *Asia*, I, 177–78.

[19] This rare 1531 edition is reprinted in Charles Schefer (ed.), *Le discours de la navigation de Jean et Raoul Parmentier* (Paris, 1883), pp. 117–37.

and country.[20] In a *chant royal* Parmentier relates how a cosmographer prepares
to search for the gold of India:

> Du chef de Caulx, provide nation
> Ung cosmographe, expert en la marine,
> Emprint la Routte et navigation
> Du Caillicou [Calicut] pour trouver l'or en myne.[21]

Although he died at a young age, Parmentier enjoyed the high esteem of his
contemporaries, especially of Jean Ango and the citizenry of Dieppe. His
enthusiasm and zeal for discovery were shared by Margaret of Navarre (1492–
1549), the king's sister and an avid reader of cosmographical and geographical
literature.[22] Parmentier named one of the islands he visited after *La Marguerite*.
In her later poems the queen of Navarre shares the inquiring spirit of the Norman
poet about the sea and distant lands.[23]

Among the pilots and navigators of Francis I the best known and most
influential was Jean Fonteneau, called Jean Alfonse de Saintonge (d. *ca.* 1544–45).
Probably of Portuguese origin,[24] Jean Alfonse evidently took service in France
around 1531. Thereafter he wrote two works based on his own overseas
experiences. His *Voyages aventureux*, probably written around 1536, was circulated in manuscript before being printed in 1559.[25] His *Cosmographie*, prepared
sometime later, also circulated in manuscript but was not printed until 1904.[26]
The latter work, which deals more extensively with the East, owes a certain debt
to the *Suma de geografía* (Seville, 1519) of the Spanish cosmographer Martín
Fernández de Enciso. But it also includes materials on the East drawn from
other sources and possibly from his own early experiences while in the service
of the Portuguese.[27]

---

[20] See K. von Posadowsky-Wehner, *Jean Parmentier: Leben und Werk* (Munich, 1937), pp.
27–41; also J. C. Lapp, "An Explorer-Poet: Jean Parmentier," *Modern Language Quarterly*, VI (1945),
83–89.

[21] Schefer (ed.), *op. cit.* (n. 19), p. 94.

[22] She wrote:

"Je m'envoloys par la philosophie
Par tous les cyeulx, puis la cosmographie
Que me monstroit la terre et sa grandeur,
Faisant mon cueur courir de grand ardeur
Parmy l'Europe et l'Afrique et l'Asie,
Où sans cesser couroys par fantaisie."

A. Lefranc (ed.), *Les dernières poésies de Marguerite de Navarre* (Paris, 1896), p. 197.

[23] For a comparison of their poetical offerings see Lapp, *loc. cit.* (n. 20), pp. 90–92.

[24] This is a much disputed question, but now it appears that he was a native of the Algarve in
Portugal rather than of Saintonge in France. For details see the excellent analysis of Luis de Matos,
Les portugais en France au XVIe siècle (Coimbra, 1952), chap. i.

[25] First printed at Poitiers, it was reprinted five times during the sixteenth century.

[26] Jean Alfonse, *La cosmographie*, "Recueil de voyages et de documents pour servir à l'histoire de la
géographie," edited by C. Schefer and H. Cordier, Vol. XX (Paris, 1904); also see Georges Musset
(ed.), *La cosmographie . . . par Jean Fonteneau dit Alfonse de Saintonge* (Paris, 1914), pp. 7, 9.

[27] Pierre Margry (*Les navigations françaises et la révolution maritime du XIVe au XVIe siècle* [Paris,
1867], pp. 229–30) was the first to suggest that he used Enciso as a model. L. Sainéan ("La cosmo-

The *Cosmographie* calls upon the French to participate more actively in overseas discovery. It is full of praise for his own age as the "mistress of all things" and as superior to all previous ages in knowledge of the world. In his descriptions of coastal regions in the East, Jean Alfonse seems to rely on personal experience or on the accounts of his contemporaries.[28] His remarks on the interior of India are drawn occasionally from classical and medieval sources, but his references to *satī*, cow worship, Malabar Christians, and the tomb of St. Thomas seem to come from later sources. East of India he continues to rely in substantial measure upon the older sources, though he mentions using the report of a person who had actually been to the Moluccas, Java, China, and Cathay. His description of Cathay, probably based on Marco Polo and Mandeville, pictures its people as living in a "better fashion than we do" and in being "better governed than we are." He believes that New Spain lies close to Cathay and that the Pacific, if there at all, is a narrow stretch of water. He incorporates a number of other unfounded claims, including a reference to Cathay as the home of the unicorn, a beast which he saw with his own eyes![29] Although Jean Alfonse's writings went unpublished in his own lifetime, they nevertheless influenced some of his contemporaries. About 1546 Jean Mallart, a minor Norman poet and royal scribe, composed in verse a description of the seaports of the world based on a close paraphrase of the *Voyages aventureux*.[30]

The most popular writer of the age of Francis I was François Rabelais (*ca.* 1490–1553), the ribald physician in clerical garb who produced the immortal "histories" of *Gargantua and Pantagruel*. This gigantic work of humor, philosophy, and satire is Rabelais' personal rendition of the traditional popular legend of Gargantua. It centers on the feats of the beneficent giant and of Pantagruel, a character whom Rabelais created to be Gargantua's son. In 1532 Rabelais published his first book on Pantagruel, followed several years later by his incomparable life of Gargantua. Both books ran into difficulties with the censorship, so Rabelais waited until 1546 before publishing another installment in the series. In the year before his death (1552) he published a fourth book on the "noble Pantagruel." The fifth and final book, over which there is still some debate as to authorship, appeared posthumously in 1562. A definitive edition of the five books, in which the history of Gargantua was incorporated as the first book (even though it was originally the second of the series to appear), was

---

graphie de Jean-Alfonse Saintongeais," *Revue des études rabelaisiennes*, X [1912], 19–67) accuses him of plagiarizing Enciso. Matos (*op. cit.* [n. 24], p. 45) concludes that his works, despite their obvious borrowings from Enciso, furnish details on the discoveries and the conquests which are not to be found in Enciso's or in the French works of the day. On Enciso see above, pp. 169–70. Jean Alfonse might have obtained some Portuguese book or maps through his compatriots. See Amy Gordon, "The Impact of the Discoveries on Sixteenth-Century French Cosmographical and Historical Thought" (Ph.D. diss., Dept. of History, University of Chicago, 1974), pp. 32–33.

[28] See Musset (ed.), *op. cit.* (n. 26), p. 21.

[29] For more details see Gordon, *op. cit.* (n. 27), pp. 38–41.

[30] Mallart's unpublished poem is entitled *Premier livre de la description de tous les portz de mer de l'univers* . . . (Bibl. nat., MSS fran., 1382, 25375, and 13371). Also see Matos, *op. cit.* (n. 24), pp. 62–64, 72–76.

first issued in 1567. No fewer than sixty editions of Rabelais' *Gargantua and Pantagruel* rolled off the presses before the close of the sixteenth century.[31]

Any reader of this great satire will at once feel Rabelais' sensitivity to the vibrant life, intellectual debate, mores, and social values of his day. He will also notice that the author is responsive to the fact that the map of the world was then being unrolled. Like Ariosto, Rabelais brought the overseas discoveries into his romance almost as quickly as he learned about them. Like the great Italian poet, he was also uncertain and vague in his geographical knowledge. In his references to the voyages and to distant lands he unhesitatingly mixes fact with fable and old sources with new. A more critical attitude could hardly be expected in a writer of romance since the geographical authorities themselves were similarly confused when they attempted to incorporate the new knowledge of the world into traditional conceptions and frames of reference. Still, Rabelais' picture of the outside world changes in response to the infiltration into France of newer information and to the evolution of contemporary ideas about navigation and discovery.

In the prologue to the first book of Pantagruel (1532) he cites among others the *Orlando furioso* (definitive edition, 1532) and the travels of Mandeville as popular books of "luxuriant growth" which are similar to the *Chronicles* of Gargantua in possessing "certain occult properties."[32] Pantagruel, the natural son of a princess of the Amaurots in Utopia, leaves Paris on hearing that the Dipsodes had invaded the Utopia of his parents. He boards a ship at Honfleur for a voyage around the Cape to the East. Utopia, a word and a mythical place borrowed from Sir Thomas More, Rabelais locates somewhere to the east of India.[33] His invading "Dipsodes" are possibly the Scythians of Central Asia, a people who had a reputation among the Ancients for dipsomania.[34] The itinerary that Pantagruel follows from Honfleur to the port of Utopia Rabelais

[31] The scholarship on Rabelais and his book is vast, much of it having been produced only in the twentieth century. Impetus to modern study of the book's realistic features has come from the Société des études rabelaisiennes founded in 1903 with Abel Lefranc as its first president. The best biographies are those of J. Plattard (Paris, 1928) and G. Lote (Aix-en-Provence, 1938); in English the best are the work of Arthur Tilley (London, 1907) and the translation of Plattard. The standard critical edition of his writings is A. Lefranc, R. Marichal *et al.*, *Oeuvres de Rabelais* (7 vols.; Paris and Geneva, 1912–65). The most recent English translation is that in the Penguin Classics by J. M. Cohen (trans.), *The Histories of Gargantua and Pantagruel by François Rabelais* (London, 1957). It is based on the text and commentary by Plattard published in *Les textes français* (5 vols.; Paris, 1929). For a summary of recent scholarship see V. L. Saulnier, "Position actuelle des problèmes rabelaisiens," *Actes du congrès de Tours et Poitiers* (Paris, 1954), pp. 83–104, and L. Schrader, "Die Rabelais-Forschung der Jahre 1950–1960: Tendenzen und Ergebnisse," *Romanstiisches Jahrbuch*, XI (1960), 161–201.

[32] Cohen (trans.), *op. cit.* (n. 31), p. 168. For the identification of Rabelais' "Monteville" with Mandeville see L. Sainéan, "Rabelaisiana—Le Monteville de Rabelais," *Revue des études rabelaisiennes*, IX (1911), 265–75. On Mandeville see *Asia*, I, 77–80.

[33] More places Utopia somewhere between America and Ceylon, while Rabelais seems to put it in Polo's northern China, or Cathay. See A. Lefranc, *Les navigations de Pantagruel: Étude sur la géographie rabelaisienne* (Paris, 1905), pp. 9–17. For the view that Utopia is an ideal rather than a real place and that it is meaningless to try to locate it geographically see H. de Bouillane de Lacoste, "La première navigation de Pantagruel," *Mercure de France*, CCCXX (1954), 604–29.

[34] See Lefranc, *Les navigations* (n. 33), pp. 21–23. Also see Plattard's review of Tilley's *Rabelais* in *Revue des études rabelaisiennes*, V (1901), 430–35.

derives in large part from the introduction to the *Novus orbis* (1532) written by Sebastian Münster.[35] While some of the places named are imaginary, others are either imperfect spellings of actual places or anagrams of genuine names. Rabelais' "Meden" and "Udem" represent Medina and Aden while his "Gelasim" is probably an imperfect anagram of "Zeilam" or "Seyla," two of the then common spellings of Ceylon.[36] Even though this itinerary is certainly based upon specific knowledge of the Portuguese route to the East, Rabelais places Utopia in a mythical East created by medieval travelers and romancers, a region where monsters, giants, and miracles might safely be expected.[37] In the final chapter of this book, Rabelais promises the rest of Pantagruel's story by "the very next Frankfurt book-fair." In it he will undertake to recount how Pantagruel "crossed the Caspian mountains, how he sailed across the Atlantic Sea, how he defeated the cannibals and conquered the Perlas Islands[Antilles], how he married the daughter of the King of India, Prester John."[38]

Rabelais failed to keep his promise to produce within six months (the Frankfurt book fairs were held twice annually) a new narrative of Pantagruel's exploits. Perhaps his default can be accounted for by the fact that his first effort at romance was condemned as obscene by the Sorbonne in 1533. Nonetheless the popular success of *Pantagruel* led him to compose his own version of the Gargantua legend and to use it as a vehicle for attacking his enemies in the Sorbonne and for setting forth his own ideas on education. In the *Gargantua*, first published in 1534, Rabelais has nothing to say directly about the overseas voyages or distant places. His references to India are limited to the exploits of Bacchus there, to its precious stones and strange animals, and to its wise Brahmans. In chapter xxxiii he gives what amounts to a summary of the prevailing state of French geographical knowledge but without references to places east of Turkey. Here he, like many contemporary poets, seems to delight in the strangeness and euphony in lists of geographical names.[39] In his famous description of the imaginary Abbey of Thélème, Rabelais depicts an institution and a way of life

[35] For a comparison of the two passages see A. Tilley, *Studies in the French Renaissance* (Cambridge, 1922), pp. 31–33.

[36] See Lefranc, *Les navigations* (n. 33), pp. 18–19; also Tilley, *Studies* (n. 35), p. 32. Lefranc even argues that the Fairy Isles ("Iles des Phées") may be a reference to the Sunda archipelago. It is certainly possible that he is here referring to the islands which he could have read about in Varthema's account included in *Novus orbis* or in the truncated French version of Pigafetta's narrative of Magellan's voyage published at Paris in 1525.

[37] See G. Chinard, *L'éxotisme américain dans la littérature française au XVIe siècle* (Paris, 1911), pp. 51–52.

[38] Cohen (trans.), *op. cit.* (n. 31), p. 277. Lefranc and Tilley agree that Rabelais was here outlining a southwest route to India. I am inclined, however, to agree with Plattard that he is merely listing a series of exploits which Pantagruel will perform. His reference to Prester John as king of India rather than as king of Ethiopia, the designation usual in the maps and writings of the early sixteenth century, was probably derived from Mandeville (see Sainéan, "Le Monteville de Rabelais," *loc. cit.* [n. 32], p. 272). In his *Cosmographie* Jean Alfonse likewise seems to have accepted Mandeville's identification (see Sainéan, "Cosmographie" [n. 27], p. 59). For the suggestion that he was referring to the reigning negus of Ethiopia rather than a mythical ruler see M. Françon, "Pantagruel et le Prestre Jehan," *Studi francesi*, IX (1965), 86–88.

[39] See L. Sainéan, *La langue de Rabelais* (2 vols.; Paris, 1922–23), II, 517.

that is utterly foreign to Europe and reminiscent of the descriptions of the lavish palaces of Asia in the medieval travel books and in those of his own day.[40] The "views of the world" (maps ?) and the "horns of stags, unicorns, rhinoceros, and hippopotami, with elephants' tusks" which decorated the abbey's galleries likewise add to the exotic atmosphere of the author's dream.[41]

The third book continuing the "history" of Pantagruel was published only in 1546, eleven years after the work to which it is the immediate sequel. The principal theme of this book is built upon Panurge's decision to marry and his perplexity as to how he should know in advance whether or not his wife will be faithful, and whether or not she will beat and rob him. After consulting sibyls, numerologists, wisemen, and many others, Panurge decides to seek the counsel of the Oracle of the Divine Bottle and Pantagruel agrees to accompany him on the journey. Panurge, often identified with Rabelais himself, has a friend called Xenomanes "who knows the place, the land, and the country where this temple and oracle are."[42] Modern scholars identify Xenomanes with Jean Alfonse de Saintonge, the navigator and cosmographer.[43] While most of the references to India in the third book are taken from classical sources,[44] it is clear from Rabelais' reference to the coins called "seraphs" that he still had in mind the travel accounts of his own century. Seraphs were common exchange in the Levant, North Africa, and the Portuguese East, and are mentioned repeatedly by Varthema in the account of his travels published in the *Novus orbis* that was consulted by Rabelais.[45] In preparation for the voyage, Pantagruel collects a supply of the plant "Pantagruelion" which the less imaginative call hemp. He extols it as being superior for making cloth to the cotton produced by the trees of the Seres.[46] Indispensable to the weaving of sail cloth, the herb "Pantagruelion" has enabled Taprobana to see Lapland, and Java to see the Riphaean mountains.[47] In a concluding verse to the third book, Rabelais advises "Arabians, Indians and Sabeans" to cease vaunting "incense, myrrh and ebony" and to

---

[40] Suggestion of Chinard, *op. cit.* (n. 37), pp. 54–56. Also see Lote, *op. cit.* (n. 31), pp. 115–28.

[41] Cohen (trans.), *op. cit.* (n. 31), pp. 152, 155. The idea that the galleries were decorated with maps is suggested in Charles Lenormant, *Rabelais et l'architecture de la Renaissance* (Paris, 1840), as quoted in Tilley, *Rabelais* (n. 35), pp. 154–55.

[42] Cohen (trans.), *op. cit.* (n. 31), p. 416.

[43] Identification first worked out by Margry, *op. cit.* (n. 27), pp. 339–41. Also see Lefranc, *Navigations* (n. 33), pp. 65–78. It has been accepted by most students of Rabelais, the notable exception being Sainéan ("Cosmographie de Jean-Alfonse Saintongeais" [n. 27], pp. 63–65). Also see above, pp. 258–59.

[44] For exact references see Cohen (trans.), *op. cit.*, (n. 31), pp. 285, 286, 332, 365.

[45] For example, Rabelais mentions (*ibid.*, p. 292) "seraphs" in his discussion of the revenues received by Panurge as Warden of Salmagundia in Dipsodia. For commentary on his use of "seraph" as an exotic word see Sainéan, *Langue* (n. 39), I, 195. The word itself is a transcription of an original Arabic-Persian term.

[46] See Cohen (trans.), *op. cit.* (n. 31), p. 428. "Seres" here probably means northern India. References to the "cotton trees" of the East occur in many medieval travel accounts. His source is probably Mandeville. For commentary see H. Yule and H. Cordier (eds.), *The Book of Ser Marco Polo* (2 vols.; London, 1938), II, 394n.

[47] Cohen (trans.), *op. cit.* (n. 31), p. 428. The first reference to the name "Java" in European literature appears in Marco Polo (see *Asia*, I, 587). But it is also mentioned in Varthema.

obtain from France the seed of this marvelous plant and to try growing it themselves.[48]

The fourth book, first issued in an incomplete version in 1548, was published in its definitive form in 1552. The subject of this and the posthumously printed fifth book (1563) is the voyage of twelve vessels by an imaginary northwest route to Cathay, the homeland of the Oracle of the Divine Bottle.[49] The pilot of the fleet is Xenomanes (Jean Alfonse) and its captain Jamet Brahier, identified as the Breton sailor Jacques Cartier whom Alfonse had served as pilot on the voyage to America of 1541–43.[50] The first Frenchman to make important Atlantic voyages, three in the decade from 1534 to 1544, Cartier was a firm believer in the existence of a northwest passage to Cathay and had convinced his countrymen to support efforts to locate it. A narrative of Cartier's second voyage by an anonymous writer appeared in 1545, a work which Rabelais probably read. This book may have been published as part of Cartier's promotional campaign, and the second voyage of Pantagruel may have been intended as support of the crown's decision to sponsor Cartier's efforts. Certainly Rabelais, in other connections, had performed notable service as a publicist for the policies and programs of the crown.[51] His decision not to fulfill the promise given at the end of Book II (1532) to follow Pantagruel on a southeast voyage to India, but rather to dispatch him on the northwestern voyage to Cathay, coincides exactly in time and in change of route and destination with the maritime policies being followed by his king.

Rabelais' own words constitute the best basis for such a conclusion. He states that Xenomanes and Brahier agree that "since the Oracle of the Holy Bacbuc [princess and guardian of the Bottle] lay near Cathay, in Upper India, they should not take the ordinary Portuguese route" for it is too lengthy and dangerous. He is also convinced that the route by the northwest passage "was the one followed by those Indians who sailed to Germany . . . at the time when Metellus Celer was Proconsul in Gaul."[52] Thus he was able to support his personal decision to change routes with the authority of the ancient writers (Cornelius Nepos, Pomponius Mela, and Pliny) who report the occurrence of such a visit. It may also be surmised, from the manner in which he handles the voyage, that Rabelais, as the author of an imaginary peregrination, decided to follow an unknown route rather than one on which the documentation was becoming specific around mid-century.[53]

In the course of the voyage Panurge, Pantagruel, and their friends call at a

---

[48] Cohen (trans.), *op. cit.* (n. 31), p. 432.

[49] For the possibility that Peru was its homeland see E. von Telle, "La situation géographique (?) de la Dive Bouteille," *Bibliothèque d'humanisme et renaissance*, XIV (1952), 329–30.

[50] For this identification see Margry, *op. cit.* (n. 27), p. 388; Lefranc, *Navigations* (n. 33), pp. 55–64; and Tilley, *Studies* (n. 35), pp. 61–65.

[51] See Lote, *op. cit.* (n. 31), p. 100.

[52] Quotations from Cohen (trans.), *op. cit.* (n. 31), p. 453. Cf. the ideas of Peutinger on this point (see below, p. 333).

[53] See Lefranc, *Navigations* (n. 33), p. 51.

series of fantastic islands, on each of which abuses are found in their "purest form." This literary device enables Rabelais to satirize allegorically some of the evils of Europe that most perturb and annoy him. The voyage itself gives him an opportunity to write an exciting and dramatic passage on a storm at sea, to describe the giant size and antics of a whale, and to display his thorough personal command of nautical terms, ship construction, and navigational problems.[54] After landing on Medamothy (Nowhere) island Pantagruel "looked at various pictures and tapestries, various animals, fish, birds, and other strange and exotic merchandise, displayed along the harbor road and in the markets of the port. For it was the third day of the great annual fair, which brought all the richest and best-known merchants of Africa and Asia to this place each year."[55] One of the "exotic" paintings he purchased on this island may be seen in his fanciful Abbey of Thélème "on the right hand wall, as you enter the high gallery."[56] Pantagruel also purchased and sent to Gargantua a Scythian tarand, a kind of chameleon, and three young unicorns along with a promise "that any strange animals, plants, birds, or stones that I may find and collect during the course of our voyage, I will, with God's aid, bring back to you."[57]

In the fifth book the travelers arrive in Satinland, where Pantagruel observes "Hearsay" explaining a chart of the world to a group of onlookers. Pantagruel remarks:

There, as I believe, I saw Herodotus, Pliny, Solinus, Berosus, Philostratus, Mela, Strabo, and a great number of other ancients, together with Albertus Magnus the Dominican, Peter Martyr, Pope Pius the Second, Rafael de Volterra, Paulus Jovius the Valiant, Jacques Cartier, Chaiton [Hayton] the Armenian, Marco Polo the Venetian, Ludovico Romano [Varthema], Pedro Alvarez, and I do not know how many other modern historians, hiding behind a piece of tapestry and stealthily writing down the grandest stuff—and all from Hearsay.[58]

Whether this was written by Rabelais or by an anonymous continuator, it is nevertheless an unfair characterization of the last five authors listed. They were all travelers and first-hand observers. Seven of these twelve authors are represented in the *Novus orbis*, a work Rabelais certainly depended upon.[59] Whatever else this list discloses, it is clearly an enumeration of his main geographical sources.[60] That he feels free to present them to his reader without further

[54] See L. Denoix, "Les connaissances nautiques de Rabelais," in "François Rabelais, ouvrage publié pour le quatrième centenaire de sa mort (1553–1953)," *Travaux d'humanisme et renaissance*, VII (1953), 171–80.

[55] Cohen (trans.), *op. cit.* (n. 31), p. 454. This is, I believe, the earliest usage in European languages of the word "exotic" with reference to Asian products. See below, p. 531 n.

[56] *Ibid.*, see above, p. 262, for Thélème and exoticism.

[57] *Ibid.*, p. 459. It was not utterly fantastic for Rabelais to imagine that Asian goods and merchants might be found in America, since he and his contemporaries thought of Canada as an island separated from Cathay only by a narrow strait. See Chinard, *op. cit.* (n. 37), p. 60. Also see below, pp. 456–57.

[58] Cohen (trans.), *op. cit.* (n. 31), p. 678.

[59] See Tilley, *Studies* (n. 35), pp. 36–39.

[60] See Sainéan, *Langue* (n. 39), II, 518–20. Interestingly, Mandeville does not appear in the list of "Hearsay" sources, possibly because Rabelais believed that Mandeville had actually traveled in the East.

explanation constitutes an indication of the popularity of these writers in mid-century France.

India and Cathay capture Rabelais' imagination because they are the Asian regions most adequately represented in his sources. To the Ancients and to Rabelais, the Brahmans of India are exemplary wisemen. From Marco Polo, Mandeville, and Ariosto he obtained his impressions of India and Cathay as rich and highly developed countries where marvels are to be expected. His rich embroidery of detail on the flora and fauna of India is drawn from the tales of the ancient and medieval authors as well as from the travelers of his own day.[61] His description of the elephant is borrowed directly from the writings of Cadamosto and Varthema, both of which are included in the *Novus orbis*.[62] According to Rabelais' own testimony Hans Kleberger, a Nuremberg merchant who resided in Lyons, showed him a picture of a rhinoceros, probably a copy of Albrecht Dürer's woodcut.[63] In 1536 Rabelais visited the Strozzi menagerie at Florence where he, like Montaigne a half-century later, saw many rare beasts and birds.[64] Aside from the authentic animals he mentions, Rabelais repeatedly refers to fabulous animals to which tradition assigned an Indian origin.

Analysis of *Gargantua and Pantagruel* shows clearly that Rabelais was in touch with the geographical explorations and discoveries being carried out in his day. He, like his contemporaries elsewhere, was unable to learn much more about the East than could be found in Marco Polo, Mandeville, Varthema, Pigafetta, Peter Martyr, and the *Novus orbis*. In other words he consulted all the readily available sources from Antiquity, the Middle Ages, and his own century. The Portuguese policy of control over more recent information operated effectively throughout Rabelais' period of gestation and writing. His countrymen, unlike the Italians, were not directly involved in the spice traffic. Consequently he was apparently able to learn very little from oral reports. The failure of the French to find the northwestern passage to Cathay also slowed down temporarily the quest for information on the East. Dependent as he was upon the reports of foreigners, it is hardly surprising that Rabelais expresses skepticism about the "hearsay" reports to which he is limited. He gives no evidence of knowing the poems of Jean Parmentier, except perhaps in his description of the storm at sea and of the fears of men aboard ship. He certainly may have borrowed a few tales of Indian origin from the collections that were available to him.[65] But it is

[61] See L. Sainéan, "L'histoire naturelle dans l'oeuvre de Rabelais," *Revue du seizième siècle*, III (1915), 210–11.

[62] See Cohen (trans.), *op. cit.* (n. 31), p. 675. For the parallel accounts see Tilley, *Studies* (n. 35), pp. 35–36.

[63] See Cohen (trans.), *op. cit.* (n. 31), p. 675. For commentary see R. Salomon, "A Trace of Dürer in Rabelais," *Modern Language Notes*, LVIII (1943), 498–500; and *Asia*, II, Bk. 1, 158–72. There was also a painting of the rhinoceros in the Abbey of Thélème.

[64] See Sainéan, "L'histoire naturelle" (n. 61), pp. 223–24. Also see below, p. 293.

[65] His educational program in the *Gargantua* appears to parallel the education of Bharata in the *Ramayana*. The charming fable of "The Fool and the Meat-Roaster" (III, 37) may have its origin in a tale from the *Avadanas* (apologue XXV). See E. Levêque, *Les mythes et légendes de l'Inde et de la Perse* . . . (Paris, 1880), pp. 547–49.

clear that he had no personal interest in their Indian provenance. Limited as his sources on the East were, he was obviously aware of its importance since he places Utopia in India and sends Pantagruel to Cathay. But for the countries, peoples, and animals of the East he is forced by circumstances to obtain his materials from the older sources. As a result his picture of Asia, in contrast to his view of the maritime routes, is essentially that conveyed by Mandeville and Marco Polo with but few additions from later materials. Perhaps nothing illustrates the poverty of his sources as much as the description at the end of the fifth book where he talks about the mosaic located in the "temple of the Bottle" in Cathay showing Bacchus' victory over the Indians![66]

Rabelais was left unmoved by the Portuguese "discovery" of Japan around 1543, by the Jesuit missionary enterprise in the East under Xavier's leadership (1542–52), and by the Jesuit letters and letterbooks which were beginning to be circulated in Europe during the last decade of his life.[67] But others were challenged, particularly his younger contemporary Guillaume Postel (1501–81). A "Gaulish cosmopolite," as Postel styled himself, he was notorious as a precocious Humanist, linguist, traveler, Orientalist, mystic, religious reformer, and nationalist. In his numerous writings, popular lectures, and extensive correspondence he involved himself in most of the knotty problems of the age and often sponsored and advocated radical ideas and remedies which shocked the orthodox and eventually got him into trouble with both religious and state authorities. Still, as a rabid crusader and zealous propagandist for various causes, he won a following among intellectuals and literati which kept alive his name and influence until long after his death.[68]

Postel's formal education began before 1530 at the Collège de Sainte-Barbe in Paris. Here he was exposed to the thought of Aristotle and Erasmus. He also quickly exhibited to his masters and fellow students an almost incredible preciosity in learning languages. Because of the special relationship obtaining between the Collège and the Portuguese crown, Sainte-Barbe in Postel's day was dominated by masters and students from Iberia.[69] Through them he learned about the Portuguese East and began to share their enthusiasm for foreign missions. The eager intellectuals who became the founders of the Society of Jesus met at Sainte-Barbe, and it was undoubtedly their influence upon the youthful Postel that first awakened and later kept alive his interest in the activities of the Society in the East. In 1536, possibly because of his linguistic abilities, Postel accompanied the French mission to Constantinople. Here he studied Arabic and began to take an interest in propagating Christianity in the Islamic Levant. At Venice in 1537 on his way home, Postel became associated with the printer Daniel Bomberg, the leader of a group interested in sponsoring publica-

[66] See Cohen (trans.), *op. cit.* (n. 31), pp. 691–94.

[67] For the Christian mission see *Asia*, I, chap. v.

[68] The most comprehensive and penetrating study of his life and ideas is W. J. Bouwsma, *Concordia mundi: The Career and Thought of Guillaume Postel (1510–81)* (Cambridge, Mass., 1957). For his biography see chap. i. For a portrait see pl. 93.

[69] For details see above, pp. 11–12.

tions on and in Eastern languages.[70] From 1538 to 1542, by royal appointment, Postel lectured at Paris on mathematics and philology. Overly enthusiastic about advancing his own ideas for training students in Arabic to prepare them as missionaries to Turkey, Postel so embarrassed the king that he was dismissed from the lectureship. In 1544, free to pursue his own interests, Postel published his first major work, a manual and an inspirational tract for missionaries called *De orbis terrae concordia* (Basel).

Once this work was in print, Postel sought to promote his own missionary program by going to Rome. Here he applied for admission to the newly created Society of Jesus.[71] At first the Jesuits welcomed him, but it soon became apparent that he was unwilling to support their program when it came into conflict with his own. In these years he also became ever more firmly attached to the idea that the unity and concord of the world could only be won by the French king. Unwilling to acknowledge the absolute authority of the pope or to accept the evangelizing priorities of the Society, Postel was reprimanded by Loyola and finally expelled from the Society at the end of 1545. Although he was always bitter about his expulsion, Postel continued to follow with great interest the activities of the Society. He soon became an avid student of the *cabala* as he gradually incorporated aspects of Jewish mysticism into his thought. In Venice from 1547 to 1549, he convinced Bomberg and others to finance another trip to the Levant to give him the opportunity to improve his knowledge of Near Eastern languages and to acquire religious texts for printing in Europe.

Postel returned to France in 1551. Over the next four years, as he sought to spread his teachings, he published twenty-three books as well as numerous pamphlets and letters. One of the most important and influential of his books first appeared in 1552 under the title *Des merveilles du monde* (Paris) and was reissued in 1553(?), 1560, 1562, and 1575.[72] In this book, more than in any of his others, he stresses the superiority of East over West in material prosperity, human excellence, civilization, wisdom, and religion. He elevates Japan, in particular, to the lofty status of an edifying example, as a living model to a Christendom disinclined to follow the teachings of Christ.

Postel was an avid reader of travel literature and cosmographies,[73] and among his friends and admirers were André Thevet, the royal cosmographer, and Johann Widmanstetter, Orientalist and chancellor of the University of Vienna. In

---

[70] Cf. below, pp. 509–10. For a summary of his travels see E. Vogel, "Ueber W. Postels Reisen in den Orient," *Serapeum*, XIV (1853), 51–53.

[71] For details on his novitiate and his relations with Loyola see H. Bernard-Maitre, "Le passage de Guillaume Postel chez les premiers Jésuites de Rome (mars 1544–decembre 1545)," in *Mélanges . . . offerts à Henri Chamard* (Paris, 1951), pp. 227–43.

[72] The initial date of publication is uncertain, though it probably first appeared at Paris in 1552. One of the few surviving copies is in the Bibliothèque nationale (Rés. D. 2.5267). Undated, but probably of 1553, this edition has 28 chapters in 96 folio pages. The printed text is studded with emendations in the author's hand. I have used a microfilm of this work kindly supplied to me by Mrs. Carol Flaumenhaft. For the other editions see G. Atkinson, . . . *Repértoire bibliographique* (Paris, 1927), pp. 84–85.

[73] See Bouwsma, *op. cit.* (n. 68), p. 58.

preparing *Des merveilles du monde* Postel used as sources for Tartary the books of Prince Hayton of Armenia and Marco Polo, two thirteenth-century contemporaries. Other materials, probably from the accounts reprinted in the *Novus orbis*, he derived from Varthema, Pigafetta (French ed., 1525), Oviedo y Valdes, and Peter Martyr. He cites the travels of Josafat Barbaro published in the *Viaggi fatti alla Tana* . . . (Venice, 1543). His major sources of current information were the Jesuit letters, including those of Xavier, Francisco Perez, and "innumerable others."[74] He employed these materials for the declared purpose of showing "clearly how Divine Providence takes care of mankind . . . by continually intervening in human affairs through miracles," and of pointing up "the travels and rare things by which it has pleased God to render admirable the lands and different provinces of the world."[75]

Through his travels and reading, Postel found evidence of true religion and human understanding in every corner of the earth. Christianity, like the primitive language, was universal before the dispersal of Babel. The vestiges that remain of a primitive, universal Christianity are particularly impressive in the East. Asia remains physically greater and more populous than Europe.[76] Originally the site of the earthly paradise and the fount of wisdom, Asia preserves traces of its earlier perfection.[77] East and West, according to God's plan, complement each other: the East is masculine, spiritual, ascendant, supernal, and unchanging; the West is feminine, declining, temporal, and capricious.[78] The Japanese, the most eastern of all peoples, are the best the world knows. The French, at the opposite end of the Eurasiatic continent, are likewise distinguished. The reunion of the peoples of the world is being undertaken by the Society of Jesus through Xavier, who received his divine vocation while studying in Paris.[79] God's purpose will be accomplished when the Turks accept Christianity and when the world finally realizes its divine destiny by accepting the sway of the king of Gaul.

In referring to the superiority of Eastern civilization, understanding, and reason, Postel accounts for the excellence of Asia's religious and moral life. Through natural reason alone the peoples of the East have followed a straight path to religious truth.[80] Of all the Asian religions he understands most about the faith of Japan, a nation that he unhesitatingly identifies with Marco Polo's "Zipangu."[81] His more recent information on Japan he obtained from a letter of Xavier written from Cochin on January 20, 1548.[82] Postel translated this letter into French, interlarded it with his own comments, and used it as the basis

---

[74] Postel, *Des merveilles du monde* (Paris, 1553?), p. 83ʳ.

[75] *Ibid.*, p. 4ʳ.

[76] *Ibid.*, pp. 7ᵛ–8ʳ.

[77] *Ibid.*, pp. 45ᵛ–60ʳ.

[78] *Ibid.*, p. 92ʳ.

[79] *Ibid.*, p. 80ʳ.

[80] See Bouwsma, *op. cit.* (n. 68), p. 210.

[81] Postel, *op. cit.* (n. 74), p. 9ʳ.

[82] For its text see G. Schurhammer and J. Wicki (eds.), *Epistolae S. Francisci Xaverii* . . . (Rome, 1944), I, 390–92.

for his discussions of the political and religious life of Japan.[83] Much of Xavier's information in this letter was extracted from a summary narrative by Yajirō, a Japanese convert known as Paul of the Holy Faith. A native of Kyūshū, Yajirō gave to the Jesuits in India the best insights they had yet obtained into Japanese government and the Buddhist religion.[84] Postel, in turn, used this new material to paint a Utopian picture of Japan as a model country governed in politics and religion by natural reason. Its rational administrative order is surpassed only by its exemplary religious life: "Nowhere else in all the world can be found so perfect an image of the primitive church."[85] He equates Buddha with Jesus Christ and Buddhism with a Christianity obscured. The Japanese, because of their devotion to a latter-day Christianity, lead an orderly social existence in which the scandals and corruptions so common in Western society are notable by their absence.[86]

For Postel the revelation of the East, particularly the recent uncovering of Japan, constitutes vivid proof of God's immediacy, of the continual renewal of the miracle of creation, and of the divine plan laid out for mankind. The discoveries themselves God apparently left to selfish men impelled by "avarice, curiosity, desire for glory, sensuality, and, in sum, human and corporal pleasures."[87] But it was also God himself who vouchsafed to Postel's age the marvel of seeing in Asia the vestiges of a pristine past and a new hope for world concord and order. Clearly God had favored the East in the past when he located there the terrestrial paradise, the magi, marvelous plants and beasts, and rich and enduring empires studded with great cities. But now God's favor has evidently shifted to the West as he permits the missionaries of the "Gallic" Company of Jesus to make an incredible number of conversions throughout the East. As God's chosen instrument the Jesuits will continue their work of evangelizing while the "most Christian" king of France, like the Japanese emperor, takes over a combined political and religious leadership. The monarch-reformer of France will finally act as God's instrument by restoring religious and cultural unity to the world.[88]

Such radical ideas, zealously promoted by their author, were predestined to cause Postel trouble. His earlier difficulties with the Jesuits and his frank interest in Islam, the *cabala*, and Protestantism aroused the ire of churchmen. In 1555 he was tried by the Venetian Inquisition, convicted of heresy, and sent to prison for four years. After wandering from place to place in an effort to rehabilitate his reputation, Postel was confined in 1563 as a lunatic in the Priory of St. Martin near Paris. His confinement was gradually relaxed to protective custody and Postel was again permitted to correspond, to teach, and to visit with friends

---

[83] For the portions excerpted from Xavier see Henri Bernard-Maitre, "L'orientaliste Guillaume Postel et la découverte spirituelle du Japon en 1552," *Monumenta nipponica*, IX (1953), 83–108.

[84] For a summary of Yajirō's narrative based on a later letter by Xavier see *Asia*, I, 660–63.

[85] Postel, *op. cit.* (n. 74), p. 82ᵛ.

[86] *Ibid.*, pp. 38ᵛ–39ʳ.

[87] *Ibid.*, p. 93ᵛ.

[88] *Ibid.*, pp. 39ᵛ, 82ʳ–84ᵛ.

and admirers. Among his disciples were many illustrious scholars and writers, such as Jean Boulaere, Guy and Nicholas Le Fèvre de la Boderie, Blaise de Vigenère, and Claude Duret. Of particular interest is the correspondence he carried on in his later years with Christopher Plantin, the enterprising Antwerp printer, and with Ortelius, the Antwerp geographer. That he retained throughout these years his curiosity about Asia is revealed most strikingly in a letter of 1567 to Ortelius in which he thanks the geographer for sending him a map of Asia and complains that Barros refuses to publish much of the information on Africa and Asia in his possession.[89] Postel died at St. Martin's on September 6, 1581.[90]

While Postel was a perfectly serious advocate of world concord, his *Des merveilles* (1552) inspired a contemporary book which ridiculed religious orthodoxy and satirized the credulity of the reading public. Jean Macer (possibly the pseudonym of Jean Le Bon called Hétropolitain), a native of Santigny in Auxois (Burgundy) and professor of canon law at Paris, published in 1555 (Paris) a Latin history of the Indies[91] in three books which he almost immediately translated into French. *Les trois livres de l'histoire des Indes* (Paris, 1555)[92] deals in ten short chapters with Japan (Bk. I), in twenty-four longer chapters with Asia in general (Bk. II), and in twenty-six chapters with India, Cathay, and the natural wonders of the East (Bk. III). The French translation is dedicated to the sisters Michele and Anne Bebrien. For their edification Macer discusses Japan, a timely and captivating subject for contemporary consumption. He uses Japan as a vehicle for satire because paradoxically it is "still an unknown land, which nonetheless, contains the most admirable things in the world." By examination of this unknown but exemplary society, he will show "in what ways we resemble and differ from the Japanese."[93]

The first book is clearly based on factual detail from Postel's *Des merveilles*,[94] though Macer claims as a source a traveler who had spent thirty years in the Indies and who told him many curious things when they met at Avignon.[95] While the Japanese emperor is the supreme authority in spiritual and temporal affairs, Macer observes, he never conducts war himself but wisely leaves that responsibility to a temporal lord. In this the Japanese are obviously much more intelligent than European Christians, who confound war with religion. "It is a marvelous thing," he cuttingly remarks, "that God has taught them through

[89] See J. H. Hessels (ed.), *Abraham Ortelii . . . epistulae* (Cambridge, 1887), pp. 43–44.

[90] On his later years see Bouwsma, *op. cit.* (n. 68), pp. 19–29.

[91] The original *Indicarum historiarum . . . libri tres* may be found today in the Bibliothèque nationale and the British Museum.

[92] I have used a photostatic copy of the original in the Huntington Library (San Marino, Calif.) that is held by the Newberry Library (Chicago). The original edition was published by Guillaume Guillard.

[93] *Les trois livres* (Paris, 1555), pp. 7ᵛ–8ʳ.

[94] For a few parallel passages see Atkinson, *Répertoire* (n. 72), pp. 173, 267. Like Postel, Macer follows Xavier's spelling of "Vous" (Voo), "Coxio" (Go-sho), "Deniche" (Dainichi) and other Japanese names.

[95] A claim made in the dedication to the Latin original, but omitted from the French translation.

nature alone what we know through grace and nature together."⁹⁶ The authority of the Japanese emperor is so absolute that a subject may be put to death for uttering a displeasing word. The Japanese are happy with this rule because they esteem all crimes to be equal in seriousness; this is a concept which resembles the evangelical belief that he who is unfaithful in small matters will be easily unfaithful in greater things and that he who errs in one thing will be guilty of everything.⁹⁷ The lawyer in Macer also leads him to point out that the Japanese possess legal remedies for resolving questions arising from adultery which cannot obtain in a society holding that no man can put asunder those whom God had joined together.⁹⁸ The Japanese, like the Christians, believe in one God, but on their idols they place three heads on a single body. They do this because they think that the more heads it has, the more it is the man of mercy and virtue.⁹⁹ The Japanese exorcise evil spirits by invoking the name of "Deniche" (Buddha) as we call out the name of Jesus.¹⁰⁰ Like orthodox Catholics, the Japanese are deeply opposed to magicians and miracle workers and to those other practitioners of the black arts specifically condemned by the constitutions of the popes.¹⁰¹ The Japanese have periods of fasting too, but theirs are strictly enforced and not lax like ours.¹⁰² The Japanese emperor as pontiff marries and has heirs. Such a system of hereditary succession in the governing of the church, forbidden in Europe, possesses the virtue of preventing schisms.¹⁰³ Finally in the administration of justice the Japanese are superior in not postponing trials indefinitely, "the evil that is today the most pernicious and shameful that there is in France."¹⁰⁴

Macer's second and third books deal with the rest of Asia. His sources here include a mélange of the ancient, medieval, and sixteenth-century writings on India, Cathay, and the islands of Southeast Asia. His sixteenth-century sources are limited to *Novus orbis*, Maximilian of Transylvania, and the writings of Postel. In treating the religions, customs, flora, and fauna of these Asian regions he is less interested in satirizing the institutions of France than he was in the first book. He treats caustically on occasion the practices of the Asians, but never forgets to attribute their general superiority to the fact, advanced so strongly by Postel, that Asia is the locale of the terrestrial paradise. As a rule, however, he is not so concerned in these pages with drawing explicit parallels or with making invidious comparisons. He does remain a rational commentator who is highly

⁹⁶ Macer, *Les trois livres* (n. 92), pp. 8ᵛ–9ᵛ. For commentary see F. Secret, "Jean Macer, François Xavier et Guillaume Postel, ou un épisode de l'histoire comparée des religions au XVIᵉ siècle," *Revue de l'histoire des religions*, CLXX (1966), 47–60; also see Atkinson, *Les nouveaux horizons* (n. 6), pp. 237–40.
⁹⁷ Macer, *op. cit.* (n. 92), pp. 10ᵛ–11ʳ.
⁹⁸ *Ibid.*, pp. 11ʳ–12ᵛ.
⁹⁹ *Ibid.*, p. 15ᵛ.
¹⁰⁰ *Ibid.*, p. 20ᵛ.
¹⁰¹ *Ibid.*, pp. 21ᵛ–22ʳ.
¹⁰² *Ibid.*, p. 25ʳ.
¹⁰³ *Ibid.*, pp. 26ᵛ–27ᵛ.
¹⁰⁴ *Ibid.*, pp. 28ʳᵛ.

skeptical about and often openly critical toward assertions in his sources which stretch too far the bounds of reason or experience.

Asia upsets the eternal and inviolable natural order of the universe with its monsoons and by having a winter season while Europeans are having summer.[105] Its peoples are likewise perverse in their determination to hold to false religions. The Indians worship devilish idols and resist conversion because the Devil punishes them for disloyalty by sending destructive hurricanes. Were they wise enough, both the Indians and the Protestants would accept the miracle of the Mass, for where the Holy Eucharist reposes the hurricane (Devil) has no power.[106] Gentiles as well as Christians understand that the terrestrial paradise is located in the East Indies. This is a land where the climate is perfect, the fruits numerous and beneficial, and the spices abundant. In Asia the story is commonly told that the "Manucodiata," or bird of paradise, dies when it leaves the salubrious air of its homeland; for this reason its plumage is revered throughout the Orient as a divine relic.[107]

The peoples of the region east of India likewise profit from its perfect climate, for they are healthy, vital, and virtuous. Their achievements in the manual arts testify to their imaginative spirit and to their perfect control over their bodily members. The Three Kings, natives of Tharse (Tarsus), Turkestan, and Cathay, knew from their superior astrology and insight what the Jews themselves never understood, namely, that Christ is king.[108] Even in India, where the Brahmans command utmost respect, the good and intelligent workers of the lower classes enjoy esteem. This is contrary to what obtains in France, where the poor pay such heavy taxes in kind, labor, and money that they revolt from misery.[109] The East is said by sailors to be peopled with sorcerers and magicians who conjure up frightening marine monsters.[110] Macer is unwilling to believe these stories, but he has no trouble crediting the stories of Mandeville and others about the marvelous trees and plants of Asia which are partly animal and fish. He is impressed by the number, size, and wealth of Asia's cities. Like Postel, he remarks on the great number of Christians or Christian-like people found everywhere except in Muslim lands.[111]

For his period Macer is unusual in his sharp and highly critical spirit and tone,

[105] *Ibid.*, pp. 32ᵛ–35ʳ.

[106] *Ibid.*, pp. 29ʳ–31ʳ.

[107] *Ibid.*, pp. 41ᵛ–43ᵛ. From his use of this Malay word for bird of paradise, it may readily be concluded that his ultimate source was Maximilian of Transylvania. See *Asia*, I, 598 n. 545. Postel also located the terrestrial paradise in the Moluccas, and was greatly impressed by the plumage of the bird of paradise, one of which he brought back from Constantinople to Francis I. His disciple, Guy Le Fèvre de la Bodérie, wrote a ballad on the bird of paradise in which he ascribes its coloring to the Holy Spirit! Also see below, p. 281. Atkinson (*Les nouveaux horizons* [n. 6], pp. 239–40) considers this reference an attempt at humor. Perhaps it is a bit of drollery, but not necessarily so. The Europeans of this period were very much impressed by the spirituality of a bird which reputedly had no feet or wings and lived on the dews from heaven. See *Asia*, II, Bk. 1, 181–82, and pl. 8.

[108] Macer, *op. cit.* (n. 92), pp. 47ʳ–50ʳ.

[109] *Ibid.*, pp. 54ʳ–55ᵛ.

[110] *Ibid.*, pp. 67ʳ–69ʳ.

[111] *Ibid.*, pp. 95ᵛ–96ʳ.

a veritable *philosophe* of the sixteenth century. While Macer may be viewed as an author whose spirit was of the eighteenth century, the same might also be said of Postel. Like many later writers, Postel sought to confront the revelation of the East directly and to bring it boldly into his own program for world peace and order. Utterly serious, perhaps even rabid, in what he was proposing, Postel was recognized by both the secular and religious authorities as a purveyor of dangerous thoughts. While Macer was a frondeur, Postel was a revolutionary. Rabelais, an equally free spirit, was likewise captivated by the opening of the overseas world and convinced of its ultimate importance to France. But as a writer of romance, he sees the distant East as an actuality still remote enough to be stocked with marvels and fables. Like Ariosto, he sent his heroes on marvelous voyages to distant places where they could perform feats of magic and daring that were impossible at home. Three French writers, each in his own different way, conceive of the East as a part of their own expanding horizons. They all see it as a challenge to existing institutions, traditional ways, and orthodox views. And all three study the East for the purpose of helping their countrymen perceive their own foibles and delinquencies, a literary response that came earlier in France than elsewhere perhaps because so few Frenchmen were themselves directly involved in Asian enterprises. For those countries with a stake in the opening of Asia, the absorption with commerce and war was of paramount concern; in France noninvolvement permitted more detachment. In this benign atmosphere the commentators were able freely and safely to begin examining the distant challenge by comparing the new knowledge of Asia to the old, and the peoples and practices of Asia to those at home.

2

THE "NEW WORLD" OF THE POETS

Documentation on Asia increased rapidly in the latter half of the century and its effects became increasingly perceptible in poetry and history, and in scientific, didactic, and popular literature. But that these changes were slow in reaching the public is illustrated by the following example. A popular geography by Jacques Signot called *La division du monde* appeared in five editions between 1539 and 1560. Only 12 of its 160 pages deal with Asia and there is no mention of recent discoveries.[112] The names "China," "Japan," and "Goa" do not even appear. The treatment of India is so traditional as to make it seem as if nothing had occurred in the sixteenth century to change Europe's picture of the East. Such omissions are particularly difficult to understand when it is recalled that

[112] J. Signot, *La division du monde, contenant la déclaration des provinces et regions d'Asie, Europe, et Affrique* . . . (Lyons, 1555), pp. 17–29. America is not even mentioned in this volume.

Xavier's letters from India were printed in French as early as 1545,[113] that a letter of King John III of Portugal on the Indies had been published in French translation in 1546,[114] and that Postel's *Des merveilles* had become available in editions of 1552 and 1553. The only conclusion possible from such evidence is simple: Signot's book remained unrevised and an uninstructed public continued to purchase it.

Most of what Frenchmen knew about the East had come to them through translations. While the poets of the Pléiade often deprecated the art of translation and urged their fellows to produce original creations in French, they nonetheless were all translators themselves and relied heavily on translations. The decade of the fifties saw the appearance of many new translations on the discoveries that would be required reading for later generations. Translations were made from Latin of Giovio's *History of His Own Times* and Münster's *Cosmographia*. Books I–X of Oviedo's history of the Indies were translated in 1555 from Castilian by Jean Poleur. In 1556 Marco Polo, Varthema, Ramusio, and a Jesuit letterbook were translated from Italian.[115] An anonymous work appeared in the same year called *L'institution . . . du royaume de la Chine* (Paris), essentially a collection of Jesuit letters in French translation, which includes favorable comments on the good government and religious tolerance of the Chinese.[116]

Especially influential was the translation by Nicolas de Grouchy of the first book of Castanheda's *História do descobrimento e conquista da India pelos Portuguezes*.[117] While at Coimbra from 1548 to 1550, Grouchy had become acquainted with Castanheda and had learned the Portuguese language.[118] On his return to France, Grouchy settled down in a Norman town near Dieppe. Here Castanheda sent a copy of his first book, shortly after its publication in 1551, with a request for translation. Although Grouchy was apparently reluctant to translate Castanheda's work into French, he was prevailed upon by his Norman friends

---

113 *Copie d'une lettre . . . des Indes* (Paris).

114 See Atkinson, *Les nouveaux horizons* (n. 6), p. 439. The king's letter addressed to Pope Paul III was written around 1545. The catalog of the British Museum (3901.2.1) mistakenly lists it under King Manuel (Emmanuel). For discussion see F. Leite de Faria's review of *Asia* (Vol. I) in *Studia* (Lisbon), No. 23 (April, 1968), p. 301.

115 Marco Polo was translated by F. G. L. and published at Paris. Varthema is included in Vol. II of the translation of Ramusio's Volume I in J. Léon, *Historiale description de l'Afrique* (2 vols.; Lyons, 1556). Despite the title the materials on Asia predominate; for a summary of its contents see Le Président Baudrier, *Bibliographie lyonnaise . . . quatrième série* (Lyons, 1899), pp. 385–87. The publisher was Jean Temporal. The letterbook was almost certainly a French version of one of the *Avisi particolari*.

116 The only extant copy of this rare book is in the British Museum (4767.2.4). I have not actually seen it myself, so here I rely on the comments of Atkinson, *Les nouveaux horizons* (n. 6), pp. 143, 174, 241, 441. This is possibly the letter of Father M. N. Barreto (November 23, 1555) discussed in *Asia*, I, 796, or the Coimbra collection in Spanish of 1555 discussed *ibid.*, p. 317.

117 On Castanheda see *Asia*, I, 187–89. The title of Grouchy's translation is *Le premier livre de l'histoire de l'Inde . . . faict par Fernand Lopes de Castanheda . . .* (Paris, 1553). On its importance as a source see P. Villey-Desmeserets, *Les sources d'idées au XVIᵉ siècle* (Paris, 1912).

118 On Grouchy in Portugal see above, pp. 31–32. For his work as the translator of Castanheda see Georges Le Gentil, "Nicolas de Grouchy, traducteur de Castanheda," *Bulletin des études portugaises et de l'Institut français au Portugal*, N.S. IV (1937), 31–46. For the influence of his translation on the French vocabulary see below, pp. 536–37.

and patrons to undertake the task. As enthusiastic maritime explorers, the Normans were naturally eager to learn all they could about the beginnings of the Portuguese enterprise. That was all they could find out from Castanheda's first book since it dealt only with the initial phase (1497–1505) of the discovery of the sea route to India.[119]

The translation from Portuguese was extremely difficult to make because Grouchy possessed no dictionaries or other technical aids. Castanheda's book was also full of nautical terms and strange names for which there were no French equivalents. As the first work translated from Portuguese into French, Grouchy's book is still of great interest to historians of language. To contemporaries his translation was important since it brought into French for the first time a systematic description of the early Portuguese discoveries in the East. Grouchy's translation, first issued at Paris in 1553 by Michel de Vascocan, was reprinted at Antwerp in 1554 and 1576, and was itself translated into Italian in 1556 and into German in 1565. Moreover, since Castanheda was forced to withdraw his first version from circulation and to revise it, the various editions of Grouchy's translation kept in circulation the uncensored account of the Portuguese overseas expansion.[120]

George Buchanan (1506–82), the Scottish Humanist, was like Grouchy a refugee from Coimbra and the Portuguese Inquisition.[121] After a brief visit to Scotland, Buchanan returned in 1552 to Paris and remained there over the next eight years. At first he taught classics in the Collège de Boncourt, where he became acquainted with Ronsard. A former student of Saint Barbe, Buchanan renewed this and other important friendships in the literary circles of Paris. Earlier, when teaching at Guyenne, he wrote four Latin tragedies. While at Coimbra he composed a liminary Latin poem for Diogo de Teive's *Commentarius . . .* (1548).[122] In Paris he wrote poems inspired by his sojourn in Portugal and circulated them in manuscript to his friends. He was on particularly good terms with Joachim du Bellay and other members of the Pléiade, but they respected him more as a student of Greek than as a Latin poet. He was also known to Louis Le Roy, the classicist, who later put into print his high opinion of the Scottish scholar.[123]

Buchanan, perhaps as a result of his stay in Portugal and of his acquaintance

[119] It should be recalled, however, that the only other systematic account of the voyage then available in France was the book of Varthema, first published in 1510, which was written by an Italian interloper rather than an experienced Portuguese. *Les voyages aventurex* of Jean Alfonse was not published until 1559.

[120] For further detail on the translations of Castanheda see *Asia*, I, 189, and Le Vicomte de Grouchy and E. Travers, *Étude sur Nicolas de Grouchy et son fils Timothée de Grouchy* (Paris, 1878), pp. 90–91, 106. Mention should also be made at this point of the short history of the Indies published in 1578 and attributed to Joachim de Centellas. See Atkinson, *Les nouveaux horizons* (n. 6), p. 452.

[121] On his career in Portugal see above, pp. 31–32.

[122] For discussion see I. D. McFarlane, "George Buchanan's Latin Poems from Script to Print," *Library*, 5th ser. XXIV (1969), 283.

[123] See I. D. McFarlane, "George Buchanan and French Humanism," in A. H. T. Levi (ed.), *Humanism in France at the End of the Middle Ages and in the Early Renaissance* (New York, 1970), pp. 299, 302–3. On Louis Le Roy see below, pp. 309–12.

with Teive, continued to take more than a passing interest in geography, navigation, and scientific poetry. While in Paris he began to prepare his long didactic poem, *De sphera*, in which he gives an account of the Iberian voyages.[124] In Book I, he depicts the Portuguese as inspired by the fiend "Avarice" to dream in their poverty-stricken land about sailing abroad to quench an insatiable thirst for riches: "The spoils of Ethiopia are not good enough. . . . India alone ravishes their hearts; only India, rich in resources, seems able to fill the gaping maw and set a limit to the hopes they entertain."[125] While love of gold led them into unknown parts and dangerous adventures, their awesome voyages "showed concretely . . . that the earth, water, and air are spheres." The French poet Ian Edouard du Mouin later translated and imitated in his *L'uranologie* (1583) some of Buchanan's Latin verses, particularly those which comment on the tropical climes and the customs of Asian peoples.[126]

Buchanan, during his stay in Paris, was acquainted with Jean Nicot (1530–1600), a native of Nîmes who first arrived in the capital in 1554. In his *Dialogues* (1556) Guy de Bruès includes Nicot in the company of Ronsard as one of four interlocuters.[127] A Ronsard poem addressed to Nicot appeared in the *Bocage* of 1554. It deals spiritedly with the relative endowments bestowed by nature upon man and the animals. Nicot, who in 1556 became the Maître des Requêtes of the royal court, clearly had close connections with ruling circles. It was probably at court that he learned to know the eminent Humanist Pierre Danès (1497–1577), then the confessor to Prince Francis.[128] In 1559 Nicot was sent to Portugal as royal ambassador to arrange a marriage and to work out certain problems arising from encounters at sea between Portuguese and French ships. He spent two years (September, 1559–October, 1561) at Lisbon, but apparently saw very little of the Portuguese literati. He was certainly in the company of Damião de Góis, who possibly presented him with a specimen of the tobacco plant. He seems, however, to have spent most of his spare time learning the

---

[124] Cf. the story of Élie Vinet (1519–87), also a professor at Coimbra with Grouchy and Buchanan. He returned to Bordeaux in 1549 where he edited and translated many classical and medieval authors. In the introduction which he wrote to his edition (1556) of Sacrobosco's treatise on the sphere, Vinet also describes the Iberian voyages.

[125] Quoted from J. R. Naiden (trans. and ed.), *The "Sphera" of George Buchanan (1506–82), a Literary Opponent of Copernicus and Tyco Brahe* (Seattle, 1952), pp. 98–99. The first two books of the *Sphera* were published at Paris in 1585; the first complete edition was published in Denmark in 1586. Buchanan, who was tutor to James VI of Scotland after his Paris days, helped to collect the king's library. See above, p. 69.

[126] For example

> Ore le mol Indois leur montre ses barrieres
> Les tirant à l'odeur des friandes poiurieres
> Et du Zezembre sec . . .

For this and other examples see the parallel passages given in A. M. Schmidt, *La poésie scientifique en France au XVIe siècle* (Paris, 1938), pp. 337–39. Facsimile edition of 1970.

[127] On Nicot's contacts with Ronsard and his group see P. Laumonier, *Ronsard, poète lyrique* (3d ed.; Paris, 1932), pp. 130, 137, 138.

[128] See Matos, *op. cit.* (n. 24), pp. 134–35. For relevant remarks on his correspondence see E. Falgairolle (ed.), *Jean Nicot, ambassadeur de France en Portugal au XVIe siècle: Sa correspondance diplomatique inédite . . .* (Paris, 1897), pp. cv–cvi.

Portuguese language and gathering materials on the Portuguese empire and on navigation.[129] He also sent many curiosities home to his friends in France, including the text of Pedro Nunes' *Tractado da sphera* and a French translation of King Manuel's letter of 1508 directed to Pope Julius II.[130] When Nicot himself returned to his friends in Paris, he carried in his baggage a number of Portuguese books, including the first two of Barros' *Décadas*.[131]

The France to which Nicot returned in 1561 was on the brink of civil war. Paris itself came under siege from Huguenot forces in 1562, and royalist sympathizers like Ronsard and Nicot were increasingly forced to turn their attention away from poetry and scholarship to the miseries of the day. Still the youthful band of literati had found time before the outbreak of the wars of religion to make the French language illustrious and to create a new school of poetry.

French poets from Parmentier (1520) to Ronsard (1550) were occupied in their consideration of nature with the development of themes, the isolation for description of certain elements of landscape and seascape, and the invention of the requisite vocabulary.[132] In the descriptive poems called *blasons* the predecessors of the Pléiade had spent their poetic energies in attaching to their subjects a list of evocative qualifiers. For example, Giles Corrozet (1510?–68) in a poem of 1539 lists every detail about an exotic cabinet down to its coverings of cloth of gold and its decorations of Oriental pearls, amber, and rubies.[133] Jean du Thiers (d. 1559) in his French translation and adaptation published in 1541 of *La Pazzia, stampata in India* introduced a theme that becomes increasingly important in later poetical works. He compares the happy peoples of the "New World" to the men of the Age of Gold and deplores the ravages which have been visited upon the natives by Europeans.[134] Ronsard himself, who worried constantly about finding the exact word, compared in 1547 a maiden's breath to "all the perfumes of India." He changed "India" to "Arabia" three years later,[135] probably for reasons of euphony rather than of new or contradictory knowledge. In the meantime, Joachim du Bellay in his revolutionary *Defence . . . of the French Language* (1549) remarks, in one of his most eloquent sentences, on "the spices and other oriental riches which India sends to us [that] are better known and better treated by us, and held of higher price, than in the place of those who sow or gather them."[136]

---

[129] Nicot was especially well versed in linguistics, his greatest claim to scholarly renown being his *Thresor de la langue française* (1606). In this work he repeatedly displays his command of Portuguese in the etymologies he gives.

[130] See Matos, *op. cit.* (n. 24), pp. 115–34.

[131] On his library see above, p. 67.

[132] See D. B. Wilson, *Ronsard, Poet of Nature* (Manchester, 1961), p. 17.

[133] See G. Corrozet, *Blasons domestiques* (Paris, 1865).

[134] The Italian work was itself an adaptation of Erasmus' *In Praise of Folly*. For discussion see R. Armstrong, *Ronsard and the Age of Gold* (New York, 1968), pp. 139–40.

[135] Pointed out in Cameron, *op. cit.* (n. 5), p. 4.

[136] G. M. Turquet (trans.), *The Defence and Illustration of the French Language by Joachim du Bellay* (London, 1939), pp. 46–47.

The decade from 1550 to 1560 was an intensely creative epoch in the history of French poetry, both in theory and practice. The poets of the Pléiade experimented freely with language, form, and imagery. In the conduct of their revolution, Ronsard and his circle enjoyed the protection and support of the Valois-Medici court. While Ronsard urged his associates to open their minds and their hearts to the world about them, he was himself cautious about accepting ideas that were too extraordinary. In 1553 Postel published both his *Des merveilles* and *La doctrine du siècle doré*, the latter, on the Age of Gold, dealing with a subject that fascinated Ronsard. In *Les Isles Fortunées*, also published in 1553, Ronsard refers antagonistically to Postel and inveighs against his influence.[137] Jean Macer, a reader of Postel, later charged the Pléiade with immorality and paganism.[138] Possibly because of their hostility to Postel and his ideas, the school of Ronsard apparently paid no attention to the discovery of Japan and the opening of the East.

To shed as much light as possible upon the Pléiade's view of the world, it is perhaps best to look at what has been called the "scientific" or cosmological poetry of the sixteenth century.[139] Efforts to reconcile the pagan with the Christian world and the old philosophy with the new learning produced this speculative genre of poetry. Later it also became impregnated with seeds from Neo-Platonism, occultism, and Calvinist theology. Peletier's *L'Amour des amours* (1555), Ronsard's *Hymnes* (1555–56), and Scève's *Microcosme* (1562) were conscious attempts to provide a coherent vision of the universe by bringing together in long poems all that the Renaissance knew or thought important in the realms of philosophy and science. Scève, in particular, was enchanted by the sound of geographical names and receptive to the discoveries as a manifestation of humanity in movement.[140]

A new sensitivity to the import of the discoveries developed with the publication in 1557 of André Thevet's cosmographical *Singularites de la France Antarctique*.[141] Etienne Jodelle (1532–73), a member of the Pléiade, contributed an ode to the *Singularites* in which he points out that Frenchmen are no less barbarous than Thevet's Brazilians in their falseness to one another, in their disdain of piety, and in their misuse of God-given talents.[142] For his voyage to America and his *Singularites* Thevet was celebrated as a new Jason and received the plaudits of Du Bellay, Ronsard, and Antoine de Baif.[143] Nor was the "New

[137] See Armstrong, *op. cit.* (n. 134), pp. 152–53.

[138] See M. Raymond, *L'influence de Ronsard sur la poésie française (1550–85)* (Geneva, 1965), I, 350–51.

[139] For general definitions see H. Weber, *La création poétique au XVIe siècle en France, de Maurice Scève à Agrippa d'Aubigne* (Paris, 1956), chap. vii; O. de Mourgues, *Metaphysical, Baroque and Précieux Poetry* (Oxford, 1953), pp. 31–41.

[140] See V. L. Saulnier, *Maurice Scève (ca. 1500–1560)* (2 vols.; Paris, 1948–49), I, 459–63; and Schmidt, *op. cit.* (n. 126), p. 170.

[141] For more detail on Thevet and his work as a cosmographer see below, pp. 302–5.

[142] Also see Armstrong, *op. cit.* (n. 134), pp. 138–39.

[143] See J. C. Lapp, "The New World in French Poetry of the Sixteenth Century," *Studies in Philology*, XLV (1948), 154.

World" limited to America in the view of these men. Like Sebastian Münster, Pontus de Tyard (1521–1605), another of Ronsard's "Brigade," is quite explicit in defining the "New World" as those lands which the Ancients had not known and which their geographers had declared nonexistent. In his prose discourse called *L'Univers* (1557) Tyard includes "New Asia," or the islands of Southeast Asia visited by Magellan, as a division of the "New World."[144] Such a designation was warranted because the natives of Southeast Asia, like those of America, were primitives in the eyes of Europeans.[145] But China and India continued to be ancient, civilized, and wealthy lands whose products Peletier and others rated exotic and expensive merchandise.[146]

The outbreak of the wars of religion in 1562 brought a sudden drop in poetic production and a swift change in content. Preoccupied by religious problems, some poets turned for solace and certainty to the occult and to secular science. As a result the poetry of this era became less lyrical and more descriptive— sometimes even intentionally obscure. Baïf turned to the description of planetary and atmospheric phenomena in his *Le premier des meteores* (1567) and Remy Belleau (1528–77) to lapidary science in *Les nouveaux eschanges des pierres precieuses* (1576). The literary traditions stemming from Ronsard and Postel finally merged in the erudite and esoteric poetry of Guy Le Fèvre de la Boderie (1510–98), Scève, Peletier, and Tyard.[147] La Boderie's *L'Encyclie* (1571) elaborates a general psychological theory which revolves around the profound difference between animal instinct and human reason as he seeks to reveal the diverse aspects of the soul. But his work also contains a few lyrical and exotic elements, such as the following excerpt from his description of a beautiful seascape:

> Puis voyez comme elle est de vaisseaus decorée
> Chargés d'Or, de Joyaus, et parfums precieus;
> Comme la Terre on void reluire en villes belles,
> La Mer on void aussi reluire en caravelles.[148]

As a close student of Pico della Mirandola and Postel, La Boderie infused his later works with Neo-Platonic abstractions in his effort to find a new Christian-French cosmology. His hymn (1578) to the bird of paradise and his adulation of the wise Brahmans in *La Galliade* (1578) both show traces of his debt to Postel

---

[144] *L'Universe, ou discours des parties et de la nature du monde* (Lyons, 1557), pp. 102–3. On Münster, see below, pp. 339–41.

[145] On the treatment of the Pacific region in Spanish literature, and particularly in Oviedo, see above, pp. 168–70.

[146] *Ca.* 1563 he wrote:

> "j'e vu le siège ou le marchand étale
> Sa soie fine e perle orientale."

As quoted in C. Jugé, *Jacques Peletier du Mans (1517–82): Essai sur sa vie, son oeuvre, son influence* (Paris, 1907), p. 75.

[147] See F. Secret, *L'ésotérisme de Guy Le Fèvre de la Boderie* (Geneva, 1969), p. 11, and Schmidt, *op. cit.* (n. 126), pp. 237–38.

[148] As quoted in Wilson, *op. cit.* (n. 132), p. 86.

and to the latter's ideas about universal concord. The Postel tradition was also continued in the writings and linguistic studies of Blaise de Vigenère and Claude Duret.[149]

The decade from 1568 to 1578 is studded with new translations and compilations pertaining to the discoveries. Gomara's Spanish history of the New World appeared in a French version in 1568. Two years later François de Belleforest, a friend and associate of Nicot, began to publish his universal history, and in 1575 he issued a new and amplified translation of Münster's *Cosmographia*. In 1571 Jesuit letterbooks once again began to appear in French translation; in that same year Edmond Auger, the Jesuit, brought out at Lyons a French version of Maffei's *Rerum a Societate Jesu in Oriente gestarum commentarius* (Dillingen, 1571).[150] In 1575 Thevet published his *Cosmographie universelle*, an enormous compendium of materials, derivative and original, on all parts of the world. As a work of vulgarization, it was an immediate success with both the public and the literati.[151]

The trend in descriptive poetry toward an elaborate cosmography finally reached its apex in the *Première Sepmaine* (1578) and in the *Seconde Sepmaine* (1584) of Guillaume de Salluste, Sieur du Bartas (1544–90).[152] A Gascon gentleman in the diplomatic service of Henry of Navarre, Du Bartas was also the most important Protestant poet of the century. His long narrative poem in Alexandrine couplets uses the first two weeks of the world's Creation as a frame for a poetic encyclopedia of scientific knowledge as well as an early history of mankind. It is his religious as well as his poetic objective to show the richness and variety of the divine Creation. In his poem the world itself becomes a cabinet of curiosities assembled by the Creator to stimulate man to wonder and speculation. He prays: "Graunt (gracious God) that I record in verse, The rarest beauties of this Universe."[153]

Du Bartas follows the admonition of Ronsard and Du Bellay to be learned in all branches of knowledge.[154] His *Première Sepmaine*, though it is but one in a long line of poems giving an allegorical twist to the story of Creation, is possibly an attempt to give France the epic that Du Bellay had called for. In his taste for the unusual and bizarre Du Bartas differs from the poets of the Pléiade, especially when he follows overzealously Ronsard's teaching encouraging the creation of new words. He differs also from the Catholic poets in his concentration upon the omnipotent God of the Old Testament and in his Protestant abandonment of the intermediaries between God and man. The God of Du Bartas produces wonders in all parts of the world and at all times in history. In the third day of the

---

[149] See below, pp. 521–23.
[150] For details on Maffei's book see *Asia*, I, 324.
[151] See below, pp. 304–5.
[152] For his biography see Urban T. Holmes *et al.* (eds.), *The Works of Guillaume de Salluste, Sieur du Bartas* (3 vols.; Chapel Hill, N.C., 1935), I, 3–27.
[153] From the 1605 translation (p. 2) by Joshua Sylvester in the facsimile reproduction introduced by Francis C. Haber, *Bartas His Devine Weekes and Works* (Gainesville, Fla., 1965).
[154] See Raymond, *op. cit.* (n. 138), II, 281–83.

first week he catalogs the wonders of nature, including this reference to the spices of the East:

> Heere, the fine Pepper, as in clusters hung
> There cinamon and other Spices sprung
> Heere dangled Nutmeggs, that for thriftie paines,
> Yearly repay the Bandans wondrous gaines.[155]

On the basis of the spellings in the original French version, it is clear that he obtained his material on spices from the French translation of Gomara and his reference to "the Bandans" from Thevet.[156]

The fifth day of Du Bartas reads like a poetic treatise on animals, especially the bizarre and mythological fish and birds of distant climes. Of the mysterious bird of paradise he writes:

> But note now, towards the rich *Moluques,*
> Those passing strange and wondrous *Mamaques,*[157]
> (Wond'rous indeed, if Sea or Earth, or Skie,
> Saw ever wonder, swim, or goe, or flie)
> Non knows their nest, non knows the dam that breeds them,
> Food-lesse they live, for th' Aire alonely feeds them
> Wing-lesse they flie, and yet their flight extends,
> Till with their flight, their unknowne lyves-date ends.[158]

The sixth day is filled with descriptions of the larger animals and of their relations to humanity. His picture of the elephant comes from both ancient and modern sources and is particularly reminiscent of the elephant of the cosmographies. On the seventh day, when God rested to survey his works, Du Bartas counsels his readers to learn of things living and dead while seated at home in quiet contemplation. Too often, however, this advice is not followed:

> But (Reader) wee resemble one that winds
> From *Saba, Bandan,* and the wealthie *Indes,*
> (Through threatening Seas, and dangers manifold)
> To seeke fare-off for Incense, Spice, and Gold.[159]

---

[155] Sylvester (trans.), *Bartas His Devine Weekes* (n. 153), p. 93.

[156] See K. Reichenberger, *Die Schöpfungswoche des Du Bartas. Themen und Quellen der Sepmaine* (2 vols.; Tübingen, 1963), I, 120.

[157] On the history of this word for the bird of paradise see C. P. G. Scott, "The Malayan Words in English," *Journal of the American Oriental Society,* XVIII, Pt. I (1897), 74–80. Du Bartas may have derived this spelling from Gomara. See Reichenberger, *op. cit.* (n. 156), p. 217. Also see pl. 8.

[158] Sylvester (trans.), *Bartas, His Devine Weekes* (n. 153), p. 180.

[159] *Ibid.,* p. 254. Reichenberger (*op. cit.* [n. 156], p. 274) suggests that the poet is here also trying to show how the names *Saba, Bandan,* and the *Indes* evoke images of or correspond to their treasures: incense to Arabia, spices to the Moluccas, and gold to Spanish America. On the Neo-Platonic idea of the relation of names to their objects see below, pp. 502–3.

In his own contemplation of the world, however, Du Bartas does wander far from home; an analysis of the *Première Sepmaine* reveals that he was probably familiar with the writings on the "New World" of Marco Polo, Vespucci, Gomara, and Thevet.[160]

A new figure appears at this point in the Du Bartas' story in the person of Simon Goulart (1543–1628). A native of Senlis, Goulart studied law in Paris and there became a convert to Calvinism. Early in 1566 he emigrated to Geneva where he became a pastor. He began a long pastorate at Saint-Gervais in 1571 as well as a prolific career in publishing. Of the seventy-five titles which bear his name, most are works of vulgarization. High on this list both in number and influence are his translations and compilations of contemporary materials. Worried by family problems between 1574 and 1576, Goulart distracted himself by studying and translating Osório's Latin history of Portugal first published at Lisbon in 1571. At the urging of his friends in Geneva, he finally agreed to publish this translation and to add to it materials on the Portuguese empire from Grouchy's translation of Castanheda and other writings.[161]

Goulart's *Histoire de Portugal* . . . (Geneva, 1581) is a combination of translations: the first twelve books, his version of Osório; the final eight, his adaptation of Castanheda and other historians. Goulart's history begins in 1496 and ends in 1578 and is, like its sources, mainly concerned with the Portuguese empire in the East.[162] In the year of its publication Goulart also prepared an alphabetical index for Du Bartas' *Première Sepmaine*. This was in fact a learned commentary whose object was to render the poem "more agreeable to persons less exercised in the knowledge of things." Goulart's commentary was first published in the Chouët edition of the *Première Sepmaine* published at Geneva in 1581. The Paris editors of Du Bartas subsequently broke up the commentary and scattered it through the text at appropriate places, a technique which Goulart himself adopted in some later commentaries.[163]

In the meantime Du Bartas was preparing the *Seconde Sepmaine*, his effort to depict mankind in its infancy. The first eight episodes were published in their entirety in 1584, including the one entitled *Colonies* which deals with the "New World."[164] Here he follows the biblical division of the world in which the East is awarded to Shem, son of Noah. It extends from the Perosite

[160] See Holmes *et al.* (eds.), *op. cit.* (n. 152), I, 121, as well as those sources identified here. For references to the East in other poems by Du Bartas see Lapp, "The New World" (n. 143), p. 159. Also see H. Perrochon, "Simon Goulart, commentateur de la première semaine de Du Bartas," *Revue d'histoire littéraire de la France*, XXXII (1925), 397–401, and Mary Paschal, "The New World in *Les Sepmaines* of Du Bartas," *Romance Notes*, XI (1969–70), 619–22.

[161] See L. C. Jones, *Simon Goulart, 1543–1628, étude biographique et bibliographique* (Geneva, 1917), especially pp. 2–29, 572–74.

[162] For its full title see the bibliography. It was reprinted at Paris in 1587 and translated into English in 1607. A revised and augmented edition which carries the history down to 1610 was published at Geneva in that year by Samuel Crespin. On Osório's and Castanheda's histories see above, pp. 139–41.

[163] See Holmes *et al.* (eds.), *op. cit.* (n. 152), I, 25.

[164] For its publication history and for details on the uncompleted episodes see *ibid.*, pp. 83–93.

promontory in the north to the fabled Anian Strait in the south. On the way one goes

> To *Malaca: Moluques Iles*, that beare
> Cloves and Canele [cinnamon]: well tempered *Sumater*
> Sub-quinoctial: and the golden streames
> Of *Bisnagar*, and *Zeilan* bearing gemmes.[165]

He sees man as originating in Asia and as migrating to Europe and America. The sons of Shem likewise peopled "China, Cambalu Cathay" as well as other eastern regions.[166]

> Their offspring then, with fruitfull stems doth stoare
> *Bisnagar, Nayarde* [probably a misspelling of Narsinga], and either shoare
> Of famous *Ganges; Ava, Toloman,*
> The Kingdome Mein, the Muske [Muscovy], Charazan.[167]

Like other poets of his age, Du Bartas enumerates place names as if bewitched by their music. Nor was he unaware of the maritime lanes of the East, or of the fifteenth-century Chinese voyages to India:

> Who maketh doubt but yerst [formerly] the *Quinzay* Fraights
> As well might venture through the *Anian Straights*
> And find as easie and as short a way
> From the East Indies to the *Tolguage Bay*
> As usually the Asian ships are wont
> To passe to Greece a-crosse the *Hellespont*.[168]

Nature is wonderful in the variety that it provides. Men themselves differ markedly from place to place in physical features, manners, and humours.[169] Each clime is likewise blessed with its own products.

> In briefe, each Country (as pleas'd God distribute)
> To the Worlds Treasure payes a sundry Tribute.[170]

Du Bartas died in 1590 before finishing the *Seconde Sepmaine*. Others quickly published the unpolished poems he had left.[171] In 1601 Goulart published a final edition which included his own annotations to the first eight poems of the *Seconde Sepmaine*. These commentaries, and those of others like Claude Duret, were far more erudite and recondite than the poems themselves. Goulart's

---

[165] Sylvester (trans.), *Bartas Devine Weekes* (n. 153), p. 439.

[166] *Ibid.*, p. 445.

[167] *Ibid.*, p. 448. From these names, and others in this passage not here cited, it is clear that he is referring to places, important and unimportant, in India and Southeast Asia mentioned by Osório and Castanheda in Goulart's rendition. Other Asian names, particularly of unexplored regions, he derives from maps and atlases which usually retained the Ptolemaic designations when no others were available. In his commentaries Goulart places "Toloman" north of Siam and "Mien" in the valley of the Ganges. "Charazon" is a region of northern Asia noted for its elephants.

[168] *Ibid.*, p. 452.

[169] *Ibid.*, p. 456.

[170] *Ibid.*, p. 460.

[171] Holmes *et al.* (eds.), *op. cit.* (n. 152), I, 26.

notes to the exotic references in the *Sepmaines* constitute a thesaurus of ancient and Renaissance learning. His gloss on the peopling of Asia by Shem and his descendants (twenty-two lines in the poem on *Colonies*) runs to more than four pages of tightly printed text. He identifies the various places named, gives the sources that the poet possibly used, indicates what the state of learning is on the place and its region, and for good measure often comments on its products, flora, and fauna. For example:

Bisuagar [Vijayanagar], is a Kingdome also, between that of Decan and Narsingue [so shown on many sixteenth-century maps], between the Mountains of Calicut, and the Sea, which we call the great Gulf of Bengala. It is rich in gold, which is found there in the Rivers. See the situation thereof in the Card of the East Indies, and in *Asia*, in the great Theater of Ortelius, and in *Asia* of D. Cellarius.[172]

Goulart's citations indicate how comprehensive and thorough his researches were on Asia. In addition to many ancient authors, he cites Boaistuau, Blaise de Vigènere, Buchanan, De las Casas, Clusius, Gomara, Gesner, Monardes, Osório, Ortelius, Oviedo, Orta, Paulus Jovius, Peter Martyr, Pigafetta, Postel, Ptolemy, Porcacchi, Thevet, Vasaeus, and his own book on Portugal.[173] The most striking omissions from this list are Polo, Mandeville, Barros, Ramusio, and Mendoza.

That materials on the discoveries and Asia were of interest to other French poets at the end of the sixteenth century can be shown by a few scattered references. The India of the Ancients with its wise and virtuous Brahmans was kept alive in the poems written for court entertainments. In the laudatory poems prepared for ballets, India is included in the program as the place where Bacchus danced.[174] To Latin and French poets, especially among the Protestants, the "New World" is a place of refuge from the turbulence of life in France.[175] Of utmost interest is the dramatic poem called *Les Portugaiz infortunés* (1608) by Nicolas Chrétien des Croix (*fl.* 1608–13) which was published at Rouen.[176] This play is based on the story of the shipwreck suffered by Manuel de Sousa de Sepúlveda and Leonor de Sà on their return from India, one of the earliest and most influential of the Portuguese maritime tragedies. Originally published at Lisbon as a pamphlet around 1555, this story inspired the long narrative poem of Jerónimo Côrte Real called *Naufragio de Sepúlveda* (1594).[177] It was probably

---

[172] From the English translation called *A Learned Summary upon the Famous Poems of William of Saluste Lord of Du Bartas . . . trans. out of French by T. L. D. M. P.* (London, 1621), p. 206.

[173] He lists a total of more than three hundred authorities in his commentaries. See Holmes *et al.* (eds.), *op. cit.* (n. 152), I, 122–25.

[174] See F. A. Yates, *The French Academies of the Sixteenth Century* (London, 1947), pp. 269–70.

[175] "Providisse novum populis fugientibus orbem," wrote Estienne de la Boëtie (1530–63), the friend of Montaigne. See L. Feugère (ed.), *Oeuvres complètes d'Estienne de la Boëtie* (Paris, 1846), p. 359. Also see for French examples, Lapp, "The New World" (n. 143), p. 156.

[176] Cf. the drama in verse by Jacques du Hamel called *Acoubar ou la loyauté trahie* (Rouen, 1603). Its story is based on Anthoine du Perier, *Les amours de Pistion* (Paris, 1602), a prose romance set in Canada. Some of the names in both the romance and the play (i.e., Acoubar suggests Akbar) may be of Asian provenance. For the play see M. A. Adams (ed.), *The Earliest French Play about America . . .* (New York, 1931).

[177] See above, pp. 131–32.

from the account included in Maffei or in another summary of it that Chrétien received the inspiration to put Sepúlveda's dramatic story on the French stage.[178]

The French poets of the sixteenth century were generally most interested in mythology, Greek and Roman heroes, and strictly national events. But the scientific and cosmological poets exhibited a growing interest in the discoveries. Most of their information and ideas came through translations of foreign or traditional writings and from the cosmographies, particularly those of Thevet. A few looked to the products of the East as inspiration for their lines. The poets were particularly interested in the "New World" and, like some of their sources, they included in its definition the insular region of Southeast Asia. They almost completely ignored the new information being circulated in France on the opening of China and Japan. Their references to China, like many of their allusions to India, derived from the materials of Antiquity and the Middle Ages. Thiers, Ronsard, and many others denounced the European explorers for their greed and their mistreatment of the natives;[179] others applauded Thevet as an exemplary traveler-scholar. The poets often related the happy primitives of the "New World" to the unspoiled innocents of the fabled Age of Gold.[180]

Ronsard would certainly have achieved his reputation as the greatest French poet of the century even if the discoveries had never occurred. But the works of Du Bartas and Goulart owe a substantial debt to the opening of the "New World." For most of the poets India remained a symbol of mystery and magic, and nothing in the newer sources disabused them of this traditional belief. The Moluccas as the terrestrial paradise, symbolized by the bird who lives on its salubrious air, fascinated the esoteric poets. The metaphysical poets, particularly Scève and Du Bartas, saw in the discoveries an example of God's continuing revelation of his works. Like other European poets, the French were bewitched with the magical sound of new geographical names. Though Du Bartas did not produce the French epic, his *Sepmaines* brought the overseas world directly into the mainstream of French poetry and Goulart's commentaries provided for future generations a vast repository of exotic materials that they would draw upon freely.[181]

[178] For a summary of the play see Lapp, "The New World" (n. 143), pp. 161–64. Lapp was evidently not aware of the importance of this story in Portuguese literature. See above, p. 134. Chrétien's play was first published at Rouen in 1608. A microfilm copy of *Les portugaiz infortunez* is in the library of the University of Minnesota. The story of Sepúlveda was related in Maffei's work (Bk. II) and passed from it into other works. See, for example, the summary in P. Camerarius, *The Living Librarie, or, Meditations and Observations Historical* . . . (London, 1621), pp. 38–39. The Latin original of this work was published in 1602 and could have been used by Chrétien as his source. For further discussion of his possible sources see F. Parfaict, *Histoire du théâtre françois, depuis son origine jusqu'à présent* (15 vols.; Paris, 1735–49), IV, 116–17. The reference in this discussion to "Massée" is probably a misspelling of "Maffei."

[179] That French poets saw in the mariners nothing but avaricious merchants is commonly asserted by literary historians. A recent example of this unqualified and undocumented assertion may be found in J. Dawkins, "The Sea in Sixteenth-Century French Poetry," *Nottingham French Studies*, IX(1970), 10.

[180] See R. Gonnard, *La légende du bon sauvage* (Paris, 1946), pp. 52–53.

[181] On the role of the epic-like poem as a source for exoticism see R. C. Williams, *The Merveilleux in the Epic* (Paris, 1925), pp. 138–39.

3

CULTURAL RELATIVISM IN POPULAR AND DIDACTIC PROSE

The translation movement of the sixteenth century contributed substantially to the development of popular literature and especially to the production of "prodigy" books, or collections of monstrous tales. From time to time, especially in the period of civil war from 1562 to 1594, these entertaining books were published in large numbers. Generally they were digests or adaptations of stories extracted from learned and literary sources. They continue and amplify the tradition of Boccaccio and Boemus whose collections in translation had been a source of themes in the first half of the century. To an age constantly disrupted by war and misery, grotesque and marvelous tales, whether fabulous or true of distant times or foreign places, provided a means of escape for the ordinary reader from the horrible realities of everyday life in France.[182]

One of the first contemporary miscellanies translated was the *Silva de varia lección* (1540) of the Spaniard Pedro Mexía.[183] In 1552 it was issued at Paris as *Les diverses leçons* of Claude Gruget. Over the remaining years of the century this book was repeatedly reissued, often in enlarged and improved editions.[184] Though Mexía himself had paid little or no attention to "lessons" from the overseas world, his French continuators gradually added stories to their publications extracted from later travel books and cosmographies. The best enlarged edition, *Les diverses leçons* (Lyons, 1604) of Loys Guyon, includes a variety of new references to the products and marvels of the East.[185]

Pierre Boaistuau (1520–66), who published the *Heptameron* of Margaret of Navarre,[186] was also a collector of "prodigies." In 1560 his *Histoires prodigieuses* appeared in forty-one chapters illustrated by forty-nine woodcuts.[187] It includes mainly stories about specters, phantoms, ghosts, demons, devils, and werewolves—horror stories which Boaistuau frequently makes illustrate a moral. He claims to have used no fabulous tales but only those which could be verified in Greek and Latin writings, both sacred and profane. Many of his sources are cited in the margin or in the text, and while most of his authorities are biblical or ancient, he is also clearly indebted to medieval and contemporary writers on the East. In his earlier *Le théatre du monde* (Paris, 1558), when talking about monstrous births, he refers to "those who have written histories of the Indies."[188] He tells stories in the *Histoires* of ghosts and magic which might have

---

[182] See Schenda, *op. cit.* (n. 15), pp. 137–39.
[183] See above, p. 173.
[184] To date there have been at least twenty editions of this work. See Schenda, *op. cit.* (n. 15), pp. 14–15.
[185] For example, see chap. iii for his remarks on Chinese porcelains.
[186] He published her stories as *Histoires des amans fortunez* (Paris, 1558).
[187] I have used the Paris edition of 1561, a reprint of the first edition. See pls. 7, 8.
[188] Fol. 24ᵛ.

been extracted from Hayton of Armenia or Marco Polo. His chapter on Satan is illustrated with a woodcut of the "devil of Calicut" taken from Münster's *Cosmographie*.[189] From the same author's history of birds he derives his entire chapter (xxxiv) on the bird of paradise. Clearly to Boaistuau the East was mainly the habitat of strange beasts, sinister spirits, and horrible demons. Some of the continuators of his *Histoires* added newer stories of strange phenomena to his collection which they extracted from later travel books. In most of the revised versions his moralizing remarks are amplified and sometimes modified by the continuators.[190]

The moral tales of Matteo Bandello (*ca.* 1485–1561), some of which were based on Indian originals, began to appear in Italian at Lucca in 1554.[191] Five years later six of these stories were translated into French by Boaistuau. The work of translation was continued by François de Belleforest, the cosmographer and historian;[192] by 1568 eighteen of Bandello's stories were printed in French. Belleforest, in particular, added remarks and digressions of his own to Bandello's stories on the history and customs of distant peoples in the Portuguese empire. Four years later (1572) a French version of G. B. Gelli's *Circe* (1549) was published and dedicated to Catharine de' Medici. In this philosophical dialogue the elephant of India is touted as having been a philosopher in his former life. Translation of this popular Italian discourse was followed (1577–81) by the translation of the Italian series (Bks. 15–21) of the *Amadis* cycle, stories in which personages from the East began to figure.[193]

In 1582 Gabriel Chappuys, translator of the Italian *Amadis*, brought out his *Hexameron*, an adaptation of the *Jardím de floras curiosas* (1570) of the Spaniard Antonio de Torquemada. What distinguishes Torquemada's work from previous compilations of prodigies is the number of examples he derives from the Portuguese historians Castanheda and Barros and their recitals of Eastern wonders.[194] This tendency to cite more frequently the travelers to the East is continued by Belleforest in his *Histoires prodigieuses* (Antwerp, 1594).[195] Four years later Jean Pillehotte, a Lyons publisher, issued in a single, thick volume a compilation of the prodigy stories from Boaistuau, Belleforest, and their imitators.[196] In 1600 Simon Goulart, the polygraph of Geneva, began to publish his two-volume collection of *Histoires admirables* at Paris which includes, according to his own claim, all the noteworthy stories of the previous century and a half. Naturally

[189] Schenda, *op. cit.* (n. 15), p. 44.

[190] For the many French editions and the ten translations of this collection see Schenda, *op. cit.* (n. 15), p. 34.

[191] See discussion of Boccaccio and Bandello above, pp. 112–13, 211.

[192] Cf. below, p. 306.

[193] On the continuations of Mambrino Roseo see above, p. 210. For a discussion of the French translator see Pierre Geneste, "Gabriel Chappuys, traducteur de Jerónimo de Urrea," in *Mélanges offerts à Marcel Bataillon* ... (Bordeaux, 1962), pp. 448–49.

[194] See above, p. 187.

[195] See especially pp. 229, 246.

[196] Entitled *Histoires prodigieuses* ... (Lyons, 1598), its six books include the collections of Boaistuau, Tisserant, Belleforest, Hoyer, Sorbin, and a miscellany of anonymous stories.

Goulart, like Torquemada and Belleforest, included stories about the Portuguese adventures on the sea and in the East derived from his perusal of the Portuguese historians.[197]

All these collections were extremely popular in their day and were used freely by others as sources. Writers on cities and costumes, like Antoine du Pinet and François Deserpz, turned to these histories of curiosities for information about their subjects.[198] Even Montaigne was an avid reader of this form of literature and his *Essais* are dotted with references to the stories in print before his death.[199] But most interesting in the use he makes of prodigy literature is Guillaume Bouchet (1513–93), book merchant of Poitiers and friend of the poets Jacques Tahureau and Jean de la Péruse.[200]

The only literary work of Bouchet that remains is his amusing and satirical collection of short stories called *Les serées* (*Evenings*).[201] In 1584 the first book of *Les serées* was published; the entire work in three books, and with substantial additions to the first book, did not appear in print until 1608. The second and third books had, however, appeared separately in 1597 and 1598. Presented in an unaffected and familiar style, Bouchet's characters are members of a closed group which meets in the evenings to tell stories. Everybody, including the host and the ladies, sits comfortably about a round table to discuss a particular theme. The stories, numbering about eight hundred, are told with brevity and wit. While popular at the time for entertainment, they are read today for the light they throw on sixteenth-century thought, manners, and morals.

Les serées is also valuable as a reflection of the state of knowledge on the overseas world. Bouchet was clearly a voracious reader of prodigies, romances, cosmographies, and history. In a discourse "on water" he cites Jean Bodin to the effect that the peoples of Africa and Asia never drink wine for their waters are so good that the Ganges is held to be sacred.[202] In the Indies, he claims, a law ordains that widows who remarry before the expiration of a year after the husband's death suffer the loss of their inheritance.[203] In his discourse "on fish" he refers to a story told by Marco Polo to the effect that the Brahmans of India bewitch the great and dangerous fish to prevent them from harming the divers after pearls.[204] In discussing "cuckolds" he tries to account for the idea that they wear "horns" by reference to Thevet's story about the importance of rhinoceros

---

[197] See above, pp. 138–48.

[198] See A. du Pinet, *Plans ... villes ... Europe, Asie, Afrique* (Lyons, 1564), and F. Deserpz, *Recueil de la diversité des habits qui sont de present en usage, tant es pays d'Europe, Asia, Affrique et Isles sauvages* (Paris, 1567).

[199] See Schenda, *op. cit.* (n. 15), pp. 102–7.

[200] For his biography see Sally Rabinowitz, *Guillaume Bouchet: Ein Beitrag zur Geschichte der französischen Novelle* (diss., University of Leipzig, Weida, 1910), pp. 9–15.

[201] The standard version is C. E. Roybet (ed.), *Les Serées de Guillaume Bouchet, sieur de Brocourt* (6 vols.; Paris, 1873–82).

[202] *Ibid.*, I, 63–64, 66.

[203] *Ibid.*, p. 220.

[204] *Ibid.*, II, 27–28. For Polo's account of pearl diving in south India see Yule and Cordier, *op. cit.* (n. 46), II, 331–32.

horn as a sexual stimulant in the East.[205] He relates a story first told in writing by Castanheda of a meeting in 1536 between the viceroy of India and a man who claimed to be 340 years old.[206] He repeats in his discourse "on soldiers" the opinion commonly held in Europe that the warriors of the East are weak, timid, and cowardly, overly devoted to carnal pleasures, and in war too inclined to depend on overwhelming numbers rather than individual acts of courage.[207] The discussants debate whether painters and sculptors should represent distant peoples as they would Europeans. One of them holds tenaciously to the idea that they should be painted the color they really are and with the features they really possess; he even points out that the Africans themselves paint as black as possible those whom they think of as being beautiful.[208] "We call Moors," he continues, "all men who are black like Ethiopians, and the Indians of the torrid zone, and of other newly found lands."[209] Bouchet obviously sees the East in medieval terms as a source of riches as well as the home of monstrous peoples who follow extraordinary laws and customs.[210] But he is also beginning to perceive that they belong to mankind and that their practices, while perhaps strange and amusing, may be seriously compared to European customs. Their ideas, in short, require understanding as well as ridicule.

French sentimental novelists, as well as writers of the short story, also began in the last years of the sixteenth century to exhibit an awareness of the overseas world as part of the human community. The French, except for Rabelais, were traditionally less concerned than the Spanish and Italians with themes of adventure.[211] They were more preoccupied with the expression and analysis of individual feelings, especially love. Perhaps it was because of the numerous translations of Italian and Spanish romances that the French were slow in working in this genre. Certainly the wars of religion had the effect of turning French thought to controversial, didactic, and escapist literature, instead of sentimental novels. While literary production continued during the years of civil war, no new work appeared between 1562 and 1593 to which the name "novel" could be assigned.[212]

It was in the relatively peaceful reign (1593–1610) of Henry IV that the novel became a major literary form[213]—almost one hundred new ones were produced. *Le desespere contentement d'amour* (Paris, 1599), an anonymous historical and sentimental novel, tells the story of two Calvinist brothers, the younger of whom flees France for the Levant. He suffers shipwreck and is rescued by a Spanish vessel bringing missionaries back from Asia. They succeed in converting him and he

---

205 Roybet (ed.), *op. cit.* (n. 201), II, 84–85.

206 *Ibid.*, III, 262.

207 *Ibid.*, IV, 140–41.

208 *Ibid.*, pp. 215–16.

209 *Ibid.*, p. 256.

210 For his discussion of precious stones and their symbolism see the discourse "On Churchmen," *ibid.*, V, 18–19, 24.

211 See G. Reynier, *Le roman sentimental avant l'Astrée* (Paris, 1908), p. vii.

212 *Ibid.*, p. 155.

213 *Ibid.*, p. 176.

returns to France a Catholic, a story which again illustrates the connection that contemporaries saw between the overseas missions and the struggle against Protestantism.[214] Nor is the exotic East completely absent from these novels. *Les pudiques amours de Calistine avec ses disgraces et celles d'Angelie* (Paris, 1605), composed by "a young damsel," includes as characters two small princesses, daughters of the kings of Cochin and Cannanore, who live at the court of Lisbon.[215] An anonymous play, *L'Ile des hermaphrodites* (Paris, *ca.* 1600), includes a bit of chinoiserie in a tantalizing reference to cabinets decorated "in the style of China on which there are represented all kinds of birds and animals."[216]

François Béroalde de Verville (1556–1629), a writer with universal interests, was particularly fascinated by the East, its stories, and its products.[217] Béroalde's works—thirty-three titles in poetry and prose—show that he dabbled in alchemy, astrology, linguistics, theology, philosophy, politics, and in the collection, imitation, and translation of tales. In 1594 he published in four parts a collection of love stories, *Les aventures de Floride* (Tours), in which he weaves contemporary names and events into a *Decameron*-like collection of tales. He followed this in 1597 with *Le cabinet de Minerve* (Rouen) which was intended to be the fifth part of the *Floride*. It is, however, quite an independent work, for he sets the scene in a palace where the nymphs of Minerva explain chemical and mechanical procedures or describe the products of the arts and crafts. In 1600 he published a book of verse advocating the revival of the French silk industry, a project dear to the hearts of Barthélemy Laffemas and Olivier de Serres.[218] Essentially this is a call for France to stop paying tribute for silk to the Orient and Italy and to develop its languishing independent industry.

Béroalde's passion for collecting tales brought him into touch with the Venetian *Peregrinaggio di tre giovani, figliuoli del re di Serendippo* (1557).[219] Using this work as a model, he published his own version of the adventures of the three princes called *L'histoire véritable, ou le voyage des princes fortunez* (Paris, 1610). He takes great liberties with his model in rearranging its order and in embellishing its parts and events with his own philosophical observations, digressions into the occult, and discourses on love.[220] Many of its plots and themes, those imitated and those added, were originally part of the European repertory of stories derived from Eastern prototypes.[221] He divides the work into four

[214] *Ibid.*, pp. 281–83.

[215] *Ibid.*, pp. 268–69, n. 5.

[216] As quoted in H. Honour, *Chinoiserie* (London, 1961), p. 44.

[217] For his biography see V. L. Saulnier, "Étude sur Béroalde de Verville," *Bibliothèque d'humanisme et renaissance*, V (1944), 209–326.

[218] Entitled *L'histoire des vers qui filent la soye. En cette Serodokimasie ou recherche de ces vers est discourse de leur natures, gouvernement, utilité, plaisir et profit qu'ils rapportent* (Tours). For commentary see H. Clouzot, "La sériculture dans Béroalde de Verville," *Revue du XVIe siècle*, III (1915), 281–86. For the development of silk manufacturing see H. Vaschalde, *Olivier de Serres . . . , sa vie et ses travaux* (Paris, 1886), chaps. vii–viii.

[219] For discussion of this work see above, pp. 212–13.

[220] See E. Vordemann, *Quellenstudien zu dem Roman, "Le Voyage des Princes Fortunez" von Béroalde de Verville* (Göttingen, 1933), p. 21.

[221] *Ibid.*, pp. 56–110.

voyages and provides a map showing the routes followed by the princes. On the first voyage they are driven by the southwind into the harbor of Calicut. There they superintend the construction of a ship made of pure gold in the form of a lion. When the princes go their separate ways, they undertake an overland trek disguised as Oriental merchants, even as Varthema had done at the beginning of the century. Nymphs and fairies figure prominently in the second voyage and one of the sibyls, a daughter of the king of Calicut, marries the "king of Asia." One of the queen's officials is sent to China from whence he returns with printers who are then assigned the task of restoring the king's library. In the course of the third voyage an emissary from China is asked to explain the meaning behind all the wonders they have seen and the adventures they have experienced. The queen in these stories, and the heroine of the piece, is Marie de' Medici who had just become the ruler of France after the assassination (1610) of Henry IV.[222] Béroalde evidently knew that Marie, like the members of her illustrious family, was a connoisseur of porcelains and an admirer of the arts and wisdom of China.[223]

Throughout his writings Béroalde repeatedly refers to China as a source of wisdom and occult understanding as well as the homeland of printing and book-making. In his encyclopedic, enigmatic, and erotic novel called *Le moyen de parvenir* (ca. 1610) he claims to have learned from a Chinese sage the secret of how to determine whether a girl is really a maiden.[224] He relates the secret in obscene detail. Like Postel and many others of his intellectual forefathers, Béroalde likes playing with words and their etymologies. In discussing humor-ously the origin of *putain* (whore), he observes parenthetically that St. Barlaam had remarked on it "in his etymologies printed more than one thousand years ago in China." [225] In this work, and in many of his others, he introduced many Oriental touches which lend an air of mystery and superior wisdom.[226] He also uses these touches for making invidious comparisons with respect to two of his favorite targets, the stuffy learned world of Europe and the Catholic Church.[227]

While both popular prose and scientific poetry included comparative, satirical, and didactic elements, several prominent literati of the latter half of the century directed their attentions explicitly to the problem of extracting lessons from the "New World" for the benefit of Europe. Pontus de Tyard, a member of the Pléiade, became absorbed from 1557 onward with natural science and comparative religion rather than pure literature.[228] He made it clear at the outset that in talking of the "New World" he included in that

---

[222] *Ibid.*, p. 54.

[223] On Marie's interest in curiosities see *Asia*, II, Bk. 1, 33; on the Medici porcelains see *ibid.*, pp. 107–8.

[224] See C. Royer (ed.), *Le moyen de parvenir* (reprint of Paris ed. of 1896, 2 vols. in one; Geneva, 1970), I, 90.

[225] *Ibid.*, p. 286.

[226] See J. L. Pallister, *The World View of Béroalde de Verville* (Paris, 1971), pp. 79, 89.

[227] *Ibid.*, pp. 136, 143.

[228] See above, p. 279. Also see K. M. Hall, *Pontus de Tyard and His "Discours philosophiques"* (Oxford, 1963), p. 110, and S. Baridon, *Pontus de Tyard* (Milan, [1950]), chap. iii.

designation not only the Americas but the entire overseas world unknown to the geographers of Antiquity. To enlarge and support his knowledge of natural science and the overseas world he collected a substantial personal library of contemporary books.[229] In his prose writings over three decades (1557–87) Tyard stresses the value of learning by experience and points repeatedly to the fact that the new scientific observations being made in Europe and the "New World" are helping to widen the cracks appearing in the edifice of traditional learning.

Eclectic in his interests and powerful in his influence at court, Tyard was a philosophical theorist and spokesman for the French academies of the sixteenth century.[230] His several prose dialogues, encyclopedic in their range, were compiled and published in a single volume called *Discours philosophiques* (Paris, 1587). Like many other contemporary writings, his various discourses include acknowledged and unacknowledged translations of various sources. From perusal of this anthology and commentary it is clear that Tyard felt the study of geography had to be assiduously cultivated and the authority of Ptolemy constantly questioned.[231] He amplifies his discussion of oceanic tides in one of his earlier discourses by adding a description of the tides of the New World borrowed from Oviedo.[232] In his review of opinions on the nature of the Deity, he points out that the Brahmans say that God is light or "that reason by which the wise man understands high things and secret mysteries."[233] His account of worship in the West Indies derives directly from the chronicle-narrative of Gomara.[234] Aside from giving him new comparative detail, Tyard contends that the voyages of discovery prove that the world is round and that the tides of the sea are not everywhere the same. The conclusion is therefore inescapable that new information and observations must be collected and cataloged, that comparisons must be consciously sought, and that new general theories must be postponed until the new and the old learning have been weighed in the same balance.

The most judicious weighmaster of the century was Michel de Montaigne (1533–92), the brilliant, charming, and wise essayist.[235] Born at the family château in Périgord, Montaigne spent most of his life in Bordeaux and its

---

[229] See S. F. Baridon, *Inventaire de la bibliothèque de Pontus de Tyard* (Geneva, 1950), especially pp. 34, 35, 40. Also see above, p. 67.

[230] See Yates, *op. cit.* (n. 174), p. 77.

[231] See J. C. Lapp, "Pontus de Tyard and the Science of His Age," *Romantic Review*, XXXVIII (1947), 17–18.

[232] See J. C. Lapp, *The Universe of Pontus de Tyard: A Critical Edition of "L'Univers"* (Ithaca, N.Y., 1950), pp. xl–xli.

[233] As quoted in Yates, *op. cit.* (n. 174), p. 90. This is a traditional view, possibly derived from Giraldi, to which he gives a Neo-Platonic twist. But cf. the remarks in 1560 of the Swiss Protestant Pierre Viret (1511–71) on the religious practices of the natives of the Caroline Islands as quoted in Atkinson, *Les nouveaux horizons* (n. 6), pp. 399–400.

[234] See Hall, *op. cit.* (n. 228), p. 110.

[235] Biographies of Montaigne are innumerable. The best and most recent in English is Donald M. Frame, *Montaigne: A Biography* (New York, 1965); in French the most useful is A. Thibaudet, *Montaigne* (Paris, 1963).

vicinity. His father was the scion of a prominent and wealthy Catholic family; his mother was a daughter of the Lopez de Villanueva, a prosperous family of converted Iberian Jews who had settled in Toulouse. As a child, Montaigne learned Latin before he knew French. He spent seven of his most impressionable years, from ages six to thirteen, at the Collège de Guyenne in Bordeaux. Among his teachers before they left Bordeaux for Coimbra were Nicolas de Grouchy and George Buchanan. His principal, Andrea Gouvea, of the famous Portuguese family of educators, was in Montaigne's estimation "the greatest principal of France."[236] Under the tutelage of these Humanists he learned to love and appreciate the classics. He then turned to the study of law, probably at Paris and Toulouse. From 1554 to 1570 he worked as a magistrate under the jurisdiction of the Parlement of Bordeaux, and in these years became the boon companion of Etienne de La Boétie (1530–63), a gifted writer and a friend of the Pléiade. After his father's death in 1568, Montaigne retired from his magistracy and took up life as a country gentleman with leisure for reading, reflection, and writing.

The decade from 1570 to 1580 constituted for Montaigne a period of intellectual gestation and sporadic writing. His longest essay of this period, called "Apology for Raymond Sebond," was prepared as an exploration and statement of the case for intellectual skepticism. His first book of *Essais*, published in 1580, concentrates upon human limitations, inconstancy, and variety. Weary of reflecting in solitude upon the deficiencies of man and suffering from ill health, Montaigne traveled abroad in 1580–81. In France, Switzerland, Germany, Austria, and Italy he was to find plenty of visual confirmation of the variety in the world. With the aid of his secretary he kept a journal of his experiences and his impressions of the people and the sights he saw.[237] While much of the journal is devoted to trivialities, it is revelatory of his wonder and sometimes his disdain for the unfamiliar. In Italy especially, which was the objective of the tour, Montaigne saw much that was new to him. At Florence he inspected the palace where the duke worked at counterfeiting Oriental stones,[238] and visited the gardens and grottoes of Castello with their statues of strange animals.[239] In Rome at the Vatican library he saw "a book from China in strange characters."[240] At the baths of La Villa he learned of a marvelous, green, pain-killing stone which had been brought from India by a monk.[241] In Pisa he bought a bamboo cane, a little vase, and a "cup of Indian nut."[242] Indeed, throughout the trip he "did not lack matter," as he remarks, "to feed my curiosity."[243]

[236] On this group of educators see above, pp. 11–13.

[237] It remained in manuscript until the eighteenth century. The best edition in English is included in Donald M. Frame (trans.), *The Complete Works of Montaigne* (Stanford, 1958), pp. 861–1039. For the relationship between his readings and his travels in enlarging his world view see J. Barrère, "A propos d'un épisode du voyage de Montaigne," *Revue historique de Bordeaux*, XXVIII (1930), 145.

[238] *Ibid.*, p. 930.

[239] *Ibid.*, p. 932. Also see *Asia*, II, Bk. 1, 166.

[240] See Frame (trans.), *op. cit.* (n. 237), p. 950.

[241] *Ibid.*, p. 997.

[242] *Ibid.*, p. 1011.

[243] *Ibid.*, p. 1014.

While at Rome, Montaigne was notified by the municipal council of Bordeaux of his election as their mayor. He hurriedly returned home and acted in this capacity over the next four years, emerging from this experience with a much higher regard for his fellow man and more satisfaction with himself. Montaigne returned to his solitude and to his writing in 1585. At this point he began to revise his earlier efforts and to compose new essays. In these compositions he reflects on the best ways to acquire and hold a life of wisdom and happiness, and on how to die gracefully. About mankind as a whole he stresses the qualities of frailty and goodness common to all. A printed version of the new and revised *Essais* appeared at Paris in 1588; they were at once greeted with acclaim. Throughout the last four years of his life, the celebrated author continued to revise the *Essais* and to amplify them. The final edition of his great life work was published posthumously at Paris in 1595.

When at home, Montaigne spent most of the daylight hours in his book-lined study located in a tower that commanded a view of his property. He boasted that the curved bookshelves of the study held a thousand volumes.[244] About one hundred of this collection were works in Italian, the only modern language other than his native French that he read with ease. Today at least seventy-six autographed copies are extant of books which once belonged to Montaigne. One of these is a 1565 edition of Münster's *Cosmographie universelle* with numerour passages underlined, evidently the book that he regretted not having in his baggage on the trip to Italy.[245] He was also an avid reader of the deeds of Alexander in India as is revealed by an examination of his marginal annotations to the Latin edition (Basel, 1545) of Quintus Curtius which he owned.[246] He also possessed a copy of Grouchy's translation of Castanheda which had been put into Spanish and published at Antwerp in 1554. It is not likely that he actually used this Spanish version, for he also owned an edition (Cologne, 1574) of Osório's *De rebus Emmanuelis* that covers much the same material and is in the Latin language that he knew so well.[247] Whatever he quotes that is traceable to Castanheda probably came to him through Goulart's translation of Castanheda's first book. Montaigne also owned a copy of the work written and published under a pseudonym by Jean de Silvá, count of Portalegre, which purports to tell the true story of the union between Spain and Portugal.[248] It was possibly because of his mother's Iberian background and of his own relations with the Humanists at the Collège de Guyenne that Montaigne collected materials on

[244] See P. Bonnefon, "La bibliothèque de Montaigne," *Revue d'histoire littéraire de la France,* II (1895), 327–33.

[245] *Ibid.,* p. 353. For the reference in his *Travel Journal* see Frame (trans.), *op. cit.* (n. 237), p. 892.

[246] See Bonnefon, *loc. cit.* (n. 244), p. 341. The copy now in the library of the Château de la Brède contains 168 marginal comments in Montaigne's hand and a final note dated July 3, 1587, summarizing his impressions.

[247] See *ibid.,* pp. 340, 355–56.

[248] Entitled *Dell'unione del regno di Portugallo alla corona di Castiglia, istoria del Sig. Ieronimo de Franchi Conestaggio, gentilhuomo genovese* (Genoa, 1585). For discussion of this book see Bonnefon, *loc. cit.* (n. 244), pp. 344–45, and above, p. 36. Also cf. G. Norton, *Studies in Montaigne* (New York, 1904), pp. 234–36.

Portugal and its empire.[249] In addition to the extant books, he owned copies of other relevant works, such as Paolo Giovio's history of his own times, Goulart's translation of Osório and Castanheda, Gomara, the French translation of Mendoza on China, and Gasparo Balbi's *Viaggio* (Venice, 1590).[250]

In the *Essais* published before 1588 Montaigne is moved by the import of the overseas discoveries in general but shows only a limited interest in Asian peoples and customs. Even so he is far more aware of the progress in overseas discoveries than in the changing astronomical conceptions of his era. His sources for the essays of this period are restricted to the relevant writers of Antiquity and to the general history of Gomara. He refers to the areas newly discovered as being nearly equal in size to the world Ptolemy knew. Then he observes that the geographers of his day are as certain as Ptolemy had been that "now all is discovered and all seen." But the skeptic in Montaigne queries: "if Ptolemy was once mistaken on the grounds of his reason whether it would not be stupid for me to trust to what these people say about it."[251] He remarks on the abundance of food in tropical regions and concludes that they "have now taught us that bread is not our only food, and that without plowing, our Mother Nature had provided us in plenty with all we needed."[252] While he draws from Gomara a few specifics about American customs, his references to *satī* and the tradition about the Indians eating their dead are derived from classical sources.[253] He is certainly aware that beauty is in the eye of the beholder and that "in the Indies [they] paint it black and dusky, with large swollen lips and a wide flat nose."[254] Even with such a limited view of the overseas world, he comes readily to the relativistic conclusion that "each man calls barbarism whatever is not his own practice."[255]

Relevant revisions and additions to the editions of 1588 are scattered and few. Perusal of these indicate that he borrowed very little from newly available materials, except perhaps from the Jesuit letterbooks and the cosmographies of Belleforest and Thevet. He deplores the price paid in destruction and human misery "for the traffic in pearls and pepper" and denounces the conquests as "bare and mechanical victories."[256] While nations had been found that "never, so far as we know, had heard anything of us," the Europeans "found in them" a very clear likeness of "our shriving priests . . . , the system of writing in pictures, [and] belief in a single first man."[257] He adds a few details to his earlier examples,

[249] See P. Villey-Desmeserets, *Les sources et l'évolution des Essais de Montaigne* (Paris, 1908), pp. 269–70.
[250] Cf. above, pp. 282–83.
[251] From "Apology for Raymond Sebond," in Frame (trans.), *op. cit.* (n. 237), p. 430.
[252] *Ibid.*, pp. 334–35.
[253] See "Of Custom," *ibid.*, p. 84, and "Of Virtue," *ibid.*, p. 534.
[254] In "Apology for Raymond Sebond," *ibid.*, p. 355.
[255] See "Of Cannibals," *ibid.*, p. 152. For commentary see B. Weinberg, "Montaigne's Readings for *Des cannibales*," in G. B. Daniel, Jr. (ed.), *Renaissance and Other Studies in Honor of William Leon Wiley* (Chapel Hill, N.C., 1968), pp. 261–79. Also see P. Vivier, *Montaigne, auteur scientifique* (Paris, 1920), pp. 11–12.
[256] See "Of Coaches" in Frame (trans.), *op. cit.* (n. 237), p. 695.
[257] See "Apology for Raymond Sebond," *ibid.*, pp. 431–32.

particularly with respect to the infinite variety that exists in the world.[258] But then he remarks "how puny and limited is the knowledge of even the most curious," for "there escapes us a hundred times more than comes to our knowledge." While Europeans pride themselves on inventing artillery and printing, "other men in another corner of the world, in China, enjoyed these a thousand years earlier." The conclusion follows that "if we saw as much of the world as we do not see, we would perceive a perpetual multiplication . . . of forms."[259]

Montaigne himself began to see after 1588 a great deal more of the East than he ever had before. His horizons were broadened by having the opportunity and time in his last years to consult the literature that was then becoming more readily available. While in Paris in 1588 on a mission for Henry of Navarre and seeing to the publication of the *Essais*, he certainly ran across the numerous Jesuit letterbooks in the book stalls. Nor could he have escaped the stir of interest in the East provoked by the Japanese mission of 1585 and by the publications in Latin, Italian, and French reporting on its progress and activities. Even while he was seeing his book through the press, the French translation (1588) of Mendoza appeared. The work of Luc de la Porte, this translation was dedicated to Monseigneur Philippe Herault, the chancellor of France and its chief justice, since it treats of the "most notable and rare matters of a nation reputedly wise and prudent."[260] In the following year Maffei's history of the Jesuit mission in the East was published in Latin at Lyons, thus bringing down to date for Montaigne and his contemporaries the story of the opening of China.

The additions to the *Essais* produced in the last four years of Montaigne's life are dotted with references to books on Portugal and the East. Osório, he maintains, is the "best Latin historian of our era."[261] Certainly most of what Montaigne adds to the essays about India and its customs comes from Osório directly or from Goulart's French translation. A few supporting or amplifying details he derives from Balbi whom he refers to as "a man of this day."[262] Most of the material added is designed to lend support to his opinions and to reinforce, extend, or refine the examples given in the earlier versions of the essays. The custom in "Narsinga" (Vijayanagar) of royal servitors burning themselves on their deceased master's pyre supports the argument "that the taste of good and evil depends in large part on the opinion we have of them."[263] The tradition in Ternate of declaring war before striking illuminates his discussion of "whether a governor of a besieged place should go out to parley."[264] On the question of voluntary death he cites the custom followed by Hindus who gain holiness by being crushed under the wheels of the juggernaut.[265] The examples

---

[258] For examples see *ibid.*, pp. 80, 355, 432, 654, 666.
[259] See "Of Coaches," *ibid.*, pp. 692–93.
[260] From dedication to *Histoire du grand royaume de la Chine* (Paris, 1588).
[261] See Frame (trans.), *op. cit.* (n. 237), p. 36.
[262] *Ibid.*, p. 355.
[263] *Ibid.*, pp. 34–35. Also see "Of Virtue," *ibid.*, pp. 534–35.
[264] *Ibid.*, pp. 16–17.
[265] *Ibid.*, p. 261. Cf. pl. 30.

could be multiplied, but it appears that for Montaigne "India" was merely a treasure house of peculiar customs which illustrate both the infinite variety in manners and morals and the universal validity of his fundamental precepts.[266]

China, as he read about it in Mendoza's adulatory book, truly astounded Montaigne. In the Vatican he had earlier looked studiously and raptly at a Chinese book.[267] He had already read about the independent Chinese invention of artillery and printing. Mendoza taught him about the sophisticated administrative and governmental organization of China. From China there must be much to learn, for it is "a kingdom whose government and arts, without dealings with and knowledge of ours, surpass our examples in many branches of excellence and whose history teaches me how much ampler and more varied the world is than either the ancients or we understand."[268] Although he has very little else to say directly about China, it probably was his discovery of its high civilization which led him late in life to conclude that "the world is something quite different from what we judge."[269] Nor does he hesitate to take the necessary next step. "As everyone would admit," he opines, "if everyone knew how, after perusing these new examples, to reflect on his own and compare them sanely."[270]

Montaigne uses the East to support his beliefs about the uncertainty of knowledge, the infinite variety in the world, and the universality of moral precepts. With the passage of time he becomes more interested in resemblances than in differences, in common than in opposing beliefs. But to avoid exaggerating the importance to him of the opening of the overseas world, a few statistics are necessary. In the first book of the *Essais* he makes no mention of America, Asia, or the Africa of his day in thirty-eight of its fifty-seven chapters. In the following two books his proportion changes sharply and in favor of the East over all other parts of the overseas world.[271] But such data are only of limited value. He makes at least fifteen extended references to India and the East Indies and but two substantial references to China. Nonetheless he is clearly much more impressed by China, a nation about which the Ancients knew little and contemporaries much more. In China he saw an example for Europe that he never discerned elsewhere in the overseas world. The primitive regions of America and the Indies stirred his sympathy and interest; China awakened his admiration.

Around 1580 Montaigne had made the acquaintance of Pierre Charron (1541–1603), a canon of the cathedral of Bordeaux, an eloquent preacher, and a

266 For further pertinent examples, see *ibid.*, pp. 168, 258, 419, 513, 626, 647, 654, 740.

267 For his very full description of it see *ibid.*, p. 950.

268 See "Of Experience," *ibid.*, p. 820. Also cf. the French translation of Mendoza, *op. cit.* (n. 260), pp. 70–72.

269 Frame (trans.), *op. cit.* (n. 237), p. 430.

270 See "Of Custom," *ibid.*, p. 80.

271 See Atkinson, *Les nouveaux horizons* (n. 6), p. 325. Strangely he has not a single reference to Japan.

learned theologian and Humanist.[272] Born in Paris, Charron commenced his studies at the Sorbonne and in 1571 received a degree at Montpelier in canon and civil law. The practice of law not appealing to him, Charron entered the priesthood. He quickly won renown for his sermons and from 1576 to 1594 was known as a leading preacher of southwestern France. His reputation then became national and he was soon embroiled in theological controversy. A first major literary effort was written in reply to Philippe Du Plessis-Mornay's *De la vérité de la religion chrétienne* (1581),[273] an attempt to validate Christianity on the basis of reason and to attack doubters, Jews, Muslims, and other infidels. Charron, as spokesman for the Catholics, published *Les trois véritéz* (1593)[274] to rebut the unorthodox assertions of "the Pope of the Huguenots." In the process he was required to take into account the best way for Christians to deal with pagans and other nonbelievers. While he is perturbed about the stubbornness of non-Christians, he is even more determined to prove the superiority of Catholicism to Protestantism. He therefore stresses the fact that Catholicism, unlike Protestantism, is a universal faith and is now rapidly spreading to all parts of the overseas world and into regions where other non-Christian religions were previously well established.[275] His inclusion of Japan in the list of regions being Christianized is certainly a reflection of the fervor for missions excited in Catholic Europe by the Japanese embassy (1584–86) to Rome.[276]

While *Les trois véritéz* enjoyed a certain popularity as a controversial tract, Charron was busily preparing a major philosophical work, *De la sagesse livres trois* (Bordeaux, 1601), which has been called "the most important Renaissance treatise on wisdom."[277] Fundamentally it categorizes "wisdom" as a moral virtue naturally acquired. The book is also a call to intellectuals and Christians to transform contemplation into action and knowledge into virtue. Charron tries in the first book to teach men how to know themselves by means of thorough self-examination; the second stresses the importance of self-discipline; the third sets up the moral virtues which should govern life: Prudence, Justice, Strength, and Temperance. Most of the work is concerned with individual self-knowledge and self-cultivation. But Charron also feels obliged to see man as a social and political being. In doing so he follows closely the ideas of Montaigne and Bodin.[278] He glories in an encyclopedic organization of data and in presenting it in tabular form. While he tends like Montaigne toward skepticism, he constantly seeks for a connection between natural and Christian morality, a search that the orthodox of his day and since have labeled unsuccessful.

---

[272] For his biography see J. D. Charron, *The "Wisdom" of Pierre Charron* (Chapel Hill, N.C., 1960), chap. iv.

[273] Subtitled *Contre les Athées, Epicuriens, Payens, Juifs, Mahumedistes et autres Infideles.*

[274] Subtitled *Contre les Athées, Idolatres, Juifs, Mahumetans Hérétiques, et Schismatiques* (Bordeaux).

[275] See *Les trois véritéz*, p. 351.

[276] See Atkinson, *Les nouveaux horizons* (n. 6), p. 339. On the mission itself see *Asia*, I, 668–706.

[277] For this estimate see E. F. Rice, Jr., *The Renaissance Idea of Wisdom* (Cambridge, Mass., 1958), p. 178.

[278] See below, pp. 306–9, for discussion of Bodin.

One of the best ways to study the *Sagesse* is to start by examining the *Traicté de sagesse*, a summary and a reply to his critics, written a few months before Charron's death.[279] In it he indicates points on which the "hypocrites" disagree with him. Most interesting are a few of his replies pertaining to relativism. The wise man, according to Charron, rejects ethnocentrism in all its forms and respects the laws and customs of the place in which he happens to be. "I doff humbly my hat... before my superiors," he claims, "because the customs of my country so ordain." Equally, "were I in the Orient I would eat my meal seated on the earth."[280] The sage will courageously admit that "among Indians, Chinese, cannibals, Turks and other nations which are generally considered barbarian there are often laws, institutions, customs and manners as good or better than our own."[281] He will open his mind to new concepts, however shocking they may be, to make himself capable of progress. To convert the Chinese "they should be taught that worldly knowledge is only vanity and dupery" and "to rid themselves of all opinions and belief" so that "they may very humbly admit to the creator a bare and immaculate soul."[282] The assumption here seems to be that the Chinese, whatever their own religious beliefs, should open their minds for the purpose of accepting absolute Christian truth, a viewpoint that can only be appreciated by recalling how vast was the separation in Charron's mind between the secular and the Christian. He simply was not able to see for himself the inconsistency of this position.[283] Like that of most of his contemporaries, Charron's relativism breaks down on the problem of religion. Christianity still remains the true faith which all men must finally accept.[284]

In the *Sagesse* itself Charron sets down his ideas more systematically. Borrowing notions of environmental determinism from Bodin, he declares that "the whole essence of man is taken and drawn from the divers sites of the world."[285] Diversities in physical appearance, manners, and "faculties of the soul" emanate from the "influence of heaven, and the sun, the air, the climate, the country." To illustrate his point he divides the world into three parts: south, middle, and north. In the eastern segment of the southern division he locates "Arabia, Calicut, the Moluques, Iaves, Taprobana"; in the middle "China, Iapan, and America"; and in the north Tartary. He provides a table to show graphically the "divers natures of these three sorts of people" with respect to "qualities of

---

279 This contention, which I follow, is advanced by Charron, *op. cit.* (n. 272), pp. 101–2.

280 Charron, *Traicté de sagesse* (Bordeaux, 1606), pp. 27ʳ–27ᵛ. This is a summary of the larger *Sagesse* written before his death as a rebuttal to critics.

281 *Ibid.*, p. 78ᵛ.

282 From his discussion of "pyrrhonisme," *ibid.*, pp. 73ʳ–74ʳ.

283 On the inconsistency of his general argument see Tilley, *Literature of French Renaissance* (n. 13), I, 277–78.

284 Botero (see above, pp. 248–49) is the only sixteenth-century philosopher who does not stress the superiority of the Christian revelation. He avoids the issue by confining his comments to secular questions.

285 I have used the English translation of *Sagesse* by Samson Lennard, *Of Wisdom* (London, 1651). These quotations are from pp. 153–54.

soul," planets, and activities in which each excels.[286] The northerners, whose planets are Mars and the Moon, are warlike, forceful, and endowed with the gift of common sense. The middlers, whose planets are Mercury and Jupiter, are reasonable, just, and prudent, and prefer discourse to action. The southerners, whose planets are Saturn and Venus, are contemplative, philosophical, and religious and doubly blessed with the quality of understanding. Individually northerners are tall, strong, and hairy; southerners are little, black, and feeble; middlers are of both types but are most like those "of that region to which they are neerest neighbors."[287] The middlers likewise share to a degree the other qualities of northerners and southerners. In spirit northerners are heavy, obtuse, and stupid while southerners are ingenious, wise, and subtle. Northerners have little regard for religion or piety while southerners are superstitious, contemplative, and devout.

After cataloging these characteristics he makes only slight distinctions between the peoples of East and West in the accompanying textual discussion. Later, following the *Essais* of Montaigne, he rejoices in the overseas discoveries for revealing "another world, almost such as ours" and queries, "who doubteth but that in time hereafter there will bee discovered divers others?" Almost everything "which we so much esteeme of heere" was in use "a thousand yeares before we heard any tidings of them." From what has so recently been revealed it may readily be concluded "that this great bodie which wee call the world is not that which wee thinke and judge it to be" for in all its parts it is "in perpetual flux and reflux."[288] Law and custom, which are the authorities in all countries, are constantly changing and extremely diverse.[289] In examining and judging the customs of others the wise man proceeds slowly and judiciously. For no matter how savage or irrational particular customs might appear to be, "yet at the least they would not bee without some reason and defence," even including the horrible custom attributed to the Indians of eating their dead parents.[290] With Charron the trend toward tolerance, comparison, self-criticism, and cultural relativism reaches its apogee.

From the popular literature of the era of religious and civil war a taste grew in France for a literature of escape. Stories of monsters, miracles, and strange and abhorrent customs were read for entertainment. The mere cataloging of customs old and new, familiar and foreign, implicitly introduced a note of ethnic comparison. Gradually, as in *Les serées* of Bouchet, customs were consciously compared for humorous, satirical, or didactic ends. Debates arose over how best to represent distant peoples in painting. Asia in both the short story and the sentimental novel continued to be a homeland of prodigies. But, as in Béroalde de Verville, it also became a backdrop for adventure stories and an

---

[286] See *ibid.*, p. 157, and pl. 17.
[287] For this second table see *ibid.*, p. 164, and pl. 17.
[288] Quotations in this paragraph to this point are from *ibid.*, p. 257.
[289] See *ibid.*, p. 325.
[290] *Ibid.*, p. 327.

unequaled source of manufactured products: artillery, printing, porcelain, and silk. China appeared not only as an exotic land but as a repository of ancient wisdom and modern technical superiority.

Pontus de Tyard, like some other philosophical writers, realized that the opening of the overseas world revealed the inadequacy of Europe's ancient learning. He urged his contemporaries to study the new geography to broaden their own intellectual horizons. He himself conscientiously studied the cosmographies to locate stories of religious practices abroad to compare to those at home. Montaigne in his early essays clearly expresses his skepticism about the certainty of given knowledge. He drew freely upon the compilations of prodigies for examples of customs which would exhibit dramatically the diversity of the world. As a critic of his own society, he was more tolerant than others of the strange practices and morals of distant peoples. Late in his life he saw China as a land from which Europe had much to learn. The intellectual relativism of Montaigne was structured by Charron into a systematic treatise on wisdom which called upon men to free their minds of preconceptions and to eschew contemplation and satire for moral action. While Montaigne thought Europe had something to learn from China, Charron actually integrated Asia into his universal schema of characteristics based on environment. Montaigne and Charron agreed that tolerance and comparison might raise questions that would ultimately lead to a deeper understanding of European civilization and thought. Neither was willing to include the Christian faith among the subjects he thought of in relative terms.

4

FROM COSMOGRAPHY TO UNIVERSAL HISTORY

The decade of the 1550's was both a period of feverish internal literary and intellectual activity and of discovery of the outside world. The investigators of the Levant sent out by Francis I returned to Paris at this time and began to publish the reports of their experiences. Postel, as we have seen, published his *Des merveilles du monde* (Paris) in 1552.[291] In the next year Pierre Belon issued his popular *Les observations de plusieurs singularitez et choses memorables... en Grèce, Asie... et autres pays estranges* (Paris), one of the most readable travelogues to appear in the sixteenth century. André Thevet (1504–92), who had visited the Holy Places and had traveled in the eastern Mediterranean region in 1549–50, issued his *Cosmographie du Levant* at Lyons in 1554. In 1559 the *Voyages aventureux* of Jean Alfonse finally appeared in print for the first time.[292] In the meantime King Henry II was preparing to send Durand de Villegagnon (1510–71) to

[291] See above, pp. 267–70.
[292] See above, pp. 258–59.

Brazil to set up a French colony where Protestants and Catholics would, it was hoped, live side by side in peace. While looking eastward to the Levant and westward to America, the French also continued to watch the progress of the Portuguese in both America and Asia.

In 1556 the Paris bookseller Estienne Denyse published a small book of thirty-two pages called *L'histoire du nouveau monde descouvert par les Portugalois, escrite par le seigneur Pierre Bembo.*[293] In the salutation to "readers desiring knowledge of foreign lands," it is alleged that this is a brief discourse by Pierre Bembo not previously published. A comparison with Pietro Bembo's *Della historia vinitiana . . . libri XII* (Venice, 1552) reveals that this Paris book is certainly not a simple translation of Book VI in which Bembo deals with the overseas discoveries of the Iberian nations.[294] The form is similar to Bembo's and the substance is not dissimilar, but the French book omits many aspects of Venetian history included in Bembo's account and brings in more details on the features of the New World. Perhaps the bookseller was here merely using Bembo's name as a pseudonym for one of his hack writers.[295] Certainly the great Venetian's name had sales value in mid-century France. The French book was evidently intended to be the first of a series, for at the end the reader is promised a continuation of the story in the next installment.

Whatever else this small book may be, it certainly is a straightforward history of the opening of the overseas world from the first voyage of Columbus to the circumnavigation of Magellan's crew. Details of natural history and exotic customs, some genuine and others fictitious, enliven the narrative. It is clearly pointed out that the Portuguese have control of the Indian Ocean and that the trade of Egypt and Venice has consequently diminished in volume and value. The Portuguese, after conquering Diu, Cochin, Quilon, and Calicut, ventured further to the East "where man had never before entered."[296] Magellan, who sailed around the world to reach the odoriferous Moluccas had the misfortune to be killed there in battle. When the "Victoria" returned, its logbook was a day off, a primitive indication of the crossing of the international date line. Many of the points here adverted to also occur in Bembo's Venetian history, but others do not. It is reasonable to conclude therefore that this is an imitation of Bembo's Book VI embellished with fascinating and lascivious detail to enhance its appeal for the reading public. Like other writers, its author treats the Portuguese conquests in Asia and Magellan's voyage to the Moluccas as integral parts of the opening of the "New World."[297]

When this book was put on sale at M. Denyse's book stall in 1556, André Thevet had just returned from his second voyage to America. A Franciscan monk, Thevet had spent most of his earlier life in travel. He took his first

---

[293] A copy of this rare work is in the Huntington Library. For its title page see pl. 6.

[294] On Bembo, see above, pp. 200–201.

[295] The suggestion of Atkinson, *Les nouveaux horizons* (n. 6), p. 44. Though he lists the book in his chronicle of geographical literature, he does not discuss it in his text.

[296] P. 30.

[297] Cf. the definition of the New World in Pontus de Tyard, above, p. 279.

Atlantic voyage in 1540 en route to Lisbon. From there he intended to depart in 1541 for the Moluccas, but fell ill with the fever and had to forgo this adventure.[298] Four years later he visited Bizerte in North Africa where he began his lifelong project of collecting ancient coins and medals, both for their value as portable art objects and as sources of the portraits of great men.[299] While in the Levant in 1549–50, Thevet continued collecting, kept notes on his experiences, and made drawings on the spot of its native peoples and places. In Europe he also collected strange objects, sketched oddities, and tirelessly recorded stories told him by people whom he met or sought out. Appointed Catholic chaplain to the colonizing expedition of Villegagnon, Thevet went to Brazil in 1555. He spent just six weeks there before illness forced him to return to France.[300] Once back home he never traveled abroad again. The remainder of his long life was spent in collecting a library, organizing his own and the king's chamber of curiosities at Fontainebleau, and compiling and writing the books on which his reputation rests.

Thevet's *Les singularités de la France antarctique* (Paris, 1558) was immediately acclaimed by French literati, especially by members of the Pléiade. Its author was congratulated for being willing to travel, for making records and sketches of his personal observations, for taking down the stories told to him by others, and for collecting samples of curiosities from the New World. In part he was himself responsible for the tone of this reaction, since he denounces in his writings the armchair travelers of Antiquity and his own day for perpetuating misleading facts and ideas. He complains about the confusion produced by the name "Indies" in its application to America, a term that correctly belongs, he argues, only to those regions east of the Indus River. A six-weeks' "wonder" himself, he had little reason to complain of the inaccuracies of others, for he uncritically accepted and recounted a host of stories worthy of being called "prodigies." But it is perhaps because of the fables he relates that his *Singularités* was long popular in France and translated into Italian (Venice, 1561) and English (London, 1568). Although Jean de Léry bitterly attacked Thevet for the inaccuracies in his stories about Brazil, it is only fair to point out that Thevet never intended to write an account of the Villegagnon expedition, a history of the colony, or a geographical description of America.[301] The *Singularités* is essentially a collection of astounding observations and stories which purport to recount the actual experiences of Thevet and others. It is his stubborn insistence upon the authenticity of these tales which eventually brought the *Singularités* into disrepute.[302]

[298] See J. Adhémar, *Frère André Thevet: Grand voyageur et cosmographe des rois de France au XVIᵉ siècle* (Paris, 1947), pp. 14–15.

[299] *Ibid.*, p. 16.

[300] See *ibid.*, pp. 31–44.

[301] See Chinard, *op. cit.* (n. 37), pp. 84–85. It should be noticed that Léry waited for eighteen years to publish his *Histoire d'un voyage fait en la terre du Brésel* (1578).

[302] Thevet even transposed animals that he had actually seen into the traditional creatures of medieval legend. See R. Wittkower, "Marvels of the East: A Study in the History of Monsters," *Journal of the Warburg and Courtauld Institutes*, V (1942), 195.

After his return from America, Thevet himself became an armchair cosmographer. He continued after 1558 to collect curiosities, books, and notes taken down from the observations of others. From these materials, and those derived from his earlier travels, he composed *La cosmographie universelle* in 1575. An enormous compendium in two volumes it numbers more than two thousand folio pages of text. Thevet's *Cosmographie* immediately won public interest, despite its author's tarnished reputation for veracity. Numerous woodcuts and four maps undoubtedly contributed to its popular appeal.[303] Its usefulness to students was greatly enhanced by the inclusion of an alphabetical table at the end of Volume II which lists the names of the places and persons cited.

Asia is the subject of Book II in Volume I.[304] After describing India's geography, Thevet attacks the authority of the ancient authors. Alexander had not gone as far to the East as history and legend claim. The stories of the Indians being monsters are untrue, even though Münster accepted them. He denies Pliny's assertion that hot climates produce tall men, for from his own experiences he found the reverse to be true. He is fascinated by what he has read about the Brahmans and their reverence for animal life. The St. Thomas Christians of India are prosperous pepper merchants and firmer in their faith than many European Christians. He links ritual bathing in the Ganges to the sacrament of baptism and, like Postel and others, views it as a relic of a past age when Christianity was the universal religion.

About China he is most eager to refute the fabrications perpetrated by Münster and Belleforest, Thevet's personal enemy. His own knowledge of China came allegedly from a prisoner of the Arabs whom he had met in Palestine.[305] This individual had spent fifteen years in China and had denied vehemently the common European opinion that the Chinese live on a certain apple-like fruit and the salubrious air of the country. In reality China is one of the greatest and most fertile lands of the East. Its king, one of Asia's potentates, holds dominion over fifteen provinces and is able to raise vast sums in gold without increasing taxes. His grandeur is so overwhelming that he can be approached only by one man. Still, he is a subordinate or vassal of the Great Khan of Cathay, an empire of which China is evidently just a part. The Chinese long to live on the water in boats. The men are brave, the women beautiful, and each man has the right to as many wives as he can support. The Chinese eat well and imbibe a wine made from rice and spices. Their language is brusque and rude and sounds like German. They are not Christian, but believe in the reincarnation of exemplary individuals as minor deities. As a consequence they are very moral in their behavior, especially in the respect they show for ancestors and family. Thevet's informant may have provided him with some of this information, but the accuracy of certain details—fifteen provinces, boat life, rice wine, vassalage to Cathay— indicate that he probably also consulted literary sources: Marco Polo, Barros in

[303] For his woodcuts of Asian scenes and activities see *Asia*, II, Bk. 1, 88, and pls. 5, 38, 39.
[304] The following summary is based on the excellent analysis in Gordon, *op. cit.* (n. 27), pp. 74–93.
[305] See Adhémar, *op. cit.* (n. 298), p. 68.

Italian translation, and the available Jesuit letterbooks. Even some of his stranger assertions—that the Chinese language sounds like German and that the Chinese are very moral—can be found in the best written sources of his day.[306]

That he was a student of the older literary sources is clear from his account of Tartary based on Marco Polo, Conti, and Poggio. He was also familiar with the Jesuit letterbooks and Postel's ideas, as can be seen from his discussion of Japan ("Giapon"). Like his sources, he is most interested in Japanese religious concepts and practices. According to their own beliefs, the Japanese hold that they were enlightened and saved by "Xaqua" (Buddha). Thevet doubts this, for he believes that the memory of Xaqua's acts is but further confirmation for his belief that the Japanese had once been Christians. He argues that the presence in Japan of monks and monastic institutions bears out this theory. For Thevet, as for Xavier, the Japanese are ready historically and intellectually to accept the Christianity of the European missionaries.

Thevet, like Münster and Belleforest, also accepts as factual a number of unfounded stories gathered from earlier authors. The people of "Taprobane" (Sumatra, to Thevet) are Christians who recognize none of the Patriarchs. An island near Ceylon is inhabited by women who visit their men on a neighboring island, a story borrowed from Jean Alfonse. "Zipangu" is not another name for Japan to Thevet, even though he is conscious that certain of his contemporaries have so identified it. Rather it is an island in the Indian Ocean which sends annual tribute to the Great Khan. Other stories, authentic and fabulous, lead him to draw comparisons. He reports, probably on the authority of Pigafetta, that certain of the islanders in the region of the Moluccas interchange blood as a symbol of brotherhood. He then goes on to preach that it is not right to condemn such practices since the European forefathers also possessed customs now deemed barbaric. He concludes his discussion of Asia by claiming to have sailed along most of its coasts, and in the process defines its configuration.[307] In his collections of portraits and lives of illustrious men, Thevet intended to include Asians as well as Europeans. He reproduces portraits of Albuquerque, Magellan, and Montezuma, but he was evidently not able to find anything on "Triumpara," king of Cochin.[308] Of relevant European intellectuals he includes portraits of Osório and Postel, and notes on the lives of Belleforest, Gomara, King Manuel, and Fernão Corrêa.[309] For Thevet, who had traveled much himself, no question existed about the importance of the overseas world and its peoples to his century, its men, and its beliefs.

François de Belleforest (1530–83), Thevet's rival, was an armchair cosmographer and polygraph who also enjoyed great popularity. Patronized by Margaret of Navarre, Belleforest studied at Bordeaux and Toulouse under

[306] On the image of China in Europe before 1575 see *Asia*, I, 731–41. Also cf. Anania's *Cosmographia*, above, pp. 231–33.

[307] P. 466ᵛ.

[308] *Les vrais portraits et vies des hommes illustres, grecz, Latins, et payens* (2 vols. in 1; Paris, 1584), pp. 420ᵃ–422ᵃ, 528ᵃ–529ᵇ, and pls. 13, 15, 68, 93.

[309] *Ibid.*, pp. 420ᵇ, 469ᵇ, 560ᵃ, 643ᵃ, 588ᵃ–590ᵇ.

Buchanan and Vinet. He soon gave up the rigors of study to embark upon a career as a dilettante of letters and poetry and as a flatterer of the great. At Paris in the late 1550's he sought to attach himself to the Pléiade; he did succeed in becoming a friend of Nicot when the latter returned to France in 1561. Once having won a few acquaintances among the court literati, Belleforest began to compose prose pieces for publishers. He was not a common hack, but an assiduous collector of material and a critical user of sources. He was a better historian than many of his contemporaries and a stylist of consequence. But his history was far from objective. In studying and organizing history he sought to demonstrate the validity of his own Neo-Platonic conception of the world and its workings.

Belleforest's *L'histoire universelle du monde* (Paris, 1570) was probably his most original contribution to historical study. Book II deals with Asia and includes everything from Turkey to China.[310] But his treatment of China and the other countries of the Asiatic continent is dependent upon traditional sources. Like Postel he spends much of his time looking for the vestiges of a primitive Christianity in Asia: Nestorians in Turkey, St. Thomas Christians in India, and the followers of "Xaqua" in Japan. He also believes that the Cathayans, because they are fair-skinned, literate, and imbued with a sense of superiority, are probably European in origin. In India, where Christianity remains firmly rooted, the missionaries should continue to work for conversion even if they run the danger of martyrdoms. He includes Japan in Book IV which is devoted to the "New World" as a place that was discovered even *more recently* than America. Japan was not discovered until 1550 (*sic*), because it is not rich in gold. Its people are fair like Europeans, discreet, virtuous, learned, and noble. Like Xavier, he concludes that Japan is the best of the nations discovered since Antiquity. In Belleforest's translated and revised version of Münster's *Cosmographie* (1575) he added material on the "New World," a mute testimonial to the importance he now attached to the newly discovered lands, and excised substantially the account on Germany. At no point in his writings does he equal Thevet in his understanding of China. Traditional India, as exemplified in his *Histoires prodigieuses* (1594), remained for Belleforest little more than the homeland of wonders and tales.[311]

The transition from cosmography to universal history was initiated by Jean Bodin (1530–96), a Parisian lawyer and political theorist. In the early years (1561–66) of the religious wars, Bodin began to see that tolerance of religious diversity was a prerequisite for the achievement of peace. He also began to reach out for an understanding of human, secular history in its worldwide ramifications. His first literary contribution to universal history was his Latin *Method for the Easy Comprehension of History*, first published at Paris in 1566.[312]

[310] Here again I follow Gordon, *op. cit.* (n. 27), pp. 117–28.

[311] See above, p. 287.

[312] *Methodus ad facilem historiarum cognitionem.* The modern English translation is B. Reynolds (trans.), *Jean Bodin, Method for the Easy Comprehension of History* (New York, 1945). The best commen-

[306]

Unlike the cosmographers and traditional historians of his day, Bodin in this work is rigorous in excluding natural and divine history from his considerations. He proposes to study history as the past of all human societies. To achieve this end he clearly recognizes how important to his analysis are the raw materials available in the geographies and the cosmographies. "For such is," he asserts, "the relationship and affinity of this subject [cosmography] to history that the one seems to be a part of the other." [313]

Bodin learned about the overseas world, its geographical divisions and its peoples, from his perusal of the cosmographies and the travel literature of the Middle Ages and his own day. Among the trustworthy narrators of the East who wrote informatively and disinterestedly he lists Francisco Alvarez on Ethiopia and Varthema on Asia.[314] He considers Boemus' collection of customs to be a valuable but meager source, primarily a help in differentiating one set of people from the other.[315] He unjustly criticizes Paolo Giovio for inventing his descriptions of countries and peoples.[316] He spurns all accounts of the Tartars except for the first-hand reports of Hayton and Marco Polo. Nor does he accept everything in their narratives. He contends that it is important to reject stories which overtax reason and the imagination as he endeavors to derive from Marco Polo a true outline of the customs, laws, and institutions of the Tartars.[317]

In the *Method* Bodin's conception of Asia is limited by the sources he used. He refers only in passing to India and not at all to China or Japan. He concentrates upon Tartary, Ethiopia, and the Levant. Most of what he reports about these areas and India comes from Marco Polo, Alvarez, Damião de Góis, and the cosmographies.[318] In his division of the world Bodin identifies America as the place where East and West meet "because this region is removed by boundless distances from India and Africa." [319] The equator in his definition divides North from South. Human beings and the societies in which they live are conditioned by geographical location and climate.[320] Tropical peoples are typically black, strong in holding to their languages and religious beliefs, and possessors of a calendar in which the year begins in the autumn.[321] Modern historians, primarily because of their better knowledge of geography and its effects, have

---

taries are J. L. Brown, *The Methodus . . . of Jean Bodin* (Washington, D.C., 1939), and J. H. Franklin, *Jean Bodin and the Sixteenth Century Revolution in the Methodology of Law and History* (New York, 1963). For Bodin's place in French historical thought of the sixteenth century see G. Huppert, *The Idea of Perfect History* (Urbana, 1970), pp. 99–105.

[313] Reynolds (trans.), *op. cit.* (n. 312), p. 25.

[314] *Ibid.*, p. 47.

[315] *Ibid.*, pp. 54, 85.

[316] *Ibid.*, pp. 60–61.

[317] *Ibid.*, p. 78.

[318] See list of materials, *ibid.*, pp. 367, 377–79.

[319] *Ibid.*, p. 87.

[320] For commentary see A. Meuton, *Bodins Theorie von der Beeinflüssung des politischen Lebens der Staaten durch ihre geographische Lage* (Bonn, 1904), pp. 29–30, 55–56.

[321] See Reynolds (trans.), *op. cit.* (n. 312), pp. 87, 127, 325, 340. For the argument that Bodin owed a heavy debt to medieval conceptions of climate and history see M. J. Tooley, "Bodin and the Medieval Theory of Climate," *Speculum*, XXVIII (1953), 64–83.

surpassed and improved upon the Ancients in their understanding of the diversities and unities in human society.[322]

In their analysis of political forms the Ancients were misled, according to Bodin, by their ignorance of the rest of the world. Plato, Polybius, and Cicero were wrong in asserting that monarchy must change to popular government, for the Scythians, Asiatics, and Americans have reportedly never had an aristocratic or popular form of government.[323] Aristotle was mistaken in equating hereditary monarchy with uncivilized societies, for it is impossible to argue that India and many other nations are uncivilized merely because they possess dynasties.[324] Civilization is universal and appears in various places and endures for differing periods of time. The Turks, Persians, Indians, and Tartars have established and maintained great empires whose history is not yet entirely clear.[325] Bodin derides the idea that the Holy Roman Empire is a continuator of the Roman Empire, or the last of the Four Monarchies of the periods into which world history was generally divided in his day.[326] The Tartar empire has a better claim to this role since it overthrew Babylon by itself.[327] In determining the antiquity of a nation and its civilization, it is necessary to look at language. By this measure the Oriental clearly antedate the Western nations.[328] From ancient times the various tribes of Asia have been migrating, colonizing, and intermingling. He discerns four motives for emigrating and colonizing: defeat by an enemy, surplus population, expansion to protect the domain, and penetration of the overseas world. The Spanish and Portuguese colonies are of a new type, but he foresees the day when the Iberian colonists will fuse with the natives.[329]

The *Method* is a call to study history in universal rather than national terms, to focus on problems of general import, and to include within its embrace all aspects of life.[330] The unity of mankind is a fundamental postulate of Bodin's viewpoint. The study of history is tied to geography as he accounts for change and variety in secular rather than in divine terms. By identifying certain common elements, such as religion and disease, as universal in scope, he sets the stage for comparative studies.[331] To make comparison possible it is necessary to study the

[322] See Reynolds (trans.), *op. cit.* (n. 312), p. 302.

[323] See *ibid.*, p. 216.

[324] *Ibid.*, p. 283.

[325] *Ibid.*, pp. 266–67, 273.

[326] On this traditional periodization of world history and its meaning for sixteenth-century French historians see G. Huppert, "The Renaissance Background of Historicism," *History and Theory*, V (1966), 55–57.

[327] Reynolds (trans.), *op. cit.* (n. 312), pp. 292–93.

[328] *Ibid.*, p. 340.

[329] *Ibid.*, pp. 361–62.

[330] On Bodin's place in "le mouvement de curiosité," presumably German in origin, see J. Moreau-Reibel, *Jean Bodin et le droit comparé dans ses rapports avec la philosophie de l'histoire* (Paris, 1933), pp. 85–87. Also see L. Febvre, "L'universalisme de Jean Bodin," *Revue de synthèse*, XXXVII (1934), 165–68, for a review of Moreau-Reibel.

[331] For example, see his remarks on the origin and spread of leprosy in Reynolds (trans.), *op. cit.* (n. 312), p. 107.

history of all known societies and their interconnections and interpenetrations. Bodin is also self-consciously preparing an approach which goes beyond the histories of Antiquity and the Renaissance in completeness by including the non-European world as an integral part of history and by making it subject to the same problems, changes, and motive forces that characterize Europe's history.

A contemporary of Bodin was the scholarly Louis Le Roy (1510–77), Humanist, translator, and historian of note. Born at Coutances in Normandy, he first appeared at Paris in 1530. After attending lectures there, he went to Toulouse in 1535 to study law. He returned to Paris in time to follow Guillaume Budé's body to its final resting place in 1540. An ardent admirer of the great classicist, Le Roy wrote Budé's biography in excellent Latin. The success of this work won him a court sinecure. Over the next twenty-five years he devoted himself to translating the great writers of Greek prose into French. In 1572 he became royal professor of Greek at Paris and died five years later. While Le Roy had traveled in Germany, Italy, and England, he was primarily a closeted scholar and writer. Nonetheless he probably felt more keenly the impact of the discoveries upon his thought and his historical work than did most of his better-traveled contemporaries. His prose works in French, written in an elegant style, also contributed significantly to the establishment of the vernacular as a respectable medium of scholarly expression.

An avid student of the classics and of Greek civilization, Le Roy throughout his scholarly life was nonetheless a modernist in outlook. In his biography of Budé, he stresses the uniqueness of modern men and their superiority to ancient men. Like Vives, Le Roy supports his assertion of superiority by reference to the discoveries overseas of lands, seas, men, plants, and animals unknown to the Greeks and Romans.[332] It is, however, in his historical works published between 1567 and 1572 that he most clearly indicates how he sees the effects of the overseas discoveries upon European thought. In a treatise on the history of political theory, he points out how it is possible for Europe to learn from the advanced as well as the primitive societies recently discovered. For example, to study and understand India is to see how philosophy itself developed.[333] In a pamphlet on religion he observes that religious diversity is a prime source of hostility and war. But he is hopeful that the missionaries will be able to spread Christianity to the entire world and thereby bring about religious unity and peace.[334] From these isolated comments it is already clear that Le Roy, like Postel before him, saw history as following a pattern of ascent or progress.[335]

---

[332] Pointed out in Kinser, *loc. cit.* (n. 8), pp. 744–45. On Vives see above, p. 173.

[333] *De l'origine, antiquité, progres, excellence, et utilité de l'art politique* (Paris, 1567), p. 10ʳ; as a contrast see the work of Guillaume de la Perrière published in the same year and entitled *Le miroir politique . . .* (Paris). In speaking of India he cites Solinus on Taprobane and barely mentions the spice traffic between Calicut and Europe.

[334] *Des troubles et differens advenans entre les hommes par la diversité des religions* (Lyons, 1568), p. 6ᵛ. For commentary see B. L. O. Richter, "The Thought of Louis Le Roy according to His Early Pamphlets," *Studies in the Renaissance*, VIII (1961), 173–96.

[335] On Postel's idea of progress see Bouwsma, *op. cit.* (n. 68), pp. 286–87.

Le Roy began to pull together his ideas about historical process in his popular *Considerations par l'histoire française, et l'universelle de ce temps . . .* (Paris, 1567).[336] While this work centers on the year 1559 in France, it contains in embryo many of his ideas about world history later documented in more detail. The problems afflicting France are universal in scope and illustrate the interrelatedness of the world. Actions in the most distant places produce reactions in Europe, as for example the strife over the Moluccas which impairs relations between Spain and Portugal.[337] The historian must, however, be equally conscious of the interrelatedness of the world through time. Had not modern man recovered the learning of Antiquity as well as acquiring a superior knowledge of the vast extent and multitudinous variety of the world? To see the world in all its dimensions the historian must tower above it and have intellectual dominion over it. He must see that Cathay as well as Rome was a great empire in Antiquity. He must also understand that modern man in Asia surpasses his forefathers. To write true history he must comprehend all aspects of the past and present and transmit to his readers a sense of the complexities reflected and produced by historical interaction and change. He will notice that empires regularly rise and fall but that the pattern of history is nonetheless a spiral of gradual ascent.[338]

Le Roy's major work on universal history is called *De la vicissitude ou varieté des choses en l'univers* (Paris, 1575).[339] Through it run two basic themes. The first is the rather simple proposition that change is constant and that as one empire or nation falls from predominance another rises to take its place. The second is an assertion to the effect that in any nation great achievements in arms and letters take place concurrently. He assumes that men everywhere are the same and like Bodin accounts for diversity by reference to the effects of climate upon places, peoples, and institutions. Men are naturally restless and bent on conquest and change. Great cities which did not exist in ancient times have since grown up in the East and elsewhere.

But material civilization is not the only aspect of life that changes constantly. The arts and sciences are likewise always in flux, witness the revival of ancient learning in the Renaissance. Languages like Latin decline, become corrupt, and are replaced by dynamic vernaculars which reflect a nation's character and answer its peculiar needs. New inventions, like printing, raise questions for him of independent development versus diffusion, and receptivity versus nonreceptivity. For example:

This is that which wee have understoode of this Art [printing] unknown heretofore amongst Greek and Romains; whereof the Almains [Germans] attribute the invention to themselves. Notwithstanding the Portugals trafiching on the farthest parts of the East, and the North, into China and Cathay, have brought there hence books printed in the languag, and writing of that contrey, saying that they have used it there a long time:

---

[336] Reissued seven times between 1567 and 1588. See Atkinson, *Les nouveaux horizons* (n. 6), p. 22.
[337] On this problem in the 1560's see above, pp. 33-34.
[338] Analysis based on Gordon, *op. cit.* (n. 27), pp. 152-56.
[339] Reprinted four times between 1575 and 1583. See Atkinson, *Les nouveaux horizons* (n. 6), p. 22.

which have moved some to thinke, that the invention hath bin brought out of that Countrey through Tartaria and Moscovia, into Germany, and so after communicated to the rest of Christiandome: and yet not received of the Mahometistes; who superstitiously account it a great sinne to write their Alcoran by any other means but by the hand of man.[340]

He might also have noted, though he does not, that other intermediary groups likewise failed to borrow the Chinese invention on its trip to Europe.

The voyages of discovery in the sixteenth century also put the Roman empire into a new perspective. However mighty Rome had been, it never possessed more than one-twelfth of the earth. It knew nothing of the land mass of America and had no control whatever over the great states of Asia. The rise of the Tartar empire with its many vassal states is astounding, particularly when one recalls that it originated with rough and rude nomadic tribes.

The great Cham of Catay is also a Tartarian, descended of the race of Changuis [Genghis Khan]. . . . It is not without cause that he exceedeth in politiche government, power, wisdom, revenew, and Magnificence, all the Princes of Europe, Asia, and Afriche; yea even the Turke himself. And if all the Christian and Saracen Seegnories were reduced under one obedience, yet they could not be compared unto his.[341]

This vast and beautiful empire boasts many talented artisans. Then, as he continues to confuse Cathay with China, he notes that its people excel in learning and in the sciences, and that public offices are neither inherited nor purchased. "They respect not nobilitie, nor riches; but learning and vertue onelie"[342] in awarding offices. This empire, like that of "Narsingue" (Vijayanagar) and Prester John, supports his argument for the concurrence between superiority in armed strength and excellence in learning.[343]

In his last three books, Le Roy discusses the problems and achievements of his own century. Instead of organizing these books along national lines, he treats his own day in terms of movements and topics. His object is to show the world as an interdependent commonwealth and to point out the similarities and differences which provide it with variety and interest. The peoples of the world suffer in common from the affliction of war. The kings of Castile and Portugal receive special mention because they carried forward the overseas conquests and discoveries. Like Thevet, he seems to be particularly impressed with the achievements of Albuquerque and Magellan and classifies them as two of the most illustrious men of the age. The historians of the expansion movement likewise receive special recognition: Peter Martyr, Paolo Giovio, Francisco Alvarez, Damião de Góis, João de Barros, Oviedo, and Münster. The three greatest inventions of the century—printing, the compass, and artillery—all with Chinese antecedents, were helpful in exploring and conquering the overseas

---

[340] From the English translation called *Of the Interchangeable Course, or Variety of Things in the Whole World* (London, 1594), p. 22.

[341] *Ibid.*, p. 104^v.

[342] *Ibid.*

[343] On this point see Gordon, *op. cit.* (n. 27), pp. 167–69.

world. The artisans of China he recognizes as the best in the world for they approach the Ancients in some skills and surpass them in others. He concludes by exhorting his contemporaries to add to human knowledge. Although Le Roy clearly recognized the temporary and changing character of knowledge, he did not despair about the future. God in his mercy might suspend his laws about the decline and fall of empires and great ages if he saw men diligently applying themselves to the task of improving their own lot upon this earth rather than reveling in and squandering their riches.[344]

Bodin, like Le Roy, was also interested at this time in universal themes and in comparative history. Greatly perturbed by the revolutionary activities set in motion by the massacres of St. Bartholomew's Day (1572), Bodin published in 1576 a thorough and elaborate justification of absolute and indivisible sovereignty. In *Les six livres de la république* (Paris) he insists that monarchs are subject only to the laws of God and nature.[345] He claims that monarchy is the most natural form of government and that all countries had kings in the beginning.[346] One of his prime examples is Tartary, which he praises as being one of the "greatest and most flourishing monarchies and kingdomes that now are, or ever were in the whole world." [347] After the election of a Tartar king, the new ruler tells his subjects that they must be "readie to performe whatsoevere I command." [348] Furthermore, should the king fail to fulfill his duties, he will be removed by God and not by his subjects. Whatever the historicity of these assertions, Bodin envisages the Tartar political system as a model of absolute sovereignty. The negus of Ethiopia, on the contrary, is the model of the ruler whose claims to absolute sovereignty are invalid because he does homage to the Portuguese.[349] But no matter where he looks, Bodin finds no kingdom as ancient or with as continuous a line of succession as France.[350] Consequently, there is every reason for the kings of France to reject all rationales and claims which seek to impose limits on their sovereignty.

Bodin asserts that many princes in Asia and Africa possess absolute power over the bodies and goods of their subjects.[351] Despotic monarchy, like slavery, arises primarily from conquest and runs counter to the law of nature. While he recognizes it as a legitimate form of monarchy, Bodin associates despotism with the East and warns that most despots abuse their power and their subjects. In a

[344] For a general discussion of the optimism of certain writers of this age see H. Baron, "The *Querelle* as a Problem for Renaissance Scholarship," *Journal of the History of Ideas*, XX (1959), 3–22.

[345] For an analysis of his doctrine of sovereignty see J. H. Franklin, *Jean Bodin and the Rise of Absolutist Theory* (Cambridge, 1973), pp. 23, 41.

[346] See K. D. McRae (ed.), *Jean Bodin: The Six Books of a Commonweale* (a facsimile reprint of the English translation of 1606; Cambridge, Mass., 1962), p. 719.

[347] *Ibid.*, p. 485.

[348] *Ibid.*, p. 89.

[349] *Ibid.*, p. 147.

[350] *Ibid.*, p. 150. Clearly, Bodin had no knowledge at this time of the history of the Chinese empire.

[351] *Ibid.*, p. 201. See commentary in F. Venturi, "Oriental Despotism," *Journal of the History of Ideas*, XXIV (1963), 134–35, and R. Koebner, "Despot and Despotism, Vicissitudes of a Political Term," *Journal of the Warburg and Courtauld Institutes*, XIV (1951), 275–302.

number of these countries, including India, a people weary of repression will choose a new form of government, rather than just a new despot, when the line of succession fails.[352] In almost all the states of Asia it is unlawful for subjects to revolt against a legitimate sovereign.[353] In certain of them the subjects are forbidden to emigrate for any reason whatsoever.[354] The Chinese ruler even ordains that his subjects may not receive strangers, and the king of Tartary has no hesitation in confiscating the goods of strangers who die there.[355] The Eastern kings expect servile obedience and even whip their nobles.[356] The ruler should not hide himself from the people as the king of Borneo reputedly does; it is better to follow the example of the ruler of Tartary and to appear only infrequently and then in a pompous display of majesty and power.[357] To prevent sedition the king should follow the example of those rulers of the East who take away the subject's arms, prohibit his building and maintaining of castles and fortresses, and forbid the use of bells to arouse the people to revolt.[358]

Rulers, like others, must realize that environment helps to shape the special practices prevailing in different places. While it is true in general that wives derive their status from husbands, the Nāyars of Calicut receive theirs from the noble women who bear them.[359] The Tartars permit fathers to sell their sons four times, "after which if he shall redeeme himself he is for ever free."[360] In the East the fathers recognize all their children, legitimate and illegitimate, and all share in the inheritance.[361] Throughout the East (he refers to the Islamic East here) it is a capital crime to draw the portrait of any living plant or creature.[362] Location and climate also affect "civilitie," particularly as between the peoples of East and West.

For although there is not any certaine place [like the equator], whereas we may distinguish the East from the West, as we may the South from the North: yet all ancients have held, that the people of The East are more mild, more courteous, more tractable, and more ingenious than those of the West, and less warlike. ... The Spaniards have observed that the people of Sina (the which are the farthest Eastward) are the most ingenious and courteous people in the world.[363]

Bodin is aware that the Iberians in the East have raised new problems of importance to international law. He lists many places which give fealty and pay tribute to Portugal, and stresses the point that no feudatory kings of Asia are

---

[352] McRae (ed.), *op. cit.* (n. 346), p. 206.
[353] *Ibid.*, p. 222.
[354] *Ibid.*, p. 60.
[355] *Ibid.*, pp. 66–67.
[356] *Ibid.*, pp. 121, 202.
[357] *Ibid.*, pp. 506–7.
[358] *Ibid.*, pp. 541–42, 605.
[359] *Ibid.*, p. 20.
[360] *Ibid.*, p. 23.
[361] *Ibid.*, p. 29.
[362] *Ibid.*, p. 400.
[363] *Ibid.*, p. 562.

exempt from paying tribute to Lisbon.[364] He notes that the Portuguese concluded alliances sealed in blood with the princes of the East, and accepted the idea of negotiating with other Eastern sovereigns on a basis of equality.[365] After commenting on the miserable conditions of slaves in the East, he laments that the Portuguese are reintroducing slavery into Europe.[366] In discussing the question of wealth in a state and its relation to international trade, he notes that the Portuguese "have for these hundred yeares [1475–1575] traded without reproach, and to the great enriching of their states."[367] As a consequence they "filled Europe with the treasures of the East,"[368] and undermined the commerce of the Turks, Egyptians, and Venetians. Italy, he asserts, suffered as much from the loss of Eastern trade as it had from the wars of Louis XII. More than a decade later, in one of his major works on economic theory, Bodin accounts for the growing wealth of France by reference to its increased share of Oriental commerce.[369]

Clearly the East played a role in the historical, political, and economic thought of Bodin. His use of the available sources is selective rather than exhaustive. The materials on the overseas world provide him with many examples of diversity and comparison as well as models for certain of his ideas on absolutism and international trade. In the *République*, for example, there are 146 references to contemporary non-European peoples in its 739 pages.[370] He was certainly conscious that he was dealing with advanced civilizations in Asia and was especially aware, without being condemnatory, of their traditional customs and morals. He even knows that they rely on a different calendar, and later he learned that the chronologies of the Egyptians and Chinese are longer than those of the Christian nations.[371] In almost all his comments about the differences between the religions of Asia and Europe he exhibits restraint and tolerance.[372] Bodin, like Montaigne, was more inclined to be critical of his own society than of those he knew only partially and by the reports of others.

That French interest in the East was not exclusively the province of Catholic scholars, and that it was of substantial general interest, is best illustrated by the

[364] *Ibid.*, pp. 147–48.

[365] *Ibid.*, p. 631. For comment on this and other theoretical questions of international law raised by the expansion into Asia see C. H. Alexandrowicz, *An Introduction to the History of the Law of Nations in the East Indies* (Oxford, 1967), pp. 30–31.

[366] McRae (ed.), *op. cit.* (n. 346), pp. 36, 44.

[367] *Ibid.*, p. 660.

[368] *Ibid.*

[369] In a tract written as a refutation of the views of Malestroit, comptroller of the mint. The *Reponses aux paradoxes de M. de Malestroict* (Paris, 1588) is his explanation of the price revolution of the sixteenth century in terms of the amount of money in circulation, the variation in general prices, and the relations among money, prices, and wages.

[370] Count of Atkinson, *Les nouveaux horizons* (n. 6), p. 322.

[371] J. Bodin, *Universae naturae theatrum* . . . (Lyons, 1596), p. 560. First edition appeared in 1590.

[372] Bodin's most interesting piece on religious toleration is the *Colloquium Heptaplomeres de abditis rerum sublimium arcanis*. Written in 1588, it was not published until the mid-nineteenth century. One of his major sources for this work was the unpublished papers of Guillaume Postel. For examples of his numerous references to Asian religious beliefs, practices, and ceremonies, see R. Chauviré (trans. and ed.), *Colloque de Jean Bodin* . . . (Paris, 1914), pp. 2, 55, 56, 67, 89, 106.

writings of the Huguenot Henri Lancelot Voisin, sieur de la Popelinière (1541?–1608). Born in Poitou, La Popelinière received an education in classical letters at Paris and in law at Toulouse. For a time he served in the naval and armed forces of the Huguenots. But in 1571, the year following the appearance of Bodin's *République*, he retired from military life to devote his remaining years to writing and publishing. His first book was a lengthy history of the civil wars in France from 1555 to 1581.[373] Thereafter he devoted himself mainly to less controversial topics and soon won a reputation for being a dispassionate, objective, and creative historian.

La Popelinière's *Les trois mondes* (Paris, 1582) is a call to his countrymen to take a more active role in overseas expansion, conquest, and colonization.[374] Like Jean Alfonse forty years earlier, he also wishes to record for posterity the exploits of the voyagers. He sees discovery and exploration as in themselves important contributions to human knowledge. He is an advocate of southward expansion, especially in America; here there remain untapped resources and possibilities for colonial plantations. He buttresses his arguments by recounting the history of expansion and questions the current assumption that the countries recently discovered were completely unknown to the Ancients. He points out that the Mediterranean nations of the past carried on a substantial trade with distant peoples and that they might have known about the Atlantic islands, even the West Indies. Certainly the writings of Herodotus and Pliny are full of stories about Asia, its products and peoples. The vestiges of early Christianity discovered in distant places like India and Japan reinforce his argument that the Ancients knew much more about the outside world than many of his contemporaries believed.

Most of his comments on Asia appear in Book I in the discussion of the Portuguese expansion movement. Here he concludes that the ancient geographers knew nothing of the islands of Southeast Asia and Japan that appear on the maps of Mercator and Thevet.[375] The Portuguese in the East, unlike the Spanish in America, ran into heavy resistance and were consequently unable to carry out a complete conquest. The peoples of the East were able to fend off the Portuguese because of their military organization and their valor. Climate and geographical isolation had also permitted the nations of the East to develop independent civilizations of great sophistication. Like Postel, La Popelinière is mightily impressed by Asia as a source of culture and suggests that the foundations of Western learning might have been laid in the East. The Portuguese, when

[373] *Histoire des troubles et guerres civiles en France pour le fait de la religion, depuis 1555 jusqu'en 1581* (2 vols.; La Rochelle, 1581).

[374] There are two editions of the same year which differ in organization and content. See Atkinson, *Répertoire bibliographique* (n. 94), items 291–92. I have used the one published by Olivier de Pierre L'Huillier which is in the Newberry Library (Chicago).

[375] *Les trois mondes* (Paris, 1582), p. 47^v. For his remarks on Chinese merchandise in America see p. 24^v. His account of Magellan's voyage (Book III, pp. 37^r–37^v) stresses the importance of keeping records. Probably he had Pigafetta's diary in mind. This work also includes a map of the world, probably based on Ortelius'.

confronted by the superior power and high civilization of the Eastern nations, wisely decided to support the Jesuits and their policies of peaceful penetration and of religious persuasion.[376]

New information on Asia flowed into France in a swelling stream after the publication of *Les trois mondes* in 1582. La Popelinière sagely continued to read, digest, and evaluate it as he contemplated the problem of writing universal history.[377] He was convinced that the Moderns who had surpassed the Ancients in several ways, especially by the invention of printing, ought to be able to surpass Herodotus in writing history. In his *L'idée d'histoire accomplie* (Paris, 1599) La Popelinière sets forth his thoughts on the scope and emphasis of universal history. It should be comprehensive enough to treat adequately the past and present of all peoples. The "curiosities" of the overseas world are not important in themselves but for what they reveal about the world and its historical evolution. A satisfying history should be far more than a chronicle of events; it should explain how and why particular happenings occurred, including the causes of the European expansion overseas. Study of the peculiar characteristics of the Oriental nations should shed light on the origin and development of highly civilized peoples. An examination of the materials on the societies of America should reveal how men pass from the primitive to the civilized state. He later (1604) wrote to J. J. Scaliger in an effort to obtain help in getting passage to America to study its society at first hand.[378] Throughout his writing La Popelinière stresses the common humanity of man and the universal attributes of his societies. He believes with Bodin that universal history begins wherever there is found the first evidence of an organized life beyond the state of nature. To express this idea of origins and to bring out the elements typical of society's evolution he was one of the first to formulate a conception of *civilization* and to advocate studying history in terms of its development.[379] The study of the origin and development of civilization through history would, he suggests, reveal the evolutionary process by which men passed from primitivism to *civilité* and by which civilization itself progressed toward higher levels of refinement and sophistication.[380]

The genres of contemporary history and chronicle, or "history of one's own

[376] For a complete summary and analysis of the relevant parts of this work see Gordon, *op. cit.* (n. 27), pp. 184–98.

[377] He includes a brief bibliographical essay and critique on sources for the history of overseas discoveries in *L'Histoire des histoires* (Paris, 1599), pp. 487–90. Here he criticizes the cosmographies of Belleforest and Thevet for being unreliable.

[378] For Scaliger's interests in Asia see below, pp. 358–59.

[379] He gives his first definition of "civilization" in *L'Amiral de France* (Paris, 1585), p. 14. For commentary on his refinement of the idea see C. Vivanti, "Alla origini dell'idea di civiltà: le scoperte geografiche e gli scritti di Henri de la Popelinière," *Revista storica italiana*, LXXIV (1962), 225–49; and F. Papi, *Antropologia e civiltà nel pensiero di Giordano Bruno* (Florence, 1968), pp. 334–35 for the relation of his thought to those of his contemporaries with similar ideas.

[380] The word *civilisation* was not in the vocabulary of the sixteenth century. For a history and an interpretation of the word *civilité* as a synonym for *civilisation* see G. Huppert, "The Idea of Civilization in the Sixteenth Century," in A. Molho and J. A. Tedeschi (eds.), *op. cit.* (n. 8), pp. 757–69.

times," likewise tend more and more to be universal rather than merely national or European in scope. The traditional chronicle was almost always a compilation of data which purported to be universal; in actuality exclusively European, the chronicles glorified the noble, Christian, and patriotic traditions of France and its neighbors. Those which treat the first years of the sixteenth century faithfully record battles and skirmishes in Europe and mention neither the Turks nor the overseas discoveries. Events in the eastern Mediterranean begin to creep into the chronicles after France allied itself with the Ottoman state in 1535. After mid-century, however, particularly as the *Histoires de notre temps* became more common, a few references are insinuated into the general chronicles about activities overseas. Retrospective chronicles likewise broaden their horizons enough to include the early discoveries of moment. Nicolas Vignier's *Biblio-thèque historiale* (Paris, 1588), for example, which deals with the period from 1095 to 1519 repeatedly notices the conquests overseas after 1492 and concludes with a reference to Magellan's trip around the world.[381] By the end of the century Palma Gayet was beginning to collect systematically everything news-worthy on overseas activities. His *Chronologie septenaire* (Paris, 1605), which went through six editions over five years, is a chronicle of the events of impor-tance that took place in Africa, Asia, and America from 1593 to 1604.[382] In the meantime the Jesuit letterbooks and the translations of their chronicles of secular and ecclesiastical enterprise in the East continued to be sold in the book stalls of Paris to the public at large.[383]

The best example of the universal chronicle of recent and contemporary events to appear at the turn of the century was Jacques-Auguste de Thou's *History of His Own Times* in Latin.[384] A courtier, diplomat, and bibliophile of great importance, De Thou was a participant in and recorder of the most dramatic events to rock France in the latter half of the century. He traveled extensively outside of France, but never ventured overseas. He was in Bordeaux when Montaigne was its mayor, and the two men of affairs and great intellect quickly came to realize they had much in common. De Thou, like Montaigne, was a sympathizer of and eager participant in the rise to power of Henry IV. Once the king was established in Paris, De Thou took charge of the royal library and accepted a number of special assignments, including the drafting of the Edict of Nantes (1598) by which the Huguenots received official toleration. In the

---

[381] Pointed out in Huppert, *loc. cit.* (n. 380), pp. 131–32.

[382] See Atkinson, *Les nouveaux horizons* (n. 6), p. 23.

[383] For example, in 1608 Pierre de L'Estoile bought a copy of the letterbook of Jacques de Pantoie on the successes of the Jesuits in China. See G. Brunet *et al.* (eds.), *Mémoires-journaux de Pierre de L'Estoile* (12 vols.; Paris, 1875–96), IX, 179.

[384] *Historiarum sui temporis* (Paris, 1604–17). De Thou constantly revised and added to this text in the editions which appeared during his lifetime. His literary beneficiaries made revisions and additions of their own in the posthumous editions. The *Historiarum* has never been published in its entirety. The most complete edition, and the one now most frequently cited, is the French translation called *Histoire universelle de Jacques-Auguste de Thou, depuis 1543 [sic] jusqu'en 1607* (16 vols.; London [Paris], 1734). For a thorough bibliographical analysis of De Thou's work and its many editions and trans-lations see S. Kinser, *The Works of Jacques-Auguste de Thou* (The Hague, 1966), *passim*.

meantime, beginning in 1591, he put together and wrote the *History of His Own Times*, a huge work of almost five thousand printed folio pages.

De Thou chronicled over sixty years (1545–1607) of contemporary history. In the introduction he provides a brief synthesis of background material on the years from 1494 to 1545. Here he gives a resumé of the progress of the Portuguese in the East and avers that their government of Asia has been "gentle and humane and always free of rapine, plunder and civil war." [385] For the period from 1545 to 1607 he presents his material in an annalistic order. He has almost nothing to report about Japan until he reaches 1585, the year when the young Japanese emissaries presented themselves at Rome. He reports in lavish detail on this spectacle and takes it as an opportunity to describe Japan itself. He cuts short his digression on the climate and geography of Japan by stating that he does not want to bore the reader "who expects other things of me, and is able, if he desires to, to find in others enough on these matters to satisfy himself." [386] One of these "others," whom he later cites himself, is the Portuguese João de Barros,[387] whose volumes he probably had at this time in his magnificent personal library.[388] He is particularly moved by the voyages of the Dutch to the East Indies at the end of the century. In recounting their activities he digresses on the geography, history, manners, plants, and animals of insular Southeast Asia and of the Portuguese activities there prior to the arrival of the Dutch in 1596. Bantam (Java) he judges to be as large as Amsterdam, and provides details on its markets, houses, mosques, and trade. He even describes in some detail the emu which the Dutch brought back with them.[389] Later he records other Dutch voyages to the East, includes comments based on Linschoten about manners, discourses on battles among the Europeans in the region, and provides lengthy descriptions of Ceylon, the Moluccas, Malaya, and Siam.[390] He reports almost nothing on China, perhaps because no European events occurred to permit a digression on the progress of the Jesuits there.[391]

The chronicle, one of the earliest forms of French historical writing, was the latest in broadening its perspective to admit the East as an integral part of universal history. De Thou, for example, concentrates his attention on Southeast Asia and Japan as lands first discovered in the sixteenth century and consequently as parts of the "New World." He follows the lead of the French cosmographers in stressing the geographical and physical in his vignettes of the "New World." [392] References to India and China in most of the histories pass lightly over topography and center on customs, dress, religious beliefs, technical advancement, and

[385] *Histoire universelle* (n. 384), I, 72.

[386] *Ibid.*, IX, 342.

[387] *Ibid.*, p. 344.

[388] On his library see above, p. 68.

[389] See *Histoire universelle* (n. 384), XIII, 57–61. On this emu see *Asia*, II, Bk. 1, 182–83.

[390] *Histoire universelle* (n. 384), XIV, 222–43.

[391] He records only that Xavier carried the Gospel to China and died off its coast. See *ibid.*, IX, 342–43.

[392] See B. W. Bates, *Literary Portraiture in the Historical Narrative of the French Renaissance* (New York, 1945), pp. 102, 116–17.

governments. In terms of detailed descriptions the cosmographies include more from the traditional sources, geographies, travel accounts, and ethnohistories than is to be found in the writings of the universal historians and chroniclers. La Popelinière, in particular, urged that the travel accounts should be respected as genuine contributions to knowledge, that they should be examined critically in the light of traditional and recent knowledge, and that they should be proved out and supplemented by travel on the part of the historian himself.

Cosmographers, chroniclers, and historians held in common the strong conviction that Moderns were superior to Ancients in their knowledge of the world and in their invention of printing and artillery. They shared an enthusiasm for new information of the kind that Gargantua advised Pantagruel to cultivate:

Keep your memory well stocked with every tale from history, and here you will find help in the cosmographies of the historians. . . . All the birds of the air, shrubs and bushes of the forest, all the herbs of the field, all the metals deep in the bowels of the earth, the precious stones of the whole East and the South—let none of them be unknown to you.[393]

A growing consciousness of the tumultous variety in the world was accompanied by a sturdy sense of tolerance for diversity, even in religion. It was clear from the vestiges that remained that Christianity had once been the religion of Asia as well as Europe and that the missionaries might be successful in reestablishing it as the universal faith. Comparisons between Europe and the overseas world, as well as comparisons among the various parts of the non-European world themselves, were implicit in even the most encyclopedic and noninferential of the historical works.

The historians, in contrast to the cosmographers and chroniclers, sought self-consciously to examine the implications of the discovery of the world for historical thought. In his *Method* Bodin identified history as a discipline which should be secular rather than religious and should focus on the study of all human societies and institutions. He accounted for diversity by reference to climate and geography. But within diversity he perceived unity in the problems common to all societies: governmental institutions, religion, emigration, and colonization. Within his argument the idea was budding that the histories of all peoples are subject to the same motive forces. Le Roy and La Popelinière were impressed by the interrelatedness of the world and by the effects of events in distant places upon Europe itself. Both clearly understood that Europe had much to learn in practical and intellectual matters from the high civilizations of Asia.

Theoretical principles also emerged in the considerations of the historians. Bodin stressed the importance of studying common problems comparatively as he does with the idea of monarchy in the *République*. Le Roy was impressed by the coincidence in time between the rediscovery of Antiquity and the exploration of the overseas world. The discovery of printing in China raised for him the problems implicit in cultural diffusion. In his observations on empire

393 Cohen (trans.), *op. cit.* (n. 31), p. 195.

he perceived a pattern of rise and decline and concluded that change is constant. Great imperial power is accompanied, he believed, by superlative achievements in the arts. The history of mankind, though it records the decline and fall of empires, nonetheless follows a spiraling ascent. To him and to La Popelinière the discoveries were important for the light they shed on historical evolution and on the perspective they provided for the study of general movements and ideas. It was obvious to La Popelinière, as it had been to Postel, that religious persuasion rather than arms would help to restore world unity. Since persuasion involved understanding of the foreign, it was necessary to study the foundations, evolution, and preconceptions of the civilizations being approached. Indeed, history itself, he suggested, should most properly be concerned with study of the process we call civilization.

The French learned about Asia mainly from translations of classics, geographies, romances, satires, cosmographies, ethnohistories, and chronicle-narratives. Naturally, many of the literati, like Montaigne, read Latin as well as they did French so that they also had access to relevant Latin materials that went untranslated. In the first half of the century most of the works translated were Latin writings, both classical and recent; a number of romances and satires were also translated into French from Italian and German before 1550. In the latter half of the century, a much higher percentage of the translations were of works originally written in vernacular languages, including Spanish and Portuguese.

Because they learned of the East through intermediaries, the French writers of the first half of the century were often vague about its placement and geography. They were unresponsive or slow to react to great new achievements, as Rabelais was to the discovery of Japan. Dependent upon traditional geography, the French tended to divide the world sharply into what the Ancients knew and what had but recently become known. As a consequence they were more explicit than others in putting Japan and insular Southeast Asia into the "New World." For most writers India retained its traditional delineation as a magical and marvelous land, a backdrop for romance. Tartary received an astonishing amount of attention, especially from Bodin, because of the continued reliance of the French upon medieval sources. China was initially respected for its invention of printing and artillery, a discovery which profoundly shocked orthodox believers in European superiority. At the end of the century Charron and others suggested that China's priority in these discoveries should lead not to the humiliation of Europe but to new certitude in the enduring value of the new techniques. China, in a word, was thought of as a secular and peaceful society, a model for what Europe might hope to become.[394]

Most of the basic literary forms, except the historical, were not changed appreciably as they accommodated themselves to the new knowledge of the outside world. The revelation of the East and America provided mainly a new,

[394] Cf. A. Du Pront, "Espace et humanisme," *Bibliothèque d'humanisme et renaissance*, VIII (1946), 40–50.

exotic subject matter which helped to accelerate the trend away from religious to secular themes. Maritime voyages and overseas places, both fabulous and real, figured more prominently than before in both poetical and prose writings. Some of the authors also called for France to participate more actively in the exploration and opening of the overseas world. Primarily, however, a new tone, anticipatory of the eighteenth century, entered French literature. While continuing to see Asia in traditional terms as the seat of religion, magic, and the occult, the literati also began to see it as a real place comparable to Europe. Macer and Bouchet satirized Europe's own institutions and practices by comparing them to what they had learned about the customs of India, China, and Japan. A tendency to Encyclopedism, especially in the compilations of prodigies and in the cosmographies, implicitly promoted comparison by placing alongside one another the descriptions of manners, morals, and customs in distant places with those of Europe itself. If Encyclopedism evokes Diderot, then certainly Montaigne anticipated Voltaire's skepticism and Bodin the geographical determinism of Montesquieu. The analogy could be pushed further, but it is probably sufficient to conclude it by reference to the Sinophilism common to both centuries.

The sixteenth-century poets were the least responsive of all French literary groups to the opening of the world. Except for Parmentier early in the century, they were only faintly curious about the voyages of exploration. A number of the poets of the Pléiade were moved by Thevet's cosmographical works and Grouchy's translation to comment on the discoveries. As a rule they, like Buchanan, deplored the avarice of the Portuguese and the cost in human suffering exacted by the spice trade and the long and sometimes disastrous maritime voyages. Accordingly, they pointed out that Europeans are no less barbarous than Brazilians; Ronsard and others compared the natives of the New World before the coming of the Europeans to the happy people of the mythical Golden Age. In their definition of the "New World," the poets, like the cosmographers, included those parts of Asia that were as unknown as America to the Ancients. In his *Sepmaines* Du Bartas brings the Asia of the cosmographers into the mainstream of French poetry; in his commentaries on the *Sepmaines* Goulart prepared a thesaurus of the new learning that was to become a repository of exotic matter for later poets to draw upon. All the poets—lyrical, metaphysical, and cosmographical—were impressed by the variety of the world as it opened before them and were bewitched by the strange euphonious names of distant places and peoples.

Writers of popular prose responded somewhat more positively than the poets to the maritime and overseas ventures. Rabelais, in particular, was fascinated by the voyages, attracted by the sea, and sensitive to the challenge to Europe implicit in the opening of Asia. The translations and imitations of Boemus, the "curious histories," and the romances aroused a profound popular interest, as reflected in the multiple editions of these works that were actually printed, in diverse manners, morals, and ideas. While foreign and "barbarian"

ways were tidbits of entertainment to the parochial, they provided more sophisticated readers with food for thought. While both Macer and Bouchet ridiculed
certain alien practices, they likewise debated quite openly their relative worth.
They exhibited an amazing degree of tolerance toward differences in religious
practices, possibly a reflection of the divided religious condition of France itself.
Ordinarily they did not endeavor to probe behind the outward aspects of strange
customs, but Bouchet advocated painting people the color they really are. At
the end of the century the novelists and dramatists began to employ overseas
locales, characters, and strange names and practices in their literary pieces.
Comparisons between European and alien practices generally remained implicit
rather than explicit in all forms of popular literature.

The challenge to Europe of the opening of the world was explicitly recognized
and assessed by writers of didactic prose from Postel to Charron. A contemporary
of Rabelais, Postel hurled the challenge forcefully to the middle generation of
the century. He forthrightly proclaimed the superiority of East over West as
the homeland of religion, wisdom, and language. The Japanese, the people
farthest to the East and the nation most recently discovered, he pronounced a
model for Europe. He was also the most assured advocate of the universality of
Christianity before the dispersion after Babel. His contemporaries, completely
unprepared as they were for such radical ideas, were often convinced that
Postel was not quite sane. Postel himself contributed to the growth of such an
idea by his irascibility and his open flirtation with Jewish and Protestant beliefs.
A few other unorthodox spirits, particularly among the poets, occultists, and
linguists, continued to respect Postel and to learn from him. Others either
ignored or denounced Postel's works and unconsciously or semiconsciously
began to examine timidly the breach that he had opened in the edifice of Europe's
belief in the superiority of Western learning and accomplishment.

Pontus de Tyard and Montaigne shared a healthy skepticism about the
sanctity of European learning, whether of Antiquity or of their own era. Both
were perturbed by the limited character of human understanding, especially
with regard to alien places and peoples. Both believed strongly that the new and
the old learning had to be scrutinized carefully, viewed without prejudice, and
weighed in the same balance. The Moderns, they concluded, are clearly superior
to the Ancients in knowledge of geography and technology. Montaigne denounced the European idea of branding everything alien as "barbaric." The
ideas and practices of others must be understood in their own terms and not by
European standards. Even good and evil, Montaigne avowed, is determined in
large part, by "the opinion we have of them." Nor was he convinced that the
entire world in all its variety had been seen by the men of his day. Charron
likewise believed that new discoveries would be made. Consequently, he argued
that it was essential to human progress for men to keep their minds open.
Charron, unlike Montaigne, was an advocate of action and impatient with contemplation. Since all customs, however strange, are what they are for some good
reason, Charron was convinced that Europe should make an active effort to

learn for itself from the experiences of others. He, like Montaigne, saw China as the nation from which Europe had most to learn.

The historians, too, were impressed by the infinite variety of the world, by the host of implicit and explicit comparisons in terms of both space and time that it contains, and by the relativism that must obtain in making objective judgments about manners, morals, and beliefs with respect to all places and times. But in no instance do they subject the Christian faith to their new objectivity. To solve the problem of writing universal history they tried several approaches. De Thou, like the Portuguese historians, converted the traditional chronicle of recent history into a broadened chronicle-narrative that included descriptions of the new places and peoples discovered in the sixteenth century. Bodin, extremely sensitive to diversity, sought unity for history by directing attention to the problems confronted at all times by all nations: economy, sovereignty, migration, urbanism, etc.[395] Le Roy sought to analyze history in terms of the interrelatedness of the world in both space and time, the rise and fall of empires, and the notion of historical progress. La Popelinière directed the attention of history to the study of civilization: the transformation from primitive to civilized societies and the evolution of civilized societies themselves in their relations one to the other. While no historian actually wrote a universal history in the sixteenth century, the would-be practitioners of the craft had seriously begun to speculate on how best to do it. They were moved in these new directions by the realization that the existing historical methods and forms were not adequate to the task of bringing all parts of the world in both their present and past dimensions within a unified history.[396]

The revelation of the East had a more profound impact upon French thought, especially history, than it had elsewhere in Europe. This may perhaps be accounted for by the fact that Frenchmen were not as directly involved in Asia as other western Europeans. They were therefore forced, as Rabelais said, to rely on "Hearsay." While being aware that momentous events were occurring, it is conceivable that distance from the scene of action lent French thinkers a perspective from which they could more quietly and detachedly contemplate the implications of the discoveries for European civilization. But it is certainly true also that the religious wars shook profoundly the faith of Frenchmen in traditional religion, politics, and thought. Disturbed as they were by the conditions of France, they were perhaps more inclined than others to look elsewhere for answers to agonizing questions. Whatever reasons may be adduced to explain it, the simple fact is that the French writers were more sensitive than most others to the ultimate meaning for European civilization of the overseas expansion of the sixteenth century.

---

[395] Botero follows Bodin's suggestion by studying the problem of the city in all societies. See above, pp. 237-40.

[396] Cf. Gordon, *op. cit.* (n. 27), pp. 302-4.

CHAPTER VIII

The Germanic Literatures

The states of northern and Germanic Europe were involved in the expansion movement mainly through participating in the spice trade. Initially the commercial cities of southern Germany and the Netherlands played a major role in the financing and supplying of fleets as well as in distributing the spices. For a long period the English remained content to let others take the initiative and pay the price in money and human misery for opening the overseas world. The spread of the Reformation in northern Europe, beginning in the 1520's, diverted attention to the more pressing and dangerous internal problems of religious struggle. Between 1530 and 1570 the northern countries took little notice of the victories being claimed by the Iberian states and their clerics in distant places, and a strict censorship, in both Catholic and Protestant states, impeded the exchange of information. It was only after a stalemate developed in the religious struggle that the northern states again cast covetous eyes upon the acquisitions of the Spanish and Portuguese. At this juncture the Protestant states were confronted by the new and powerful international complex of possessions controlled by King Philip II following the union in 1580 of the Spanish and Portuguese crowns. Blocked in his efforts to suppress the rebellious Dutch, Philip determined to reestablish his position in northern Europe by controlling the seas with a huge Armada and by sweeping them clean of English and Dutch marauders. The defeat of his naval efforts and the dispersion of the Spanish Armada in 1588 led directly to the demise of the Iberian monopoly and to the beginning of direct participation by the Dutch and English in trade with the East.

Learning and literature in Germanic Europe remained for a long time peripheral to the swirl of intellectual activity sweeping sixteenth-century Italy and France. Humanism in the north had as its proponents the towering figures of Erasmus, Reuchlin, and More. But imaginative literature in the vernacular could boast no comparable giants before the end of the century. German popular literature received a great impetus from Sebastian Brant's *Ship of Fools* (1494) and the myriad songs and poems of Hans Sachs. Literary talent of equal stature did not appear in England until the later years of the century when Sidney and Spenser strode upon the stage of history. In the Netherlands a substantial literature in the Flemish and Dutch vernaculars did not emerge until the end of the century. The very cosmopolitanism of the Low Countries helped to delay the growth of a national language and literature; Flemish was in constant competition with Spanish and French and the learned in the universities of the Lowlands continued to uphold the primacy of Latin. In Germany more than two-thirds of all books published in the latter half of the century were Latin editions.[1] The more isolated English had less trouble, particularly after the Reformation took hold, of releasing their literature from the stranglehold of Latin. The political unity of England also contributed greatly to the quick flourishing of literature in the age of Queen Elizabeth. The exuberant growth of a secular literature in England was unique in Germanic Europe; the drama of Shakespeare's day was rivaled in Europe at large only by the Spanish theater of Lope de Vega and his contemporaries.

The initial response in Germanic Europe to the revelation of the East was spasmodic and intimately related to involvement in the spice trade. The popularity of Mandeville as a folkbook helped everywhere to fix a picture of the East as the supreme source of riches and marvels. This traditional East was never completely repudiated by the Germanic literati of the sixteenth century. In every country there were those who questioned it or sought to reconcile the East of Mandeville with the newer information published in the more recent travel accounts. A more nearly contemporary view of Asia appears with greater frequency in the allusions found in the earlier writings of the century than in those of its middle and later years. Mandeville, like the Bible, was too rich a source of literary ideas to be cast aside. And there were those, even among the critical collectors of travel literature and the skeptical historians, who continued to believe that the more recent accounts confirmed rather than invalidated the assertions of Mandeville. In the north of Europe, by contrast to the south, the medieval conceptions of Asia remained firmly embedded in all forms of literature to the end of the century.

I

GERMAN LITERATURE

The Holy Roman Empire, unlike England and France, lacked a coherent political constitution in the sixteenth century. A multinational structure

---

[1] See K. O. Conrady, *Lateinische Dichtungstradition und deutsche Lyrik des 17. Jahrhunderts* (Bonn, 1962), p. 29 n. 72a.

governed by a thousand-year accumulation of legal and historical traditions, the empire possessed no institutional focal point. As a political entity it has therefore successfully defied all efforts to diagram its workings. At the beginning of the sixteenth century it was nominally governed by an elected emperor from the House of Habsburg who shared his powers and responsibilities with thirty secular princes, fifty ecclesiastical lords, three thousand cities and towns, and legions of knights, counts, and prelates. Though several nationalities were technically subject to the empire, its institutions were dominated by the German majority. Efforts to reform its constitution along national lines were stifled or circumvented in the sixteenth century by particularistic interests jealous of traditional privileges and suspiciously hostile to centralization. The coming of the Reformation strengthened localism and regionalism and frustrated the last hopes of those who were intent upon founding a German nation.

Despite its tangled constitution, the Holy Roman Empire was in many ways the dominant power of Europe. It possessed traditional rights and claims of universal political authority not belonging to any other secular entity. In area and population it was the largest country of Europe, even before Charles V added his inheritance to it. The agricultural productivity of its land was relatively high and its mineral deposits the richest in Europe—especially in silver and copper. In the industries of mining, metal working, and textile production, Germany and Bohemia led the way on the Continent. Most of the empire's important urban centers were strategically located for trade between east and west, and north and south. The cities and towns of the south and west, especially those located between the Rhine and the Danube, were the brightest spots on the imperial landscape, for they dominated commerce, industry, banking, and the arts throughout most of the sixteenth century.

The cities of the empire were usually quite independent politically and self-sufficient economically. They were strikingly different from the city-states of Italy in that they were governed by patrician families of merchants rather than by princes. Vienna, Prague, and Regensburg were the cities most closely associated with the court and the imperial administration. The metropoles of commerce and crafts were Ulm, Cologne, Nuremberg, Strassburg, Augsburg, Basel, and Frankfurt; they were rivaled in the north only by Hamburg and Lübeck, the port cities. But most of the German population continued to live outside the cities, almost 85 percent of the total. Cologne, the largest of the German cities, had a population of 30,000 at a time when Naples, the largest city in Europe, counted 230,000 inhabitants.

The south German towns were nonetheless important in international trade, industry, and finance, owing in large measure to their strategic locations, their control of valuable minerals, and their advanced craftsmanship in metals, textiles, and printing. Augsburg and Nuremberg, both Imperial Cities, played especially prominent roles in the spice trade.[2] The agents of their merchant and

---

[2] For discussion see *Asia*, I, 107–12.

banking families operated at Venice, Lyons, Seville, Lisbon, and Antwerp throughout the sixteenth century. As the centers of the spice traffic moved, their agents moved too. The mercantile cities were also quick to make readjustments in their imports and exports as the focus of commercial activity shifted from the Mediterranean region to the Atlantic seaboard. The German port cities in the north profited directly from supplying timber, ships stores, and grain to the Iberian states.

The rural population of the empire suffered losses as a result of the overseas discoveries because of the general inflation in prices and because of their inability to profit as the cities did from the expansion of commerce. This variation in economic adjustment tended to produce wide divergencies in perceptions about the meaning of the overseas discoveries. The gradual exclusion of the Germans from direct participation in the ventures of the Portuguese smothered the enthusiasm of the German towns for overseas trade, and the Reformation with its tensions and wars finally forced Germans of all walks of life to concentrate upon problems at home rather than distant events.

The story of Nuremberg's response to the opening of the overseas world is particularly instructive when considering how time and circumstances altered viewpoints in Germany.[3] Located midway between the Rhine and the Danube, Nuremberg by 1500 was an established point of transit boasting a population of 20,000 souls. Twelve major trade routes converged upon it, and the agents of its family firms conducted business in marts from Spain to Poland. Its merchants had bought Oriental wares at Lemberg and Venice long before they became available at Lisbon and Antwerp. Once the sea route to India was opened, the Nurembergers began to sell spices to Lemberg itself which they purchased through Antwerp or in Iberia.[4] The craftsmen and artisans of Nuremberg produced metalworks for outfitting the ships and for stocking the cargoes of the Portuguese fleets to the East. Its bankers provided financing for some of the voyages, and its artillery experts and gunners went to sea with the fleets. Nuremberg's scholars and artisans provided the Portuguese with navigational instruments, astronomical charts, clocks, globes, and maps of high quality.[5] Nuremberg, like Augsburg, was a leading center of printing, especially of geographical and astronomical books and of newsletters and other materials on the overseas discoveries.

Through their travels and letters the Nurembergers kept one another informed, as well as many of their correspondents elsewhere in Germany, of the Portuguese achievements. Martin Behaim, scion of a patrician family, went to Portugal in 1477 as an agent of the Hirschvogel firm. He traveled with the Portuguese to the Azores and in 1483 made a brief trip down the African

---

[3] See the excellent study by Gerald Strauss, *Nuremberg in the Sixteenth Century* (Bloomington, Ind., 1967).

[4] See F. Lütge, "Der Handel Nürnbergs nach dem Osten im 15/16 Jahrhundert," in *Beiträge zur Wirtschaftsgeschichte Nürnbergs* (2 vols.; Nuremberg, 1967), I, 344-49.

[5] See T. G. Werner, "Die Beteiligung der Nürnberger Welser und Augsburger Fugger in der Eroberung des Rio de la Plata . . . ," *ibid.*, I, 506-8.

coast. When he returned to Nuremberg in 1490, he was commissioned by the city to complete his world map and famous globe (*Erdapfel*). The globe enabled his fellow townsmen to study the world, as it was then known, on a pedestal placed in their own town hall. Behaim also probably sought financing and support for further voyaging while he was in Nuremberg.[6] He was certainly successful in stimulating local interest in Iberia, for in 1494 the physician and geographer Hieronymous Münzer (1437–1508) left for a trip to Spain accompanied by the sons of three rich merchants.[7] Nuremberg merchants corresponded with Valentim Fernandes, the printer, after his arrival at Lisbon in 1495, and the Imhof and Hirschvogel firms participated in the German pepper syndicate put together at Lisbon in the early years of the sixteenth century.

It was not only Nuremberg's merchants who watched with interest and concern the economic ascent of Portugal. In 1506 Christoph Scheurl (1481–1542), Humanist and lawyer, wrote from Bologna to Nuremberg that the Portuguese had struck a serious blow to the economy of Nuremberg because the eastern Europeans would soon be able to buy spices more cheaply at Leipzig (through Antwerp) than at Nuremberg (through Venice). For Nuremberg to prevent its losses from becoming too severe it would be required, Scheurl shrewdly observed, to export its own manufactures to the new spice marts.[8] In 1519 Scheurl was sent to Spain by the council to extend officially the congratulations of the city to Charles V on his accession as emperor and to offer him its formal allegiance.[9] A warm reception converted Scheurl into a great admirer of Charles. Upon his return to Nuremberg in 1520, he began to follow avidly the emperor's career. Over the next decade, Scheurl became an intermediary correspondent for Germans wanting to learn of their emperor's activities elsewhere. Scheurl boasts at one point that information sent him will eventually reach six hundred people.[10] Among other matters he informed his correspondents about overseas trade and the Portuguese victories in Asia.[11]

Nurembergers retained a lively interest in distant events throughout the 1520's. In 1520–21 Albrecht Dürer traveled to the Low Countries, where he collected information about and curiosities from the East.[12] Part of the cargo of the "Victoria" from Magellan's fleet was purchased by a German group and the spices were marketed at Nuremberg.[13] Johann Schöner (1477–1547) in 1523 prepared maps and globes which included new information brought back by

[6] See H. Kellenbenz, "Die Beziehungen Nürnbergs zur iberischen Halbinsel . . . ," *ibid.*, I, 468–71.

[7] See above, p. 27.

[8] Text of his Latin letter to Sext Tucher of December 1, 1506, in F. von Soden and J. K. F. Knaacke (eds.), *Christoph Scheurls Briefbuch* (2 vols. in 1; Potsdam, 1867, 1872), I, 41.

[9] See W. Graf, *Doktor Christoph Scheurl von Nürnberg* (Leipzig and Berlin, 1930), pp. 73–74.

[10] *Ibid.*, pp. 107–8.

[11] For example, he wrote to George, duke of Saxony, in 1536 about the successful Portuguese action in defending the fortress of Diu. See Soden and Knaacke (eds.), *op. cit.* (n. 8), II, 154.

[12] For details see *Asia*, II, Bk. I, 17–18.

[13] See H. Kellenbenz, "Os mercadores alemães de Lisboa por volta de 1530," *Revista portuguesa de história*, IX (1960), 127–28.

the survivors of the Magellan expedition. Most of the Germans left Lisbon in 1518 when an epidemic hit the city. Jörg Pock, however, remained in Portugal and eventually sailed for India in 1520. On January 1, 1522, he wrote a letter to Nuremberg from Cochin giving information on the diamonds of Vijayanagar. He alleged that Krishna Deva Raya's collection of precious stones far surpassed in number and value those possessed by the emperor or any other European ruler.[14] The Germans in Lisbon and elsewhere thereafter began increasingly to purchase the precious stones from India and to learn Portuguese cutting techniques. The Augsburg house of Herwart bought more than six hundred-weights of pearls in one year and its Lisbon agent owned a diamond valued at 160,000 ducats. Another outbreak of the pest at Lisbon in 1530, followed by an earthquake the next year, brought an abrupt halt to German activity there. In literature the jewel trade at Lisbon was adopted by Jörg Wickram as the main theme for his novel *Von güten und bösen Nachbaurn* (Strassburg, 1556).[15]

Only a few Germans, and even fewer Nurembergers, had connections with the spice trade of Asia in the years from 1530 to 1579. Bartholomaeus Khevenhüller (1539–1613), scion of the famous Austrian family, visited Lisbon in 1557; with youthful enthusiasm he exclaimed, after seeing the *näus* in the harbor, that he would certainly have embarked for India himself if only he had brought enough money along.[16] The decline of the Portuguese crown and the economic losses suffered in the latter half of the century produced a second opportunity for the Germans to participate directly in the spice trade. Representatives of the south German firms, such as Ferdinand Kron (1559–1637) of Augsburg, were sent to India to watch over the interests of the merchant families in the spice trade. Between 1589 and 1591 Georg Christoph Fernberger (d. 1594) traveled throughout Portuguese Asia and ventured as far east as Malacca.[17] The Saxon traveler Bernhard von Miltitz (1570–1626) arrived at Goa in 1595 but failed in his efforts to get to Malacca.[18] Over the course of the sixteenth century thousands of Germans were involved in the spice trade as merchants and investors, and in the overseas voyages as sailors, gunners, and pilots. But no trace remains of many of their names or their activities, for they kept no records. Even those about whom there are a few facts, or from whom letters or other notices exist, have been all but forgotten. In spite of their traveling and trading, the Germans produced no books on the East comparable to the accounts of Varthema in Italian or Linschoten in Dutch. What the Germans at home knew about Asia came mainly though translations of classical, medieval, and

---

[14] See H. Kömmerling-Fitzler, "Der Nürnberger Georg Pock (d. 1528–29) in Portugiesisch-Indien und im Edelsteinland Vijayanagara," *Mitteilungen des Vereins für Geschichte der Stadt Nürnberg*, LV (1967–68), 139–68.

[15] For its text see Hans-Gert Roloff (ed.), *Georg Wickrams sämtliche Werke* (Berlin, 1969), IV, esp. 28, 54, 143.

[16] As quoted from his diary in V. Hantsch, *Deutsche Reisende des sechzehnten Jahrhunderts* (Leipzig, 1895), p. 93.

[17] *Ibid.*, pp. 118–19.

[18] *Ibid.*, pp. 122–23.

contemporary writings that the printing presses regularly turned out, or from the reports written by German travelers to the Levant.[19]

A. FIRST REACTIONS

In German literature of the pre-discovery era the Orient and its peoples are mentioned in chronicles, romances, and court poetry. The "Seres" of the Romans appear in Notker's tenth-century Germany commentary on Boethius and in Rudolf von Ems' *Weltchronik* (*ca.* 1240).[20] A fabulous India was kept alive for Germans by the various renditions of the Alexander legend in poetry and prose.[21] During and after the Crusades the tendency grew among poets to provide Oriental backgrounds and to introduce exotic Asian persons and products into their creations.[22] But the places and peoples of Asia remained mere names to Germans until the Mongol invasion and the consequent devastation of Silesia and Moravia in 1240-41. Knowledge of the East thereafter came to German intellectuals mainly through the accounts of Marco Polo and other medieval travelers. Around 1400 Otto von Diemeringen, canon of Metz, translated Mandeville into a lively German version from the Latin and French texts.[23] Mandeville was probably more popular in Germany than elsewhere before the age of printing for sixty-five of the three hundred extant manuscripts are in German.[24] In popular literature also, for example in the adventures of *Herzog Ernst* (fourteenth century), numerous incidents take place in the "ferren India" and references are frequent to the princes and princesses of India and to their wonderful magic rings, precious stones, and cloth of woven gold. The name "Cathay," like other words from Marco Polo's and Mandeville's texts, were well enough understood in the fifteenth century to appear in popular verse.[25]

The most influential of the German translations of Marco Polo was the incunabulum which Fritz Creusser, the printer, published at Nuremberg in 1477 (see pl. 2). To judge from its dialectical peculiarities and spellings, this

[19] For an example of a traveler to the Levant who also learned many items of interest about the more distant East see K. H. Dannenfeldt, *Leonhard Rauwolf, Sixteenth-Century Physician, Botanist, and Traveler* (Cambridge, Mass., 1968).

[20] See E. H. von Tscharner, *China in der deutschen Dichtung bis zur Klassik* (Munich, 1939), p. 8.

[21] See above, pp. 93-96. Also K. Bertau, *Deutsche Literatur im europäischen Mittelalter* (2 vols.; Munich, 1972), I, 352-60.

[22] See A. F. J. Remy, *The Influence of India and Persia on the Poetry of Germany* (New York, 1901), p. 6.

[23] This was the translation most frequently published, though there are two other important translations by Hans Bart and Michael Velser. See W. Stammler, *Von der Mystik zum Barock (1400-1600)* (Stuttgart, 1950), p. 267.

[24] See *Asia*, I, 80.

[25] For example, see the excerpt from a "Weinsegen" by Hans Rosenplüt as quoted in Berlin, Ausstellung . . . im schloss Charlottenburg, *China und Europa* (Berlin, 1973), p. 118.

anonymous translation was probably made at Nuremberg. A new and independent translation was printed at Augsburg in 1481 by Anton Sorg.[26] A Latin version of the reigning Pipino text of Marco Polo's book was included in the *Novus orbis* (1532) edited at Basel by Simon Grynaeus from materials collected by Johann Huttich. Two years later a free translation of it appeared at Strassburg in the German of Michael Herr, a physician and writer.[27] Simon Schwartz, city secretary of Schraubing in Bavaria, between 1574 and 1582 prepared a new and careful German translation of the Pipino text; although commissioned originally by Duke William of Bavaria, it was never printed.[28] Hieronymous Megiser (*ca.* 1553–1618), the lexicographer, later published his own German translation of the Pipino version in his *Chorographia Tartariae* (Leipzig, 1610).[29] From this brief review of the German translations of the Polo text it is clear that his account of Asia retained its prominence in Germany throughout the sixteenth century.

The printed *Travels* of Mandeville meanwhile became popular enough to rank as a *Volksbuch*,[30] those renditions in prose of traditional stories and poems which were read for entertainment. Originally prepared in lavish editions for the nobility, the German printers of the sixteenth century began to issue beautiful illustrated editions of the *Volksbücher* for sale to the public at large.[31] The first illustrated *Mandeville* was published in 1481 by Anton Sorg of Augsburg, the printer of Marco Polo. Between this date and 1507 eight other printings appeared in German.[32] A gap opened thereafter in the sequence of German editions, possibly because the Protestants thought that Mandeville's concern with pilgrimages and miracles was too "popish." In 1560 a *Volksbuch* was published which satirized derisively the Mandeville book.[33] After 1580 the old Mandeville story again began to be issued in new illustrated printings, possibly to replace those earlier versions which had been destroyed.[34]

According to the Augsburg edition of 1509, Fortunatus, the traveler in search of riches and material gain, visited the India of Mandeville. On a brief stop there, he explains that Asians never voyage to Europe because they would be foolish to leave their warm and fruitful country for a cold and inhospitable

26 On the relation of these two incunabula to the German manuscript version see A. Hoffmann, *Untersuchungen zu den altdeutschen Marco-Polo Texten* (Ohlau in Silesia, 1936), pp. 2–7. Also see Moule-Pelliot, *Description of the World* (London, 1938), pp. 509–16, for a list of the manuscript and printed editions; for a comparison of the incunabula see L. Benedetto, *Marco Polo: Il Milione* (Florence, 1928), pp. cxiv–cxvii.

27 For details see M. Böhme, *Die grossen Reisesammlungen des 16. Jahrhunderts und ihre Bedeutung* (Strassburg, 1904), pp. 60–64.

28 See Hoffmann, *op. cit.* (n. 26), pp. 7–10.

29 For further information on Megiser's works see below, pp. 516–17.

30 For its appearance in German libraries see above, p. 61–62.

31 For a brief history of the *Volksbuch* see H. Rupprich, *Das Zeitalter der Reformation*, Pt. 2 of *Die deutsche Literatur vom späten Mittelalter bis zum Barock*, Vol. IV in H. de Boor and R. Newald (eds.), *Geschichte der deutschen Literatur von den Anfängen bis zur Gegenwart* (Munich, 1973), pp. 184–85.

32 For a listing see Appendix II in J. W. Bennett, *The Rediscovery of Sir John Mandeville* (New York, 1954), pp. 364–70.

33 See Rupprich, *op. cit.* (n. 31), p. 187.

34 See *ibid.*, p. 243.

land.[35] Mandeville's stories also acquired a fresh credibility in Germany by the appearance at the beginning of the century of newsletters (*neue Zeitungen*) announcing the fabulous discoveries being made by the Portuguese and Spanish in India and America. These brief announcements were soon supplemented by German translations of lengthier travel accounts.[36] Jobst Ruchamer, physician of Nuremberg and friend of Pirckheimer, published in 1508 his *Neue unbekanthe Landte*, a translation of Montalboddo's *Paesi novamente retrovati* (1507). In the following year Balthasar Springer published at Augsburg *Die Merfart*, his personal account of the voyage to India and back which was richly illustrated by Hans Burgkmair.[37] The *Itinerario* (1510) of Varthema (more often "Barthema" or even "Vartomann" in German) was translated in 1515 by Michael Herr. Becoming one of the most popular books of the day, it was quickly reprinted in 1516 and 1518. The ninth and last printing of this German version appeared in 1556. That Varthema soon became a symbol of the traveler for German readers is indicated by the appearance of his portrait on world maps.[38] He was, indeed, a kind of latter-day Mandeville and his book was more likely to be found in contemporary book shops and libraries than any other travel account of the sixteenth century.[39]

German and Czech literati and Humanists reacted questioningly and hesitantly to the first spate of news about the momentous discoveries of the years from 1492 to 1515.[40] The story of Sebastian Brant (1457–1521), a native of Strassburg and resident of Basel from 1475 to 1501, illustrates the point.[41] A lawyer by training, Brant was a close student of Latin literature and interested in translating it. When Johann Bergmann von Olpe opened his printing shop at Basel in 1493, Brant became his literary adviser. Such a post was to Brant's liking, for he had long been anxious to write more than broadsides in German to convey to the public his deep concern for the future of the empire and the Catholic religion. In 1493 Bergmann published a pictorial edition in Latin of Columbus' letter announcing the discovery of America. The following year Brant edited for Bergmann a Latin book on the Spanish conquest of Granada to which was appended a reprint of the Columbus letter and a Latin poem by Brant praising Ferdinand the Catholic, the sponsor of Columbus, and expressing the heartfelt

[35] See H. Günther (ed.), *Fortunatus: Nach dem Augsburger Druck von 1509* (Halle, 1914), pp. 82–83. Thomas Dekker published a comedy, *Old Fortunatus* (1600), that was based on this folkbook.

[36] For further detail on these early reports see *Asia*, I, 161–63. Also see P. Roth, *Die neuen Zeitungen in Deutschland im 15. und 16. Jahrhundert* (Leipzig, 1914), p. 17.

[37] For Burgkmair's part in preparing "The Triumph of Maximilian I (1519)" see *Asia*, II, Bk. 1, 79–80. For an English translation of the verses attached to these woodcuts see Stanley Appelbaum (trans. and ed.), *The Triumph of Maximilian I* (New York, 1964).

[38] Suggestion of L. D. Hammond (ed.), *Traveler in Disguise* (Cambridge, Mass., 1963), p. xx.

[39] See above, pp. 61–62.

[40] For Czech reactions see B. Horák, "Ohlas zámořských objevů v české literatuře" ("Responses to Overseas Discoveries in Czech Literature"), in his *Historie o plaveni se do Ameriky kteráž i Brasilia slave* (Prague, 1957), pp. 27–28.

[41] What follows is based upon E. H. Zeydel, *Sebastian Brant* (New York, 1967). Also see the same author's "Sebastian Brant and the Discovery of America," *Journal of English and Germanic Philology*, XLII (1943), 410–11.

wish that Germany might have such a king. "Then," he exclaims, "the whole world would soon be subject to our laws."[42]

Brant, like many of his German contemporaries, was a staunch proponent of cultural nationalism and strove through his writings in the vernacular to win others to his viewpoint. His most famous work, *Narrenschiff* or *Ship of Fools*, published by Bergmann in 1494, is a collection of satirical verses in which he denounces the follies of men. Brant's purpose in these moral preachings is to make plain his belief that the German people will never be able to carry out their divine mission of maintaining the Roman imperium so long as they wallow in sin. Moral reform is necessary to the security of the empire and for a renewed Christian crusade against the Turkish hordes threatening it. About the decline of the faith he writes:

> Our faith was strong in the Orient
> It ruled in all of Asia
> In Moorish lands and Africa
> But now for us these lands are gone
> 'twould even grieve the hardest stone.[43]

Considering his grave fears about affairs at home, it is not hard to understand why, despite his recognition of Columbus' achievement, Brant expressed no enthusiasm for overseas ventures. In writing "of experience of all lands" Brant concludes:

> Some have explored a foreign land
> But not themselves can understand,
> . . . .
> For those ay longing to depart
> Cannot serve God with all their heart.[44]

Brant's friend and correspondent, Conrad Peutinger (1465–1547), the Humanist of Augsburg, illustrates another aspect of the early reaction to the discoveries. As a relative of the Welsers, Peutinger was able to collect information and oddities directly from Portugal. He was also proud that his townsmen in 1505 were among the first Germans to visit India.[45] But, despite his enthusiasm for collecting curiosities and gathering data relative to the voyages and to India, Peutinger was intellectually unable to accept the idea that men of his own day knew more about the world than his beloved Ancients. In one of his *Table-Talks*, or *Sermones Convivales*, published at Strassburg in 1506, Peutinger ruminates on the sea route to India discovered by the Portuguese.[46] In the course of this

---

[42] As quoted in Zeydel, *op. cit.* (n. 41), p. 71.

[43] E. H. Zeydel (trans.), *The Ship of Fools* (New York, 1944), pp. 316–17. On the belief in the universality of Christianity in earlier times see above, pp. 268–70.

[44] *Ibid.*, p. 225.

[45] See *Asia*, I, 159, 162.

[46] Entitled "De Lusitania nautis que in Indiam navigant" (pp. bii^v–biii^r). For commentary see M. Weyrauther, *Konrad Peutinger und Wilibald Pirckheimer in ihren Beziehungen zur Geographie: Eine geschichtliche Parallele* (Munich, 1907), pp. 7–9.

discussion he raises the question whether the Ancients knew about the route around Africa to India; he concludes that Cornelius Nepos, Pliny, and Pomponius Mela were probably aware of it. To arrive at his conclusion he uncritically accepted a story from Nepos to the effect that seafarers from India were once swept by storms to the shores of Germany.

Historians, cosmographers, and geographers were more inclined than other German intellectuals to welcome news about the discoveries and to accept it at face value. Hartmann Schedel (1440–1514), physician and bibliophile of Nuremberg, published a *Weltchronik* (Nuremberg, 1493) which sharply departs from the traditional chronicle by its heavy dependence on recent and contemporary materials. Educated at Padua, Schedel was acutely aware of the grand achievements of the Italian Humanists and well versed in their historical methods. For the *Weltchronik* he took as his model the *Supplementum Chronicarum* (Venice, 1483; 2d ed., 1485), of Foresti da Bergamo, an Augustinian Eremite. Schedel adopted Bergamo's division of world history into six ages, the last era beginning with the birth of Christ.[47] His choice of Bergamo as his model led Schedel to include more information on India in the *Weltchronik* than might be expected there, for Bergamo's text, particularly the second edition, is noteworthy for the unusual attention it pays to the traditional tales about India and to Poggio's relation of Conti's travels in the East. Schedel supplements Bergamo's materials with references to the *Asia* (Venice, 1477) of Aeneas Sylvius Piccolomini (Pope Pius II), the most influential and revered in Germany of all foreign cosmographers and Humanists.[48] Since Schedel's *Weltchronik* appeared in richly illustrated editions in both Latin and German, it quickly became popular with scholars and the general public alike.

The geographers and cosmographers of Alsace-Lorraine responded quickly, openly, and with astonishing impartiality to the news coming to them from Iberia by way of Paris and Antwerp. In 1505 Matthias Ringmann (1482–1511), a young poet and geographer, published at Strassburg the letter written by Amerigo Vespucci in 1503 to Lorenzo de' Medici reporting on his third voyage to America.[49] Two years later (1507) Ringmann migrated to St. Dié in Lorraine where Duke René II, the titular king of Jerusalem, sponsored a group of geographers and printers who were busy revising Ptolemy. At St. Dié, Ringmann collaborated with Martin Waldseemüller (*ca.* 1470–*ca.* 1522) and others in preparing the famous *Cosmographiae introductio* (1507) in which the Western

---

[47] For an analysis of Schedel's sources see M. Haitz, *Schedel's Weltchronik* (Munich, 1899), pp. 11–37; for a discussion of Bergamo's *Supplementum*, see Francis M. Rogers, *The Quest for Eastern Christians: Travel and Rumor in the Age of Discovery* (Minneapolis, 1962), pp. 74–78. On Conti and Poggio, see *Asia*, I, 59–63.

[48] On the great authority of Aeneas Sylvius in Germany see G. Strauss, *Sixteenth-Century Germany: Its Topography and Topographers* (Madison, Wis., 1959), pp. 12–13. Also see *Asia*, I, 70–71.

[49] Printed by Matthias Hupfuff, its dedication expresses clearly the great astonishment felt by Ringmann. It also includes an engraving of four savages and five ships. See C. G. A. Schmidt, *Histoire littéraire de l'Alsace* . . . (2 vols.; Paris, 1879), II, 87–89, 398n.

Hemisphere was first given the name "America."[50] In the part dealing with geography, Waldseemüller lists the islands unknown to Ptolemy, including therein Java and "Zipangri" (Japan) located "in the Western Ocean."[51] Waldseemüller at this point in his career, though he later changed his mind, was so impressed with the achievements of Amerigo Vespucci that he also included as the second part of the *Cosmographiae* the Florentine's letters on his four voyages in Latin translation. On his fourth voyage, Vespucci set sail in 1503 for Malacca, "a stopping place for all ships coming from the Gangetic and Indian seas, precisely as Cadiz is the port for all vessels going from east to west, or in the opposite direction."[52] Although his ship was not able to complete the voyage to the East, Vespucci certainly let the Germans know about the strategic location of Malacca several years before the Portuguese conquered it. The Vespucci letters were soon translated into German along with a separate booklet entitled *Der welt kugel Beschrybung* (1509). Clearly its printer, Johann Grieninger of Strassburg, was beginning to see the commercial possibilities in publishing geographies and cosmographies in German; about the same time, his colleagues in Nuremberg and Augsburg were investing in translations and in editions of the materials coming to them by way of Italy.[53]

Not all the early cosmographers were equally open to newer ideas about the earth. Conrad Celtis (1459–1508), the wandering Humanist and patriotic geographer, was too preoccupied with the Greeks and Germans to react positively to the overseas discoveries. On geography outside central Europe his remarks are brief and traditional. To him India is but a distant land desiccated by heat, and China little more than the homeland of silk.[54] But Joachim Vadian (1484–1551) of St. Gall believed in challenging the authority of the Ancients and eagerly accepted the stories of Moderns who had traveled further and seen more. In his Latin edition (1518) of Pomponius Mela's geography, Vadian amplifies the original by including references to the geographical discoveries of the contemporary Spanish and Portuguese.[55] Willibald Pirckheimer in his Latin Ptolemy published at Strassburg in 1525 completely ignored the new information circulating there. But he collected books on the voyages for his library.[56] And to his *Germaniae* (1530) he added an appendix in which he tries to equate the Ptolemaic names with those used by the Portuguese of his day.

---

[50] For the Latin text and an English translation see C. G. Herbermann (ed.), *The Cosmographiae introductio of Martin Waldseemüller in Facsimile* . . . (New York, 1907). For discussion of Waldseemüller's maps and globes see below, pp. 454–55. Also see pls. 56 and 57.

[51] *Ibid.*, pp. 75–76.

[52] *Ibid.*, p. 145.

[53] On the cartography of St. Dié see below, pp. 453–54.

[54] See L. Geiger, *Conrad Celtis in seinen Beziehungen zur Geographie* (Munich, 1896), p. 5.

[55] *Pomponii Melae Hispani. Libri de situ orbis tres* . . . (Vienna, 1518), pp. 3ʳ–7ᵛ, and the letter to Rudolf Agricola, p. 124ᵛ. For commentary see W. Näf, *Vadian und seine Stadt St. Gallen* (St. Gall, 1944), p. 268, and Strauss, *Sixteenth-Century Germany* (n. 48), pp. 5, 33. Also see the appendix of the *Reportorium* . . . (1519) of Jacobus Stoppell for another example of how commentators on geography were adding the new to traditional knowledge. For Vadian's place in geography see below, p. 389.

[56] See above, p. 57.

In a second appendix Pirckheimer, possibly inspired by Peutinger's earlier attempt, tries to show that ancient seafarers had rounded Africa. He does not, however, claim that the Ancients had circumnavigated the world before Magellan's men.[57]

While attempts were being made to reconcile the new with the old geographical learning, efforts were undertaken to compile collections of manners and customs from all parts of the world. The Ulm patrician Johannes Stammler (d. 1525) published a work of comparative religion called *Dialogus de diversarum gentium sectis* (1508) which includes impartial references to Tartar religious beliefs and practices.[58] It was perhaps this work which inspired Johannes Böhm (1485–1535), usually called Boemus, to compile his popular collection of folklore and customs, *Omnium gentium mores* (Landshut, 1520).[59] A canon of the cathedral at Ulm and a Hebraist, Boemus put together from ancient, medieval, and fifteenth-century sources an orderly ethnological compendium laced together by his own comments on the great variety in human behavior and on the laws and governments of alien nations. By assembling the available accounts he hoped to encourage his readers to form intelligent judgments on what customs could be best adopted in their own lands for the promotion of general tranquility. The nations, peoples, and customs most fully described are those located farthest from Europe. His comments on India include almost everything ever written by the Ancients about the subcontinent. For the Mongols and the Cathayans he relied on the descriptions of John de Plano Carpini, the thirteenth-century traveler. Neither in the original version nor in the expanded edition of 1536 are stories included from the reports of the Spanish and Portuguese.[60] Nor, strangely enough, was Boemus' book translated into German during the sixteenth century.

This is not to say, however, that Germans went unaffected by Boemus' work. Sebastian Franck (1499–1542), an esteemed German stylist, historian, and religious controversialist, was a close student of it. A native of Donauwörth, Franck was ordained a Catholic priest in 1524 and soon thereafter became a Lutheran minister. In 1528 at Nuremberg he married Ottilia Behaim, a daughter of the well-known patrician family of that city. About this time, Franck received from the Swiss Lutheran Andreas Althamer a copy of Boemus' book. With it as his inspiration and with the library resources of Nuremberg at his disposal, Franck seriously began to plan his major historical work, the *Hauptchronik*. He appar-

[57] For commentary see Weyrauther, *op. cit.* (n. 46), pp. 20–28, 36–37. On Peutinger see above, p. 333.

[58] It was quickly translated into Italian by Mathias Gurgense and published at Venice. A separate manuscript is also extant by Stammler called "De Tartarorum sectis" (Cod. 806, Stiftsbibliothek, St. Gall). See W. Stammler, *op. cit.* (n. 23), pp. 76, 546.

[59] Three Latin editions in revised and expanded form were published in 1536. From 1536 to 1611 there appeared no fewer than twenty-three reissues in Latin, Italian, French, English, and Spanish. William Waterman translated it into English in 1555 and called it *The fardle of facions*. See M. T. Hodgen, *Early Anthropology in the Sixteenth and Seventeenth Centuries* (Philadelphia, 1964), pp. 132–33. For its place in early literature of this type see R. Schenda, *Die französische Prodigienliteratur in der zweiten Hälfte des 16. Jahrhunderts* (Munich, 1961), pp. 9–11.

[60] Hodgen, *op. cit.* (n. 59), pp. 137–38.

ently visualized a large work in three or four parts: a profane history in annal form running to 1529 or 1530; a religious and ecclesiastical chronicle; and a *Weltbuch* describing all the important countries and peoples of the world. A projected but unrealized fourth part would presumably have dealt with the customs and beliefs of all peoples.[61]

Franck's *Weltbuch* was first published separately at Tübingen in 1534.[62] It follows Boemus' book in general structure and in the basic organization of individual chapters. Franck makes no secret of the fact that he is a compiler of materials as well as a commentator on them. His translated portions of Boemus are stylistically sprightlier than the original and his additions more religious in tone. Rather than treating non-Christians with secular impartiality, he is inclined to look upon them as children of the Christian God equal to all others. In his depiction of overseas peoples he adds to Boemus the latest information at his disposal from contemporary sources. He specifically excludes Mandeville's book as being too fabulous. In the preface he complains how difficult he finds it to get the story straight on distant places, for "99 out of 100 places bear names different from those current in Ptolemy's time." When conflicts in the sources appear, he forthrightly proclaims that he will place his trust in recent travelers rather than in the ancient or medieval scribes. He warns his readers not to hate strange peoples or to denounce their customs. Rather he counsels them to remember: "When Gentiles who have not the law do by nature what the law requires, they are a law to themselves, even though they do not have the law. They show that what the law requires is written on their hearts" (Romans 2:14–15).

The *Weltbuch*, like Boemus' compendium, is divided into four geographical sections: Africa, Europe, Asia, and a brief account of America. Franck gives more pages to Asia than to Africa and America combined. In his survey of Ethiopia Franck admits following Varthema's description.[63] In his depiction of India, though he does not indicate it, he also depends upon Varthema for his itinerary of the coastal cities and his account of the places where the spices grow. Textual comparison reveals that he copied Varthema's spellings of Indian places exactly and concluded his account of Portuguese activity in India with 1506, the date when Varthema left India. For his discussion of Cathay he depends upon medieval travelers, but does note that rhubarb comes from "Kini" and that Malacca pays tribute to the king of "Cini."[64] On Malacca itself he includes references from the letter of King Manuel to Pope Leo X that had been published in *Novus orbis* (1532) and points out that among the merchants there may be found "Chineser."[65] Franck concludes the section on Asia by praising

[61] See W. E. Peuckert, *Sebastian Franck, ein deutscher Sucher* (Munich, 1943), pp. 153–59.

[62] I have consulted the version, identical to this first edition, which is included in the work entitled *Warhafftige beschreibungen aller theil der welt* ... (Frankfurt-am-Main, 1567). In all, there were four sixteenth-century editions of the *Weltbuch*.

[63] *Ibid.*, p. 3ʳ.

[64] *Ibid.*, pp. 207ᵛ, 211ʳ.

[65] *Ibid.*, p. 240ᵛ. On Manuel's letter see *Asia*, I, 167n.

its heathens for their stoic virtue in nobly bearing ills and in showing contempt for death. Through Franck the Asia of tradition, heavily reinforced and ampli-fied with newer materials, first entered German historical thought and writing. It could hardly have occurred under better auspices, for he is still recognized as a master of German prose and a pioneer in the writing of universal history.[66]

Shortly after the publication of the *Weltbuch*, the German *Lucidarius* in prose was substantially altered in content. A *Volksbuch* dating from the end of the twelfth century, the *Lucidarius* was originally designed as a brief instructional manual for the laity in the prevailing religious beliefs and in the knowledge of the world locked in the Latin texts of the learned.[67] Divided into three books, symbolizing the Trinity, the traditional *Lucidarius* provided in its first book a description of the three parts of the known world. This little medieval miscel-lany pictures Asia, the first part of the world, as a land rich in treasure and peopled by marvelous and fabulous men and animals. With the advent of printing, the religious content of the *Lucidarius* was gradually reduced in favor of secular materials, especially geography and natural history. At Strassburg around 1534–35, a "reformed" *Lucidarius* was printed at the instance of Jacob Kammerlander that was designed as reading for Protestants.[68] It was also the first of the editions to include materials from contemporary writings. On Asia and Africa it follows Franck's *Weltbuch* rather than the traditional account pre-served in the earlier manuscript and printed versions of the *Lucidarius*.

The Frankfurt editions of the *Lucidarius* which soon predominated followed Kammerlander's revision with regard to geographical description. The printers also added cosmographical features of their own devising to their editions, which serve to illustrate the greater attention they and the public were paying to the overseas discoveries.[69] A wind-rose engraving began to appear on the title page in 1549, a "Farmer's Compass" was appended to the editions published from 1566 to the end of the century, and from 1580 onward a world map became a regular feature of the illustration program.[70] The German *Lucidarius* in prose traveled to neighboring countries where it appeared in Danish, Czech, and Dutch versions. In Germany the succinct comments of the *Lucidarius* on geo-graphy were often repeated in the calendars and chronicles prepared by the printers for popular consumption. Materials from it were also included in the *Faustbuch* of 1587.[71]

Contemporary with the "reformed" *Lucidarius* there appeared, also at Strassburg, the German translation by Michael Herr of the *Novus orbis* called

---

[66] For Franck's place in German historiography see H. Oncken, "Sebastian Franck als Geschichts-schreiber," *Historisch-politische Aufsätze und Reden* (2 vols.; Munich, 1914), I, 273–319, and F. Gundolf, *Anfänge deutscher Geschichtsschreibung* (Amsterdam, 1938), pp. 49–52.

[67] See K. Schorbach, *Studien über das deutsche Volksbuch Lucidarius* (Strassburg, 1894), pp. 2–5.

[68] See *ibid.*, pp. 140–48. The first dated incunabulum is the one published in 1479 at Augsburg by Anton Sorg, the printer of Marco Polo and Mandeville.

[69] The Oporin edition of 1568 prepared at Basel was the first to include a reference to America.

[70] Beginning in 1655, the *Lucidarius* title was replaced by *Kleine Kosmographia*, a general designation which appeared on books of this genre to 1806. See Schorbach, *op. cit.* (n. 67), p. 124.

[71] See below, pp. 343–44.

Die New Welt (1534).[72] In his preparation of the original Latin edition (1532), Simon Grynaeus (d. 1541) of Basel was aided by Johann Huttich (1480–1544), and Sebastian Münster (1488–1552), author of an introduction to this joint enterprise. These colleagues possessed a common interest in cosmography and in the collection of geographical and historical materials relating to all parts of the world. In their era Basel was a lively center of mercantile, religious, and scholarly activity. It was central to the trade on the Rhine between the Netherlands and Italy, and a shelter for religious refugees from less tolerant places in its environs. Münster, who probably got many of his ideas as well as information from Grynaeus, began as early as 1524 to prepare the *Kosmographie* that would finally appear in print twenty years later. In his work of compilation he was aided by scores of interested scholars including Peutinger, Beatus Rheanus, Bonifaz Amerbach, and Konrad Gessner.[73]

Initially Münster was most devoted to the geographical aspects of his work. He was apparently inspired by the Lorraine editions of Ptolemy and the maps and historical chronicle of Waldseemüller to think of his *Kosmographie* as a kind of atlas which would include brief descriptive texts as well as maps. After a short interim (1527–29) during which he devoted himself to Hebrew studies, Münster evidently began to work out the plan for his ambitious and elaborate description of the world. The outlines of his project show up clearly for the first time in the *Typi Cosmographici* (1532), his contribution to the *Novus orbis*. Münster clearly expresses in this text his pride in the progress being made by his contemporaries in uncovering land and peoples unknown to Ptolemy and Pliny. With a world map as his focus of discussion, Münster depends on the travel accounts in the rest of the book for his commentary on the "New World." His conception of the "New World," all those newly discovered places unknown to the Ancients, became as broadly influential as his writings. Like others of his time he included within this conception the newly discovered places of Asia as well as America.[74]

Münster worked for a time with Christian Egenolf (1502–55), the Frankfurt printer of a variety of popular books in German. About 1535 Egenolf himself published a chronicle and a description of various parts of the world.[75] His annalistic history concludes with the year 1525 and records what he knew about Calicut and the early Portuguese wars in India.[76] While he designates America as the "fourth part" of the world, Egenolf strangely makes no reference to the circumnavigation of Magellan's men. The book includes many woodcut

[72] For contents of this compilation see *Asia*, I, 179–80.

[73] See K. H. Burmeister, *Sebastian Münster: Versuch eines biographischen Gesamtbildes* (Basel and Stuttgart, 1963), pp. 135–40.

[74] *Ibid.*, pp. 111–14. Cf. above, pp. 279–80, and below, pp. 456–57.

[75] This work exists in several editions. I have used the one entitled *Chronica von an uñ abgang aller Welt wesenn. Ausz den glaubwirdigsten Historien beschriben* ... (Frankfurt, [1553?]); the title more commonly cited is *Chronica, Beschreibung und gemeyne Anzeyge, vonn aller Welt herkommen* ... Frankfurt, [1535]).

[76] *Chronica von an uñ abgang aller Welt*, pp. xxxi^r and ^v.

illustrations, including a print of the Portuguese fighting the Indians at Calicut. It becomes obvious from the accounts in this book that Münster was dealing with a printer who was himself informed on the opening of Asia.

In 1536 Egenolf published Münster's *Mappa Europae*, an amplified version in German of his earlier *Germaniae descriptio* (1530). Especially remarkable is his inclusion in this picture of Europe of a description of Tartary and the Tartars based on the texts of Hayton and Marco Polo published in the *Novus orbis*. The popular success of the German *Mappa Europae* probably convinced Münster that he should publish his *Kosmographie* in both Latin and German versions, but initially in the vernacular. Before he actually began preparation of his life's work for the press, he edited and published in Latin between 1538 and 1540 the geographical works of Pomponius Mela, C. Julius Solinus, and Ptolemy.[77]

Beginning in 1540, Münster finally began to assemble and organize the vast quantity of materials incorporated in the first edition of the *Kosmographie* that went on sale in 1544 at the autumn book fair in Frankfurt. Through his long-standing relations with printers and his own considerable talents in engraving, Münster had on hand a large number of engraved maps and other illustrative materials. As he had done in the past, Münster composed his text as a commentary on the maps and illustrations. The first edition, put together hurriedly to beat the competition and therefore full of errors and omissions, quickly sold out. Over the next five years, as seven new printings came out, Münster constantly improved and expanded his text and added to his work many new and better woodcuts. Others were engaged to find and prepare better illustrations, and Hans Rudolf Manuel Deutsch, the engraver, played a singularly important role in improving the entire illustration program as well as the individual woodcuts. Münster and his Basel publisher, Heinrich Petri, had become convinced that plates would sell books. And in this judgment they were proved right. Münster's definitive German and Latin editions were published in 1550; by 1638 thirty-five editions in all, some revised and expanded by others after Münster's death, had appeared, in German, Latin, French, Italian, and Czech, as well as abstracts and epitomized versions in English.[78]

Examination of the *Kosmographie* itself reveals that Münster was more concerned to preserve *all* the available sources on Asia than to decide whether to favor ancient or contemporary materials.[79] Like many of his contemporaries, he was aghast at how much of the knowledge of the past had been lost through

[77] See Burmeister, *op. cit.* (n. 73), pp. 115–18, 138. Münster used Franck's *Weltbuch* as a source in this study, but scarcely at all in the *Kosmographie*.

[78] See G. Strauss, "A Sixteenth-Century Encyclopedia: Sebastian Münster's Cosmography and Its Editions," in C. H. Carter (ed.), *From the Renaissance to the Counter-Reformation: Essays in Honor of Garrett Mattingly* (London, 1966), pp. 145–46. For an analysis of the Czech edition of 1554 prepared by Zikmund of Puchov see Horák, *loc. cit.* (n. 40), p. 29.

[79] Many previous commentators wonder why Münster failed to cite the Portuguese sources, particularly in the light of his close association with Grynaeus and the *Novus orbis*. See especially C. Kollarz, "Die beiden Indien im deutschen Schriftum des 16. und 17. Jahrhunderts" (Ph.D. diss., University of Vienna, 1966), pp. 61–62. Such questions evidently arise when the perusal is limited to the oldest editions, for he does use Portuguese materials in the later editions.

the disappearance of the original texts and of how much had fortunately been preserved in the encyclopedic works of Antiquity and the Middle Ages.[80] He is consequently much more concerned about completeness than about selectivity. He rarely differentiates among his authors in terms of chronology or authority but only in light of the subject matter they treat. On India, Strabo and Pliny are cited along with Hayton and Varthema. Traditional stories about the Indians appear next to the most recent information available. His contemporary sources on Asia are limited to the travel accounts in the *Novus orbis* and to fragments of information acquired elsewhere.[81] That he was concerned to bring everything he knew into his encyclopedia is supported by the additions he made to the revisions prepared during his lifetime. For example, he added new materials to the second German edition of 1545 on Sumatra and China.[82]

For Münster nothing is irrelevant, whether factual or fabulous. Sumatra is the island that grows quantities of the lac from which a beautiful red dye is made; Java is the island where they cannibalize the old and the useless.[83] While the East hardly existed as a reality for Münster, a number of later editors of his cosmography, especially François de Belleforest, improved vastly on the realism of the descriptions, excised traditional myths, and pointed out contradictions in the sources.[84] But for Münster and his publisher, the book proved, despite its poor German style, limitations, and distortions, to be a smashing financial success. It was probably its encyclopedic and uncritical spirit, as well as its lavish use of illustration, that appealed to the substantial burghers of Germany, who rapidly adopted it as a *Hausbuch* and cherished it as a conversation piece. Also there was very little in the book to disturb a reader's complacency. Münster's conception of history is theological in essence without being controversial in tone. In a number of Catholic countries the work was permitted to circulate freely or in only slightly expurgated versions. While he worked as a historian, Münster does not concern himself with theoretical questions and remains satisfied to describe or narrate without passing moral judgments.[85] He is generally unaware of the possibility of historical change in distant places, but he points out to his German readers how vastly northern Europe has improved and how civilized it has become since Roman times. In short, he wrote for his readers and showed himself to be a shrewd and discriminating judge of their tastes.

[80] The remarks that follow are based on an analysis of Book V of the definitive German edition, entitled *Cosmographei oder Beschreibung aller Länder-Herschafften . . .* (Basel, 1550). For its title page see pl. 70. Also see Burmeister, *op. cit.* (n. 73), pp. 159–63. The first German edition (1544) ran to more than 650 folio pages; by 1598 it had reached 1,461 pages.

[81] He apparently used Poggio's account of Conti's travels which was published at Basel in 1538.

[82] See Strauss, *loc. cit.* (n. 78), p. 154. For examples of his illustrations see pls. 3, 4, 7.

[83] *Cosmographei* (1550), pp. 1, 178–79.

[84] See Burmeister, *op. cit.* (n. 73), pp. 159–63. Though Münster and his associates sought everywhere for illustrative woodcuts, they were evidently unable to extract any substantial number from the fine collections of Theodor de Bry of Frankfurt or of Levinus Hulsius of Nuremberg. See V. Hantsch, *Sebastian Münster* (Leipzig, 1898), p. 68.

[85] On his place in German historiography see Gundolf, *op. cit.*, chap. vi.

Other mid-century writers of popular literature adopted similar tactics. Hans Sachs (1494–1576), the *Meistersinger* and leading poet of the school of Nuremberg, was one of the most prolific versifiers ever to set pen to paper. He was apparently also a reader of travel books, for he owned the account of Breydenbach (Mainz, 1486), "Ludovicus Vartomanus [Varthema] der lant farer," and Schiltberger (Nuremberg, 1542).[86] But in his songs, fables, tales, and plays, almost no trace appears of these works, perhaps because of Protestant hostility to Catholic pilgrimages and victories overseas. The "India" which he writes about is the marvelous land of the ancient and medieval writers. Since he often cites his sources in the poems, he appears to have in mind the viewpoints and sentiments of his largely Protestant audience. He certainly has no hesitation in drawing upon the tales from the *Gesta Romanorum* or from the fables in the *Book of the Seven Wise Masters*.[87] He likewise draws upon the bank of information in the natural histories for his poems on animals and fish.[88] In his play celebrating "Wilhelm von Orlientz," Sachs adopts a plot from Rudolf von Ems, the *Minnesinger*, which relates a lengthy tale of the efforts of the king of England to marry his daughter to Helmo, the king of India.[89] But nowhere does he use contemporary sources, even though he had certain of them in his personal library, for his references to the East.

B. PROTESTANTS VERSUS CATHOLICS

The conclusion of the Schmalkaldic wars (1555), the abdication of Charles V (1556), the peace of Cateau-Cambrésis (1559) between France and Spain, and the death of Suleiman (1566) combined to produce a respite in domestic and international tensions and to open a new opportunity for Germans to turn their attention again to cultivation of the arts of peace. Since Germany remained religiously divided, relations became increasingly close between Catholic Bohemia, Austria, Bavaria, and Spain, and between the southwest German courts and France. Instead of traveling only to Italy as before, the German knights, burghers, and students of the western and southern towns increasingly gravitated toward France and Switzerland. The spread of Calvinism naturally contributed greatly to this shift.[90] When the Dutch began their struggle for independence in 1568, many German Calvinists supported their cause and

[86] See R. Genée, *Hans Sachs und seine Zeit* (Leipzig, 1902), pp. 464–68.
[87] For example, a poem of 1559 begins:

> "Gesta Romanorum genant
> Das buch macht unns noch leng bekant."

A. Keller and E. Goetze (eds.), *Hans Sachs: Gesamtausgabe* (26 vols.; Stuttgart, 1870–1908), VII, 302.
[88] On the rhinoceros, elephant, and other Asian beasts his sources are mainly ancient and medieval stories. See *ibid.*, pp. 450–51, 456–63.
[89] *Ibid.*, XVI, 77–78.
[90] See W. Stammler, *op. cit.* (n. 23), pp. 469–70.

established closer ties with Netherlandish intellectuals. Dutch printers, geographers, and writers also emigrated from their war-torn homeland to Frankfurt and other German towns. Germany itself enjoyed a period of uneasy peace in the last forty years of the sixteenth century while wars raged on the peripheries of Europe from the Mediterranean to the North Atlantic.

The Germans who traveled abroad in this era brought back with them a variety of materials relating to the overseas world and to the literary activities of their European neighbors. At Rome in 1555 Frederick of Wirsberg, afterwards Bishop of Würzburg, met the Japanese convert Bernardo, who gave him certain writings in Japanese. They were still on display at Würzburg in 1568 when the Jesuit Jeronimo Nadal visited there.[91] The book trade also began to revive in Germany, the first catalog for the Frankfurt fair being produced by Georg Willer in 1564.[92] In the following year Grouchy's French translation of Castanheda's first book was translated into German and published, probably near Frankfurt.[93] In 1573 an unknown translator published a German version of Quintus Curtius' history of Alexander. Sigmund Feyerabend (*ca.* 1527–90), the publisher and collector of Frankfurt, contemporaneously began to issue in German translation a variety of materials on the overseas discoveries. The most comprehensive of these publications is his *General chronicon . . .* (1576),[94] a compendium of travel accounts and geographical writings from a number of authors, including Andrea Corsali of Florence on the voyage (1515) to India, the work of Maximilian of Transylvania on the voyage of Magellan, and Osório's history of Portugal.[95] A few years later Johann Wetzel translated into German the Italian romance of Christopher "the Armenian" relating the voyages of the three princes of "Serendip," or Ceylon.[96]

Johann Spies, a Frankfurt printer, published the first *Faustbuch* in 1587. Tales of the deeds of the learned Dr. Johann Faust (d. 1541) had circulated in Germany even before his death. An unknown author compiled and wrote down these tales for publication and in the process furnished the popular stories with a modicum of factual material gathered from classical authors, the *Lucidarius*,

---

[91] See P. d'Elia, "Bernardo," *La civiltà cattolica*, CII (1951), No. III, 531–33. Also see *Asia*, I, 673.
[92] On Willer's activities see above, pp. 59–60, and below, pp. 476–77.
[93] Typographically a duplicate of Grouchy's it was probably printed by Nicolas Heinrich of Ober-Ursel near Frankfurt. No place of publication or even the name of the translator appears in the book. The translator confides in his preface that he originally undertook the translation as an exercise in translating French, but was prevailed upon by his friends to publish it in spite of the imperfections. It is entitled *Wahraftige und volkomene Historia von erfindung Calecut und anderer Königreich, Landen, und Inseln . . . Auss Frantzoesischen Sprach jetzt newlich ins Teutsch gebracht, Anno 1565*. For details see Vicomte de Grouchy and E. Travers, *Étude sur Nicolas de Grouchy* (Paris, 1878), pp. 106–8.
[94] His *Weltbuch* (Pt. I) is a reprint of Franck's earlier book. The *General chronicon* is Pt. II of what is often referred to as Feyerabend's *Weltbuch*. See Kollarz, *op. cit.* (n. 79), pp. 51–52.
[95] For Feyerabend's business career see H. Pallmann, *Sigmund Feyerabend, sein Leben und seine geschäftlichen Verbindungen* (Frankfurt, 1881). Vol. VII in New Series of the *Archiv für Frankfurts Geschichte und Kunst*.
[96] For discussion of this original work see above, p. 212. For the German translation see H. Fischer and J. Bolte (eds.), *Die Reise der Söhne Giaffers, aus dem italienischen des Christoforo Armeno ubersetzt durch Johann Wetzel 1583* (Stuttgart, 1896).

and Münster's *Kosmographie*. Among other spectacular acts, the sorcerer Faust flies over many places, including India, while seeking the earthly paradise. For his description of India the anonymous author depends on the legends of Solinus for general materials but turns to Münster for comments on India's cities.[97] In the *Lalebuch* of 1597, the first comic novel in German, the city of Laleburg is located "behind Calicut" in the powerful kingdom of Utopia! The preface to the reader in Schiltbürger's 1598 edition explains that the stories of the Laleburgers remained so long unpublished because of the city's remoteness and the peculiarity of its language. Throughout the century "Calicut" and "India" remain in German imaginative literature little more than synonyms for the most remote places conceivable.[98]

Stimuli from abroad nonetheless brought with them a measure of interest in the East. Duke Christopher of Würtemberg, for example, sponsored the translation of the popular French *Amadis* cycle, a task that was finally completed in twenty-four books published between 1569 and 1595, with its references to Asian places, kings, and peoples.[99] One of those involved in this translation project was Johann Fischart (*ca.* 1545–*ca.* 1590), the foremost German satirist of the day. Trained at Siena and Basel as a jurist, Fischart traveled from about 1570 to 1572 in Flanders, England, and France. In addition to Latin, he was proficient in French, Italian, and Dutch. He spent most of his productive years in Strassburg, though he traveled and lived in other German towns as well. A publicist for Protestantism, especially Calvinism, he reserved his most pointed barbs for the Jesuits, the Spanish, and their German allies. But he was also highly critical of all Germans for their adulation of foreign lands and practices, and for their addiction to traveling abroad. He claimed that Würtembergers travel about the world so regularly that when a Swabian arrives in Asia he invariably asks if his good friend from Beblingen is not also on the scene.[100]

Fischart became acquainted with the first book of *Gargantua* (1534) in 1572 and was thereafter bent upon becoming the "German Rabelais." Three years later, he published his major work, the first version of his *Geschichtklitterung*, a rendering of the first book of the heroic deeds of Gargantua.[101] Revised versions of this grotesque classic appeared in 1582 and 1585. Though he hoped to "translate" the other books of Rabelais, he never attained this goal and so never became involved in the imaginary voyages of Pantagruel. He evidently found the colossal Gargantua sufficient to his needs for satirizing the Germany of his day. He used the French tale merely as a frame on which to hang stories and

[97] See A. Kühne (ed.), *Das älteste Faustbuch: Wortgetreuer Abdruck der editio princeps des Spies'schen Faustbuches vom Jahre 1587* (Zerbst, 1868; reprint of 1970), pp. 75–77; and G. Ellinger, "Zu den Quellen des Faustbuchs von 1587," *Zeitschrift für vergleichende Literaturgeschichte*, I (1888), 158–62.

[98] See K. von Bahder (ed.), *Das Lalebuch (1597) mit den Abweichungen und Erweiterungen der Schiltbürger (1598) und des Grillenvertreibers (1603)* (Halle, 1914), pp. 8, 147–48.

[99] On the Eastern references in the *Amadis* see above, pp. 210–11.

[100] On the nature of his satire see H. Schneegans, *Geschichte der grotesken Satire* (Strassburg, 1892), p. 382.

[101] On *Gargantua* see above, pp. 260–66. For an analysis of the *Geschichtklitterung* see H. Sommerhalder, *Johann Fischarts Werk: Eine Einführung* (Berlin, 1960), pp. 52–80.

comments from the German past and present. His references to Asia are incidental and limited to mentions of the heavenly odor of Indian spices, the Indian custom of wearing nose gems, and the worship of the devil in Calicut.[102] Picrohol's (or Buttergroll's) plans are much more colossal in Fischart's rendition than in Rabelais' original. He does not want, like Hercules, merely to erect two stately pillars at Gibraltar but strives to be more "practical." He aims to fill in the strait so that one might walk with dry feet from Europe to Africa to Asia. To link the individual countries more closely, he would throw up bridges over the seas. Should the seas resist being bridged he would make short shrift of the whole matter by emptying them through an old diversionary canal onto the moon![103]

From the evidence in Fischart's poems it emerges that he was acquainted with the Jesuit letterbooks circulating in Germany during the 1570's. In the *Nachtrab* (1570–80) he bitterly attacks the Jesuits for their activities in both Europe and Asia. To those who doubt their claims of success in Asia, the Jesuits responded by telling the disbelievers to go there and observe for themselves. Fischart's reply is to remark that the Jesuits lie about matters much closer to home so it is to be assumed that they also lie about distant affairs.[104] He is especially vehement in his attack on the miracles and successes of Xavier. He predicts that the Jesuits with their mass and forced conversions in Asia are building an edifice of straw bricks that will soon crumble.[105] He laughs at their hope of compensating in Asia for the losses suffered by the church in Europe, and jibes that nobody in Germany will take umbrage if they should simply decide to remain with the "cannibals" permanently.[106] In other poems he praises the virtues of rural life and extolls the farmer who takes no interest in the rich cargoes coming from the East to Portugal and remains content to tend his own garden.[107] His last poems warn about the disastrous consequences for northern Europe of the union of the Spanish and Portuguese crowns. He rejoices ghoulishly in the defeat of the Spanish Armada and claims that the English victory proves that the Spanish cannot crush northern Europeans as simply as they do the peoples overseas:

> Here it is not as in India,
> Where they regarded your ships as so many birds.[108]

Certain Latin poets also responded positively to the news of the overseas world they read about in the compendia of the printers. The humanistic genre

---

[102] From the synoptic reproduction of the versions of 1575, 1582, and 1590 of A. Alsleben (ed.), *Johann Fischarts Geschichtklitterung (Gargantua)* (Halle, 1891), pp. 19–20, 393, 412.

[103] For commentary see Schneegans, *op. cit.* (n. 100), p. 383.

[104] See H. Kurz (ed.), *Johann Fischart's sämmtliche Dichtungen* (3 vols.; Leipzig, 1866–67), I, 63–64.

[105] *Ibid.*, pp. 83–84.

[106] *Ibid.*, p. 93.

[107] *Ibid.* See *Aus XV. Bücher vom Feldbau, ibid.*, III, 308–9.

[108] Hie gings nit wie in India
Da man jhr Schiff für Vögel ansah.

See *ibid.*, III, 375.

of travel and topographical literature called *Hodoeporicon* began to include more references to the Portuguese in Asia. Nathan Chytraeus (1543–98), professor of classics and poetry at Rostock, makes reference in his *Hodoeporica* . . . (Frankfurt, 1575) to the new importance of Leipzig as a spice market. He also indites a Latin poem on Calicut and another on Lisbon as he works out the spice itinerary for his readers.[109] Martin Chemnitz (1561–1627), while a law student at Leipzig, celebrated in a long narrative poem the heroic story of the Portuguese conquest in Asia to the circumnavigation of Magellan's men.[110] Like Camoëns, he concentrates on the voyage of Vasco da Gama. Like poets everywhere, he details one after the other for the euphony in their names the places of Portugal's conquests. Both of these Latin poets were clearly responding in their works to a new interest in Asia generated in northern and central Germany by Leipzig's strategic but short-lived role in the spice trade.[111]

The Latin poets were not the only German Protestants stimulated by these new developments. Georg Rollenhagen (1542–1609), a Lutheran teacher and preacher of Magdeburg, wrote poetic dramas of an edifying and amusing kind for his students to perform. Most of these were based on themes or episodes introduced from secular sources, both ancient and contemporary. In his play called *Tobias* (1576) Rollenhagen introduces a story derived ultimately from Varthema. The Italian traveler recounts a tale, quite in the literary tradition of the saga of the *Giftmädchen* (poisonous damsel), of the sultan of Cambay in India who has a breath so deadly that it kills people. For Rollenhagen this story is a source of amusement and a warning to the audience of the danger involved in getting too close to foreign peoples and ideas—especially those associated with Catholics.[112]

While still a student at Wittenberg, Rollenhagen learned about the pseudo-Homeric poem of the battle between frogs and mice. It had been translated in 1549 from the Greek *Batrachomyomachia* into Latin and quickly came to be popular reading in academic circles.[113] As a portrait of human life in animal form, it soon became a vehicle for satire. From 1565 to 1595 Rollenhagen worked on his own version of this Greek tale and finally published it under the title *Froschmeuseler* (1595). A moralistic satire in which the men wear animal disguises, *Froschmeuseler* was popular in Germany until the eighteenth century. The first two parts of the poem are based on a frame borrowed from the

[109] *Hodoeporica; sive Itineraria* . . . , pp. 290–91, 298–99, 304. For later works of this genre see the writings of Matthias Quad (1557–*ca.* 1610), polygraph and engraver of Cologne. Cf. pl. 81.

[110] *Navigatio Lusitanorum in Indiam Orientalem, heroico carmine descripta* . . . (Leipzig, 1580). I have consulted the copy of this rare poem in the *Bibliothèque nationale* (YC. 2526).

[111] For the establishment of the Thuringian Company see *Asia*, I, 134.

[112] Rollenhagen has "Memia" tell the story in Act I, scene 2. See J. Bolte (ed.), *Georg Rollenhagens Spiel von Tobias 1576* (Halle, 1930), p. 20. Rollenhagen might have used Franck's *Weltbuch* as his immediate source, but in any case Franck obtained it from Varthema. See J. Bolte, "Quellenstudien zu Georg Rollenhagen," *Sitzungsberichte der preussichen Akademie der Wissenschaften* (Berlin), *philoso-phisch-historische Klasse*, 1929, p. 675. For the relationship of the tale to the saga of the poisonous damsel see W. Hertz, *Gesammelte Abhandlungen* (Stuttgart and Berlin, 1905), pp. 261–66.

[113] W. Stammler, *op. cit.* (n. 23), pp. 445–46.

Panchatantra as relayed through the German version of the *Seven Wise Masters* published by Anton von Pforr (Ulm, 1483).[114] A number of the chapters, or moral tales, in the poem itself refer to traditional fables or beliefs about India. What makes Rollenhagen different is his acute awareness of the falsity of these old stories. As a consequence he employs them satirically and didactically. For example, he repeats the story of the gold-mining ants of India to ask where their holes lead to and whether or not they end up in Saxony.[115] In the meantime he had his son Gabriel prepare as a Latin exercise a list of thirty-five "true lies" or superstitious beliefs held by the learned with regard to fabulous animals in distant places.[116]

The Protestant historians were, like Fischart, reluctant to believe the testimony of the Catholics, secular or Jesuit, about their progress in Asia or even about its countries and peoples. In Philip Melanchthon's (1497–1560) lectures on world history delivered between 1555 and the date of his death, no place is reserved for or mention made of America or Asia.[117] A member of Melanchthon's circle at Wittenberg, David Chytraeus (1531–1600) the historian, included information on Tartary in his Saxon chronicle and reported on the basis of the writing of Damião de Góis on the state of Christianity in Ethiopia.[118] But nowhere in his works is reference made to the progress of the Portuguese and the Jesuits in Asia. Though hopes ran high around 1580 of Leipzig becoming a staple in the spice trade, this episode evidently left no significant imprint upon Protestant historians. It was the appearance of the Japanese mission (1584–86) in southern Europe which finally convinced the skeptical Protestants of the general truth of the Jesuit claims. In the *Flugschrift* literature of the 1580's directed against the Spanish claims of universal monarchy, a number of the pamphlets grudgingly recognize that Philip was the only European ruler with overseas possessions.[119] An anonymous pamphleteer of 1585 even called upon the Lutherans to begin sending missions of their own to Japan.[120] Four years later at Frankfurt there appeared German and Latin translations of Mendoza's book on China, the latter being dedicated to Anton Fugger. But to all this evidence the Protestants deep in Saxony reacted only suspiciously and slowly.

[114] Bolte, *loc. cit.* (n. 112), p. 481. Also see above, p. 99.

[115] In the chapter called "How Reinecke was betrayed by the mountain ants" in K. Goedeke (ed.), *Froschmeuseler von Georg Rollenhagen* (Leipzig, 1876), Pt. I, Bk. 1, chap. 14, p. 111.

[116] Called "Wahrhaffte Lügen" this exercise was appended to Gabriel Rollenhagen's collection of ancient sources on India in *Vier Bücher wunderbarlicher indianischer Reisen* (Leipzig, 1717).

[117] See Samuel Berger, "Melanchthon's Vorlesungen über Weltgeschichte," *Theologische Studien und Kritiken*, LXX (1897), 781–84. An examination of his correspondence also reveals that Melanchthon, even though Góis had once visited with him (see above, p. 17), apparently remained entirely preoccupied with other matters.

[118] See Chytraeus' lecture on the land of Prester John in *Was zu dieser Zeit in Griechenland, Asien, Africa unter des Türcken und Priester Johans Herrschaften ... der Christlichen Kirchen zustand sey ...* (Frankfurt [?], 1581). On his use of oral and written sources see D. Klatt, *David Chytraeus als Geschichtslehrer und Geschichtschreiber* (Rostock, 1908), p. 87.

[119] See H. Tiemann, *Das spanische Schrifttum in Deutschland von der Renaissance bis zur Romantik* (Hamburg, 1936), pp. 35–36.

[120] Details in *Asia*, I, 702.

The Protestant reaction is well illustrated by reference to Matthias Dresser (1536–1607), after 1581 the eminent professor of classics and history at Leipzig. His career and writings are utterly representative of what might be expected from an orthodox Lutheran Humanist of his day. By 1590 all his writings were on the papal *Index*. As a historian he was responsible for teaching the entire range of history following the traditional periodization of the "four monarchies" prescribed by the *Book of Daniel*. Possibly because he became aware of the inadequacy of these divisions, he suddenly published in 1598 a German translation of Part I of Mendoza's book on China to which he wrote a preface.[121] In Dresser's introductory remarks he records the grave doubts he originally felt about believing the current reports on China because that country was not known to either Ptolemy or Strabo. He put his doubts aside, however, upon reflecting that it was probably known to the Ancients under another name, even as America was known to the kings of the Old Testament as the land of Ophir.[122] He recalls that the historians of the past, especially Herodotus, refer to Asian peoples, particularly the Scythians, who might well be identified with the Chinese. He insists that it is possible for vital information of this kind to remain long hidden as is illustrated by the story of Japan. Marco Polo knew Japan, but this knowledge remained hidden until the island kingdom was opened by Portuguese merchants in 1543. The Jesuit letters, he admits, have also revealed much about Japan. Chinese are not known in Europe, because they are forbidden by their own laws to leave their country. Still, he acknowledges, it is not impossible that the Chinese have for centuries practiced the art of printing. He also observes that the systematic uncovering of the overseas world began around the time of Martin Luther's birth in 1483 and was mostly completed by his death in 1546, an indication, he implies, that God undertook simultaneously two aspects of his continuing revelation. More pragmatically, he concludes that he has republished this book because copies of it are not available in Frankfurt or Leipzig though many still ask for it. Despite Dresser's relative openmindedness as expressed in his preface, it should be noted that Mendoza's name never appears in this book. In his own world history published three years later, Dresser includes nothing on the discoveries, even when discussing Portugal.[123]

In Catholic Germany, particularly at Vienna, Munich, and Ingolstadt, the clergy dominated education, printing, and court life in the latter half of the sixteenth century. The censorship was extremely severe, especially in Bavaria, in dealing with unauthorized or suspect books. From their presses at Dillingen,

---

[121] *Historien und Bericht von dem newlicher Zeit erfundenen Königreich China* . . . (Leipzig, 1598). The preface is dated 1597. I have established its identity with Part I of Mendoza's book by textual comparison. The translation is word for word except for the omission of about four pages near the end where Mendoza writes in the first person summarizing the conditions under which he was supposed to go to China. For a map of China based on Mendoza see pl. 78.

[122] On the location of Ophir see below, p. 386.

[123] On India his account is completely traditional; he also recounts the Tartar depredations in Europe. See *Isagoge historica, Historische Erzehlung der denkwürdigsten Geschichten von Anfang der Welt, biss auff unsere Zeit* . . . (Leipzig, 1601), pp. 134, 137–38, 717–19, 774.

Cologne, Mainz, Ingolstadt, and Munich, the Jesuits regularly issued their letterbooks in German and Latin over the last generation of the century.[124] In 1585 Renward Cysat, the municipal secretary of Lucerne, published a survey in German of what he had learned about Japan from the Jesuit letterbooks.[125] At the turn of the century the Jesuits themselves began to compile selections from the letters into "histories" of their conquests in the East that included what was then known about China and Japan.[126] At the Catholic courts everything from Spain became fashionable whereas in the Protestant towns and states the French and Dutch exercised the chief influence.[127] Books were regularly imported from Spain for the collections of the Catholic princes and prelates. Since northern Europe knew so little about Spain, the printers began in the early years of the seventeenth century to compile and publish between two covers most of what had been written about Spain (and Portugal) over the preceding century.[128] Conrad Löw, an amateur historian of Cologne, even sought to keep alive and fresh the biographies and deeds of the discoverers. In 1598, the centennial of Vasco da Gama's first visit to India, he issued a collection of excerpts from the voyages of the Iberians and the Dutch whom he labeled "maritime heroes."[129]

The Jesuits were not the only missionaries who kept Catholic Germany informed about events in Asia. In 1588 Valentin Fricius, a Franciscan and confessor of Archduke Matthias of Austria, published a German translation with commentary of Francisco Gonzaga's Latin history of the Franciscan Observants in the missions of America and Asia.[130] In talking about their activities in Malacca, Fricius stipulates that it cannot be "noticed enough how many of these idolatrous heathens have been inscribed by our brothers in the register of believers."[131] The following year the Augustinian Mendoza's book on China appeared in German at Frankfurt. In 1599 the Franciscans at Munich published in German the account of Francisco Tello, first issued the year before in Italian at Rome, of the martyrdoms suffered by their brothers in Japan in 1597.[132] Despite such efforts to win recognition of their trials and sacrifices in Asia, the other orders were unable to capture the limelight from the Jesuits in Catholic Germany.

[124] For representative titles of the German letterbooks see the *Bibliotheca exotica* (2 parts; Frankfurt, 1610–11), II, 458, 487.

[125] For details see *Asia*, I, 702–5.

[126] For example, Gotthard Arthus, *Historia Indiae Orientalis, ex variis auctoribus collecta* . . . (Cologne, 1608).

[127] See W. Stammler, *op. cit.* (n. 23), pp. 473–74.

[128] For example, see above, pp. 23–24.

[129] It was entitled *Meer oder Seehanen Buch*. A copy is in the British Museum. For commentary see Kollarz, *op. cit.* (n. 79), pp. 54–55, 174.

[130] Gonzaga (1546–1620), Bishop of Mantua, published at Rome in 1587 his *De origine seraphicae religioniis Fräciscanae*.

[131] *Indianischer Religionstandt der gantzen newen Welt, beider Indien gegen Auff und Niedergang der Sonnen* . . . (Ingolstadt, 1588), pp. 151–52.

[132] For its lengthy title see *Bibliographischer Alt-Japan Katalog* (Kyoto, 1940), p. 358, no. 1479. On the martyrdoms see *Asia*, I, 717.

In their teaching of students the Jesuits were inclined to use the letterbooks for secular readings.[133] Beginning in 1555 they also began to use the drama for instructional purposes. In their morality plays prepared in Latin for students to perform, they celebrated the deeds of Loyola in Rome and Xavier in the East; India and Japan sorrow at the sight of Xavier for he will die and the waves will not swallow his ship. These plays purport also to show him working with the natives as he travels in the East from place to place.[134] In the dramas and tales of Jakob Bidermann (1578–1639) a few themes from Marco Polo's materials appear.[135] Bidermann also favored the story of Josaphat, upon which he based a play later to become standard in the Jesuit repertory.[136] Before the sixteenth century ended it had been performed at Vienna (1571), Munich (1573), Graz (1599), and probably many other Jesuit centers.[137] It was not until the seventeenth century that plays on the martyrdoms in Japan began to appear on the Jesuit stage.

Aegidius Albertinus (1560–1620), secretary and librarian to Duke Maximilian of Bavaria, was a great friend of the Jesuits and the Spanish as well as a leading figure in the cultural life of Catholic Germany. At Munich he was associated with Johann Baptist Fickler (1533–1610), tutor of the heir-apparent and curator of the ducal collections of coins and curiosities.[138] Both men, like the ducal family itself, watched closely the activities of the Jesuits in the East. But the German Jesuits themselves, preoccupied as they were with the spread of Protestantism, took no part directly in the missions to Asia. Albertinus translated a number of the letterbooks into German, particularly those relating to China and Japan. In 1611 he translated Giovanni Botero's *Relazioni*, one of the first chronicles to bring the East into the mainstream of history.[139] In the meantime Johannes Mayer, with the encouragement and support of Albertinus, had prepared a chronological compendium of manners and morals reminiscent of but far more recent in its data than the collection published by Boemus in 1520.[140] Despite such efforts the German Catholics, like their Protestant co-nationalists, failed to produce important new interpretations of their own. They relied entirely upon translations and compilations; as a result they did not create historical syntheses comparable to those of Botero or Louis Le Roy.

The direct involvement of Germans in the spice trade was limited to the first and last generations of the sixteenth century. In the intervening forty years

---

133 On their use in the Jesuit colleges of France see below, pp. 480–81.

134 Only a few Jesuit dramas of this sort were played in the sixteenth century. See K. Adel, *Das Wiener Jesuitentheater und die europäische Barockdramatik* (Vienna, 1960), pp. 6–7.

135 See J. Müller, *Das Jesuitentheater in den Ländern deutscher Zunge vom Anfang bis zum Hochbarock* (2 vols.; Augsburg, 1930), I, 44–45.

136 For the Josaphat story see above, pp. 101–3.

137 See Müller, *op. cit.* (n. 135), I, 46, 54.

138 For details see *Asia*, II, Bk. 1, 24–25.

139 See above, pp. 243–48.

140 Entitled *Compendium cronologicum . . . ; Das ist: Summarischer Inhalt aller gedruck und glaubwirdigen Sachen . . . mit kurtzer Beschreibung etlicher Völcker und Länder mancherley sittin und gebräuchen ausz ansehelichen authoribus zusamb getragen und in dise formb verfasset* (Munich, 1598).

(1530–70) they were preoccupied with domestic problems, especially those stemming from the religious conflicts. While the early literati were stimulated by the revelation of the East, they had difficulty in reconciling the new information with their desire to recover the learning of the Ancients. The Reformation heightened German skepticism about the opening of the overseas world because the reports came through Catholic writers about the successes of Catholic nations and missionaries. The costliness of the spices turned the rural populace against the spice merchants and their foreign associates. The end of direct German contact with Lisbon around 1530 and the collapse of the spice monopoly at Antwerp in 1549 had the effect of making even more remote and unbelievable the overseas activities of the Iberians and the Catholic missionaries. The resumption of German participation in the spice trade after 1570, the production at Frankfurt of new collections of travel literature, the union of the Spanish and Portuguese crowns (1580), and the appearance in southern Europe (1584–86) of the Japanese envoys gradually reawakened the Germans to their own stake and their own possible involvement, directly or indirectly, in the expansion movement.

The cosmographers, geographers, and historians, along with the printers, were the German literati most attentive to the new knowledge of Asia in their own works. But they were completely dependent upon the reports which came through foreign writings. Only a few of the German participants in the spice trade actually traveled to the East, and but one of them, Balthasar Springer, prepared and published (1508) the story of his voyage. Still, the geographers sought to revise Ptolemy and other Ancients in light of the new information; a few historians, especially Sebastian Franck, tried to broaden world history enough to take account more adequately of the new discoveries. But it was the cosmographers, in their determination to preserve *all* knowledge, who brought the new materials most fully into their vast compendia. The cosmographies also, like the compilations of Boemus and others, were organized to invite comparison of both substance and sources. These encyclopedic works were among the most popular books of the day both in Germany and in western Europe at large.

Few German literati, as compared to the Italian and French, were either ready or able to begin drawing implications for their own society from the discoveries. The poets, especially Brant and Fischart, were skeptical or hostile to the claims that the Catholics were successfully opening the world for the greater glory of the Christian God. Hans Sachs refrained from antagonizing his audience by ignoring in his innumerable writings the new picture of the East. Like his public, he retained intact the traditional view of Asia preserved in the universally popular histories, travel books, and collections of fables inherited from the Middle Ages. To the Protestants, even certain of these folkbooks, for example Mandeville, were too full of materials on pilgrimages and miracles to be regarded as safe reading. In the Catholic areas the censorship was so rigorous that most of the literati opted for noncontroversial plaudits of sea heroes or openly polemical tracts. In such circumstances it is hardly surprising that but few Germans were moved enough by the revelation of the East to think of it as one of the greatest achievements of their age and to glorify it in their writings.

2

NETHERLANDISH LITERATURE

At first glance it might appear that Dutch and Flemish literati must have responded more sensitively and dramatically to the discoveries than their colleagues of Germany and France. Antwerp throughout the first half of the sixteenth century was the northern European outpost of the spice trade and played host to merchants of all nationalities. This thriving metropolis was also a leading center of printing and engraving to which scholars, artists, and writers were drawn magnetically. By comparison to other cities of the time Antwerp was prosperous, stimulating, and cosmopolitan—the hub of a vigorous southern Netherlandish region that was itself a meeting ground for the luminaries of government, commerce, education, and printing. Charles V held his court periodically at Brussels and always attached to it were men of distinction from all parts of his dynastic empire and France.[141] Louvain in the early sixteenth century (1517–50) became the home of the Collegium trilingue, a university of international reputation and influence. Cities like Bruges and Ghent, which were beginning to experience a decline, were nonetheless still far better known than Amsterdam and other towns of the northern Netherlands. Culturally the southern towns were also much more advanced than the isolated centers of the north. Limburg, Flanders, and Brabant easily outstripped Holland before 1550 in their individual contributions to the development of a literature in the vernacular. But, even though conditions apparently favored cultural flowering in the south, the innovations in literature were few and unremarkable. Instead of responding creatively to the challenges offered by Humanism and the discoveries, the Flemish and Dutch literati continued for a long time to confine their experimentation to reforming and refining traditional literary forms.

Independent literary works in Dutch began to appear in the twelfth century.[142] Religious writings and romances of chivalry derived from French originals were the most characteristic products of these early endeavors. Jacob van Maerlant (*ca.* 1235–91), the father of Dutch poetry, chose as the subject for his first romance the heroic deeds of Alexander the Great (*Alexanders Geesten*). A few writers translated or adapted French and Latin sources which included stories of Eastern origin. Maerlant and others called in their writings for a new crusade against the Turks. But most early writers of prose and poetry preferred

---

[141] On the impact of the New World on his court see M. Bataillon, "La cour découvre le nouveau monde," in J. Jacquot (ed.), *Fêtes et cérémonies au temps de Charles Quint* (Paris, 1960), pp. 13–27.

[142] See R. P. Meijer, *Literature of the Low Countries . . .* (Assen, 1971), chap. i.

stories of religious and moral import to romances of chivalry. It was the invention of printing and the growth of literacy that brought about a vogue for the romance in prose. One of the most immediately successful of the secular romances was *De Reis van Jan van Mandeville*, a version of which was in print before 1470. Over the course of the next century, Mandeville's book retained its popularity and was printed in at least six separate editions.[143] Strangely, the travels of Marco Polo seems not to have been translated into Dutch until the seventeenth century.

Accounts of the maritime voyages of the late fifteenth and early sixteenth centuries quickly appeared in Flemish versions. The printers of Antwerp, especially Jan van Doesborch, began to print newsletters describing the voyages to the East, some of which were illustrated with woodcuts. The first to appear was the *Calcoen (Calicut)*, a 1504 rendition by a Dutch sailor who had accompanied Vasco da Gama on his second voyage to India.[144] This was followed around 1506 by Doesborch's compilation of materials on the land of Prester John.[145] Two years later he published a Dutch version of the German newsletter first printed in 1505 at Nuremberg describing the route from Lisbon to Calicut.[146] Doesborch was also acquainted with the German accounts of the India fleet of 1505, for he utilized them in the preparation of the Latin, English, and Flemish versions of his *Of the newe Landes* which he published around 1511. In the English and Latin editions of this work he included seven woodcuts adapted from the originals prepared by Hans Burgkmair for *Die Merfart* of Balthasar Springer, first printed in 1509.[147] Perhaps most striking here is Doesborch's dependence upon the Germans for both his textual and illustrative materials. It is also worth noticing that he, like other Antwerp printers, prepared cheap, popular books in English for sale in a country where the art of printing was less advanced at this time.[148]

But such productions in foreign languages were the exception rather than the rule. Of the more than twelve hundred editions published at Antwerp between 1500 and 1540 relatively few were printed in foreign vernaculars. More than half of those issued were in Latin, about five hundred in Flemish, and sixty-five in French.[149] Most of the Latin editions were liturgical or theological works intended for clerics, or editions, translations, and commentaries on the classics

---

[143] For a listing of the early Dutch editions see J. W. Bennett, *op. cit.* (n. 32), pp. 371–73. The most important are those of Brussels of 1550 and Antwerp of 1564, 1578, 1586, and 1592.

[144] For further detail see *Asia*, I, 160.

[145] *Pape Ians landen* (ca. 1506). A facsimile of this work was issued by Frederick Müller at Amsterdam in 1873.

[146] *Die Reyse van Lissebone*. For discussion of the original see *Asia*, I, 161–62.

[147] For discussion of Springer's account see *Asia*, I, 162–63; for analysis of Doesborch's books see M. E. Kronenberg (ed. and trans.), *De novo mondo. Antwerp. Jan van Doesborch* [*about 1520*] (The Hague, 1927), pp. 10–14.

[148] See R. Proctor, *Jan van Doesborgh, Printer at Antwerp: An Essay in Bibliography* (London, 1894), p. 4.

[149] Based on an examination of W. Nijhoff and M. E. Kronenberg, *Nederlandsche bibliographie van 1500 tot 1540* (3 vols.; The Hague, 1919–61). Antwerp produced 56 percent of all editions printed in the Netherlands at this time.

intended for Humanists and students. The predominance of Latin editions may also be accounted for by the presence of a large international community in the Netherlands most of whose members were unacquainted with Flemish and other northern vernaculars.[150] The strict surveillance of book production inaugurated in 1521 by Charles V to check the spread of Protestantism in the Netherlands also contributed to the reluctance of the printers to issue contemporary materials in the vernacular languages. Most of the Flemish editions after 1521 were therefore limited to official publications, Catholic tracts, and folkbooks. Almost all information on the overseas discoveries appeared in Latin editions after 1530. A few of the cosmographies, such as that of Apian, appeared in Flemish translation, and finally in 1544, and again in 1563, Varthema appeared in Dutch. Around mid-century, with the decline of the Portuguese factory at Antwerp, a number of works relating to Asia, such as Gomara (1552) and Castanheda (1554), began to be printed at Antwerp in Spanish.[151]

The publication of such materials evidently made little or no impression upon the writers of popular Dutch literature. The Chambers of Rhetoric (*Rederijkerkamers*) which began to flourish in the fifteenth century were organized like urban trade guilds and were delegated to present pageants and plays on festive occasions.[152] A considerable proportion of the literary, dramatic, and musical talent of the Netherlandish towns in the sixteenth century was involved with the preparation of poems and plays for the productions and contests of the *Rederijkers*. Their efforts were generally directed to the celebration in extravagant pageants of important events and the achievements of individual rulers, or to the preparation of simple mystery, miracle, and morality plays designed to edify a lay audience. Most of these productions went unpublished until they were collected and printed by entrepreneurs like Jan van Doesborch. In a poem celebrating Charles V, the emperor is compared to the Grand Khan, a reference familiar to readers of Mandeville. But perusal of other *Rederijker* poems reveals no references to contemporary Asia and but few to the spices from which Antwerp derived so much profit.[153] Nor does this condition change as popular poetry began about 1566 to become less religious and more secular and contemporary in its orientation.[154] This omission can be accounted for in part by the broadening of the censorship to include surveillance of folkbooks in the vernaculars. Were one to judge by the *Rederijker* poetry alone, one would conclude that the people of the southern Netherlands were totally unaware of Asia.

[150] See F. Prims, *Geschiedenis van Antwerpen* (13 vols.; Antwerp, 1941–43), VII, Bk. iii, 316–17.

[151] See J. Peeters-Fontainas, *Bibliographie des impressions espagnoles des pays-bas méridionaux* (Louvain, 1933), p. 82. Also note that Francisco Tamara's *De las costumbres de todas las gentes* was published at Antwerp in 1556.

[152] For their relation to literary development in general see G. Kalff, *Geschiedenis van nederlandsche Letterkunde in de 16de Eeuw* (2 vols.; Leyden, 1889), I, 86–186.

[153] See A. H. Hoffmann von Fallersleben, *Antwerpener Liederbuch vom Jahre 1544* (Hanover, 1855), pp. 163–69.

[154] See Prims, *op. cit.* (n. 150), VIII, Bk. iv, 11.

Humanistic controversy too, relating particularly to the ideas of Erasmus, kept most Netherlandish intellectuals absorbed in European affairs. Educational theory and experiment were stimulated by the Brethren of the Common Life, Erasmus, and Luis Vives. Latin poets played a major role in the development of the school drama as a teaching device. In higher education the center of gravity increasingly became the Collegium trilingue at Louvain. Students from all over Europe, including Iberia, were attracted to Louvain. Included in their number were the Portuguese André de Resende and Damião de Góis. It was here that the two Portuguese Humanists published their Latin works on the victories of the Portuguese in the East.[155] And it was from Louvain that a number of Netherlandish scholars, including Clenardus and Vasaeus, went to Iberia to forward their careers.[156] Another Netherlander, Gaspar Barzaeus (or Barzée), journeyed to Portugal in 1546 to enter the Society of Jesus and two years later went to India to work with Xavier. The Netherlandish Jesuits, like their German colleagues, were ordinarily much too involved in local problems to enlist in the mission to Asia.

Religious and civil wars tore the Netherlands apart from 1566 to 1609. Philip II's ascent to power in 1555 was followed by a Spanish effort to suppress militarily the rise of Protestantism and the spread of insurgency in the Low Countries. Antwerp, the richest and most cosmopolitan of its cities, was at the center of the religious and political struggle. As control of the city changed hands periodically, its leading citizens began to emigrate to escape the terror and the blood-letting. After the "Spanish fury" of 1576, the decline of Antwerp was precipitous. Its losses of trade and citizenry became Amsterdam's gain. In the period of uneasy peace which prevailed after 1576, the lines solidified between the southern and northern provinces. Spain's resumption of control over Antwerp was not fully achieved until 1585. Thereafter the cities of Holland and Zeeland slowly replaced Antwerp in commerce and in most of the related activities that had first brought renown to the city on the Scheldt.[157] In literature the Amsterdam Chamber of Rhetoric became the leading center of poetry and Leyden with its new Protestant university became the nexus of Humanistic studies.[158]

The printers of Antwerp were among those groups most buffeted by the religious and political strife of the latter half of the century. Christopher Plantin (1520–89), the printer to King Philip II, provides a case in point.[159] A native of the Touraine in France, Plantin learned his trade with the best masters of Lyons, Paris, and Antwerp. In 1550 he opened a book store in Antwerp and five years

---

[155] On the details see above, pp. 19–20.

[156] On these men and others see Henry de Vocht, *History of the Foundation and Rise of the Collegium Trilingue Louvaniense, 1517–1550* (4 vols.; Louvain, 1951–55), II, 220–24, 474–76. Also see A. Roersch, *L'Humanisme belge à l'époque de la Renaissance* (Louvain, 1933), pp. 87–93.

[157] For a summary discussion see J. J. Murray, *Antwerp in the Age of Plantin and Brueghel* (Norman, Okla., 1970), pp. 37–42.

[158] See Meijer, *op. cit.* (n. 142), p. 100.

[159] For his life and times see Colin Clair, *Christopher Plantin* (London, 1960).

later began to print books there under his own imprint. His success as a book-seller helped to finance his early, modest ventures in printing. Although Plantin was outwardly a devout Catholic and a close associate of numerous prelates, he became suspect as a heretic as early as 1562 for his personal interest in mystical sects and for publishing books deemed to be dangerous by the censor. Despite such difficulties, Plantin succeeded in building a thriving business at Antwerp, which ultimately outlived many other less controversial and more orthodox enterprises. Local Calvinist merchants provided the capital for many of his early ventures by investing in his printing business. Once his popular series of emblem books and liturgical editions had helped the business to prosper, Plantin began to issue more extravagant scientific, technical, and scholarly books. He also began printing in foreign languages and types, his greatest achievement being the preparation of the famous Antwerp Polyglot Bible completed in 1572. Eight years later the Jesuits in India presented a copy of the Antwerp Bible to Akbar. Despite such spectacular achievements for Catholicism and Spain, Plantin like other booksellers and printers in the Netherlands continued to be closely supervised by the suspicious censors of church and state. Philip II appointed Plantin in 1570 to the honorary post of proto-typographer of the Low Countries, an office which the printer only reluctantly accepted because it involved him personally in administering the royal censorship.[160]

Artists, linguists, botanists, and geographers of international renown belonged to Plantin's circle of associates and co-workers. Early in his career Plantin the bookseller built up a reputation for himself as a specialist in maps. Gemma Frisius, Gerald Mercator, and Abraham Ortelius supplied him with maps and globes which he sold in his shop and had engraved for inclusion in his books.[161] The "Spanish fury" of 1576 brought an end to Plantin's greatest period and thoroughly disrupted his flourishing business. The city of Antwerp hereafter allied itself with those fighting the Spanish. In an effort to recoup his losses, the printer prudently shifted his allegiance in the religious and national wars from one side to the other as the tides of battle ebbed and flowed. He even printed some of the Calvinist attacks upon the church and the Spanish empire. From 1583 to 1585 he moved temporarily to Leyden to act as printer to the university, probably at the suggestion of his Latinist friend, Justus Lipsius. Plantin returned to Antwerp in 1585 when the Spanish regained control of the city and spent there three of the four remaining years of his life in a successful effort devoted to piecing together the remnants of his business and in providing for its future. During his thirty-four years of publishing in Antwerp, Plantin managed to issue more than fifteen-hundred books, a phenomenal achievement in the face of the difficulties he confronted.

Plantin's hectic career illustrates how complex it was for Netherlandish printers and their clients to carry on creative work. Most of the works published were liturgical books and safe popular books which appealed to a broad public.

[160] See *ibid.*, chap. vi.
[161] See below, p. 466.

The more prestigious enterprises, the Antwerp Polyglot or the *Theatrum* (1570) of Ortelius, were scientific in character and noncontroversial. The work of Ortelius, since it was not likely to offend the sensibilities of the authorities, was translated into various vernaculars and produced for the mass market in cheap, epitomized editions. For example, Michel Coignet, the Antwerp intrument maker and mathematician, produced in 1601 a Latin epitome of Ortelius' *Theatrum* which was quickly translated into French and English. Coignet added a map and literary description of Japan derived from the Jesuit letterbooks.[162] Ortelius himself referred his readers also to the popular book of "Iean Macer, a civilian, [who] hath written bookes of the history of India in which he hath much of the ile Iava."[163] Plantin meanwhile published a revision of the *Theatrum orbis terrarum* (1585) which includes a collection of small engraved maps by Philippe Galle and descriptive materials in Latin verse collected by Hugo Favolius.[164]

The Humanists were among the first Netherlanders to awaken to the importance of Asia for European civilization. This was perhaps because they had close connections with colleagues in Iberia or visited Spain. Clenardus and Vasaeus were followed to Spain and Portugal by Clusius (*ca.* 1570) and Andreas Schott (1552–1629). A Jesuit and philologist, Schott was a native of Antwerp who spent the years from 1579 to 1594 in Spain. Like other Netherlandish intellectuals, he originally went abroad to escape the troubles at home. While in Spain he studied the ancient geographers and prepared his own edition of Pomponius Mela which Plantin published in 1582. While teaching and studying classical philology in Spain, Schott corresponded with Lipsius, Hugo Grotius, Ortelius, and J. J. Scaliger as well as many leading Jesuits.[165] The most important monument to his fifteen years in Spain was the collection of writings about the Iberians which he compiled and published as *Hispania illustrata* ... (4 vols.; Frankfurt, 1603–8).[166] In addition he published a companion volume called *Hispania bibliotheca* (3 vols. in 1; Frankfurt, 1608), an encyclopedic and bibliographical work of great importance. Seven years later at Antwerp he translated from Italian into Latin a Jesuit letterbook containing the missives sent from Japan in 1609–10 to Claude Aquaviva.[167]

---

[162] See *Abraham Ortelius His Epitome. Supplement Added by Michel Coignet* (Antwerp, 1603), pp. 11–12. This English translation is dedicated to Sir Walter Raleigh.

[163] See *The Theatre of the Whole World* (London, 1606), p. 105. This is probably a reference to the Jean Macer discussed above, pp. 270–73.

[164] *Theatri orbis terrarum enchiridion, minoribus tabulis per Philippum Gallaeum exaratum: et carmine Heroico, ex variis Geographis et Poëtis collecto, per Hugonem Favolium illustratum* (Antwerp, 1585).

[165] See Léon Maes, "Lettres inédites d'André Schott," *Le Muséon*, N. S.VII (1906), 67–102, 325–61; IX (1908), 368–41; XI (1910), 239–70; and L. Maes, "Une lettre d'A. Schott à Abr. Ortelius," *Musée belge*, IX (1905), 315–18.

[166] The full title reads: *Hispania illustrata: Hispania illustratae seu rerum urbiumque Hispaniae Lusitaniae, Aethiopiae, et Indiae scriptores varii. Partim editi nunc primum, partim aucti et emendati.* For discussion of its contents see above, p. 24 n.

[167] Entitled *Rodriguez Giram literae japonica ex italicis lat. factae* (Antwerp, 1615). This translation was dedicated to his nephews, one of whom was David Haex (b. *ca.* 1595), later a lexicographer and compiler of a Malay-Latin dictionary first published in Rome in 1631.

The Humanists, unlike the artists and naturalists of the Netherlands, remained singularly unimpressed by the novel flora and fauna entering Europe from the East. Justus Lipsius (1547–1606), the celebrated historian of Rome, openly derided the Indian elephant that so delighted the people of Antwerp in 1563.[168] Recruited by the new Calvinist university of Leyden to lend glory to its Humanistic faculty, Lipsius concerned himself mainly with history, theological controversy, and political theory. He was honored as a sage even after he left Leyden in 1592 to return to Catholicism and to the university of Louvain. His only notable contribution to the scholarly controversies provoked by the overseas discoveries was the rejection of the notion that the New World should be identified with Plato's "Atlantis."[169] In his letters to Prince Philip before he became Philip III of Spain in 1598, Lipsius addressed the heir-apparent as "Hispaniarum et Indiarum Principi" and urged him to become in reality a new Alexander in Asia.[170]

Lipsius was replaced at Leyden by Joseph Justus Scaliger (1540–1609), the French Protestant scholar who was known to contemporaries as "the bottomless pit of erudition." As a young man, Scaliger attended the Collège de Guyenne at Bordeaux where the Portuguese teachers were so prominent. Later he studied at Paris with Guillaume Postel, the linguist and Orientalist.[171] Upon his arrival in the Low Countries he became associated with its leading scholars, including the natural scientists. He helped Clusius to prepare his botanical editions based on Orta's book of the "simples" of India.[172] He collected geographical materials and learned whatever he could about the languages of Asia. In his funeral oration for Scaliger, Daniel Heinsius remarked:

There was, there was that time when the house of one man in this city [Leyden] was the Museum of the whole world: when distant Maronites and Arabs, Syrians and Ethiopians, Persians and some of the Indians had in this city the man to whom they could unfold their thoughts through the interpretation of language.[173]

Nor were these merely rhetorical words of praise coined for the occasion. In his will Scaliger left the plumages of two birds of paradise to Clusius, a large quire of China paper to Franciscus Gomarus (1563–1641), the leader of the orthodox Calvinists, two large globes to the library of the university, and two others to a friend.[174] Scaliger's books and manuscripts in Oriental languages were left to the university library. They included five Chinese books, a Japanese book printed at Amakusa by the Jesuits, and a *Doctrina Christiana* printed at Goa

---

[168] See *Asia*, II, Bk. 1, 151.

[169] In his *Physiologa*, II, 19, as reproduced in *Opera* (4 vols.; Antwerp, 1603), IV, 946–50.

[170] See A. Ramirez (ed.), *Epistolario de Justo Lipsio y los Españoles* (St. Louis, Mo., 1966), pp. 123, 125.

[171] On Postel see above, pp. 265–68.

[172] See J. Bernays, *Joseph Justus Scaliger* (Berlin, 1855), p. 291. For his portrait see pl. 36.

[173] From G. W. Robinson (trans.), *Autobiography of Joseph Justus Scaliger* (Cambridge, Mass., 1927), p. 85.

[174] *Ibid.*, pp. 66–67, 69.

in the "language of Malabar."[175] His other books, numbering 1,382, were sold at auction by Louis Elzevir. The catalog of the sale lists among the offerings some globes, maps, Chinese books, and Gomara's history of the Indies in Spanish.[176]

Despite the presence of and the interest in such materials, the Humanists of the Low Countries made but few serious efforts to reckon intellectually with the discoveries or to assess their impact upon European life, history, and thought. An exception was Martin Antoine del Rio (1551–1608), the Christian Humanist of Antwerp.[177] The son of a respected Spanish official in the Netherlands, Del Rio was educated at Paris, Louvain, and Salamanca. From 1575 to 1580 he was an official in the government of Brabant. Thereafter he went back to Spain and entered the Society of Jesus at Valladolid. In Bordeaux during 1585–86 he started to write his *Syntagma tragoediae Latinae* which Plantin finally published in 1593. Though this is an orthodox Christian effort to explain Latin tragedy to the faithful of the sixteenth century, it is also a critique of the morals and an attack on the ignorance of the Ancients. Curious about natural marvels and foreign practices unknown to the Ancients, Del Rio chose as sources the cosmographies and Jesuit letterbooks of his day and used them to correct the Ancients. He rejects the marvelous geography and fabulous creatures of the classical authors and seeks to explain the existence of strange phenomena in natural terms. From reading the Jesuit letterbooks he became convinced that people universally believe in the immortality of the soul and that the name of God (*Deus*) is everywhere mystically written in four letters.[178]

The union of the Spanish and Portuguese crowns in 1580 had a far greater impact upon the United Provinces than it had upon the Spanish Netherlands.[179] Antwerp was left to wither on the vine after its recapture by Spain in 1585. The initiative in maritime enterprise was quickly grasped by the "Beggars of the Sea" based at Amsterdam and in smaller ports such as Middleburg and Enkhuizen. These towns, except for Amsterdam, were not centers of learning or publishing even though they were flourishing commercial places.[180] Still, the citizens of these smaller towns evidently read with interest and understanding the numerous romances and histories which were part of the general fare

[175] Listed in the Spanheim (1674) *Catalogus* of the library. Bernardus Vulcanus, Leyden's professor of Greek, left three Chinese books to the library. See E. Hulshoff Pol, "The Library," in Th. H. Lunsingh Scheurleer and G. H. M. Posthumus Meyjes (eds.), *Leiden University in the Seventeenth Century: An Exchange of Learning* (Leyden, 1975), p. 429. Also see pl. 37.

[176] See Baron de Reiffenberg, "Bibliothèque de Joseph Scaliger," *Le bibliophile belge*, IV (1847), 229–33. For Scaliger's use of these materials in his scientific works see below, pp. 414–15.

[177] For his biography see the University of Paris thesis by M. Dréano, *Humanisme chrétien: La tragédie latine commentée pour les chrétiens du XVIe siècle par Martin Antoine del Rio* (Paris, 1936).

[178] For references see *Syntagma*, III, 43, 193, 379, 445.

[179] See *Asia*, I, 198–203.

[180] On Enkhuizen see G. Brandt, *Historie der vermaerde zee-en koop-stadt Enkhuizen . . .* (2 vols.; Hoorn, 1747), especially the discussion of Lucas Janszoon Waghenaer and Paludanus, I, 310–17. See, facing p. 312, the portrait of Paludanus holding a pepper(?) plant. On the relations of Paludanus to Linschoten's book see *Asia*, I, 201; and C. M. Parr, *Jan van Linschoten: The Dutch Marco Polo* (New York, 1964), pp. 190–205.

provided to the public by the big printing concerns. Later in life Jan van Linschoten, a native of Enkhuizen and the greatest Dutch traveler to the East, recalled:

Being young, and living idelye [to 1576] in my native Countrie, sometimes applying my selfe to the reading of Histories, and straunge adventures, wherin I tooke no small delight, I found my minde much addicted to see and travail into strange Countries, thereby to seeke some adventure.[181]

While testimonies to the influence of literature upon men of action are few and far between in this period, Linschoten was certainly not unique in his appreciation of stories about distant places. Mandeville's and Varthema's voyages, when the censors did not prohibit their printing and distribution, continued to be of general interest. For those who could read Latin, French, or Spanish, there were available the histories of Gomara and Castanheda and the cosmographies of Münster, Thevet, and Belleforest. Martin Duncan (1505–90), pastor of Saint Hippolytus in Delft and an inveterate opponent of the Calvinists, printed at Leyden in 1567 a translation into Dutch of a collection of thirteen Jesuit letters telling about the great numbers of converts being made in America and Asia.[182] Latin, French, and Italian editions of the Jesuit letters, including a tract on the Japanese embassy, appeared at Antwerp with some regularity.[183] The first publication in 1594–95 of Linschoten's volumes in Dutch provided a wholly new reading experience. Two editions of Mendoza's book on China appeared in Dutch translation in 1595, one at Hoorn and the other at Amsterdam.[184] A new Spanish version of Mendoza was printed the following year at Antwerp. In 1598 Willem Lodewijcksz published his account in Dutch, Latin, and French of the itinerary followed by the Dutch voyagers to the East.[185] Nor was romance far behind genuine travel literature. In 1596 the *Amadis* began to be translated from French into Dutch, a project which took the following

[181] From the English in John Wolf (publ.), *Iohn Huighen van Linschoten, His Discourse of Voyages into ye Easte and West Indies* (London, 1598), p. 1.

[182] For Duncan's biography see *Nieuw nederlandsch biografisch Woordenboek*, III, 310–11. His unpaged translation, probably of the *Epistolae Indicae* . . . (Louvain, 1566), is entitled: *Die vruchten der ecclesie Christi. Van wöderlicke Wonderheyden dwelcken geüonden eñ gedaen wordē met Godts gratie in veel eñ grootelanden van Indien* . . . (Leyden, 1567). For the contents of the Louvain Latin edition see R. Streit, *Bibliotheca missionum* (21 vols.; Aachen, 1916–55), IV, 915; Streit evidently was unaware of Duncan's translation. A copy of this rare Dutch book is in the Bancroft Library at the University of California.

[183] The edition on the embassy is entitled: *De trium regum Japoniorum legatis* . . . (Antwerp, 1593). It should be recalled (see *Asia*, II, Bk. 1, 89) that Philips van Winghe of Louvain was in Rome between 1585 and 1592 sketching scenes from the Japanese screens presented to the papacy.

[184] Entitled *D'Historie ofte Beschrijvinghe van het groote Rijck van China*, it was translated from the Italian version. See G. J. Geers, "Invloed van de Spaansche Literatur," in G. S. Overdiep *et al.* (eds.), *De letterkunde van de Renaissance* (Antwerp, 1947), p. 66.

[185] He was often listed as G. M. A. W. L.[odewijcksz], and his work was entitled *D'Eerste Boeck. Historie van Indien, waerinne verhaelt is de avonturen die de Hollandtsche Schepen bejegheut zijn* (Amsterdam). A second book in French was published at Calais in 1601 (Paris, Bibliothèque nationale, o²k. 20).

twenty-five years to complete. While such publishing events indicate a quickening interest in secular literature about the East, nothing appeared in the sixteenth century to forecast how deeply the Dutch would become involved during the following century in the trade and civilizations of Asia. That story, in all of its ramifications, will appear in the volumes of this series devoted to the seventeenth century.

3

ENGLISH LITERATURE

Unlike their Continental neighbors, the English refrained during the first half of the sixteenth century from becoming involved in the voyages to the East or in the spice trade. In his search for Asia John Cabot had sailed westward in 1497 under patent from King Henry VII. But this initial foray was not followed up. Overseas expansion was quickly abandoned in favor of programs of economic and commercial development closer to home. While Germans and Netherlanders participated in the Portuguese voyages and in the distribution and sale of spices, the English remained sideline observers. In contrast to the French, the English throughout the long reign (1509–47) of Henry VIII meticulously avoided challenging the claims of the Iberian states to supremacy in the overseas world. As in times past they continued to fish off Newfoundland and remained content to have others carry on the expensive and dangerous business of overseas discovery and conquest.[186] Some English merchants traded legally and peacefully at Antwerp and Seville while others sought to promote and extend the vital wool and cloth trade in the Baltic and Mediterranean regions. Henry VIII was meanwhile involved in costly intermittent wars with France and with extravagantly ambitious diplomatic adventures on the Continent. The king's break with Rome in 1534 opened England to the Reformation and to its attendant controversies and rebellions.

Despite England's intense preoccupation with domestic and Continental problems, Henry VIII sought at times to keep abreast of the expansion movement. He commissioned maps, talked to navigators, and listened to proposals for northwest and northeast voyages to Cathay and the Moluccas. In 1541 when Portugal was forced by shortages to try buying grain in England, the king sought, though unsuccessfully, to include as part of a bargain the dispatch of Englishmen on the next voyage from Lisbon to Calicut.[187] But there was apparently no substantial support for such moves. The London merchants continued to the end of Henry's reign to be most concerned to find new

[186] See D. B. Quinn, *England and the Discovery of America, 1481–1620* (New York, 1974), pp. 160–61.

[187] See V. M. Shillington and A. B. W. Chapman, *The Commercial Relations of England and Portugal* (London, 1907), p. 136.

markets for English cloth and to be only secondarily interested in circumventing the Portuguese monopoly of the spice trade.[188]

A. FROM HUMANISM TO COSMOGRAPHY

The knowledge of Englishmen about the East remained traditional and derivative throughout Henry's period. Most of the information available in English was to be found in versions of medieval cosmographies, pilgrimage literature, and travel books.[189] William Caxton published in 1481 an encyclopedic work called *The myrrour of the worlde*, a translation of a French prose manuscript of 1464 whose author was probably Gossouin. This work, like other contemporary books in English, gave a description of the world and of Asia based entirely upon ancient and medieval materials. Even after the great voyages had brought new knowledge to Europe these earlier works were reissued without alteration and without recognizing that a geographical revolution was in progress.[190]

The *Travels* of Mandeville enjoyed a renewed popularity, possibly because of an awakening interest in distant places. Between 1496 and 1510 it went through at least four English editions, two of which were adorned with woodcut illustrations.[191] At Antwerp in 1503 a miscellany of general reference called Richard Arnold's *Chronicle* was printed in English; it was reprinted in London around 1521 along with the spurious claim that it was an essential handbook for merchants and navigators.[192] In 1511 Jan van Doesborch, the Antwerp printer, finally published the first English translations of some of the travel accounts circulating on the Continent.[193] Nine of the ten narratives included within *Of the newe landes and of ye people founde by the messengers of the kynge of portugale named Emanuel* relate to the exploits of the Portuguese in sailing to India. But there is little in this collection on Asia itself or on its peoples; it was never reissued. The best description of Asia's geography and peoples published in English before 1550 is contained in the introduction to the translation of the medieval account of Prince Hayton the Armenian, published in 1521.[194]

A few reflections nonetheless can be found in English literature of a growing consciousness about the overseas world. William Dunbar (*ca.* 1460–*ca.* 1522),

---

[188] See W. Foster, *England's Quest of Eastern Trade* (London, 1933), pp. 5–6.

[189] For Asian references in Chaucer see *Asia*, I, 77.

[190] For a listing in chronological order of the books printed in English from 1481 to 1620 relating to the overseas world see John Parker, *Books to Build an Empire* (Amsterdam, 1965), pp. 243–65. Caxton's translation was reprinted without changes in 1490 and 1527.

[191] See J. W. Bennett, *op. cit.* (n. 32), pp. 346–47.

[192] See Parker, *op. cit.* (n. 190), pp. 17–18; and H. S. Bennett, *English Books and Readers, 1475 to 1557* (2d ed.; Cambridge, 1969), p. 121.

[193] One-third of Doesborch's total production was composed of editions in English. Also see *Asia*, I, 164, and above, p. 353. On this particular book see E. G. R. Taylor, *Tudor Geography* (London, 1930), p. 7, and Parker, *op. cit.* (n. 190), pp. 21–22.

[194] The English translation was the work of Richard Pynson. Also see *Asia*, I, 42, 60; and Parker, *op. cit.* (n. 190), p. 26.

the Scottish diplomat and poet, addressed a complaint to King James IV regarding a benefice he had long been anticipating:

> It micht have cumin in schortar quhyll
> Fra Calyecot and the new fund Yle,
> The partis of Transmeridiane;
> Quhilk to considder is ane pane.
>
> It micht, be this, had it bein kynd,
> Cumin out of the desertis of Ynde,
> Our all the grit se occeane;
> Quhilk to considder is ane pane.[195]

In a later poem called "Of Content" (*ca.* 1511) Dunbar avers that the covetous individual lives in poverty when he is one

> Quho [Who] had all riches unto Ynd,
> And wer not satefeit in mynd.[196]

In 1509 Henry Watson and Alexander Barclay translated into English Sebastian Brant's *The Ship of Fools* from the Latin and French versions of the original German poem. Like most translators of that day, Barclay felt free to add verses of his own composition. One of those interspersed in the original reflects Barclay's lively, personal interest in the revelation of the world:

> For now of late hathe large lande and grounde
> Ben found by maryners and crafty governors
> The whiche landes were never knowen nor founde
> Byfore our tyme by our predecessors;
> And here after shall by our successours
> Parchance mo be founde wherein men dwell
> Of whome we never before this same harde tell.[197]

The staider literati of England also reacted quickly to the revelation of the outside world, especially Thomas More (1478–1535). The greatest of England's Humanists, More was employed as a diplomat in 1515 to aid in working out an agreement between his king and Charles of Castile (later Emperor Charles V) about the trade in English wool and Flemish cloth.[198] While on a six-month mission to the Netherlands, More personally observed the operation of the spice trade at Antwerp and consciously sought to extend the range of his own geographical knowledge. He became the close friend of Peter Giles (Aegidius),

---

[195] From "Of the Worldis Instabilitie," in W. Mackay Mackenzie (ed.), *The Poems of William Dunbar* (Edinburgh, 1932), p. 30. This is presumably the first literary usage of "Calicut" in English.

[196] See *ibid.*, p. 144. For discussion consult J. W. Baxter, *William Dunbar: A Biographical Study* (Edinburgh, 1952), p. 197.

[197] Watson and Barclay's translations were based on the *Stultifera navis* (Basel, 1497) of Jacob Locher and Pierre de Riviere's French translation (Paris, 1497). For the quotation from Barclay see A. Pompen, *The English Versions of the Ship of Fools: A Contribution to the History of the Early French Renaissance in England* (London, 1925), pp. 225–26. For discussion of Brant's original poem see above, pp. 332–33.

[198] For details see R. W. Chambers, *Thomas More* (New York, 1935), pp. 122–25.

town clerk of Antwerp and an eminent literary figure. More wrote his *Utopia* ("Nowhere") while in the Netherlands and had it printed on the insistence of Giles and Erasmus at Louvain in 1516. More's classic picture in Latin of the ideal commonwealth immediately became popular on the Continent; in the next two years it appeared in four editions and was translated into French, Italian, and Flemish. It was not translated into English until 1551, possibly because of More's personal involvement in politics and his execution in 1535 for refusing to follow Henry in breaking with Rome.

Giles evidently introduced More to a knowledgeable Portuguese, called Raphael Hythlodaeus in the *Utopia*,[199] who talked to him about the overseas world. According to More, Raphael had accompanied Amerigo Vespucci on the last three of his four voyages. On Vespucci's final voyage Raphael and twenty-three others remained behind at a fort in America when their leaders returned to Europe. After making friends with the natives, Raphael and five of his companions left the fort and began traveling over land and sea. "By strange chance," More observes, "he was carried to Ceylon [Taprobanen], whence he reached Calicut [Caliqut]."[200] There he conveniently found a Portuguese ship which carried him back to Europe. Whether Raphael actually circumnavigated the world before Magellan's men is a subject that has been debated.[201] There can be no question, however, that he at least performed this remarkable feat in More's mind. While Mandeville and others had certainly believed in the possibility of sailing around the world, More produced a character who seriously claims such a momentous accomplishment.[202] The likelihood is that More had read of Vespucci's intention of sailing on his fourth voyage directly to the East.[203] Even though this ill-fated voyage ended in Brazil, More for his own literary purposes had to get Raphael to the East, a possible locale of Utopia.

Raphael spent five years in Utopia, an ideal land whose name appeared on no world maps and in no cosmographies. Both More and his contemporaries claim that they never learned "in what part of the new world Utopia lies."[204] But they do concede that it lies in the New World, at a position directly antipodal to Europe, and in those regions not known to Antiquity. While it is still not possible to place Utopia on a map, it appears from the two verses that prefix the early editions that More had in mind a re-creation of the ideal state

[199] "Hythlodaeus" is Greek for "an expert in trifles." See. E. Surtz and J. H. Hexter (eds.), *The Complete Works of St. Thomas More* (New Haven, 1965), IV, 301.

[200] *Ibid.*, p. 51. This approximates the spelling ("Calliqut") on Waldseemüller's world map, possibly one of More's sources for the new names; cf. pl. 56. Waldseemüller himself copied this name from the Canerio Chart (see below, p. 452). More's precise spelling appears on the *Indiae tabula moderna* in Ptolemy's *Geographia* (Strassburg, 1522).

[201] An advocate of Raphael's priority is G. B. Parks, "More's *Utopia* and Geography," *Journal of English and Germanic Philology*, XXXVII (1938), 224–36. Also see A. R. Heiserman, "Satire in the *Utopia*," *PMLA*, LXXVIII (1963), 170.

[202] On Mandeville's ideas about circumnavigation see J. W. Bennett, *op. cit.* (n. 32), pp. 231–33.

[203] See Vespucci's letter on his fourth voyage in C. G. Herberman (ed.), *op. cit.* (n. 50), pp. 145–51.

[204] Surtz and Hexter (eds.), *op. cit.* (n. 199), IV, 43. On Asia as part of the "New World" see above, p. 279, and below, pp. 456–57.

of the Gymnosophists of India celebrated in medieval and contemporary writings. The tradition was still powerful in his time that Alexander had consulted Brahmans at Taxila in A.D. 326 who lived in a commonwealth of virtue.[205] Viewed from this angle, the *Utopia* can be seen as an effort to reproduce from classical, medieval, and contemporary sources an ideal society similar to but more credible than the serene and sinless world of the Gymnosophists.

Such a conception is supported by the assumption common at the time that India was endowed with inexhaustible riches, a silent testimony to the belief that its society was one in which peace, order, and tolerance reigned. Its people, however, were thought to despise gold, silver, and precious stones, though the state accumulated them to use when necessary to spread dissension among its greedy enemies. Utopia is situated close to other advanced nations "from which our own cities, nations, races and kingdoms may take example for the correction of their errors."[206] If any factual prototype for Utopia exists, it must then be found in a civilized and serene Asia rather than in an America on whose primitive character all the existing sources of the time agree.[207]

An understanding of the conceptions of More's associates lends further substance to the argument that More regarded Asia as possessing an advanced society. John Skelton (1460?–1529) was attracted like More by the great maritime enterprises of his day; he nonetheless retained a traditional view of the East. While he mentions the contemporary instruments of navigation, he takes no notice of the new places being found.[208] He relies entirely on Ovid and the legend of Alexander when he refers to India in the opening stanzas of his allegorical poem, "Speke Parrot," written about 1521.[209] Parrot, like man himself, was born in the earthly paradise and was nourished "with dyvers delycate spyce." Parrot was driven into India by the Euphrates, one of the four great rivers of paradise. Found and captured by the "men of that countre," Parrot was sent to Greece as Skelton follows the story in Arrian and the Pseudo-Callisthenes to the effect that Alexander brought parrots to Greece that had been presented to him by Candace, queen of India. At no point in Skelton's works can there be found any references to the great voyages or to the activities of his contemporaries in the East. Asia is still an ideal place both for him and for More.[210]

[205] See the note in Surtz and Hexter (eds.), *op. cit.* (n. 199), IV, 585. For this general argument see J. D. M. Derrett, "Thomas More and Joseph the Indian," *Journal of the Royal Asiatic Society*, April, 1962, pp. 20–22.

[206] Surtz and Hexter (eds.), *op. cit.* (n. 199), IV, 55.

[207] For discussion of the Utopian alphabet and its possible relationship to Malayālam see below, pp. 530–31.

[208] See M. Pollet, *John Skelton, Poet of Tudor England* (London, 1971), p. 184.

[209] For the text see the critical edition of R. S. Kinsman (ed.), *John Skelton. Poems* (Oxford, 1969), pp. 77–95.

[210] See Pollet, *op. cit.* (n. 208), pp. 182–83. Also H. L. R. Edwards, *Skelton: The Life and Times of an Early Tudor Poet* (London, 1949), p. 185; and F. W. Brownlow, "The Boke Compiled by Maister Skelton, Called Speake Parrot," *English Literary Renaissance*, I (1971), 8–10. On the legend of Alexander see above, pp. 91–94.

Closely connected to More's circle was John Rastell (d. 1536), distinguished printer and producer and writer of dramas.[211] Rastell was married to More's sister and was certainly well acquainted with his brother-in-law's experience in the Netherlands. At the beginning of 1517, with More's encouragement and financial aid, Rastell outfitted an expedition to America. Perhaps Rastell had in mind the adventures of Hythlodaeus and intended like More's character to establish a foothold in America from which to find a route to Asia and its wealth.[212] Whatever his hopes may have been, they were dashed when Rastell's crew revolted. Rastell himself ended up in Ireland and did not return to England until 1519.[213]

Evidently Rastell spent a portion of his time in Ireland writing a play in rhymed verse which he entitled *The Nature of the Four Elements*. Here he put on paper his feeling of personal enthusiasm for exploring the opportunities offered by his age:

> Studyous Desire:
>> Syr, I understonde that ye have be,
>> In many a strannge countree,
>> And have had gret fylycyte
>> Straunge causes to seke and fynde.
> Experyence:
>> Right farr, syr, I have ridden and gone,
>> And see straunge thynges many one,
>> In affryk, europe, and ynde.[214]

A perusal of his later lines shows plainly that Rastell was well acquainted with much of the recent Continental writing on world geography and cosmography. On the overseas world he obtained a substantial part of his data and his basic conception of the map, as More probably did, from Waldseemüller's *Cosmographiae introductio* (1507).[215] With respect to Asia he displays much of the ignorance and many of the traditional notions common to his day. He evidently knew nothing of the East Indies or of the Portuguese activities there. Most of his

---

[211] See E. M. G. Routh, *Sir Thomas More and His Friends, 1477–1535* (London, 1934), pp. 43–45.

[212] Suggestion of A. W. Reed, *Early Tudor Drama* (London, 1926), pp. 11–12; also see Quinn, *op. cit.* (n. 186), p. 63.

[213] For details on Rastell's attempted voyage see Appendix I in Reed, *op. cit.* (n. 212), pp. 187–201.

[214] From J. S. Farmer (ed.), *The Tudor Facsimile Texts: The Nature of the Four Elements* (London, 1908), unpaged. This poem is sometimes classified as a piece of topographical poetry, or an English imitation of the *Hodoeporicon* poems of Humanism. See H. Taylor, "Topographical Poetry in England during the Renaissance" (Ph.D. diss., Department of English, University of Chicago, 1926), p. 129. On this genre in Germany see above, p. 346.

[215] M. E. Borish ("Sources and Intentions of the *Four Elements*," *Studies in Philology*, XXXV [1938], 151) denies this assertion and contends that Rastell depended more on the popular encyclopedia by Gregor Reisch called *Margarita philosophica*. But it has since been shown by careful textual comparisons how heavily he drew upon Waldseemüller's text and map; see pls. 56, 57. See E. M. Nugent, "Sources of John Rastell's *The Nature of the Four Elements*," *PMLA*, LVII (1942), especially pp. 80–81. For suggestions as to a few other pertinent and contemporary texts from which Rastell might have borrowed details see J. Parr, "More Sources of Rastell's *Interlude of the Four Elements*," *PMLA*, LX (1945), 48–58.

references to Asia seem to derive from medieval sources, such as Mandeville, rather than from recent maps or cosmographies.[216] Still, he understood that America lies between Europe and Asia and, surprisingly, postulates that it is separated from Cathay by more than one thousand miles:

> Experyence:
> But estwarde on the see syde,
> A prynce there is that ruleth wyde,
> Callyd the Cane of catowe.
> And this is called the great eest see,
> Whiche goth all a longe this wey
> Towardes the newe landis agayne;
> But whether that see go thy ther dyrectly,
> Or if any wyldernes bytwene them do ly,
> No man knoweth for certeyne:
> But these newe lands by all cosmografye,
> Frome the Cane of Catoue's lande can not lye,
> Lytill paste a thousand myle,
> But from these new landes men may sayle playne
> Estwarde and cum to Englande agaie,
> Where we began ere whyle.[217]

Rastell probably intended his *Four Elements* as a call to the court and the public to begin taking more seriously the ideas of More and his circle about participating actively in overseas discovery and commerce. While More's influence at the court mounted throughout the 1520's, the king and the London merchants passively resisted all efforts to lure them into overseas enterprises. When Wolsey proposed a northwest voyage to Cathay in 1521, the response was negative. When Robert Thorne, an English merchant resident in Seville, sent a petition to the king about 1530 proposing a northern voyage to the Moluccas, it was ignored.[218] To counter this apparent apathy, Rastell prepared his *New Boke of Purgatory* (1529?), which stresses how much merchants can learn from travel in distant places. He addressed it to the merchants because he hoped that More, who became chancellor in 1529, would by himself be able to win over the court to a more active interest.[219]

When More retired to private life several years later, he entertained visitors from the Continent who shared his enthusiasm for overseas expansion. Simon

216 G. B. Parks ("The Geography of the *Interlude of the Four Elements,*" *Philological Quarterly*, XVIII [1938], 261–62) concludes that Rastell was not as well informed about geography as More. J. Parr ("John Rastell's Geographical Knowledge of America," *Philological Quarterly*, XXVII [1948] 239–40) disputes this conclusion and contends that his knowledge, particularly his conception of the New World, is essentially equal to that of the cosmographies.

217 Farmer (ed.), *op. cit.* (n. 214). On the distances between Asia and America in the maps of the time see below, p. 456. For the first English world map (1527), see pl. 60.

218 On the very complex matter of Henry's involvement in the pawning of Charles V's interest in the Spiceries and of Thorne's part therein see Taylor, *op. cit.* (n. 193), pp. 46–51.

219 See A. W. Reed, *op. cit.* (n. 212), pp. 217–19.

Grynaeus, the Basel printer, visited with More in 1531.[220] Immediately after his return home from England in 1532, Grynaeus published his *Novus orbis*, one of the most influential collections of travels ever published. In the dedicatory letter to this book, Grynaeus echoes More's ideas when he expresses the hope that his collection will open the eyes of those who remain blind to the discoveries of science and philology. Damião de Góis, the Portuguese publicist of empire, had possibly visited More in 1528. At any rate in 1533 the young John More, Thomas' only son, translated from Latin into English Góis' highly favorable account of the social and religious systems of Abyssinia.[221] The following year Henry broke with Rome. More and Rastell defied the king, and both lost their lives as a consequence. All immediate hopes for overseas voyages perished with More. The few voices hereafter raised in behalf of foreign trade were drowned out for the duration of Henry's reign by the tumult produced by ecclesiastical and religious controversies.

In England, as elsewhere, the regulation of the book trade was closely related to the rise and spread of heresy and sedition. The statutes enacted around 1410 to deal with Lollardy were revived in 1525 and applied to Lutheran books.[222] The writings of Luther and his followers were brought into London by German merchants. Many of these heretical books were confiscated and burned in the 1520's. Booksellers were forbidden to sell them and printers were ordered not to reprint them. The infant printing industry meanwhile gradually passed out of alien into English hands as foreigners were excluded from it for both economic and religious reasons. About six thousand books were published in English before 1557, a testimony in itself to the existence of a considerable reading public.[223] Most of these publications were of a religious or devotional type, for the printers could rely on a steady demand for such books and pamphlets.[224] The requirement that licenses had to be obtained prior to printing was enacted in 1538. Popish books were thereafter subjected to increasingly tight surveillance and included therein apparently were books relating to the successes of the Catholic powers in the overseas world.[225] No translations of foreign books about the overseas world were printed between John More's translation of Góis' book in 1533 and the translation in 1551 by Ralph Robinson of the elder More's *Utopia*. Mandeville's *Travels*, so immensely

---

[220] On Grynaeus see above, pp. 339–40.

[221] On Góis see above, p. 17. Young More's translation of Góis was printed by William Rastell, the son of John. In 1536, his brother, John the Younger, went off on a semi-scientific voyage to Labrador. For speculation on the relationship, if any, between this translation and More's *Utopia* see Reed, *op. cit.* (n. 212), pp. 79–80. More's translation is entitled *The legacy or embassate of prester John unto Emanuel Kynge of Portyngale.*

[222] See Reed, *op. cit.* (n. 212), pp. 161–65.

[223] Figure based on H. S. Bennett, *op. cit.* (n. 192), p. 20; for a general discussion of European literacy in the sixteenth century see C. M. Cipolla, *Literacy and Development in the West* (London, 1969), pp. 52–60.

[224] See H. S. Bennett *op. cit.* (n. 192), p. 65.

[225] See Sir Paul Harvey (ed.), *The Oxford Companion to English Literature* (4th rev. ed.; Oxford, 1969), p. 911 (App. I).

popular at the beginning of the century, was evidently not reprinted between 1510 and 1568.

Native English writers on geography and cosmography were likewise kept out of print until mid-century. But this is not to say that the government was as uniformed as the reading public. In 1540–41 Roger Barlow, an associate of Sebastian Cabot, wrote a *Geographia* which he dedicated to the king. The first geographical work written in English after the great discoveries, Barlow's book existed only in manuscript in the sixteenth century.[226] Much of it was translated quite literally from the first edition (1519) of Enciso's *Suma de geografía*.[227] Barlow's original contributions relating to Asia are limited to a discussion of Magellan's voyage, to a description of Calicut excerpted from Varthema's book, and to an appeal for the king to prosecute the northern voyages and the search for Cathay.

The decade of the 1550's inaugurated a new era in England's perception of the overseas world. It was marked especially by a number of translations related to the rising interest of both the government and the merchants in overseas ventures. A growing belief in the feasibility of a northeast approach to Asia led to the dispatch of expeditions charged with finding a passage through northern Europe to China and the East Indies. In connection with the effort to penetrate Russia and continental Asia on the route to China, retrospective and contemporary writings about the Asian mainland began to appear in English translations. Quintus Curtius on Alexander the Great in India appeared in 1553 in an English text, and four years later the medieval *Gesta romanorum* with its tales from the East went through a second English printing.[228] William Waterman in 1555 translated from French the Africa and Asia sections of Boemus' collection under the title *The fardle of facions*.[229] Its description of Tartary is based on Vincent of Beauvais; Waterman, following Boemus, describes India and the rest of the East as if the Portuguese had never been there. Waterman's work, like Boemus' original, provided the public with a broad range of ethnological materials which enabled thinking men to make explicit comparisons between their own manners and morals and those of distant and different peoples.

The reign of Queen Mary (1553–58) saw the rehabilitation of many English Catholics and the conclusion of closer relations with Spain and its overseas endeavors. Ralph Robinson in 1551 had translated More's *Utopia* into English for the first time, possibly because the Protectorate government of the duke of Northumberland had reawakened interest in overseas ventures. Richard Eden, shortly before King Edward's death in 1553, published a translation of a portion of Sebastian Münster's cosmography and dedicated it to Northumberland. A

---

[226] See Taylor, *op. cit.* (n. 193), pp. 45–54. For the modern edited version see E. G. R. Taylor (ed.), *Roger Barlow: A brief summe of geographie* (London: Hakluyt Society, 1932).

[227] On Enciso and the *Suma* see above, pp. 164–65.

[228] On these two traditional works see above, pp. 96, 110. The first English translation was printed by Wynkyn de Worde around 1510.

[229] On Boemus see above, p. 336.

treatyse of the newe India, as Eden entitled his version, depicts both Indies but pictures the East Indies as being wealthier and more agreeable than the West Indies—a conclusion that was certainly welcomed by Sebastian Cabot and the other advocates of a northeast passage.[230] As a propagandist for overseas ventures, Eden reached the zenith of his influence under Mary's reign. To celebrate the marriage of Mary to Philip of Spain in 1554 Eden prepared his translation of the first three *Decades* of Peter Martyr under the title *Decades of the New World.*[231] In this work Eden urged his countrymen to reject Protestantism and to follow Spain's lead by exploiting overseas navigation.

By the end of Mary's reign a few English intellectuals had begun to incorporate the new knowledge of the East into their own collections of materials and into their literary creations. In 1556 Sir William More of Loseby in Surrey possessed two maps of the world, one globe, Münster's *Cosmographia,* More's *Utopia,* and Eden's *A treatyse of the newe India.*[232] Robert Recorde (1510?–58) in *The Castle of Knowledge* (London, 1556) has a "master" reply to a "scholar" by asking (p. 65), "who is it hath not hearde of the isles of Molucca, and Samatra, where the Portingales gette the greate plentye of rich drugges and fine spices?" He also includes a moderately sophisticated map of the Eastern Hemisphere and writes familiarly of Calicut. Much less acquaintance with the East is exhibited by William Cunningham in *The cosmographical glasse . . .* (London, 1559). He is even confused about the great discoveries, for he attributes the navigation to Calicut to Vespucci and Columbus. Although himself quite unclear on the places and peoples of Asia, Cunningham does not hesitate to denounce the Asian prototypes of the Mandevillian heritage. The newer knowledge of the East had thus begun to infiltrate English learning, but the occurrences are still rare, and any influences are strictly confined to those intellectuals primarily concerned with geography, cosmography, and navigation.

B. THE ART OF POESY

Over the first two decades (1558–77) of Queen Elizabeth's reign little was added to England's store of knowledge about the East. In part this can be attributed to the relatively small number of editions printed in these years. History, geography, and news constituted only about 10 percent of the new titles.[233] Still, in 1566 there were complaints that itinerant peddlers of books

---

[230] See Parker, *op. cit.* (n. 190), p. 40.

[231] For detailed analysis see *Asia,* I, 209–10. Eden made his translation from Martyr's *De rebus oceanis et orbe novo decadas tres* (Basel, 1533), a copy of which has his autograph on the title page and his handwritten notes in the margin. See E. Baer, "Richard Eden's Copy of the 1533 *Decades* of Peter Martyr," in *Essays Honoring Lawrence C. Wroth* (Portland, Me., 1965), p. 3.

[232] See John Evans, "Extracts from the Private Account Book of Sir W. More," *Archaeologia,* XXXVI (1885), 288–92.

[233] See H. S. Bennett, *English Books and Readers, 1558–1603* (Cambridge, 1965), p. 269.

were selling "Newes out of India," possibly Jesuit letterbooks, at stands in the village marketplaces.[234] No substantial works on Asia can be identified from these years, and most of the new material was limited to what could be garnered from translations of Continental sources, old and new. Pliny's wonders of the world appeared in an English summary in 1566 and Mandeville was reissued two years later for the first time since 1510. Current writings on America included a translation of Thevet's *Antarctike* (1568). A translation from about 1569 of the prose romance of the Greek Heliodorus called *Aethiopica* provided an ancient model for Englishmen interested in writing romances of chivalry and adventure as well as a basis for stories with an Eastern romantic background.[235] E. Fenton translated the French collection of stories by Pierre Boaistuau as *Certaine Secrete Wonders of Nature* (London, 1569). From Italian Sir Thomas North in 1570 translated *The moral philosophie of Doni*, a book of didactic episodes based on Indian stories.[236] In 1571 Thomas Fortescue issued a translation of the "curious history" of P. Mexía called *Silva* which became extremely popular.[237] Thomas Marshe culled extracts of strange and memorable things from Münster's *Cosmographie* and published them in 1572 and 1574. Although individually none of these contributed to the development of a new literary outlook, they provided collectively a repository of exotic material for the literary giants of the century's last generation to draw upon.

Richard Willes (1546–91?), who is best known as the continuator of Eden, also contributed significantly to English geographical and literary advances.[238] While living abroad as a Catholic exile from Elizabethan England, Willes studied languages at Louvain and Mainz. He entered the Society of Jesus in 1565, taught Greek at Trier for a time, and then set off for Italy in 1570. After a short stay at Perugia, he arrived at Rome in 1572. Here for some unexplained reason he was discharged from the Society, possibly because of his eccentric views about the Society and its mission.[239] While in Italy he became acquainted with Giovanni Pietro Maffei, the official historian of the Jesuit mission in Asia. He also came to know Guillaume Postel, Piero Valeriano, and François de Belleforest. On his return to England in 1573 or 1574, Willes published his *Poematum liber*, a selection of Latin verses written during his years on the Continent. This collection was dedicated to the scholars of Winchester school with the idea of bringing to their attention "a new and more subtle (abstrusius) form of verse not hitherto made known."[240]

[234] *Ibid.*, p. 267.

[235] See D. B. J. Randall, *The Golden Tapestry: A Critical Survey of Non-Chivalric Spanish Fiction in English Translation, 1543–1657* (Durham, N.C., 1963), p. 95.

[236] Complete title is: *The moral philosophie of Doni: drawne out of the auncient writers, first compiled in the Indian tongue, and now englished out of the Italian.*

[237] On the Spanish original see above, p. 173. In English it was entitled *The Forest, or Collection of Historyes No Lesse Profitable Then Pleasant and Necessary, Done out of French into English.*

[238] On his geographical activities see below, p. 482.

[239] For a biography of Willes see A. D. S. Fowler (ed. and trans.), *"De re poetica" by Richard Wills* [*Willes*] (Oxford, 1958).

[240] As quoted by J. W. H. Atkins, *English Literary Criticism: The Renascence* (London, 1951), p. 103.

The hundred Latin poems prepared by Willes include a variety of different verse forms not ordinarily used by Elizabethan poets. The literary community of the Continent which Willes had moved in was dedicated to the exchange of verses in which the poet made a display of his ingenuity and innovative skills. All sorts of "conceits" were devised by the practitioners captivated by this literary fashion. The most precious and contrived of these verse forms were the pattern and puzzle poems and those written in many languages or in hieroglyphs.[241] Contemporaries evidently valued such poems more for their symbolic than for their literary value. Although the pattern poem had antecedents in the West going back to the Hellenistic age, tradition has it that this type of verse which forms a picture or a design by the varying length of its lines was imported from Asia at some point in the past. Willes contributed his share to the perpetuation of the tradition by making it clear that many of his Continental associates—Postel and Maffei especially—were close students of Asia and its mysteries.[242] Poetry, he explains, "improves the mind and understanding with a manifold erudition, enriches it with many branches of knowledge."[243] For Willes, as later for Puttenham,[244] the pattern poem splendidly concealed meaning, invited esoteric speculation, and brought physical shapes into a harmonious relationship with the words themselves. But there was little in all this literary mystery to enlighten the reader about the East. That revelation came much more directly from the navigational achievements themselves.

George Gascoigne (1542?–77) was one of the first Elizabethan poets to allude to the East and its products in his literary creations. From 1572 to 1575 he saw military service in the Netherlands under the command of Sir Humphrey Gilbert and was for a time held captive by the Spanish.[245] It was possibly through his Continental experience and his association with Gilbert that the East came within the range of his vision. In 1575, shortly after his return to England, Gascoigne pronounced before the queen at Woodstocke "The Tale of Hermetes the Heremyt," a story set in the country of "Cambaya which is scytuate neere the mouth of the riche ryver Indus."[246] In his poem called "Don Bartholmew of Bathe" Gascoigne exclaims:

> For sugar and for sinamon I call
> For Ginger, Graines, and for eche other spice,
> Wherewith I mix the noble Wine apace.[247]

---

[241] Poem 57 called *Litteris Aegyptiacis* shows five different animal drawings in two parallel lines. See R. Willes, *Poematum liber* (London, 1573), p. 43.

[242] See Poem 32, Nos. 3 and 7, which are *encomia* to Postel and Maffei, *ibid.*, pp. 26–27.

[243] Fowler (ed. and trans.), *op. cit.* (n. 239), p. 85.

[244] See below, pp. 375–77.

[245] See R. R. Cawley, *The Voyagers and Elizabethan Drama* (Boston, 1938), p. 123; and C. C. T. Prouty, *George Gascoigne, Elizabethan Courtier, Soldier, and Poet* (New York, 1942), pp. 49–55.

[246] See J. W. Cunliffe (ed.), *The Complete Works of George Gascoigne* (2 vols.; Cambridge, 1907–10), I, 479–80. Also see J. W. Cunliffe, "The Queenes Majesties Entertainment at Woodstocke," *PMLA*, N.S. XIX (1911), 92–141, and Prouty, *op. cit.* (n. 245), pp. 227–28.

[247] *The Poesies* (London, 1575), p. 113.

When Gascoigne visited Sir Humphrey at Limehouse in 1576, he noticed a copy of a letter in his study written ten years earlier, telling of the discovery of a new passage to Cathay. Gascoigne borrowed the letter, compared its assertions to the materials in the atlas of Ortelius and to other cosmographical works and charts, and published it without the author's permission. In the prefatory epistle to *A Discourse of a discoverie for a New Passage to Cataia* (1576), Gascoigne claims kinship to Sir Martin Frobisher, the explorer and adventurer, and reveals that John Dee in his preface to H. Billingsley's English *Euclid* (1570) commends as sound the geographical ideas of Sir Humphrey. Gascoigne's prophetical sonnet which precedes Gilbert's text denominates Sir Humphrey as "Neptune the fifth" and places him in the company of Columbus, Vespucci, and Magellan.[248] The following year Gascoigne published *The Steele Glas* (1576), one of the earliest original nondramatic poems in blank verse composed in the English language. In his dedication to Lord Gray of Wilton, Gascoigne refers to the qualities of "magnanimitie" and "industrious diligence" as "two pretious Spiceries."[249] But his admiration for the spices did not extend to the merchants who seek "to make *Monopolyes*, Of every ware that is accompted strange." It is not for the advantage of the country but for the private enrichment of the merchants

> For whom al seas, are tossed to and fro,
> For whom these purples come from Persia,
> The crimosine, and lively red from Inde:
> For whom soft silks, do sayle from Sericane
> And all queint costs, do come fardest coasts.[250]

Gascoigne's unauthorized publication of Gilbert's treatise had a more immediate influence on practical affairs than his personal literary works. Gilbert's *Discourse* with the support it received from Dee helped to convince Frobisher and his financial supporters of the "Cathay Company" of the existence of the northwest passage to China. Frobisher's unsuccessful voyages (1576–78) convinced others to carry forward the earlier efforts to open the southwest passage to Asia and its wealth that Magellan had reconnoitered. In connection with this shift in attention to the route pioneered by the Spanish, the English merchants resident in Seville began to translate into English the Spanish materials on the East, especially those relating to China. From 1577 to 1579 an entirely fresh documentation on the East appeared in English with Thomas Nicholas' *Newes Lately Come from . . . China* (1577) and John Frampton's translations of Marco

---

[248] See Cunliffe (ed.), *op. cit.* (n. 246), II, 562–67, and Prouty, *op. cit.* (n. 245), p. 13. On John Dee see below, p. 471.

[249] Cunliffe (ed.), *op. cit.* (n. 246), II, 135.

[250] *Ibid.*, pp. 162–63. Later poets continued to attack the merchants for their greed and rapaciousness. For example, see Joseph Hall's "The Kings Prophecie: or Weeping Joy (1603)," in A. Davenport (ed.), *The Collected Poems of Joseph Hall, Bishop of Exeter and Norwich* (Liverpool, 1949), p. 117.

Polo (1579) and the discourse (1579) of Escalante on China.[251] Further enrichment of the English materials on the East was to be found in Richard Willes' revision of Eden's collection published in 1577 which included the account of Varthema's travels and materials on Japan from the Jesuit writings.[252]

Sir Francis Drake's circumnavigation of the earth (1577–80) launched a new English policy of boldly defying Philip II's claim to a monopoly over the entire overseas world. The literary response to the return of Drake was slow and uncertain. Stock references to India as a land of wealth remained predominant in the poetic inventory of the dramatists.[253] John Lyly (1554?–1606) in *Euphues and His England* (1580), a didactic narrative, was one of the few influential literary figures of Drake's time to underline the importance of travel experience. Callimachus, the old hermit, observes in Lyly's words:

Ulisses was no lesse esteemed for knowledge he had of other countryes than for ye revenewes he had in his own and wher in ye ende, you seeme to refer me to yt viewing of Maps, I was never of that minde to make my ship in a Painters shop, which is lyke those, who have great skill in a wooden Globe, but never behold the Skie. And he that seeketh to bee a cunning travailer by seeing the Mappes, as an expert astronomer, by turning the Globe, may be an apprentice for *Appelles* [most celebrated of Greek painters and contemporary of Alexander the Great], but no Page for Ulisses.[254]

From this work the English literary world also derived the peculiar and high-flown style to which the name "Euphuism" has been assigned and which was fashionable among writers of the last generation of the sixteenth century. The euphuistic authors placed many of their most incredible inventions in Asia, the region where marvels were to be expected.[255] Even Nicholas Breton's little book called *A Discourse in Commendation of . . . Master Francis Drake, with rejoysing of his happy adventures* (1581) was written as if it were a romance in euphuistic prose.[256]

War with Spain and Portugal became a reality in the 1580's. It was accompanied by the appearance in London bookshops of a new series of important translations of classical and modern writings. The twelve books of the *Aeneid* had been translated in 1573 and in 1584 a spurious thirteenth book was added to a new edition. Sir Thomas North had translated Plutarch's *Lives* from French in 1579; this was followed two years later by a poor translation of the *Iliad*. From Spanish, Frampton and Nicholas respectively translated Thamara's work

---

[251] For a reprinting of Nicholas' text with a critical introduction and notes see R. McLachlan, "A Sixteenth-Century Account of China . . .," *Papers on Far Eastern History* (Canberra), No. 12 (1975), 71–86.

[252] For details on these translations see *Asia*, I, 211–12, and Parker, *op. cit.* (n. 190), pp. 76–81.

[253] See Cawley, *op. cit.* (n. 245), p. 113.

[254] See R. W. Bond (ed.), *The Complete Works of John Lyly* (3 vols.; Oxford, 1967 reprint of 1902 edition), II, 28.

[255] See Cawley, *op. cit.* (n. 245), p. 100.

[256] See H. P. Kraus, *Sir Francis Drake: A Pictorial Biography* (Amsterdam, 1970), p. 82. In 1587 a topographical poem by Thomas Green was written to honor Drake, but it is one of the very few literary works celebrating his deeds. See H. Taylor, *op. cit.* (n. 214), p. 129.

on the northeast passage to Cathay (1580) and the first book (1582) of Castanheda's authoritative history of the southeastern discoveries and conquests of the
Portuguese navigators. Richard Hakluyt, the pioneer collector of travel narratives, also became more active in this decade. He corresponded with the
Continental geographers, interviewed Portuguese in exile in France,[257] and
encouraged his countrymen to undertake travels and to write down their
observations. Thomas Cavendish, following the lead of Drake, circumnavigated
the world between 1586 and 1588.

With Hakluyt's encouragement and with the inspiration of Cavendish's
successful voyage to spur him on, Robert Parke published his translation of
Mendoza's *China* in 1588. He dedicated it to Cavendish and urged him in the
future to seek a northern route to China.[258] Sensitive to the anti-Spanish and
anti-Catholic feelings of his readers Parke advised them that the favorable
accounts of missionary achievements in the East were the responsibility of the
author and not due "to any fault of mine." In 1588 Thomas Hickock published
his translations of the travels to the East of the Venetian Cesare Fedrici. The
following year (1589–90) brought the appearance in print of Hakluyt's collection
entitled *The principall Navigations*. For the first time in the sixteenth century the
English reader now had available a substantial documentation on the East. The
most important materials not yet translated into English were the Jesuit letterbooks that circulated on the Continent in most of the vernacular languages as
well as in Latin. Thomas Stevens, the sole English Jesuit in Asia, wrote from
Goa to Hakluyt and others but mainly about language.[259]

The increase in knowledge of China immediately produced, according to
their authors, a pair of startling new ideas for language and literature. Timothy
Bright, the father of modern shorthand, was possibly stimulated by reading
about the Chinese system of writing to invent his *Characterie* (1588).[260] George
Puttenham (d. 1590), the first of England's great literary critics, brought his
interest in the overseas world into *The Arte of English Poesie* (1589). Here he used
his knowledge of alien and distant peoples to support his argument that poetry
in the vulgar tongue is natural to all peoples of the world and is older than the
artificial creations of the Greek and Latin writers. Although he was a well-
versed student of European poetry in all its dimensions, Puttenham was aware
that the high civilizations of Asia had poetic traditions of their own rivaling the
European in sophistication. More specifically than Willes he credits the Asians
with inventing pattern poetry.

In his chapter entitled "Of Proportion in Figure," Puttenham discusses that
form of poetry which "yields an ocular representation" and which is usually

[257] On the Portuguese in France see above, pp. 10–14.
[258] See George T. Staunton (ed.), *The History of the Great and Mighty Kingdom of China and the
Situation Thereof. Compiled by the Padre Juan Gonzalez de Mendoza and Now Reprinted from the Early
Translation of R. Parke,* "Publications of the Hakluyt Society," Nos. XIV and XV (2 vols.; New York,
1970 reprint). Also see pl. 78.
[259] On his letter see below, p. 529.
[260] For discussion see below, p. 523.

reduced to "certaine Geometricall figures."[261] He asserts, somewhat inaccurately, that pattern poems of this sort except for oval shapes ("Anacreens egge") were not composed by Greek, Latin, or vernacular poets.[262] Then he reports in this manner on his personal discovery of them:

But being in Italie conversant with a certaine gentleman, who had long travailed the Orientall parts of the world, and seene the Courts of the great Princes of China and Tartarie. I being very inquisitive to know of the subtillities of these countreyes, and especially in matter of learning and of their vulgar poesie, he told me that they are in all their inventions most wittie, and have the use of Poesie or riming, but do not delight so much as we do in long tedious descriptions, and therefore when they will utter any pretie conceit, they reduce it into metrical feet, and put it in forme of a Lozange or square, or such other figure, and so engraven in gold, silver, or ivorie, and sometimes with letters of ametist, rubie, emeralde or topas curiously cemented together, they sende them in chaines, bracelets, collars and girdles to their mistresses to wear for a remembrance. Some fewe measures composed in this sort this gentleman gave me which I translated word for word and as neere as I could followed both the phrase and the figure, which is somewhat hard to performe, because of the restrainte of the figure from which ye may not digresse.[263]

After commenting on the "Lozange" as a "most beautiful figure," Puttenham provides two examples which he allegedly translated "into the same figure observing the phrase of the Orientall speach word for word."[264] The first of his Lozanges, he claims, was presented by the "Lady Kermesine" to the "Can" (Khan) of Tartary surnamed "Temir Cutzclewe" on his return "fro the coquest of Corasoon (a great kingdom adioyning)."[265] The second pattern poem is the Khan's reply. Puttenham's second set of two poems deals in triangular form with the sultan of Persia and his love, the "Lady Selamoour." Although he never indicates precisely what Oriental language he is translating, it is certainly possible that his poems are in some obscure way related either to Chinese or Persian prototypes. Puttenham's pattern poems correspond to the genre called "games of words" in traditional Chinese poetry and to similar creations in

[261] See G. D. Willcock and A. Walker (eds.), *George Puttenham, The Arte of English Poesie* (Cambridge, 1936), p. 91.

[262] George Puttenham, *The Arte of English Poesie* (London, 1589), p. 75. The pattern poem first appeared in the West in Greek bucolic literature of around 300 B.C., perhaps as an import from the Orient. The Planudean version of *The Greek Anthology* was the chief vehicle by which it was carried from Antiquity to the Renaissance. *The Greek Anthology* circulated widely on the Continent where it was revised and amplified by sixteenth-century poets. The first pattern poem known to English literature is included in Stephen Hawes' *The Convercyon of Swerers* (1509). See M. Church, "The First English Pattern Poems," *PMLA*, LXI (1946), 636–39. Also see discussion of Willes, above, p. 372.

[263] Willcock and Walker (eds.), *op. cit.* (n. 261), pp. 91–92.

[264] *Ibid.*, p. 93. See pl. 23.

[265] *Ibid.*, pp. 93–94. On these names: both Marco Polo and Mandeville write it "Caan" or "Can". Mandeville (1588 edition, ed. John Ashton, p. 177) writes: "In ye land of Corosayan. Yt is at the north side of Cathay". Khorosan is a region of northern Asia where elephants were to be found.

Persian poetry which were in existence when he wrote.[266] His other characterizations of Oriental poetry, particularly his references to its suggestiveness and brevity, ring remarkably true even yet.

Puttenham thinks of the pattern poem as a device in which a necessary and mystical relationship exists beween the figure and the poem. An example emerges from his discussion of the emblems and arms of various world rulers. He is particularly interested in and impressed by the "imperial arms" of China: "two strange serpents [dragons?] intertangled in their amorous congresse the lesser creeping with his head into the greaters mouth, with words purporting [*ama* and *time*] love and fear." He asserts that this "poesie with marvelous much reason and subtillity implieth the dutie of every subiect to his Prince, and of every Prince to his suiect . . . for without fear and love the soveraigne authority could not be upholden." He is most impressed that this imperial insignia is used as a symbol of the Chinese ruler's authority and is even embroidered upon the vestments of his officials who "may not presume to be seene in publick without them." Finally he confesses:

I could not forebeare to adde this forraine example to accōplish our discourse touching devices. For the beauty and gallantness of it, besides the subtellitie of the conceit and princely pollicy in the use, more exact then can be remēbred in any other of any European Prince.[267]

Whether or not Puttenham is correct in his understanding of the pattern poems and devices of China, he is clearly impressed with the achievements of the Chinese and has sought to find in their civilization literary techniques and ideas worth emulating. The search for symbols, particularly of distant provenance, was pursued tirelessly during the sixteenth century.

[266] On the possible relationship see Ch'ien Chung-shu, "China in the English Literature of the Seventeenth Century," *Quarterly Bulletin of Chinese Bibliography*, N.S. I, No. 4 (December, 1940), 355–56. For an evaluation of these two claims see A. L. Korn, "Puttenham and the Oriental Pattern Poem," *Comparative Literature*, VI (1954), 289–303. Professor Chow Tse-tung (Wis.), in a letter dated December 12, 1974, informs me: "I believe some of the Chinese pattern poems might have developed during the second century. . . . A pattern poem composed by Mrs. Su Po-yü of the later Han dynasty (A.D. 23–220) is extant. . . . Wang An-shih and Su Shih (Su Tung-p'o) of the 11th century are [also] among such poets." In China the Buddhists wrote picture poems. For examples see S. W. Williams, *The Middle Kingdom* (2 vols.; London, 1883), I, 708.

[267] Quotations from Willcock and Walker (eds.), *op. cit.* (n. 261), pp. 106–7. Mendoza (Staunton [ed.], *op. cit.* [n. 258], I, 97; II, 62, 168–69) refers to the king's arms as being serpents entangled or knotted together. But I have so far been unable to locate the source for the words which Puttenham associates with this device or with the interpretation he attaches to it. Ample evidence exists in Mendoza's China (*ibid.*, I, 103; II, 45) to support Puttenham's claim that this insignia is embroidered on the robes of imperial officials and on other official cloths. This is certainly a correct reference to the "dragon robes" worn by Ming officials. They were also presented as gifts to foreign emissaries and many even got to Europe. Gaspar da Cruz wrote in 1569 that the Chinese officials "do wear for a badge the King's arms on their breasts and on their backs which are certain serpents woven with golden thread many of which have come to Portugal and which are often presented to churches to serve to ornament them." See C. R. Boxer (ed.), *South China in the Sixteenth Century*, "Publications of the Hakluyt Society," 2d ser., No. CVI (London, 1953), p. 156. For illustrations and for pertinent discussion of these "dragon robes" see S. Camman, *China's Dragon Robes* (New York, 1952), pp. 13, 16, 78–79, 112, 157.

C. DRAMA AND SATIRE

The traditional East as well as the opening of the overseas world both figure prominently in the dramas of the young Christopher Marlowe (1564–93). In his *Tamburlaine the Great,* written about 1587, he reveals both a fascination for the historical Timur Khan (1336–1405) of Tartary and a preoccupation with the overseas discoveries of his own century. Marlowe derived his information on Tamburlaine and his activities mainly from the accounts included in George Whetstone's 1586 translation of Pedro Mexía's *Silva* (1543), the 1553 Latin biography of Petrus Perondinus, and the 1521 translation of Hayton.[268] Throughout the play, but especially in Part II, he also depends for geographical details on Belleforest's *Cosmographie* (1575) and Ortelius' *Theatrum* (1570).[269] The two parts of this play first printed in 1590 intermingle the historical and imaginary deeds of a ruler who sets out to conquer the world as Alexander had in ancient times. Marlowe possibly was inspired by the spirit of empire-building that animated him and the others who belonged to the group about Sir Walter Raleigh.[270]

The scene of the play is laid in Asia, specifically in the Scythia and western Tartary of Ortelius and the other geographers of Marlowe's day. The cast is completely Asian, most of the characters being the rulers and nobles of their respective nations: Persia, Turkey, Egypt, etc. From the first act on, Marlowe, without much regard for history and without deference to chronology, does not hesitate to put the present into the past. He has Prince Cosroe of Persia, the contemporary of Timur, recognized as "Monarch of the East," even including "East India and the late discovered Isles."[271] He also takes the opportunity here to list the resonant and evocative names of Eastern places as his contemporaries were doing in other European literatures.[272] And he has Cosroe complain:

> Men from the farthest Equinoctial line [equator],
> Have swarm'd in troopes into the Eastern *India*:
> Lading their shippes with gold and pretious stones
> And made their spoiles from all our provinces.[273]

[268] The title of Perondinus' book is *Magni Scytharum Imperatori Vita* (Florence); for Silva see above, pp. 173–74, and for Hayton see above, p. 307. For discussion of Whetstone's translation from the French see T. C. Izard, "The Principal Source for Marlowe's Tamburlaine," *Modern Language Notes,* LVIII (1943), 411–17. Also see pls. 12, 13.

[269] See E. Seaton, "Marlowe's Map," *Essays and Studies by Members of the English Association,* X (1924), 13–25, and U. M. Ellis-Fermor, *Tamburlane the Great in Two Parts* (London, 1930), pp. 34–48.

[270] For further discussion see E. G. Clark, *Raleigh and Marlowe: A Study in Elizabethan Fustian* (New York, 1941), pp. 396–97, 407–8. For an effort to relate the rise and decline of Elizabethan drama to overseas discoveries see W. Holzhausen, "Übersee in den Darstellungsformen des Elisabethanischen Dramas," in W. Horn (ed.), *Beiträge zur Erforschung der Sprache und Kultur Englands und Nordamerikas* (Breslau, 1928), pp. 156–65.

[271] See Fredson Bowers (ed.), *The Complete Works of Christopher Marlowe* (2 vols.; Cambridge, 1973), *Tamburlaine,* Pt. I, Act 1, scene 1 (Vol. I, p. 84). Cf. pl. 14, on the rulers of the East.

[272] See above, pp. 120–21, 283.

[273] Bowers (ed.), *op. cit.* (n. 271), Pt. I, Act 1, scene 1 (Vol. I, p. 83).

Later he has Cosroe assure Tamburlaine:

> Then will we march to all those Indian Mines,
> My witlesse brother to the Christians lost;
> And ransome them with fame and usurie.[274]

Marlowe's Tamburlaine boasted of conquests he would make in regions that the historical Timur could not have known about. Being a world conqueror, he circumnavigates the earth, reversing the direction followed by Magellan, Drake, and Cavendish, to extend his rule even to America:

> Until the Persian Fleete and men of war,
> Sailing along the Orientall sea,
> Have fetcht along the Indian continent
> Even from Persepolis to Mexico,
> And thence unto the straights of Jubalter.[275]

To appease his personal wrath Tamburlaine vows to take the Indian gold mines and to make the kings of India work them for his benefit. Orcanes, king of Natolia, lends support to these boasts by telling of Tamburlaine's bloody conquests:

> He brings a world of people to the field
> From *Scythia* to the Oriental Plage
> Of India, wher raging *Lantchidol*
> Beates on the regions with his boysterous blowes,
> That never sea man discovered:
> All *Asia* is in Armes with *Tamburlaine*.[276]

Finally Tamburlaine cries "Give me a map" to see how much of the world remains unconquered so "that these my boies may finish all my wantes." Marlowe, who had probably heard of the Venetian proposals then current, also has Tamburlaine talk in terms of cutting a canal at Suez "that men might quickly sail to India."[277]

---

[274] *Ibid.*, Pt. I, Act 2, scene 5 (Vol. I, p. 101). Notice that he is not referring (as suggested by Ellis-Fermor, *op. cit.* [n. 269], p. 106, n. 41) to the pre-Christian conquests of India. He specifically refers to "Christians" in what is certainly a reference, however anachronistic, to the Portuguese in India.

[275] Bowers (ed.), *op. cit.* (n. 271), Pt. I, Act 3, scene 3 (Vol. I, p. 120).

[276] *Ibid.*, Pt. II, Act I, scene I (Vol. I, p. 154). In Ortelius' *Theatrum* the "Lantchidol Mare" borders a promontory of unexplored land. See E. Seaton, *loc. cit.* (n. 269), p. 31. Eden in his translation of Pigafetta mentions "Lantchidol" as a great sea. It was written "Lant chidol" in the epitomized Paris version of 1525 of Pigafetta's account. See P. S. Paige (trans.), *The Voyage of Magellan: The Journal of Antonio Pigafetta* (Englewood Cliffs, N.J., 1969), p. 146. On Ramusio's map (1554) "Mare Lantchidol" appears to the north of Java between Sumatra and Celebes. For the Ortelius map see *Asia*, I, end-paper; for the Ramusio map see *ibid.*, following p. 528. These are probably all misreadings of the "Laut Chidol" of Pigafetta. For this reference see C. E. Nowell (ed.), *Magellan's Voyage around the World: Three Contemporary Accounts* (Evanston, Ill., 1962), p. 254. "Laut" is the Malay word for sea. There is also the island of Laut at the southern entrance to the Strait of Makasar, and a Little Laut to the south of it in the Java Sea.

[277] Bowers (ed.), *op. cit.* (n. 271), Pt. III, Act 5, scene 3 (Vol. I, p. 48).

Throughout his brief but active life, Marlowe evidently sought information on Asia and its products from his books and his acquaintances. A friend, Robert Hues, sailed around the world with Cavendish as mathematician and geographer. It is likely that Marlowe was also acquainted with Hawkins and Hakluyt.[278] Like most of his contemporaries, Marlowe was fascinated by the wealth of "golden India."[279] Determined to control the spirits for his own service, Marlowe's Doctor Faustus declares:

> I'le have them flie to India for gold,
> Ransacke the Ocean for Orient pearle,
> And search all corners of the new-found-world
> For pleasant fruites and princely delicates.[280]

The "wealthy Moore" finds precious stones in India and sells

> Bags of fiery *Opales, Saphirs, Amatists,*
> *Jacints,* hard *Topas,* grasse-green *Emeraulds,*
> Beautious *Rubyes,* sparkling *Diamonds.*[281]

In 1593 Marlowe was accused, shortly before his death, of holding "monstrous opinions" about religion. Allegedly he had shocked the conscience of proper Elizabethan society and its police by declaring "that the Indians and many authors of antiquity have assuredly writen of above 16 thousand yeares agone whereas Adam is proved to have lived within 6 thousand yeares."[282]

Despite Marlowe's difficulties with the authorities, the religious climate in Elizabethan England was not repressive of secular literature. Total book production increased substantially from 1580 to 1603. The proportion of religious literature declined to about 40 percent of the whole while secular literature constituted 25 percent and history, geography, and travel about 10 percent.[283] Beginning with Marlowe's *Tamburlaine* (printed 1590) the number of important plays produced and published increased markedly. The Orient as the scene of action and the cast of Oriental characters became more common in Elizabethan drama. The plays set in the Orient are uniformly tragedies which portray Orientals as warlike, fratricidal, and lustful.[284] This conception of the Oriental was probably derived from the stories that circulated widely about the ravages of the Tartars, Mongols, and Turks. Indeed, the word "Tartar" was generally employed as a synonym for the "devil." But these were the neighboring Orientals of the Continental tradition, the arch-enemies of Christian Europe. They were not the Orientals newly discovered in places remote from Europe.

[278] See A. D. Atkinson, "Marlowe and the Voyagers," *Notes and Queries,* CXCIV (1949), 247–49.
[279] See "Dido Queen of Carthage" in Bowers (ed.), *op. cit.* (n. 271), I, 49.
[280] *Ibid.,* II, 164.
[281] From "The Jew of Malta," *ibid.,* I, 264. Here again the names are cataloged for sonority.
[282] As quoted in J. E. Bakeless, *The Tragicall History of Christopher Marlowe* (2 vols.; Cambridge, Mass., 1942), I, iii.
[283] See Bennett, *op. cit.* (n. 233), p. 269.
[284] See Louis Wann, "The Oriental in Elizabethan Drama," *Modern Philology,* XII (1912), 423–47.

The Elizabethan conception of the East Indian was formed in large measure by the Alexander legend, Polo, and Mandeville. In this tradition the East bred monsters and miracles, and its people enjoyed abundant wealth and lived in numerous, great cities. Very little was published in England during the sixteenth century that openly questioned these premises about Asia. Indeed many of the most popular books—*The fardle of facions* and the travel collections of Eden and Willes—seemed to substantiate and to fix the earlier portrait of Asia as a land of unbelievable wealth, mystical marvels, and demoniacal magic. The stories about wealth were confirmed by trade, and exaggerations about places and peoples were both substantiated and amplified by returning eyewitnesses who enjoyed shocking the stay-at-homes.[285] Sir Philip Sidney who kept himself abreast of the opening of the overseas world was as impressed as others by the riches of India. He remarked:

> Be your words made (good Sir) of Indian ware
> That you allow me them by so small rate?[286]

A play called *Sir John Mandeville* was still current in 1592.[287] Eight years later a translation was published from the Spanish of Antonio de Torquemada and entitled in translation *The Spanish Mandevile*.[288] In the popular drama the character of the East and its people remained fundamentally unchanged to the death of Shakespeare in 1616.

The bard himself best exemplifies the place of India and the East in Elizabethan drama. Twenty-four allusions to the *Indies*, *Indian*, *Ind*, and *India* appear in Shakespeare's plays.[289] Of these references six definitely refer to America, three certainly to the East, and the remainder are ambiguous.[290] Like his contemporaries, Shakespeare uses both Indies as a metaphor for riches but in his earlier plays the references are almost always to the India of Asia. He mentions *spice* and *spicery* on twelve occasions but generally without much specificity about the islands from which the spices came. In his several references to *Tartars* Shakespeare mentions their bows and arrows and their talents as archers, but otherwise regards them as being cruel and uncivilized. Both of his allusions to *Cataians* are clearly synonyms of dishonesty and chicanery.[291] In his numerous references to precious stones he certainly has those of India—especially diamonds

---

[285] See Cawley, *op. cit.* (n. 245), pp. 1, 107, 112.

[286] From "Astrophil and Stella" (XCII, 1–2), written *ca.* 1584, as reproduced in W. A. Ringler, Jr. (ed.), *The Poems of Sir Philip Sidney* (Oxford, 1962), p. 225.

[287] See F. E. Schelling, *Elizabethan Drama, 1558–1642* (2 vols.; London, 1911), I, 291.

[288] *The Spanish Mandevile of Miracles. Or the Garden of Curious Flowers Wherein Are Handled Sundry Points of Humanity, Philosophy, Divinitie, and Geography. Beautified with Many Strange and Pleasant Histories* (London, 1600).

[289] See J. W. Draper, "Indian and Indies in Shakespeare," *Neuphilologische Mitteilungen*, LVI (1955), 103, 111.

[290] For a summary of these references see C. Clark, *Shakespeare and National Character* (New York, 1932), pp. 293–94.

[291] See Chan [Ch'en] Shou-yi, "Influence of China in English Culture" (Ph.D. diss., Department of English, University of Chicago, 1928), p. 8.

and rubies—in mind. Just one reference in all of Shakespeare appears to have a degree of special knowledge regarding India. It is Bassanio's comparison in *The Merchant of Venice* (III, ii, 99) of "the beautious scarfe Veiling an Indian beauty," a reference possibly to the custom of purdah.[292] In *Measure for Measure* (II, i, 92–94) Shakespeare reveals something about how common porcelain was in his day when he has Pompey remark about a three-penny prune dish: "Your honours have seen such dishes; they are not China dishes, but very good dishes."

Shakespeare and his fellow dramatists of the turn of the century were generally unresponsive to the rich contributions being made by their contemporaries to knowledge about the East. While the Globe Theatre had inscribed above its entry *Totus mundus agit histrionem*, very little about the Eastern world then being revealed actually appeared on its stage. This omission may possibly be accounted for by the effort of dramatists to observe the Aristotelian unities or by the limits imposed by the stage itself.

Againe, many things may be told which cannot be shewed: if they know the difference betwixt reporting and representing. As for example, I may speake though I am here, of *Peru*, and in speech digresse from that, to the description of *Calecut*: But in action, I cannot represent it without *Pacolets* Horse.[293]

Shakespeare, like Hakluyt of the first edition, was more interested in the sea, navigation, trade, and national expansion than in learning about Asia. References to ships, and to their parts and sailing them, outnumber by far Shakespeare's allusions to India.[294] While he obviously paid very little attention to the publication of Hakluyt's second amplified edition (1598–1600), Shakespeare noticed Edward Wright's Map of the World that appeared in 1600. In *Twelfth Night* (III, ii, 82) Maria remarks of Malvolio: "he doth smile his face into more lines than are in the new map, with the augmentation of the Indies."

Information on the East was being augmented substantially at the turn of the century by a rash of translations mostly inspired or published by Hakluyt. Thomas Hickock's translation of Cesare Fedrici (1588) was included in Hakluyt's new edition. The itinerary of Jan van Linschoten in the English version of John Wolfe was published separately in 1598. Hakluyt's second edition also included an "excellent treatise" on China that had been prepared by the Jesuits at Macao as well as Ralph Fitch's narrative of his travels in Asia. In 1601 Hakluyt published the English translation from Portuguese of Antonio Galvão's (Galvano's) *The Discoveries of the World*, a chronological epitome of all noteworthy travels undertaken to the year 1555. In the same year Robert Johnson published *The Travellers Breviat*, an epitome of Giovanni Botero's famous

---

[292] See Draper, *loc. cit.* (n. 289), p. 105. But it should also be noticed that a great scholarly debate goes on about the proper reading of this line. See H. H. Furness (ed.), *A New Variorum Edition of Shakespeare* (Philadelphia, 1871–1919) VII, 145–46.

[293] Words of Sir Philip Sidney, commenting upon *Gorboducke* in his *Defense of Poesie* (London, 1595), sig. H⁴ᵛ-II.

[294] For such references see A. F. Falconer, *Shakespeare and the Sea* (London, 1964), *passim*.

Relazioni of all countries.[295] In the meantime the early voyages of the new East India Company (1600) led to the production of travel narratives which effectively and quickly widened the horizons of Englishmen with respect to Asia and its peoples.[296]

Writers of nondramatic literature tended to be more responsive than the playwrights to the overseas achievements of their contemporaries. While a few popular balladeers celebrated the return of Drake from his world voyage, others damned the Spanish for planning cruelties against the English "even as in India once they did against those people there."[297] Edmund Spenser (1552?–99) sketched in *The Faerie Queene* his dreams of conquest in America, while remaining utterly traditional in his references to Asia.[298] In Sonnet XV of his *Amoretti* (1595) Spenser reveals something about his interest in Asia in his treatment of the merchants and the rare stones of India:

> Ye tradefull Merchants that with weary toyle
> do seeke most pretious things to make your gain
> And both the Indies of their treasures spoile,
> what needeth you to seeke so farre in vaine?
> For loe my love doth in her selfe containe
> All this worlds riches that may farre be found,
> if Saphares, loe her eires be Sapher plaine,
> if Rubies, loe her lips be Rubies sound:
> If Pearles, her teeth be pearles both pure and round;
> if Yvorie, her forehead yvory weene.[299]

Other poets of Spenser's day looked to Hakluyt for information and inspiration. In one of his madrigals written around 1600, Thomas Weelkes sings:

> The Andalusian merchant that returns
> Laden with cochineal and China dishes,
> Reports in Spain how strangely Fogo burns
> Amidst an ocean full of flying fishes.[300]

---

[295] On Botero's original work see above, pp. 245–49.

[296] For a listing of the relevant travel narratives of the early seventeenth century see B. Penrose, *Travel and Discovery in the Renaissance, 1420–1620* (Cambridge, Mass., 1955), p. 322.

[297] For the poem celebrating Drake's return written by the scholars of Winchester School see J. E. Gillespie, *The Influence of Overseas Expansion on England to 1700* (New York, 1920), p. 278; for "A new Ballet on the cruelties planned by the Spanish of the Armada," see F. O. Mann (ed.), *The Works of Thomas Deloney* (Oxford, 1912), p. 481; also see A. Esler, "Robert Greene and the Spanish Armada," *Journal of English Literary History*, XXXII (1965), 314–32.

[298] Spenser relies for his references to the East entirely upon the medieval travelers and upon the poetical references in Ariosto and Tasso.

[299] E. Greenlaw *et al.* (eds.), *The Works of Edmund Spenser: A Variorum Edition* (8 vols.; Baltimore, 1932–47), VIII, 201.

[300] *Madrigals of 5 and 6 parts apt for the Viola and voices* (London, 1600), Pt. II (six-part madrigals), pp. vii–viii. Based on the account of Drake's voyage of 1579 in which the English report on a volcanic island ("ila del fogo") and on capturing "a ship laden with linnen cloth and fine China dishes of white earth and great store of China silks." See D. B. Quinn and R. A. Skelton (eds.), *The Principall Navigations . . . by Richard Hakluyt Imprinted at London, 1589* (2 vols.; Cambridge, 1965), II, 643B, 643F.

The euphuistic writers of the era in their preoccupation with similes and antithesis found a valuable source in Mandeville's stories. For example, Thomas Deloney in *Jack of Newberry* (written by 1597) describes Master Benedicke as "saying nothing, as if he had been tongueless like the men of *Coromandae*," and his maiden lover as being as deaf to his moans "as if she had been borne (like the women of *Taprobana*) without ears."[301] That Sir Philip Sidney was aware of the appeal of Asia to the euphuistic authors becomes plain when he attacks those writers who play with comparison:

> Or with strange similes enrich each line
> Of herbes or beastes, which *Ind* or *Afrike* hold.[302]

In the earlier writings of Thomas Lodge (1558?–1625), especially the romance called *Euphues his Shadowe* (1592), the literary device of antithesis continues to derive support from the popular stories about Asia.[303] This work was published while Lodge was on a voyage with Cavendish that was bound for China by the southwestern passage. Lodge never got farther than Brazil. It was probably after returning home that he wrote his Arcadian romance called *A Margarite of America* (1596).[304] The scene of this poetic romance, nominally laid in Muscovia, has nothing to do with America.[305] Of the margarites (small pearls) he wrote:

> Ye gentle pearles where ere did nature make you?
> Or whether in Indian shores you found your mould.
> Or in those lands where spices serve for fuel:
> Oh if I might from out your essence take you
> And turne my selfe to shape what ere I would
> How gladly would I my Ladies Iewell?[306]

Lodge and many of his contemporaries also had a more realistic view of the meaning to Europe of the opening of the East. The new geographical names, especially China, begin to replace or to accompany the older names in their writings. A growing sense of the qualities common to mankind everywhere begins to appear in poetry and prose. Lodge notes that "good husbandmen thrive in America as in Asia."[307] And in *A Fig for Momus* (1595) he philosophizes:

[301] See Mann (ed.), *op. cit.* (n. 297), p. 47.

[302] From "Astrophil and Stella" (III, 7–8) (n. 286), p. 166.

[303] For examples see The Hunterian Club edition of *The Complete Works of Thomas Lodge* (4 vols.; Glasgow, 1883), II, 13, 64, 70, 75.

[304] See C. J. Sisson, *Thomas Lodge and Other Elizabethans* (Cambridge, Mass., 1933), pp. 106–8. Also see D. B. Quinn (ed.), *The Last Voyage of Thomas Cavendish, 1591–92* (Chicago, 1975), p. 23.

[305] For commentary see N. B. Paradise, *Thomas Lodge: The History of an Elizabethan* (New Haven, 1931), pp. 122–31.

[306] See The Hunterian Club, *op. cit.* (n. 303), III, 16. Cf. the description of margarites as "little pearls found in shell fish, especially in oysters, whereof some have holes in them, and some have none, the best are brought out of India, yet they are also found in our English seas" in H. Platt, *The Jewell House of Art and Nature* (London, 1594), p. 221.

[307] See The Hunterian Club, *op. cit.* (n. 303), II, 102.

And what impression we in youth retaine
In age, our reason hardly will restraine:
The idle *More*, the *Turke*, the *Saracine*,
The *Chinois*, and the wealthy *Abissine*:
Observe that custome and idolatrie
Which was ingrafted in their infancie.[308]

And something of the same sort of cultural relativism appears in Samuel Daniel's (1562–1619) *Defence of Ryme* (*ca.* 1602) when he writes:

Will not experience confute vs, if wee shoulde say the state of *China* which neyer heard of anapestiques, trochies, and tribraques, were grosse, barbarous, and vncivile?[309]

A growing preoccupation with China and the preparations for the formation of the East India Company led to an open repudiation of Mandeville and his tales. Sir Philip Sidney, in a letter to his brother Robert, remarks that from China "good lawes and customes are to be learned, but to knowe their riches and power is of little purpose to us, since it can neither advantage us, or hinder us."[310] Samuel Rowland (1570?–1630?) in his satires on the manners of Londoners called *The Letting of Humours Blood in the Head-Vaine* (1600) uses Mandeville as a prime example of the teller of tall tales.[311] Joseph Hall (1574–1656) avowedly disapproved of the travelers though he was himself an avid reader of their works while still studying at Cambridge at the end of the century. So his attack on the travel account in *Virgidemiarum* (published in 1597–98) is at least partly autobiographical:

The brainsicke youth that feeds his tickled eare
with sweet-sauc'd lies of some false Traveiler
Which hath the Spanish Decades [Eden] red a while
Or whet-stone leasings of old Maundevile
Now with discourses breakes his mid-night sleepe
Of his adventures through the *Indian* deepe
Of all their massy heapes of golden mines
Or of the antique Toombs of Palestine
. . . .
Of the bird Ruc that beares an elephant:
Of Mer-maids that the Southern seas do haunt;
Of head-lesse men; of savage cannibals.[312]

---

[308] *Ibid.*, III, 37.

[309] A. C. Sprague (ed.), *Poems and a Defense of Ryme* (Cambridge, Mass., 1930), p. 140. This was possibly written in response to George Abbot's remark in *A Brief Description of the Whole Worlde* (London, 1599), fol. B2: "The [Chinese] people are not much learned, but more civill than the Tartars."

[310] Albert Feuillerat (ed.), *The Prose Works of Sir Philip Sidney* (4 vols.; Cambridge, 1963, reprint of edition of 1912), III, 126.

[311] The Hunterian Club, *The Complete Works of Samuel Rowlands* (2 vols.; Glasgow, 1880), I, 48.

[312] Book IV, Satire 6, in A. Davenport (ed.), *The Collected Poems of Joseph Hall, Bishop of Exeter and Norwich* (Liverpool, 1949), p. 71. On the "Ruc" or "ruch" see *Asia*, II, Bk. 1, 92.

Hall was writing at about this same time his clever *Mundus alter et idem*, a burlesque aimed at the credulity of Hakluyt, the cosmographer, and Sir Thomas More, the Utopian. Translated by Healey as *A Discovery of the New World* (1609), this book is an ingenious satire of people and their habits which rivals in tomfoolery the *Pantarguel* of Rabelais.[313]

But Mandeville and the other travelers easily survived the barbs of the satirists. Samuel Purchas, the seventeenth-century continuator of Hakluyt and original student of travel literature, praised Mandeville for being "the greatest Asian traveler that ever the world had." The stories derived from the Bible continued also to be of moment, especially regarding the location of Ophir, from whence King Solomon's Tyrian sailors brought the gold to adorn the temple of Jerusalem. In the appendix to his 1574 edition of the Vulgate, Benito Arias Montano identified Ophir with Peru because the Bible (2 *Chron.* 3:6) speaks of the "gold of Parvaim." Most of the Elizabethan writers, including Linschoten and Galvano, were convinced that its true location was in the East Indies.[314] Sir Walter Raleigh, England's famous colonial planner, became involved in the Ophir question while writing *The History of the World* (1614). Although he never progressed beyond Antiquity in his history, Raleigh brought his new knowledge of navigation and the overseas discoveries to bear upon his analysis of the remote past. About Ophir he observes:

Now although there may be found gold in Arabia itself (towards Persia) ... and all along that East Indian shore; yet the greatest plenty is taken up at the Philippines, certain islands planted by the Spaniards from the East Indies.[315] And by the length of the passage which Solomon's ships made from the Red Sea (which were three years in coming and going), it seems they went to the uttermost, as the Moluccas or Philippines. Indeed these that now go from Portugal, or from hence, finish that navigation in two yeares, and sometimes less; ... But we must consider, that they evermore kept the coast and crept by the shores which made the way exceeding long. For before the use of the compass was known, it was impossible to navigate athwart the ocean; and therefore Solomon's ships could not find Peru in America. Neither was it needful for the Spaniards themselves had it not been for the plenty of gold in the East India islands, far above the mines of any one place of America, to sail every year from the west part of America thither, and there to have strongly planted and inhabited the richest of those islands, wherein they have built a city called Manilia.[316]

At the end of the century Raleigh, like Sir Thomas More at its beginning, was still seeking to reconcile the traditional with the new learning about the East.

---

[313] See H. Brown (ed.), *The Discovery of a New World (Mundus alter et idem)* (Cambridge, Mass., 1937). For a contrast see the high praise accorded Hakluyt and others in William Warner, *Albion's England* (1602).

[314] See R. R. Cawley, *Unpathed Waters: Studies in the Influence of the Voyagers on Elizabethan Literature* (Princeton, 1940), pp. 32–33. For the Jesuit view that the land of Ophir is in the East Indies see L. Kilger, "Die Peru-Relation des José de Acosta 1576 und seine Missionstheorie," *Neue Zeitschrift für Missionswissenschaft*, I (1945), 24–38.

[315] Pigafetta and the early Iberian authors had reported on Luzon and Mindanao in the Philippines as sources of gold. See *Asia*, I, 626, 628, 642.

[316] *History of the World* in *Works* (8 vols.; Oxford, 1829), II, 334–35.

Each man was at the center of a circle of literati who sought to encourage and extend England's participation in overseas discoveries. More, through his contacts on the Continent with Giles, Góis, and Grynaeus, hoped to keep abreast of the progress being made by others in the opening of the overseas world. Both More and Rastell clearly understood that America blocked the westward sea route to Asia, but both were nonetheless convinced before Magellan had done it that the world could be circumnavigated. Despite the best efforts of More and his circle, Henry VIII and the London merchants continued to remain aloof from the spice trade while concentrating on the trade in woolens and on Continental policies. Knowledge of the East in these early years was thus limited to what could be learned in England from the translation of Mandeville and from other, more recent Continental cosmographies and travel accounts. Henry's break with Rome in 1534 severed even this connection, for Mandeville and the Iberian accounts became suspect in Reformation England.

The isolation of England and its temporary relief from Continental interference ended at mid-century. A growing interest among English merchants in the possibility of a northeast passage to Cathay had the effect of focusing attention on materials old and new about Tartary and Muscovy. The Marian period (1553-58) with its Catholic and Spanish connections permitted the publication—especially in Eden's collection—of hitherto untranslated accounts of the Iberian conquests. In the first two decades of Elizabeth's reign little new material was published relating directly to the discoveries. A number of "curious histories," such as those by Mandeville and Mexía, were reprinted or translated into English for the first time. To the literary giants of the last generation of the century these "curious histories" were important as source books.

A brief revival of interest around 1575 in the hopeless possibility of the northwest passage to Cathay was followed by a determined effort to defy the Spanish and to open to English navigation the southwest passage to Asia. In connection with this new orientation of interest the English merchants at Seville began translating the newer Spanish materials into English, especially those dealing with China. The successful navigations of Drake and Cavendish, as well as other English and Dutch oceanic forays, inspired Spain to build an Armada to attack England directly; in England the circumnavigations stimulated pride in the national achievement and a determination to pursue it to the end. The defeat of the Armada in 1588 left the opportunity open for the English to begin sending their own fleets to the East by any route whatsoever. At the same time the translation and publication of Mendoza's *China* (1588) and Fedrici's travels in Asia (1589) vastly improved documentation on the East.

The literary imaginations of the poets quickly responded to this new concentration of the national effort. Many of the poets themselves—Gascoigne and Lodge among them—were directly involved in one aspect or another of overseas navigation or had close friends who had "crossed the Line." John Lyly, the father of Euphuism, was, like many of his contemporaries, an ardent advocate of travel as experience. Lyly and the later Euphuists delighted in using as sources for their antitheses the grotesque stories in Mandeville and other "curious histories." The travel books and collections seemed clearly to substantiate Mandeville's stories, and Hall even accused their writers of having copied the medieval accounts. The travel books certainly helped to preserve the fabulous vision of Asia represented in Mandeville. When Hall and the other satirists attacked Mandeville, Hakluyt, and other "travelers," they were also indirectly deriding the credulity of the Euphuists.

The years immediately following the Armada's defeat were notable in literature for innovation. Puttenham, like Timothy Bright, apparently saw that China had much to teach the European literati. He recognized China as the homeland of the pattern poem, a poetic form he tried to emulate. On the basis of Mendoza's account of China, Puttenham contends that the insignia, or arms, of the Chinese emperor is superior to those of European princes for it is used practically as the symbol of "love and fear," the qualities necessary to the maintenance of authority and stability in the realm. Marlowe, who depends upon earlier sources for his *Tamburlaine*, also used innovatively the new materials on the overseas discoveries. Like Raleigh, he employed the recent materials to help illuminate the past. Marlowe wrote about the East with Ortelius' world map at hand and by his perusal of it was able to suggest the idea that canals at Suez and Panama might facilitate navigation.

Marlowe's successors in the field of drama were not so imaginative in their reactions to overseas expansion. Shakespeare and his contemporaries treated the East in traditional fashion as the source of abundance, magic, and mystery. While they were all aware of the sea and navigation, they limited their references regarding maritime exploits to brief allusions. India and the East were similarly treated. From this observation it need not be concluded that they were unaware of the new spirit of discovery that was sweeping the land. It is more reasonable to conclude, as Sir Philip Sidney suggested, that they were limited by their concern for the unities of time and place and by the requirements of dialogue written for performance on the stage.

The authors of nondramatic literature were more responsive to Asia in the last two decades of the century. Hakluyt, for example, amplified his initial travel collection (1589) by adding to the second edition (1598–1600) a number of substantial new accounts of the East. China especially, as it became better known, made a reality out of the myth of the East, and poets and writers of romance began to refer to it and its people in more realistic terms. While the Chinese were recognized as different, they were not stigmatized as devils, as were the Tartars. It was obviously impossible, after seeking so long for the route to the riches of Cathay or China, to think of its inhabitants as barbarous and backward. By the turn of the century the Chinese had become a real and accomplished people for the English, one whom they were about to encounter directly for the first time. Most of the writers anticipated the meeting with unconcealed curiosity.

Throughout northern Europe the sixteenth century saw a regular increase in total book production and a substantial rise in the proportion printed in the vernaculars. In the last quarter of the century the number of books and pamphlets directed to religion and to theological controversy declined and the percentage of books of secular learning and literature increased appreciably. Censorship in these countries was aimed mainly against works that were thought to challenge either directly or indirectly the major tenets of Protestantism or Catholicism. Most northern European states considered heresy tantamount to sedition; as a consequence, praise of the Iberian and Catholic overseas achievements was viewed in the Protestant states as a threat to the political order. Fortunately, in a few relatively independent towns, such as Basel, Frankfurt, and later London, a measure of tolerance enabled printers to turn out the newer materials in the language of the original, in translation, and in collections. The fortunes of the travel accounts varied, however, in relation to changing times. Protestants often suspected Mandeville, Marco Polo, and Varthema of being the purveyors of "popish" ideas,[317] but since no Protestant travel accounts were published in the sixteenth century, the Catholics had nothing to which they could take exception. No travel account in a Germanic language approached Varthema's book in authority until the appearance of Linschoten's work at the end of the century.

Perhaps it was because they produced so few noteworthy or reliable travel accounts of their own that the northern Europeans were great collectors and publishers of accounts by others. All the important travel collections of the sixteenth century, with the sole exception of Ramusio's stupendous pioneering compendium, were produced by collectors and printers of northern Europe. The book dealers of Antwerp, Basel, and Frankfurt, in particular, produced illustrated travel collections, encyclopedias, and atlases. These were evidently sold at good prices to the burghers of northern Europe, who valued them as "conversation pieces" and as sources of strange lore. Hakluyt's collecting and publishing activities were designed less for personal gain and more to stimulate the English nation to emulate the successes of their Continental neighbors to the south by undertaking overseas enterprises at their own expense and for their own profit. In England, as opposed to the Continent, the Jesuit letterbooks with their rich materials on Asia, never circulated widely and were only infrequently translated. Apparently only two northern European Jesuits, Gaspar Barzaeus (Barzée) of the Netherlands and Thomas Stevens of England, were active in the Portuguese East before 1600.

In Germany the first important literary reactions to the new discoveries came from geographers, cosmographers, and historians. The pioneering works of Waldseemüller and Vadian were immediately disseminated in the Netherlands and England as well as in Germany itself. Humanists like Peutinger, More, and Pirckheimer responded to this new information, each according to his own particular bent of mind. Peutinger was determined to look for and to find

---

[317] Popular interest in Marco Polo was much less than that in Mandeville. Polo was not translated into Dutch during the sixteenth century; it was first translated into English only in 1579.

antecendents for the most recent discoveries in his beloved classical epoch. More was inclined in his *Utopia* to place the new in juxtaposition to the old without prejudice to either. Pirckheimer, while upholding the priority of ancient discovery, seriously tried in his works on geographical nomenclature to reconcile the old with the new. Some writers of vernacular literature, like John Rastell and Sebastian Franck, preferred the new sources to the old and were not apologetic about saying so.

The great cosmographers of Basel, especially Grynaeus and Münster, were dedicated to the idea that their major task was to catalog and preserve *all* the sources by including them in their encyclopedic cosmographies. They unhesitatingly and uncritically placed ancient and recent sources together without comment or criticism. Often they did not even bother to point out obvious contradictions in the sources. It was this Basel group, in particular, which defined the "New World" as including all places recently discovered that were unknown to the Ancients, including the islands of East and Southeast Asia. Ceylon, for example, was a part of the "New World" in this conception until it was definitely identified as the Taprobane of Ptolemy. Since Münster took no firm position on controversial religious or political issues of the day, his cosmography was permitted to circulate freely throughout Europe and thereby became one of the most influential books of the century.

In Germany a concern for world history developed along with the growth of geography and cosmography. Under the influence of the Italian historians Schedel was the first to bring Asia into the world chronicle. Other Germans soon began to collect materials on the folklore and customs of distant peoples from all the available sources and to compare and contrast them with one another and with European beliefs and practices. Boemus' collection, especially in its numerous adaptations and translations, commanded a European audience before the middle of the century. Boemus particularly influenced Franck in the organization and emphasis of his world history. A strong Protestant and a German stylist of stature, Franck excluded Mandeville from his sources as being too fabulous, and probably too Catholic, and enlivened his world history with ethnological materials reminiscent of those in the Spanish histories of the New World. He specifically urged his readers to keep their minds open when evaluating the customs of alien peoples. Franck's efforts to produce a world history were not followed by others, and Raleigh's ambitious but uncompleted history of the world was his work's only lineal descendant in northern Europe.

The poets, especially in Germany, were among the first of the northern literati to react to the overseas expansion. Brant and his English adapters differed in their views: the German author of *The Ship of Fools* considered exploration an undesirable distraction while the English clearly thought its revelations important. But most of the poets ignored the most recent sources and confined their allusions, as Hans Sachs did, to a traditional Asia of wealth, mystery, and magic. They employed, as their colleagues did elsewhere, the place names of

Asia, as well as the names of precious stones, in a sonorous catalog designed to evoke exotic feelings. In their references to the spice trade they sometimes departed from the exotic to launch out indignantly against the monopolists and their exploitation of others. In the poetic dramas played in the Continental schools the allusions to Asia derived almost always from Mandeville or Varthema. The proponents of Euphuism in England also helped keep Mandeville alive by their generous employment of his tales. Varthema's book was never as popular in England as it was on the Continent.

The English exhibited a number of other tendencies which set them apart from their Continental contemporaries. Most striking was their interest, both literary and practical, in the circumnavigation of the world. Mandeville, if he may be considered English, was among the earliest to suggest circumnavigation as a realizable goal. More in the *Utopia* created a character who claimed to have accomplished this feat before Magellan set out, and Rastell appeared to share a belief in his credibility. Drake and Cavendish were the only two to follow in Magellan's wake across the Pacific to the East. Marlowe's *Tamburlaine* with a Persian fleet allegedly sailed around the world in the opposite direction. In his great play Marlowe had no hesitation about introducing anachronisms as when he had Tamburlaine comment on events which occurred two hundred years after his time, especially those events referring to the Portuguese conquests in India. This practice of using contemporary information on Asia to illuminate the past was also followed by Raleigh in his history of the world.

Marlowe was certainly one of the most innovative in his responses to the opening of the overseas world. Like Ariosto, he wrote with the map of the world within easy reach. His fellow countryman, Puttenham, studied Mendoza and introduced into his literary criticism the idea that pattern poems had originated in the East. He was also much impressed by the device of the king of China and accorded to its entwined dragons a rank superior to the arms of European princes. The traditional German folkbook called the *Lucidarius* was revised over the course of the century in deference to Protestantism and to the overseas discoveries. Popular calendars and almanacs in all parts of northern Europe underwent similar revisions in the direction of a greater cosmopolitanism. Matthias Dresser, a spokesman for the Lutherans, sought to make the discoveries more palatable to his fellow believers by pointing out that they occurred mainly during Luther's lifetime and that they, like the reformer himself, were but aspects of God's continuing revelation. The Catholic literary critic, Martin Antoine del Rio, used similar materials from the Jesuit letterbooks to denigrate the geographical conceptions of the Ancients and to explain strange phenomena in natural rather than supernatural terms.

Toward the end of the century a new realism with reference to Asia also entered Germanic literature. While certain Latin poets celebrated the achievements of the Portuguese, Fischart condemned the Jesuits for lying about their overseas exploits and railed against Philip II for thinking that he could subdue northern Europe as easily as he had extended his sway over the Indies. The English satirists, especially Hall and Rowlandson, repudiated Mandeville and laughed at the credulity of Hakluyt and others for their willingness to accept the travel narratives as true and even suggested that contemporary travelers copied their stories from Mandeville. Such attacks were combined everywhere with a general condemnation of the merchants and all others connected with the spice trade. The Rollenhagens, father and son, revealed in their own ways how the learned world stubbornly continued to believe the "true lies" of the Alexander stories.

The skepticism and hostility of the satirists was balanced by a newer and deeper appreciation of China. The translation of Mendoza's highly laudatory work into German, English, and Dutch brought home to northern Europeans for the first time the magnificence and antiquity of China's civilization. Mendoza's account was generally supported by Linschoten's work, a patent fact since the Dutch traveler clearly used Mendoza as one of his major literary sources. Poets, literary critics, and historians all came to agree that Europe had much to learn from China. But in northern Europe the impact of China ended there. No master works were produced comparable to the history of Louis Le Roy, the *Divine Weekes* of Du Bartas, or the theoretical studies of Botero on China's cities and political organization.[318] The Dutch and the English, who were involved in direct economic and military competition with Spain, wanted data on Eastern navigation and trade rather than speculation about what Europe might learn from China. The Germans were likewise more involved in trade, or the prospect of reviving it, than they were in deciding how best to compare China to Europe or how to bring the East into world history. Such speculative activities were left to the Italians and the French who had no immediate hope of partaking directly of the riches of Asia.

[318] Botero's *Relazioni* was translated into English piecemeal beginning in 1603. Du Bartas' complete poem was translated into English by Joshua Sylvester in 1605. On the English translation of Le Roy see above, p. 311.